THE
GOOD SCHOOLS
GUIDE

www.goodschoolsguide.co.uk

AMANDA ATHA

Amanda, who died in April 2000,
founded the Guide with Sarah
Drummond in 1984. Her spirit,
her style, her wit and combativeness
still infuse this edition – despite
the howls of protest from
offended heads.
We miss her every day.

THE
GOOD SCHOOLS
GUIDE

Seventh Edition

www.goodschoolsguide.co.uk

LUCAS PUBLICATIONS

Seventh Edition published 2001
by
Lucas Publications

Bowland House, West Street, Alresford, SO24 9AT

ISBN 0 9532659 2 7

A CIP catalogue record for this book is available from the British Library

Every care has been taken that all information
was correct at the time of going to press.
The publishers accept no responsibility
for any error in detail, inaccuracy
or judgement whatsoever.

Designed and typeset by Atha Bellman Associates

Printed and bound in Great Britain by The Bath Press

Contents

Editors:
Caroline Brandenburger
Sarah Drummond
Sue Fieldman
Elizabeth Lawrence
Felicity Lees Schoeman
Patrea More Nisbett
Beth Noakes
Sarah Norton
Stephanie Page
Brandon Robshaw
Jenny Steeples
Jenny Swann
Anthony Verity
Janette Wallis
Sue Wood

Editorial Assistants:

Helen Carpenter-Couchman

Ben Chambers

Jacket design by Ivor Claydon

ACKNOWLEDGEMENTS

We should also like to thank the countless friends, pupils, parents, staff (not to mention moles because they would rather we didn't) who have contributed enormously valuable information and to whom we are deeply indebted.

The delightful line illustrations in the text have been contributed by the pupils of The Edinburgh Academy. We are most grateful for their permission to reproduce them in this edition.

Introduction

Hardly a day goes by without education hitting the news headlines. Schools are constantly in the news. We have become used to government ministers bleating away daily on radio and television, to teachers being taken to court, to schools' performances being exposed, to expulsions, to reports of bullying. We have had the private/state schools entrance to Oxford and Cambridge furore and the Laura Spence debate. There have been reports on teachers' pay, and teachers' performance, and acres of league tables – 'education, education, education.'

On our rounds re-visiting schools for the seventh edition of the Good Schools Guide we have observed some significant trends. Boarding numbers are down again, and most boarding schools also take day pupils. There are only fifteen schools left with 100 per cent boarders (including seven prep schools). It is now relatively easy to get a place in even the most academic boarding establishments. There are larger numbers of foreign children in our boarding schools today, (8,000 enrolled last year, 10 per cent upon the previous year, four out of ten coming from the Far East). Weekly boarding is ever more in demand. Meanwhile the pressure on places at the strongest day schools – state and private – gets fiercer. This is most noticeable in large cities, and is worst in London. The knock-on effects of competition for senior schools are to make the junior schools choosier and tougher about which pupils they accept and, we note, place more emphasis on learning at an earlier age. Whatever happened to childhood? Tests and 'assessments' are now the norm for four year-olds in the fee-paying

sector, and pushy parents demand special coaching from tutors – who usually refuse. Parents are uncomfortably aware of a disdainful arrogance among some of the most fashionable sought after schools, who can pick and choose their intake.

Private schools are moving in on the childcare market in a big way. We observe an increased demand from parents for 'daily boarding' – schools which offer supervision from 8 o'clock in the morning, before school starts, until at least 6, sometimes, 8 o'clock at night in the case of boarding plus day schools. They give the pupils tea after school, supervise homework and then provide supper if required. A few day schools are discovering this is a vote winner for working parents. More prep schools have added on a feeder pre-prep, and there appears to be a trend for these to sprout a nursery (nappies no longer necessarily barred) – for three-month-old babies in at least one case.

In London, several co-ed prep schools have grown upwards to cover GCSEs, or even, in one case A levels as well. Cuts down on the marketing costs, and keeps the school run simple – but is it really best for the kids?

Some areas report increasing numbers of parents who could (just) afford private schooling, now opting for senior state schools, especially where there are selective state grammar schools. Fee-paying senior school heads are now to be found trawling state primaries and hoping to attract the brightest pupils.

Co-ed is much in demand, particularly at the pre-teen stage. But now that the latest showing of exam results have demonstrated that boys and girls do better separately will there be a sudden rush to single sex schools? We note a certain rubbing of the hands among schools who have solidly remained single sex in the face of changing fashions. There is a new trend, as yet in an experimental stage, in a few brother/sister schools (some of them previously co-ed), for boys and girls to be taught separately at senior level.

On the academic front, yet more coursework and modules at GCSE, and parents report their children tackling increasing mounds of homework. Tutor groups tell us there is a hugely increased demand for coaching in study skills, with pupils wanting help on essay planning and exam techniques. A levels have now given way to A2s, preceded by AS examinations – a new phase that is being watched with interest. Heads report that this means far harder work for pupils in their penultimate year - often a time when teenagers have managed to coast along and slack off: no longer. For all the talk, so far there has been only a small take up of the International Baccalaureate, though we suspect more schools will opt for IB in time.

Pressure is a word you hear all too often in school circles – alas. We have heard of children having mini nervous breakdowns at the age of ten. Teachers at the highest performing schools have complained that pressure to stay at the top end of the league tables means they have to spend more time teaching to the exams. – allowing less room for creativity. Parents are more league table conscious than ever (so are schools) but parents now appear slightly more realistic about them, recognising that as long as their school is within fifty places of its previous position it is probably doing well.

We found bigger and better IT rooms, computers everywhere, though teachers are discovering serious problems of authenticity with work done on computers, including the downloading of entire essays. Laptops in classrooms are still relatively rare. More and more children are in need of help with learning difficulties – but this need is not always well met. Dyslexic children – from the brightest to the dumbest – are often lumped together. Help for dyspraxics is still thin on the ground.

Finding places for non-academic children gets harder by the term, and even heads of some hot-house schools have commented that parents today are increasingly interested in extra-curricular activities – is this the natural backlash to so much pressure? All-round schools with a broader intake and curriculum are seeing their numbers of academic pupils increasing, and the danger is that these schools could get over-run with academic children and become the very cloistered, elitist institutions that parents and pupils want to escape from. It is a truly strong-minded head who turns away bright pupils in favour of a mixed intake.

Other trends we note: more anorexia, particularly among the high powered girls schools – and we wonder whether schools are observant enough of the early signs. It is heartening to know/hear that a few schools now invite experts on eating disorders to talk to pupils.

Parents, we note, have become more litigious – whether over money, bullying, teachers or teaching. Is this the American influence at work? Parents demand 'inspirational' teaching for their children – that is almost the most frequent request of parents seeking help via the Good Schools Advisory Service. Parents are getting beadier about their choice, and we are hearing reports from schools that parents tend to visit a school several times. They are, by the way, increasingly fed up with the school run – and schools that offer proper transport covering a large area are becoming increasingly popular. Mind you, currently the favourite way for scores of younger children to get to school is by scooter.

As usual, large numbers of heads have been on the merry go round. Governors report they are having a harder time finding really top class heads, and they are getting younger. It is not infrequent to hear complaints from parents that they don't think the head is up to the job, or is not a patch on the previous person. Selling the school and public relations is blatant in both sectors and at all ages.

Pastoral care is as much of an important issue as ever. Bullying is bad all over the place, it is sad to report. Drugs ditto. Drink poses a perennial problem – not just the post exam. high spirits (the Euan Blair factor), but as a common or garden problem in a lot of schools. Heads, like parents, find today's young hard to handle: how do you teach freedom and responsibility? Heads will tell you that they deal with problems of good order and discipline that parents don't always want to face at home. Recently staff stuck their heads above the parapet to demand that more is done to help 'tweenagers' – in other words, problems are starting younger. The sub-language of school children is foul and shocking nowadays, even in the toffest establishments. Pupils who look smart are the exception rather than the rule: scruffiness is particularly noticeable at schools without uniforms.

Mobile phones are with us – schools have had to accept them, however unwillingly, it seems. In any break time now you are likely to see hordes of children talking on their mobiles: only a few schools restrict use to before lessons start and after the school day finishes. Chat lines on the internet are another menace. It's worth asking your child's school spell out the school policy, since we have heard some hair-raising stories of the young spending hours chatting on line, unsupervised and unsuitably.

Money: fees at private schools have gone up again, the record being set last year by a demand for a forty per cent rise in one school (a week after the new crop of pupils had signed up). Scholarships continue to be spread broader and thinner, and several fee-paying schools, hard-hit by the loss of assisted places, have set up their own bursaries and scholarship funds. One or two remarkable philanthropists have set up trusts to help the needy obtain private education.

At *The Good Schools Guide* we have embarked on two years of expansion and improvement. As boarding declines, schooling is becoming a much more local affair; we are increasing our coverage of local schools, and in particular state schools, throughout the UK. We shall remain selective – do not expect to find all the good but ordinary schools in the Good Schools Guide – but will aim to cover the best of each type of school in each local area, rather than setting a national standard for inclusion. We will, though, judge schools against a common standard. If you know good schools that you think should be in the guide, please tell us about them. New schools are being added to the web site all the time, as are updates on the schools that we cover now; the depth and range of information on the site are increasing too.

There is no such thing as the perfect school, as we all know – but there is a huge breadth of variety and no two schools are quite alike. What matters is to find the school that really suits your particular child. Small wonder, then, that more and more families move house in order to be near their children's school.

How to read this book

Read between the lines. For obvious reasons we have had to be mealy-mouthed at times. For example, 'keen' could mean just that, or it may mean enthusiastic but not actually very good.

The curate's egg is still with us. 'Sport not worshipped' could mean they don't play games when it's wet and couldn't care less when they lose.

If you are looking for the junior department of a senior school and don't find it in the prep section, look at the end of the relevant senior school.

If a school is not included in the book this does not necessarily mean it is not a good school – our selection is a personal one.

Sussing out a School and Horses for Courses

Every single reference book on schools indulges in advice on this. Lists of questions tend to make heads bristle, but going in as a parent can be daunting. The following is a list of guidelines we drew up as we went around. Obviously not all are applicable to every school: ask even half these questions and you will probably never be invited back again, but it does no harm to take them along for prompting.

ACTION

1. Send for the prospectus, a copy of the school magazine, list of governors, and ask for the last three years' results (for senior schools) and leavers' destinations (for junior schools), the latest Ofsted or ISC inspection report (and the school's reply to it), and any other bumf – and read it. This saves time on crucial matters such as registration, subjects offered, exeats, though some of the information may be out of date. NB Ofsted reports, good as they are, are written in obscure language by educationalists, can be hard to penetrate, and may entirely fail to see the school from a parental point of view; ISC reports are too cosy by half – read with a large pinch of salt.

2. Make an appointment to see the head and to see round the school. You may find you are fobbed off with an open day, registrars, etc, and for big schools with large numbers of applicants this is an understandable way to start. It is, however, time-consuming for you: remember you have to meet the head – no amount of wonderful buildings make up for a rotten one.

3. What to wear? Projecting the right image – not too smart (particularly if you are looking for a cut-price offer), but not dowdy either. No school wants to feel they are attracting dull people, and if you have something to offer, however humble, tell them.

4. On the day of your visit, get to the school early in order to sniff around. Approach children/staff and ask them anything (eg where is the main school notice board?). It's amazing how telling their replies can be.

WHAT TO LOOK OUT FOR

What are the pupils like? Do you want your child to be like that? Bearing of pupils – politeness, neatness. Bearing of staff, ditto. Do they look clean, bright-eyed and bushy-tailed (or whatever you like)? Attitude of pupils to staff and vice versa. Does the head know who they all are (you'd be surprised)? Do pupils flatten themselves against the wall as the head passes? Do they flatten him/her against the wall as they pass. (If so, do they stop and say sorry?) Is self-confidence universal, or confined to just some kids (and if so, which ones?) Is the atmosphere happy? Fraught? Coerced or co-opted? Do you fall over pupils smoking in corners? How many are slumped in front of the television (key question when visiting around 1.30pm especially)? Do the drains smell? What is the state of the paintwork, etc – a glance at the ceiling will usually tell (not that it matters per se).

Grab an exercise book or three in passing and look at the standard of work and the standard of marking – this can tell you an enormous amount. Check the size of teaching groups – it's amazing how often numbers do not tally with the official version. What is the average age of the staff? All old can mean not enough dynamic new ideas or energy; all young can mean too inexperienced and also, possibly, too transitory. Ask if you can pop in to a class, or have a good long look through the peep holes, and see what is really happening: are the children dozing, is the teacher dozing, is there rapport between the teacher and the taught?

What's on the walls – look for evidence of creativity and the celebration of pupils' achievements. Observe the state of the library: rows of dusty tomes look impressive but bright, new and dog-eared is healthier. Where is the library – is it in a useful position, do the troops use it? What is the annual book budget? And, incidentally, where is the head's study: is he in the thick of things, ie finger on the pulse, or is he still in his ivory tower? Look at notice boards for signs of plenty going on, and names you know

(for grilling later).

What are the computer facilities like? Are there enough for all the kids all the time (according to the school? According to the kids?) – go-ahead schools are starting to use a laptop each. (Alternative view: Image-conscious schools are using a laptop each. Lap tops are a pain in the fundament to most schools, parents and even pupils who have to worry about losing them and – if their parents are buying them rather than the school supplying them – have to worry about whether their model is sufficiently cool.) Are keyboarding/typing skills universal? Is good use made of the internet, and is the internet access fast? Do all teachers use computers in class as an integral part of lessons, or just some of them? Is the school proud of its imaginative use of computers?

Finally, do you like the look of the parents, and would you be happy for your children to mix with theirs?

QUESTIONS TO HAVE UP YOUR SLEEVE

1. What are the results like? This is one for the head. Watch the whites of his eyes as he gives you the answer – and see section on What the League Tables Don't Tell You.

2. What are the 'value added' scores like? Most schools now use one system or another of monitoring value added – the improvement in pupils' performance over the years. Very few publish it (yet), but you should be allowed a glimpse.

3. How does the school monitor progress (pupils and, indeed, staff?) School reports? Point systems? Incentives? Regular tests? The best will be integrated with the value added system.

4. How much does the school spend on staff training, and what do they train them

to do? Do any of the staff write school books or work as chief examiners?

5. What is the size of the classes – biggest and smallest? (Though NB a good teacher teaches any class size competently; bad teachers do not become good teachers by reducing class size.)

6. What is the ratio of full-time teaching staff to pupils? How many part-timers are there? How part-time are they?

7. What is the turn-over of staff – do too many stay too long? NB you are unlikely to get a straight answer on this.

8. Which exam boards are taken? (This doesn't help, but shows you are on the ball.)

9. What is the size of the library budget? What arrangements are there for getting hold of new books, papers?

10. What special projects are currently on the go?

11. Does the school have special help on tap for special learning difficulties? If so, how much help, in what form, and is it going to cost you extra? If this is of particular interest to you, see Dyslexia, Dyspraxia and Other Special Needs. NB mainstream schools that do well by children with SENs are often excellent places for all sorts too – the systems of individual attention and understanding that support SEN pupils mean that any child in any trouble is picked up quickly and dealt with sympathetically. Also nurtures 'diagnostic teaching' – not 'it's wrong' but 'what's wrong.'

12. Does the school feel responsible for pupils once they are accepted – or will it fire misfits/slow learners if they don't shape up quickly? How many pupils leave after GCSE and why? Are any encouraged to leave then (as not up to A levels, etc? V bad

news) (They may not be honest about this.)

13. How many are imported into the sixth form from outside? NB this probably will affect the school's results and needs to be looked at with a beady eye, ie they may be reaping the benefits of another school's hard work.

14. How is the school coping with the new A level system? Do pupils have more or less work to do, more or less time for extras, a more interesting spread of choice of courses? None of this will show in results until 2002. Talk to some sixth formers about how they are finding it.

15. What is the pressure of work? Amount of work? Homework? Setting? Streaming?

16. How involved are parents with the school? Can parents talk to (or email) teachers when they want to? Is there special provision for parents on the school website? How does the school report to parents? How often are school reports issued? Monthly? Termly? You would be surprised how many fee-paying schools only provide one written report a year.

17. What emphasis is there (if any) on religious teaching? Daily chapel? Daily assembly? Weekly chapel? Are special arrangements made for any other faiths – and what are they? Some schools claiming to cater for eg RCs make it quite hard for them to get to mass. How many of each faith are in the school?

18. How are pupils selected? What is the school looking for in the pupils it takes?

19. Is there automatic promotion from the Junior School to the Senior? If not, under what circumstances are pupils rejected, and how many each year?

20. Who are the pupils and where do they

come from? (Both geographically and socially?) How many Brits and in particular how many non–Brits whose first language is not English? Too many of the latter can grind teaching to a halt – very few schools can afford to cater for them separately.

21. Where do pupils go on to?

22. What is the careers advice like?

23. What scholarships are available and won? What bursaries and funding are available when finances come adrift?

24. The cost: fees, plus real cost, ie size of bill? Some schools quote an 'all-in' fee, others quote tuition fees only and charge massively for extras (such as lunch!) 'Extras' are usually listed on a separate sheet of paper (because they constantly rise) and tucked into the back of the prospectus.

25. Are games compulsory? CCF?

26. What subjects and extras are on offer? Can they really deliver? Beware: schools are inclined to pay lip-service. A small school offering dozens of extras is probably doing none of them very well.

27. What languages are genuinely on offer (ie without having to import the local Chinese take-away man)?

28. How many learn a musical instrument, and for how long? Are practise sessions time-tabled? What proportion of these are taught privately outside the school? This can be quite telling if you are trying to suss out the strength of a school's music department. Also: what does music tuition cost? The price of a half-hour piano lesson can vary by a hundred per cent from school to school.

29. Who owns the school? If privately owned – though few are – are there any checks and balances, eg governors, PTA, etc, and to whom do you make out your cheque? Who takes over when the current owner calls it a day?

30. How does the head run the school? As a Thatcher, as a Major, as a Blair?

31. What are the head's ambitions for the school and for him/her self? What is his/her history? What does he/she regard as most important? What does he/she really want for the pupils in the long run?

32. Until when is the head 'contracted'? (ie is he/she about to leave)? Is he/she married, with children (ie hands-on experience)?

33. What is the head's attitude to discipline? Drugs? Sex? Alcohol? Homosexuality? Stealing? Bad language? Breaking the more petty school rules? What form do punishments take? Are prefects allowed to mete it out? Ask for a copy of the school rules – this can be illuminating – and ask how they have been established (from on high? With pupils?)

34. What does the school do about bullying? Bullying is universal, so 'we don't have it here' probably means they don't look, and there's lots of it. A good sign – frequent examples of dealing well with it. Who chooses the prefects? 'The boys alone' is an invitation to bullying, 'the staff alone choose the nicest boys' the kindest.

35. How many people have been expelled, asked to leave, suspended in the last two years? (This could pinpoint specific major problems.)

36. Who would not be happy at the school?

37. What is the pastoral care like and who is responsible to whom and are problems spotted early? Is there a tutorial system

(moral or academic)? What special arrangements are there for boarders (and what are the housemasters / house parents like?)

38. How good is the health care? Do they notice if pupils skip meals? How aware is the school of the dangers and signs of anorexia? Is there a cafeteria system or a table laid and 'table talk'? How much fresh raw food is there?

39. What are the present numbers in the school? What has the trend been like over the last five years, and why? (NB you need to look at the trend within age groups to see which bits of the school are popular, and also factor in any change to co-ed.) What is the school's capacity?

40. What is the acreage? Or square metreage (NB there are government guidelines on the minimum amount per child, but not all schools meet them)?

41. What is the structure of the school What houses are there, if any? What is the school hierarchy?

42. For boarding schools, how do parent and child communicate? Weekly letter? A phone for each fifty pupils? Or nightly emails and a mobile phone?

43. Is there any privacy for boarders?

44. What happens in the school at weekends? How many pupils are around then?

45. How often are boarders allowed home? Are there weekends when they have to go home (and what are overseas parents supposed to do about this?)

46. Are boarders allowed up to town at weekends? How does the school control what they get up to? How can parents ditto?

47. Is there a shadowing system for new pupils? Any special arrangements in place to welcome pupil who comes in at an odd moment, eg the middle of term?

48. How much pocket money is suggested? A vital question this.

49. What is the temperature at the school in the winter? (a question for Scottish and seaside schools particularly).

50. Is there a second-hand shop?

51. Is this a Neighbours watching school, and what is the school's attitude to watching television?

52. Is there a holiday reading list, and is there holiday homework ever? Never?

53. What are the strengths of this school – and weaknesses? (Always interesting to hear the answer to this.)

54. For boys' schools which have gone co-ed in the last 20 years: How many female academic staff are there? How many girls are there? What provision is there for them to play games (small numbers mean no hope of making up teams)? What facilities are there for them? What is the school's policy on boy/girl relationships?

55. (At prep/junior schools) do staff sit with pupils at meal times and supervise table manners, etc or is lunchtime intended to be a break for the teachers?

QUESTIONS FOR PUPILS

1. What is the food like?

2. What subjects do you like best? (This often reveals the most popular members of staff.)

3. What do you like best about the school?

4. What do pupils value / care about / look up to pupils for being good at (in rank

order) – eg work, sport, social life, drama, art?

5. What changes would you make if you were in charge?

6. Where is the head's office?

7. Are you happy here? What sort of kid would not fit in here?

8. Are you allowed to get on with your own thing without teasing or bullying? (This might flush out peer group pressure to conform.)

9. Boarding school question: what do you do at weekends? (Does this correspond with what the school says happens?)

10. Have you got a brother or sister in the school, what does he/she think?

11. Why did you choose this school, and what do you think of the others that you might have chosen?

QUESTION FOR THE LOCAL SHOP/TAXI DRIVER/ESTATE AGENT

What is the school like? This can produce a flood of enlightening comment.

What the League Tables Don't Tell You

League tables have caused a lot of agony and misunderstanding. As we have said elsewhere, as raw statistics, they are more or less meaningless. You will observe, for a start, that results swing wildly according to which newspaper you happen to look at. Among other things they don't tell you:

1. The pupils' IQ: two Ds for some pupils is a triumph of wonderful teaching.

2. The pupils' background: how much help/support are they getting at home?

3. The school's background: is it academically selective or mixed ability? How many are on Assisted Places/scholarships (abolition of the former will change the profile of some schools out of recognition, but this will not show in the results yet).

4. The school's policy towards A levels: do they allow pupils to 'have a go' or to take an extra A level (for stretching/breadth). Do they operate a policy of dissuading borderline candidates from taking a subject?

5. The school's policy at sixth form? Are they pinching, for example, bright girls from neighbouring girls' schools? Or are they turfing out their less able pupils? Do they insist on very high (A grade) GCSEs in proposed A level subjects for those coming into the school at sixth form?

6. Good years and bad years: is this a blip, a one-off? There may be exceptional circumstances, eg death of a teacher six months before the exam.

7. What subjects are taken. Some are considered easier than others, eg business studies, classical civilisation. The league tables do not tell you (at the time of writing) which schools are taking general studies at A level: A level general studies can push league table ratings up no end.

8. What is the spread of subjects at A level? Which are popular, which neglected? Does that profile fit your child – it may reflect the relative quality of teaching, or just the spirit of the school.

9. Is there a large enough number of children doing really well, especially in subjects that you are interested in, to form a cohort of excellence that will give leadership and confidence to the rest of the school? Are sufficiently few pupils failing altogether to avoid the reverse effect?

10. The quality of education overall: depth, breadth, all-round, music, debating, etc, etc – can he/she think for him/herself? By sheer swotting, exams can be successfully passed – but at the expense of what?

11. The reliability of the figures: the more pupils there are, the more statistically significant the results are.

12. Also, watch out for Scottish schools lurking in among the English league tables. Many Scottish schools offer two systems, ie Scottish Highers (usually for the weaker brethren), and A levels. Only the A levels show up in the league tables.

13. The results of children who took the exam late. Schools that encourage pupils to polish off GCSEs as and when the kids feel ready may come off looking worse than they should – the separate Year 11 column in the tables may be a better indication of their quality.

INTERPRETING RESULTS
(as best you can)

This is what you need to ask the school:

1. Have they anything to declare – any special circumstances?

2. Ask for a complete breakdown of exam results for the last three years, ie a complete list of subjects taken showing the number of pupils taking each subject and the number achieving each grade from A to U. If you are fobbed off with a 'summary' of results,

be indignant and suspicious – they are asking you to trust them with your child, so why won't they trust you to react sensibly to the results. Ask also which year group took the exams – make sure that retakes and early examinations are listed separately.

3. With all this in front of you and a cold towel wrapped around your head, look to see where the weaknesses/strengths are to be found. Which are the popular and successful subjects? Is one subject pulling the overall results up? Or down? Or is 100 per cent A-grade pass in Norwegian translated as one pupil (with a Norwegian mother)?

4. How many pupils are taking exams over all? A school with a sixth form of 40 (three children doing each subject) should find it considerably easier to come up high on the league tables than larger schools. The larger the number taking any one subject, the more commendable when the results are strong, and the wider the scope for failure. (Watch out for sudden improvements, particularly in main stream subjects, and look warily at the numbers of candidates: if the number has halved from one year to the next, could it be that the school policy has been to force out the weaker candidates and so manipulate the results?)

5. This will give you some idea of what is going on and where the weak teaching might be (or perhaps it is just that the less academic children tend to take that subject – there is no way of knowing without asking). Now you are in a position to ask the head to explain those appalling geography results, and to explain what he is doing about the situation. Listen carefully, because all schools have weaknesses, and the important thing is what is being done to remedy them. Ask for the ALIS/MIDYIS or other value added data, which should show how

good the results really are allowing for the quality of individual pupils. But at the end of the day, remember that league tables are only one often unreliable indicator of how a school performs. And, of course, this still won't tell you which is the right school for your child.

Entrance

Fee-Paying Schools

As a rule of thumb this is what you do:

1. Visit the schools you have short-listed, take a tour round them and talk with the head and/or housemaster or whoever is appropriate. (V time-consuming, but infinitely less so than making the wrong choice.)

2. Register the child's name in the school(s) you have chosen. Telephone the school and they will send you an application/registration form. (If your child is still in the cradle, and the schools you have your eye on are v oversubscribed, you may decide to register before visiting.)

3. Fill it in. This has to be done at the right moment or the 'list' may be 'full'. Embryos are acceptable at some schools. It will usually cost a registration fee (usually non-returnable) ranging from £25 to £200 or more.

4. The school will then contact you and your child's current school about the next stage (it doesn't hurt to telephone and check, though, if you think they may have forgotten you — and don't forget to tell them if you change your address). They will usually get a report from the head of your child's current school and attention is usually paid to that.

5. The child is usually, though not always, put through his/her paces, which might mean an exam, a test or two, or 'meaningful' play or whatever. (NB you might also — openly or surreptitiously — be put through your paces as well: are you good parents, is there discipline in the home, are you educated, have you some wonderful attribute the school might be able to use?)

6. All being well, the school will then offer a firm place. You must write and confirm acceptance of this place or it may be offered to someone else. NB you will probably be asked for a large non-returnable deposit at this stage (can be hundreds of pounds). Those public schools that require boys to attend an exam/assessment when they are ten/eleven may require a massive cheque when the child is still years away from leaving prep school.

7. Pay school fees — in advance of the term is normal practice, alas.

8. Read any contract you have to sign carefully: if in any doubt eg what do they mean by 'a term's notice' a little legal advice at this stage can save you a lot of agony later.

There are a few variations on this theme. For example, grammar schools will often accept entries up to the last minute, though there will be an official date for closing the 'list', from about three weeks to three terms before the exam.

TIP

All things being equal, always have a go at

the school you think is right for your child. Even those schools you have been told are jam packed may have a place. Don't restrict yourself to trying at the 'normal' entry periods. Dare to try mid-term, and mid-academic year, or even the day before term starts. If you get a no, don't be afraid to try again.

State Schools

Since the 1980 Education Act, you, the parent, have been able to express a preference for the school at which you wish to have your child educated, and the local authority or school in question has a duty to comply with any preference expressed unless:

a) compliance with the preference would prejudice the provision of efficient education or the efficient use of resources or b) the school is an aided or special agreement school, or compliance with the preference would be incompatible with any arrangements that have been made between the governors and the local education authority in respect of admission of pupils to the school or c) the arrangements for admission to the preferred school are based 'wholly or partly on selection by reference to ability or partly on selection by reference to ability or aptitude and compliance with the preference would be incompatible with selection under the arrangements'.

This system needs to be understood in the light of the particular admissions criteria of each school, ie it is a complicated mess. Geographical location can be particularly important though, and parents have been known to rent houses within the catchment area of the school in order to establish residence there. Many good schools have special admissions arrangements for particular talents – they may specialise in languages, science or sports, or they may admit a few

talented musicians; if so, consider some targeted coaching.

You may also be faced with arrangements that require you to state your preferences in order of priority. You may need to do some careful research to decide which schools to put on your list. Top comprehensives in areas that have grammar schools may refuse to consider your child if you have also applied to a grammar school; you may not be considered by your local school if you have put another as your first choice. The threat you are faced with is that if you aim for the best and miss, you may only be offered a sink school miles away. This makes life easy for schools and difficult for parents. We (but not this government or most LEAs) think that this is entirely the wrong way round – but it's unlikely to change. It makes it essential that you find out how the rules work in your area, and are realistic about your first choice.

If you get what appears to be a 'No' on any count you have the right of appeal, stating to an Appeal Committee why you think little Edna should go to Grunts and not St Dumps. One of the most successful reasons seems to be health: if you can get a doctor's letter stating that your ewe lamb gets asthma and will only flourish in the pure air of Grunts, you are half-way there. Like any other appeal you need to lobby like mad – the head, the governors, the doctor, the local authority, your MP, the lollipop man – whoever seems good to you.

Thoughts for Parents

FIRSTLY and most importantly, what is your child really like? This is your starting point for finding the school to suit him/her rather than you.

SECONDLY, what do you want for your child? It helps to have a game plan, even if you change it at a later date, eg state or fee-paying? Day or boarding? Single sex or co-ed?

THIRDLY, what do you want from the school? Make an honest list for yourself of everything that occurs to you, however ambitious, frivolous or peripheral it may seem. You must both do this. Your list may include, for example: happiness, safety, beauty of architecture, a stepping stone to university, social status, very local, very convenient, exeats that fit in with your career, offers Japanese, doesn't cost too much (if anything). Are you looking for a traditional approach, or something totally different? What do you really feel and think about co-education?

Beware the danger of judging a school exclusively by the bottom end because your child is young – look at the end product. How and where do you want your child to end up? Is there a member of staff at the school who is on the same wavelength as yourself? There must be someone you can turn to (particularly true of boarding).

See several schools – it's a process of elimination, and comparisons are vital to make. Go by your gut reaction. Were you impressed with the head (you don't have to like him/her, but it helps)? Did he/she appear in control of the situation? The head really does make or break a school.

Finally, did you come out feeling good?

Notes for Foreign Parents

Most UK schools are now genuinely thrilled to welcome in foreign students, and no longer regard a cosmopolitan mix as a matter for shame (that they cannot fill the school with home-grown products). Foreign students are perceived to add breadth, excitement, new horizons, not to mention fantastic exam results in exotic languages (Turkish, Norwegian, Polish, Mandarin, Japanese, Gujerati, Urdu among the most common), high intelligence (often), motivation – and last but not least, cash.

The best schools in this country are outstanding by any standards. Beware, though, of being fobbed off with second-rate places.

Here are a few thoughts from overseas parents who are already in the UK system:

1. Be on the look out for academic schools which pay lip service to 'potential' but in reality they are usually only interested in performance on the day of the entrance exam. No use explaining your child is trilingual and English is his/her fourth language – they do not want to take the risk or have the bother.

2. The majority of schools in this country are not geared to teaching the English language to pupils who don't know it. Beware of schools which have a high proportion of foreigners, but no real way of teaching them English. (Schools which have very few foreigners in the school are another matter – being immersed in a language without the option is the quickest way to learn, particularly for younger children.)

3. If a school says it has got 'provision' for teaching English as a Foreign Language (EFL), ask exactly what that provision consists of, and whether it will cost extra. EFL teachers need to have a proper teaching degree/diploma as well as an EFL qualification. (The latter means very little.)

4. Don't ask the impossible. Do not, for example, expect an English academic secondary school to cater at public exam level for a pupil whose English is almost non-existent. However quick at learning your child is, he/she will certainly struggle at this

stage – the pressure of work is just too high.

5. Be prepared to 'sell' yourself a bit to the school. Private schools in this country have a tendency to ask what you can do for them, rather than what they can do for you. This shocks parents from other countries, but it is a fact.

6. Ask what arrangements a boarding school has for exeats (weekends when the pupils are allowed away from the school premises). There is an increasing tendency in the UK towards 'weekly' and 'flexi' boarding where pupils can go home any weekend they want. If you live overseas, this is obviously bad news. It is best, if you can, to opt for a 'full' boarding school, which has a proper programme of activities at the weekend, and one or two pre-arranged exeats per term.

7. Ask what the school would do if your child were to be found guilty of a serious misdemeanour (drugs etc). You do not want to find him/her ejected from the school at a moment's notice.

8. Ask what arrangements are made at the end of public exam terms. There is an increasing tendency to send pupils home early once they have finished their exams – sometimes weeks and weeks early. Again, not good news for overseas parents. You need to know that the school has a proper programme of activities to keep pupils occupied until the last official day of term.

9. Beware of 'international centres' which have just been set up. They may one day be good, but meanwhile, your child is a guinea pig while the new centre learns the ropes.

10. Do not assume a school is good simply because it is famous (an obvious point, but you would be surprised how many people believe famous equals good).

11. If – once your child is in a school – he tells you he is miserable/homesick/being bullied – believe him. Act at once by telephoning the school and explaining the problem. If the problem persists, consider taking your child out of the school and finding another, more compatible one. Better a temporary disruption to your child's schooling than permanent damage.

12. Consider doing a summer/holiday course before opting for main stream schooling. There are courses which take place in British public schools, for example, which will give your child a 'feel' for what's in store – and get the English up to scratch. The British Council vets most such courses, and lists the ones that it approves of.

13. Always go and see a school you are interested in yourself – or at least send someone whose judgement you trust (and who knows your child). You will be surprised how much you can learn about a place from even a brief look.

14. Look for a school that is popular with the British as well as with foreigners – talk to personal contacts if possible. The British Embassies abroad – www.tagish. co.uk/ – and British Council – www.britcoun.org/ –are both often useful initial points of contact, but don't rely on their advice over particular schools.

15. UK 'placement' agencies will give you a list of schools in the UK which have places available when you ask – beware, though, as these are usually no more than lists, and do not differentiate between the good, the bad and the ugly. Such agencies are usually paid fat commissions by the schools they recommend, and may be reluctant to mention those schools that do not pay them a commission (this includes many of the more famous ones).

Money Matters

Schools in this country are mostly state funded, ie paid for by the government and local authorities from taxes. A small proportion are private, funded mostly from fees paid by parents, but also indirectly by the state, given that most private schools enjoy charitable status. (Approximately 7 per cent of children in education are at fee-paying schools.) Fees range from under £1,000 per term to almost £4,000 per term for a day pupil – with wide variations depending on the age of the child, the staff/pupil ratio and so on – and £1,500 (if you're v lucky) to £5,000++ per term for boarding.

FEE-PAYING SCHOOLS: BARGAIN HUNTING

SCHOLARSHIPS: These are to attract the academically bright or specifically talented child (art, music, science, sports, all round – and one or two amazing ones for eg chess) and they vary in amount. Girls' schools, alas, offer fewer and less valuable scholarships. As a rule of thumb, the old famous foundations are the richest. (They may well disclaim this, but all is relative.) The largest scholarships awarded by HMC and GSA schools are now normally 50 per cent of the full fees, which was a policy decision made a few years ago to spread the bunce around. However, we note that almost all schools are now breaking ranks on this and offering to 'top up' your 'scholarship' with a means-tested 'bursary'. (There are also, NB, schools offering scholarships which hardly cover the cost of extras.) There are also some schools which have a statutory number of full scholarships to offer (eg Eton, Westminster, St Paul's) – and from them 'full' may include the cost of uniforms and travel to school.

Watch out for esoteric scholarships, eg sons and daughters of clergy, medics, single mothers, etc. If your name is West and you live in the parish of Twickenham there could be a bursary waiting for you (at Christ's Hospital). Scholarships to choir schools are worth thinking about, but they will not cover full fees and the children work incredibly hard for them (and it is worth asking what happens when their voices break?). But NB this could well be the beginning of a music scholarship into public school.

If you are after a musical scholarship then 'Music Awards at Independent Schools' from the Music Masters and Mistresses' Association, by Jonathan Varcoe, may be just what you need.

Keep your eyes open for internal scholarships which run at various stages, sixth form especially. Of course, there are also increasing numbers of schools luring pupils in at sixth form with generous scholarships: might be worth moving schools for.

USELESS SCHOLARSHIPS: Don't fall for them. It is a false economy to be flattered into going to the wrong school for £200 off the bill. You may be much better off with a school with slightly lower fees to start with but no scholarship on offer. By the way, it is well worth lobbying for 10 per cent off in any case – if you have three children you should be able to negotiate a job lot. (Heads are used to this, wary of it – but take courage: this is the way the world now is. Of course, you may get a raspberry.)

BURSARIES: Usually for helping out the impoverished but deserving and those fallen on hard times. We have listed them as far as possible under each school, but a more complete collection will be found in the Independent Schools Yearbook (see Useful Addresses and Books).

ASSISTED PLACES: These were offered by the government for children of impoverisheds who were judged to 'benefit' from private education (ie, usually bright ones). They have now been abolished, but we have noted their existence under Money Matters for individual entries, because their abolition has had serious repercussions for many schools, and, as the existing assisted place pupils work their way through the system, there could well be a dip in league table standings as schools are forced to fill their places with less able children.

CHARITABLE TRUSTS: Charitable grant-making trusts can help in cases of genuine need. ISIS (the Independent Schools Information Service) warns parents considering this route: 'Do not apply for an education grant for your child unless the circumstances are exceptional. The grant-giving trust will reject applications unless their requirements are satisfied. The genuine needs recognised by the grant-making trusts are:

a) boarding need, where the home environment is unsuitable because of the disability or illness of the parents or of siblings,

b) unforeseen family disaster, such as the sudden death of the breadwinner when a child is already at school,

c) need for continuity when a pupil is in the middle of a GCSE or A level course and a change in parental circumstances threatens withdrawal from school,

d) need for special education where there is a genuine recognised learning handicap which cannot be catered for at a state school.'

If you want to explore this road, the key books are: The Educational Grants Directory (specifically directed at funding for schoolchildren and students in need), The guide to the Major Trusts (in three volumes), The Directory of Grant Making Trusts and the Charities Digest – most come out annually with a year suffix to the title, and you should be able to find one or more in your local library.

OTHER CHEAPOS: Certain schools are relatively cheap. The Livery Companies, eg Haberdashers and also Mercers etc, fund various schools, eg Haberdasher's Monmouth, Gresham's. Such schools are usually excellent value – not only cheap(er), but good facilities.

Also cheap, but with fewer frills, are The Girls' Day Schools Trust (GDST) schools – see Useful Addresses and Books.

Take great care in comparing fees between schools. Some quote an all-in fee, others seem cheaper but have a load of unavoidable 'extras' – school meals, trips, insurance, etc, etc that can add up to 25 per cent to the bill.

It may well be worth considering sending your child as a day pupil to a big strong boarding school. This way you will reap the benefits at a lesser price (though sometimes the day fees are ridiculous).

PAYING THE FEES

There are any number of wizard wheezes on the market. The schools offer 'composition fees', which means, in a nutshell, you put a sum of money down one year and get a sum of money back later. The 'school fee specialists' offer endowment-backed, mortgage-backed schemes, etc, which, in effect, do the same thing. Either way, you are stepping into deep waters. Unless you totally understand what you are doing and all the implications – how the money is being invested, what the returns are, how it compares with any other investment, what the charges are, hidden and otherwise, etc, etc, we think it might be safest to avoid such schemes.

This does not mean you should not plan, ie save and invest. The earlier you start, the better – obviously enough.

Given the astronomic sums involved, it is worth looking very carefully at what you are actually buying. Most good schools have viable numbers, but there are still those that are struggling, and you need to know that the school you are interested in is in good financial health. This is easier said than done. A good indicator is to compare the number of pupils this year with last year and indeed the year before that. The numbers should not show too marked a dip (though NB watch out for schools whose numbers are now topped up with their new nursery/pre-prep). You can find out exact statistics through the Department for Education and Employment.

Other indicators of financial problems are: not sacking trouble makers – one sacking can mean the loss of £15,000 a year, ('This can be the difference between profit and loss', said a bursar); cutting corners in the curriculum, eg offering German one year, Spanish the next; the head being away too much drumming up business; cheap labour – Gap year students can be wonderful, but they are inexperienced and they don't last. Also look out for dilapidated buildings, dirty decor, unkempt grounds, teeny libraries, scarcity of computers.

If possible, pick a blue chip school with a rich foundation: they are better positioned to ride out any storms. Look at the Money Matters section of individual entries in this guide.

Scrutinize your bill carefully. We have noticed an increasing tendency to pop in items with a footnote (inertia selling) saying that 'unless you notify the school and deduct the amounts mentioned, it will automatically be charged to you'. For example, the Old Boys/Girls society; the ISIS membership, your 'contribution' to charities? Do not be shy about deducting these sums from your cheque.

Insurance needs particular care. Often policies are taken out automatically unless you say otherwise – and we know of for example sickness policies on offer that only pay up once the child has been ill for at least 8 days, but don't pay up for illnesses lasting longer than a term.

Getting in and out of financial difficulties

If you do get into financial difficulties, you will not be alone, and schools are very used to this. Their attitude to bill-paying and money varies hugely. The best schools are wonderful and increasingly flexible over payment – and allow, eg, monthly instalments. Bursars are expecting this request – no shame attached. Indeed the bursar has changed from the enemy to being the father confessor (with some notable exceptions – best description this year 'the bursar is a most evil toad').

A lot will depend on how well funded the school is: it is worth investigating this before you go any further. Some well-funded rich schools will pick up the tab until further notice if you fall on hard times and your child is a good egg. Most of them will do their very best to see you through exam periods, but some poor schools simply cannot afford this, however much they may wish too.

Don't assume that because they are called 'charities' that they will be charitable to you. Some may send out the debt collectors. They will hold you to the small print – ie one term's payment or one term's notice to quit really means it. They may well threaten to take you to court – though of course it will be an extremely different matter if your child is especially bright (see What the League Tables Don't Tell You).

ACTION

1. Speak to the head. Mothers and New Fathers may burst into tears at this point.

2. The head will immediately direct you to the bursar.

3. Explain your position – as optimistically, positively and realistically as possible.

4. Hope for flexible arrangements, eg monthly payments, or deferred payment.

5. Have all the scholarships gone? Is there a spare bursary?

6. Assess the situation: how vital is it to keep your child in this school? Will the world fall apart if he/she leaves now?

7. If you really feel it is vital the child stays put, try touching a relation for a loan/gift. Grandparents are still the number one source of school fees. Investigate the possibility of an extra mortgage.

8. And if it is not vital, start looking for state alternatives. See Playing the System.

Playing the System

It helps, when planning your child's journey through the maze of state and private schools, to know the main stages of jumping from one to another.

Advantages of state education are: usually it's close by, and part of community. Free school bus operates in country areas (often but by no means always) avoiding need to become full-time driver, broad social mix, no school fees, a slight edge on the private sector when it comes to Oxbridge entrance (if your child has the determination and confidence to get straight As in the state school), often greater understanding of the wide world at the end of it.

Advantages of the private system are: (usually) a better chance of doing well in public exams, especially for an average child, though there are many exceptions; often better academic (as opposed to pastoral) care; a wider range of extras; smaller classes; the opportunity to start modern languages earlier, the opportunity to board.

Age 2+-4+. Kindergarten/nursery, particularly in the private sector.

Age 4. 'Pre-prep' starts in the private sector.

Age 5. Education is compulsory in the UK. Year 1, in the English state system, is the year beginning in the September following the child's fifth birthday.

Age 7-8. 'Prep' school starts in the private sector. If you have a boy headed for the private system, you may need to take him out of the state system at this stage in order to get in enough coaching to pass the entry exam (see below).

Age 11. State secondary schools and grammar schools usually start ie in year 7. Grammar schools are by definition selective and a wheeze used by some parents is to put children into private schools until the age of 11 in order to train them up for getting into the state grammar of their choice – thus avoiding the fees thereafter. The important thing here is to be in the right geographical place at the right time to qualify for entry to good/popular ones, which are increasingly oversubscribed (and be prepared for inflated house prices). However, in some areas secondary schooling starts at 12 or 13.

A few private prep schools open up a new class for very clever ten/eleven-year-olds from state schools to coach them up for entry to their senior schools at 13 CE.

Girls may move from the state system to the private one at the age of 11, which can work well as there is a 'break' in both state and private systems for them. Extra tuition may be needed in English and maths if moving to the private sector – coaching after school is the answer.

Age 13 (or thereabouts). Move to most private secondary (public) schools for boys, and to private co-educational establishments, though NB some have lowered their entry age to eleven.

Age 16. Once GCSE is over, all change is possible: boys and girls may move from state schools to private ones (almost all now have entry at 16+, sometimes with scholarships), or from private schools to eg state sixth form colleges as petty restrictions begin to irk. You may want to leave for a school that offers International Baccalaureate.

Entry at sixth form increasingly depends on GCSE results. Check with the school when applications need to be made. Girls applying to the sixth form of boys' or co-ed schools may expect toughish competition.

NB if it looks as though A level may be a struggle for your child and he/she has set his/her heart on university, it is possible (though the logistics may defeat you, and it will almost certainly mean going to school in Scotland) to change from the English exam system to the Scottish one of Highers. This is much more broadly based – more subjects at a slightly lower level – and is now accepted by most English as well as all Scottish universities.

Another possibility for the less academic is to find a school or college that offers GNVQs. Many universities are now happy to admit students with GNVQs (particularly business).

Useful Names and Addresses

A much more extensive list of information sources is available on our website – www.good-schoolsguide.co.uk/links

The Department for Education, Sanctuary Buildings, Great Smith Street, London SW1T 3BT. Tel: 0870 0002288. Fax: 01928 794248. Web www.dfee.gov.uk. Has an information division which will give you the names of schools, pressure groups and leaflets, Tel: 0870 0012345. There is also a publications division on Tel: 0845 6022260.

The Scottish Executive Education Department, Victoria Quay, Edinburgh, EH6 6QQ. Enquires: 08457 741741. Web:

www.scotland.gov.uk Not an easy site to navigate, but if you persevere the information's there. Schools performance tables, for instance, can be found at www.scotland. gov.uk/library/documents-w4/erss-00.htm Reached by clicking on 'what we do', 'school education', 'publications' and then 'more', and then browsing.

The Welsh Assembly, The Public Information and Education Service, The National Assembly for Wales, Cardiff Bay,

Cardiff, CF99 1NA. For School Performance Division contact, Tel: 02920 825111. Fax: 02920 826016. Web: www.wales.gov.uk Now has more useful education data on its site. The Welsh schools performance tables can also be found on Web: www.totalwales.com

DENI – the Northern Ireland Department of Education, Department of Education, Rathgael House, Balloo Road, Bangor, County Down, BT19 7PR. Tel: 02891 279279. Fax: 02891 279100. Web: www.deni.gov.uk

The Independent Schools Information Service (ISIS), 35 Grosvenor Gardens, London SW1W 0BS, Tel: 020 7798 1500; Fax: 020 7798 1501, Web www.isis.org.uk/. This is the information and propaganda arm of the private sector (though NB not all schools belong).

For information on charities for parents who wish to send their children to fee-paying schools but cannot afford the fees, contact ISIS.

For lists of all schools registered in your area (state and private) telephone the County or Borough concerned (eg Westminster City Council, Suffolk Education Authority). Local Authority websites can be traced through Web: www.tagish.co.uk

The Advisory Centre for Education, Department A, Unit 1C Aberdeen Studios, 22 Highbury Grove, London, N5 2DQ. Tel: 020 7354 8321. Fax: 020 7354 9069. Web: www.ace-ed.org.uk A charity founded in 1960. Publishes guides on such subjects as how to approach primary schooling, UK school law, and how to deal with the bureaucrats on Special Educational Needs, school choice and appeals, home education, bullying etc etc.

DRUGS:

ISDD, Dcost, PO Box 105, Sandwich, Kent, C213 9BR. Tel: 01304 614 731 for publications and their CD-ROM. The Health Education Authority's (ISDD) drugs website www.trashed.co.uk

National Drugs Helpline: 0800 776600.

Adfam National , Waterbridge House, 32-36 Loman Street, London, SE1 0EE. Helpline: 020 7928 8900. Fax: 020 7928 8923. The drugs advice charity.

Parentline, 3rd Floor, Chapel House, 18 Hatton Place, London, EC1N 8RU. Helpline: 0808 800 2222. Advice over the telephone on problems at school and of parenting

USEFUL LAWYERS:

Mr Peter Woodroffe, Woodroffes, 36 Ebury Street, London SW1W OLU, Tel: 020 7730 0001; Fax: 020 7730 7900. Specialises, among other things, in advising parents about legal matters concerning fee-paying schools.

The Education Law Association, 39 Oakleigh Avenue, London N20. Tel/Fax: 0130 3211570. Network of solicitors who are experts on educational law.

And for home study, Independent Schools Law Custom and Practice by Robert Boyd. Written by a partner at Veale Wasbrough (a firm with much schools experience, but which acts mostly for schools rather than against them) in magnificently plain English. Intended as a guide for schools and their governors, but it's so clearly and readably set out that it should prove an invaluable aid to parents brewing up for a dispute with a school, or just wanting to know where they stand.

BOOKS

The private schools' 'bible' is The Independent Schools' Yearbook (A&C Black). Covers around 1,500 schools for children between the ages of 3-18. Like a huge collection of prospectuses. Beware in general of books with entries written by the schools themselves.

Much comfort may be had from Molesworth by Geoffrey Willans with illustrations by Ronald Searle. A timeless companion for little mites sent off to boarding school, and for their parents.

CONGLOMERATIONS OF SCHOOLS

The Woodard Schools Started in 1848 by the Rev Nathaniel Woodard when he founded Lancing (qv) to promote (muscular) Christianity, and offer Christian worship and values. There are now 37 schools. For more information, Tel 020 7222 5381. Web: www.woodard.co.uk Fax: 020 7222 7502.

The Girls' Day School Trust, (formerly The Girls' Public Day School Trust), 100 Rochester Row, London, SW1P 1JP Tel: 020 7393 6666. Fax 020 7393 6789. Web: www.gdst.net Set up at the end of the last century to provide no-frills academic education for girls as cheaply as possible. Concentrates on getting pupils through exams. Has been very dependent on government-funded 'assisted places'. Now the government is phasing these out, it is raising money to fund its own scholarships – aiming for £70 million.

CIFE: the Conference for Independent Further Education, Web: www.cife.org.uk The crammers' professional association and your first port of call for advice on which might, for instance, be persuaded to take on little Johnny when he's been sacked from school for drug taking. Also covers summer schools and revision courses.

The Good Schools Guide on the Web

Books are best – best for reading in bed, best for making notes in, best for taking round schools with you. But there are things that we just can't do in a book:

We update the guide on the web weekly

We are adding new schools to the guide all the time

You can have access to additional information at a click of a mouse:

E-mail the school

Look at the school's web pages

Look at the school's data on the ISIS site – for current fees, etc

many other features, such as schools' exam results in full, are planned for introduction in 2001.

We also have extensive links pages: sources of advice; information on FE, universities, the gap year, summer schools; and links to all our competitors on the web.

Take a look at us at www.goodschoolsguide.co.uk

As a purchaser of the seventh edition, you are entitled to access to the Good Schools Guide Online for half price. Have your Guide with you when you subscribe – you will need to refer to it to prove your purchase.

The Good Schools Guide Advisory Service

is a consultancy run by The Good Schools Guide to advise parents on choosing the best schools for their children.

We are in a unique position to do this because we have visited hundreds of schools over the past fifteen years, and have gathered an enormous reservoir of information and experience. The Guide is only a glimpse of this. We would be happy to put our knowledge and our wide network of personal contacts to work for you.

We are, in effect, highly experienced parents, and offer our advice on that basis. If you are looking for something more than this, you might like to consider Penrith Associates (see opposite)

Not even the best school is perfect. Good schools differ enormously in what they offer and in the kind of child they suit best. We specialise in:

Matching the child with the school;

Inside information on what a particular school is really like;

Suggesting good schools that you may not know about;

Checking out specific schools for you;

Information on strong specialist departments and unusual features;

Advice on how to get in.

All information is treated in the strictest confidence.

Tell us what you need, and we will tell you if we are able to help. If we can, the next step is to arrange for a consultation with you, ideally in person, but alternatively by email, fax or telephone. If we cannot help we may be able to suggest someone who can.

Contact us at:
2 Craven Mews, London SW11 6PW, UK.
Tel: +44 (0)20 7733 7861
Fax: +44 (0)870 052 4067
E-mail: editor@goodschoolsguide.co.uk
or
27a Warwick Square, London, SW1V 2AD, UK
Tel: +44 (0)20 7828 1052
Fax: +44 (0)20 7932 0747
E-mail: sarahdrummond@gsgas.fsnet.co.uk

Penrith Associates, run by Anthony Verity – a former headmaster of Dulwich College, and an editor of this Guide – offers a more comprehensive (and expensive) personal school location service. Contact them at

The Readings
Cliburn
Penrith
Cumbria CA10 3AL

Telephone and Fax: +44 (0)1931 714 625
Email: a.verity@snuffmills.freeserve.co.uk

Can You Help Us?

The Good Schools Guide is written by parents for parents. We do not take money from schools in any shape or form, either directly or indirectly – no fees, no commissions for 'introducing' pupils to particular establishments, no retainers. We do not take advertising from schools, nor are we affiliated to any organisation (such as a newspaper) that does. We are therefore in a position to be outspoken, to write and to advise you impartially, without fear of being biased or having a conflict of loyalties.

We visit all the schools ourselves and – since we were first published in 1986 – have visited most of them several times over, both formally and informally. We are a small team, and are therefore able to compare the strengths and weaknesses of one school with another – to put them into context.

Visiting is of course only a start. We also spend many happy hours talking to pupils, staff, heads, educationalists of all sorts, matrons – even the school dog. Last, and most importantly, we listen to you, the consumer.

We would like to know what you think of the schools in this edition. All information will be gratefully (and confidentially) received – no detail is too slight to mention. Suggestions for schools to be included in the next edition would also be welcome.

Please write to us at:

2 Craven Mews,
London SW11 6PW

Or e-mail: editor@goodschoolsguide.co.uk

Glossary & Abbreviations

A level   General Certificate of Education, second public exam in the UK, taken at age 18

AS level   Advanced Supplementary level public exam equivalent to half an A level, formerly taken as a supplement to A levels but now forming the first year of a standard A level course

A2   The examinations at the end of the second year of an A level course

ALIS   A system of value-added measurement used by many schools to compare their GCSE and A level results

ARCM   Associate of the Royal College of Music

Assistant   A young person from abroad, usually French or German, who helps teach the language (not to mention taking rugby, etc)

Assisted Places   Government-backed scheme, whereby bright children of impoverished parents can be educated in fee-paying schools. Means-tested – the government pays the short fall. Being phased out by the Labour Government

BA   Bachelor of Arts. University first degree

BD   Bachelor of Divinity

BEcon   Bachelor of Economics

BEd   Bachelor of Education. A teaching qualification

BHSAI   British Horse Society Assistant Instructor – the lowest qualification needed to be a riding instructor

BLit   Bachelor of Literature. University qualification

Brill   Slang for brilliant

BSc   Bachelor of Science

BTEC   A vocational qualification – alternative to A level – awarded by the Business and Technology Education Council

Bursary   Contribution to the school fees, usually given to those who are poor

CAD   Computer-aided design

CAE   Computer-aided engineering

Cantab   Cambridge

C of E   Church of England

C of S   Church of Scotland

CCF   Combined Cadet Force. Para-military training corps for the young (boys and girls)

Combined Sciences   GCSE exam covering Biology, Chemistry and Physics, counts as one GCSE

CDT   Craft, Design and Technology

CE   Common Entrance. Qualifying exam taken usually at 11, 12 or 13 in the private sector for entry to senior schools

Cert Ed   Certificate of Education. A teaching qualification

CLAIT   Computer Literacy and Information Technology

CReSTeD   Council for the Registration of Schools Teaching Dyslexic Pupils

CSYS   Certificate of Sixth Year Studies (used occasionally in Scotland)

DfEE (Government)   Department for Education and Employment

DT   Design Technology

Dip Ed   A teaching qualification

DPhil   Doctor of Philosophy

Dual Award (Science)   GCSE exam in Science covering Biology, Chemistry and Physics – counts as two GCSEs.

D of E   Duke of Edinburgh Award Scheme. A combination of various different activities, including demanding physical exercise, culminating in a medal

EAL   English as an Additional Language – the latest and PC acronym

EFL   English as a Foreign Language

Eisteddfod   A Welsh festival of music, poetry etc

ESL   English as a Second Language

Fab   Slang for fabulous

FP   Former Pupil (Scottish expression)

FRS   Fellow of the Royal Society (v grand)

FRSA Fellow of the Royal Society of Arts (not grand)

Gap   Work experience projects in year between school and university. Also (when in capitals) name of organisation specialising in this

GCSE   General Certificate of Secondary Education. First public exam in the UK

GNVQ   General National Vocational Qualification. A system of vocational qualifications

GDST   Girls' Day School Trust (Formerly called the Girls' Public Day School Trust) A foundation of private schools

Grammar school   A type of school which selects pupils on academic merit and provides a rigorous academic education (and often not much else)

Grant-maintained   State schools that have 'opted out' of local education authority control and are directly funded by the government

GSA   Girls' Schools' Association. Female equivalent of HMC. See below

Highers   Higher Grades. Scottish public exam, usually taken one or two years after 'Standard Grade' (qv)

HMC   Headmasters' Conference. A sort of headmasters' trade union (and now one or two headmistresses), mostly for public schools, whose heads belong and are considered 'top' by those in it

IAPS   Incorporated Association of Preparatory Schools. Organisation of prep schools. Again, generally considered the 'top' ones by those in it

IB   International Baccalaureate. A public exam at secondary level, increasingly recognised for entry to university in the UK

ICT   Information communications technology

IGCSE   International GCSE

ILEA   Inner London Education Authority – local administration of state schools, now defunct

Independent   Word used by fee-paying schools to describe themselves – erroneously

Inter-denom   Inter-denominational (refers to religious affiliation)

IQ   Intelligence Quotient

ISC   Independent Schools Council – inspects independent schools

ISCO   Independent Schools Careers Organisation

ISI   Independent Schools Council's inspectorate – inspects independent schools

ISIS   Independent Schools Information Service

IT   Information Technology

JMB   Joint Matriculation Board

L es L   Licencie es Lettres. French university degree

Lab   Laboratory

LTA   Lawn Tennis Association

MA   Master of Arts. University degree

MEd   Teaching qualification

MIDYIS   See ALIS, but this measures value-added up to GCSE

MoD   Ministry of Defence

MSc   Master of Science. University qualification

NB   Nota Bene

NFER   National Foundation for Educational Research

NNEB   Nursery nurses official qualification

Non-denom   Non-denominational (refers to religious affiliation)

OB   Old Boy (ie former pupil of a school)

OED   Oxford English Dictionary

OG   Old Girl (ie former pupil of a school)

Opt(ed) out   See Grant-maintained

OSB   Order of St Benedict

OTT   Over the top, as in eg (unacceptable) behaviour

Oxbridge   Short for Oxford and/or Cambridge universities

Oxon   Oxford

Pastoral Care   Care of pupil on matters not related to their work, eg personal and social ones

PE   Physical education

PGCE   Postgraduate Certificate of Education.

A teaching qualification

PS(H)E   Personal, Social (and Health) Education (courses)

PTA   Parent-Teacher Association

qv   quod vide

RC   Roman Catholic

RE   Religious Education

RI   Religious Instruction

RSA   Royal Society of Arts

San   Sanatorium, sick bay

Scotvec   A Scottish vocational qualification

SEN   Special Educational Needs

Set   A group of children of similar ability within a form (setting is a way of sorting children by ability for more effective teaching in specific subjects)

Six-inch rule   Rule applied at some co-educational schools whereby boys and girls may not come closer to each other than six inches (in case they get over-excited)

SSSI   Site of Special Scientific Interest – designated as such by the government and, as such, protected

Standard Grade   The Scottish equivalent of GCSE

Stooge   A foreign gap year student employed by a school

Stream   A form of children of similar ability

Suss   Slang for find out, get to the bottom of, investigate, sniff out

TLC   Tender Loving Care

V   very

Vibes   Slang for vibrations

VIP   Very Important Person

VR(Q)   Verbal reasoning (quotient)

YE   Young Enterprise. A hands-on business studies course

YELLIS   See ALIS, but this measures value-added at primary level

YMCA   Young Men's Christian Association (Youth Hostel organisation)

Dyslexia, Dyspraxia and other Special Needs

Special Educational Needs ('SEN') come with a wide variety of labels, spring from a wide variety of causes, and can be very mild, very severe, or anything in between.

Some SEN are obvious: physical disabilities, or gross misbehaviour from an early age. Others are not – children are extremely adaptable. We have come across cases where severe dyslexia has been diagnosed in mid-A level, even at degree level, when the adaptability finally ran out. Some symptoms to look out for are a lack of pleasure in reading, problems with writing, clumsiness, not enjoying school, disorganisation, easily distracted and generates distraction, reluctance to do homework, not getting on with other children, not thriving at school – and

having parents with these symptoms. All are also symptoms of normal childhood – which is why SENs can be hard to spot and the abler the child the more concealed they may be.

If you suspect an SEN, take your child to an educational psychologist (or other appropriate professional) for a diagnosis. A diagnosis makes it much easier for everyone – you, the school, and above all the child ('thank goodness, I thought I was stupid') – to deal with the problem.

Finding a good EP is not simple. It is a bit of a black art, and the quality of practitioners is variable to say the least. Ask those you trust or who see a lot of EPs – the school perhaps, or local arms of support groups like the British Dyslexia Association, or even the Local Authority. If in doubt see two of them.

It is the duty of Local Education Authorities to assess pupils with SEN, 'statement' them if substantial support is required, and to provide and pay for such support as they may need. This can be extremely expensive, and not unsurprisingly some of them have developed ways of not paying, from delay to a denial that any provision is appropriate – 'we are not sure that statements help'. Some LEAs are terrific – computer assistance on demand for dyslexics, etc – but if yours is one that you may have to fight, arm yourself with a good support group, and an EP who is prepared to fight alongside you in the tribunals (not all will). You may need a specialist solicitor too (some suggestions below).

There is always a large number of claimed cures for any SEN – eg for dyslexia coloured lenses, covering one eye, stimulating changes in reflexes, fish oils, seasick pills etc. Some of them work to some extent for some pupils, but there is a general lack of properly conducted and reported trials. They often cost a lot too. Don't be put off trying one, or more – but remain at all times sceptical of the possibility of improvement, and paricularly cautious about how much of any improvement you ascribe to the cure.

Choosing a School

1. Be honest with yourself. Neither over emphasise your child's problems nor diminish them. Be honest with the school too.

2. Get as good a professional assessment as possible. For a child who has a physical problem it is likely you will have much useful information from the clinicians who have worked with him or her. For the child who has a learning difficulty, be it specific or global, get as much up to date advice as you can. The more a school knows about your child the more easily they can be sure of their ability to do well by him or her.

3. Make use of an appropriate support group, such as those listed below, who will be able to recommend professional people who can give you a frank description of your child's needs.

4. Think of the end point. What would you expect your son or daughter to be doing in twenty years time? Education must be challenging, bringing out a child's full potential, and, if possible, going beyond what the potential is currently perceived to be.

If you are looking at mainstream schools, for a child with a relatively mild degree of need:

5. Ask if the school tests all children on entry – there are lots of ways of doing this, and most will do as long as the assessor is SEN-aware. If a school is really switched on to SEN they will be testing.

6. Ask if the school's special needs support is an integral part of the school, with a two way flow of information between specialist teachers and subject teachers. Schools where SEN support is an 'add on', with help found when needed and specialist teachers having little contact with the school, are really only suitable for very mild cases. Ask a teacher or two where they turn to for advice, and how often, and how good it has been.

7. Ask how many pupils in the school have special needs like your child's and how many teachers offer specialist support. A sizeable peer group will ensure that support is there in depth, and that your child's difficulties are not misunderstood or looked down on by staff or pupils.

8. Are teaching methods appropriate for SEN children – worksheets always provided, lessons in relatively short sections – or are there long periods of dictation / copying off the board, or half an hour's chat and then 'now make notes of what I have said?'

9. What do pupils miss in order to receive extra help? Do you mind?

10. What is the head's attitude to special needs? Does he have high expectations of them? Does he celebrate their successes? A head who is not enthusiastic about helping SEN children may mean that staff are not as supportive or understanding as they should be. Be sure that your child will never be asked 'is this the best you can do?'

11. Do the school make use of concessions for public exams, such as providing a laptop, or an amanuensis – and is a full degree of training available for your child in how to make best use of these aids?

12. Talk to some pupils with the same diagnosis as your child – are they bubbling with pride and confidence?

13. How much extra will you have to pay for the support that you want?

If you are looking for a school for a child who needs a high level of support, or specialist facilities:

14. When it comes to choosing a special school beware of those schools that offer all things to all men.

15. Remember that headteachers of special schools, like their mainstream counterparts, need to fill places in order to 'balance the books'. Be wary of those schools who say they will take special measures for a child who is obviously going to be treated differently from the other children in the school.

16. If a child has a substantial learning difficulty exam results may not be particularly useful to measure the success of a school (though they will give an indication of how well it is possible to do in that school). Try to find another base line from which to work. See if you can discover what the typical child has in terms of both emotional and educational status on arriving at the school, and see if you can determine what value has been added to that child when he/she leaves. What success do the school have in getting their students into further education, or employment, and how successful are they in keeping a relationship with their ex-students to see if they are successful in their chosen field of work? Look for signs of confidence in the older children, and see what help they are given with 'life skills', either formally through programmes in the curriculum, or informally in the way the pastoral side of the school is run. Ask for contacts with existing parents of children like yours, and make your telephone calls to three or four across the age range.

17. And again, what is the head's attitude, and what are the kid's like? There is simply no excuse for a school with low expectations and dulled kids.

For Help on Learning Difficulties

AUTISM/ASPERGER'S:

AUTISM Independent UK (formerly SFTAH) The National Autistic Society, The Centre for Autism.
Tel: 01536 523274. Fax: 01536 523274.
Web: www.autismuk.com

DYSLEXIA/DYSPRAXIA:

The British Dyslexia Association, 98 London Road, Reading, Berkshire RG1

5AU, Helpline: 01189 668271; Office Tel: 01189 662677 Fax: 01189 351927. Web: www.bda-dyslexia.org.uk A helpful and well put-together site. Good links. Has associations for assessing and teaching dotted around the country. Contact them to find your local branch.

The Dyslexia Institute, 133 Gresham Road, Staines, Middlesex TW18 2AJ. Tel: 01784 463851; Fax: 01784 460747. Web: www.dyslexia-inst.org.uk Also has member groups around the country.

The Dyslexia Teaching Centre, 23 Kensington Square, London W8 5HN, Tel: 020 7937 2408; Fax: 020 7938 4816. Web: www.arkellcentre.org.uk Has visiting educational psychologists, and recommends others, and has a large team of specialists trained to help (adults and) children. Also offers private tuition early in the morning and after school hours.

Helen Arkell Dyslexia Centre, Frensham, Farnham, Surrey GU10 3BW, Tel: 01252 792400; Fax: 01252 795669. Web: www.arkellcentre.org.uk 'Excellent,' comments a nearby prep school head.

The Dyspraxia Foundation, 8 West Alley, Hitchin, Hertfordshire SG5 1EG. Helpline:01462 454986. Fax: 01462 455052. Web: www.emmbrook.demon. co.uk/dysprax/homepage.htm Explains the condition well; has national network of 35 local groups giving information and support for the dyspraxic.

GENERAL:

The Advisory Centre for Education, Department A, Unit 1C Aberdeen Studios, 22 Highbury Grove, London, N5 2DQ. Helpline: 020 7354 8321. Fax: 020 7354 9069. Web:

www.ace-ed.org.uk A charity founded in 1960. Publishes guides on such subjects as how to approach primary schooling, UK school law, and how to deal with the bureaucrats on Special Educational Needs, school choice and appeals, home education, bullying etc etc.

Independent Panel for Special Education Advice (IPSEA), 6 Carlow Mews, Woodbridge, Suffolk, IP12 1DH. Helpline: 0800 0184016. Tel/Fax: 01394 380518. Web: www.ipsea.org.uk A charity offering free advice and assistance to parents of children with 'special educational needs' in their negotiations with schools and LEAs

The Tavistock Clinic, 120 Belsize Lane, London NW3 5BA, Tel: 020 7435 7111. Fax: 020 7447 3733. Web: www.tavi-port.org

The National Association for Gifted Children, Elder House, Elder Gate, Milton Keynes, MK9 1LR, Tel: 01908 673677. Fax: 01908 673679. Web: www.rmplc. co.uk/orgs/nagc Gives advice to parents with exceptionally bright children.

SOLICITORS:

Specialising in fighting special needs cases: Robert Love of A E Smith & Sons, Frome House, London Road, Stroud, Glos. GL5 2AF. Tel: 01453 757444. Fax: 01453 757 586. E-mail: AE.Smith.Stroud@cwcom. net

Jack Rabinowicz of Teacher Sterne Selby, 37-41 Bedford Row, London, WC1R 4JH. Tel: 020 7242 3191. Fax: 020 7242 1156. Email: j.rabinowicz@tsslaw.com Web: www.tsslaw.co.uk

How to Find the Right Sort of School

For mild SENs there's a good deal of information in this Guide.

CReSTeD, The Council for the Registration of Schools Teaching Dyslexic pupils, produces a register of schools that have been through a registration procedure, including a visit by a CReSTeD selected consultant. CreSTeD does not inspect a school for aspects not connected to dyslexia – eg many of those covered in the Good Schools Guide. Many such schools will cater for other SENs too.

The register is updated twice a year and schools are normally revisited at three yearly intervals. Some schools may have chosen not to be listed , though their teaching provision may be of an equally high standard.

CReSTeD publish a list of registered schools, which may be had from them at Greygarth, Littleworth, Winchcombe, Cheltenham, Gloucestershire GL54 5BT, Tel/Fax: 01242 602689, Web:www.crested.org.uk – where you can find a list of schools online.

CreSTeD categorises schools as follows:

Category A: The school provides a total learning environment for dyslexic pupils where the specialist support is integrated in all teaching. Assessment for admission to the school includes Educational Psychologist reports.

Category B: The provision for dyslexic pupils is in a dedicated centre. The centre will have a significant input for literacy and numeracy for the pupils attending the unit. The head of the centre must have head of department status with an input into curriculum development and planning. There is an awareness by other members of staff of the necessity to adjust their teaching to meet the needs of dyslexic pupils and this is evident across the curriculum. The majority of staff and all English and specialist language teachers are qualified in the teaching of dyslexic children or are undergoing training.

Category C: There is awareness by other members of staff of the needs of dyslexic pupils. There is a base with appropriate resources which is used for timetabled specialist classes and individual tuition.

Category D: There is some provision for individual lessons on a withdrawal basis. The specialist teachers are qualified in the teaching of dyslexic pupils or are undergoing training.

A school's inclusion in one category may or may not mean that it additionally offers the sort of care offered by schools in a different, less intensive category. For example, a category B school may also offer care of a category D type.

Some Special Schools

We have visited several special schools in preparing this edition –
others will be covered on the website.

FAIRLEY HOUSE SCHOOL

30 Causton Street, London SW1P 4AU

TEL: *020 7976 5456* FAX: *020 7976 5905*

E-MAIL: nr@fairleyhouse.rmplc.co.uk

✦ PUPILS: 95 boys and girls (70 boys, 25
girls); all day ✦ Ages: 6/7-12, 13 from 2001
✦ Inter-denom ✦ Fee-paying

Head: Since September 2000, Mr Nicholas
Rees NPQH MA PGCE DipRSA(SpLD)
(forties) who originally came to the school
in January 1987, becoming deputy head in
1995 after a year's sabbatical during which
time he liaised with the architects to put
together the fantastic purpose-reconstruct-
ed (it used to be the diocesan office) building in Causton Street.

Educated in Germany and Singapore (his
father was a teacher so teaching is in the
blood), he got his NPQH (National
Professional Qualification of Headteachers)
in London, the MA in education at the
Open University, studied for his PGCE at
Portsmouth, and did his RSA at the
Hornsby Centre in London. He previously
taught in prep schools in Bath and in
Germany. Gassy, fun, and very pleased to be
head of Fairley House; he is unusual in that
not many men who teach have an interest
in remedial education.

In September, 2001 the Principal of
Fairley House School, Mrs Jacqueline

Ferman BA MEd DipRSA(SpLD), will
return to the school after a year's sabbatical
training as an educational psychologist. Mr
Rees will move to be head of Fairley House
Upper School, catering for pupils up to 13
from newly acquired premises.

Entrance: Entry is by a serious (and expensive – currently £525) assessment with an
educational psychologist, a speech therapist
and an occupational therapist – and if the
child is border-line then they spend an
entire day at school. Building no good for
the physically handicapped but otherwise
most special learning needs catered for,
including ADHD (as long as the child is not
disruptive in class) and mild Asperger's
(ditto).

Exit: Currently most pupils leave either to
go back into the state sector, London day
schools, or to eg Bruern Abbey, Shiplake,
Millfield, Stanbridge Earls, Frewen or
Sibford.

Remarks: This a CReSTeD category A
school, founded twenty years ago, a school
that other schools look up to. Not cheap,
fees currently run just under sixteen grand
a year. Pupils come from all over and spend
two, three or four years at the school: whatever is beneficial. About twenty five per
cent are statemented, with eighty per cent
of those being paid for by their LEAs – but
of course it varies. Very occasional exclusion
if child totally disruptive, but usually only
for a day or so.

Adjustable desks to improve posture; max
class size 12, with masses of tinier groups,

one to six for reading (no coloured lenses, but some use of coloured transparencies if it helps), literacy, maths; proper science, art, design technology, drama important. No languages, but masses of multi-sensory activities. Good library, reading and social skills important, plus study skills. Games nearby (with swimming in the Queen Mother's Sports Centre), massive hall which doubles for PE, assembly and lunch (great emphasis on healthy eating – no E numbers if at all possible). Hugh gang of teachers, plus some part timers, occupational therapists and speech and language experts; annual ed psych's report for all.

Children come as young as six, but the school profile broadens at nine and ten. Huge computer room (with annual computer expert on sandwich secondment from Hertfordshire University), all networked, as are the photocopying machines. Laptops (provided by the school) for all at nine.

MARK COLLEGE

Mark, Highbridge, Somerset TA9 4NP

TEL: *01278 641 632* FAX: *01278 641 426*

E-MAIL: post@markcollege.somerset.sch.uk

WEB: www.markcollege.org.uk

✦ PUPILS: 80 boys ✦ Ages: 11-16
✦ Non-denom ✦ Fee-paying

Principal and Proprietor: Since 1986, Dr S J Chinn BSc PhD PGCE DipEd AMBDA (fifties). Read chemistry at Leeds, then a PhD in applied physics. Head of three schools specialising in dyslexia before founding Mark. Lectures worldwide on dyslexia and maths. A spare, energetic man, a long distance runner, full of smiles and interest. Married with three children.

HEAD: Since 1999, Mrs J Kay BEd (late thirties). Joined Mark College in 1990, and became assistant head in 1994.

Academic Matters: Takes boys of 'average to above average ability' with severe dyslexia, and gets them (by and large) good GCSEs. Achieves the national average in English (from an average reading age at entry of 7 years), well above in maths and humanities. Offers the full national curriculum – no sheltering the boys from the need to shape up for the world outside. Doesn't, on the whole, believe that dyslexics can be cured, but majors on coping strategies – all teaching materials and methods have been adapted for dyslexics; much use of voice recognition computers that speak back to the boys – highlight a word and you hear it.

Staff interesting and highly qualified – Dr Chinn says that all he needs to do is advertise 'class size 8' and the best come running. Boys treat staff as friends but call them 'Sir.' Chosen as a Beacon School by the DfEE for excellence with dyslexics – a thoroughly deserved accolade.

Games, Options, the Arts: Sports hall, tennis courts, playing fields. V good rugby (runners up in ISA sevens) and athletics (gold and other medals in ISA national championships) – typical dyslexic sports, says Dr Chinn, as no dual tasking is involved. All encouraged to do bronze D of E, some do silver. A good range of activities generally, but the weekends are not packed. General studies course centres on dealing with the world after school.

Background and Atmosphere: A Georgian house with new and old outbuildings, within easy range of the M5 (junction 22). College named after the village – a quiet place with several shops, where news of misbehaviour by the boys would quickly get back to the school; half a mile up the road and the school would have been called Splot College. Boarding houses in age groups, two to a room and then one. Facilities generally not plush, but everything thought through for dyslexics – eg clothes on open shelves not hidden in drawers. With the prospectus (small and grey) you get a CD-ROM containing a virtual tour of the college – another example of their excellent provision for dyslexics. Food leaves substantial room for improvement.

Pastoral Care and Discipline: No concessions made to dyslexics' difficulties – organisation, memory, etc – boys have to learn to survive outside the school by outside standards – but difficulties are well understood, and much help is given to help boys improve. A lot of boys arrive at the school with attitude problems – many have been bullied (and so may want to bully), many have had their self confidence shaken – and close attention is paid to clearing these up. Boys agree that after the first year all is well. Boys stand up when you enter a classroom, neat and alert, smartly dressed and with regulation haircuts.

Pupils and Parents: Parents high society and paying the fees to ordinary mortals on LEA grants. Schools aims to make its pupils confident, articulate and at ease with relationships; and indeed they are a very pleasant and open lot. 'They don't fail interviews,' says Dr Chinn.

Entrance: At 11, 12 or 13. Must have been diagnosed as severely dyslexic, with average intelligence or above, have no 'primary behavioural or emotional problems' ie those not resulting from dyslexia and peoples'

reaction to it, and must want to learn. Apply up to two years in advance.

Exit: To schools that can offer continued support – the school keeps a list of recommended ones.

Money Matters: Fees £5,000-ish per term, pretty all-in.

Remarks: As good as you get for those with severe dyslexia.

MORE HOUSE SCHOOL

Frensham, Farnham, Surrey GU10 3AP

TEL: *01252 792 303* FAX: *01252 797 601*

E-MAIL: MoreHouseSchool@hotmail.com

✦ PUPILS: 165 boys, 54 board✦ Ages: 9-18
✦ RC foundation but all welcome
✦ Fee-paying

Head: Since 1993, Mr Barry Huggett (fifties), experienced scientific research and the City before moving into education. Previous job director of studies at a large prep school. Currently teaches 'maths and some RE'. Married to Gerry, a physiotherapist who now works in the school office as admissions registrar, as well as headmaster's wife. Two children, their daughter is headmistress of a large primary school, and their son is a medical student. Mr Huggett is available day and night for pupils, parents and staff.

Julia Rowlandson, who trained ten years ago with the Helen Arkell dyslexia centre prior to becoming deputy head in 1994, set up special needs departments in two schools. In 1998 she was asked (by Cherie Blair) to chair, in Downing Street, a discussion about children with special needs with the Prime Minister's wives who had accompanied their husbands to the Asia Europe (ASEM) meeting held in London. She constantly researches all new teaching methods including alternative treatments.

Academic Matters: This is a specialist school, with a very supporting, caring ethos. The staff, work very hard to bring out the best in every boy, all of whom will be of average intelligence but have a specific learning difficulty. Every boy has an individual education plan (IEP) with targets monitored weekly, and a full 'review' each year. The school has an enviable reputation for anything creative, art & design, sculpture; 3D studies and drama are all very good – and good exam results too. Pik 'n mix-GCSEs depending which boards/subjects suites best. Computers everywhere and used in GCSEs if necessary. GCSE results improving each year with many boys who had not expected to take the exams on enrolment gaining good passes. Because of their specific learning difficulties, English and history cause the boys much difficulty, but in summer 2000 the number of boys approaching the magic 5Cs and above was close to the national average. All pupils take a course in 'life skills', which leads to a certificate of achievement and helps boys with interview techniques, financial matters, CVs, body language and other inter personal skills. A CReSTeD category A school.

Games, Options, the Arts: Rugby, football, cricket, athletics and swimming plus others. Adventure training, Duke of Edinburgh, ceramics, CDT, music. There are also several school pets around including a couple of pot-bellied pigs, goats, geese, ducks, reptiles and an aviary of birds.

Background and Atmosphere: Close to Farnham set in woody yet spacious grounds. New IT block and agreed plans for further expansion to cover art and sports. Small dorms, senior single and double dorms, live in qualified care staff. In '00 the head boy's speech at founders day included the following: 'I remember my first day here very well. For once in my life I wasn't called names, wasn't being teased in class, and wasn't desperately wishing that I was somewhere else. I had found a place where everyone seemed to understand, and was willing to help. At any time of the day or night, there was always someone there who cared about me and, in my book that makes this place special.'

Pastoral Care and Discipline: Boys demonstrate genuine and great care for each other backed up by staff. Only one case of drug taking in many years that anyone can remember.

Pupils and Parents: Broad spectrum of society many living locally, all of whom are uncomfortable or failing to achieve at other schools, and who may have specific learning difficulties. Lots of weekly boarders with a strong cadre of full time boarders (who have organised activity at weekends); several expats, FCO and Services families.

Entrance: Parents send any reports that there may be on a boy, and talk to Gerry Huggett on the phone. They are invited for an interview, without their son, and assuming all goes well, the boy is then invited for an assessment day. If it is a boarding place this also involves an overnight stay. The boys are very welcoming and Mr Huggett says that 'everyone enjoys their assessment'; during which an up-to-date reading age, maths age and spelling age are obtained. But the main purpose is to see how the child fits in to the school environment and to make sure his total needs can be met at the school.

Exit: Up until 1999, most boys left at 16 and went into further education, predominantly with a vocational bias, especially in art & design. However, more boys are now staying on post-16 and from '00 the school has a proper sixth form with its own building for tutorials, senior art and a social area.

Money Matters: Very strong learning support throughout but extra one to one tuition is available at a reasonable cost. School will try to help whenever with financial crisis/difficulty. Good value for money, no hidden extras.

Remarks: Super confidence-building in caring environment.

THE OLD RECTORY SCHOOL

Brettenham, Ipswich, Suffolk IP7 7QR

TEL: *01449 736404* FAX: *01449 737881*

E-MAIL: theoldrectoryschool@talk21.com

✦ PUPILS: 38 Boys (of whom 30 board, the rest day) and 12 girls (of whom 8 board, the rest day) ✦ Ages: 7-13 ✦ Inter-denom ✦ Fee-paying

---

Head: Since April 1999, Miss Ann Furlong MA CertEd SpNeedsEdDip SpLD (forties), who first came to the school in January 1981 with the founder, Dr Martin Phillips. Educated at the Catholic Bonus Pasteur in Bromley, she got her Cert Ed at Gloucester College of Further Education, followed by an MA (in special needs educa-tion) at the Open University and further qualifications at Chelmsford Hall, Eastbourne. She previously taught at Sinden College in Sussex, followed by a spell at Chelmsford Hall, then Sinden again, plus Bruern Abbey and five years as head of remedial teaching at King's College, Cambridge and back to The Old Rectory as head designate for a couple of terms. Quite.

Incredibly well qualified in a number of disciplines, Miss Furlong is a quiet, thoughtful and engaging character, rather self-effacing, and perhaps not as full of exuberance as many of the heads whom we have met. Knows the children and their problems well and takes regular classes.

Remarks: This is indeed an old rectory, next to the church which is used for daily assemblies and set in five acres of deep Suffolk – with another two tennis courts' worth of land coming on stream shortly. The fabric of the school was bought from the Phillips' by Michael Murphy (whose role appears to be that of interested bene-factor) in 1999. Since then dormitory accommodation has been revamped and plans are afoot to extend the girls' accom-modation in the Coach House over the duck pond and double the number of (cur-rently rather cramped) bedrooms.

Boys live in the main house, in immacu-late tidiness (can this really be so?) with lessons either taken in a large room subdi-vided into four class rooms with cunning folding screens (The Arches which was opened by Lord Archer) or in portacabins outside. Lots of English, maths and all the other trad subjects taught in tiny classes (max size 8), according to ability rather than age. The school follows a modified national curriculum, with German rather than French. An impressive computer room, with children taught touch typing early, but no laptops; two handwriting lessons a week match the two keyboarding lessons.

Music and drama important. Games on site, and masses of extra-curricular activity, including karate, target shooting and fire crew – the school has five fire engines which specially selected pupils can help 'crew', usually putting out controlled fires only. All the extra-curricular activities are chosen to improve motor skills.

Children come from all over, often only for a year or two to get them up to speed; they then return to normal mainstream schools, be it state, prep, or senior schools: Wellington, Stowe, Merchiston Castle in Scotland, Framlingham, Gresham's, Oakham. Most come around 11 or 12, but there is no provision for CE. This is a school for the dyslexic, the dyspraxic, those with dyscalculia and the occasional fragile child. The school does not take any child with behaviour problems, nor any child on Ritalin, though there are several on efalax oil, and several wear coloured spectacles – deep pink, mauve, dark blue which are often promoted as remedial aids.

Twelve children are currently statement-ed, of whom three are paid for by their LEAs. Many of the children do not come from a boarding school background and their parents 'may have sold their house or gone without holidays' to send them here; female staff are invariably called Miss, and the few men Sir. No real problems in get-ting staff, but the head feels that it is impor-tant to have more than just the very popu-lar groundsman as the token male role model and takes time to find men with the right qualifications – and if staff do not come with suitable dyslexia training they train at the Hornsby Centre. Occupational and speech therapists on hand.

Entrance is by an educational psycholo-gist's report (and there is a twice yearly visit by the ed psy to all children. Plus points for good behaviour, and once a fortnight all those with the best grades for effort have a party in the jacuzzi and sauna chalet; bad points for rotten behaviour, really disruptive children can be sanctioned, involving loss of privilege and occasionally suspended or expelled.

This is a helpful little school, which kicks children with special needs back into main-stream education. Worth considering if your child falls into its particular criteria.

STANBRIDGE EARLS SCHOOL
Romsey, Hampshire SO51 0ZS
Tel: *01794 516 777* Fax: *01794 511 201*

E-MAIL: stanearls@aol.com

✦ PUPILS: 160 Boys, 35 girls; 175 board, 20 day✦ Ages: 11-18✦ Size of sixth form: 35 ✦ Inter-denom ✦ Fee-paying

Head: Since 1983, Mr Howard Moxon MA DipEd (sixties) who was educated at Ecclesfield Grammar School, read geogra-phy at Downing, Cambridge, and came to Stanbridge Earls via Highgate and Forrest Schools. Mr Moxon, who retires July 2001 to take on the secretary-ship of Deal golf club, still teaches geography 'a little'. New head not yet appointed.

Academic Matters: This is a CReSTeD category B school, and whilst a mainstream curriculum is (more or less) followed, and children take A levels, Stanbridge Earls has one of the more important accelerated learning centres and mathematics skill centres in the country. The school was originally founded in 1952 by refugees from the London world of creative arts, as an 'alternative to the conventional public school' and is renowned for its early recognition – by Dick Cuvet, in 1963 – of the condition then known as 'word blindness'.

Described by the outgoing head as 'a recovery school', 112 out of the 196 pupils at Stanbridge Earls need some form of remedial teaching for 'all sorts of learning difficulties': ranging from mildly 'fragile' pupils to dyslexia, dyspraxia, dyscalculia, dysgraphia, autism, Asperger's syndrome and ADHD. Mrs Edwina Cole runs the remedial department with a large dedicated staff. Tiny classes, staff/pupil ratio of 1:6, max class size 14, but mostly eight or nine. Remedial classes are either for children withdrawn from class on a one to one basis, or for small groups; many subjects are also taught with a support teacher in class. Occupational and speech therapists are on call and their time greatly over-subscribed; this is a school which treats the whole child. Impressive.

Thirty-eight pupils are currently statemented, of whom 33 are paid for by their LEAs (often after Tribunal). GCSEs, A levels, NVQs, Certificates of Achievement are the norm though most take the exam at modular level; and most children are 'double entered' with the chance of at least one qualification. English lit and lang, French, Italian, maths and sciences are de rigueur at GCSE, though some take and indeed achieve, A level. Courses are tailored to the child's interest and ability with pupils attending classes at local colleges where appropriate. It would be unfair to judge this exceptional school against the 'normal' academic. This is a school which does well by its pupils and 'the vast majority get academic GCSEs', though most get extra time for exams. School has scribers, readers, writers, and computers, though we would like to see more than 78 computers. As the forerunner in the IBM BECTa voice recognition programme (one of the pupils was the prototype) perhaps more will come on stream shortly! Keyboarding skills on hand, and taught early. Some pupils take English GCSE in the November before the rest of their exams. Wide range of subjects available at every level, including automotive engineering, and creative, business and general studies. Sixth form studies include A or AS levels (not really much take up here), GNVQs, City & Guilds, Certificate of Extended Studies (CES) and GCSE retakes – no shame here.

Games, Options, the Arts: Usual collection of games on offer, excellent and well used swimming pool, games hall, plus riding, judo, air rifle shooting etc, forty different activities on offer post class – pupils must opt for five, of which three must be of a physical nature. D of E and a challenging 24 hour marathon plus leadership training.

Home economics popular and fabric design. Drama strong, and music on stream, though having said that, perhaps not as much emphasis on these two disciplines as one might expect, but both available at exam level. And on Tuesdays all the staff listen to any child who wants to perform anything – even if it's only a one finger exercise on the piano. One of the ponds is well stocked for fishing, and a tributary to the nearby river Test runs through the grounds.

Art very strong and popular, but with the art department currently designing a web site, one felt that CAD or even a computer would be handy. CDT well supported, again there was a lack of computers. Lots of successful entrants in all subjects at national competition level.

Background and Atmosphere: Charming, much altered sixteenth century manor house set in fifty acres of delightful parkland, with streams and ponds and mature trees. The grotty collection of elderly and dying temporary buildings that house the classrooms are due to be replaced this summer and not before time. And whilst such special schools do not run on computers alone, it is to be hoped that the promised internet/intranet/network is indeed put in place. There seems no point in having some of the best remedial teaching in Britain and not using every conceivable aid. The new complex should be in use by Summer 2002 and will include snazzy new library as well as all the ancillary subject rooms. Some rather dismal old dorms in original house at odds with spankingly luxurious new houses.

Pastoral Care and Discipline: Horizontal tutor groups for all, but if personality clashes are inevitable, then pupils can chose their own tutor – matron, gap year student, whatever. Pupils call teachers 'Sir' and 'Miss.' School bends over backwards to be a 'happy school', but normal school rules in place: smoking = fines, drinking = counselling and gating as a last resort. Drugs testing in place, random if any suspicion (and there is apparently no danger of any prescription drugs fouling up the test itself, but if the result is queried then school tests on the expensive Unilab system which is legally binding), plus lectures from Phil Cooper the (reformed) druggy poet. Though pupils 'do get forced to leave if things don't improve.' Sex = out.

Pupils and Parents: Fairly middle to lower middle class on the whole. Guy Ritchie (of Madonna fame) is an old boy.

Entrance: Previous head or educational psychologist's report plus interview. School not equipped for wheelchairs, though the new build may go some way to improve matters. Children with specific learning problems come from all over; around 25 per cent leave and 25 per cent join at 13, ditto after GCSE – many come from the state sector. But children arrive and leave throughout, and can come mid-term if space (and particularly space in the boarding houses) is available. Small number from abroad who combine EFL with remedial treatment for learning difficulties.

Exit: At 13 to more mainstream boarding schools (Stowe is a popular choice), post GCSE to vocational training. Post sixth form to colleges usually for vocational training, occasionally to university. Quite a number to sporting universities abroad – basketball strong.

Money Matters: Help from LEAs for some statemented pupils, some bursaries and scholarships available, but this is not a rich school.

Remarks: V good for dyslexics. Great emphasis on raising pupils' self esteem, pupils badly bullied elsewhere often go back to their original school with coping strategies in place. However buildings well below par, and pupils a bit hodden doon too – did not stand up straight, look you in the eye or display as much self confidence as one might have hoped.

SENIOR SCHOOLS

ABINGDON SCHOOL

Abingdon, Oxfordshire OX14 1DE

TEL: *01235 849 078* FAX: *01235 849 085*

E-MAIL: registry@abingdon.org.uk

WEB: www.abingdon.org.uk

✦ PUPILS: 795 boys 662 day, 133 board (including 64 weekly boarding)
✦ Ages: 11-18 ✦ Size of sixth form: 257
✦ C of E ✦ Fee-paying

Head: Since 1975, Mr Michael St John Parker MA (fifties), read history at King's College, Cambridge, formerly head of history at Winchester and also taught at King's Canterbury and Sevenoaks. Married, with four children. Something of a stickler for discipline, a traditionalist. Fondly referred to as 'our eccentric headmaster' by some of his staff. Very fast talking, humorous but stands no nonsense. Liked by the boys; occasional mutterings about 'high-handed' style of management from parents and staff. Highbrow. Comments that he hopes boys leave 'knowing how to think' and 'happy with themselves'. Retiring December 2001, and will be much missed.

Academic Matters: GCSE profile brill. Maths very popular and outstanding A level results. Sciences also impressive. Some other mainstream subjects less so. Geography, economics and English the other popular subjects – v v few take languages, though lots on offer. 50 per cent A grades in '00, then a long tail – this school does not chuck pupils out if they shape up less than perfectly at GCSE. Large classes (25 in lower school, decreasing to 20-21 in GCSE years), and staff adept at drawing boys in. Good general studies programme (non-examinable) for sixth form. Fine modern teaching block (opened '94), with 15 classrooms and departmental suites (generous help given by the Mercers' Company). Stunning hi-tech, huge IT centre, all departments making use of it, networking, CD-ROMs, plus computers increasingly dotted about classrooms. Teaching interfaced with research, masterminded by David Haynes, considered to be a 'bit of a whizz'. Not a place for dyslexics.

Several staff changes and additions, a lively bunch, some serving for two decades and more, leavened by interesting new young recruits.

Games, Options, the Arts: Rowing especially strong, and has regular successes. Boat club generates huge enthusiasm. Plenty of sport available (compulsory twice a week right through to sixth form), though pupils don't live or die by it. Not brilliant (heated) outdoor pool; sports hall used by local community. Strong music tradition with 30 peripatetic teachers, numerous orchestras and chamber groups (National Youth Orchestra and National Jazz Youth Orchestra players), and good choral work. Concerts and plays, especially in conjunction with St Helen's and St Katherine's school. Super theatre. Energetic charity fund raisers.

Background and Atmosphere: Ancient foundation, ex-direct grant school which has grown to become one of the largest schools in the region. Sprawling, redbrick Victorian Gothic, with steep roofs and turrets and new complex built in the vernacular. Recent addition, in executive homes style, Mercers' Court, built at a cost of £2.5 million. This now houses the Head's offices – posho. Whole school is psychologically separated from Abingdon, although practically in the town square. Morale high. Terrific sense of purpose. Feels – and operates – like a boarding school (though boarders are a minority), with Saturday morning school, matches on Saturday afternoons etc. Houserooms the centres of social life, featuring lockers, toasters, pool tables. Separate houses for day boys and boarders, whose accommodation has much improved with creation of study bedrooms (singles for upper sixth).

Pastoral Care and Discipline: 'Far more sensitive to bullying issues nowadays', commented a parent. Thorough-going pastoral care system, with regular reporting between tutors/housemasters and pupils. Poor work means detention. Head hot on pastoral care going far beyond the school gates – advises on Saturday parties etc and describes parents as 'responsive'.

Pupils and Parents: Popular with business, Oxford gown, professional and Service families, and plenty of first-time buyers. Some M4 corridor computer-sophisticated parents attracted by computing facilities. Boys are unpretentious, lively, relatively well-groomed and industrious. 40-50 ex pats and foreigners, including Hong Kong and Malaysian scholars. Boys living over 45 minutes' bus ride away must board. Twelve buses to fetch and carry.

Entrance: Increasingly popular choice for day pupils, particularly at 13. From primary schools at 11 via examination; from prep schools at 13 by CE (with a pre-test at 11). Lots from The Dragon, a few from Chandlings. 15-20 at sixth form (including some refugees from other public schools).

Exit: 97-100 per cent go on to degree courses, some after a gap year. 20 the norm to Oxbridge. Engineering popular, also geography. Slight bias to science subjects.

Money Matters: Good value – 'We're cheaper than a lot of other schools', says the head – but school may be affected by abolition of assisted places (had dozens). Means-tested bursaries, and several status-only scholarships – so it's those who need the fee concession that get it. Enjoys some Mercers' Company funding.

Remarks: Academic boys' school, currently the flavour of the month, with good facilities and some fizzing staff. One or two parents still complain it's a bit of a swot shop, particularly at the top.

ALLEYN'S SCHOOL
Townley Road, London SE22 8SU

Tel: *020 8557 1500* Fax: *020 8557 1462*

E-mail: alleyns@rmplc.co.uk

Web: www.alleyns.org.uk

♦ Pupils: 430 boys, 497 girls, all day
♦ Ages: 11-18 ♦ Size of sixth form: 241
♦ C of E ♦ Fee-paying

Head: Since 1992, Dr Colin Niven MA (Cantab), DipEd, Dr de L'Univ (Lille) (fifties). Dulwich man and boy. Has taught in France, Sedbergh, housemaster at Fettes and head of modern languages at Sherborne. Principal of Island School, Hong Kong and St George's English

School, Rome. Former chairman of the European division HMC etc. Single, he still teaches modern languages.

Academic Matters: All three science departments boast published authors amongst their teachers, and science in general is popular. Dual award for the majority, three separate sciences for high-fliers at GCSE. Everyone does one year of Latin. French in first year and German and Spanish introduced in second year. Wide variety of design GCSEs taken – including food. League table talk: results are now more respectable for the intake and size of school. NB boys' and girls' results listed separately – useful detail – girls do best. Head claims 'we've become more academic without losing the ethos'. Member of staff comments 'we are not as selective as people think. We take a pretty wide ability range, wider than, say, Dulwich.' General studies examined.

Reports are still reaching us from one or two disgruntled parents that slack work is not picked up early enough; some parents worry that their children might have achieved better results elsewhere against a more formal background. 'Some' specific learning difficulties support is available, including allowing the use of laptop computers, although the school 'does not (in general) promise SEN provision'.

Games, Options, the Arts: One afternoon a week is devoted to sport – not enough, say parents – in the 20 acres of grounds surrounding the school, including netball next to the parked staff cars. In the first and second years girls and boys have some combined games. Sports hall, girls' gym, badminton, serious hockey, cricket, basketball (v popular), netball, fencing (sadly no longer coached by Professor Moldovanyi, said to be the last person alive to have seen a duel to the death). Strong swimming tradition, girls take on JAGS and St Paul's girls and beat them regularly (though results in other matches not staggering).Voluntary and popular CCF, D of E. Otherwise conservation work, gardening or helping with disabled children. Workshop and Saturday literacy and numeracy schemes with primary schools, and work shadowing in fifth and sixth forms.

Fantastic drama everywhere (the National Youth Theatre was founded at the school), particularly popular in the 'Bear Pit' in the old gym. Outstandingly successful art and design department – lots taking both GCSE and A level, unbelievable results, and 13 leavers in one year recently went on to art college. Terrific pottery. Photography offered at GCSE. Excellent music in spectacular converted brewery which links with junior school. Has produced choirboy of the year; some children play in the National Youth Orchestra, 3 Oxbridge choral scholars in '97. Lots of lunchtime and after-school options. Music, table tennis. Field centre at Buxton in Derbyshire. Staff attend regular Institute of Education refresher courses in their subjects (school keeps fund for such training).

Background and Atmosphere: Connected to Dulwich College via the Elizabethan actor-manager Edward Alleyn, under royal charter of 1619. Became fully independent of the other two schools in 1995 (the 375th anniversary of the Alleyn Foundation), and now has its own board of governors etc. Was a bit in the shadow of nearby Dulwich College until it went fully co-ed in September 1979. Large Victorian building in South London redbrick, surrounded by higgledy-piggledy collection of purpose-built blocks. New maths and business 'suite' etc. Still retains the atmosphere of a direct grant school: committed staff, intelligent children from a wide variety of backgrounds and nationalities but strictly unsmart. Fairly laid back atmosphere, but uniform to sixth form and then 'formal dress of their choice'. Extremely friendly place – this may be the first thing you observe.

Pastoral Care and Discipline: Tutors for all, strong house system and good links with head, deputy head and head of lower school (first two years). Staff committed to pastoral care, attending counselling courses, etc. Drugs on campus = instant dismissal – the school has been known to sack in run up to exams on this front – suspension for fags and booze. Pupils may drive to school with parents' and house master's permission.

Pupils and Parents: Wide cross-section. 'Loyal following.' 'More Dulwich than Dulwich' but then again a conscience-stricken socialist can say 'it's not really a public school like Dulwich'. Enormously strong Alleyn's Association and sports club etc . Some parents really struggle to keep their children here. Lots of first-time fee-payers, and huge ethnic mix. Several hundred primary schools have submitted pupils for entrance, and pupils have been known to come from as far away as Sevenoaks and Knockholt. Shares buses with Dulwich College, Dulwich College Preparatory School and JAGS.

Lively pupils, friendly, bright-eyed, a tendency to scruffiness. Former pupils include Professor R V Jones, C S Forester, V S Pritchett, Julian Glover, Simon Ward, Micky Stewart and Jude Law.

Entrance: From Alleyn's Junior School (qv), on site. Some from Dulwich Hamlet and from Wandsworth schools. Oversubscribed (some 550 candidates sit for 130 places at 11) and selective. Entrance exams:

'What we are looking for is an enquiring mind and potential. We see all parents too, and there we need support.' Around 10 children are accepted at 13; 20 or so pupils come in at sixth form – '3 viable A levels and 14 points from GCSE' needed. Home-grown pupils need 10-12 GCSE points to go on to A level.

Exit: Over 90 per cent to universities – a mixture of old and new. 9-14 to Oxbridge annually. One or two straight into employment. Also a good number to art college.

Money Matters: Twelve Saddlers' and foundation scholarships at 11, one at 13 and two for the sixth form. Had 212 assisted places – privately-funded scheme in place to offer similar means-tested deal to 10 pupils. Extra bursaries can often be found for genuine cases of hardship.

Remarks: Still the only major private co-educational day school in sight of London. Breeds tremendous loyalty; parents fight to get their children in. Given the selectivity and potential strength of the place, it could do better in some areas on the academic front, but as one of the very few London senior schools with a 'liberal progressive' ethos it makes no academic claims. Like a very good curate's egg.

AMPLEFORTH COLLEGE

York YO6 4ER

TEL: *01439 766000* FAX: *01439 788330,*

E-MAIL: admiss@ampleforth.org.uk

WEB: www.ampleforthcollege.york.sch.uk

✦ PUPILS: around 500 boys, 8 girls in the sixth form (all board, except for 40) ✦ Ages: 13-18 ✦ Size of sixth form: around 240 ✦ RC ✦ Fee-paying

---

Head: Since 1992, Father Leo Chamberlain MA (sixty). Clear-sighted Father Leo cuts a generous figure 'not unlike Friar Tuck', commented a parent not unkindly. He has been man and boy at the college since the age of nine (his great-grandfather started here in 1835) with a brief interlude as a scholar of University College, Oxford, where he read modern history (he teaches an A level set). Comments on the defection of RCs elsewhere, 'We must respond to the needs of the present day. Catholic boys should go to Catholic schools and our job is to be so good that they would want to come to us.' NB nice new abbot – Fr Timothy Wright – a former housemaster and cricket master here, elected '97.

Academic Matters: Top of the Catholic league but makes no bones about non-elitist intake – from A stream scholars to fifth stream IQs of around 105 who get extra help with English and maths. NB 90 per cent of this bottom stream achieve three A levels: 'That the strong should be given something to strive for and the weak should

not be over-burdened', is Father Leo's statement of purpose. 'They never discard,' says a parent, 'the boys gain self-respect, the monks have an ability to home in on potential, to unlock talent to achieve.' Core curriculum plus compulsory Christian theology throughout (at which they do very well); most take three separate sciences at GCSE although the lower stream take the combined award. Liberal arts have traditionally had the edge here but science and maths continue to strengthen. History, English lit and Christian theology still very popular. Greek and politics among the options. Two-thirds of the staff are lay (a number are women), 20 are monks.

NB boys are allowed to try an A level subject, even if only from a pretty modest grade obtained at GCSE. Dyslexics taught 'for the most part' in the mainstream, but there is some additional specialist one-to-one teaching available. TEFL sets also in place.

Games, Options, the Arts: Powerful games school (games are compulsory, including rugby); strong first XV. 'We have a depth of expertise,' says head. Also cricket, cross-country, hockey, athletics, squash, golf, fly-fishing, renowned beagling. Twelve rugby fifteens, seven cricket elevens, four tennis teams, 25-metre swimming pool, sports hall. Strong CDT (centre includes photography and electronics). Excellent drama, main and studio theatres. CCF now voluntary. D of E awards, scouts now taken over by Outdoor Activities Group, and clubs for everything from debating to bee-keeping. Annual pilgrimage to Lourdes for senior boys.

Background and Atmosphere: Founded in 1902. Fine setting in lovely Yorkshire valley – very isolated, but, as Father Leo points out in his drive to attract day boys, 'the half hour it takes to get boys here daily from

York is as long as many London day-school runs'. NB the fast train from London to York takes less than two hours. Rather austere 1861 Victorian Gothic main wing plus Giles Gilbert Scott's huge abbey church and school buildings (1930s) with late '80s additions: 'the Benedictines have joined forces with Holiday Inn', commented an architect, though the school points out indignantly 'There are other views!' Huge central hall 'rather like a liner' according to a pupil, and study hall with carrels (individual study desks). Much building in hand. Houses are autonomous and vary considerably in character with deliberate spread of ability throughout, run by ten housemasters, 'deeply thoughtful men, they've seen it all before' – 7 are monks, 3 are married laymen. No choice here, boys are allotted houses.

Though remote and very much a country school, Ampleforth has links with the outside world via excellent and regular lecturers, and far-away projects eg Chile and Eastern Europe (on which Father Leo has been described as 'mustard-keen'). 'It's perfect for parents abroad,' says one such, 'so much going on at weekends there and too far away for exeats.' No exeats except for the winter term, otherwise half terms. Handy list of local hotels, restaurants and B & Bs is sent out to parents in the v comprehensive book 'Confirmation of Entry – Your Questions Answered'. Not unknown for parents to rent a cottage in the area during their son's school years. The warmth of welcome is legendary: 'It's part of the Rule of St Benedict to welcome guests as Christ welcomed his guests', comments Father Leo.

Central feeding sadly now in operation – at a cost of £2.4 million – but pupils are at least seated by house for supper in subdivided areas within the main dining hall. The monks of Ampleforth singing plain chant are now known to millions via Classic FM – a nice little earner.

Pastoral Care and Discipline: Pupils have a slight reputation for wildness. Father Leo's clamp down appears to be having effect – no shock horror headlines recently. Consciences still worked on rather than harsh restrictions imposed. 'The philosophy is absolutely right,' says a parent, 'it is no good succeeding in life if you fail yourself.' The school's 'Handbook for Parents' spells out clearly what the policies are – tough, while bending over backwards not to hurt the offender's academic career. Fine for smoking (£7.50 for first offence). Lower sixth upwards can have two pints of beer with a meal in local market towns eg Helmsley – a suspension for spirits. Bad language censored: 'they see tennis stars disputing, footballers spitting, we ask for standards to be different.' Pastoral care, say parents, is 'unique'. 'The housemaster is a priest and a friend, there is a loyalty from boys in return, who come back to the Abbey to be married and to have their children christened.'

Pupils and Parents: Scions of top and middle Catholic families from all over the place. Lots of Forces children. Notoriously untidy-looking boys now stick somewhat closer to the no-uniform 'dress code' of jacket and trousers with black or sports colours ties. Old Boys include Rupert Everett, Hugo Young, Christopher Tugendhat, Lord Nolan, James Gilbey.

Entrance: Common entrance, with exceptions always allowed, especially 'for reasons of faith or family', or simply because boys have come up through the junior school. Entrants to sixth form are 'expected' to have at least 6 GCSEs at C or above, but pupils are taken in from outside the British system so 'each case on its merits'.

Exit: 90 per cent to university, on average 15-18 to Oxbridge (21 conditional places in '98). Popular subjects include history, classics, theology, music, medicine, estate and business management.

Money Matters: A generous 17 major and minor scholarships available, and others internally awarded. Seven music scholarships of varying value. Had 51 assisted places.

Remarks: Unfailingly kind and understanding top Catholic boys' boarding school that perhaps unnecessarily suffers from time to time as a result of its long-standing liberal tradition. Deserves more loyalty from the parents who form its traditional (potential) intake. Now taking day girls in the sixth form (and boarding from 2001). Beginning of the end of a great tradition, though the school points out that there have been one or two girls over the years, mostly daughters of lay staff.

AYLESBURY GRAMMAR SCHOOL

Walton Road, Aylesbury, Buckinghamshire
HP21 7RP

TEL:*01296 484545* FAX: *01296 426502*

E-MAIL: office@ags.bucks.sch.uk

WEB: www.ags.bucks.sch.uk

✦ PUPILS: 1,271 boys, all day ✦ Ages: 12-18
✦ Size of sixth form: 390 ✦ Non-denom
✦ State

Head: Since 1999, Mr Steve Harvey MA MSc, educated at Cambridge. Took over from Mr Ian Roe, who was here from 1992.

Academic Matters: School became a technology college in '97 with strong links to British Aerospace. Gets excellent GCSE and A level results year after year. The school is outstanding in computer science – v v popular, regularly has pupils in top 5 A level results and over 50 per cent grade As. General studies taken by all and very well taught – this boosts the general picture no end. Large numbers doing maths and the sciences. Few take modern languages.

New IT network (linked to the Internet) links computer block, library, science departments and new sixth form centre. Some pupils have e-mail addresses for sending work back and forth between school and home. Markets own programs. Computers with everything, even Latin. Groups of pupils can be found engaged on projects such as making a flight simulator or designing an aircraft wing. The school regularly looks after a handful of real high fliers – eg achieving first place out of 47,000 candidates in business studies/computer science at A level; a few get 5 or 6 As at A level, and not so long ago a 13-year-old got into Oxford. Extra learning support available in the shape of a part-time specialist – comes out of school budget.

Games, Options, the Arts: Particularly strong on sport – one of 30 schools nationally to be awarded Sportsmark Gold Status. Tennis teams have won the Buckinghamshire competition every year since '85. County champions at cross-country and football. Strong rugby. Basketball teams reached the last 8 in national championships, and has a member of the national squash team. That's for a start. Streams of teams for most sports. Swimming if wanted before school in the morning. Hot on sports abroad – skiing in Maine, football tour to Spain, rugby tours to South Africa and France.

Much less energy expended on art and music, and results reflect this. New centre for art, design and ceramics just built, though, which might help. School timetable linked with (very good) girls' high school next door, so increasing numbers of joint clubs and activities. The schools combine for drama and choir. Masses of orchestra, and clubs for everything. Masses of visits, trips and exchanges. Remarkably successful at public speaking events – the school has produced 3 individual world champions in recent years.

Background and Atmosphere: School founded in 1598, and moved to present site in 1907; an oasis of green in town. Original school building now surrounded by mass of specialist (some rather ugly) buildings. Boys tidy and uniformed. Occasional ponytail. Photographs of achievements everywhere, school constantly being revamped – special environmental team for plants and paintings, and wizard ceramic tile composition

by juniors in main hall showing life at the school.

Pastoral Care and Discipline: Boys relate to head of year and head of house, who report serious misdemeanours to head. Expectations high on this front.

Pupils and Parents: Half from Aylesbury, half from surrounding areas. Middle-class parents without capital still move here in droves. Mix well, helpful and supportive.

Entrance: Highly competitive. Via school reports and examination. Around 95 per cent from state schools, rest from prep. 20 boys in sixth form come in from public school and roughly the same from the state sector. Top 30 per cent of ability range. Relatively modest requirements for taking A level: 6 A–C GCSE grades with Bs in A level subjects needed for both internal and external applicants. Top 30 per cent of ability range. Pupils can come in at other times, but stringent entrance test. Waiting lists.

Exit: Around 20 a year to Oxbridge, and the rest to other universities, particularly those with scientific, business and/or computer leanings, eg Southampton, Keele, Brunel, Imperial College, Bournemouth. Boys join the professions, become engineers, business managers etc . Serious counselling for universities and careers.

Money Matters: Extra help available for extra-curricular activities – eg trips, exchanges. Recent appeal raised £400,000 for buildings etc. Not rich though.

Remarks: As we have said before, this is one of the few, old-fashioned 'free' grammar schools. Run on the lines of traditional public school, and the occasional criticism is that it is 'more like a public school than a public school'. Absolutely the place to send your computer-mad son.

BADMINTON SCHOOL

Westbury-on-Trym, Bristol BS9 3BA

TEL:*0117 905 5200 (Junior School 0117 905222)*

FAX: *0117 962 8963*

E-MAIL: registrar@badminton.bristol.sch.uk

WEB: www.badminton.bristol.sch.uk

✦ Pupils: around 290 girls, 160 board, 130 day. Plus junior school on site, 20 board, 75 day ✦ Ages: 11-18; junior school 4-11 ✦ Size of sixth form: 88 ✦ C of E ✦ Fee-paying

---

Head: Since 1997, Mrs Jan Scarrow BA (Manchester) PGCE (forties), previously deputy head at Stonar School (qv), including 6 months as acting head. Married, keen on keep fit, theatre and travel. States she is totally committed to single-sex education – boarding school ethos – girls develop as confident individuals etc etc. Took over from Mr Gould, who put the school back on the academic map.

Academic Matters: Superb results: 60 per cent get A grades at A level and close to 90 per cent get A★/A at GCSE – consistent across the subjects and along the years. Maths popular and well taught. Sciences ditto; ditto art and design. Humanities slightly squeezed. Most staff female (35 women, 8 men), more young ones than there were. Teaching staff go home by 7pm 'that way they're far more willing to come in over the weekend and do D of E or whatever.' Seriously good advice on universities and careers.

Games, Options, the Arts: Music continues to be a real strength – there is a long tradition of this in the school: 90 per cent of pupils learn an instrument, choir practice (twice a week), all manner of good interesting concerts and string quartets, with four orchestras, four choirs, numerous ensembles – quite something for a school this size. Good drama, sports matches kept to day schools 'to avoid two-hour drives'. Excellent batik and textile department, enthusiastic jewellery making, keen art and super art centre (completed '95) – a few go on to art college. Lots of options and activities often purposefully clashed with prep times during the day. Very successful European Youth Parliament speakers, also model UN (unusual in a small girls' school). Arts circus for junior girls, whereby they move round art and technology departments. Home economics examined (it's in among the A level statistics). Good on trips and outings at all levels. 'Key skills' excellent, much of it examined (spoken English, IT, languages).

Background and Atmosphere: Founded in 1858, as a place where girls would learn to compete with men in a man's world, and has been through ups and downs. Fashionable Fabians. After a blip, went up the fashion stakes again, though sadly numbers of boarders still dropping. Moved to present site, pebble-dashed 19th-century seaside-style hotel architecture, set in 20 acres on the fringe of the suburbs of Bristol, encircled by stone walls, with curiously bent yew hedges. Many new rather ugly buildings including excellent indoor pool, a pleasantly painted yellow sixth form house (extended and refurbished '99) and fine light library (with classrooms below) designed by Sir Hugh Casson (an ex-parent). Junior school and playgrounds also on site; overall sense of muddle in lay-out with not much space in a campus which feels a bit claustrophobic by boarding school standards. Strong work ethic firmly in place. School feels a bit bleak at weekends, but there is a 'weekend programme' offered. Prevalent no-nonsense attitude. Team of three head girls (elected by pupils). Super jolly, bright, busy junior school with its own pre-prep (girls now come aged 4) on site.

Pastoral Care and Discipline: Fairly tight rules (sixth form booklet mentions school's emphasis on 'moral, intellectual and social welfare' in that order). Pupils friendly and everyone knows everyone else. 'We're not wild on parties here.' Boarding staff are teachers (now the majority) plus 19-year-old Australians, plus French, German and Spanish 'assistants'. Discipline not much of a problem (occasional drinking misdemeanours). 'The strip' (the bright lights of Bristol) about a mile way.

Pupils and Parents: Mixed. Fields a nice collection (around 7 per cent) of appreciative foreigners (Malaysians, Kenyans, Hong Kong Chinese etc), and families from Devon, Cornwall, Hereford and Worcester and also London M4 corridor. Professional parents. Girls are distinctly articulate, very busy and stretched, well motivated. Very career minded. Naff baby-blue jerseys. Some complaints from boarding parents over inflexibility of exeat rules, 'at variance with weekly boarders and day girls' freedom'. Day and boarding pupils well integrated.

Entrance: At 11 (many from junior school); also at 12 and 13 (one of the first girls' boarding schools to offer places at 12 and 13 in order to cater for girls from co-ed prep schools). Also at 16 (regularly from the traditional girls' boarding schools and the Far East). Old girls include Iris Murdoch, Indira Gandhi, Claire Bloom.

Exit: Leakage to co-ed (usually) schools post GCSE, 80-90 per cent stay on to sixth form. Almost all who apply to university get into their first choice. Increasing numbers do gap year. Art college popular in some years – the majority to places of excellence. A few to Oxbridge every year. Medicine a particularly popular subject, also engineering, and an unusually wide variety of subjects and careers followed.

Money Matters: Careful with money, 10 per cent of fees are spent on the buildings, so the school is well maintained with constant improvements. Had no assisted places; 'help is available'. Variable scholarships – 24 awarded last year (academic, music and art, and general all-round) worth between 10-50 per cent of fees.

Remarks: Strong all-round small girls' school, more aggressive than the 'nice' little all-girls' schools, with a lot to offer. Still suffering from the anti-boarding fashion, but Mrs Scarrow points out that overall numbers are up. Useful place to include on your short list, especially if you want a non-institutional school that caters for the individual.

BANCROFT'S SCHOOL
Woodford Green, Essex IG8 0RF
TEL: *020 8505 4821* FAX: *020 8559 0032*

✦ PUPILS: 788 boys and girls (equal numbers). Plus prep school on site, about 200 boys and girls ✦ Ages: 11-18; prep school 8-11 ✦ Size of sixth form: 206 ✦ C of E, but Jews and Muslims properly provided for ✦ Fee-paying

Head: Since 1996, Dr Peter Scott. A graduate of St John's College, Oxford, he taught for 17 years at Charterhouse, where he was a housemaster, and was deputy head at the Royal Grammar School, Guildford. He has also been an inspector of schools and has written 8 textbooks on chemistry. A youngish, energetic head with a frequently-deployed smile and a firm handshake, he states that he is 'committed to getting the best out of every individual in the school'. Bancroft's seems to attract, or perhaps create very loyal headmasters; Dr Scott was only the sixth head to be appointed in the twentieth century.

Academic Matters: The record here is verging on the stupendous. 100 per cent of pupils achieve 5 or more GCSEs at grade C or above; 50 per cent achieve at least 8 A grades; it is in fact the highest-achieving co-educational school in the country, in terms of GCSEs and A-levels, and has been for the last 2 years. Pupils are repeatedly reminded of this fact, and it's fair to say that a pretty academic atmosphere reigns. Latin is compulsory for the first 2 years and ancient Greek is an option. Some interesting AS levels on offer, including critical thinking and philosophy of religion. There is a teacher with responsibility for diagnosing and helping dyslexic pupils; but if you had dyslexia in any but its mildest form, you simply wouldn't be at this school.

Games, Options, the Arts: A strong tradition of drama. Every year there's an interhouse drama competition, as well as a junior play, a middle school play and a senior play (last year's senior play was *Murder in the Cathedral*; the year before that, *The Crucible*). Rugby, hockey, cricket, netball and tennis are the principal sports; there are squash courts and a swimming pool. John Lever, ex-England bowler, is on the PE staff.

The school orchestra puts on a concert once a term. The school choir puts on a big annual concert at the Drapers' Hall. Wide variety of clubs to join: the electronics club boasts 3 winners of the Young Electronic Designer Award. 10 gold and 22 silver D of E awards last year. There's a Sea Scouts troop and CCF. Pupils produce an annual magazine, *The Bancroftian*. Also hot on trips and exchange visits. There are annual exchanges with France, Spain, Germany, Greece and even New Zealand.

Background and Atmosphere: Founded in 1737 by the Drapers' Company on behalf of Francis Bancroft as a school for poor boys. The original site was in Mile End; the school moved to leafier Woodford in 1889. The building is a redbrick Victorian pile with towers and crenellated walls, a large quadrangle with a war memorial in the middle, playing fields, a chapel and a wood-panelled library: all in all a reasonable imitation of a minor Oxford college. It is surrounded by Epping Forest on two sides with busy roads on the other two, lined with large, expensive houses.

Pastoral Care and Discipline: The school is 'very keen on mutual respect', says the head. There is a written anti-bullying policy, but in fact bullying isn't a problem here. There's a general atmosphere of good behaviour and politeness. All sixth form pupils are monitors, with responsibility for ensuring orderly lunch queues etc. They have the power to give detentions, but this hasn't been done within living memory.

Pupils and Parents: There's quite an ethnic mix here. About 30 per cent of pupils are of Asian origin; there's also a strong Jewish contingent. Chapel is attended by most pupils, but there is also a Jewish assembly and Moslem prayers. Pupils mainly drawn from affluent Essex suburbs rather than from East London. The boys wear dark grey suits and the girls wear maroon skirts. It's a crowded, bustling school – not quite enough space, really, but it's a good-natured sort of bustle. Kids are feisty but friendly. A parent remarks: 'There's a feeling of oneness about the school, from the prep school to the sixth form'. Alan Davies, the comedian and actor, is an Old Boy. So is David Pannick, Britain's youngest ever QC.

Entrance: Competitive entrance exam along the lines of the 11-plus. Of about 400 candidates, about 60 are selected (the rest of the annual intake is drawn from the prep school). The exam is on a Saturday but there is an alternative Wednesday evening sitting for the benefit of Orthodox Jewish candidates.

Exit: Almost all pupils go on to university. 20 or so to Oxbridge.

Money Matters: Bancroft's has a strong link with the Drapers' Company, which offers a number of scholarships, usually for half or a third of the full fee. The school also awards six of its own assisted places each year. In total, about 170 pupils receive financial support.

Remarks: There's a certain amount of pressure to succeed academically, but it would not be fair to call it a hothouse. The school does encourage plenty of interests besides academic ones. If your child is bright, they'll probably enjoy themselves here. If they're not, they probably won't get in.

BEDALES SCHOOL
Petersfield, Hampshire GU32 2DG

Tel: *01730 300 100, admissions 01730 304 274*

Fax: *01730 300500*

E-mail: registra@bedales.org.uk

Web: www.bedales.org.uk

✦ Pupils: around 400, boys and girls, in approximately equal numbers (around 75 per cent board) ✦ Ages: 13-18 ✦ Size of sixth form: around 170 ✦ Non-denom ✦ Fee-paying

Head: Since 1995, Mrs Alison Willcocks MA BMus (forties). Educated at Cambridge and Birmingham. Previously taught at Portsmouth High School, and was housemistress then deputy head at Bedales – an appointment from within the school. A very capable lady, whose interests include literature, music, history and child psychology. Immensely articulate. Fabulously convinced and convincing about co-education – 'boys and girls are wired up differently'. A few parents complain that she does not listen. Large family; husband, David, used to be admissions tutor. Mrs Willcocks is a member of the HMC and chaired their co-educational group in '98.

Retiring September 2001, to be succeeded by Mr Keith Budge MA CertEd (forties). Educated at Rossall, read English at University College, Oxford, PGCE at Edinburgh. Rugby blue. Previously a housemaster at Marlborough, and then (from '95 to '00) head of Loretto. Married to Moony, three young children.

Academic Matters: Operates very much on university lines – broad curriculum, pupils learn to organise themselves and work on their own – working habits taught in the junior school. This can be tricky for pupils coming in from schools taught by more straight up-and-down methods.

Some outstanding staff, some of very long standing. Parent commented school had 'given my daughter a love of English and theatre which will last her for the rest of her life'. Voluntary extensions in several subjects for pupils who want to be stretched beyond exam courses. 9–11 GCSEs the norm. Dual award science for all at GCSE. Setting in maths, science and French. French results quite good by public school standards – large numbers taking it perhaps reflect Foreign Office parents. English by far the most popular A level subject and the school gets solid results in this: biology, history, economics come next. Subjects more or less balanced between boys and girls – including science. Pupils encouraged to do arts with science. Exceptionally strong, stable common room. Two part-time qualified special needs teachers help fiftyish pupils, all staff trained to help with special needs pupils.

Games, Options, the Arts: School has had reputation of having a strong art department, and 10 or so go on to art foundation courses each year – and it still attracts much pupil talent. Music, under Nick Gleed, v v good and has produced some outstanding work, and NB there are good opportunities for the less skilled too. Drama also lively – a good place for budding thespians, particularly after the building of the Olivier Theatre.

Sport. We have been taken to task again for suggesting that sport at Bedales consists of happily making daisy chains on the boundary during cricket matches. A spokesman says this is no longer so, and points to the school's current achievements: 3 county players at netball, under 15s won the South East Hampshire tournament, and the under 14s were runners up in the South of England netball championships; hockey: Bedales 'won more matches than it drew or lost'; football: played 14, won 8, drawn 3 which, writes the captain, is 'possibly as good as it gets'. We stand corrected, but still humbly suggest that serious sportspeople might do better elsewhere. The alternative to games is Outdoor Work (ODW) – hands-on farm and conservation work on the school's estate – and this is taken up by many. Strongly imaginative and green environmental policy.

Background and Atmosphere: A way of life school, which attracts like-minded staff and parents, who are on the whole very loyal to the place. Started in 1893 by J H Badley in an attempt to retain the best features of traditional public schools, while reforming the narrow bias towards classics, muscular Christianity and rugby. One of the oldest co-educational boarding schools – a true mix, in which boys and girls relate to each other on equal terms and, much more unusual, on equal terms with the staff. Pupils all call staff by Christian name (including the head), and this, says a pupil who has also been in a school where more conventional modes of address are used, 'has the immediate effect of putting them on the same footing as you. They cannot be stuffy, and you cannot be in awe of them.' Present head considers communication 'a vital aspect of school'.

School has reputation of being liberal and let-it-all-hang-out, but this has been a surface impression, more or less confined to clothes, which give pupils an illusion of freedom, while allowing staff to run the place with a firm structure. No uniform – school is contender for scruffiest in the country, all clothes go in washing machine and come out grunge-coloured. Pupils go round like walking rag-bags, 'it's the fashion now', said one. Hair is also freedom city – you can dye it sky blue pink if you wish.

Mish-mash of mostly jolly old and new buildings, including fine example of arts and crafts through to 1960s utilitarian structures. Glorious mellow library, well stocked (40,000 books). Barns restored by students for ODW centre. Girls, excepting upper sixth, are all housed under one roof (Steephurst) – giant rambling building with corridors, annexes – quite ghastly for newcomers, and gives school a feeling of being very large and soulless, though a new pupil commented that she was reassured on entering the place to 'see it filled with smiles'. Smart new(ish) boys' boarding house, the school's pride and joy, looks like a ski chalet. Three main boarding houses, with upper sixth now in the recently refurbished house, which aims to provide 'good pre-university atmosphere of controlled co-ed boarding'. Until upper sixth, boys and girls in mixed-age dorms. Food not brilliant but the few complaints of hunger appear a thing of the past.

Pastoral Care and Discipline: School famous for the strength of its pastoral care – staff highly experienced at watching for and sorting out problems and handling rebels with the lightest of touches. Excellent house staff. School has various customs which bring unruly into line ('abuse freedom, lose freedom'). Everyone shakes everyone's hand at the end of assemblies (three times a week) and at 'jaw' on Sunday evenings (the nearest the school appears to get to the high moral ground). Punishments can be based on labouring for the commu-

nity. Large numbers of pupils go home at weekends. Excellent relationship with the village of Steep, in which school is – a good test of how a school is functioning. Discipline on 'issues that really matter' can be tough but fair. Students (NB they are not referred to as pupils here) know where they stand. Firm emphasis on self-discipline, with scope for making mistakes and – hopefully – 'growing through them'.

Pupils and Parents: Famous for its arty media parents, but also lots of Foreign Office and large numbers of sons and daughters of luvvies. Some a bit brittle, a bit cliquey. Two of Pink Floyd were parents here, as were Peter Hall, Princess Margaret and Ted Hughes/Sylvia Plath. Most pinned-up famous OB is still Daniel Day-Lewis.

Entrance: Half from Bedales' own junior school, Dunhurst (qv), the rest from over 100 preps in London and the south west, including co-ed ones such as Windlesham. Entry at 11, 13, and into sixth form. 6 'good' GCSEs minimum, but according to the admissions tutor, 'present competition for sixth form places demands A grades in A level subjects to be considered for the sixth form' (now the norm at the fashionable sixth forms).

Potential pupils come down for civil service-type two-day residential tests over a wide range of subjects and performance – excellent also for pupils to get to know and judge the school.

Exit: Many do gap year – and some travel scholarships are available. 'Nearly all get to first or second choice of university.' A good number to art college. A few to Oxbridge.

Money Matters: During a previous reign, school built up excellent reserves, and so has developed its facilities; while not among the ritzier of establishments, it isn't missing anything important. School bends over backwards to help parents in financial distress and on this score alone earns its charitable status. Had 5 assisted places in each year, but poverty is not something associated with Bedalian parents. Scholarships available for general excellence at 13+, for music throughout, and for art and design and academic excellence at 16+.

Remarks: Genuine co-ed boarding school. Once highly fashionable, now less so. A one-off. You either like it or loathe it. Can justifiably claim to 'educate for life'. Will be watched with interest, post-Willcocks .

BEDFORD SCHOOL

Burnaby Road, Bedford MK40 2TU

TEL: *01234 362 200* FAX: *01234 362 283*

E-MAIL: registrar@bedfordschool.org.uk

WEB: www.bedfordschool.org.uk

✦ PUPILS: around 660 boys (226 full boarders, 40 weekly) plus prep school, with 450 boys ✦ Ages: 7-18 ✦ Size of sixth form: around 280 ✦ C of E ✦ Fee-paying

---

Head: Since 1990, Dr I P Evans OBE MA PhD FRSC (early fifties). Educated at 'a maintained grammar school' in North Wales, then got a first in natural sciences at Cambridge, followed by PhD at Imperial College, London. Came via St Paul's where he was head of chemistry and chief examiner for A level at University of London Examining Board. Keen committee man. An enthusiast: keen on cricket, the organ (which he plays), poetry and a Welsh-speaking Celt whose non-conformist views ('caring communities are important in educating the young') are reflected in his passion for pastoral care. 'Good civilized values are supported by the power of working together.' Teaches chemistry. His wife also has a PhD in chemistry. A fast talker; his eyes twinkle only slightly more than his watch chain. Bubbly, caring and urbane (for all his Welsh lilt).

Academic Matters: Impressive – computers throughout, myriad labs and language labs – separate buildings for science, IT etc . Latin and a little Greek. 'High degree of scholarship among the staff.' Marvellous facilities: fully networked, 200 computers in all; full-blown weather station incorporated into geography department. Much use of visual aids. Classes of 18/20 throughout GCSE programme, 10-12 at A level. Uses all three exam boards (one of the many schools which have opted for this).

Games, Options, the Arts: Superb design technology building still a little under-used, marvellous wood-working (sorry, natural materials technology), electronics, pneumatics facilities etc . Art room burgeoning with ideas – though v few take it at A level – and own library and slide dept. Music department well equipped, with children working quite late on their own compositions. Impressive standards, with a large batch of grade 8 players of various instruments. The recreation centre combines a purpose-built theatre (huge depth of stage) attached to a seven-badminton-court-sized games hall, vast swimming pool (canoes). Keep fit room. Games taken very seriously, hockey and rugby still strong, also basketball. CCF very popular. Leadership values are strongly emphasised. The school makes full use of river, rowing is popular, and they usually thrash all comers in local regattas.

Background and Atmosphere: Letters Patent 1552, endowed by Sir William Harpur 1566, moved to present site 1891. Main school burnt down in March 1979 and internal structure radically reshaped, with mega hall on first floor. Good feeling of space. 50 acres of playing field-filled campus, dominated by G F Bodley-designed school chapel (newly restored) – God is strong at Bedford. Hotchpotch of ancillary buildings, culminating in the building of a 500-seater hall, attached to prep school and much used by them.

Revamped Victorian boarding house near campus. Boys move from small dormitories to study bedrooms: all very cosy with carpets and duvets and occasional poster. Day boys are allotted to same six houses: there is no apparent rivalry between the two. One smart boarding house for sixth formers only. NB the International Study Centre for boys and girls aged 11-17 is steaming ahead.

Pastoral Care and Discipline: Relies on houseparents and tutors – same tutor throughout. 'Discipline not a problem.' Based on co-operation. Drugs: 'no problems in school'; but would sack if discovered, cigarettes totally banned anywhere in school – staff as well as pupils. Very strong anti-bullying programme. Children helped write the policy document.

Pupils and Parents: Much loyalty to school and most UK boarders have strong Bedford connections or live within a 50/60-mile radius. Buses all over Bedfordshire and to Milton Keynes and beyond: wide net. Around 20 boarders have Service connections (mostly RAF). 10 per cent overseas pupils, mainly at sixth form, including boys from Hong Kong, Japan, Thailand, Malaysia and Brunei, also Germans, some Spaniards and other Europeans. Paddy Ashdown an OB, also H H Munro (Saki), John Fowles.

Entrance: From own prep school, and elsewhere by CE at 13 with pre-testing at 12 as well. Own exam for boys entering from state schools.

Exit: 99 per cent go to universities; 16 to Oxbridge in '00.

Money Matters: The well-endowed Harpur Trust helps out generously. Had a large number of assisted places; will feel their loss, but bursaries coming in to replace some.

Remarks: Gritty and purposeful traditional boys' school with a good following, good social mix and outstanding facilities. Low profile, but much admired by educationalists and now becoming well-known for its International Study Centre.

JUNIOR SCHOOL: Bedford Preparatory School, Tel: 01234 362274, Fax: 01234 362285. Head: Since 1997, Mr Christopher Godwin BSc (Loughborough) MA (Durham) (late late thirties). Came to the school in '93, was director of studies at the prep school until his appointment as head. Super, highly regarded prep school, self contained but can use facilities of the senior school. Strong on games and music. French from 7; German, Spanish and Latin from 11. Five star hotel-esque boarding house. All boys go on to the senior school with rare exceptions (logistical, financial, occasionally they don't make the grade).

BENENDEN SCHOOL

Cranbrook, Kent TN17 4AA

TEL: *01580 240592* FAX: *01580 240280*

E-MAIL: registrar@benenden.kent.sch.uk

WEB: www.benenden.kent.sch.uk

✦ PUPILS: 442 girls, all board
✦ Ages: 11-18 ✦ Size of sixth form: 149
✦ C of E ✦ Fee-paying

Head: Since 2000, Mrs Claire Oulton (late thirties). Taught history at Benenden before becoming head of history at Charterhouse and then head of St Catherine's, Bramley. Married to Nick, a publisher – two daughters aged 9 and 7. We hear good things of her. Took over from Mrs Gillian duCharme, who was here from 1985.

Academic Matters: Very strong A level results. Popular subjects English, maths, biology, economics (consistently impressive but responsible for too many of the very few Ds and below), chemistry. A few doing 'Chinese'. Setting in maths, Latin, French. GCSEs now taken early in maths, French and Latin. Inspiring English master, Dutch–Welshman Nicholas van der Vliet, still doing his stuff. All 11 to 13-year-olds now do two modern languages on entering the school. Design technology and theatre studies on offer. 'Limited' amount of extra support for specific learning difficulties and EFL.

Games, Options, the Arts: Traditionally hot on these: lacrosse, 15 tennis courts (including all-weather), squash etc – lots of inter-house matches. Strong tradition of riding at the excellent nearby stables (see Old Girls). Also, judo, dance. Indoor swim-ming pool (25 metres), plus dance studio and area well thought out for seminars. Technology centre opened 1991. Lots of music and drama. Holds regular arts festival, for which they manage to get top writers, designers, etc to participate. Art not notably popular. Whole campus now networked with e-mail for staff and students.

Background and Atmosphere: Founded in 1923 by three mistresses from Wycombe Abbey. Huge, elegant and slightly gloomy Victorian mansion built by Gathorne Hardy, first Earl of Cranbrook, set in 244 acres, with lots of rhododendrons. Generally dormies are now arranged by year group in six 11-16-year-old houses, plus sixth form centre. Rogues' gallery close to staff room with named photograph of every pupil, ditto staff. Isolated position makes the school self contained, and life is a bit boyless – not good news for sixth formers. A fourth sixth form house opened in 1997. £6 million study centre under construction. In the traditional all-girls' boarding school manner, crushes and passions still run high – shades of Angela Brazil. General atmosphere on the steamy side. Few comparable boys' schools nearby, but most houses now twinned with houses in boys' schools, especially Tonbridge.

Pastoral Care and Discipline: New policy on television watching, following parental angst. No set night for television: the thinking behind this is that they will watch less and 'must learn to budget their time'. Houses now smaller, with more married housemistresses and also housemasters. Atmosphere less institutional and more family life-like, a fact that was amply demonstrated in the rosy-tinted television programme on the school, which showed happy matrons cheerily coming in and drawing back the curtains. But 'It's not like that at all', say pupils. The new uniform is considered boring.

Academic tutors attached to each house – 6 to 8 students each. Smoking not allowed (fixed penalties). Sixth formers may drink limited amount of alcohol with 'specific permission'.

Pupils and Parents: Interesting and rich geographical and social mix – new money, first-time buyers, overseas pupils and some upper crust. Three-quarters UK residents (most from quite close), the rest half ex-pats and half foreign (from 26 different countries). Most famous Old Girl HRH Princess Royal; also Charlotte Brew (the first lady to ride in the Grand National), Liz Forgan, Joanna Foster (Chairman of the Equal Opportunities Commission), the Reverend Angela Berners-Wilson (one of the pioneer women priests) and – wait for it – Lady Moon (founder of worldwide Old Bags' Society for rejected wives – following the wonderful headline case in which she cut off sleeves of her erring husband's suits and distributed his cellar of chateau-bottled clarets about the village).

Entrance: By CE and interview – from 60 different preps at 11+, 12+ and 13+. A few at sixth form – keen to have fresh blood at this stage. Competitive exam for external sixth form entrants, plus 'at least' 6 grade C GCSEs including As or Bs in A level subjects. Home-grown pupils need at least 6 GCSEs at grade C or above, and 'at least' Bs in A level subjects. £50 registration fee; also 20 per cent of a term's fees on acceptance of a place (ie just under £800 at time of writing).

Exit: A good number do a gap year. Then on to degree courses. London v popular, also Bristol, a handful to Newcastle, Edinburgh and Oxbridge (but 18 per cent

in '00), otherwise everywhere from Bath to Surrey and the USA.

Money Matters: Sixth form (academic, music and art) and lower school (academic and music) scholarship exams are held at the school in January. Major (up to 50 per cent of fees) and minor awards. Don't hold your breath though – school not well endowed. Some bursaries for hard times, with priority normally given to students about to sit public examinations.

Remarks: Traditional girls' country boarding school. No longer a fashionable choice for English pupils, but this could be a strength. Institutional and appearing slightly old-fashioned in today's climate, but see what the new head can do.

BIRKDALE SCHOOL

Oakholme Road, Sheffield S10 3DH

TEL: *01142 668409 Fax: 01142 671947*

E-MAIL: birkdalesc@aol.com

WEB: www.isis.org.uk/data/0115.htm

✦ PUPILS: 725 boys, including prep and pre-prep school; around 25 girls in the sixth form, all day ✦ Ages: 4-18 ✦ Size of sixth form: 160 ✦ Christian ✦ Fee-paying

---

Head: Since 1998, Mr Robert J Court MA (late forties). Educated at St Paul's and Clare College, Cambridge (physics). From 1974 a master, housemaster and (in 1994) second master at Westminster School. Married to Andrea. Took over from The Rev M D A

Hepworth, who built the school up into the success story it is today.

Academic Matters: The school has built up a good design technology department (working on a project to replant the centre of Sheffield when we visited, as part of an A level course) and art department. Good staff here, moved into new buildings in 1998. Everyone does general studies at A level and lots get A grades. Only the most mainstream subjects currently being studied, though one or two more exotic ones – politics, and music for example, are offered. Few doing languages – though the school has wonderful assistants to help – but numbers increasing and more now doing physics or art at A level too. English (lang and lit), geography, maths, history and biology currently the most popular A level subjects, with OK results. All do double award science at GCSE. Currently 34 per cent of the staff are female – unusual in a boys' secondary school, but, of course, standard in a prep school. Class sizes are a maximum 24, but average 15 in the senior school, and staff:pupil ratio is a respectable 1:10.

Games, Options, the Arts: The school buses pupils to sports fields. There aren't enough girls to do much within the school, but they take part in the local netball league, hockey is 'also available', and swimming – that is, said one or two of the boys darkly, 'when they are not shopping'. Traditionally the school has not set a lot of store by games success, but head points to their '96 and '99 South Africa tours, to triumphs in cricket (under 12's) and football (1st XI) and to the sixth formers who are currently playing for Yorkshire and Derbyshire under 19s in rugby and cricket. Team games compulsory for the first two years of the senior school. Everyone in the lower sixth does a week's work experience

(good contacts with industry, not least among the current parents) and 'leadership training'. Strong outward-bounding.

Background and Atmosphere: The school was founded at the turn of the century as a private prep school, and remained that way until 1978. The school then took in pupils to 16, then in 1988 started a sixth form, sharing teaching with the nearby girls' school. For various reasons this did not work out, and Birkdale now successfully runs its own sixth form. The school acquired a new 2.3 acre site in '97 and burst out of its hitherto cramped quarters into it in '98. There is a very nice octagonal sort of gazebo for concerts. The main school hall is shrill and much too small for current numbers (extension planned). There is a separate sixth form block – the Grayson Building (named after a governor), which has lots of little boxes opening off narrow corridors, but running into a nice old house which used to be offices. It was cold when we visited, and the pupils acknowledged this was a problem. Atmosphere lively, scruffy and quite fun however, and the actual site of the school is in one of the nicest parts of Sheffield – education corner, up by the university, and near the other schools.

Pastoral Care and Discipline: The school's policy statement reads: 'It is the policy of Birkdale School to promote a Christian lifestyle…any illegal use of controlled drugs by either staff or pupils will be treated as serious misconduct'. The school is structured into five age 'layers', with a head for each layer, there are also form tutors. School uniform (black and grey with vying red striped ties) right the way through the school. Girls wear neat jackets and skirts with white blouses.

Pupils and Parents: Local lads, many first

generation in private education. Large catchment area. OBs: Michael Palin, a brace of judges, lawyers, an MP, etc.

Entrance: The school is not selective at the age of 4 – although there is a testette to go into the senior school – but boys coming straight to the senior school are tested; so it's semi-selective.

Exit: Ex-polys the most popular (De Montfort, Leeds Met etc); Leeds the most popular university: a few to Oxbridge. Business, engineering, computing and law are popular degree subjects (most of the pupils we talked to wanted to become lawyers).

Money Matters: Coining in money from fees (which are reasonable). Was given assisted places just before they were phased out, so this should not cause a problem. Academic scholarships of 25 per cent of school fees are on offer – which can be topped up in case of need.

Remarks: Junior school which has grown at lightning pace into a full-blown boys' private secondary school, serving a great need in the area. Outgrew its strength for a time, building up numbers too fast rather than stopping to consolidate departments and smooth out rough edges. The situation is now settling down and Birkdale looks set to become part of the Sheffield educational scenery in its current incarnation.

JUNIOR SCHOOL: On separate rather nice site, overlooking the Botanical Gardens, in what was once the family home of the Osborn family. Compared with the senior school, the prep school feels vast – big corridors, rooms with space, music rooms in the basement, and its own noisy gym. Not a cosy place, even in the pre-prep forms, which are in their own wing.

BLACKHEATH HIGH SCHOOL

Vanburgh Park, London SE3 7AG

TEL: *020 8853 2929* FAX: *020 8853 3663*

E-MAIL: info@bla.gdst.net

WEB: www.gdst.net/blackheathhighschool

✦ PUPILS: 360 girls, all day, plus 295 in junior school and nursery
✦ Ages: 11-18, juniors 3-11 ✦ Size of sixth form 45✦ Non-denom ✦ Fee-paying

---

Head: Since 2000, Mrs Elizabeth Owen BA MA PGCE (forties). Read geography at Liverpool, taught at St Christopher's Beckenham, Old Palace School Croydon, and Cator Park. Joined Bishop Challoner as deputy head, then became head, and hence here. Believes that praise is more motivating than punishment. Took over from Miss Rosanne Musgrave, who left 'to strike out on her own'.

Academic Matters: Strong, traditional grammar-school teaching. Gap between project- and subject-based teaching bridged by sending girls to eg study life in St Omer, visit London museums, make scale drawings in maths and geography, print their own reports, and make and fire their own bricks for building models in technology. Three separate sciences taught to half at GCSE, with combined science for the rest. Around 23 to a class, 1:3 male:female teacher ratio: 9 GCSEs the norm 'There's no point in doing too many, I want them to go on playing the tuba and swimming.' There is lots of good advice on A levels. maths and English are most popular subjects with economics on offer. Homework not unduly heavy – school is conscious that some pupils get a huge amount of help at home, others none.

Games, Options, the Arts: Bus to 5-acre site at Kidbrooke Park for hockey and netball. Popular rowing for sixth form at Royal Victoria Docks. Bizarre listed '50s 'gull-wing' former chapel serves as music centre. Flourishing music department, two-thirds learn an instrument, three choirs, orchestra, traditional jazz band, recorder groups. Plays, poetry competition, keen art (life class offered) with trips to European cities. Active social services programme: girls 'adopt' and visit local OAPs, funding an annual party for them by means of discos and socials.

Background and Atmosphere: GDST school. Moved in '94 to imposing Victorian brick pile across the Heath in Vanbrugh Park, formerly a Church Army training college, with renovated rear annexes. 'But it's not all roses', muttered a member of staff of the school move. A hall is badly needed. A new multimedia resources centre recently opened. Bustling, friendly, unsnobbish girls in navy-pinstriped blouses; no uniforms in sixth, lots of trousers on show as they sit chatting over coffee in sixth form common room. Morning assembly 'generally uplifting monotheistic, so as not to offend'. Cafeteria-style food and vending machines. Good careers advice.

Pastoral Care and Discipline: Strong policy centering on form tutors, joined by older girls who help in junior classes – 'they love it', comments head. Homework books sent home for parents to sign or comment on, lots of space for these, target attainment ratings. PSHE classes. Immediate expulsion for drugs, suspension for drinking.

Pupils and Parents: Ethnic and social melange drawn from gentrified Blackheath, also from Rotherhithe, Deptford and Catford. One-third black and Asian. Friendly parent body, ranging from top professional classes to blue-collar, raises £5,000 each year for the school. OG Baroness Jay.

Entrance: From state primary and local preps at 11. Exams in maths and English, plus Mrs Owen's Blackheath Paper III surprise, 'might be a design problem – build a paper platform – or questions on a video. It's to see how they reason. Prep schools hate it', enthused head. Interview to suss out 'a good sense of humour and enthusiasm for life – we don't want little silent gnomes'. School is part of the South London Consortium (pioneered by Mrs Owen.

Exit: Almost all to higher education. Around 2-5 to Oxbridge. Old girls include Margaret Jay, Katie Stewart, Mary Quant, Helen Lederer.

Money Matters: Very reasonable fees (about £6,000 per annum), paid mostly by monthly direct debit. Had many assisted places and may eventually feel their loss, depending on success of the GDST's Minerva fund in replacing them.

Remarks: Strong, unpretentious, multi-ethnic, expanding city school turning out confident, realistic girls for bargain outlay.

JUNIOR SCHOOL: Wemyss Road, SE3 0TF Tel: 020 8852 1537. Head: Mrs Nicola Gan CertEd. Moved into the refurbished premises which recently housed the senior school: 1880s fine purpose-built premises with Palladian-style hall and balustraded double staircase. A good move for the juniors, lovely place, now expanding from 250 to 300 3-11 year olds. Active after-school care caters for girls who are collected late. Most girls go on to the senior school.

BLOXHAM SCHOOL

Banbury, Oxfordshire OX25 4PE

TEL: *01295 720206* FAX: *01295 721897*

E-MAIL: registrar@bloxham.oxon.sch.uk

WEB: www.bloxham.oxon.sch.uk

✦ PUPILS: 340; 263 boys, 97 girls (70 per cent board) ✦ Ages: 11-18 ✦ Size of sixth form: 155 ✦ C of E ✦ Fee-paying

---

Head: Mr David Exham MA (Cantab) PGCE (fifties). Unmarried, educated at Radley and read maths at Christ's College. Came here via St Peter's York, King's Taunton where he was housemaster and head of maths (he still teaches it), and Repton where he was deputy head. Has overseen a considerable building programme since our last visit – the school went totally co-ed in 1998 with an increase in numbers plus a very snazzy lower school; boarders on the increase as well, and boarding age now dropped to 11.

Affable and avuncular, he reckons to turn out 'friendly individuals, not clones; contributors who have achieved their academic potential'. His contract has five years to run.

Academic Matters: Results good, given the intake. GCSE has few A*s, but very few below C either – good teaching (though science seems to lag). A level results consistent – German seems to do well. Favoured subject is business studies (originally introduced for the less able and now fervently studied by all abilities). Huge spread of languages (though less now than previously, as the number of exotic foreigners decreases).

School uses the modular exam system to full advantage. Staff say, 'it's not an easy school to leave'. Computers everywhere, networked with printers throughout, no keyboarding taught as such, the head wonders if 'voice recognition' programmes will make basic keyboarding skills redundant.

Superb remedial facilities for dyslexia under Hugh Alexander (still), though school is anxious not to be known as a school for dyslexics and says it 'only accepts children with an IQ in the high 120s as members of the dyslexia unit'. Not as many laptops as one might expect, but scribing and 'translating' for exams (ie a teacher who knows the pupil's work and writing will transcribe his or her answers into 'proper' English).

Games, Options, the Arts: The advent of girls throughout the school has hammered the rugby teams, no longer trailing clouds of glory. But lots of good variety remains – tennis/hockey Astroturf, huge modern gym, two charming little cricket grounds and great indoor swimming pool, much used by locals (there was a geriatric swim-in when we visited). School good at individual sports. The boys were national champion clay shots for the second year running, and the girls were second. Expected to wipe the board at the schools' polo championship

Music perhaps not as blox-swinging as it was before – new head of music who does not add 'blox' to everything. Art department open at weekends, much improved since our last visit; some exciting ceramics and textiles, lots of As at A level. Drama in The Wesley, the old converted chapel, popular and thriving. Young Enterprise, D of E etc. Staff put in a lot of extra hours here, and it's not so easy to get good staff; those that come must 'live in the parish of Bloxham' and are certainly not the huntin' shootin' brigade, says the head.

Background and Atmosphere: Founded in 1860 and given to the Woodard Foundation in 1896. Handsome building of Horton stone, quarried from below the foundations (very economical), with stunning chapel on first floor. Glorious re-shaping of dining room and kitchen area has released the basement to business studies; the TV monitor displays the financial channel and clocks on the wall tell the time in New York and Tokyo. Fabulous new IT building, the top floor floats above the lower, joined by an alarming glass staircase. New lower school opened in May 2000 – a palatial transformation of the White Lion pub, feels just like a ship with decking and portholes, though some of the passages seem a little narrow to accommodate two chattering creatures carrying books.

School proper is contained in playing field-filled eighty-acre campus with quite a lot of out-houses and buildings; a lot of walking. Boys and girls allowed a certain amount of free visiting between houses; girls' houses much posher. All graduate from dorms to study bedrooms by fifth form. Sparkling new furniture everywhere.

The school went totally co-ed in 1998. Day and boarding numbers on the increase, and boarding age now dropped to 11. School is essentially a boarding school, weekly boarding OK, and the odd flexi-boarding but head 'not prepared to become the Bloxham travel lodge'. Days are long, from 8.30am–9pm.

Pastoral Care and Discipline: Strong tutorial system via houses; children stay with same tutor throughout. Each house has five tutors who are often on hand during prep in the evening. 'Brilliant' new chaplain recently appointed. Discipline 'not as big a problem here, we're a small school where you feel you might be letting someone down'. Drugs policy: urine testing on demand if drug use suspected, followed by probable rustication and random testing. No pupil is automatically expelled, though they would be for repeated offences.

Booze not a major problem, head usually suspends 'it puts the others off'. The school bar is pupil controlled and leads to a lot less over-boozing than if staff were in charge. Fags the biggest problem ('it comes and goes'), pupils suspended if caught smoking in the building, villagers complain if they drop fag ends in the (very pretty) village, and the campus is too busy to find a quiet corner. Head tightened up on visits between the sexes – 'before, you didn't worry about a girl coming out of a boy's study, now intra-house contact is fairly controlled'.

Pupils and Parents: Lots of first-time buyers. Parents with children in the state sector come to the school because they see it as 'an upmarket alternative to the state system' and parents from the independent prep sector come to the school because they see it as 'a gentler school for the less able'. Basically North Oxfordshire farmers, businessmen, the Services – a good mix. Forget Range Rovers, green wellies and huskies; these children are neither street-wise nor Sloane.

Entrance: Takes a wide range of abilities. At 11 own test and assessment, at 13 from trad prep schools; Bilton Grange, Swanbourne, Winchester House, New College etc. At sixth form by interview and report from previous school.

Exit: Small leakage after GCSE. Majority go on to higher education – ex-polys and universities favouring practical hands-on courses, eg Southampton, Loughborough, Harper Adams (for agri/land management), Bristol (UWE).

Money Matters: Parents in real need still

get helped via the 'dreaded blue form'. Woodard Foundation can give help in an emergency for children of old Bloxhamists. Huge collection of scholarships for everything from music, sport, DT, art and academic ability, at 11+, 13+ and sixth form; take as many as you want, as often as you want. Amazing.

Remarks: A thriving school with Christian values, academically more challenging than before. Very strong dyslexia unit.

BLUNDELL'S SCHOOL

Tiverton, Devon EX16 4DN

TEL: *01884 252543* FAX: *01884 243 232*

E-MAIL: registrars@blundells.org

WEB: www.blundells.org

✦ PUPILS: 519; 330 boys, 189 girls (two-thirds board/weekly board, one-third day)
✦ Ages: 11-18 ✦ Size of sixth form: 165
✦ C of E ✦ Fee-paying

Head: Since 1992, Mr Jonathan Leigh MA (late forties), educated at Eton and a Cambridge choral scholar; historian – teaches the first-year sixth. Married with two children. Previously second master at Cranleigh. A housemasterly head – holds the reins but delegates; often to be seen with his equally approachable black labrador. Hot on pastoral care, and still remembered with admiration by those in his house at Cranleigh. We would not be surprised to find him moving to somewhere more glamorous.

Academic Matters: GCSE results solid in most subjects, with consistently good modern languages. Maximum class size 20, four ability bands and some setted subjects. Smart computer room. Full-time EFL specialist teacher, who is backed up by two part-timers. 'Some' special provision for dyslexia.

Of the A level results the head comments that 'we have a broadly comprehensive intake, and our results are uncomfortably close to some of our selective friends. At the lower end of the scale we are similarly delighted that several candidates with relatively weak GCSEs, who might not have been allowed to sit A levels at many schools, have secured them successfully.' Good consistent performance across the board.

Games, Options, the Arts: Lively music department – particularly creditable given that Wells Cathedral School attracts the musical talent – with good and full programme of concerts. Currently stronger on choral work than orchestral. The choir tours central Europe each year. Good workshops (textiles, silver-smithing, cabinet-making, engine repairs and so on). CCF is compulsory for one year; fairly strong community involvement. Ten Tors taken seriously. Highly enthusiastic mainstream sports (rugby, cricket, hockey etc) – the school magazine is crammed with the results of all the matches. Astroturf pitch.

Background and Atmosphere: On the edge of Tiverton, on 100-acre site, calmly set in the most beautiful country. Dignified collegiate main blocks, cloister and chapel; over the road the newer music block, huge dining hall, excellently designed Ondaatje Hall housing theatre plus photography, art, pottery, named after its Old Blundellian benefactor, the richissimus successful businessman, Christopher Ondaatje (brother of the Booker Prize winner). Typical public school redbrick boarding houses (spacious, carpeted study beds for groups of six, working up to singles for top-year pupils). Notably unpressurised atmosphere and ethos. New sixth form centre. Still gingery brown tweedy jackets, with patched elbows, for 13 to 16-year-olds, that add to the comfortingly homely feel of the place; sixth form boys now wear navy blazers, with the girls in red jackets and navy skirts. School founded in 1604 through the will of a local clothier, Peter Blundell. Long association with the Amory family, whose endowments have been generous. Went fully co-ed in 1993. New house for 11 to 13-year-olds opened in '96 – lively and full already (115 pupils). School mentioned in Lorna Doone.

Pastoral Care and Discipline: Good supportive care; work and motivation well monitored. Occasional misdemeanours over drink, but nothing too alarming. Daily meeting between head, (new) deputy and heads of school. Head meets pupils at breakfast and lunch.

Pupils and Parents: Parents working in the professions (probably also looking at King's Taunton); radius is closing in, but a few far-flung pupils, including Londoners with West Country connections; gentle middle class plus a sprinkling of landed families (who have often sent boys for many generations). A fair number of Forces children. 10 per cent foreign nationals, including Germans, pupils from the Eastern bloc, Japanese, Canadians. Strongly loyal and supportive Old Boys. OBs include Christopher Ondaatje, Donald Stokes, Michael Mates MP, Anthony Smith. Pupils are pleasant, unpushy, unspoilt.

Entrance: Not a problem. CE at 11+ and 13+ from traditional prep schools (eg Mount House) and a good sprinkling from local state schools. Also at sixth form – 5 C grades at GCSE needed for internal and external candidates. Entrance test for those outside the mainstream private sector.

Exit: 95 per cent go on to further education. Sports science a popular subject. The school has traditional links through Peter Blundell with Sidney Sussex, Cambridge and Balliol.

Money Matters: Generous number of scholarships, academic and also for music, art, sport and drama, at different ages – well worth enquiring about. Approximately one-third of entrants hold awards of some sort, up to 50 per cent of fees. Foundation places for some day boys.

Remarks: Popular, truly rural, fully co-ed public school with charm, where pupils will not sink without trace. Gentle and kindly. Academic results strong for a comprehensive intake.

BOLTON SCHOOL

(BOYS' DIVISION)

Chorley New Road, Bolton BL1 4PA

TEL: *01204 840201* FAX: *01204 849477*

E-MAIL: hm@boys.bolton.sch.uk

WEB: www.boys.bolton.sch.uk

+ PUPILS: 1025 boys, all day; plus own Junior School with 150 boys, all day
+ Ages: 8-18 + Size of sixth form: 220
+ Non-denom + Fee-paying

Head: Since 1983, Mr Alan W Wright BSc

(fifties), educated at Manchester Grammar School and Birmingham University. Arrived via King Edward's Birmingham, then head of chemistry and sixth form supervisor at Newcastle-Upon-Tyne Royal Grammar School. Married, three grown-up children. Approachable and understanding, Mr Wright has transformed the school (he would say allowed it to evolve) during his time in office. He comments that there has been an 'enormous amount of adapting to modern needs'. Beady-eyed. Deals with problems with great sensitivity.

Academic Matters: No streaming or setting – not necessary as pupils all bright. Science reigns supreme here both at GCSE (separate sciences for all) and A level. Huge numbers taking chemistry, biology and physics at A level and getting excellent results. Maths also popular. French good at GCSE but take-up tails right off at A level. Superb Russian teaching (from second form): they write their own textbook that is sold to other schools and have regular trips to Russia. Popular up until GCSE with good results, but very few take it at A level. History and English lit the most popular arts subjects, but these are poor relations compared with science. Art and design hardly taken as exam subjects. All do general studies.

Excellent careers dept. Staff high powered, lots of PhDs etc. Inspired computer/technology department, with designs being patented and sold: everything to a truly professional industrial standard, building a 45ft yacht the latest project. IT transformed from within the school, lots of serious machinery. Complete refurbishment of the technology department in '94 under the innovative Mr Whitmarsh. Computers everywhere; the geography department sports a popular satellite weather station

Games, Options, the Arts: Surrounded by pitches: a soccer school. Matches near and far. Rugby gaining in popularity; also hockey, cross-country. Games hall the size of four badminton courts. Tennis. Multi-gym and fitness training centre. Water polo popular. Regular timetabled residential holidays at hostel operated by the school in a former Victorian lakeland mansion, Patterdale Hall, Ullswater. Parents contribute towards food and travel. Sailing, abseiling, rock-climbing, etc. Strong scout and cub scout troops. Music and music technology, arts centre attached to 25-metre swimming pool – shared with the girls' division (qv). Clubs for everything during lunch hour, shared with the girls' school. Shares theatre with girls, and linked design technology courses at A level, also economics and classics.

Background and Atmosphere: Private since 1524, with links going back to before 1516, the school was re-endowed in 1913 as a single foundation by the first Viscount Leverhulme in equal partnership with the girls' division (founded in 1877). Set in 32 acres on the western edge of Bolton, with excellent motorway links. There are 22 school buses (for girls too) criss-crossing the local countryside.

Collegiate Edwardian sandstone structure, with oodles of passages and modern buildings, surrounded by playing fields. Impressive 'chained library', as well as an operational one.

Pastoral Care and Discipline: Yearly form tutors, who report to year head. Form tutors meet with class twice a day and do mega termly interviews with each boy – and also deal with any crisis. One official counsellor, the art mistress, plus several otherspecially trained staff in a small team led by the second master, Doug Wardle. Sackings for involvement off-campus with drugs (drugs counsellor on staff). Immediate expulsion for drugs in school or dealing. Drink less of a problem than in previous years. 'No vast smoking problem.' Expulsion if name of school brought into disrepute.

Pupils and Parents: From far and wide, and include lots of merchants' and local businessmens' sons. Enormous parental support: 95 per cent regularly turn up for year meetings. Not many 'non-professional, non-white pupils': 15 per cent, very few, if you think of the catchment area. Unsophisticated by London standards.

Entrance: Oversubscribed. 350 interview for 120 places. Four- or five-form entry, depending onstandard of applicants, and no automatic entry from junior school. Each child is tested on their own merits and no preference is given to siblings.

There is sixth form entry at least to balance the books (around 15 each year). All candidates (including those already in school) must normally get As or Bs at GCSE in subjects they want to study at A level, and not less than C in maths and English and one other.

Exit: Some 5-10 post-GCSE. Otherwise 95+ per cent to universities, old established northern ones such as Leeds, Manchester, Liverpool, Sheffield particularly favoured. 10+ to Oxbridge. Engineers, accountants, doctors, etc and business.

Money Matters: Can and will help if real need arises. Did have some assisted places, and feels the loss of those, though bursaries are available on same basis. Student, travelling and 'initiative' grants available.

Remarks: Currently strong boys' day school majoring on science. Good work ethos.

JUNIOR SCHOOL: Bolton Junior School

(Boys' Division) Master in Charge: Since 1990, Mr Michael Percik, BA PGCE (forties). Entrance via test, with no automatic entrance from the school's own pre-prep, Beech House (with 200 boys and girls 4-8, on Junior School site). Strong feeder prep, just across the road from the senior school, to which virtually all boys progress.

BOLTON SCHOOL

(GIRLS' DIVISION)

Chorley New Road, Bolton BL1 4PA

TEL: *01204 840201* FAX: *01204 434710*

E-MAIL: info@girls.bolton.sch.uk

WEB: www.girls.bolton.sch.uk

✦ PUPILS: 1055 girls, all day ✦ Ages: 11-18, plus own junior school, with 150 girls ages 8-11. (Also a pre-prep dept, ages 4-8, 200 boys and girls) ✦ Size of sixth form: 210 ✦ Non-denom ✦ Fee-paying

Head: Since September 1994, Miss Jane Panton MA (Oxon). Formerly of The Merchant Taylors' School, Liverpool.

Academic Matters: Strongly academic and results reflect this. 'All year groups are unstreamed', but maths is set from second year. Curriculum elastic enough to allow a good number of options at GCSE. All taking 4/5 AS levels, including general studies. Dual certificate or separate sciences at GCSE. All pupils must do one modern language (French, German or Spanish) and one humanity at GCSE. English and history currently the most popular A level subjects by miles, then geography, maths, psychology and the sciences (physics a relatively poor relation.) Those who take languages do well in them.

Wide range of optional subjects in sixth form studies. Girls and boys join up for specialist courses. Computers are everywhere; some now networked, girls and staff can take them home for weekends and holidays.

Games, Options, the Arts: Lacrosse, netball, swimming, all strong. Large sports hall, 18 tennis courts, swimming pool and sports pavilion plus arts centre and language bureau all shared with the boys. Lots of minor sports: golf, squash. Fabulous textile projects. Good music, with lots of children taking associated board exams at all levels – impressive results. Regular to-ing and fro-ing with boys, lots of joint clubs (usually at lunch time – little such activity after school). Senior girls help with juniors, and Beech House, and do odd reading practice. Outdoor pursuits centre in the Lake District.

Background and Atmosphere: Founded in 1877, under the auspices of the first Viscount Leverhulme (soapsud king), who endowed the school in 1913 as a single Foundation in equal partnership with the Boys' Division, moved with it to its present site of 32 acres on the western edge of Bolton. Cloned with Boys' Division (qv).

Pastoral Care and Discipline: Yearly form tutors, who report to heads of school. Form tutors meet with class twice a day and do termly interviews with each pupil – and also deal with any crisis. Sixth formers allowed considerable latitude, clocking in each morning and afternoon. Five hours' homework per subject per week: may either be done at school or at home. Detention,

letters home for repeated minor offences. Drugs: educational specialists on call.

Pupils and Parents: As per boys' division. Old girls include Ann Taylor MP, Harriet Steele MP and Dame Janet Smith QC.

Entrance: Highly competitive. Own exam at 11+ (pupils from 60 different state schools currently applying), no automatic entry from junior school. Test and interview. Enormously oversubscribed with about three girls trying for each place. Entry at sixth form, test again; and As at GCSE in A level subjects 'generally preferred'.

Exit: Trickle after GCSE. Almost all to a wide variety of universities, both old and new, north and south, studying variety of courses, everything from communications studies, to food management, to law, oceanography, countryside management, psychology – a truly impressive collection. Around 15 to Oxbridge.

Money Matters: Had huge number of assisted places and the loss of these may be felt. Bursaries in keeping with the 'principal objectives of the first Lord Leverhulme – that no boy or girl of potential who qualified on academic grounds but whose family were able to offer limited support would be debarred from entry to the school' – 26 'foundation grants' a year. Now has four Ogden Trust bursaries for 'above-average children from a state primary school of limited or no parental means'. Can and will help in unexpected financial crisis.

Remarks: Still a top class, well-endowed, sought after academic city girls' day school, with a strong work ethos and high aspirations. Worthy.

JUNIOR SCHOOL: Bolton Junior School (Girls' Division). Pupils: around 150 girls, ages 8-11, plus 200 boys and girls in Beech House, the pre-prep. Head of lower schools: Mrs H Crawforth: Mistress in charge of lower schools: Mrs K M Critchley. Entrance via test at 8, also for children who have been at the pre-prep. Shares the campus with the senior school and uses some of its facilities. Thriving on all fronts: French starts early, lots of computers, good library, superb cooking and fabric facilities. Most girls transfer to the senior school via tests.

BRADFIELD COLLEGE

Bradfield, Reading, Berkshire RG7 6AR

TEL: *01189 744203* FAX: *01189 744195*

E-MAIL: headmaster@bradfieldcollege.org.uk

WEB: www.bradfieldcollege.org.uk

✦ PUPILS: around 500 boys; 80 girls in sixth form (mostly boarding, about 30 day pupils) ✦ Ages 13-18 ✦ Size of sixth form: about 280-90 ✦ C of E ✦ Fee-paying

---

Head: Since 1985, Mr Peter Smith MA (early fifties). educated at Magdalen College School and Lincoln College, Oxford. Previously housemaster at Rugby. Married with teenage daughters. Known in the Thames Valley, says a parent as 'the chief executive'. Former Oxfordshire cricket captain. Affable, thoughtful, laid-back, possibly shy. Plays cards close to chest. Headmaster's office feels slightly isolated, given the sprawl of the school, but head assures us this is not so.

Academic Matters: Some unusual and excellent teaching. Severe streaming. Girls no longer bump up results, according to head. League table results reasonable, given the level of academic ability at intake.

Games, Options, the Arts: Seriously sporty – turns in solid wins in cricket and soccer and in major block football fixtures. 'Games and games players are worshipped at Bradfield', sighed a sixth form girl. Terrific sports complex, built at a cost of £3 million, officially opened by OB Lord Owen, huge and impressive. Girls also play a mean game of cricket, not to mention lacrosse, tennis, sailing, riding (riding school nearby), hockey. Own golf course. All manner of extras also on offer such as fly-fishing, clay pigeon shooting. Has one of the most beautiful cricket pitches in the country, The Pit. Keen CCF.

School perennially famous for its open-air classical Greek theatre, in which is performed every three years a Greek play, in (ancient) Greek and draws enthusiasts from all over the world. Play performed by the best thespians (rather than the classicists – there aren't a lot), with drama coach, and input from classics masters. Theatre has amazing atmosphere, stone seats surrounded by bosky glades, also used for speech day picnics etc , as can hold the whole school – definitely worth a detour. Excellent art department – atmosphere conducive to inspiration, and showing good work. Music on the up. Good school mag – the *Bradfield College Chronicle* – worth a browse to give some idea of strength of extras.

Background and Atmosphere: Place occupies a whole village just off the M4 and pupils constantly walking up and down the road from one building to another. A lovely setting. Founded 1850. Three purpose-built girls' houses – ritziest we've seen, with en-suite bathrooms which, according to housemaster, only cost an extra £30k or so to do – well worth it. Most of houses – particularly the girls' houses – in super sunny positions with views, French windows opening out on to lawns. Boys' houses were generally tougher in aspect, but most now upgraded. Choose house with care. Compulsory chapel once a week – was three times, and pupils no longer wear gowns. Beer available in Blundell's the school bar. Numbers have grown with the addition of girls and opening of the third girls' boarding house in '96.

Pastoral Care and Discipline: School freely offered us a copy of local authority report. Head says he welcomes the inspection, to alert him to possible problems.
NB given the geographical layout of the school, it is difficult for head, or indeed anybody, to keep tabs on everything at the same time.) Every family regularly handed a large questionnaire to fill in by parents after consultation with pupls, giving, eg rating of communication with housemaster from 1-5. Gives a v good chance to spot problems. Machismo still alive and well in one or two houses. 23 female members of staff at last count (ie gradually increasing). Has not always been an easy school for boys to settle in at 13+: 'It's tough', said one; all new boys now in separate boarding house for their first year. Looks after girls vv well.

Pupils and Parents: Jolly good chaps. Mostly from business and high-tech industries in the M4 corridor. Around 15 per cent from overseas, some Services parents. 10 per cent sons of OBs. Famous OBs include Lord Owen, Richard Adams, Nobel-prizewinner Martin Ryle, Leslie Glass and Stephen Milligan. Girl Talk: second choice for some – who then love it; first choice for others not seeking high-powered co-education at sixth form. Girls given pep talk early to join in everything – 'then you'll meet everybody'.

Entrance: By CE or scholarship exam. Sixth form entry for girls and boys (10-20 of latter at sixth form) on interview, IQ test, assessment and school report (and expectation of 'good grades' in five GCSEs). Draws pupils from 40 different prep schools (Elstree, Brockenhurst, St Andrew's Pangbourne, Papplewick, Hall Grove, King's House Richmond, Pilgrim's, St Neots's Twyford etc regularly), but keeps in touch with 80 preps.

Exit: Virtually everyone to higher education, most to degree courses, a few to drama college, Royal Academy of Music, art college etc. A handful to Oxford, lots to Edinburgh and other places north. Produces engineers and businessmen and a small percentage to the Services.

Money Matters: Up to 15 scholarships between 10 and 50 per cent of the fees, with provision for upping this to 90 per cent in case of need. Up to 4 music scholarships of 20-50 per cent of fees plus free tuition.
NB had assisted places at sixth form, and their loss may begin to colour the results. Parents who fall on hard times asked to fill in financial circs form, then school does what it can to see pupil through to a sensible moment. Endowment=freehold of 200 acres in Bradfield.

Remarks: Strongly traditional public school that somehow fails to catch the fashionable selector's eye. This could be to do with prep school heads' perception of the school as academically second division. 'I send lots of parents to see it', lamented one who recognises the school's many strengths, 'and they never come back enthusiastic.' Which is a pity: boys who arrive and survive to the top are, on the whole, charming, and well-prepared for life. Head comments the school is 'not for non-doers'.

BRADFORD GRAMMAR SCHOOL

Bradford BD9 4JP

TEL: *01274 542 492* FAX: *01274 548129*

E-MAIL: hmsec@bgs.bradford.sch.uk

WEB: www.bgs.bradford.sch.uk

✦ PUPILS: 755 boys and 95 girls, plus 180 boys and 25 girls in the Clock House (the junior school) ✦ Ages: 11-18, Clock House 7-11 ✦ Size of sixth form 235 ✦ Non-denom ✦ Fee-paying

---

Head: Since 1996, Mr Stephen Davidson BSc PGCE (forties), educated at Tynemouth Grammar School, and read metallurgical engineering at Manchester University. Previously head of the middle school at Manchester Grammar School. Married, with one young son. Getting into his stride (the previous head was a daunting act to follow), described as popular in the recent inspection report.

Academic Matters: A powerful academic school, with strong traditions across the board – sciences especially so. GCSE results as you would expect. A levels – an exciting collection, and with generally good results. A fair number of lower grades, especially in maths – accounted for half the failures in '00 from one sixth of the attempts, following similar results in earlier years. The school attributes the spread of their results to their entrance policy (see below) and to standing by pupils even if they are not making the Bradford Grammar School grade. Business studies, economics and politics the most popular non-traditional choices. Small classics department which consistently gets As. School keen on AS, 'good for stretching'. Expectations incredibly high, and pupils work hard. Staff 'amazingly devoted and committed' – and teach sixth formers 'as if they are university students', said a parent. Pupils are highly competitive, 'but not necessarily when we arrive here', confided one – and thrive on it. The '98 ISC inspection report notes though that 'evidence of independent learning is thin: pupils prefer to do what they are told.' Head says, 'this is a grammar school', and points out that the ability to do what you are told is not evidence of lack of independence, but of independence under control. Low turnover of staff.

Games, Options, the Arts: Very strong, successful rugby sides and cross-country. Both the 1st XV and the U15 sides were beaten semi-finalists in the Daily Mail National Schools' Cup recently. Cricket good too, and some outstanding results for tennis and table tennis teams. Rowing. Keen drama, Three full-time teachers for design and technology (and the numbers choosing it as an exam option both at GCSE and A are still increasing). Art in somewhat cramped rooms, and few take it at exam level. Inspectors criticised lack of breadth at sixth form and below, and said that 'the development of spiritual values is not much in evidence'. Head disputes this strongly. Visiting speaker every Friday. Half day each week is given over to sport, drama, music. Music lively.

Background and Atmosphere: School

dates back to the 16th century. Formerly a free grammar, became direct grant, then private. Pleasant setting on the outer edge of Bradford, in 20 acres of grounds and all classrooms, games etc , on the site – present sandstone buildings planned with 'incredible foresight'. Pleasing feel of space to corridors and quads between buildings. Subjects grouped together in classics 'row', geography ditto – rather like prison corridors ('refurbished departmental suites'). Large modern library and well-equipped IT rooms. Huge indoor swimming pool in the midst of the class blocks. No pre-fabs, though new(ish) science block extra-ordinarily badly designed. Pupils and staff all purposeful and fully stretched. Faint sense of production line. There is a traditional morning assembly three days a week. Very traditional, the school is quite hierarchical. Co-education began in earnest from '99.

Pastoral Care and Discipline: Lack of self-discipline is heavily frowned upon – and relatively rare. Northern hard-working ethos very much in place – and plenty of space to let off excess steam. Well structured pastoral care system. Good peer support.

Pupils and Parents: Sons – and now daughters – of local businessmen, professionals, 15 per cent Asians (usually bright and hard working – 'It suits us well here', said one sixth form Asian girl.). Old Boys include David Hockney (who comes back to the school and is president of the current appeal – a source of inspiration), Denis Healey, Adrian Moorehouse. Pupils courteous and self-confident, and neatly dressed. Lively Old Bradfordian Society.

Entrance: 50 per cent from state school, average IQ is 120; selective exam, but any candidate showing any 'sparkle' in any part of the exam is interviewed with a view to selecting on potential rather than performance. Over half the 11+ entry come in (also via exam) from the Clock House (for 7–10 year olds), which has expanded in recent years and is going strong, tucked away at the side. Sixth form candidates need 20 GCSE points (4 for an A* to 1 for a C) plus interview – 18 points for internal candidates: a high hurdle.

Exit: 20 or so annually go to Oxbridge, it used to be between 40 and 50, but now 'the competition [from other universities] is greater'. The Bradfordian, the school's magazine, is full of interesting charts on, amongst other things, university choices, subject choices and the current swings in these. Durham, Newcastle, Bristol, Nottingham, Edinburgh, Liverpool, Newcastle, Manchester, and Birmingham are all popular choices.

Money Matters: Fees kept purposely low – a bargain. NB 20 per cent of pupils were on assisted places, and their abolition has hit hard here, though school comments that these are 'being replaced by the school's own bursary scheme – about 20 per annum', and 'we are determined to retain our all-round social ethos'. Could do with a new benefactor.

Remarks: First-class, outward-looking boys' grammar school having to face up to the challenges of co-education and the modern world.

BRISTOL GRAMMAR SCHOOL

University Road, Bristol BS8 1SR

TEL: *01179 736006* FAX: *01179 467485*

E-MAIL: headmaster@bgs.bristol.sch.uk

WEB: www.bgs.bristol.sch.uk

✦PUPILS: 1060 boys and girls in the main school, plus another 270 juniors; all day ✦ Ages: 11-18, juniors 7-10 ✦ Size of sixth form: just under 300 – one of the biggest academic sixth forms in the south-west ✦ C of E ✦ Fee-paying

---

Head: Since 1999, Dr David Mascord. Read chemistry at York, PhD at St John's Cambridge. Previously deputy head here. Took over from Mr Charles Martin, head from 1986, who presided over a significant rise in numbers.

Academic Matters: The head is anxious to disperse the perceived view of the school as a home from home for geniuses – 'your good average child will do well here', he says, and points to the good academic results, in the light of this comment. The grammar school has some outstanding staff in all departments, putting in good rigorous teaching while at the same time – so it seemed to us – putting life into things. Regularly produces a clutch of students studying Russian (the head of modern languages is married to a Russian and writes Russian textbooks), and the school does an exchange with St Petersburg. Classics is also alive and very well here and very well taught; indeed, year 7 – the youngest – nominated Latin as one of their two fav-ourite subjects. Class sizes are a maximum of 30 at the bottom of the school, 15 at the top (but often far fewer); the average is 20.

GCSE results are usually excellent – though on a declining trend over the last three years, and economics seems to be a perennial source of low grades. A level strong and has been on an improving trend over the same period, with maths, English and the sciences the most popular subjects. Offering expanding beyond main stream traditional subjects to include eg theatre studies and psychology.

No streaming or setting when pupils first enter the main school, first setting is in maths at 12. The school has recently appointed a special needs co-ordinator, and can provide support for mild learning difficulties – there are 'little groups' all over the school doing extra lessons in eg the lunch hour.

Games, Options, the Arts: Strong no nonsense DT department. Boys play rugby, hockey, cricket; girls hockey and netball, tennis and athletics. PE is mixed. The school owns large acres of playing fields over the river at Failand (as do other Bristol schools) and pupils are bussed out – it's part of Clifton school life. There is a sports hall on the site, much used (a large fencing class was in progress when we visited, both girls and boys). Inter-form competitions are held at lunch-time ('we eat quickly', commented a pupil). Over 140 pupils are 'going through to gold' in the D of E award scheme – an amazing number for a school without an outward bound tradition. Public speaking is a popular option. Stunningly good library – county standard, and with a £15,000-a-year budget, beautifully catalogued and laid out, and a joy to use – brilliant librarian.

Background and Atmosphere: Founded in 1532 as a boys' grammar school with the usual worthy objectives by the Thorne brothers – hence the school's puzzling motto – *ex spinis uvas*. The school is dominated by the huge hangar-like gothic old school hall, which has wooden seats carved into the walls where masters sat, warming their feet on the (only) hot pipe, with assorted pupils ranged in front of them. Today the old hall is used for concerts, for lunch etc and provides a good focal point. All around this the school has mushroomed out, perched up the hill, just beside the university (sixth formers sometimes use the university labs). The school has even gone into 'layers' with IT underneath and a grassy walkway on top.

Pastoral Care and Discipline: The first two years are housed in the Princess Anne Building (so called because she opened it), under the care of Mr Huckle, who, said one parent, is 'tremendous ...he treats each child as if his own'. Before the new children come to the school, the staff go out to the children's previous school to introduce themselves, and generally go out of their way to make new pupils feel at home. Each pupil is given a booklet which looks modelled on many state sector booklets we have seen, full of simple, useful reassuring information, such as what you should do if you're feeling unwell. Thereafter, each year has its tutor groups (house based), and an overall head of year. Bullying is reacted to fast, and although some drugs must be expected on an inner-city site not far from a notoriously druggy area, our impression is that the school is too open (every corner being used for legitimate purposes) and too busy for the drug culture to get much hold. Has gone co-ed over the past 20 years, with all the changes this entails. Sixth formers say they are so at ease that they literally have to think twice before working out how many of each sex is in any particular set.

Pupils and Parents: Sons and daughters of Bristol businessmen, lots of first-time buyers, and a fair number of shell suits. A few famous old boys: Tom Graveney the cricketer, also Sir Oliver Franks, Allen of Penguin fame, John Pople (Nobel prize for chemistry), Robert Lacey – but mostly it's clergymen, doctors, solicitors, solid citizens etc.

Entrance: Entry exam at 11+ (earlier, if 'mature') in January for September – the exam is held in conjunction with several other Bristol private schools. A third of pupils come up from the grammar school's own junior school (on the same site, but separated by high wire fence), the rest from schools not just all over Bristol, but as far flung as Weston-super-Mare. Typical feeds are Henleaze, Elmlea and Stoke Bishop primaries, Colston's Primary in Cotham, Westbury Park, Westbury C of E, plus Clifton, Redmaids, Redlands, Clifton High etc. 20-25 pupils join at 13+. Entrance to sixth form: 6 GCSEs at A–C required, including A or B grades in subjects to be studied.

Exit: Mostly to the strong popular redbrick universities – everywhere but Bristol, really. For a sixth form of this size the number of pupils going to Oxbridge is small.

Money Matters: Fees just over £5,160 a year, as we write. School had a huge number of assisted places – difficult to assess how much their loss will affect the school, probably quite a lot, but on the other hand, Bristol is a rich city. The school now offers 'its own assistance'. A few academic and music scholarships (the latter paying for music tuition only). Some Ogden Trust bursaries. The school is part of the Bristol Municipal Charities.

Not a rich school, but selling land in the city has produced capital for endowment, and, given the large growth in numbers, the school does not have a serious problem finding the money it needs from fees.

Remarks: Once the 'direct grant' grammar school catering for the academic cream of Bristol's male youth. Now a private-sector grammar producing a good academic grounding for boys and girls, with a less selective intake. In most respects BGS comes top of the 10 private schools in Bristol. Not the place for social climbers.

BRYANSTON SCHOOL

Blandford Forum, Dorset DT11 0PX

TEL: *01258 452411/484664* FAX: *01258 484661*

E-MAIL: admissions@bryanston.co.uk

WEB: www.bryanston.co.uk

✦ PUPILS: around 370 boys, 270 girls; around 600 board, the rest day ✦ Ages: 13-18 ✦ Size of sixth form: 260 ✦ C of E ✦ Fee-paying

---

Head: Since 1983 (and says he's staying till 2005), Mr Tom Wheare, MA (fifties), educated Magdalen College School and Cambridge, where he read history. Married with two daughters, both ex-Bryanston. A professional front man for the school, easy to talk to. Hobbies music and drama – sings in school, and occasionally directs plays. Wife, Ros, is one of the school's counsellors – someone to talk to in confidence – and also runs the fortnightly Over 60s Club (at the school). A zealous PR head, some would say too zealous. Cultivated, witty, slightly eccentric. No, eccentric.

Academic Matters: Pupils assigned an academic tutor on entering school and usually keep the same tutor all the way up the school. Much made of the school's use of the American Dalton system of time-tabling – lots of chart filling, and free periods in which weekly projects 'must be done', with tutors on tap at specific times. This is meant to give a little preparation for tutorial-based system at university. Some parents slightly nervous about the temptation for pupils to pull wool over staff's eyes. All academic subjects setted. Brilliant CDT Centre designed by Piers Gough (observe the column on entrance – large left-handed screws). Size of classes 20–12. Staff:pupil ratio 1:10. English still by far and away the most popular subject at A level, and does reasonably well; biology, geography, history, physics and art history come next. Maths results good – but much less popular here. Results overall seem OK. School has active exchange programme with schools in Europe, plus American links. A fair number of AS levels taken but NB no examined general studies. Provision for children with learning difficulties has increased enormously – one full-time specialist member of staff assessing etc, and four part-time specialists. No special time-table arrangements.

Games, Options, the Arts: All staff take three afternoons of games or pioneering work a week, and are supposed to be available to pupils three evenings a week. Pupils must do something sporty three times a week, and there are any number of success stories here, but essentially this is still not a school which worships the team game. Rowing school, with glorious River Stour flowing at the bottom of the games fields. Enthusiastic reports of the riding. Huge holiday-camp-like range of extras from bell-ringing to mountain biking.

Strong tradition of community service. Art making a comeback after its depressing years in the doldrums, with new ('97) art building and new head of art. Drama good and enthusiastic – '60s Coade Hall and Greek theatre – school now has a director of drama/theatre studies.

Background and Atmosphere: Norman Shaw house for Viscount Portman is 'more like a town hall than a private house', to quote John Betjeman. Grand buildings make it a great favourite with staff and parents to visit for summer ball etc . Stunning grounds, with approach by long drive which always wows the parents – 'by the time they get to the front door they are sold on the place', said the previous bursar. Rudimentary house system – school is centrally run from huge notice board in the 100-yard front hall (parquet flooring everywhere), and much lingering about goes in and around there. Some boys and all girls live in purpose-built blocks (girls' houses all have hair-dryers). New boarding accommodation for boys, though some live in the main building.

Excellent food from self-service in basement, with omelette bar capable of flipping out omelettes at a rate of 150 in 40 minutes. Atmosphere of je m'en fiche and let-it-all-hang-out vis-a-vis appearance appears to be still in evidence. The laid-back image of the school is at odds with the formality of the surroundings. Sixth form common room can provoke strong parental reaction: 'Cosy atmosphere would be putting it mildly – it's like a fairly sleazy night club', said a father, adding, 'but they love it.'

Pastoral Care and Discipline: Heavily into the outward trappings of pastoral care. Not so heavily into discipline. Slightly obsessive, American-style preoccupation with relationships, feelings etc   (though it pales beside Bedales). Given the liveliness of the place and the trickiness of some of the inmates, it's a difficult place to manage. Head comments that the Children Act has given them the 'opportunity to be positive' – and set up intricate system for complaints, problems etc, which, he said, were well patronised to start with, but have now dwindled as the novelty wears off.' Pupils caught in bed together and those committing drugs offences are liable to be expelled' (note that word 'liable'). Tiered system of punishments for smoking (many parents in despair over this), drinking etc – gatings, warnings etc .'Night wandering' – climbing on to the roof and racing round the parapet – still the occasional excitement. Head must consult chairman of governors for a pupil to be 'withdrawn out-of-time', and if they have to let a pupil go he does his utmost to find another school. School has chapel in the grounds, but not much evidence of organised religion. Alarming shooting accident in '98.

Pupils and Parents: Middle-class arts and trendies' children, and media. About 50 ex-pats, including lots of Service families (though numbers of Services' children have dropped spectacularly since last count), and wide selection of foreigners. Articulate. Tendency to self-obsession can result in slight gracelessness. OBs include Quinlan Terry, Lucien Freud, John Eliot Gardiner, some Conrans, Phil de Glanville, Frederick Sanger, Emilia Fox and Mark Elder.

Entrance: Via scholarship exam, CE, or school's own entrance exam. Well worth trying for a place at the last minute. Pupils come from prep schools all over the country, particularly co-eds. Useful entry at sixth form – qualification has tightened up from 'they need to be capable of taking A levels' to 6 A-C GCSEs.

Exit: Some leakage post-GCSE. Edinburgh and Oxford popular in '96, followed by Manchester, Bristol, Leeds etc and a fair number to ex-polys eg Oxford Brookes, 4 to USA. NB school good at relocating pupils kicked out for drugs.

Money Matters: Around 8 per cent of fee income goes on bursaries. If the parents are in genuine financial difficulties, school tries to work out something; 'if I can help, I will', says head. Also, academic, music, sport, scholarships, and one art scholarship at 13; one or two at sixth form.

Remarks: All-round genuine co-ed liberal education. In its heyday one of the three top co-ed boarding schools in the country. This is no longer the case. We are getting two distinct types of reports: from parents who are deeply disappointed, and point to specific departments which they consider not up to scratch, and from those (mostly local) who report their children 'having a wonderful time'. Remedial department increasingly sought after.

BURFORD SCHOOL
AND COMMUNITY COLLEGE
Cheltenham Road, Burford, Oxfordshire
OX18 4PL

Tel: *01993 823303* Fax: *01993 823101*

E-mail: burfordschool@rmplc.co.uk

Web: atschool.eduWeb.co.uk/burford

♦Pupils: 1,100, boys and girls (approx 85 board, the rest day) ♦ Ages: 11-18 ♦ Size of sixth form: about 220 ♦ Inter-denom ♦ State (boarding fees approx £1,650 a term)

Head: Since 1995, Mr Patrick Sanders BA FRSA (fifties), with a degree in English and American Studies from Hull, (PGCE from Bristol). Teaches English in the lower school. Previously head of the Cotswold School, Gloucestershire, and before that deputy head of Wallingford School. Married, with two children; a keen family man, and an enthusiastic sportsman.

Entrance: Comprehensive intake. Siblings get priority, then locals, and of those from further afield, boarders will get priority – for obvious financial reasons.

Exit: Wide and interesting next steps. Large numbers to ex-polys, also to old-established redbrick universities (Newcastle, Bristol etc), some straight into employment, and some do a gap year. One or two to university abroad. Two or three to Oxbridge each year.

Remarks: Large state comprehensive with

a boarding element which should be useful to have on your doorstep, but, said a potential middle-class parent looking at the results, 'I just can't risk it'. Everything in place, with good range of subjects offered at sixth form level – not just the usual subjects, but psychology, sports studies, photography, environmental science, information technology, GNVQs etc – much wider than the average private school. Maximum class size 'average in the first 3 years is 26 or less' (good for a state school); special needs department. School farm (approximately 40 acres) – riding on offer.

Founded by Charter in 1571; beautiful surroundings, reasonably attractive front buildings. Some grammar school hangovers – including house systems, prefects, ushers, uniform. The boarding house is in the old grammar school site in picturesque Burford (Lenthall House, for both sexes, 50 per cent of boarders are Services' children), cheerful and friendly – true of the whole school.

GCSE results quite heartening – a wide spread, not top of the tables, but no obvious weak subjects – and note the large numbers of pupils at GCSE level – but A level results too low from too few pupils.

CAMDEN SCHOOL FOR GIRLS
Sandall Road, London NW5 2DB

Tel: *020 7485 3414* Fax: *020 7284 3361*

E-mail: camdeng@rmplc.co.uk

Web: www.rmplc.co.uk/eduWeb/sites/camdeng

✦ Pupils: 840, all day ✦ Ages: 11-19
✦ Size of sixth form: 370 including 100 boys ✦ Non-denom ✦ State

---

Head: Since 2000, Ms Anne Canning, previously deputy head at La Sainte Union convent school in Camden. Took over from Mr Geoffrey Fallows, a much liked head, who was here from 1989.

Academic Matters: National curriculum plus; classical studies of some sort for all, Latin and Greek both available. Setting for maths, sciences and languages mainly in Key Stage 4. Sixty-five per cent achieve five A-C grades at GCSE, almost all get five A-G. English, science, art and French have notably good results.

A levels do well – 75 per cent A–C grades – large numbers transfer from other schools including private sector, with English far and away the most popular subject, followed by art. Thirty-three subjects on offer; and GNVQ business courses. The school is a partner in the Camden Consortium at sixth form, and pupils can do one A level at a partner school or college, or transfer to them for eg vocational courses. All pupils take an exam at the end of their first year in the sixth form; those few who fail have to drop back a year if they wish to continue.

Individual departments have always had a

large measure of independence from central control, which accounts (inter alia) for the great length of time it has taken to dispose of the ghastly ILEA maths scheme. Look at individual subject areas with particular care, and beware of those with consistently disappointing results.

Pupils of widely differing abilities stretch the immensely dedicated staff, who start here early in the morning and often give girls extra tuition. High expectations, and school proudly continues founder's tradition of 'promoting opportunities for girls'.

Games, Options, the Arts: The art is wonderful: exuberant, expressive, immensely popular and successful. Music is ambitious with several choirs (Mozart Requiem, Haydn Mass etc) and orchestras, several pupils in London Schools Symphony Orchestra. Big range of drama events. Negligible sports facilities; do well with what they've got.

Broad tutorial and general studies programme at sixth form.

Background and Atmosphere: Founded in 1871 by that great pioneer in women's education, Frances Mary Buss (who also founded North London Collegiate qv). Voluntary aided, which status has enabled them to avoid the worst excesses of past governments and fashions. Hotchpotch buildings, old and new, sprawling prefabricated, generally inadequate and run down and should (but probably do not) make Camden and the DfEE blush with shame to look at. Parents and OGs now funding some much needed improvements, and at last, Camden are funding some major building works (due for completion in the Autumn of 2001). Relaxed atmosphere with buzz of excitement in some areas. No uniform (eye-catching dressers at the top end). With the great range in ability and background of its intake, the school seems to be a less coherent place in the lower forms; the presence of so many Muslim girls is reported as setting a high standard of behaviour from the outset.

Pastoral Care and Discipline: Truancy rate is average; staff 'fairly strict' about courtesy, ('but not always successfully so', notes a parent). Supportive and tight system, particularly good with children in difficult circumstances. 6th form smokers have outdoor hideaway; 'the best we can do', says the head.

Pupils and Parents: Very broad mix. 40 per cent black or Asian. Substantial numbers of well-off middle-class girls and also the socially deprived. Well-heeled middle class parents continue to opt to live in the area in order to benefit from the school.

Always turns out a bunch of talkative, independent-minded girls who know their place in the world and have the confidence to take it. Old Girls include Emma Thompson, Beeban Kidron, Arabella Weir, Ruth Evans, Jodhi May, Sara Kestelman, Kate Saunders, Deborah Moggach, Susie Boyt, Gillian Slovo. Strong informal OG network much involved with school.

Entrance: Heavily oversubscribed for year 7 entry. 112 places available. Preference for sisters, and for up to five music places, then for small number of girls granted social or medical priority; remaining places on the basis of distance as the crow flies from the school gates – in practice half a mile is often too far. From 1999 the intake was 'banded' again: all applicants take the NFER cognitive ability test, and are divided into four equal groups on the basis of their scores; 25 per cent of pupils are drawn from each of these groups, priority being given to sisters, the music students and those with social/medical claims; the balance of each group is filled on the basis of distance from the school gates (which may be different for each group). At 16+ by interview, extra-curricular achievements being particularly valued; distance not a factor at this stage; five Bs at GCSE expected for A level, less for GNVQ. 25 per cent of admissions to the sixth are boys.

Exit: Over 70 per cent continue into the sixth form (others go elsewhere in the consortium), of these, over 80 per cent continue to higher education (5-10 a year to Oxbridge), otherwise London, Sussex, Bristol etc, about one-third to read science. Art college a popular choice.

Money Matters: Parents and girls expected to help with – and good at – fund-raising to help building programme/maintenance. All parents asked to give £10 per term to supplement school funds.

Remarks: An exciting and lively London comprehensive state school, that encourages self-motivation and also feminism. Judge it by its old girls.

CANFORD SCHOOL

Wimborne, Dorset BH21 3AD

Tel: *01202 841254* Fax: *01202 881723*

E-mail: canford.admissions@dial.pipex.com

Web: www.canford.com

✦ Pupils: 370 boys, 205 girls. (250 boys board, 120 day boys; 135 girls board, 70 day girls) ✦ Ages: 13-18 ✦ Size of sixth form: 243 ✦ C of E ✦ Fee-paying

Head: Since 1992, Mr John Lever, MA (Cantab) PGCE (forties), went to Westminster, then read geography at Trinity, Cambridge. Rowing Blue. Taught briefly at St Edward's School, then to Winchester for sixteen years where he co-founded the geography department and was housemaster for eight years. Married, to Alisoun, with three young children. Hobbies: 'I enjoy my children, and I enjoy wild places…and I enjoy silence.' Has highly strategically placed elegant study (with gilt mouldings) – perfect for bouncing out of and nobbling people as they tiptoe by. Highly articulate and fun, with a good line in uplifting thoughts and bons mots. One of v few heads who systematically make a point of seeing pupils who have done well rather than badly – chatting for a few minutes, and maybe pressing into their hands a card with 'From the Headmaster, Canford School' at the top and 'My true religion is kindness' (The Dalai Lama) written on it. 'Though it's too much to hope that they actually look at it.' Mr Lever is passionate about boarding, pointing out, it 'develops unselfishness' and 'extends sense of community'. Teaches PSHE and believes that a 'positive attitude to their own talents and other people's values is absolutely critical'. Shaping up to be a five star head. Jolly new deputy head from Tonbridge.

Academic Matters: Results are amazingly good, given the relatively wide ability range and the soothing lack of obsession with league tables. Biology department hums with excitement, 'terrific place', under head of department, Andrew Powell, who 'leads from the front'; with trips to almost everywhere – deep-sea diving in Israel, visits to Costa Rica, charting flora off Old Harry (rock). Chemistry consistently strong and excellent results – chemistry teacher

Andrew Browning recently won the Salters' prize for stinks teachers.

New head of drama appointed, which will take some pressure off the head of English (work's been suffering a bit). Lots of visits and lectures to fire pupils with enthusiasm, even for potentially tedious matters. Everyone does a language to GCSE 'and they don't fail'. Unusually for a ('boys') co-ed, offers Italian to A level (along with the usual choices). Setted for maths, all languages, top movers streamed, maximum 23 per class. There are computers throughout plus a busy computer room that the staff also use. IT linked to all A level subjects.

The school now has a full-time (female) member of staff catering for dyslexics.

Games, Options, the Arts: Strong on games, particularly hockey – the school has a string of county players, often national champions. To its amazement the school won the Rosslyn Park Sevens in '97. Also plays, among other things, royal tennis. Double-sized sports hall with full sized indoor hockey pitch. Sailing on flooded quarry at Ringwood, racing at Poole Harbour, sculling on River Stour which runs right through the estate even under a very watery day house. Music v v good under Mr Warwick (former organ scholar of Merton College), who positively wills his charges to perform to the best of their ability. Weekly concert-ettes (among other things) so that everyone 'has a bash' at performing in public. Standard of music plumped up by music scholarships. New Layard Theatre – state of the art – and much increased participation at GCSE and A level. Art fun and thriving, good ceramics. The school helps with local charities, Riding for the Disabled, gives swimming lessons to local disabled children in the Canford pool and helps tinies at local primary schools with reading. Also now allows (well-vetted) locals to use the school weight-lifting equipment etc.

Background and Atmosphere: Founded in 1923 in marvellous Gothic Barry design, built, following a fire, for the Guest family (of GKN fame) on (not much visible) Norman design; ponderous 19th-century interiors. Splendid dining-hall with deeply ornate dark wood carving leading to grand carved staircase and serving hatches in separate area – reminiscent of a posh motorway self-service cafeteria. 300 acres of pleasant and well-kept park land (the head groundsman is married to a matron).

Girls have cosy, state-of-the-art new houses which feel exactly like motorway hotels (also posh), with single and double bedrooms (and sewing machines and kitchens), not to mention special areas for socialising with the opposite sex. Boys' houses have much more character, in particular School House, over the main school building, which has state bedroom, wonderful old rooms and corridors and a positive symphony of creaks and squeaks from doors and floorboards. Day houses are mixed. Canford is one of the Allied Schools (for what that is worth), with a low church foundation with 20 per cent of governors appointed by the Martyr's Memorial. Now 'broad' C of E, with chapel for all. The dear little Norman chapel in the grounds is used for service in rotation (too small for the whole school). School very security conscious, only two entrances in use. The library has been revamped, with carpet of the school's very own design, with oak tree and open book. Tres chic.

Co-ed note: School went fully co-ed in September '95, but there have been girls in the sixth form since early '70s, and this is one boys' school which actually already feels co-ed, with girls properly integrated (rather than boys with a few imported girls) – possibly because the place didn't feel aggressively male to start with.

Pastoral Care and Discipline: Some truly super matrons, and 'good mature pastoral care', commented the head of a neighbouring prep school. If you are worried whether your little lamb is going to survive boarding school at all, this is the place to look at. Housemaster/mistress plus three tutors and matron in each house. Each pupil has a tutorial (either individual or by group) each week. Anti-drugs policy is 'to keep pupils busy', and teach them 'how to say no' and 'pupils may expect to be expelled'. 'No hesitation in throwing child out for bullying if appropriate.' Prefects chosen for their moral qualities and good role model material rather than flash achievements.

Pupils and Parents: Most from within one and a quarter hours' drive; huge car park for older day pupils. A small number foreign nationals (25 at last count), who are 'very welcome'. A number of Services' children (38 at last count). Lots of children of local accountants, farmers, teachers etc – not a flash collection.

Entrance: First come, first served system, with short waiting list at time of going to press. 55 per cent CE pass-mark plus interview (pass mark has been ominously upgraded from 50 per cent). Prep school recommendation matters: 15 regular feeders, including Castle Court and Dumpton. Girls and some boys arrive after GCSE (A-Cs needed to study A levels). A large number of new sixth formers come from local state schools.

Exit: 91 per cent to universities: a steady 10–12 to Oxbridge, which is the 'favoured choice'. Formidable and wonderful head of Beaufort girls' house, Mrs Taylor, helps with Oxbridge entrance strategy (but she'll probably have been headhunted by the time you read this). School traditionally strong on engineers, professions. Southampton popular for scientists.

Absolutely no policy of kicking pupils out if they don't do well in exams. 'If one was really struggling I might suggest he would be better off doing something else, but if he really wanted to stay...'

Money Matters: This is the school that had the amazing luck to discover in '94 a 3000-year-old Assyrian bas-relief being used as the back drop to a darts board in the (now famous) tuck shop. The relief sold for £7.7 million, and ever since the school has regarded time as Before and After the Money. The money has enabled the school to do vital repair work to the extensive fabric, to build using good-quality materials and architects, and to set up a whole new scholarship fund. This is one place the loss of assisted places will not be noticed. Scholarships at 13+ for academic, art, music, and for an 'all-rounder' – which gives an indication of the head's genuine desire to more than just get the punters through their exams. Will keep child in exam year if real financial need, 'work with parents'.

Remarks: This still predominantly boarding school is currently all singing and dancing. Sound all through, hard to fault. Kind, confident, enthusiastic, unpretentious, good all-round. Quietly satisfied parents who report it's 'warm and welcoming'. It's not a place which attracts the fashionable set, but then, you might consider this a plus... .

CARDINAL VAUGHAN MEMORIAL SCHOOL

89 Addison Road, London W14 8BZ

TEL: *020 7603 8478* FAX: *020 7602 3124*

E-MAIL: mail@cvms.co.uk

WEB: www.cvms.co.uk

✦ PUPILS: 700 boys, plus 100 girls in sixth form; all day ✦ Ages: 11-18 ✦ Size of sixth form: 240 ✦ RC ✦ State

Head: Since 1997, Mr M A Gormally BA (early forties). Previously deputy headmaster here, he has been at the school for 20 years and is totally committed to its values. A likeable, hands-on head who can always be seen around the building, he teaches Latin. Very much the traditionalist, he is affable, popular with the pupils and approachable – 'a rotund and orotund bon viveur', in the words of a witty member of staff. Took over from Mr Pellegrini, who was head here from '76.

Academic Matters: Religious education considerable – at least as many take religious studies at GCSE as take English and maths. Sciences – 'we cream off our ablest scientists after the second year and they jolly well do physics, chemistry and biology as specialist subjects.' All other children are required to do 'balanced sciences' (ie dual award). In '92 increased the working week by one hour to fit everything in. Over 45 per cent female staff at the last count. There are six recently refurbished labs; recently built arts and technology centre to accommodate the grow-ing numbers. Girls biased towards arts, but go on to study sciences at eg Oxbridge. Good support for children with learning difficulties – two full-time members of staff, plus part-timers. All pupils follow school curriculum, but in-class support, plus agreed withdrawal for reinforcement; homework club specifically for children with learning difficulties – a v v good idea. Also some provision for gifted pupils.

Generally good exam results. English, maths, history and economics the popular choices at A level. Small but competent classics department.

Games, Options, the Arts: Extremely active sports – soccer and rugby the main games, and pupils are bussed to the river for rowing (strong); good fencing too. Pupils go to Kensington Sports Centre for swimming. Excellent playing fields next to the Rugby football ground at Twickenham. Pupils do one whole afternoon of games a week, plus PE in school. New IT Centre. Lots of school trips to eg Lourdes. Really strong choral music – choirs taking part in events all over London, eg the English National Opera's production of Carmen, and they also perform abroad. The choir has appeared on BBC's *Songs of Praise*.

Background and Atmosphere: Built at turn of century as memorial to Herbert Vaughan, third Archbishop of Westminster, whose chief claim to fame was the building of Westminster Cathedral. Originally a private grammar school, changed tack in 1945 following the 1944 Education Act. Super site (leafy) behind Holland Park. Upper and lower school split by a busy one-way road however. Parts warm and mellow, parts '60s functional, part hi-tech '90s. Black and grey uniform, burgundy and grey for the girls (school hot on that). Busy friendly atmosphere, and a feeling of safety, where many

Inner London state schools are jungles.

Pastoral Care and Discipline: Good: taken seriously. Sex education entrusted to the religious education department. All members of upper sixth appointed prefects – to set a good example to younger boys. A 'homework centre' is available each evening – good news for working parents. There is a daunting list of thou-shalt-nots – including, 'The use of corrective fluids and thinners is strictly forbidden'.

Pupils and Parents: School fed by 'strategically placed' RC primaries, including Our Lady of Victories Primary School, St Joseph's, Maida Vale, St Francis, Notting Hill.

Entrance: By test on application for 'balanced intake'. Primary criterion for admission = 'evidence of baptism or reception into the Roman Catholic Church'. Outgoing head points out that it is untrue to say the school creams off talent from lesser RC establishments. Always oversubscribed – heartbreaking piles of letters going out rejecting hopeful candidates. Entry at sixth form for both sexes.

Exit: About 25 per cent leave post GCSE. Lots to London University, some scattered further afield (Manchester, Bristol etc), and half a dozen to Oxbridge. Also one or two to Chelsea College of Art.

Money Matters: Voluntary aided.

Remarks: A kind religious state school with dedicated staff, and a comprehensive intake which, by national state school standards, has consistently good exam results.

CASTERTON SCHOOL
Kirkby Lonsdale, Cumbria LA6 2SG
TEL: *01524 279200* FAX: *01524 279208*

E-MAIL: headmaster@castertonschool.co.uk

WEB: www.castertonschool.co.uk

✦ PUPILS: around 350 girls (around 80 per cent in the main school board), including 30+ boys and girls in the pre-prep ✦ Ages: 3-19 ✦ Size of sixth form: around 90 ✦ C of E ✦ Fee-paying

Head: Since 1990, Mr Tony Thomas MA (Cantab) (fifties), educated at William Hulme's Grammar School in Manchester and previously housemaster and head of maths at Sedbergh. Lacrosse international (he coaches it), keen on drama. Friendly and welcoming. Very keen on single-sex schooling, 'girls work jolly hard'. Norwegian wife, Kirsti, and two sons, at Sedbergh and Shrewsbury. Mr Thomas is the third headmaster in a row at Casterton – a record for a girls' school?

Academic Matters: Consistently good at GCSE: very few grades D and lower, no obviously weak subjects, languages good. A level results seem, by contrast, a little ordinary; no evidently good or bad subjects; no-one fails, but some culling of weak candidates reported by parents. Some joint teaching with Sedbergh at sixth form. Maximum class size 20. Can deal with 'mild dyslexia'. Mixture of male and female staff, some very dedicated. Some good teaching. Planning to share some subjects and facilities with Sedbergh eight miles away – a sound move.

Games, Options, the Arts: Superb Creative Arts Centre opened in 1990, and much used for lots of jolly productions (musicals a favourite), sometimes with Sedbergh boys. Lots of pupils' work on show in the Centre, inspiring exhibitions and a great strength. Lacrosse as well as trad hockey and netball. Strong parental demand for all-weather pitches. Good music and drama. Indoor swimming pool. Impressive gym mistress. Successful Young Enterprise groups. The heart of the school seems to be in the riding stables out at the back – with lots of girls happily mucking out.

Background and Atmosphere: The Brontës' school, founded in 1823, as the Clergy Daughters' School. Set on a hill at the top of the handsome village; central house includes dining room and library, stables to the rear. The main building feels very much like a large residential house which has grown rabbit warrens of classrooms at the back; the whole is much bigger than it first appears. Nice old-fashioned feel. Safe and sensible through and through: 'They long for glamour,' says a parent. Lots of good limestone conversions. Separate boarding houses in converted stone houses dotted around and dominating tiny friendly village which is down in a hollow below the school. 18-year-olds can go to local pub. Junior boarders (including one or two 7-year-olds) housed separately, with separate enthusiastic housemistress. Slight split personality feel between boarders/day girls. Sixth formers have study bedrooms. Most do D of E. Strong links with local boys' schools – particularly Sedbergh, but also Stonyhurst and Barnard Castle. Regular trips to Manchester, Leeds, Liverpool and London plus work experience.

Pastoral Care and Discipline: Not a real problem. 'Haven't sacked for many years now.' Will expel for 'usual reasons' – drugs automatically out.

Pupils and Parents: Mostly locals, though also real foreigners, including Hong Kong Chinese contingent – this a real strength. 'Not a snobby school', with lots of first-time buyers and 'new money', said a parent. Some Forces children (29 at last count).

Entrance: Not a problem. Own entrance exam: most pupils come via Brontë (the Junior House), but entry at any time. New pre-prep started in 1993, and is going well. Sixth form entry requires six GCSEs grade C, with B in the subjects to be studied.

Exit: Tiny leakage after GCSE: Around 95 per cent go on to higher education, and NB this percentage is considerably increased since we last wrote, even taking into account national trends. Previous parental grumbles (hotly denied by the school) 'that they have to do all the work' (finding the courses available), appear to be fading and career guidance is 'getting better'.

Money Matters: Numbers OK, but school had 60+ assisted places and will feel the lack of them. Regular bursaries and scholarships (out of income) at 11+, 12+, 13+; but basically support for real emergencies, rather than on ability basis. Not a rich school.

Remarks: Friendly unpretentious girls' boarding school – cosy, happy, but perhaps lacks muscle. Popular with locals, and with girls, who pronounce it 'brilliant'.

CENTRAL NEWCASTLE HIGH SCHOOL

Eskadale Terrace, Newcastle upon Tyne
NE2 4DS

TEL: *0191 281 1768* FAX: *0191 281 6192*

E-MAIL: admissions@cnw.gdst.net

WEB: www.gdst.net/newcastlehigh

✦ PUPILS: 649 girls (all day). Plus own junior school with 335 girls ✦ Ages: 11-18, junior school 4-11 ✦ Size of sixth form: 161 ✦ Non-denominational ✦ Fee-paying

---

Head: Since 2000, Mrs L J Griffin BA BPhil (fifties). Educated at Swanshurst Grammar and King Edward VI High School, read English at the University of Wales and medieval studies at York. Taught English at a number of schools, head of English at Scarborough sixth form college, head of St Michael's, Burton Park, and the head of Bedgebury School before coming here. Choral singing a passion; values enthusiasm. Took over from Mrs Angela Chapman, head from 1984.

Academic Matters: Far and away the most academic girls' school for miles around, gets consistently super results. NB last year 78 girls opted for 70 different subject combinations at A levels. Popular subjects are chemistry, maths, English, biology, physics, history and geography – sciences notably strong. Light bright laboratories in the middle of being upgraded. Over half the girls take all three separate sciences at GCSE. Languages are also strong, with a choice of French, German or Spanish (well-run and popular exchanges to all three countries), and other languages on offer later. Latin for everyone for a minimum of two years from the age of 12. The language department has now moved into a neighbouring building which also houses IT – a serious department with masses of machines, and all girls achieving some kind of certificated course. Philosophy for all 11-year-olds, strongly supported by the present head, which the girls either love or loathe.

Sixth formers take four or five ASs and three or four A2s, and follow a general studies programme. 'There is a big emphasis on breadth', said a parent, 'sometimes I wonder if they aren't over-stretched.' Classes are a maximum of 28, though many classes are divided into smaller teaching groups. Setting for maths from year 8 and English from year 9, and the 'fast set' for languages takes the relevant GCSE early. Average staff age somewhat reduced since we last visited, 'It's good having some younger teachers now', said a sixth former.

Games, Options, the Arts: Exceptionally strong tennis – national schools tennis champions at some age group seven times in the last seven years, and the LTA tennis 'School of the Year' in 1997. Indoor and outdoor tennis courts. Squash champions. Hockey and netball also do well: the school is far more sporty than many of its sister Girls' Day School Trust schools. Music is on the up, with its own well designed building, and huge quantities of keyboards, also a recording studio. Good and varied art and design, including graphics, photography, textiles, with some whizzy new young staff. Good on debating, keen D of E award take-up, and forceful fund-raisers, with girls showing initiative; for instance, running their own successful fashion show.

Background and Atmosphere: Urban setting without much green space in sight, in a quiet road in Jesmond, one of Newcastle's 'posh' areas. Newly acquired and newly built additions are round the corner and down the road, including the one-time synagogue, for the art school and dining hall. Sixth form have now moved into their own wing, newly built, with separate entrance. Not a spacious gracious place, but space is well used, and the school generates a atmosphere of getting on with it, functional rather than aesthetically pleasing. Large hall used for assemblies and plays also doubles up as the place to sit – in serried ranks – with your break or indeed your lunch, and rather grim for this (only first years must eat in the dining hall). Outside, notice boards heaving with activities and lists, nearby tuck shop and the girls' telephone (long queues at break, so mobile phones allowed then). School founded in 1895.

Pastoral Care and Discipline: Firm and fair, strong emphasis on 'basic values'.

Pupils and Parents: Solidly middle class, lots of professionals and Asians. Articulate and friendly girls. A rich mixture of regional accents. Lots of brothers over the road at the Royal Grammar School. Fashion note: morale boosted when brown became the 'in' colour, and girls now wear their skirts very short revealing acres of bitter-chocolate tights. Miriam Stoppard is an old girl.

Entrance: Very sought after, and relatively tough, with considerable competition at 11+. Many through the school's own junior department, which has moved its 8 to 11-year-olds from Gosforth to a much closer erstwhile convent set in 5 acres of grounds. Less academic and gentler options locally are Church High and Westfields.

Exit: Medicine is regularly incredibly popular, and a regular contingent of girls go on to art colleges. Average of 10 to Oxbridge, otherwise Leeds, Nottingham, Edinburgh, Glasgow, St Andrew's and Manchester.

Money Matters: Had a large number of assisted places and GDST fund is not nearly large enough to replace all lost income yet. Three or four academic scholarships (of varying worth), one bursary.

Remarks: Powerful and deservedly popular academic girls' day school with a great deal to offer.

CHANNING SCHOOL

Highgate, London N6 5HF

TEL: *020 8340 2328* FAX: *020 8341 5698*

E-MAIL: admin@channing.co.uk

WEB: http://www.channing.co.uk

+ PUPILS: 335, plus 160 in junior school, all girls; all day + Ages: 11-18, juniors 5-11 + Size of sixth form: 100 + Non-denom (Unitarian) + Fee-paying

---

Head: Since 1999, Mrs Elizabeth Radice MA Oxon, PGCE, formerly director of studies at the Royal Grammar School, Newcastle-upon-Tyne. Educated Wycombe Abbey and Somerville, read English. Married to writer and lecturer at the School of Oriental and African Studies, two student daughters. Took over from the clear-headed, hard-fighting Mrs Isabel Raphael, who turned the school into a successful, all-round establishment.

Academic Matters: Not an academic hothouse, and has traditionally been regarded as second division, but in recent years it has been consistently turning out good solid A–C results – not a D in sight at GCSE, and very few of them at A level. A small school, so at A level there are more than ten candidates for only five subjects: English – consistently, the most popular subject, and well taught, maths, biology, chemistry and history. With the advent of the new A level regime the ranking has changed to English and biology equal first, followed by art, maths, French and economics. A reasonable range of subjects in the seventeen on offer. Several part-timers among the staff, several heads of department are men. Dual certificate science for GCSE. Classes of 18–26, shrink for GCSEs. Head of RE, a Unitarian minister, teaches comparative religion. Good library. No provision made for special needs.

Games, Options, the Arts: Good and enthusiastic art in roof-top studios; good exam results. Not really a sporty school, though there are tennis courts on the site (doubling up for hockey and netball) and over the road at the junior school (used by parents during the holidays), and playing fields near by. Which said, Channing does consistently well in matches against larger schools, including athletics. Big sports hall. No Saturday matches ('perish the thought'). Main orchestra and choral society with Highgate boys, who also join in drama. Sixth formers go over (5 minutes' walk) for lunch-time talks, and for drama. Lots of musical activity, good associated board results. Very successful D of E and Young Enterprise – girls win all manner of prizes in this. Lots of lunchtime clubs.

Background and Atmosphere: Looks and feels uninstitutional, a mixture of 18th-century and 1980s buildings. Founded in 1885 'for the daughters of Unitarian ministers and others', set in 31/2 acres (swings, playground and garden) at the very top of Highgate Hill: stunning views. Main buildings linked by curious warren of staircases; cooking smells chase all along corridors. Hugely popular sixth form centre, that is alluring enough to keep the troops here post GCSE. New lecture theatre. Morning assembly starts with singing 'because it's good for everyone to sing once a day'.

Pastoral Care and Discipline: Firm and fair. 'Every case judged on its merits'. Locals comment appreciatively that Channing girls are polite and thoughtful, and that the school really cares what goes on in the community – top marks.

Pupils and Parents: A racial and religious mix, but less so than some other schools in the area. Predominantly from professional families. Parents come in and talk and help with work experience. Old Girls include Baroness Cox, Crown Princess Sarvath of Jordan, Emma Sergeant, Peggy Vance. Girls appear slightly protected, but there is no prototype.

Entrance: One-third from the school's own prep Fairseat (used to be a higher percentage), the rest from state and private schools in roughly equal numbers. Requirements for sixth form entry are six B grades at GCSE, or above, including maths and English. External candidates also need a 'satisfactory school report' and all candidates are interviewed.

Exit: A very few to other sixth forms – eg Camden Girls which takes boys in the sixth form. Approximately 25 per cent opt for a gap year. To Oxbridge and other good universities old and new. A few to art foundation courses.

Money Matters: Had no assisted places, so

no problems here; some academic and music awards, some bursaries.

Remarks: Super small all-round girls' day school in useful London location. Excellent place for girls who seek good academic results but would rather not face the bustle and stridency of big competitive schools to get them.

JUNIOR SCHOOL: Fairseat. Head: Since 1994, Miss Elaine Krispinussen. The school is over the road from the main school with 160 girls (including new reception class), ages 4-11. Set in lovely grounds, handsome old buildings which have just undergone another round of conversion to provide performing arts block and new science/art/IT area. Beastly brown uniform. Generally more than half go on to the senior school, others all over the shop. Hugely sought after by locals – does a good job.

CHARTERHOUSE

Godalming, Surrey GU7 2DJ

TEL: *01483 291501* FAX: *01483 291507*

E-MAIL: admissions@charterhouse.org.uk

WEB: www.charterhouse.org.uk

✦ PUPILS: 620 boys, 80 girls (in sixth form all board except for 25 day) ✦ Ages: 13-18 ✦ Size of sixth form: 340 ✦ C of E ✦ Fee-paying

---

Head: Since 1996, The Rev John Witheridge MA FRSA (forties). Educated at St. Albans School, University of Kent and Christ's College, Cambridge, also Ridley Hall Theological College, Cambridge. Married with four children. Previously the Conduct of Eton. Teaches English. One visiting parent reported him as 'business-like': alas like all major schools the role is mainly administrative and it is said by one sixth former that he is 'not often seen amongst the school' – must have missed him playing Ralph Nickelby in the 1999 production of *Nicholas Nickelby*.

Academic Matters: Head of science likes taking boys on trips in the UK and abroad, 'so they really see the subject applied to industry, and it's not just theoretical'. Science labs all finely updated and modernised with their own excellent resource library – true of several departments. Economics and politics continue to have strong followings at A level – much more popular than in most schools – but they also produce far and away the most D and E grades. A good range of languages can be arranged, though you may have to pay extra if you want an exotic one eg Arabic; parents are advised to ask.

Games, Options, the Arts: Traditionally and actually a strong sporting school – read OC Simon Raven's account of glorious summer cricket matches to get the flavour of the thing. Wins majority of fixtures, one or two described as 'massacres'. Strong strong football. Lots of minor sports now on offer too – shooting, karate, canoeing, fencing, water polo, archery etc. Splendid new sports centre. One of the best public school theatres in the country – named after OC Ben Travers. Nearly 50 per cent of pupils learn an instrument. (NB Vaughan Williams was here.) Well-supported CCF, also Scouts (Baden-Powell was here). Trillions of societies: 'A good place to discover and develop interests for life', commented a parent. Girls coming here from all girls' schools enthusiastic about all this: 'I can't believe how much there is on offer', said one. Excellent post-GCSE period when pupils organise (under supervision and must have staff blessing) all manner of trips (groups of three, 'vaguely educational', boys must report on experience to school); relies much on trust and 'not often broken' said a master. Glorious main library – no expenses spared, and a museum stuffed with exciting objects. Super art studio.

Background and Atmosphere: A golden place on a good day, with idyllic grounds surrounding turreted and Gothic brickwork of the main building. Towering chapel (by Sir Giles Scott) has name upon name of OCs who fell in the world wars, and an awe-inspiring organ. Strong feeling of fellowship. Breeds tremendous loyalty (though a few, like Max Hastings, loathed their schooldays here). New houses look like ocean liners rising out of the grounds in '70s university campus style. Buildings spread far apart over much ground, 'I walk MILES every day just getting about the place', said one boy. Founded in 1611 in London by Thomas Sutton, moved to present site in 1872 and school now feels like a fully paid up member of the Victorian railway-station family. Boarding houses all very different (choose carefully), oldest with cubicles ('cubes') and rooms for sixth formers of shabby luxury. Girls have a new (boarding) 'hall', but during the day they belong to one of the boys' houses.

Pastoral Care and Discipline: The rules are clearly defined. Occasional drugs problems. Drugs policy: one strike and you may be out; two strikes and you definitely will be. Smoking is an irritant. Good staff/pupil relationships. Pupils may go home from Saturday lunch to Sunday chapel on any weekend. Appointment of Under Master to oversee the 13-16-year-olds has helped the pastoral care.

Pupils and Parents: New money (and lots of it), Surrey stockbrokers, Londoners. Also some from far corners of the UK; 50 from overseas (mainly British families), a handful of Thais, twenty or so Germans etc . Charming chaps, good at interfacing with the world; school events good for networking. Old Carthusians, a hugely interesting list, covering all walks of life – eg Joseph Addison, Max Beerbohm, Don Cupitt, John Alliot, Peter May, Archie Norman, Lords Wakeham, Prior, Griffiths – also judges, statesmen, soldiers, scholars. School has strong yuppie appeal. 'There's a brash smell of money', commented one parent.

Entrance: CE results must be good across the board for entry at 13 (reasonable average will do nicely). Entry at sixth form much tougher (all those girls to choose from): no stated policy, it is 'at the headmaster's discretion' – but, again, ask. One recent applicant told us that 'the recorder (registrar) was extremely helpful'.

Exit: Over half do a gap year, all end up at university. Usually 30 plus to Oxbridge. Currently more opting for humanities than sciences. A few go on into the creative arts.

Money Matters: Generous scholarships at 13+ and 16+. 12 academic, 3 exhibitions, 5 music, 2 art at 13+. Various academic, art, music scholarships. Continues to maintain its position as one of the most expensive schools in the country – pots of money about, mostly from the pockets of parents and grateful OCs. The school is well run.

Remarks: Super public school for the sons of stockbrokers, with five-star facilities. Slight split personality between lower school and sixth form.

CHEADLE HULME SCHOOL

Claremont Road, Cheadle Hulme, Cheadle, Cheshire SK8 6EF

TEL: *0161 488 3330* FAX: *0161 488 3344*

E-MAIL: registrar@chschool.co.uk

WEB: www.chschool.co.uk

✦ PUPILS: 1,420 boys and girls, all day
✦ Ages: 4-18 ✦ Size of sixth form: 290
✦ Non-denom ✦ Fee-paying

Head: New head, Paul Dixon, takes over in April 2001. In his forties, read zoology at Oxford – teaching career entirely in the independent sector, includes a six-year stint as second master (deputy head) at Stockport Grammar and, since 1996, as headmaster at Reigate Grammar School, Surrey. Active sportsman, married to a PE specialist who has herself taught in independent schools. Three children. Cheadle's previous head for 10 years, Donald Wilkinson, was responsible for huge changes at the school, including recruitment of new staff and massive building programme. Interregnum being managed by Mr Andrew Chicken.

Academic Matters: In the past, Cheadle Hulme has had a slightly uneven academic reputation, but in recent years – and particularly the last three – it has increasingly held its own and achieved impressive results. ISC inspection in 1995 (next one January 2001) was favourable, and the school has addressed those short-comings that the inspectors highlighted, eg new facilities.

The teaching methods are a mixture of traditional, all-class teaching and more informal approaches – not dogmatic, whatever is appropriate. A child who might shrivel up and under-achieve in a more pressurised academic environment, could well blossom and do great things here.

Of the 110 full-time staff, 33 have been at the school for over 10 years. A sizable number of new staff have been recruited from the state sector. Ratio of staff to pupils is on average 1: 13. Class size in years 7-11 is on average 25–26; sixth form, average of 9–10, with a maximum of 15. The last three years show a huge improvement in exam results; this year, 90 per cent attained grade B or above at GCSE, with coordinated science, English and maths scoring particularly well. A levels are modular. Slight bias towards maths and science. Over 80 per cent of pupils gain A–C grades at A level, excluding general studies.

Games, Options, the Arts: Games are compulsory, and under new head, for whom sport is clearly important, the signs are that the school's sporty reputation should continue. New developments are planned. Year-round indoor swimming pool since 1911. School has good reputation for music – lots of groups, concerts; head of music aims to introduce children to wide range of music, not just classical. Facilities for fine arts, ceramics, textiles are new and fantastic – but few take at A level (we suspect that the school values these subjects, but parents less so). Broad curriculum. Computer facilities and technical support excellent, under new partnership with computer firm Viglen.

Background and Atmosphere: Site large, spread out, surrounded by greenery. Main school buildings are pure Victorian splendour. Established in 1855, as Manchester Warehousemen and Clerks' Orphan Schools, for 'orphans and necessitous children'. Compassionate and co-educational origins very much alive today; the word 'progressive' slips tentatively from the lips of a member of staff. Emphasis on child as individual, not just a cog in a system. Pupils comment on flexibility within school, staff prepared to accommodate different needs, eg optional drop-in sessions at lunch-time, for children having difficulties in given subjects. The school feels it 'competes successfully with the most prestigious schools in the area, as we aim to preserve our unique focus on the individual child'. Ratio of girls to boys roughly even. Enthusiasm and happiness evident, also creativity, pride in achievement. Lots of clubs and societies run by the children. No snobbery about industry, business – on the contrary, school proud of its links.

The school has its own sixth form centre, complete with café. Lunchtime is noisy, lively, possibly slightly overwhelming for quieter pupils but full of life for the more sociable. Pupils wear different coloured uniform (blue) from rest of school (green).

Pastoral Care and Discipline: Does not consider itself, or wish to be considered, an authoritarian school. Has detailed structure for pastoral care which 'reacts quickly' to any problems. Aim is self-discipline but, if necessary, 'persuasion' is used towards that end. Bullying identified and dealt with quickly – 'if we hear about it from a parent first, then we have failed'. For school council, pupils cast votes, but staff have the final say. Pupils have recently established their own peer support scheme.

Pupils and Parents: The school aims to further values common to all – pupils are from Christian, Jewish (15 per cent), Muslim and Sikh backgrounds, and from secular homes. School takes parents' views into account – prides itself on listening to them and finding 'enough common ground', even if not total agreement on all points.

Pupils come from all over the South Manchester/North Cheshire area, from as far afield as Delamere (near Chester) and Macclesfield. Many from Stockport, Didsbury, Hale/Altrincham. Numerous school buses ferry children to and fro, in some cases leading to a rather long school day: 'it's dark when I leave home in the morning and dark when I get back…but I'm still glad I've packed it all into the day'.

Entrance: Entry is by examination (including crucial VR test) and interview. Entry requirements are not as demanding academically as some of its 'competitors' in the South Manchester/North Cheshire area – its aims are different in some respects, with a wider focus. Much trouble is taken to assess each child. Demand has increased in recent years – there are now four applicants for every place (not necessarily all first choices.) 45 per cent of senior school intake comes from state primary schools.

Exit: Many to university, particularly northern universities, some to London, Oxbridge. Old Waconians include Katie Derham (TV journalist and presenter), Lucy Ward (political correspondent with *The Guardian*).

Money Matters: School offers some bursaries, based on academic merit and financial eligibility. Two scholarships in music or creative arts available every year for applicants to sixth form. Fees represent good value for money.

Remarks: A vibrant, confident, action-packed atmosphere for children who intend to get stuck into life and make their way in the world. For quieter, introverted children it might all seem a bit too much. Not yet possible to judge the new head.

JUNIOR SCHOOL: The Junior School is housed in its own, 1970s building adjacent to the main site of the senior school, over-looking playing fields. Shares some facilities with senior school (eg swimming pool, playing fields), but is sufficiently separate to prevent small children feeling over-whelmed. Own head. Around 260 boys and girls, ages 4–11. Happy, informal atmos-phere. Computers in abundance. Good facilities for art. As with senior school, music and sport are highly valued.

CHELMSFORD COUNTY HIGH SCHOOL FOR GIRLS

Broomfield Road, Chelmsford, Essex
CM1 1RW

TEL: *01245 352592/256993* FAX: *01245 345746*

E-MAIL: cchs@rmplc.co.uk

✦ PUPILS: 745 girls; all day ✦ Ages: 11-18
✦ Size of sixth form: 232 ✦ Non-denom
✦ State

Head: Since 1997, Mrs Monica Curtis BA (fifties). Educated at Bournemouth School for Girls and Manchester, where she studied English and history of art. Has held a wide and interesting range of teaching posts including a year at Cedars Special School for Physically Handicapped and Delicate Children in Gateshead, two years at Gateshead Technical College, head of lower school at Lancaster Girls' Grammar, and head of Kesteven and Grantham Girls'. Widowed, with two children.

She took over from Mrs McCabe, who commented about the school: 'It's all about expectations, the word "weak" is not in our vocabulary here.' A difficult act to follow.

Academic Matters: Highly selective, pro-ducing chart-bursting results. Committed long-serving staff – largely female and on expensive top-of-scale salary grades. Hard driven by outgoing head; endless appraisals 'for academic success, our top priority'. Class sizes around 25 with setting in French and maths. Teaching styles vary from tradi-tional to National Curriculum require-ments for girls to take responsibility for their own learning through project and investigation (in the biology lab we found girls hatching chicks). Compulsory three separate sciences up to GCSE in new(ish) eight laboratory science block (funded by government grant of £850,000) as part of ten subject GCSE package, including French, German, (Spanish, Russian available in the sixth form), Latin (one-quarter take Latin at GCSE – no classical civilisation on the menu; no Greek and v few take Latin at A level). Nineteen subjects on offer at A level plus FLAW (French Language at Work business qualification for those not doing a language). Three weeks' post-GCSE work experience for all (Trident Project) with placings including the Cabinet Office, local accountants, a Brunei hospital.

Games, Options, the Arts: A team of games captains cover hockey (have been Eastern Counties Champions), netball, ten-nis, fencing, athletics, dance, swimming (the school has its own pool). Regular Saturday matches – three hockey pitches, five tennis courts, dance/drama studio, gym for PE, weight-training, fencing. Eleven musical groups includes choirs taught by keen sixth formers, likewise drama groups. Compul-sory community service involves each class in serious fund-raising. Home economics on offer (rare now in academic girls' schools), textiles, electronics, computing (Nimbus). D of E awards. Debates with boys' grammar school. Stunning art and ceramics – teeming art studio; art and history trips. In-house Royal Academy 'outreach' workshops, life-drawing. Good careers advice with professional parents asked to come in to give talks and interviews.

Background and Atmosphere: Solid Edwardian redbrick, ivy-clad, two-storey, purpose-built (1906) with dismal refurbished '50s extension and the odd Portakabin. Neighbouring detached villas for sixth formers with own common room, kitchens. Development appeal now almost complete for performing arts suite, artificial turf pitch etc. Buildings stand off the main Cambridge road near soulless Chelmsford centre but 'buzz with life' as previous head said – spotless corridors, gleaming lino, landings with trestles of immaculate ceramics – 'No, we have no vandalism here.'

Pastoral Care and Discipline: 'We have high expectations of our students, who are both intelligent and sensible', comments

new head. Homework 'log-book' sent home for parents to sign/comment; questionnaire on parent's views on schools 'strengths and weaknesses'. Drugs: 'any girl who brings illegal drugs on to the school premises will be liable to permanent exclusion.'

Pupils and Parents: Majority from white professional middle classes, plus a handful of ethnic minorities, 40 per cent from Chelmsford, otherwise Essex, Suffolk, Hertfordshire. Up to one third transfer from the private sector 'feeling the pinch'. Tidy, biddable, navy-blazered girls ('Latin motto, 'We carry the lamps of life') in pleated grey skirts ('dress-code' only for sixth – no extremists), smile helpfully above neatly knotted ties. Parents and Governors (including a Cambridge admissions tutor, an accountant and an MP) are 'committed to education'.

Entrance: Annual intake of the 112 highest scorers on 11-plus examination (verbal reasoning, maths and English) – no interview, IQ range 115-140; 'I get lots of calls from parents asking how to make sure their daughters get in', comments head. Appeals system for despairing near-misses. Head is careful to point out that not every able child opts for selective education. About an extra 20 taken on in the sixth form with a minimum of five or more GCSE passes at grades A–B, and 'clear evidence of strength in the subjects to be taken at A level'.

Exit: 98 per cent to higher education including a regular troupe to Oxbridge. Lots of medics, lawyers, international bankers, engineers; also the Forces, business studies, teaching, arts foundation.

Remarks: Highly selective powerful bouncy girls' grammar school delivering top-quality exam results, which they care about desperately: 'It's not a rest-cure here.'

CHELTENHAM COLLEGE

Bath Road, Cheltenham, Gloucestershire
GL53 7LD

TEL: *01242 513540* FAX: *01242 265630*

E-MAIL: registrar@cheltcoll.gloucs.sch.uk

WEB: www.cheltcoll.gloucs.sch.uk

✦ PUPILS: 365 boys, 145 girls in sixth form. (two-thirds of the pupils board, one-third day) ✦ Ages: 13-18 ✦ Size of sixth form: 290 ✦ C of E ✦ Fee-paying

---

Head: Since 1997, Mr Paul Chamberlain,BSc (early fifties). Educated at a 'now defunct state school in Cheshire', followed by zoology at Durham. Previous post, head of St Bees, Cumbria. Before that taught at Haileybury – 'something else kept coming up so I stayed' – and ended up as housemaster. Wife is a JP, one son and one daughter. Charming, thoughtful, with a sparkling sense of humour. Took over from Mr Peter Wilkes MA, whose forced resignation caused headlines and furious reaction from parents against the governors – a tricky situation to start in, but the consequent reduction in intake appears to have been contained.

Academic Matters: Good profile of results at A level. Most popular subjects maths (fine results here), English, economics, biology. German gets wonderful results, French not so. Some interesting staff, head of biology an opera enthusiast ('actually, I'm a fanatic') who regularly encourages a coach load of pupils up to Covent Garden and brings them back singing. Five or six sets for most

subjects. Traditionally excellent electronics department – huge emphasis on the subject from the start, though even girls coming in at sixth form and new to the subject have been known to win national competitions. School regularly wins all the top electronics prizes (two or three each year), with all manner of inventions, under watchful eye of inspiring head of department, who arrives in a Porsche. Big emphasis on IT throughout the school, computers all over the place. Part-time, qualified specialist for dyslexics for three days a week. Full-time EFL specialist, who teaches small groups withdrawn from French, and on a one-to-one basis. Good results for a (reasonably) broad intake (IQs from 100 to 130+).

Games, Options, the Arts: Good art, also drama (much liked head of drama; small studio theatre plus proscenium arch theatre hall), and also good music, some with the Ladies' College. A sporty school – everyone partakes of some sport on Saturday afternoon. Rugby keen and strong – results lovingly recorded in great detail in school magazine – first XV won ten out of its eleven matches at last count. Cricket the other main game, huge numbers of teams and matches. Girls' hockey. NB head groundsman was a former England fast bowler. Keen polo school, they play at Inglesham, box your own pony or make arrangements locally, particularly popular with Gloucestershire day boys.

Boat house at Tewkesbury, and some rowing alumni doing very well. Very strong CCF, unusually high standards in all departments (compulsory for most for one year). Career department has good industrial links. Many activities/clubs on offer.

Background and Atmosphere: Proud of being the oldest of the Victorian public schools (founded for 'the sons of gentlemen'), with strong army links (has its own regimental colours). Has sold much land over the years and now the A40, roaring with traffic, slices the school in two, dividing the main campus from subsidiary blocks; somewhat improved recently by re-routing of heavy lorries. Fine Gothic collegiate architecture in honey-coloured stone, dining hall (hopeless acoustics) used to be the chapel; extremely fine library (looks like a chapel). Chapel service starts with school notices (good acoustics and rousing singing) every morning at 9.10am, ie after the first lesson. On the edge of the city, fine views of Cotswolds. Now about 30 per cent girls: 'fully co-ed' says school.

Pastoral Care and Discipline: Occasional sackings for drugs. List of pubs/cafés/restaurants pupils may visit plus the forbidden places on public display. Typical house will have a married housemaster or housemistress, a younger unmarried tutor (both full-time teachers), and a foreign gap year student living on the premises – an unusual range of havens for the pupil in distress. All staff are tutors; parents 'urged' to get to know their offspring's tutor and have been known to react with 'dismay' on finding that theirs is not the one who lives in.

Pupils and Parents: Army links decreased but lingering (a mere 25 Services' children at last count). Increasingly pupils come from within a one-hour radius. Day pupils from the far side of Swindon, Gloucester, Broadway. At least 8 per cent non-Brits. Boys' hair, appearance and manners get eight out of ten. Girls wear uniform even in upper sixth – and don't complain. Old Boys include Scott of the Antarctic's companion Edward Wilson, many distinguished soldiers, eg Field Marshal Sir John Dill, General Sir Michael Rose, Lt-General Sir John Bagot, 14 VCs (the largest per capita number of any school apart from Wellington). Not to mention more Old Boys rumoured to have been eaten by tigers than any other school.

Entrance: CE not a high hurdle. Many via the school's extremely good prep school (see separate entry), but increasingly from elsewhere. Pupils in school need at least five passes at GCSE to go on to sixth form; competitive entrance exam for outside sixth form entrants (mainly girls) plus VRQ test and interview.

Exit: Numbers at post-GCSE drop out dwindling (clever locals opt for Pate's Grammar School). Most to university, occasionally into the army or art college.

Money Matters: Half a dozen or so scholarships of 50 per cent fees; others between 10-40 per cent on academic merit; help for the needy.

Remarks: Solid if still somewhat uninspiring low-profile public school (once one of the greats) with a marked technological emphasis, fighting its corner.

THE CHELTENHAM LADIES' COLLEGE

Cheltenham, Gloucestershire GL50 3EP

Tel: *01242 520691* Fax: *01242 227882*

E-mail: enquiries@cheltladiescollege.org

Web: www.cheltladiescollege.org

✦ Pupils: 850 girls (650 board, 200 day)
✦ Ages: 11-18 ✦ Size of sixth form: 300
✦ C of E but welcomes (and respects) all faiths ✦ Fee-paying

Principal: Since 1996, Mrs Vicky Tuck MA BA PGCE (forties). Came from City of London School for Girls where she was deputy head. Formerly at Bromley High. Married, two teenage boys. Cool and collected. Former modern languages teacher. Keeps in touch with what is happening in the classroom by shadowing a girl twice-a-year for the day. Size of school means that girls have very little contact with her (unusual in a girls school).

Academic Matters: Continues to be seriously strong. Over 80 per cent A*/A at GCSE. At A level over half the grades are As; maths, English, biology, chemistry, economics and history being the most popular subjects. One or two do Greek. Spanish, German, Russian, Mandarin Chinese on offer, Japanese classes available: Italian at sixth form. IT strong, and CDT much encouraged. 200 computers throughout. Internet and e-mail available to all. New art, design and technology block. The school prides itself on allowing 'any combination of subjects at every level'. Huge staff. Low turnover. Two well-equipped libraries, both with full-time librarians. Can cope with 'mild dyslexia', but this is not a place to send a dyslexic child. Superb university advice/careers department, work shadowing in holidays.

Games, Options, the Arts: Excellent 'big' school facilities. Huge gym in main building, games hall, fitness room, indoor tennis, new competition sized indoor swimming pool which generates great enthusiasm and spectacular results. Slight grouch from pupils that 'not allowed enough time for Field' (ie games). 'Lots of silverware', though. Own riding school nearby, girls are allowed to bring ponies (popular among younger children especially), and polo is an option. Teams for everything, but girls who aren't good at games 'sit around'. Immensely strong music as always – 750 music lessons weekly, all packed in round subject lessons, five choirs, three orchestras, dozens of chamber groups and lots of girls compose. New director of music and new organist. Drama strong with new 'director in residence', theatre studio revamped, and editing suite for filming etc. Cooking; excellent fabric design, pottery, and art studios now open at weekends. About 10 per cent take art at A level, and almost all get As. Debates, concerts and occasional drama with Cheltenham College (now co-ed, 'which doesn't help', said one pupil) half a mile away. Strong on charity work. D of E. New co-ordinator appointed in '98 to 'beef up provision at weekends' – lack of things to do at weekends has long been, and continues to be, a parental moan. Keen on charity work – helping in primary schools, special needs etc – 'Mrs Tuck's big thing', said a pupil.

Background and Atmosphere: Founded in 1853, granted Royal Charter in 1935, main school revolves round huge purpose-built Victorian campus, with magnificent stained glass, marble corridor, Princess Hall, vast library, in the middle of Cheltenham. Based on concept of boys' public schools, pupils go home to their house for lunch, tea and at night – pets, table napkins, pianos, and sewing machines, friendly homely atmosphere – it really works. Most houses are about 5-10 minutes walk away. Junior boarders live either in rooms converted into 'cubs' (cubicles), or in open-plan dormitories which are much preferred; 'friendlier, you get to know each other better', say the girls. Sixth formers have own houses (one day, four boarding), boarders sleep and work in charming individual rooms, each with its own panic button ('with 222 girls in the middle of town, what else can we do?' said one housemistress), but retain strong links with their junior house.

Housemistresses in junior houses are non-teaching (which works particularly well), whilst sixth form housemistresses also have academic responsibility. Sixth formers can 'have dinner in town' (taxi there and back) and invite their boyfriends back – 'the boys often become house friends'. Socialising with Radley, Dean Close etc, including plenty of 'unofficial contact'. Called 'greenflies' by townfolk, the girls wear magnificent loden coats and staff have been known to accost total strangers wearing the school coat 'on the lawn' at the National Hunt Festival. Uniform worn even by sixth formers. New uniform '98 – shapeless trousers. Food said to have improved. Few anorexics. Girls carry their books in 'sacks'; send internal messages via 'slab' and have names for almost everything: Slodge (Sidney Lodge), St Mags (St Margaret's), the bunny run. No bells, just clocks. Very highly structured, very institutional, feels big (it is) and daunting to new girls.

Pastoral Care and Discipline: Head feels that this is good and lots of safety nets have been put in place. Bullying is 'managed'. Class teachers liaise with housemistresses for junior girls, Sixth formers have tutors and all girls have a personal 'mentor'. Two day houses and a sixth form house are based at the Day Girl Centre, each with their own housemistresses. Confidential counselling service available to all girls run by professionally trained counsellors. 'No shame attached', said a girl. Very comprehensive and tough drugs policy – nothing mealy-mouthed about it. Sixth formers commented that all prospective parents ask, when being shown round, if there is a drugs problem, and wondered if any of them really thought that the girls would say 'Yes'!

Pupils and Parents: Ambitious parents of academic offspring – school has to manage the parents' expectations as much as the girls'. Broadish social mix, majority professional, not the 'posh' place the tabloid press think it is (accents are well-spoken but not smart). Lots of ex-pats. 18 per cent are foreign, mainly from Hong Kong and Singapore. Girls are good natured, bright and sensible, robust, astute and articulate. Perhaps a touch 'solid': girls' priorities in life work, sport, shopping (in that order). Old girls: Rosie Boycott, Mary Archer, Cheryl Gillan, Rachel Lomax, (Vice-Chairman of the World Bank), Katharine Hamnett.

Entrance: Fairly stiff competition, at 11+, 12+, 13+ by CE or own exam. Foreigners need to have 'fluent and accurate English' before entering. Own competitive exam into the sixth form (lots of foreigners join then, and love it).

Exit: Of 150 leavers, 50 take a gap year, around 25 offered Oxbridge places. Others to traditional universities. A handful to art colleges. 'All girls are destined to have careers'.

Money Matters: Expensive, but definitely provides value for money. Four per cent of fee income available for bursaries at last count. Large number of scholarships (by girls' school standards) available.

Remarks: Famous and strong traditional girls' boarding school, with large numbers of day girls. Impressive results as always. Offers a full and busy timetable. A strong institutional feel. Conformist. Not the place for the timid girl or the sparky rebel, however clever they may be.

THE CHERWELL SCHOOL

(CHERWELL UPPER)

Marston Ferry Road, Oxford OX2 7EE

TEL: *01865 558719*, FAX: *01865 311165*

E-MAIL: cherwell@rmplc.co.uk

WEB: www.rmplc.co.uk/eduWeb/sites/cherwell/

✦ PUPILS: approx 1025in all, boys and girls; all day ✦ Ages: 13-18 ✦ Size of sixth form: approx 350 ✦ Non-denom ✦ State

Head: Since 1981, Mr M H Roberts MA (Oxon) (fifties), educated at Christ's Hospital and Merton College, Oxford (historian). Previously taught at Leeds Grammar School, then went into state comprehensive system and has stayed in it. Married to Diana, who is a social worker, son and daughter. Lists his hobby as writing history books for schools.

Academic Matters: Good, though not considered anything out of the way by locals, who live in the academic hot house of Oxford, but fine results by any ordinary standard – and v good maths. Some reports of sloppy teaching. HMI report very complimentary. Sets for maths and modern languages. Block subjects now on timetable, so departments can organise groups as they wish. History of art is well taught. Growth at sixth form level in recent years, with two-thirds of the pupils now staying on, and up to 30 or 40 new pupils coming in.

Games, Options, the Arts: County representatives in football, netball and basketball, boys and girls. Strong and enthusiastic music department with lots of extra-curricular bands and concerts. Drama and theatre studies also strong.

Background and Atmosphere: Modern brick and prefab buildings off Banbury Road. Cramped and ugly school assembly hall seriously overused and stuffy. Some new buildings. Whole school bursting with energy, and some staff radiating interest in and concern for the well-being of their charges, like kindly shepherds. A feeling of safety and spiritual warmth. Interestingly, school started life as a secondary modern. Million-pound building programme to include three science labs, two technology labs, 12 workshops.

Pastoral Care and Discipline: Each class has the same form tutor who relates to same head of year for first three years: sixth form have own form tutors and heads of year. Pupils go 'on record' and parents are informed for slacking or truancy, disrupting lessons; fighting can 'lead to suspension'; drugs and threatening or violent behaviour lead to 'permanent exclusion'.

Pupils and Parents: Some middle class, some connected with the University, and large numbers from nearby housing estates. Seriously popular locally, buses from all over. Ability range a fair spread. Several staff have children in school. Good parental links and consultations.

Entrance: Majority from the local middle schools. (NB Oxford still has middle and first schools). Oversubscribed for all years. 40+ come at sixth form level from local private schools.

Exit: Very few into employment at 16; most do two years in sixth here or at the local FE college, and on to university.

Money Matters: Two successive years of

financial cuts ('95/6 and '96/7) in Oxfordshire mean that class sizes are larger, learning support has been cut and there are five fewer staff.

Remarks: State comprehensive with an enlarged sixth form, with reasonably satisfied parents, that could be even better.

CHRIST'S HOSPITAL

Horsham, Sussex RH13 7LS

TEL: *01403 211293* FAX: *01403 211580*

E-MAIL: adsec@christs-hospital.org.uk

WEB: www.christs-hospital.org.uk

✦ PUPILS: approx 481 boys, 328 girls (all board) ✦ Ages: 11-18 Size of sixth form: approx 220 ✦ C of E ✦ Fee-paying – but see Money Matters

---

Head: Since 1996, Dr Peter Southern MA, PhD (early fifties). Educated at The Dragon School, Magdalen College School and Merton College, Oxford, plus PhD from Edinburgh (medieval history). Previously Head of Bancroft's School, Woodford Green and before that head of history at Westminster. Married, two children. Enjoys 'tennis, golf, sailing and slaving in the garden' – and is keen on PG Wodehouse. Played Real Tennis for Oxford. Swift turnover of heads before arrival of Dr Southern entailed a period of disruption and disaffection. This appears to be settling down, but Christ's Hospital is not an easy school to run.

Academic Matters: Strong academic tradition, particularly sciences and maths. Satellites sprouting up into physics labs (weather signals feeding in) and language departments. Science at GCSE is compulsory (double award). Offers classics, Russian, Italian as well as French and German. Girls tend to do more and better in arts subjects here. Unusual subjects on offer include British government politics and archaeology. Very strong art and design, and pupils regularly score straight As.

Games, Options, the Arts: Very strong musical tradition. The school band leads the Lord Mayor's procession in London each year and hundreds of people turn up to hear the school beating the retreat – an old tradition. It also plays while school marches in to lunch and it is considered a status symbol to be in it (though it makes you late for a rather good lunch). School has five organs – a record? Good arts centre with a super theatre seating 500, said to be inspiration for the Swan Theatre, Stratford-upon-Avon. Lots of good productions, both school and professional, and theatre much appreciated by all. School now claims to have the 'best' sporting facility of any school in the country opened by its President, HRH the Duke of Gloucester, at a cost of £3 million, which includes a social centre and even disabled facilities – as ritzy as any we have come across. The school has a well-established and useful programme of community service which other schools could learn from.

Background and Atmosphere: Founded in 1552 by the boy King Edward VI for the education of London's sick and poor, and still sticks by and large to the spirit of this aim. School moved from its five-acre site in the City (good grief!) to 1,200 Sussex acres in 1902. Large complex and avenues and quads designed by Victorian architect Sir Aston Webb, looks like a huge, smart, redbrick barracks with gracious cloisters. Vast dormitories – think of Florence Nightingale and you've got the picture – now converted into units of study/bedroom accommodation. Still feels a bit institutional. Dorms are Spartan, but 'cosy psychologically' commented a mother. The best part of £60 million is to be spent on completely refurbishing boarding, and lots of new facilities – see website for latest details.

In 1985 joined forces with the sister school that moved from Hertford. Boys wear wonderful ancient uniform of floor-length blue wool coats, black breeches and saffron-coloured stockings, and tab and 'broadie' buckle on leather belt. Girls wear the same blue coats in winter, and picturesque navy suits with old-fashioned cuffs and buttons, and could all step straight into a Tudor play, without changing a thing. Parents love the flapping cassocks on November evenings. Uniform provided free, worn seven days a week – often smelly by half term – and by the way, amazing to relate, the children love wearing it.

Pastoral Care and Discipline: Things tightened up considerably under the previous head, whose message to the children on sex was 'if possible, wait'. There are still occasional outbursts of trouble (drink in particular).

Pupils and Parents: Anybody poor and deserving from miners' sons to those of bankrupt bankers and 'we even have prostitutes' children here', said a member of staff. Mostly from south-east, though school is trying to rectify this. Both working class and a few distressed gentle toffs. 38 per cent of pupils are totally supported by the school; 67 per cent of parents earn less than the national average. Largish proportion of single-parent families. OBs (Old Blues): lots of distinguished ones, as you might expect, including bouncing-bomb man Barnes Wallis, William Glock, Bernard Levin, Colin Davis, cricketer John Snow, Coleridge, Leigh Hunt.

Entrance: Very complicated, owing to ancient charitable foundation and ancient Counting House which oversees the procedure. For the majority of places the school will only consider children whose parents cannot afford boarding school fees and who have a definite 'need'. It helps to be in the Church, the RAF, a single parent or down on your luck. School sets its own exam. Places gained either by competition or by 'presentation' – governors and certain livery companies have the right to sponsor a child. (This means that the 'presentees' have to reach a minimum standard, which moves up and down depending on numbers applying, while the competitive candidates have to be brighter, and to compete.) Get the up-to-date governors' list from the school to see who may help. Or alternatively donate £12k or more to become a 'foundation governor' yourself.

Caveat: the whole process can be intensely humiliating (the head says 'interminable' would be nearer the mark). 'Now I know what it feels like to be a Third World child being patronised by the West', said a would-be Christ's parent. School says that 'the admissions process is under review to make life easier for parents' – good.

Exit: Most to university, and very widespread, though school gets some fall-out from children whose family circumstances make it impossible for them to continue.

Money Matters: School has pots of money, largely derived from property. Better endowed than Eton, says Eton. Fees assessed according to income, from nil, if family income is less than £11,361, to just under

£14k for incomes above £55k gross (not many such camels get through the needle's eye), at time of writing. You may need a good accountant. Had over 80 assisted places, but replacing them should not be a problem.

Remarks: This is an ancient foundation (now full-boarding co-ed) which, unlike most, still operates as a genuine charity, and is without the snobby aspects of the usual public school; a parent comments that the 'traditions knit the troubled backgrounds.'

CITY OF LONDON

FREEMEN'S SCHOOL

Ashtead Park, Surrey KT21 1ET

TEL: *01372 277 933* FAX: *01372 276 165*

E-MAIL: headmaster@clfs.surrey.sch.uk

✦ PUPILS: 785 pupils, 395 boys (20 board) and 390 girls (11 board). Plus 360 pupils in Junior School ✦ Ages: 13-18, junior school 7-13 ✦ Size of sixth form: 165 ✦ Non-denom ✦ Fee-paying

---

Head: Since 1987, Mr David Haywood MA (Cantab) PGCE (early fifties). His fourth appointment, previously Deputy Head of Dauntsey's School, Wiltshire. Charming and affable, Mr Haywood is married with two teenage sons. Slightly removed from the day-to-day lives of pupils (he has hands-on management team), he is nevertheless well respected and liked. 'He knows all our names', said one pupil admiringly. Called 'headmaster' by his staff.

Popular with parents. Passionate about sport, especially cricket. A great champion for the cause of co-education.

Academic Matters: Given the entrance requirements (13+ requires a 55 per cent minimum average at CE) the academic results are really good. 2000 saw 85 per cent of A level candidates gain A-C grades and a 98.7 per cent pass rate. 'Cherish the individual' is a mantra for the head, and it certainly seems to work here. The sciences are by far the most popular choice a A level. Maths also gets a good showing.

In the core subjects at GCSE, maximum class size likely to be 22 and the minimum, about 10. In the sixth form class sizes average at around 8. Average pupil/teacher ratio is about 10:1. Head does not believe in taking pupils out of class for extra lessons, so the setting system caters for this. EFL tutor for midweek and Saturday morning sessions with foreign students.

Games, Options, the Arts: A great school if you are into sports. Facilities are excellent and there are 57 acres to play with. Main winter sports are hockey (girls) and rugby (boys) and in summer are tennis (girls) and cricket (boys). Swimming is a major competitive sport all year round. Netball, golf, tennis (boys) and athletics are also played competitively. The facilities in the new (5-years old) sports hall are excellent and offer huge range of indoor sports. Outdoor playing fields are extensive and outdoor hockey facilities (floodlit Astroturf pitches) so good that county, regional and national tournaments are often held here.

Drama has been the focus of increased activity over the last few years and music plays an important role in the life of the school, with more than 20 regular musical activities each week. There are numerous choirs, orchestras, bands and ensembles –

even an African drumming ensemble. At least one-third of all pupils in senior school plays an individual instrument. The music tech department generates huge amount of interest among pupils and is housed in wonderfully atmospheric vaulted cellars which were once used for hanging venison. The existing facilities look wonderful but music pupil says 'the acoustics in the main hall (where concerts are held) are terrible'. The answer? A new multi-million pound theatre and auditorium is being built (completion 2001).

The art and design centre is stunning – wonderful light and space. It looks and feels like a gallery. With 3 full-time specialist teachers and even a special studio for sixth formers, art ought to get more exam takers then it does currently.

Pupils are generally spoilt for choice in extra-curricular activities – up to 80 each week.

Background and Atmosphere: School founded in Brixton in 1854, by the Corporation of London to educate orphans (boys and girls) of the Freemen of the City. If there are any such orphan children today, it is still possible to be educated at the school, their fees borne by a fund administered by the Corporation. The school moved to Ashtead Park in 1926 and expanded to include fee-paying locals.

The school has an enviable location set in 57 acres of woodland and playing fields. Focal point is the beautiful Main House, completed by Sir Thomas Wyatt in 1790, that houses among other things the headmaster's gracious office (with fabulous coffee machine), dining room, music department and girls' boarding accommodation.

Over the last seven years, the Corporation of London has funded a major building programme (£25 million) and the

results are modern, attractive and extremely impressive. The school's pride and joy is a state-of-the-art multimedia centre in the recently completed Haywood Centre.

Stunning new science block with state-of-the-art laboratories, prep rooms, teaching rooms and lecture theatres. Biology even has its own attached greenhouse. Excellent sixth form block which younger pupils all yearn to be part of. Says one sixth former, 'we'd walk past and see them all listening to music and drinking coffee ...we couldn't wait to be there'. Not sure how much work goes on – it has the air of a large, noisy frat house.

Unlike many other schools, sixth formers wear a uniform. Different to the rest of the school (navy jacket and trousers/skirt with choice of shirt). Pupils like it. 'no-one worries about wearing the right label.'

Food is so-so, say pupils but used to be terrible. Many still bring packed lunches. There is a strong family atmosphere about the school, 50 per cent are siblings, and pupils seem relaxed and friendly. They like being co-ed and feel it helps them see the opposite sex as people, not objects.

Pastoral Care and Discipline: Strong pastoral care system in place. Older pupils are encouraged to be role models for younger ones. New pupils are assigned a buddy to help them through first few weeks. Early in the first term, new pupils (age 13+) are taken on a weekend filled with all sorts of bonding activities.

School has a code of conduct out of which all other rules flow. As the Head says, if you adhere to this code, you will never step out of line. Not a particularly authoritarian school but encourages children to behave reasonably and responsibly with respect for fellow beings. Zero tolerance for drugs (immediate expulsion – about one every five years) but head says they do understand the enormous pressures children are under today and would try to help such pupils find alternate schools.

Pupils and Parents: Parents are predominantly middle class and as it is a day school, the main catchment areas are within a 10-12 mile radius. At 13+ most entrants come from own junior school the rest mainly from other local prep schools including Danes Hill (Oxshott). Head maintains boarders give the school its core – one suspects he'd like to see the numbers increase. Only 30-40 currently and most of them are from abroad.

Entrance: Increased popularity of school has made rumours rife as to the school raising its entrance level requirements. Not true say school, but for entrance at 13+, you need to have names down by the time your child is 11 and respond with deposit as soon as you get the letter offering you a conditional place. If you respond quickly and child passes common entrance with 55 per cent average or more, he/she should get a place. Alternately your child can also sit school's own exam (January before admission) – maths, English, French/German and science. Sixth Form entrance based on GCSE results – (at least 5 subjects at Grade C, A or B in subjects to be studied).

Exit: 98–99 per cent go on to higher education or gap year. Many traditional university choices. Broad cross-section from medicine and sports science to music, politics and languages. Excellent careers centre and full-time career advisor.

Money Matters: A seriously well-endowed school with very reasonable fees (a pleasant anomaly). The Corporation of London owns, financially supports and manages the school. Although there is a lot of red tape and teeth gnashing involved, the head is pragmatic and appreciative of the generosity of the Corporation. There are more than 26 scholarships available (usually a third, but up to a half of fees) and they attract a number of very bright pupils. There are also some bursaries in the sixth form which offer financial assistance in needy cases.

Remarks: A very attractive school that offers outstanding facilities and opportunities for all its pupils. Egalitarian in feel, it is not the place for social climbers. The sort of school that makes one believe in the benefits of co-education.

JUNIOR SCHOOL: Tel: 01372 277 933 Fax: 01372 276165. Head: Mr John Whybrow BEd (Exeter). Although seen by the outside world to be umbilically attached to the senior school, the ethos of the junior school is of a prep school in its own right. Headmaster encourages this, believing that the children need to see the senior school as a new exciting place to aspire to when they are 13. Junior school is excellent prep with superb facilities, wide range of sport and housed separately from the senior school on shared campus. Entrance at 7+ (maths, English and IQ tests) and 99 per cent of the pupils do go on to the senior school (no entrance test for them).

CITY OF LONDON SCHOOL

Queen Victoria Street, London EC4V 3AL

TEL: *020 7489 0291* FAX: *020 7329 6887*

✦ PUPILS: around 895 boys; all day ✦ Ages: 10-18 ✦ Size of sixth form: Approx 260 ✦ Non-denom ✦ Fee-paying

Head: Since 1999, Mr David Levin, BEcon MA FRSA (forties). Went to school in South Africa, read economics at the University of Natal, then a research degree at Sussex. Previous post was as head of the Royal Grammar School, High Wycombe, and before that he was second master at Cheltenham College, but started his career as a solicitor. South African in origin, with a strong interest in development economics. Keen sportsman, particularly rugby and swimming – he has swum the Channel. Tall, with charm, very able, a brilliant manager. His wife Jenny is a management consultant.

Governors are made up of representatives of the Corporation of London (not noted for being long-sighted or easy to work with) which owns the school; as such the headmaster is termed a 'Chief Officer' and as such must meet with other 'Chief Officers' of parks for example. Took over from Mr David Grossel, acting head for a year after a hiccough with the succession to the dynamic Mr Roger Dancey, who was here only three years. The head before that was here for five. School has (we feel) suffered from this fast turn-over of heads – Mr Levin determined to stay for a long time.

Academic Matters: Grammar school ethos, some setting, no specialisation below sixth form level. Poised – like many other schools – to set pupils 4 AS exams, followed by 3 or 4 A2s. Results remain steady and pleasing by and large – heavily weighted to A grades. Maths continues as the most popular A level subject, followed by history ('brilliantly taught', say boys), chemistry, biology, French and economics. Light dusting of Es and three N/Us. Pupils regularly distinguish themselves in Mathematics Olympiad. Remarkable English master, Jonathan Keates – distinguished author of biographies on Stendhal and Purcell. Staff currently looking closely at academic monitoring, to find ways of picking up problems early. Big new emphasis on modern languages, with work shadowing schemes in German and France.

Games, Options, the Arts: For a London school, this is a sporty place, with numerous teams. No pecking order among sports. Two terms of soccer – rugby has been dropped. Traditionally strong on basketball, and all the water sports (super pool on site) also badminton. Keen sailing. Lots of staff involved in games, with seventeen acres of playing fields at the school's disposal, some thirty minutes bus ride away. Real tennis sadly no longer played at Queen's, but Eton fives can be had at Westminster. Sports facilities on site are splendid and well used, and even include a sauna. CCF bristling with participants. Extremely good music department; art and design technology reveal pockets of fine work. Enthusiastic drama. Good on trips, including a reading week, very lively political debates, big programme of clubs/activities at lunch break and some after school. Boys run societies (heaps of these), and get speakers galore – a prime site for getting the great and the good and also the famous. Signs of Jeremy Paxman's recent visit on our tour. Square Mile Society newly set up (head's baby) with four or five other City schools (state and private), fruitfully netting more speakers and exchanging ideas.

Background and Atmosphere: Present school started in 1837 on medieval foundation; in 1976 moved to purpose-built high-tech U-shaped building with river frontage, just east of Blackfriars Bridge, and bang opposite the Tate Modern, right beside the (troublesome) footbridge. Terraces for the boys (one enclosed so a football can be kicked around), constant hum of boats from the river. Stunning view of St Paul's – altogether, an exciting setting. Good library, attractive small theatre and drama studio, large hall for assemblies, slightly airless locker-lined corridors, large classrooms (where you can hear the proverbial pin drop). Work hard, play hard atmosphere. Sixth form common room reeks of toast and Nescafe with pool table, and a poker game in progress at time of our visit.

Pastoral Care and Discipline: Well-developed tutor system, with all boys reporting to their tutor first thing each morning and afternoon. For all that, slightly impersonal feel. Links with parents increasingly fostered (parents mainly pleased). Good clear guidelines on drugs, bullying etc. Misdemeanours are 'discussed by reason'.

Pupils and Parents: Recent survey breaks down the pupils as about 35 per cent WASP, 22 per cent Jewish, 20 per cent Asian; 10 per cent Greek and Cypriot – probably one of the broadest social and ethnic mixes in any school. Over half come from North London; some East Enders, and a few from South London too (good trains). Handy for City yuppie parents, and increasingly for US/Europeans working there. Gritty, an edge of sophistication, quite a few mobile telephones busy at break, boys not afraid to voice their opinion, not afraid of life, by and large bushy tailed with a sense of curiosity and they know how the world works. Old Boys include: H H Asquith, Mike Brearley, Kingsley Amis, Julian Barnes, Denis Norden, Anthony Julius (Princess Di's lawyer).

Entrance: Entry (at 10, 11, 13 and 16), with the school's own exam set at three different standards according to age group. Interview lasts 20 minutes. 10 year old entry includes 8 choristers (all day boys) who sing at Temple Church and Chapel Royal, St James'; 72 come in at 11, at least 75 per cent from state schools; 48 places at 13 (well over 100 trying for places) from 23 prep schools. Sixth form takes in 12 or 13 boys – and typically between 5 and 8 leave, invariably for co-educational schools.

Exit: All to university or medical school, including nearly 20 per cent to Oxbridge, then high powered hard working careers.

Money Matters: Financially in the thrall of the Corporation of London, not short of lolly, but Byzantine system of organising it prevails. A number of the assisted places have been replaced by academic bursaries. Academic Corporation scholarships at all ages, some music. Several Livery Company scholarships. Choristers are bursaried pupils; some bursaries available for hard-pressed parents of fifth and sixth formers.

Remarks: Busy cosmopolitan urban London boys' school with an international outlook, slightly on the soulless side, but delivering the goods and with high morale.

CITY OF LONDON SCHOOL
FOR GIRLS

St Giles Terrace, Barbican, London
EC2Y 8BB

TEL: *020 7628 0841* FAX: *020 7638 3212*

E-MAIL: sampsons@clsg.org.uk

WEB: www.clsg.org.uk

✦ PUPILS: around 650 girls, all day
✦ Ages: 7-18 ✦ Size of sixth form: 154
✦ Non-denom ✦ Fee-paying

Head: Since 1995, Dr Yvonne Burne BA PhD FRSA (who requests us to omit her age), educated at Redland High School in Bristol, read modern languages at Queen Mary and Westfield College; taught at Harrow County School for Girls, moved to Washington – and elsewhere – with her diplomat husband, and worked in educational publishing. Daughter just left university, son just gone there. Head of St Helen's Northwood before coming here. A low profile lady, terrifically efficient. Busy fostering the American 'can do' attitude in City girls, and emphasises her interest in 'expanding opportunities' for girls. NB the Corporation of London appoints the governing body, which is a mixed blessing.

Academic Matters: Continues to get good results (GCSEs almost all A★ to B, over 73 per cent A–B grades at A level in 2000). Three classes of 26 per year, then numbers drop to far smaller groups in GCSE years; four divisions for maths and French from the age of twelve. Some staff changes in the last two years, with several youngsters, 'It's great', said a sixth former, 'you feel they're on our wave-length.' The school day has recently been extended, lessons elongated. Increased emphasis on modern languages, with French for everyone from the start, and Spanish or German as a second language; Latin GCSE optional. Russian and (ancient) Greek also offered at GCSE but only if the numbers are viable. Strong science teaching, with double award GCSE. Biggest A level take up is for history; English, biology, maths, art are other popular and successful subjects. Politics and theatre studies now appears on the A level menu. Work and progress carefully monitored at all stages, including sixth form. Very strong work ethic.

Games, Options, the Arts: Lovely art, up in the sky-lit attic, producing a huge variety of objects of good quality, achieving rows of A★ grades at GCSE and As at A level. Brilliantly equipped design technology department making rapid progress under its new young head of department, producing exciting work. Impressive music – a keen subject, as you would expect with peripatetic teachers from the neighbouring Guildhall School of Music and Drama, and the same is true for drama. Ambitious productions of their own by various ages/groups, new drama studio, and lots of interest. 'And we do more drama with the boys' school now', say girls happily, 'they ask us to be in their plays.' Surprisingly sporty, and, even more surprisingly, it's all done here in the concrete jungle, even athletics. Excellent swimming pool, large gym/indoor sports hall, next door to the compact well-equipped fitness room. Netball and tennis do well (two outdoor courts). Five-a-side teams for football. One small games pitch, the only grass for miles around.

Young Enterprise and D of E both very active, also fund-raising for the Third World and environmental issues are a hot subject. Careers advice strongly emphasised. Increasing numbers of girl-led initiatives these days – grunts of parental approval – among them setting up an Asian society, also a law society, with prominent figures lured in as guest speakers. New experiment for a group of sixth formers to do a two week swap with pupils at Chapin School, New York.

Background and Atmosphere: Concrete purpose-built '60s block in the centre of the Barbican, with a few ancient historical monuments peeking through and a skyline of towering glass and steel City blocks. Khaki coloured water (the lake) and well-planted tubs occasionally relieve the eye in this relentlessly urban environment. Bustling and purposeful atmosphere. The school was founded in 1894 on Victoria Embankment by coal merchant William Ward, with the express intention that girls receive a 'broad and liberal education with the emphasis on scholarship'. Entrance foyer with its waiting area feels more like a hospital than a school. Functional in layout and design, with five floors plus design technology and sport beyond the main block, making an L shape around the small lake. 'It lacks charm', is often the first impression of parents more used to traditional old-fashioned establishments ('awful' said one). That said, the place buzzes with enthusiasm and energy: girls are cheerfully noisy between classes, notice boards all bulge with information and are keenly read. Good libraries (one silent, one to talk/teach in), lots of computers, often found out on the broad corridors, 'So you learn to work with quite a racket going on around you', commented one pupil. All Acorns are net-worked and Internet is much used. Sixth form common room next to the lake is quite a haven, and a new development. Interesting history of the school recently published (James & James).

Pastoral Care and Discipline: Democratic ethos, with all sixth formers acting as prefects, active school council and suggestions book. Recently set up 'initiative course' for all sixth formers has proved popular. Discipline has not been a problem here. No sense of spiritual values.

Pupils and Parents: Lots of Jewish girls, and large numbers of Asians. Top choice for Islington and lots from NW areas; numbers from Essex (who commute to Liverpool Street). A really broad ethnic and social mix, children of ship brokers and shop-keepers, heavy on professions. Happy, confident and talkative girls, 'quite prepared to be outspoken', said one parent, 'and they are encouraged to take the initiative.' Butch uniform of black trousers and red sweatshirt, the skirt option is less fashionable. (Sixth formers are uniform-free.)

Entrance: Sharply competitive, with around 400 girls sitting the exam, which boils down to interviews for 200 for the final selection of 57, plus around 45 from the school's own prep. NB interview counts for a great deal, with beady staff seeking the X factor. Girls come from a huge number of state and fee-paying schools. Some new arrivals at sixth form, to take up additional places on offer and to fill vacancies (girls exit to Westminster, boarding school or sixth form college – some then change their minds and return to City).

Exit: 10-16 per year to Oxbridge, also Manchester, Durham, London, Leeds etc, with a handful to the ex-polys. One or two to art school or music and drama studies.

Money Matters: The school is part of the Corporation of the City of London (who are financially generous), and has established connections with the Livery Halls. Varying numbers of academic scholarships for girls at 11+, totalling five full-fees, and spread at the head's discretion. Also academic bursaries. NB the school had huge numbers of assisted places, but the better-off appear to be taking up the slack.

Remarks: Academic and hard-working day school that currently produces good results and unspoilt articulate girls, but remaining low profile. Sought after, but not among the chattering classes.

JUNIOR SCHOOL: City of London School for Girls' (Preparatory Department). Tel: 020 7628 0841, Fax: 020 7638 3212. Pupils: 107 girls ages:7-11. Head: Since 1997, Mrs Christine Thomas, MA, husband in senior management, two grown up children. Entry via whole day assessment, oversubscribed, put names down early. Umbilically attached to the senior school and a way in (with very rare exceptions), though pupils take same entrance exam as external candidates. Shares some of the facilities (pool, gym, DT) with senior school and has assembly with them twice a week. Particular focus on French and IT; termly music and drama events. A very busy and active little school.

CLIFTON COLLEGE
32 College Road, Bristol BS8 3JF

TEL: *0117 3157 000* FAX: *0117 3157 101*

E-MAIL: admissions@clifton-college.avon.sch.uk

WEB: ds.dial.pipex.com/clifton-college/

✦ PUPILS: 454 boys, 186 girls (393 board, 247 day) ✦ Ages: 13-18 ✦ Size of sixth form: 279 ✦ C of E and one Jewish house ✦ Fee-paying

---

Head: Since 2000, Dr Stephen Spurr DPhil (forties). Educated at King's Canterbury and Sydney Grammar School; studied classics at Sydney and Oxford. Taught classics at Sydney Grammar School and Australian National University, then to Eton where he became in due course a housemaster and head of classics. Interests include Italian literature, archaeology and hill walking. Married, two children (15 and 10). Reportedly a very different character from Mr Hugh Monro, who was head from 1990 and has now gone to Wellington.

Academic Matters: As usual, the 'hard' subjects are the most followed – maths the most popular, then economics (disappointing results), English, chemistry, biology, geography, physics. Tiny numbers taking quite a wide range of languages at A level – including Russian, Spanish, Polish, Greek, Latin, Mandarin, German. Increasing percentage of As, but no reduction in the Ds and Es; overall performance creditable, given mixed ability intake. Science schools in large Victorian block, ultra-modern computer system. Some subjects (eg history) away from the main campus. Director of studies meets every pupil at the end of their first year to discuss options. Good support for dyslexics available – Ofsted described this as a 'real strength'. Special needs teaching takes place in the new Percival Centre – named after the school's first headmaster and famous educationalist, John Percival. Previous head reduced average age of staff, and limited tenure of heads of departments. Effort grades for each subject publicly displayed in each house bi-weekly.

Games, Options, the Arts: Fine drama, and lots of it, splendid theatre – the Redgrave theatre (used by Bristol OldVic and visiting companies) – and theatre studies on offer at A level. Good art, enthusiastic textile department. Famous for its sporty poem, 'Play up and play the game', written by Old Boy Sir Henry Newbolt. Girls (whose numbers have now levelled off) do well at rowing and fencing ('everything' says school.) Sport studies offered at A level – sixteen taking it at last count, and ten apprentice footballers from Bristol City (football association league club) are studying for exams here. Keen CCF (girls very enthusiastic), strong D of E. Good activities programme, with a master in charge, whereby 'pupils must take part in some options'. Main games fields (86 acres) on the other side of Clifton Suspension Bridge; pupils are ferried back and forth – endless school buses are a familiar sight.

Background and Atmosphere: Huge mass of high Victorian Gothic buildings, all now a bit squished for space. The main campus overlooks the Close (as in the 'There's a breathless hush in the Close tonight' poem); school buildings spread over the road, next door to the zoo (20p entry for pupils provided they are in uniform) in Bristol's smartest residential area. School founded in 1862, by Bristol merchants, went fully co-ed in 1987. Dining hall now redecorated, has unusually small tables (for six or four). Regular compulsory chapel, day pupils included. 11 houses (three for girls, five-star of course).

The most famous house – though apparently not the one with the richest pupils – is Polack's, for Jews only, (previous head made enquiries and found 'Yes, there is still a need for Polack's', despite dwindling numbers, currently 40.) Own synagogue in house. The separateness of the house has been known to cause resentment. Jewish girls, on the other hand, are integrated into girls' houses.

Firm emphasis on inter-house competitions in every sphere. Some flexi-boarding (seen as important for the future). Slightly split-personality feel with day/boarding elements. No Saturday school for the Jewish students, so it's a bit of a treading-water day for the rest, ('absolutely not', says the head). Quite a cosy atmosphere prevails, despite the spread of the lay-out.

Pastoral Care and Discipline: Pastorally good. V good at looking after pupils from overseas. Pubs are the temptation – the Marshal makes regular raids round the likely ones on a Saturday night. Homework notebooks considered 'effective' particularly for the shambolic. Drugs policy clear and firm.

Pupils and Parents: Professional parents, hordes of 'businessmen'. From Wales, Hereford and Worcester, West Country; often from quite humble backgrounds. A fair number of Forces children. Pupils: pleasant, friendly, streetwise. Old boys include Sir Michael Redgrave, Simon Russell Beale, Trevor Howard, John Cleese, Earl Haig, Sir David Willcocks, Roger Cooper (quoted soon after his release from prison in Iran as saying 'prison experience is not unlike public school', which resulted in a large number of enquiries from potential parents). Fair number of foreign nationals. Auberon Waugh visited the school not so long ago and found the pupils 'polite, intelligent and seemed happy' – praise indeed. Pupils open-minded, encouraged to discuss all kinds of issues – a Good Thing.

Entrance: Not a high hurdle – 50 per cent at CE and NB there are always some high fliers. 75 per cent from own prep. At 13 and 16 (average 15 leave post GCSE). Three GCSE passes at grade B and three at C needed to enter sixth form.

Exit: 95 per cent to university, subjects widely varied, and pupils go on to some very exciting careers. 20 a year to Oxbridge.

Money Matters: Several scholarships (depending on calibre of pupils) of varying worth.

Remarks: Traditional public school that, after a difficult time, now appears to be emerging triumphant, despite being in a city over-stuffed with private schools.

JUNIOR SCHOOL: Clifton College Preparatory School (THE PRE), The Avenue, Bristol. Tel: 0117 3157 502, Fax: 0117 3157 504. 450 boys and girls, ages 3-13. Head: Since 1993, Dr R J Acheson MA (fifties), who has written with wonderful honesty on a day in his life for ISIS magazine. Not far from the main school, with plenty of space, kindergarten for 3-8-year-olds down the road. Boarding now down to a third of total prep children, many of the boarders are from overseas (Far East and expats). Not simply a feeder for Clifton; has a long tradition of being as strong if not stronger than its big brother.

CLIFTON HIGH SCHOOL
College Road, Clifton, Bristol BS8 3JD

TEL(UPPER SCHOOL): *01179 730201*

(LOWER SCHOOL): *01179 738096*

FAX: *0117 238962*

E-MAIL: admissions@chs.bristol.sch.uk

WEB: www.chs.bristol.sch.uk

✦ PUPILS: 355 senior girls, (5 family boarders, rest day). Plus Lower school with 365 boys and girls ✦ Ages: Upper school 11-18, Lower school 3-11 ✦ Size of sixth form: about 95 ✦ C of E ✦ Fee-paying

---

Head: Since 1998 Mrs Colette Culligan BA PGCE (forties). Previously deputy head at St Mary's Calne, Wiltshire, and before that was head of English. Currently completing final stage of MEd at Bristol University. Has also taught in the state sector, and, on a voluntary basis, in the USA. This appointment follows an interregnum, and a very brief period under the previous head (since '96). Head of Upper School: Dr Alison Neil PhD BSc PGCE. Head of Lower School Mr Tony Richards BsocSc PGCE.

Entrance: Exam at 11+, with many girls coming up through the excellent on-site Lower School. Also at 13+ and some at sixth form. Lower School entry by in-class assessment.

Exit: University (around five a year to Oxbridge); Birmingham, Cardiff, Exeter, Southampton are favourites, and usually some to art college.

Remarks: Traditional girls' day school, which used to have a boarding element but this has now all but disappeared (some 'family boarding' for overseas sixth form students.) In the poshest part of Clifton, much sought after by locals, though Clifton College down the road syphons off some potential pupils. Founded in 1877, main school building (once a private house, and seen on TV in The House of Eliot) has fine Georgian entrance and staircase. Still gets good solid GCSE results (some Ds and Es etc); A levels have improved substantially over the last three years, and are back to the strong profile that we were used to. Maths is no longer the most popular subject at A level – a decline against the national trend, though excellent results here. English and biology lead the popularity stakes. Head of classics publishes the successful 'Minimus' Latin course. One or two doing less mainstream subjects such as home economics, 'Chinese', music, theatre studies. Large numbers stay on for sixth form studies here, and new girls come in – this is good news.

Recent additions and improvements include attractive and functional sixth form facilities and technology department, including powerful computers for design. Good careers department, girls are encouraged to think boldly. Good library. Excellent textiles, and home economics department, also nice art. Drama and music are both strong (choirs in particular). A traditionally sporty school, though the main sports grounds are a bus ride away: major investment planned with Bristol University and the LTA as partners. Jo Durie is an old girl, also Sarah Keays, Mary Renault and Bernice McCabe (head of North London Collegiate). Pupils are articulate, streetwise and unspoilt. Many come in from the school's own very good on-site junior school. Uniform recently changed from unbecoming grey and green to heathery blue sweaters plus kilts. Despite recessions and hot competition from other schools, Clifton High went from strength to strength under the penultimate head, Mrs Walters, and from strength to weakness when she left; recent reports suggest cautious optimism re the new regime.

CRANLEIGH SCHOOL
Cranleigh, Surrey GU6 8QQ
TEL: *01483 276377* FAX: *01483 273696*

E-MAIL: jeh@cranleigh.org

WEB: www.cranleigh.org

✦ PUPILS: around 380 boys, 120 girls in sixth form (about 70 per cent board) ✦ Ages: 13–18, plus own prep school 7–13 (see separate entry) ✦ Size of sixth form: 220 ✦ C of E ✦ Fee-paying

Head: Since 1997 Mr. Guy de W Waller, MA MSc (Oxon) (fifty), educated at Hurstpierpoint and read chemistry at Worcester College and educational psychology at Wolfson College. Cricket and hockey blue. Former headmaster of Lord Wandsworth College, and before that housemaster/head of chemistry at Radley where he was master-in-charge of hockey and cricket and coached the 1st XV. Married with four daughters: one finishing at Cranleigh 2001, two more at the school, one at Cranleigh Prep. Admired by parents ('imposing but very approachable'). Hugely energetic and runs a tight ship. Teaches Oxbridge chemistry and 'critical thinking' –

a compulsory lower sixth AS subject (analysing writing, argument, reasoning in public discourse), that he is rightly proud of introducing to the school. Aware that he is running an educational institution and not ICI. A 'nutty Wagnerite', British motorcycle buff and sports fan.

Academic Matters: 'A mixed ability school.' Pupils work hard but without an overtly pressurised atmosphere. Head not interested in trying to smash into the A-level premier league: 'We don't want everyone to be a scholar – we just need a few each year.' An excellent, long-established scholars programme stretches cleverclogs with intellectual discussion sessions etc . Setting in maths and French from the start, and other subjects the following year. Parents say bringing in girls is raising academic standards and A-level results. ALIS figures show a significant added value achieved in the sixth form. Stunning art. Good theatre studies and German. Classics on a crawling come-back with even a couple learning Greek. Good but underused library. Librarian has put together excellent files of topical or subject-related articles for debates, research etc , but many students don't even know it exists. Subject departments in distinct zones to encourage academic exchange and togetherness.

Games, Options, the Arts: Sport for all, regardless of talent. Head keen on team values learned from games. Rugby and hockey compulsory for boys in their first year (rugby a big deal here – may not suit a football hotshot) with loads of teams and boys of many ability levels playing for the school. Lots more choice follows (but some boys unaware of this and go on grimly playing rugby for years). Boys complain that girls have far more sporting options. Nine-hole golf course, but some pupils unclear whether they can use it freely (they can). The school has its own stables. Two floodlit artificial pitches convert into tennis courts in the summer. Six other tennis courts, squash, Eton fives, shooting, indoor pool, fencing, and so on. No gymnasium but plans afoot to build a sorely needed sports hall, possibly through a big fund-raising campaign.

Lots of art, well-taught in the bright, cheerful art building – popular at A level with over 90 per cent A-B grades. Outstanding drama, with heaps of productions every term. The new Merriman Music School houses the excellent music department. Around half play a musical instrument, but surprisingly few take the music A level (only one last year). 'Protected time' after lunch each day mainly for creative and performing arts (practice, lessons, clubs, rehearsals). All juniors must attend an activity on Wednesday afternoon, eg, lifesaving, vehicle maintenance, ecology. CCF popular.

Background and Atmosphere: Strikingly friendly. Imposing redbrick building founded in 1865, set in over 250 acres overlooking rolling Surrey countryside. Originally built to educate the sons of local gentlemen farmers. Lots of mostly attractive additions, new and old. Head has brought together all the school's most important offices around the school's central quad: head and deputy, bursar, director of studies, computer room, book shop, library, careers. Moving the careers office to this august location is meant to signify its importance to the school (pupils speak of the endless stream of careers/university talks from age 13 on). Short services crammed into small but elegant chapel on Tuesdays and Thursdays (communion services for boarders on Sundays) and congregational practice on Fridays.

Admitting girls to the lower forms in

1999 reversed the declining numbers problem (sixth form co-ed since early '70s). The move vexed Cranleigh's sister school, St Catherine's, Bramley, leading to the dissolution of the schools' 100-year partnership (established by a royal charter under Queen Victoria). Ratio of boys to girls set to remain roughly 2:1 for now. Have restructured the houses, reducing the number from eight to six to improve standards of accommodation and ensure a family atmosphere through live-in housemasters and housemistresses. Fierce house loyalties made the change traumatic for many (staff had to undergo grief training). Boarding houses in good nick. Boys are never allowed in the girls' boarding houses, but the reverse not so. No gulf between day and boarding pupils. Day boys in mostly open plan, noisy studies (some a major hike from the main school) but day girls have quieter digs. Day pupils often do prep at home anyway. Day boys/girls may leave at 6pm to catch one of the school buses home but most stay later. Saturday school until 3.30pm, plus matches.

Pastoral Care and Discipline: Guy Waller has come down hard on previously sloppy discipline. Bullying 'non-existent', according to pupils, since a crackdown two years ago. Very anti-drugs; anyone involved immediately expelled and pupils are constantly reminded of this. Regard drugs as a problem for other schools. Gated for two weeks if caught smoking. Pupils allowed out into village in free time until 5.30pm (no hotbed of excitement – boys complain about having to keep their uniform on and Cranleigh pupils cannot enter a pub within three miles of the village during term, even with Mum and Dad). Sixth formers can get special permission to visit the bright lights of Guildford. 'The Buttery' serves limited beer and wine to sixth formers. Pupils like

the 'credits and commendations' system leading to tokens for the tuck shop. Boys say girls treated more leniently but starting to even out. Parents praise the 'wholesome' relationships between the boys and girls.

Pupils and Parents: A local school. Nearly all from within a 35-mile radius, 10 per cent overseas Brits (with local homes or connections) and 3 per cent overseas nationals, mostly Kenya, Nigeria and Germany. Pupils tend to be generalists rather than geniuses in one field ('specialists might not be so happy here', commented a girl). Families not as ostentatiously wealthy as at some public schools, and children accordingly less status-conscious. Parents not overly ambitious for their children – looking for a school that turns out well-rounded, interested, polite youngsters. Few are disappointed.

Entrance: From 2001, six-streams of 20/21 pupils at 13+ (up from five). 'Places are given to those who we think will make good use of what Cranleigh has to offer – they don't have to be stars.' Lots of research into pupils before they are accepted: head wants busy beavers who will be interested and involved. 55 per cent at CE expected. Boys and girls come from huge range of local schools, some from London. £800 deposit is required two years before joining. 16+ intake of about 45-50, but this number will fall as higher numbers feed through from below. Not looking for academic powerhouses: three Bs, three Cs at GCSE will do nicely.

Exit: Almost all to university. One in ten to Oxbridge (9–10 each year). A few move out to local sixth form colleges.

Money Matters: Academic, art and music scholarships ranging from half fees down to 15 per cent but not in vast quantities. Pupils can also earn honorary scholarships once at the school which carry virtually no money but give entrance to the scholars programme. Eric Abbott scholarship for an all-rounder with one particularly outstanding area of talent.

Remarks: Friendly local public school, for all-rounders. Makes the most out of each pupil while avoiding the pressures of the top-flight public schools. Parents ecstatic. Definitely on the way up since going fully co-education.

DEAN CLOSE SCHOOL

Cheltenham, Gloucestershire GL51 6HE

TEL: *01242 522640* FAX: *01242 258003*

E-MAIL: dcsregistrar@dean-close.demon.co.uk

WEB: www.deanclose.org.uk

✦ PUPILS: 248 boys (144 board) and 189 girls (117 board). Prep school 138 boys (51 board) and 99 girls (38 board). Pre-prep 66 boys and girls ✦ Ages 13-18, prep 7–13, pre-prep 3–7 ✦ Size of sixth form: 190 ✦ C of E (Anglican Foundation) although all denominations welcome ✦ Fee-paying

Head: Since 1998, The Rev Tim Hastie-Smith, MA BA (Cantab) (thirties), educated at Cranleigh, then Magdalene followed by theology at Wycliffe Hall, Oxford. Personable and fun. Taught briefly at Felsted between Oxford and Cambridge: St Nicholas Scholar, with three years curacy at St Ebbe's before coming to Stowe in 1991, where he was chaplain (and a very popular one too), also admissions tutor and head of theology. Married to Joanne, with two

young children, Hastie-Smith (nicknames Tastie-Hastie, Tastie Bits) built up a large theology department (philosophy and ethics as well as God).

Although evangelical himself, Hastie-Smith prefers to 'provide a seedbed not a hothouse for faith'. 'You cannot and MUST not impose'. Keen on sport, Hastie-Smith is 'horrendously computer literate' and wants to capitalise on the increasing academic success of Dean Close by 'creating an atmosphere within which education can flourish'. Hastie-Smith was appointed after the first batch of interviewees had been thrown out, and a notice was spotted in the kitchen of a current parent exhorting them to 'pray for a successful outcome in the search for our new head.' Took over from the previous head, the much-loved Christopher Bacon.

Academic Matters: Not notably selective, and the average ability of students can vary from year to year. This accounts, according to the school, for the '00 A level results – average point score dropped from 25.6 to 19.6, A grades halved in number – but not for the ghastly biology results in the same year (school reacted far too slowly to known problems). Class size 24, four or five streams for each year, all pupils must do RE at GCSE, plus three sciences as well as maths and English. 'Liberal' studies on offer in lower sixth including philosophy, science in the environment, electronics, astronomy, photography etc. Economics not particularly strong. French, German, Spanish, Latin, Russian and Chinese successes. Superb labs, combining practical areas with 'proper' lecture auditoria. Pupils are equipped with laptops on arrival at the school, with infra-red networking facility throughout, which should also connect to printers and the Internet – all without wire – this is cutting edge stuff. EFL and learning support throughout.

Games, Options, the Arts: Primarily a hockey school, champions at all levels, Decanians regularly feature in county, regional and national teams. Rugby, cricket, sailing, tennis etc all on offer. Two Astroturf pitches. 25 metre swimming pool and sports hall the only facilities we saw which were not state of the art. Water polo strong. Huge numbers of clubs. Superlatives fail to describe the brilliant new music wing, attached by overhead bridge to professional theatre, much used by locals. Outdoor Tuckwell theatre in the grounds. Music and drama very strong and timetabled. Art and design, CDT with CAD, and home economics for both sexes. CCF at 13, D of E.

Background and Atmosphere: School founded in 1886 in memory of Dean Francis Close, Dean of Carlisle, and earlier Rector of Cheltenham. 'Voluntary' Christian Union and Bible study feature in each house; Christian ethics important (and the word 'Christian' used in almost every other sentence when we visited). The whole school worships together three times a week in the slightly austere Chapel (porch with interesting modern stained glass.) Day children no longer have to attend morning service on Sundays.

School set in 80 acres of manicured grounds, shared with prep school, who also share sports, drama, and music facilities. Original Victorian buildings much altered, with fantastic library like an upturned boat with beech galleries and refurbished parquet flooring. Huge lofty dining room, with 'God's Word a Guiding Light' inscribed below the rafters. Café-style feeding, vegetarian option. Modern cloisters with unusual sculptures contrast with older classrooms, and boarding houses not all up to scratch – though many individual rooms have their own basins. Larger dorms have been subdivided into tiny cabins. Boarding encouraged, and flexi-boarding on offer. Strong family feel.

Pastoral Care and Discipline: Eight houses, three for boarding boys; two for boarding girls; with two day-boy houses, and one day-girl house; plus three boarding houses in junior school, two for boys, one for girls and two co-ed day houses. House parents (all married, plus ancillary tutors). 'Christian ethos prevails', but not aggressively so – 'really good pastoral care' reported one Muslim parent. Automatic expulsion for drugs and sex; warnings, followed by 'Jankers' (hard labour) for booze, fines for fags. Lookout for the 'Dean Close Hello Handshake.' Good PSHE and tutorial backup.

Pupils and Parents: Neither a Sloane, nor a yuppie school: Good middle-class ethos, local professional and businessmen, plus farmers etc, some ex-pats, one or two foreigners (who must attend chapel). Number of committed Christians, fair proportion of Clergy children, relatively large number of Services' children (54 at last count). 'Down to earth, not a snob school', said a parent. Children tidy rather than stylish.

Entrance: To prep school by own entrance exam (English, maths, VR). To Senior School by common entrance; special arrangements for children from state primaries. To sixth form via VR, plus six GCSEs at C or above, and 'special exam' in potential A level subjects.

Exit: 98 per cent to universities, with occasional gap year. Around 10 per cent a year to Oxbridge; one or two train for Holy Orders. Otherwise slight preponderance to engineering.

Money Matters: This is a rich school. Well founded with a great deal of inspired modern building. Scholarships throughout for everything. Church and Service bursaries – the former automatic.

Remarks: Inspiring Christian co-ed (predominantly) boarding school which is not even faintly perturbed by neighbouring Cheltenham College going co-ed.

JUNIOR SCHOOL: Dean Close Preparatory School, Lansdowne Road, Cheltenham GL51 6QS. Tel: 01242 512217, Fax: 01242 258005. Pre-prep School: The Squirrels. Head: Since 1997, Mr. S W Baird, BA (St David's, Lampeter) PGCE, (thirties). Educated at Colston's School, Bristol and Monkton House School, Cardiff. Married, with three young sons, all in the school. A committed Christian (not ordained) he wears a cross in his left lapel. One prep-school master commented that 'you had to swear over the 39 articles to get that job.' French from the age of 4, Latin at 11, classes streamed, with maths, French and Latin set. IT, science, masses of computers, Popular rink for roller blading and the like, good art, good drama.

DOLLAR ACADEMY

Dollar, Clackmannanshire FK14 7DU

TEL: *01259 742511/742986/743164*

FAX: *01259 742867*

E-MAIL: dollarac@aol.com

WEB: www.dollaracademy.org.uk

✦ PUPILS: around 550 boys, 550 girls (150 board, 950 day) ✦ Ages: 5-18
✦ Size of sixth form: 250 ✦ Fee-paying

Head (Rector): Since 1994, Mr John Robertson MA (forties). Formerly assistant head at Stewart Melville, and deputy at Dollar for several years. English specialist. Sits behind a huge desk beneath the glowering portrait of the school's first Rector, seems perfectly suited in looks, manner and intellect to the post he now occupies. Has made the prospectus unusually large so that it doesn't fit easily into the waste paper basket (so it stays on your desk).

Academic Matters: Scottish system (Standard Grade and Highers). Bias to science, and to business and technical subjects; notably good results (at Highers) in some of these subjects. About 80 per cent of leavers achieve 5+ Highers, most of the rest get 3+. Reasonable range of subjects and flexible timetable to fit pupils' options, rather than the other way round. French or German in junior school. Short courses in Japanese possible at sixth form – school has close ties with Japanese faculty at Stirling University; short courses also offered in Italian, philosophy, car mechanics and other jolly options. Classes of 18-26 in junior school and 5-22 in senior school: the width of the range is due to the efforts made to allow pupils to study whichever subjects they choose. Mixed ability classes; no setting. One full-time member of staff and three part-timers give learning support for dyslexics etc. Serious homework: 'we expect that all pupils in the Academy should have enough work to occupy their evenings, and any child who indicates otherwise misunderstands'.

Games, Options, the Arts: Very strong rugby – good beefy teams and some international caps; hockey for girls – not so impressive. Individual pupils regularly get through to county level in major and minor sports, and do well in inter-school competitions. Lots of extra-curricular games. Lots of games fields, plus large hall and indoor pool. CCF. Art popular and has very strong results at Highers (90 per cent grade A). Strong choral tradition and two orchestras. Enthusiastic pipe band (wears McNabb tartan) and CCF; drama, D of E, work experience in local hospitals etc, and in Germany (sponsored by Lufthansa – nicht nichts). Boarders participate keenly in ballroom dancing at weekends, and sport the badges earned thereby on their blazers. Good facilities, plenty of clubs.

Background and Atmosphere: Founded as a co-ed boarding school in 1818 by Andrew Mylne, the local minister, with legacy from John McNabb's shipping fortune (whether this came from piracy or slavery is unclear). McNabb's ashes are entombed in the wall above the main 'Bronze Doors': this is the only school in the land where pupils pass under the founder every day. Formerly direct grant, but in 1974 became private. A day school with a strong international boarding element.

Uncrowded but circumscribed grounds embedded in the northern edge of the prosperous town of Dollar. Elegant Playfair facade, but following fire in '60s, the main building was rebuilt entirely. A regular flow of new building since then. Boarding houses small: thirty pupils in each, homes not institutions. Geographically useful, given the school's position vis a vis the Forth Bridge. Wet weather a feature of the place, and matches often rained (or snowed) off.

Pastoral Care and Discipline: Firm discipline often involves cleaning up school. Lots and lots of niggly rules eg 'chewing gum is not acceptable…' 'you should walk on the left-hand side of corridors' etc. Early morning detention. Boarders complain of not wearing own clothes enough – school uniform has to be worn to all meals at weekends – but are free to go into Dollar whenever they want and have unescorted exeats to Stirling/Edinburgh when they are old enough. Instant exit for drugs.

Pupils and Parents: The vast majority from 30-mile radius; plus numbers of Forces' children and a large contingent from the Scottish diaspora world-wide: school has a long tradition of looking after the children of tea-planters and engineers. Some fourth-generation pupils. Rector says pupils are perhaps 'too conservative' and an English master said 'they would have difficulty discussing the concept of rebellion'. Exceptionally strong and active FP network: eg 72 members currently in Australia. Famous FP is Sir James Dewar (vacuum flask).

Entrance: 5, 10 or 11, the latter two by examination, which is very selective. Well oversubscribed for entry at V and V1 forms – 'each case is individually considered', 'good' GCSE/standard grades required.

Exit: 90+ per cent pursue degree courses, mostly in Scotland (Edinburgh, Glasgow, Aberdeen) though a few go on South or abroad. A very few ('the more independent and self-reliant') do a gap year: it's just not the done thing, despite all the Rector's efforts.

Money Matters: Four academic scholarships of 50 per cent of fees at 11, two at 15/16, plus a few new means-tested scholarships for boarding (ie tuition fees not paid). Very reasonable and excellent value. The school had 80+ assisted places – a place of this size and prosperity should stagger along without them.

Remarks: A large, solid, traditional co-ed school which while it is not setting the world alight, is very popular round about, and strategically placed to benefit from a wide catchment area.

DOWNE HOUSE

Cold Ash, Newbury, Berkshire RG16 9JJ

TEL: *01635 200286* FAX: *01635 202026*

E-MAIL: correspondence@downehouse.berks.sch.uk

WEB: www.downehouse.berks.sch.uk

✦ PUPILS: 530 girls (517 board, 13 day ✦ Ages: 11-18 ✦ Size of sixth form: 164 ✦ C of E ✦ Fee-paying

---

Head: Since 1997, Mrs Emma McKendrick BA (mid thirties). Nickname 'Kenny' (reference to South Park intended, but not for any obvious reason). Educated at Bedford High and Liverpool University where she read German and Dutch 'just to be difficult.' Previous post was head of the Royal School Bath ('94-'97), and head designate of the Royal School Bath/Bath High when the two schools amalgamated in 1998. This didn't work out, however and so here she is – and good, super, confident. Before that she was deputy head of the Royal School, Bath, and before that, head of sixth form. Shy and friendly. Comments that school is 'very much about preparing girls for the next stage and not an end.' Has argued in the education debate that single sex schools give the best answer. Husband is in banking. Took over from Miss Sue Cameron, who left the school suddenly in '96 (fell out with the governors) to go to North Foreland Lodge.

Academic Matters: Splendid and inspiring science block and good solid results at GCSE (single sciences); sciences the most popular subjects at A level; physics less so. A good collection of modern languages on offer (including Italian, Chinese and Russian at A level), with 'taster' club for all 11-year-olds of Spanish, German and Italian. Ecole Hampshire (in the Dordogne) has been acquired on a long lease: 12-year-olds go out for an entire term (in batches of 25), and LOVE it. 'Magic for the French, of course', says a mother. Projects, art, music etc , also benefit from the French experience. English literature the most popular humanities subject at A level (v good results). Class subject rooms rationalised, cutting down on endless movement hither and thither. Good IT. Technology fairly recently introduced ('We're starting gently'), proving popular. Can cope with mild dyslexia and dyspraxia – two qualified members of staff co-ordinate all forms of learning support, also one peripatetic. EFL undertaken by a member of the English department (qualified). General studies taken by all, which improves league table performance no end. Results good by any standard, however.

Games, Options, the Arts: Round-the-year tennis coaching (oodles of courts), strong on lacrosse, also very strong swimmers – splendid pool. Music everywhere (90 per cent of girls play an instrument), practice rooms in nuns' former cells; particularly good choir. Cookery and needlework for everyone; art (Includes textiles, screen printing and ceramics) good, but not very good. Enthusiastic drama, 'and', said one girl, 'quite a lot of it.' Good Young Enterprise, D of E, also CCF.

Background and Atmosphere: Whitewashed building in Hispano-Surrey style, disjointed and scattered (lots of to-and-fro, with the library well down the hill), set in 110 acres. Definitely a house-orientated school. First two years lead a cosy life apart, under strict management, but 'attached' for the purpose of drama, sports etc to one of five mixed-age houses which they move into in their third year. In the sixth form, the girls move into the newish sixth form block: four boarding houses (lower and upper mingled, large single rooms for upper, doubles for lower), huge common/telly viewing rooms and own dining room. Cafeteria system introduced ('We know our manners have gone downhill'), good food.

Chapel is too small for the whole school, but much used, with some complaints of 'too much.' Highly structured set-up, but subtly so, with uninstitutional buildings and atmosphere (which comes as a disappointment to potential parents who imagine it might be a really traditional girls' public school). Weekend programme with considerably increased options (Saturdays and Sundays), 'but some girls still choose to mooch around', and Oxford and Windsor are within easy reach. Strong work ethic, pleasantly non-institutional atmosphere.

Pastoral Care and Discipline: Smoking a persistent irritant 'no matter how disagreeable the evidence against it', sighs the head. Surrounding woods thick with head-high nettles appear to keep the boys at bay. Girls very much on trust. Ages mix freely, plenty of staff to turn to. Occasional drugs incident. Pupils report peer group pressure to be thin.

Pupils and Parents: Upper-class parents with cohesive backgrounds and values, some (25-ish) Forces' children. Geographically fairly widespread (Scotland, Cornwall and of course London and Thames Valley). Delightful and open girls, a good advertisement for their school, who comment on themselves, 'We're very untrendy – lessons finish at 6.30, and no one bothers to change into mufti afterwards' – though there's a strong weekend/holiday social life and an IT girl would be at ease here too. Old Girls include Baroness Ewart-Biggs, Dame Rosemary Murray, Geraldine James.

Entrance: By exam at 11+ (the bulk), 12+, quite a lot at 13+ and some at sixth form. Competitive, but not fearsomely so. Minimum of seven GCSEs at A or B grade for entry at sixth form, plus entrance exam and interview.

Exit: Some leave post-GCSE, and some come in. Almost all to university (Durham, Edinburgh and other green wellie choices), ten or so to Oxbridge (extra coaching for Oxford and Cambridge), increasing numbers take a gap year.

Money Matters: Major and minor scholarships at 11+, 12+. 13+ and also at sixth form; two open music scholarships, and two for art.

Remarks: Has enjoyed a long innings as the most popular and fashionable girls' boarding school in the country. The previous head's abrupt departure plus small exodus of staff rocked the boat (effects still visible in pupil numbers.) The new regime is succeeding in re-establishing confidence – a pretty good school, all in all.

DOWNSIDE SCHOOL

Stratton-on-the-Fosse, Bath BA3 4RJ

TEL: *01761 235100* FAX: *01761 235105*

E-MAIL: downside@rmplc.co.uk

✦ PUPILS: 291 boys, all board except for 9. Plus own Junior House, with 43 boys
  ✦ Ages: 9 –18, junior house 9-13
  ✦ Size of sixth form: approx 115
  ✦ RC and Christian ✦ Fee-paying

Head: Since 1995, Dom Antony Sutch MA (forties) aka the Monk of Mayfair, the Monk of Manhattan, also Tone. 'My motto as it were for the school is that we have been given life in abundance and should live it accordingly.' Totally in agreement with his predecessor that 'The time scale for a Downside boy should be eternity and not the passing moments.' Educated at Downside, read history at Exeter. Became a chartered accountant before becoming a monk, then went to Oxford and took a degree in theology. Taught theology and history at Downside, was a housemaster. Described by a spokesman for Virgin Records as having 'the charisma of a pop star.' Sometimes writes the Credo article in *The Times*. Appears thrilled with worldly matters, and hence good choice as head, though possibly rather wasted on monkdom. Lives with his four predecessor headmasters.

Academic Matters: Low-ish A level average and low-ish overall marks – lower, perhaps, than they should be, even given the school's very broad ability range. Modern languages have a good following and do well (Russian, Chinese, Arabic, Spanish, German, Italian, Portuguese, French – and tutors for other languages can be brought in). Sciences distinctly well taught (separately or combined at GCSE). Around 15 teaching monks, the rest lay, including a handful of women. Business studies A level introduced. School has 'someone to ensure that those who have dyslexia are not suffering in any way.' Lots of trips, eg geographers to French Alps, language exchanges all over the place, historians to Rome with insider access to Vatican museums etc .

Games, Options, the Arts: Keen sport, especially rugby (Jonathan Callard alas no longer with them, but instead a foundation with the London Irish RFC for the funding of players and coaching from current internationals), also soccer, hockey, cricket, golf, orienteering, fencing. Indoor pool, space-age sports hall. Flourishing CCF; Ten Tors walk, summer camp in Cyprus. Annual pilgrimage to Lourdes, where boys remain on helper duty throughout the night. Recently signed up with Virgin Records, jumping on the Gregorian Chant bandwagon – a triumph of marketing (and the monks at least make a marvellous noise). Slaughterhouse Seven jazz band constantly on tour, raising money for charity, often abroad. Half the boys learn an instrument and all try one out free for the first term.

Background and Atmosphere: Nicknamed 'Downslide', part of the Benedictine Monastery (which still owns the 300-acre farm). Transferred to rural Somerset from Flanders (via Shropshire) in 1814. True to Benedictine tradition as a seat of learning,

Downside Review, a slim theological quarterly, is internationally known. School buildings are a monument to Mammon. Huge hexagonal monastery library with 500,000 books – 'We have some that aren't in the British Museum' – is used by scholars from all over the world. The Abbey Tower dominates the lush landscape for miles around. Neo-Gothic architecture by Giles Gilbert Scott, plus many additions. Vast roof encompasses virtually all the Downside buildings. Six boarding houses amalgamated to four during the recession (falling numbers at the time), giving GCSE and A level boys individual study bedrooms – much welcomed. House kitchens and leisure areas now in place. 'Boys mix easily and there is a spirit of camaraderie', approves a parent who chose Downside 'campus' over the more scattered Ampleforth. Requirements of the Children Act has split larger dormitories into cubicles. Monastic and scholastic bells divide the day, and even during a cricket match play stops for prayer when Great Bede is rung. Boys 'on own request' are back in old pre- (first!) war uniform of black jackets and pinstripes – murmurings of 'media hostility to the men in grey suits.'

Tolerance a keynote.

Pastoral Care and Discipline: Discipline, say parents, has been 'the eternal problem here', and boys 'tend to go OTT.' Three lay masters act as deputies: one in charge of pastoral side (this includes discipline of both boys and staff), one in charge of studies, one in charge of the tutorial system. Rustication for drinking, expulsion if, on suspicion of drug-taking, a urine test is refused. Otherwise 'early parade' for misdemeanours – 'more of a pain for the adults supervising than for the children.' The head says he targeted foul language when he first arrived,

and has now moved on to scruffiness.

'Wonderful humanitarian approach' to foreign boys, eg Italians and Spanish, in helping them cope and settle, though some reported to have bolted initially – one recaptured at Heathrow (though NB head says he cannot remember this).

Pupils and Parents: More sons of old boys than most other public schools (30-35 per cent), often three or four generations. 20 per cent boys from overseas – widespread, and a fair number of Forces' children. Lots of Spanish with English (sherry) links, Maltese, Italian and links with Russia, Poland and sister Benedictine schools in Hungary. Handful from Hong Kong; also South and North America. Most of Catholic Western Europe represented – St Benedict is the patron saint of Europe. Old Boys (Gregorians) include Timothy Radcliffe (the first English world head of the Dominican order), the archbishops of Birmingham and Southwark, Lord Hunt of Tamworth, John Pope-Hennessy, Michael Noakes, David Mlinaric, Rocco Forte, Rupert Allason, sportsmen Simon Halliday and Richard Cohen. Also Auberon Waugh.

Entrance: No problem. At 9 to Junior House (Plunkett) , or at 13 to main school at CE. Family links can clinch a place: 'We do admit boys who haven't done so well if we know who they are.' There is a huge range of ability within the school.

Exit: Around 94 per cent to universities; eight to Oxbridge. Otherwise arts foundation, Cirencester Agricultural College, business courses, study abroad.

Money Matters: The school had a particularly difficult time in the early '90s, what with the recession and the trend for Roman Catholics to send children to non-Catholic schools. A number of major scholarships plus a number of minor ones. Maths scholarship, art scholarship, several music scholarships from half fees to instrumental cover; Choral scholarships for Junior House. Some sixth form scholarships. 'Kind' to those in financial difficulties.

Remarks: Traditional monastic boys' boarding school, enjoying life under its startling head. Now holding its own.

DR CHALLONER'S GRAMMAR SCHOOL

Chesham Road, Amersham, Buckinghamshire HP6 5HA

TEL: *01494 787 500* FAX: *01494 721 862*

E-MAIL: DCGS@educl.ftech.co.uk

♦ PUPILS: 1,200 boys; all day ♦ Ages: 11-18
♦ Size of sixth form: 382 ♦ Non-denom
♦ State – voluntary controlled

Head: Since 1993, Mr Graham Hill MA (Cantab) (fifties), educated at Bacup, Rawtenstall Grammar School, Lancashire, and Trinity College, Cambridge, where he read natural sciences, followed by PGCE and Advance DipEd. Previously deputy head, having started as assistant science teacher at Marlborough and head of science at Bristol Grammar. Came to school in '78, and is the author of several successful textbooks. Chairman of the Association for Science Education for two years (1987-1989), after a year as Fellow at York University – during which time he had secondment from the school. A no-nonsense, caring head, with clear-cut ideals and great

vision. Looks to produce boys of serious academic standing, who are involved in their community and have enjoyed the range of extra-curricular opportunities and activities of the school.

Academic Matters: Excellent GCSE results; and the school is normally to be found nestling near the top of the state schools in the GCSE league table (NB selective intake). Language laboratories v well used. Computer-linked satellite weather station in geography department. Computers throughout (two dedicated IT rooms). Fair number of pupils studying technology and electronics. CDT and IT linked to business studies, BP Link school, bursary for advice on how to build an assault course for D of E and expeditions etc . Maximum class size 30 in lower forms, down to 28 in GCSE years, 18 in sixth form. No streaming for first two years, then 'banded' rather than set: top two bands take maths a year early. Remedial help on hand.

Games, Options, the Arts: Sport amazingly successful. County and inter-counties champions at football in '96 and '97; also strong at basketball, athletics, gymnastics, cricket (African tour '98), cross-country, athletics and swimming. Have been national champions in cycling and table tennis. Desperately cramped site, small sports hall, but superb achievements: have been Buckingham County Champions in four different sports at junior level, and five different sports at senior level. Music brilliant, boys sing in Central Hall Westminster and Albert Hall. Plus two orchestras, three choirs, barber's shop group, jazz, Dixieland band, swing band, 'tremendous amount of music going on', often in conjunction with sister school, Dr Challoner's High (qv). They also combine for drama. Debating and public speaking very strong. Art rooms always open, strong ceramics and trad pottery, and photography popular. Strong exchange and work experience links with schools in France, Germany and – wait for it – Ethiopia (the first British school to link with Ethiopia – sponsored by Glaxo Wellcome). Regular expeditions to North Africa (Egypt, Morocco, Ethiopia). Work experience arranged pre-sixth form: linguists do it abroad.

Background and Atmosphere: Founded in 1624, moved to present site in 1903, co-ed till 1962. Cramped (head would rather we say 'compact') site encompasses main trad Edwardian old school building, overshadowed by '50s tower block, and enhanced by charming cloistered brick-built library and classroom extension, which also contains sixth-form common room. Well stocked senior and junior libraries New court with drama studio, departmental offices and suites for history and geography. Extended suite for music and more classrooms around a second court being built. Boys wear uniform below sixth form; thereafter dress is 'relaxed but smart and conventional': the overall impression of the pupils is neat and tidy. 'Fair number' of female staff. 12 head boys, 50 prefects, all share responsibilities. 300 metres from Metropolitan line tube station.

Pastoral Care and Discipline: There is a clear chain of command via the form tutors (division tutors in sixth form); heads of year, deputy heads have regular weekly meeting with head. All very available to parents: if head not around, deputy head, matron (SRN) or one of four trained counsellors can all be contacted IMMEDIATELY. Strong anti-bullying policy, including bully box where boys can leave notes, not necessarily signed, without feeling they are telling tales. Serious wickedness equals either temporary or fixed-term exclusion, or expulsion (ie for supplying drugs or other major misdemeanours) but boys 'usually' get a second chance. Headmaster reckons he is firm, but fair.

Pupils and Parents: 'Very much commuter country', droves of middle-class parents with perhaps 7 per cent ethnic, mainly Asian. Hard-working, conscientious and very supportive. Parents join The Friends of Dr Challoner's Grammar School, with heavy fund-raising events plus links with the school – wine tasting as well as careers advice is provided.

Entrance: At 11; 40–50 feeder schools, including fee-paying eg The Beacon, Gayhurst, Chesham Prep as well as local middle schools. By county-administered VR test, preference given to siblings and good head teachers' reports, but school has 'no say whatsoever.' Head believes that boys who arrive might be one-quarter of those who put Dr Challoner's first on their list, but no accurate info given to school. Entry to sixth form is no longer by interview: 12 GCSE points needed, including B+ grades in subjects to be studied at A level, plus a satisfactory headteacher's report. 30–40 annually; 70–80 usually apply.

Exit: Small number leave post-GCSE, either relocation, or to take up employment (two or three annually) or go to art foundation courses or co-ed grammar schools. Otherwise 95 per cent to universities (40 per cent to ex-polys), including regular 15–25 to Oxbridge.

Money Matters: State. Funds available for financially hard-up for extra-curricular activities (the latter on a growing curve); two travelling scholarships in sixth form.

Remarks: Very strong all-round selective state school – and as such, a rare beast. In

1995, the school was named as one of 30 outstandingly successful schools by Her Majesty's Chief Inspector.

DR CHALLONER'S HIGH
SCHOOL

Cokes Lane, Little Chalfont, Buckinghamshire HP7 9QB

TEL: *01494 763296* FAX: *01494 766023*

E-MAIL: staffl@dchs.bucks.sch.uk

WEB: www.rmplc.co.uk/eduWeb/sites/drchalls

✦ PUPILS: 886 girls (rising to 1030); all day ✦ Ages: 11-18 ✦ Size of sixth form: 286 ✦ Non-denom ✦ State

---

Head: Since 1993, Mrs Sue Lawson BA (forties), educated at Queen Mary's College, London, followed by Northern Counties teacher's training. Pretty and gassy (not a description she cares for), married to civil engineer, one daughter. Came to teaching via Coal Board and personnel. Previously taught peripatetically (thanks to husband's job), and came to Dr Challoner's from George Abbot's School in Guildford.

Academic Matters: Max class size 30; unstreamed except in maths, a strong department. Early language diversification with French, Spanish, or German and Latin on offer at 11, 12 or 13; girls can choose two languages for GCSE. Dual or single sciences available, large take up in all three sciences at A level. Computers throughout, and maths dept uses palm-top Hewlett Packard computers (with Derive software); keyboarding teaching in lower school. Super library, still 'about to be enlarged.' Two support lessons for those experiencing learning difficulties

Games, Options, the Arts: Superb arts and technology faculty. Good art, which festoons the building – large numbers taking it at GCSE, and goodo number at A; results in both excellent. Masses of drama, mostly via English department, and lots of competitions. Music strong, lots of peripatetic teachers, string, wind, brass ensembles, hugely adaptable. Choirs and good links with Dr Challoner's Grammar School (qv) for orchestras, societies, drama etc. Arts week in the summer term, with master classes, and artists and dancer in residence.

Sport popular, national and county level athletics, hockey and swimming (but no pool), and county level netball. Strong on extra-curricular sports clubs, and ballroom dancing option with the boys. Work experience, D of E, and masses of clubs for everything, good charity involvement.

Background and Atmosphere: Founded in 1624 by Dr Robert Challoner, becoming co-ed in 1906, the girls hived off to Little Chalfont in 1962, concentrating, in the words of the then headmistress, 'not on looking backwards, but upon a forward vision'. Splendid suburban site, with mature trees and acres of playing fields, the school is a combination of ghastly flat-roofed '60s and marvellous curving brick-built recent extensions, encompassing an outdoor amphitheatre. Library being upgraded. Very close to Metropolitan tube line station. Lots of foreign visits.

Pastoral Care and Discipline: Girls have the same form tutor from the time they arrive until sixth form level. Girl-orientated

School Council, and parents involved in pastoral curriculum – 'an awareness-raising programme.' Personal social and health education in place, little bullying, will 'probably' exclude for involvement with drugs, mutual support with all schools in area ie you exclude, they take in and vice versa. Helpful daily assembly.

Pupils and Parents: From all over Buckinghamshire and down Metropolitan line, predominantly middle class, with fair share of ethnic-minority backgrounds. Parents very supportive financially, underwrote original computer lab. Parents can visit the school at any time, with head's 'clinic' once a month for queries.

Entrance: Selective. 150 pupils each year at 12+; administered by LEA. School has no say in intake (it's done by Buckinghamshire selection procedure), though preference given to siblings and girls within the catchment (grammar schools in Bucks take approx. top 30 per cent of ability range). Sixth form entrants apply direct to school, need minimum five GCSEs at C or above, and a minimum of B in the subjects they want to do at A level.

Exit: Dribble leave after GCSE, usually to do different A levels elsewhere, otherwise 95 per cent to university. 8-12 annually to Oxbridge.

Money Matters: State funded. Parents' Association involved in fund-raising events.

Remarks: Strong and worthy academic traditional girls' state grammar school with dynamic head. Perceived as an excellent solution for impoverished middle class.

DULWICH COLLEGE
London SE21 7LD
TEL: *020 8299 9263* FAX: *020 8299 9263*

E-MAIL: *the.registrar@dulwich.org.uk*

WEB: *www.dulwich.org.uk*

✦ PUPILS: 1,437 boys. Boarders: around 80
✦ Ages: 7-18. (Divided into Junior School: 7-11; Lower School 11-13, Middle School: 13-16; Upper School: 16-18) Plus 'DUCKS' 3 months to 7 years ✦ Size of sixth form: 393 ✦ C of E ✦ Fee-paying

Head: Since January, 1997, Mr Graham Able MA (early fifties), educated at Worksop College, read chemistry at Trinity College, Cambridge. Previous post was head of Hampton School (qv). His wife is a force in the school. Two children. Direct, highly competent (able by name, able by nature), widely admired. Keen hockey player, puts a big emphasis on tolerance, and dismissive of league table 'games.' Took over following an interregnum of the Deputy Master, Mr Christopher Field, following the enforced resignation of the much-liked Mr Anthony Verity (later cleared of the sexual harassment of his secretary, and now inter alia an editor of this guide). Senior management team has terrific muscle. Governing body split off from Alleyn's recently and there are several new appointments; chairman = Robin Butler, star = Eddie George – a strong team.

Academic Matters: Strong work ethic. Distinguished academically, and, considering the school has a much wider ability range than Westminster or St Paul's, good results, though still too many Ds and Es in some subjects. Increasing number of mixed arts/sciences courses (three separate sciences or dual award at GCSE), Around one hundred and thirty five staff, very low turn over, extraordinarily committed and full of value added. Excellent careers provision – department even drums up paid jobs for pupils. National Curriculum broadly followed. There is a learning support team of three, which helps boys with dyslexia and dyspraxia. Mr Able likes to put it this way: that they help 'intelligent people who have dyslexia problems.'

Games, Options, the Arts: Famously brilliant first XV rugby side in '98 – broke every record and generated several England caps. Enormous gym, used for international basketball matches (basketball v popular), and used daily for martial arts, weightlifting, fencing etc . Huge numbers of playing fields and floodlit Astroturf (and one not floodlit). Friends of Dulwich College can use the school's sports facilities, including swimming pool and magnificent fitness centre (deep envy). Strong army, navy, air force with three over-subscribed troops of scouts, plus a venture scout unit. Many clubs, computing, biology, archery. Stunning music, all children learn a stringed instrument at eight ('sometimes it sticks'). Choir tours internationally. Drama everywhere: 'Difficult to drag Dulwich boys off the stage.' Purpose-built theatre, over 30 plays produced annually – girls come from JAGS. Field centre in Wales also used for sixth form studies.

Background and Atmosphere: Founded by Elizabethan actor-manager Edward Alleyn (1619). (School has first folio edition Alleyn's Shakespeare and diaries of Globe and Rose theatres.) 1870s stately pile not totally at odds with late 20th-century buildings. Spectacular frontage, handsome grounds with trees, parks, woods, the sheer size automatically confers a sense of considerable privilege amidst the redbrick of South London. Inside, corridors are wide and spacious and no noise or suggestion of overcrowding. Exceptional facilities, four libraries in all (one for staff only), the Wodehouse library has replica of his study. Huge dining hall with vegetarian option. Staff eat there too. Lower and junior school are self contained and set apart but still on the generously large green campus. From the age of 8 boys start using specialist facilities at the main school (eg labs, art, design and technology rooms). Day houses for competitions etc, each with its housemaster – a 'nice little safety net. Many boarders from overseas; three jolly boarding houses, all things considered, with locks on doors so pupils feel private with understanding housemasters who 'treat them specially.' Junior house – the Orchard – is over the road. 30 per cent weekly boarding. Senior boarding houses now 'en suite' (I ask you …)

Ritziest school 'magazine' in the business – hard-backed, dust-covered, landscape coffee-table extravaganza.

Flourishing offshoot in Phuket, Thailand – Dulwich International College – with 450 pupils. Staff and pupil exchanges.

Pastoral Care and Discipline: A formal contract on code of conduct to be signed on admission by parents, pupil and school has been in place for several years (and is now being widely copied). Form tutors throughout. Drugs an 'occasional problem' and instant dismissal. But for day boys 'they usually know where to draw the line; there is little overlap between parties and school.' 'Possible' sackings for theft, one or two a year on average, otherwise detention AND it's on Saturday mornings (there is no Saturday morning school). Visiting Imam,

Rabbi and Hindu priest twice a term. Occasional complaints from boys that staff 'don't even know our names.'

Pupils and Parents: Very wide but not conspicuous social and ethnic mix, including Hong Kong Chinese and other Asians, not to mention new trickles from Eastern Europe. Lots of Bank/City children. Boys are fairly street-wise as you would expect but very 'anti-attitude.' Buses with Alleyn's and JAGS from all points out, including Wimbledon. Many locals (richest and poorest eg, looking back a bit, postman's son Eddie George) – the majority (just) come from state schools. Pupils can and do drive to school. Over 25 mother tongues in the school. OBs P G Wodehouse, Trevor Bailey, Peter Lilley, Roger Knight, Sir John Willis. Also Shackleton, whose Antarctic expedition boat is on display in the entrance hall on a large pile of stones.

Entrance: At seven, 10, 11, 13 and sixth form. By exam and interview. Own entrance exam – though NB not when you'd expect it (January for 7+, 10+ and 11+;, February for 13+, 60 places, also 20 more places via common entrance): get details from the registrar, it's complicated and not like other public schools. Foreign children can sometimes be admitted throughout the term if that is when their parents hit this country. Automatic entry via Lower School. Popular 'feeds' – Dulwich Hamlet Junior, Honeywell, All Saints C of E Blackheath, Thomases, Rokeby, Dulwich Prep, Hill House. NB prep school entrants must come in at 13, ie no poaching.

Exit: More than 90 per cent to universities. Wide spread, including northern. A good number to Oxbridge, reading traditional subjects, English, history, engineering, the classics, sciences, languages. Imperial College London popular. Several to US – MIT, Harvard, Princeton.

Money Matters: A very wealthy foundation. Substantial numbers of academic scholarships (including ones for East Europeans), also for music and art. Bursaries. Sixth form scholarships and bursaries. The school had a staggering 290+ assisted place but the head says their demise has not affected Dulwich at all. On-going Bursary appeal (set up in the recession to help hard hit), with £1.6 million for bursaries for non-scholars.

Remarks: Boys' public school in London – rich, with broad based education, not a hothouse. Wonderful site which generates benign feelings. Well run, good at keeping parents informed, enviably rich social mix; general atmosphere of a proper country public school.

JUNIOR SCHOOL: DUCKS: Dulwich College Kindergarten and Infants School, 87 College Road, London SE21 7HH. Tel 020 8693 1538. Serves as a creche for teachers' children, from 8am to 4.30 pm. No right of entry to the main school.

THE EDINBURGH ACADEMY

42 Henderson Row, Edinburgh EH3 5BL

Tel: *0131 556 4603* Fax: *0131 556 9353*

E-mail: *rector@edinburghacademy.org.uk*

Web: *www.edinburghac.demon.co.uk*

✦ Pupils: 410 boys, 40 girls (all in sixth form), all day except for 20 boarders. Plus own prep school 340 boys; and nursery, 55 boys and 10 girls ✦ Ages: 11-18, prep 5-11, nursery 3-5 ✦ Size of sixth form: 160 ✦ Non-denom, ✦ Fee-paying

---

Head (Rector): Since 1995, Mr John Light MA (early fifties), who refers to himself as 'Lighty.' An inspired appointment ('decent', 'old-fashioned' comment parents). Educated at Sedbergh; and Clare College, Cambridge, where he read modern languages. This was followed by a diploma in business administration. After a period in industry, he came to the Academy (as it is known to aficionados) via Glenalmond, Uppingham, Haileybury and finally Sedbergh, where he was a housemaster. Married with four children: two at university and two working. Wife wonderful – ran in the London Marathon, among other things. Keen on sport and singing but has been relegated to the sidelines in both disciplines. An iron fist in a velvet glove, though boys approach his room with problems throughout the day. Lighty has strong policies, believes in producing individuals who are 'competitive, and realise that while their best is as good as anybody's, their second best will get them nowhere'; keen on

grades, 'but they are not an end in themselves.' 'Qualifications will get you a job, but personality will get you customers.' A lateral thinker, with a keen sense of humour, he and Campbell Paterson, head of the prep school (Arboretum) are chums outwith the confines of Academe. Both heads arrived at the Academy after a period of turmoil, when heads and deputies were replaced in the same term. There is a trenchant new board of governors.

Academic Matters: Not really selective, but is nevertheless patronised by bright children, and does well by them. The Academy still offers GCSEs, and Highers, followed by A levels, but is increasingly becoming more unusual in this approach, as progressively Scottish schools – often because of financial pressure – only offer Highers. Pupils take GCSE at 15, followed by Highers a year later, and A levels the year after; many of the courses follow on automatically, but occasionally pupils find themselves taking Highers at the start of the summer term and straightway diving into a completely different A level syllabus. Mix'n'match Boards. Expect a broad academic range of pupils in mixed-ability classes, with the exception of maths, which is set from 10 (ie in the junior school), max size of class 24, some streaming, but basically three parallel classes throughout. French, German and now by popular request Spanish. As ever, very strong science, with streams of As/Bs in both A levels and Highers – though results are strong across the board. Expect 8 GCSEs, 5 Highers, plus As. Rector comments that 'you are only as good as the next year's results.' Staff-room profile young and challenging. Good learning support throughout, with the legendary Maeve Moubray,: both one-to-one and team teaching in class. The tradition of 'dux', the brightest boy or girl in the school (Magnus Magnusson was dux in his day), has now been enlarged to include a clever group of dux-worthy pupils – the Dux Club.

Games, Options, the Arts: A seriously gamesy school – famous on the rugby field – though unusually, no FPs in the current international squad; most matches still on Saturday mornings, involving large numbers of pupils – and their parents. Main games field half a mile away. Huge new sports hall opened in '98 at Arboretum: this is a community project, so comes complete with cafÈ as well as specialist weights and gym. CCF with pipe band, keen D of E. Art still excellent (has been outstanding in the past) headed by Jonathan Ellis, son of an earlier Rector, and utterly brilliant ceramics under Ken Needle. Pupils notch up A grades galore at A level and GCSE; life class in evenings after school – a popular option. DT going well. Strong music, especially on the choral side (new CD released); also a string group, pipe band and orchestras. ('But we don't use the choir for PR'). Academy Action recently launched – involving 'Accies' in the local community, even the Rector joins the charity raising sleep-out. Also forging links outside with the great and the good of Edinburgh, 'making use of the place – it's no good just sitting on our

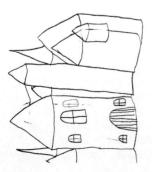

backsides', to quote a member of staff. Place used for regular Brains Trusts as well as school activities.

Background and Atmosphere: The School was founded in 1824, in trad Edinburgh classically inspired granite, Greek motto on the main portico reads 'Education is the mother of both wisdom and virtue.' Some obviously designer-inspired additions, including a fabulous oval assembly hall, plus a mass of add-ons, as well as classrooms and labs around huge tarmac yard. Smart new music department. Look for generous Edinburgher sponsored libraries etc ; successful FPs remember their font of learning with pride. Boarders live some 15 minutes' walk from the main school, near the Botanical Gardens and Inverleith Park (the green lung of Edinburgh North) and all meals are taken in the superb parquet floored dining hall at Arboretum opposite. Boarding numbers yet further down. Weekly boarding and flexi-boarding (ie bed and breakfast on a temporary basis) on offer, the latter hugely popular. School owns a field centre in Angus. Girls still in the minority, but apparently do not feel overwhelmed. Unpretentious, quietly civilised atmosphere. Boys wear tweedy jackets in winter, blazers in summer; sixth form girls look neat in navy blue blazers.

Pastoral Care and Discipline: Pupils divided into four houses. Head of year, plus form takers: good PSHE in place. Head Ephor (Prefect) is a key link with headmaster and school. Rector 'not complacent that drugs are confined to an area South of Princes Street', and maintains 'it would be foolish to believe there are no problems', and reckons that it is 'everyone's problem.' He takes tough action on offenders who must sign an agreement that they can be tested at any time. 'Not out to make victims', and keen on parent/school partnership. One of the more honest appraisals we have come across. City temptations are close, and boarding school parents have commented that this, coupled with insufficient activities for boarders at weekends, is a problem. One or two teeny reports of bullying, but not enough to be alarming.

Pupils and Parents: All sorts, with large numbers of professionals from Edinburgh and the Lothians. Not many from abroad. Rector and head keen on playing down traditional middle class image of the school – hence extended nursery hours. On the whole, pupils are pleasantly self-confident and polite; occasional lout. Sir Walter Scott was one of the school's founders and FPs include authors, Robert Louis Stevenson and R M Ballantyne.

Entrance: Special test from Arboretum, few fail (and usually the headmaster has already had 'a quiet word' with the parents about their son's future), also entry via English and maths assessment at 11+, 12+, 13+. Some boys and girls join at sixth form, more come than leave after GCSE, often from the state sector; 'a breath of fresh air' says the Rector.

Exit: 'Around 90 per cent' to various universities, with a strong preponderance to the Scottish ones. Steady trickle to Oxbridge. As ever, sciences, engineering and art feature strongly. Competent careers department.

Money Matters: Despite its protestations, the Academy is well-funded and does not expect to suffer unduly from the removal of assisted places ('not as exposed as most' – 79 at last count, however): will offer financial support in extremis, as long as parents are 'upfront' about the problem. Otherwise, tranches of scholarships for musicians and academics.

Remarks: A traditional and distinguished academic day school, which had a rough ride five years ago but is now well back on track.

JUNIOR SCHOOL: The Preparatory School, 10 Arboretum Road, Edinburgh EH3 5PL (Commonly known as Arboretum). Tel: 0131 552 3690, Fax: 0131 551 2660. Head: Since 1995, Mr C R F Paterson MA Cert Ed (forties), educated at Aberdeen Grammar, followed by Aberdeen University, and previously taught at the Nippers (Loretto Junior School) and head of Bow School in Durham. Married, with one son at the Academy and a daughter at St George's (familial discount for third children only). A historian, the head substitute-teaches and coaches games. Junior school incorporates busy and popular nursery, with tinies from 8.00 am, and after school club till 6.00 pm (on a profit sharing basis with Excel). Classes 20-24. Holiday care currently under consideration. Girls into nursery; boys only from 5. Forbidding concrete exterior, with massive modern extensions: the Denham Green (pre-prep) and Art Department gratifyingly exciting. Computers everywhere: the place buzzes with energy and enthusiasm. Brilliant art throughout; ambitious music and plays, lots of games. Junior school in general very good.

EPSOM COLLEGE

College Road, Surrey KT17 4JQ

TEL: *01372 821000* FAX: *01372 821005*

E-MAIL: registrar@epsomcollege.org.uk

WEB: www.epsomcollege.sch.uk

✦ PUPILS: 660, two thirds boys; 330 board – of whom half weekly ✦ Ages: 13-18 ✦ Size of sixth form 300+ including 100 girls ✦ C of E ✦ Fee-paying

Head: Since 2000, Mr Stephen R Borthwick (forties), previously head of Aldenham. Educated at a Surrey grammar school, then physics at the University of Wales. Previously head of physics at Marlborough, and then deputy head at Bishop's Stortford. Enjoys golf, walking, portrait photography and music. Took over from Mr Anthony H Beadles, who was head here from 1993.

Entrance: Via CE at 13, also at sixth form (30 girls – own sixth form house), 20 boys; entry requirements 'vary according to the individual'). All existing pupils expected to go on to sixth form. The Royal Medical Foundation helps 'medical practitioners and their dependants in distressed circumstances and has generous scholarships and bursaries'.

Exit: University for most, some to Oxbridge; twenty or so go on to study medicine. Art college for some.

Remarks: Founded for the sons of doctors in 1855, and claims to produce more doctors than any other school, though now largely a local school (around 100 from abroad, including Malaysians and Hong Kong Chinese). 'In the good old days medical families automatically sent sons here.' (17 per cent children of medics currently, however). Set in 80+ acres, a green oasis in a sea of suburbia, redbrick Gothic gives a homogeneous feel, even including the 1993 staff flats addition.

Strong overall performance at GCSE; very few grade Ds; consistently good A/A* performance from French, geography, maths and the (separate) sciences. A level results consistent and good, with D–Ns reflecting the intake. Maths, the sciences, economics, geography, English and history the most popular subjects. Strong learning support department for dyslexics with high IQs; small EAL (English as an Additional Language) team (one full-time, two part-time members of staff). Nice (unique?) little biology/natural history museum on site – all manner of pickled objects.

Art is exceptional: here is one of the country's outstanding art departments, under Mr G Poupart; good enough to be your reason for choosing the school. Several pupils doing three sciences take art as their fourth A level. Both Graham Sutherland and John Piper are old boys (also large numbers of medical bigwigs). Super organist. Finely equipped in all departments (far better than some more famous schools), contradicting College claims not to be well off. State-of-the-art library in the quadrangle converted from old gym, and new teaching block in 1999. Strong sports, with two sports halls, any number of squash courts, huge fencing salle, Astroturf, hockey /cricket/soccer grounds galore. Regular sports tours abroad. Revamped IT, fitted above the now outmoded swimming pool. Design technology department with shining equipment. Excellent army assault course (the army make use of it).

Sixth form girls' house (originally built

for medical pensioners) cosy and comfy.

Boys' accommodation, which was sparse, has been 'enormously improved'. Pub-like sixth form common room (leather banquettes, fruit machine). Pupils are polite, neat, friendly, middle class, and kept very busy. A few reports of bullying continue to reach us, despite head's anti-bullying policy (but bullying is not eradicated in a day); head comments that 'all who visit get the response from the boys and girls that bullying is not acceptable at Epsom College or in any way a concern'. Saturday night 'peaceful' say staff, 'dull' say some boarders, with loss of day and weekly boarding pupils, but life hums into action again on Sunday evening (concerts, prep), though the school lives well up to its claims of operating as a boarding school (and good value, especially for weekly boarders) with a six-day week in which the various categories of pupils integrate well.

Getting more popular with Central Londoners in search of weekly boarding.

ETON COLLEGE

Windsor, Berkshire SL4 6DW

TEL: *01753 671000* FAX: *01753 671248*

E-mail: admissions@etoncollege.org.uk

WEB: www.etoncollege.org.uk

✦ PUPILS: 1,284 boys (all boarding) ✦ Ages: 13-18 ✦ Size of sixth form: 510 ✦ C of E (other faiths 'excused' chapel) ✦ Fee-paying

---

Head: Since 1994, Mr John Lewis MA (fifties). Educated 'in Auckland, NZ', and Cambridge. Classicist. Previous post – head of Geelong Grammar School, Australia (one of Prince Charles' more favoured alma maters) and before that, master in college (housemaster in charge of scholars) at Eton. Quiet, dapper ('hardly', comments head) New Zealander with Antipodean drawl who loathes personal publicity and plays his cards very close to his chest. Teaches scripture to the junior boys. Danish wife, no children. We have been taken to task by Sir Antony Acland, the recently retired Provost (chairman of governors, ex-diplomat) for, among other things, likening Mr Lewis to a 'startled rabbit'. 'Of the people we interviewed (for the post of head)', comments Sir Antony, 'he was far and away above the rest'. Given the outstanding calibre of one or two of the heads interviewed, this would put Mr Lewis in the towering genius class. Staff report that, after a baffling start, they now find Mr Lewis 'slow but sure'; parents do not seem to be so positive. Mr Lewis and Sir Antony took over from Dr Anderson (who became rector of Lincoln College, Oxford) and Lord Charteris of Amisfield – an impossible act to follow. Dr Anderson has now returned to the school as Provost, which would seem to put Mr Lewis (and indeed any future headmaster) in an extremely uncomfortable position. Sarah Hogg is a fellow (governor).

Academic Matters: First-class all round. Outstandingly good teaching – Eton can pick and choose. Boys setted by ability from the first year, and all take GCSE Latin, French and science one year early, then seven or eight more the following year. Plenty of va et vient among sets, so boys are constantly changing beaks (masters) and peer groups. Very highly structured, lots of sticks and carrots, monthly order cards, show-ups and all that. Outstanding languages – one of the most successful departments in the country in terms of results – packs in talk and chalk. Japanese is an option (NB if Eton offers a subject it really happens – unlike many other schools which often have an element of window-dressing). As elsewhere, maths is a very popular A level subject. Geography is another strong department, so is history.

Choice of forty A levels genuinely on offer, and results are a joy to behold. Twice yearly internal exams ('trials'), very detailed reports to parents and work is thoroughly monitored at all stages. Boys need considerable stamina and self-discipline to cope with it all and structured academic day, and occasionally fall by the wayside. NB no quarter is given if this is the case. Increasing numbers of boys are to be found in crammers in the holidays, swotting up exam subjects. Also: this is absolutely not the school for a dyslexic – though there is some support for those who get through the net by accident. Parents still complain of the difficulty of getting at staff for information.

Games, Options, the Arts: Excellent all round: every conceivable extra-curricular activity is on offer to amazing standards in some cases (IT did trail a bit, but a massive £6 million now being poured into wiring every boy and beak to the intranet). Music under Mr Ralph Allwood generally acknowledged to be one of the best departments in the country – attracts the brightest and best in music scholarships. Very polished concerts. Wonderful chapel choir. Good art department producing some remarkable work. Very fine drama, and a lot of it, a mixture of 'traditional' and boys plus masters writing their own plays – one at the Edinburgh Festival in '00. Main games are soccer, rugby (usually trounced by Harrow), fives, hockey, cricket (very good), boats (rowing lake), plus Eton's own Wall Game

and the Field Game; good fencing, swimming, water polo, sailing etc. Also judo, polo, beagling etc etc but though still successful the school does not appear to be winning the way they once did, and sport is no longer worshipped the way it once was: but head encourages boys to continue with sports through exam terms – brownie points for this. Considerable numbers of outings, visits, field trips etc, with regular exchanges with schools in France, Germany, Japan, Spain and Russia. Good provision for amusing pupils post exams (school disputes this!). Casa Guidi in Florence recently acquired with study opportunities for boys. Vast numbers of societies (mainly run by boys, often held in the evenings).

Background and Atmosphere: Founded in 1440 by Henry VI (sister college of King's, Cambridge, which was founded a year later), and 70 King's Scholars still live in the original buildings (most elegant dining hall). Buildings of mellow old red brick, grounds run down to the Thames. Magnificent chapel built by Henry VI and a second chapel for Lower boys. Twenty-four boarding houses, including separate one for King's Scholars (single-study bed-sits for all from the start) strung out along the streets. Decor differs – a mother described one as 'like a working brothel'. Boys still wear traditional tailcoats and stiff white collars (NB good second hand trade in High Street tailors); however, much changing and half-changing throughout the day and full-fig is no longer worn out of school hours. Incidents of antagonism between Etonians and the town which were reported in our last edition are 'nil', says head. Atmosphere very much alive, not easy, and every day is highly structured and active. Everyone – boys, beaks – on the go. The school has a well-developed ancient language, which it clings to with child-like fervour, and insists you play along with (eg halves, beaks). Current slang adds '-age-' to everything, eg 'pubage', 'birdage', 'tabage' (tobacco), 'plebage' (as in pleb). In general the school has a solipsistic attitude to life. Quality school mag, *The Eton College Chronicle,* has featured inter alia a funny report on the ISC inspection and an interview with the Spice Girls – scoop.

Pastoral Care and Discipline: Broadminded and liberal in principle though is quite capable of firing a pupil at a moment's notice, often to the consternation of parents. Drink a perennial problem ('minor problem only' says school). Drugs policy 'very firm' – random drug testing introduced; head's September '00 newsletter goes into the matter in great detail – five pages on the school's policy, the law, and warning signs – very commendable. Housemaster, dame, division master, academic tutor oversee each boy, 'which means,' said a mother, 'that problems should be spotted early'. However, minimal tradition of parental involvement can and does cause Mummy angst. We have had some reports of bullying (to be expected in a school that is so much run by the boys) but head comments 'absolutely not so', and refers to the ISC inspectors' report. Boys are allowed out any Sunday (plus official exeats), which is great for going up to town and getting into mischief (eg demonstrating against global capitalism), but a considerable concern for parents without a safe London base for their adventurous young; fewer pupils from the North as a result.

Pupils and Parents: A rich mix of spivs and toffs. Currently 35 per cent sons of Old Etonians, plus first-time Eton buyers, and yuppies. Among numerous Old Etonians:

Hubert Parry, 19 Prime Ministers, Captain Oates, the poets Gray and Shelley, Keynes, Feilding. Surprisingly few real stars among the living: politicians (William Waldegrave, Nicholas Soames, Douglas Hurd, Boris Johnson), a clutch of journalists (Charles Moore, Nicholas Coleridge, Craig Brown); also Martin Taylor, Humphrey Lyttelton, Nicholas Charles Tyrwhitt Wheeler, Sir James Goldsmith, Jonathan Aitken, Darius Guppy, Matthew Pinsent and Michael Chance. NB the current entry procedure does not appear to be serving the school well – missing out on mavericks, geniuses, late developers and the less well taught, though evidence that this is changing.

Entrance: Registration by 10 years 6 months; inspection ('interview') and exam (VR) at 11 (one out of three fall at this hurdle) and conditional places offered at this stage. CE at 12+ or 13+ (6-7 per cent failure at this stage). Provost comments that the school is 'not just looking for academic ability', but 'leadership qualities, sports, artistic talent' and that sons of OEs 'are given a small weighting'. Entries for King's Scholarships (14 per annum) accepted until the beginning of May for exam in May at 12+ or 13+. Up to four junior scholarships a year for boys from state schools at 10, at which point Eton pays for three years' prep school education in traditional Eton 'feeds' for successful candidates. Four scholarships for state school pupils at sixth form.

Exit: Average of 70 boys to Oxbridge – but parental angst that political pressures result in many top candidates not getting there. Successful on organ scholarships to Oxbridge. All boys go on to university – to Edinburgh in droves, plus over 70 different institutions in the UK, 10-15 abroad. Lots of gap year pupils. Thereafter, the City, journalism, family estates, politics.

Money Matters: Pots and pots of money and assets, in particular property. It can afford to, and does, have everything of the best, and to pay its staff very well indeed. Good value. Large numbers of bursaries etc for parents on hard times. Also pots of money still in evidence among parents. In addition to scholarships detailed under Entrance, there are also eight music scholarships each year, plus exhibitions.

Remarks: Still the number one boys' public school for social status, and numbers seeking places keep increasing, but potential parents seem less obsessed with the place than they were a few years ago. Can sometimes be a hard place to be for a boy who is neither one of the lads nor a gifted sportsman – just as it was in Peter Wimsey's day.

FELSTED SCHOOL

Dunmow, Essex CM5 3LL

TEL: *01371 820258* FAX: *01371 821232*

E-MAIL: jcd@felsted.essex.sch.uk

WEB: www.felsted.org

✦ PUPILS: Around 400 pupils, 150 girls, 250 boys. (300 boarders, 100 day pupils). Also prep school of 220 pupils, and pre-prep of 110 ✦ Ages: 13-18 ✦ Size of sixth form: 170 (including 60 girls) ✦ C of E foundation ✦ Fee-paying

---

Head: Since 1993, Mr Stephen Roberts, MA (early forties), nicknamed 'Loopie'. Not one of your outgoing heads, according to pupils, but friendly withal. Educated at Mill Hill and Oxford, where he read physics. Previous post – housemaster at Oundle, where the troops had little to say about him, one way or another. Started life as a merchant banker. Married – wife Joanna helps with pastoral side of the school. Two sons. Hockey player.

Academic Matters: Solidly good performance at GCSE: very few below grade C in anything. A level results are OK overall; the popular subjects are maths, geography, the sciences, English and history. Maths results are consistently excellent, chemistry and art too (Dr Kay Stephenson, head of chemistry, awarded 1999 Salter's teaching prize); some other subjects are more variable – caveat. Girls in particular tend to 'over-achieve', according to a master – though everything is relative. Dual award and individual subjects in sciences at GCSE. Some excellent teaching staff. New system of screening for dyslexia, and remedial help in operation. One full-time EFL teacher, and additional help available.

Games, Options, the Arts: A school well known for prowess on the games field and competitive attitude of the 'professional' games players, though by no means unbeatable at present. Bruising rugby, strong hockey and cricket: only the cricket appears to be considered too rough for the girls. Lots of overseas tours (NZ, Zimbabwe etc). Shooting teams as usual distinguishing themselves: David Crisp (16) was national short-range champion in 1997. Pupils unkeen on games now have a 'rolling programme of health-related fitness'. School still in the grip of the official computer buff (head of computing) Chris Dawkins, who has more or less succeeded in his ambition to wire up the whole school into one huge network – one of the first to have done this – into which anyone can plug at any time and check on eg whether Smith is currently on a bicycle ride/ill/doing exams. 'Even the unkeenest pupil will sooner or later want to use it,' says Mr Dawkins, 'if only to look up the latest Test score on Prestel.' The school also has a wonderful old farmhouse next door (The Bury), left to the school by an OB in the '30s in which all manner of societies take place. Some distinctly good art, and school has noted director of music, Jasper Thorogood, from the Royal Academy of Music, who has galvanised the place in this direction, with lots of super and ambitious things on offer in the Felsted Arts Festival in March, from William Blake lectures to dinner with Germaine Greer; open to all. Impressive community service.

Background and Atmosphere: Set in the heart of yuppie East Anglian commuter belt, surrounded by fat Ferraris, BMWs and flitches. School is on good terms with the local village in which pupils flit to and fro. Founded in 1564 by Richard, Lord Riche, Lord Chancellor of England, who came and 'buried his conscience here' after his successful part in the decapitation of Thomas More. For 300 years thereafter, the Riche heirs were patrons of the school, which still solemnly celebrates his existence on Founder's Day. Peaceful, pleasing and quietly purposeful, almost civilised to look at, though some Dickensian horrors tucked away out of sight. Modern buildings in the grounds (diligent groundsmen), well planned and unobtrusive. Main buildings now Grade I and II listed, which has necessitated reorganisation and refurbishment. Large modern dining hall and school mostly now central feeding (alas). One sixth form house; two new houses for girls 13-18. Smallish numbers of girls below sixth form were looking a bit lost but the head says this is no longer the case – girls now 37 per cent of population.

Pastoral Care and Discipline: All members of staff are attached to a boarding house and every pupil has a tutor. Good San (also wired up to the network). School makes use of child psychotherapist for counselling expertise. Discipline and anti-bullying policies spelt out in detail: firm but rational, the only automatic expulsions are for drug dealing and bonking. Occasionally makes local headlines for live wire behaviour.

Pupils and Parents: 'Lack get up and go – motivation,' according to visiting educationalist. 'Broad' spectrum of backgrounds, from round Felsted, Hertfordshire, Southend, also London and south of London; some overseas too. Local accents predominate. Most famous Old Felstedian is Richard Cromwell, son of Oliver (a letter from him hangs in the rather static-looking library). Most famous present OB is probably Kenneth Kendall. Lots of engineers among OBs.

Entrance: By CE or exam. Special provision for pupils from state schools. School has own prep school over the road; pupils also come from other local prep schools. For the sixth form five grades C at GCSE are required (six for external candidates).

Exit: Keen gappers, then higher education (several Oxbridge, and others) business, the Services, farmers and the occasional vicar.

Money Matters: An unspecified percentage of fee income goes towards bursaries and a variety of academic, music and art scholarships worth up to 50 per cent of the fees at 13 and 16. Scholarships also for 11+, and some means-tested awards. Had around 80 assisted places (at last count). School does not have heavy endowments.

Remarks: Formerly a macho boys' public school, formidable on the sporting front. Now co-ed with rising rolls. Low profile.

FETTES COLLEGE

Carrington Road, Edinburgh EH4 1QX

TEL: *0131 311 6701* FAX: *0131 311 6714*

E-MAIL: postmaster@fettes.co.uk

WEB: www.fettes.co.uk

✦ PUPILS: 228 boys plus 177 girls (186 boys and 122 girls board, the rest day) Plus prep school: 86 boys, 75 girls (27 boys and 27 girls board) ✦ Ages: 8-18 ✦ Size of sixth form: 176 ✦ Non-denom ✦ Fee-paying

---

Head: From 1998, Mr Michael C B Spens MA (Cantab) (forties) educated at Marlborough and Selwyn College where he read natural sciences. Came to Fettes via a short spell in business followed by 20 years at Radley where he was housemaster and taught geology. Then quick switch to prep school world, and five years as head of Caldicott. The transition between junior and senior schools is always an interesting one, but Mr Spens admits he is 'glad to teach grown-ups' again, though 'it is a good hard grind'. Charismatic, vibrant, fun. Fettes and Mr Spens are zinging. There must hardly be a morning he wakes up without red ears as the Edinburgh mafia sing his praises in the hallowed dining rooms of the New Town – the self same dining rooms where disgruntled parents planned their yet to be resolved law suit against Fettes more than ten years ago.

To meet him you would hardly expect the iron fist in the velvet glove, but under his aegis (though much credit must be given to the previous head) Fettes has lost its laissez-faire druggy alcy image and is currently challenging all comers as Scotland's school of excellence. Married to Debbie, who is part-time dyslexia coach, they have three young children and two dogs. Took over from Mr Malcolm Thyne, who had a difficult row to hoe here, but hoed with a will.

Academic Matters: 'School in v good nick academically right now, morale is right up'. This is a rising plane of excellence, though league tables are misleading as the school plays the system: A levels for some, Scottish Highers (over two years) for others. Positive advice and encouragement on which route to take, 'but parents' wishes at the end of the day are followed'. This will undoubtedly become more complicated with the introduction of AS and A2s later this year. Three sciences on offer throughout, plus trad French, German and Spanish, as well as Russian, Chinese and Japanese (often taken by native Russians, Chinese and Japanese); English still strong. Good staff:pupil ratio. 'Computers zooming ahead'. School on line for total networking in September 2000, with third formers having their own laptop. This is hi-tech ex-military technology designed by ex-army experts.

NB Foreign pupils with minimal ('basic') English are accepted, with EFL marketed (not cheap this) and taught instead of French, and if necessary, English.

At the time of writing, Fettes is creaming off the academic elite of Edinburgh, be they boarder or day.

Games, Options, the Arts: Enthusiastic games, though nothing like as strong as they were when this was a single-sex school. 'Rugby is strong, though no longer a religion' – 73 Blues to date. Needle matches with Glenalmond on the rugby field, and Strathallan in hockey. Lacrosse impressive, girls play hockey as well – sixth form not forced to play games at all – 'swimming, aerobics or netball will do'. Big new sports centre in the offing and swimming pool due for a face lift (not before time – this is the favoured snogging area for the local young).

Keen drama with imaginative productions, pupils often perform at the Edinburgh Festival (and win awards). New art centre in pipe line and 'v inspirational head of art' recently appointed. Pipe band popular. CCF, granny bashing, D of E etc. Masses of trips, everywhere, for everything.

Background and Atmosphere: Vast Grimm's fairy-tale of a building, turreted and with acres of dark wood panelling (strong smell of Nitromors when we visited, so perhaps not now so dark), purpose built in 1870 by Bryce. Part of the main building still has the original steam driven heating which starts up twice-a-day with alarming groans and wheezes – ripe for the engineering museum methinks.

Various Victorian edifices scattered about the school's wonderful 90 acre grounds plonk in the middle of Edinburgh. 'School uses Edinburgh a lot, but not enough', says the head. Acres sold off to raise £3 million caused quite a stir locally, now Fettes Village, a collection of natty little boxes that splits the games field. The collection of new and converted buildings that house the new prep department are much bigger than they look from the outside, and an example of space well used.

The school has gradually metamorphosed from famous trad boys' school to genuinely co-ed. Girls have been head of school twice in recent years, and the flavour has changed from home-grown Scots to more exotic with an influx from the Far East.

Pastoral Care and Discipline: Edinburgh is the drugs capital of the North and running a school in the middle of it is no joke. Head maintains that 'he has not had a sniff of drugs since we've been here' but automatic expulsion if he did.

'Underage drinking a problem': three tier system: housemaster/deputy head/head = rustication/formal warning and suspension or expulsion. Ditto smoking. 'Prefects very responsible'; imaginative bullying (anti-bullying?) code involving culprits 'writing down what they must or must not do, and signing it'. Expulsion always an option. 'Very clear house visiting rules: no overt demonstrations of affection'; bonking equals out.

Pupils and Parents: School topped up with many non-Brits in the bad old days, now the mix is veering more towards the British norm, but still tranches of exotic foreigners, plus increasing numbers of locals and Scots from all over. 'Pupils from 34 different countries, East European connection sadly dropping off'. Very strong old Fettesian stream, plus loads of first-time buyers, intellectuals etc etc. Good vibrant mix. Old Fettesians include John de Chastelaine, Ian McLeod, James Bond, Tilda Swinton and Tony Blair (who was remembered fondly for 'his acting ability').

Entrance: CE or school's own exam for foreigners. 'Hurdle' exam from own prep; approx 15 after GCSE, currently much sought after as pupils pile in from other (mainly Scottish) schools.

Exit: University or further education the norm with 11 Oxbridge places last year, and very few taking a gap year; favoured universities are – as ever – Newcastle, St Andrews, Durham, London, Bristol and Aberdeen with half a dozen going to Edinburgh.

Money Matters: Well endowed with academic scholarships which can be supplemented with bursaries when the chips are down – if necessary up to 100 per cent: 'the level of these awards depend upon parents' financial means and can cover up to the full value of the fees'. Special (Tod) bursaries for Old Fettesians, 12.5 per cent discount for Forces (not so many of these around).

Remarks: Undoubtedly the strongest school in Edinburgh – possibly riding too high? – to quote one governor 'it is better to have a challenge, otherwise we become complacent'. Exciting cosmopolitan mix in an exciting city.

JUNIOR SCHOOL: Fettes Prep School. Head: Since 2000, Mr A G S Davies BSc CertMgmt (early forties). Formerly a housemaster in the senior school and still its deputy head. Married to Alison, who teaches EFL; one young daughter. A talented sportsman – a senior referee for the Scottish Rugby Union.

With 161 pupils during second year of its life, this newest addition to Scotland's prep schools is shaking other prep schools – particularly Edinburgh prep schools – rigid. Tiny classes, excellent remedial (Catriona Collins who also does the senior school), super facilities, and plumb in the centre of Edinburgh. Latin early, computers everywhere. Possible drawback would be the lack of stimulation for children spending 10 years in the same place.

FRAMLINGHAM COLLEGE
Near Woodbridge, Suffolk 1P13 9EY
TEL:*01728 723789* FAX: *01728 724546*

E-MAIL: info@framlingham.suffolk.sch.uk

WEB: www.framlingham.suffolk.sch.uk

✦ PUPILS: 257 boys, 148 girls (273 board, 132 day) ✦ Ages: 13-18 (Junior school, Brandeston Hall, caters for 4-13)
✦ Size of sixth form: around 195
✦ C of E – inter-denom ✦ Fee-paying

Head: Since 1994, Mrs Gwen Randall BA (forties), who studied French at Bristol University and comes here from Dauntsey's (deputy head); before that she was head of modern languages and drama at St Mary's Calne; she has also taught in Germany. A very spirited live wire (and the first woman to join the HMC). Married to a helicopter instructor, with a teenage daughter. She has set about the place like a ball in a bowling alley, but reassures OBs that, though they will not recognise the place, they will feel immediately at home.

Academic Matters: Good facilities, with well equipped labs, geography department, drama studio. The design department is inspiringly staffed and housed, and the results are excellent.

This is determinedly a school for the middle ability range, picking up the stragglers and dyslexics, and aiming to persuade everyone that they can succeed. We suspect that, by and large, pupils do better than average here (there are some good ALIS results), and the school's exam results bear this out. ESL, pastoral/academic care tailored to the various ethnic groups that come here.

Games, Options, the Arts: 'Sport is an important part of college life, and we are good at it,' crows the prospectus, and with reason. All participate. Teams regularly do well at county level, and most years one or other reaches a national finals. In 2000, 65 pupils played sport at county, national or international level. County-standard cricket pitch, all-weather hockey pitch, golf course, indoor swimming pool. CCF; D of E in spades. Plenty of music of all varieties, termly drama.

Background and Atmosphere: College founded in 1864 as 'Albert Memorial College for Sons of the Middle Class' to commemorate the Prince Consort. Long and continuing association with Pembroke College, Cambridge on whose land the school was built. Beautiful setting and well tended grounds (50 acres of playing fields) perched on one of Suffolk's few hillocks, with an inspiring view over the mere (an icy bog) to Framlingham Castle. There are some fine old buildings, and many well-designed modern ones (including boarding/day houses) replacing the ghastly collection of cabins and suchlike that used to be there. On the social side, there is a much used sixth form centre, and a covered courtyard that is a central meeting place for all.

Pastoral Care and Discipline: There is a long and unusual tradition of prefects keeping the staff informed as to what is going on. Drugs and bullying are approached seriously and with professionalism, but are rare. No cuddling on campus allowed.

Pupils and Parents: Outward-going, bouncy, relatively unsophisticated boys and girls from middle-class backgrounds. Lots of East Anglian farmers' children; a strong Forces contingent; large numbers of Germans, who integrate seamlessly, and pupils from Japan and Hong Kong, who do not yet but whose presence is generally appreciated. Increasingly popular locally with parents seeking more opportunities for daughters than are offered by single-sex schools.

Entrance: No problem – 'individuals with whom the college feels they can succeed are accepted.' Five Cs at GCSE for sixth-form entry.

Exit: Degree courses, agriculture, the Services, medicine, teacher training, business.

Money Matters: Increased pupil numbers (though not recently) and a long-awaited land sale restored the school's fortunes, though the demise of the assisted places scheme has not helped. Scholarships available for academic excellence, science, music, drama, technology, an all-rounder and locals. Reductions for siblings, HM Forces.

Remarks: Sporty boarding school full of Forces, farmers and foreigners. Continuing approving noises from locals – it is taken seriously. Mrs Randall is clearly taking this school places: so far so good.

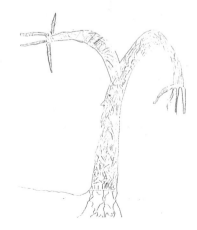

FRANCIS HOLLAND SCHOOL

Ivor Place, Clarence Gate, Regent's Park,
London NW1 6XR

TEL: *020 7723 0176* FAX: *020 7706 1522*

E-MAIL: sandybailey@fhs-nw1.org.uk

✦ PUPILS: 370 girls, all day ✦ Ages: 11-18 ✦
Size of sixth form: around 90 ✦ C of E
✦ Fee-paying

Head: Since 1998, Mrs Gillian Low MA (mid forties). Read English at Oxford, formerly deputy head of Godolphin and Latymer School. Took over from Mrs P H Parsonson, a five star head and an impossible act to follow.

Academic Matters: Refuses to publish detailed examination results – but will discuss them with a prospective parent. Twenty-nine maximum class size at the bottom of the school (taught in half classes for some subjects), 14 at the top (though most classes we went in to were much smaller). Options at sixth form – eg Spanish from scratch, drama – have had to be abandoned in the face of the new A level system, where girls will take 4 and perhaps 5 ASs in the first year. Non-examined general studies programme survives, however. Useful careers department. Some support for mild dyslexia/dyspraxia; EFL support bought in when needed.

A school where, by and large, you can count on pupils getting the results you would expect of them – if not better – in an atmosphere which feels conducive to learning. There is a pleasant, not very large, library, light and airy, well supplied.

Games, Options, the Arts: No room, no room for games – Regent's Park is about two stone throws away (for hockey, netball, rounders and tennis), and there is a 'gym/fitness room', but as usual in inner London girls' schools, there is no great feeling of enthusiasm here. Netball is perhaps the exception: since becoming Middlesex under 14 champions in '94, teams have continued to do well, and the girls now sport Virgin and Tommy Hilfiger sponsorship on their kit. More scope for swimming with the new pool. Music is another matter – the school was finalist in the National Choral Competition recently and did a concert (along with other finalist schools – and very good they all were) in the Queen Elizabeth Hall on the South Bank; they also put on ambitious musicals. Some excellent three-dimensional art – showing real imagination here – in a good light area; arts exam results mediocre at GCSE, but fine for the few who keep on to A level. Clubs in the lunch break, keen drama and debating.

Background and Atmosphere: The school was founded as a church school in 1878 by Canon Francis Holland, whose portrait hangs in the front hall (this was the first of the schools he founded). No endowment however, but the school appears to be managing its funds extremely well. This unlikely talent for making money spills over into the monies raised for various charities by the school: the noticeboards are alive with statements saying the school has raised eg £450 for the Terence Higgins Trust, and organising to supply desks to children in Kimilili, and many more. Although the school is known as 'Francis Holland, Clarence Gate' to distinguish it from the Graham Terrace school of the same name, it actually lurks on the edge of Park Road, where the traffic whistles down into Baker

Street; it is next door to the Rudolph Steiner establishment, and quite easy to miss. The building – once you find it – is a very distinctive wedge shape, like a large thin slice of cheese, and it is the thin end of the wedge that has the main door in it. No feeling of ceremony about the place, but the minute you walk in it really does feel friendly, with broad smiles and a welcome, and it is this, says the previous head, which over and over again parents give as the reason for choosing the school. Recent improvements added a whole new range of classrooms etc at the wide end of the wedge, with what amounts to an atrium at the top, making lots more room, with a sixth form centre, swimming pool (with a floating floor so the space can be put to other uses) and new labs. The school has a jolly rabbit-warreny feel to it, and it is difficult to see how this will ever change much, given the lack of space overall.

Pastoral Care and Discipline: Parents do query whether the bright lights of Oxford Street etc are a temptation, but 'it's a long walk' the girls say realistically. Drugs education taken seriously; infractions dealt with case-by-case: the needs of the child come first. No particular problems at time of writing. Former head ruled with a light touch, no stupid rules.

Pupils and Parents: Charming gentle folk, polite, kind, fun and with a good sense of humour. 15 per cent Jewish (around eight a year), 10 per cent Muslim, daughters of diplomats, and inner London parents looking for something a bit less shrill, more laid back, than some of the competition. Big plus: the enthusiasm of the girls. Famous Old Girls: Joan Collins, Jacquie Collins, Amanda Donohue, and Saskia Wickham (actress).

Entrance: Hugely oversubscribed, and at the last minute – impossible. Own exam at 11 – one of the 'North London Consortium' of schools who co-ordinate their entry for January (names down by end of November). Some spaces at sixth form to make up the numbers: six, grade C at GCSE, with B+ in proposed A level subjects.

Exit: Lots to London University, half a dozen or so to Oxbridge, most of the rest to a wide spread of other universities. A good broad strong offering of subjects, and no longer showing a bias to the arts. The usual slight exodus après GCSE – mostly to co-ed sixth forms.

Money Matters: One music scholarship at 11+. Generous bursaries for those already in the school. Had some assisted places, but at present their loss will probably not affect the school much. Fees a bit less than some comparable schools.

Remarks: A pearl of a girls' day school, tucked back from the swirling traffic. Lively and friendly, academic but without the feeling that nothing else counts in life. We have yet to hear a complaint from those who choose it.

FRANCIS HOLLAND SCHOOL

39 Graham Terrace, London SW1W 8JF

TEL: *020 7730 2971* FAX: *020 7823 4066*

E-MAIL:office@francishollandsw1.westminster.sch.uk

WEB: www.francishollandsw1.westminster.sch.uk

✦ PUPILS: around 240 in the senior school (plus 170 in the junior school, see separate entry), all girls, all day ✦ Ages: 11-18 ✦ Size of sixth form: about 40 ✦ C of E ✦ Fee-paying

Head: Since 1997, Miss Stephanie Patten-den BSc PGCE. Educated at St Anne's Sanderstead (now defunct), Durham (maths) and King's London (PGCE). Comes from South Hampstead High, where she was deputy head, and before that taught at St Paul's, Lady Eleanor Holles and Harrow County Girls' Grammar School. 'Efficient, capable, but not whizzy' say the girls. Lives locally, interested in music and hill walking. Teaches maths to year 7.

Entrance: Not difficult. From school's own junior school (qv), otherwise from local preps (used to be a half, but school set to expand). One of North London Consortium Group 1 (with St Alban's, Heathfield, Notting Hill, and South Hampstead etc). Written exam in English and maths; all who take the exam are interviewed, and must participate in a lesson to see how they react. Sixth form entrants must have minimum five Cs at GCSE; external candidates also sit subject papers.

Exit: Interesting spread in ones (including Cambridge, Durham, Oxford Brookes,

Bristol, Newcastle, Manchester, Camberwell College of Art, Imperial College) and reflects what the school is good at – finding the right course for the pupil.

Remarks: Small Church of England girls' school founded in 1881. On useful site at the edge of Belgravia – surprisingly roomy behind terraced facade, with good playground and hall (stained-glass windows of famous biblical women). Pupils are daughters of diplomats, bankers, one or two politicians' children etc. Refuses to publish detailed examination results – but will discuss them with a prospective parent. Very good computer studies under Chris Chisnall, with timetabled lessons through much of the lower school. Class size – around 24 in first two years, but subdivided for most subjects; after third year, almost all are in groups of 15. Dual award GCSE science for all.

Neat uniform. Good library. Lots of visits to galleries etc. Good careers advice. Has links with St Mary's Church round the corner and the vicar comes in on Thursdays to take prayers. That said – no particular feeling of religious propaganda – all are welcome and school has 'lots' of Catholics and Muslims. Three younger girls left in '99 after being caught with cannabis.

One or two small bursaries and scholarships, also help for clergy daughters. Much-needed new wing on adjacent site for science, technology, computing, art, gym, library in '98; sixth form centre in '99. This might give the school new impetus. Still a very small school (though two form entry working its way up the school), and rather limited with it – just not in the same category as the sister school. Feels safe; works well for children who might flounder in a larger, more demanding, establishment.

FRENSHAM HEIGHTS

Rowledge, Farnham, Surrey GU10 4EA

TEL: *01252 792134*, FAX: *01252 794335*

E-MAIL: headmaster@frensham-heights.org.uk

WEB: www.demon.co.uk/frensham-heights

✦ PUPILS: 431; half boys, half girls. Boarding from 11 (37 per cent board; 62 per cent in sixth form). ✦ Ages: 11-18, juniors 3-10 ✦ Size of sixth form: 83 ✦ Non-denom ✦ Fee-paying

Head: Since 1993, Mr Peter de Voil (pronounced like boil) MA DipEd (mid-fifties), educated at Northampton Grammar School, read classics and English at King's College, Cambridge. Married, no children. Previously a housemaster at Uppingham. Taught at Milton Academy in Massachusetts and maintains US connections. Sensitive and kindly. Likes to discuss rather than boss about ('I'm a guide, not a moulder'). Huge interest in art history (would teach it in another life). Chairman of HMC Community Service Committee and keen to start more community service at Frensham Heights. High ideals and these are shared by students: 'there are no cynics at this school'.

Academic Matters: A level pass rate respectable, but beware: A level subjects timetabled so that some conflict and students cannot always study their first choice. 46 per cent A/B passes in 2000 (a typical year). Good art, maths, design technology, dance, languages. Two (of six – drama, dance, music, art, ceramics, DT) performing/creative arts subjects required at GCSE. Setting in French and maths but not other subjects to avoid labelling perennial slow-streamers. No classics. No RE after age 14. Some good, unconventional teaching, using drama etc to get the message across. Parents concerned about class sizes creeping up.

Games, Options, the Arts: Sport is 'improving'. All the usual games are played but probably not the place to send a prep school rugby champion. Plenty of minority sports – basketball strong, fitness training popular and one pupil boasts the unusual title of British and European Wake Boarding Champion. Compulsory games twice-a-week up to end of GCSE years with, oddly for this school, no choice – the whole class plays the same game. In sixth form they choose what they like.

Intimidatingly good performing arts, with several pupils in current TV programmes and films. Award-winning dance in stunning dance studio. Music strong, with loads of opportunities to play and sing, including an annual concert tour abroad (Hungary 2000). Expeditions and outdoor education a big deal. There is a climbing wall on the back of the sports hall and a brilliant 'activity and challenge' area in the woods that would be the envy of many adventure holiday camps. Trekking, camping, mountain climbing, survival skills, first aid. A trip into Borneo's jungle last year with tales of scorpion encounters. Kyrgyzstan in 2001. Lots of weekend trips away for boarders, which day pupils may join.

Background and Atmosphere: Unusual, small, co-ed school capable of taking children virtually from cradle to university. Progressive women founders opened school in 1925 with the aim of 'avoiding a second world war'. A smaller and slightly less academic version of Bedales (staff frequently comparing the two). No uniforms, no bullying, no competition, no house points, no prize-givings. Creative learning, creative thinking. Teachers and students all on first-name basis.

Magnificent Edwardian pile, built by a brewery magnate, set in beautiful grounds with stupendous views. Many new buildings including sports hall and a magnificent theatre block that was set ablaze by an electrician's halogen light just days before it was to open (being repaired – will be fantastic). Flash library – hard to find any books published before 1990. Inviting and well-used with audio books, videos and appealing paperbacks. Hoping to build a sixth form centre, but for now they are allotted rather noisy studies. Pleasant boarding facilities. No more Saturday school, and day pupils may leave at 4.10 on weekdays. Pupils have breaks at different times and some complain of noise for those still in lessons. School canteen could win a Michelin star.

New, lovely, bright First School houses three to eight-year-olds (no longer across busy road). Confident, busy six-year-olds rushing about calling teachers 'Sue' and 'Caron'. Seven-year-olds get specialist teachers for French, drama, ICT, music and PE. The Lower School (8–12) is a collection of classrooms dotted along the ground floor of one building, cheek by jowl with hulking sixth formers. Pupils' posters displayed on the theme, 'Be an individual, be proud of who you are.' Lower School has own dinky library and hall with main school facilities on its doorstep.

Pastoral Care and Discipline: Very nurturing pupil/teacher relationships with teachers widely available out of school hours. 'If you get a bad mark it's easy to discuss it with your teacher' said a pupil. 'Mentors' instead of prefects, trained to counsel younger students ('nice and easy to talk to'). Anti-bullying student committee.

A few pupils late to lessons with a grunt of apology and no teachers in a stew. Strict about getting prep in, though, and discipline is taken seriously. Slight tension between liberal philosophy and the need for rules. Smoking mentioned by several parents and pupils as an issue where school rules (smoking is banned) and pupils' free-choice can, for a few, be in conflict – and there are all those woods to patrol! Virtually no expulsions, but a couple of worrying pupils have left through mutual agreement. Sixth form bar for pupils 17 and over. No chapel, but various assemblies, notices, 'morning talks' etc each week.

Pupils and Parents: Pupils come from state and independent schools in Surrey, East Hampshire, West Sussex and the A3/M3 corridor into South-West London. About 7 per cent ex-pat and no more than 10 per cent from overseas. Unusual international dimension, echoing the founders' international conscience, with the head keen on bringing overseas kids into a 'parochial part of Surrey'. Two free places each year for phenomenal students from abroad. Brilliant students from Ethiopia and Bulgaria, some refugees – Sir Claus Moser is an old boy (here as a refugee from Nazi Germany). 32 pupils receive support for mild specific learning difficulties; of these 25 receive extra tuition. Parents interested in personal development, not league tables. Many from the arts, publishing, film, entertainment, design etc. Also academics, professionals and IT people.

Entrance: Mainly at 3+, 11+, 13+ or 16+. Assessment, interview and school report at age 10 (or below). Entrance exam required for the older children. Need six Cs or better at GCSE. Hate to turn anyone away ('the worst thing you can say to anyone is – you failed'). A few do not pass the entrance exam, but can get extra tuition or delay entry a year. Some children come here from schools where they were not happy. This is a place which may take in your child if he/she has been sacked from elsewhere for drugs (many schools do this, but few admit to it). Those given a second chance must agree to counselling and to 'undergo periodic urine testing' – as must pupils within the school who have been caught with drugs.

Exit: Some to music conservatories, drama schools and art colleges in the UK and abroad. Most to a wide range of universities (a couple to Oxbridge).

Money Matters: The school is not endowed, but some scholarships available for academics, music and other performing arts (dance and drama). Sixth form scholarships occasionally awarded. Busy-bee development officer, helping the school to make a bob or two letting out facilities like the outdoor education centre to visiting schools. Does a brisk trade in weddings, providing essential funding for the excellent facilities.

Remarks: Friendly and inspiring school, achieving its aim of providing good alternative education with lots of freedom but no hint of chaos.

GEORGE WATSON'S COLLEGE
Colinton Road, Edinburgh EH10 5EG
TEL: *0131 447 7931* FAX: *0131 452 8594*

E-MAIL: f.gerstenberg@watsons.edin.sch.uk

WEB: www.watsons.edin.sch.uk

✦ PUPILS: 1,260; boy:girl ratio 55:45, (1,230 day, 30 board); plus own junior school (qv) ✦ Ages: 12-18 ✦ Size of sixth form: 400 ✦ Non-denom ✦ Fee-paying

Head (Principal): Since 1985, Mr Frank Gerstenberg MA (Cantab) PGCE (London) (fifties). At school at Glenalmond, and previously head of Oswestry School. 'Not a committee man', he describes himself as 'fairly shy' (outgoing and gassy would be nearer the mark), and reckons to have the 'most challenging job in Scotland – there's an awful lot happening'. He should know: since his appointment he has transformed the place. Very hot on industrial liaison and work-shadowing, now also in Europe. Aims to produce the 'best parts of a comprehensive without the worst parts'. Mr Gerstenberg teaches history 'a little', to first and last year. Retiring July 2001.

The new principal will be Mr Gareth Edwards MA (forties), from Morrisons Academy. Born in Wales and has a 'keen affinity with the Celts.' Educated at Tudor Grange Grammar, Solihull; read classics at Exeter, Oxford. Taught at King Edward's Edgbaston, was a head of department at Bolton Boys, and then vice principal of Newcastle-under-Lyme School and rector of Morrisons. Married, with one daughter.

A slow speaking, deep thinking head, he has all the Welsh charm and a quiet charisma.

Academic Matters: Enormous range of subjects, easier to get good grades in sciences than the arts ('you can't go wrong with practical stuff'). Pupils do the Scottish system, Standard Grades followed by Highers and Advanced Highers: academic results good on the whole, brightest (usually around 50 per cent for English and history and 25 per cent for maths and French) skip Standard Grades and go straight to Highers. Maths particularly popular. Modern studies on offer and keenly followed, and sixth formers can take German, Italian, Spanish and Russian as modules; also Mandarin Chinese and Gaelic. Marvellous technology building. Best dyslexia help in Scotland under Dr Charles Weedon, who was previously at Perth Grammar. Six children with specific learning difficulties taken each year for special help. Rows of computers everywhere. Enormous library.

Games, Options, the Arts: Strong games traditions: rugger good (lists of internationals), games fields on campus, refurbished swimming pool, and three gyms adjacent to sports hall. Art, pottery strong. Music everywhere, orchestras throughout with regular trips to Assisi. Wind band, Baroque orchestra, jazz band and full-blown pipe band. Clarsach popular (Scottish harp). D of E (lots of gold awards), and masses of exchanges with Europe. Lots of ancillary sports, Scouts, Guides, community service (granny bashing) and clubs for everything.

Background and Atmosphere: School founded in 1741, and moved to present site in 1932; magnificent sandstone building, purpose built, long corridored totally symmetric building sporting the Merchant Company boat. Superb hall much in demand for dances, political rallies etc. Masses of modern conversions and additions. Co-ed throughout since 1974, classes down to max 25, smaller for practical sessions. Timetabled on seven-day cycle, pupils are positive, doing things, particularly extra-curricular. School no longer fettered to Merchant Company, but loosely linked; need permission to buy and sell land, and have budgets and accounts approved, but now appoint own (v dynamic) board of governors, and have more freedom of action within the Company.

Pastoral Care and Discipline: Each year has a head of year who stays with pupils until they leave, and is responsible for pastoral care. Works well. Houses purely for competition. Deputy head in charge of discipline, 'firm but fair'. Drugs: 'sackings relatively rare.' Otherwise, detentions, occasional suspensions for second offence smoking.

Pupils and Parents: Offspring of Edinburgh professionals, from outlying suburbs and as far away as Kirkaldy and Peebles. Some boarders are ex-pats. Border farmers' children, fair quantity of first-time buyers and FPs' children. Strong Watsonian tradition (new parents conform quite quickly). FPs include Malcolm Rifkind and Chris Smith (Heritage Secretary).

Entrance: At 12 and 16 by interview, assessment and test. Straight through from the junior school. Suitable candidates can be fitted in at any time if space available.

Exit: Very occasionally to traditional public school at 13 – both Scottish and English; a little leakage after Standard Grade. Otherwise 180 per annum to university (either after Highers or Advanced Highers), about 10 to Oxbridge.

Money Matters: Nearly a fifth of the

school was on much needed assisted places; to some extent these have been replaced by the school's own foundation, with bursaries of up to 100 per cent for up to 150 pupils in the school. Twelve scholarships, both academic and music.

Regular winners of national Arkwright Technology scholarships.

Remarks: Huge co-ed day school with remarkable principal. Very commercial. The school produces friendly children, who come out as themselves, not clones.

GIGGLESWICK SCHOOL

Settle, North Yorkshire BD24 0DE

TEL: *01729 893 000* FAX: *01729 893 150*

E-MAIL: office@giggleswick.n-yorks.sch.uk

WEB: www.giggleswick.n-yorks.sch.uk

✦ PUPILS: 310 boys and girls (250 board, 60 day) Plus own junior school, with 130 boys and girls (50 board, 80 day) ✦ Ages: 13-18, junior school 3-13 ✦ Size of sixth form: 155 ✦ C of E ✦ Fee-paying

---

Head: Since 1993, Mr Anthony (Tony) Millard BSc (forties). LSE and Balliol. Economist with experience in industry and the European Commission. Previous post, head of Wycliffe College. Married to Lesley, a magistrate, has four children. Leaving August 2001 (having been selected to fight Wirral South for the Conservatives).

Academic Matters: Hard-working pupils, good solid staff. School selective, but not greatly so. Separate and combined sciences offered, setted in English, French, maths, sci-

ence. All go on to do A level; results reflect this mixed intake, but do not flatter it. Most subjects sport a few Ds and Es, but none fail altogether. Humanities a little more popular than the sciences. Full-time special educational needs co-ordinator. EFL provided by part-time teachers with two to four lessons a week, one to one, in study periods. Class sizes 22 maximum, 10-14 for A level. Lots of computers, including some in each boarding house: e-mails home. Offers tailor-made sixth form courses – could be v useful for the less academic pupil who does not know what he/she wants to do next.

Games, Options, the Arts: Art and design taken seriously – impressively ambitious design work in particular. Strong links with half a dozen large companies: lots of work experience and management courses, all gain experience with Microsoft programs, and have a go at public speaking. Sport keenly pursued: cross-country and canoeing historically their most successful team sports – a regular contributor to county teams – but international-level coaching over the last few years has led to success in hockey, rugby, cricket and athletics as well. Keen drama started by Russell Harty, and lots of OBs and OGs active in the profession. Third of pupils learn an instrument. Revamped swimming pool. Super sixth form centre. Outward bound, CCF (including girls). Exchanges with schools in France and Germany, tours (eg of drama and jazz to the US, sports to Canada and Zimbabwe). Glorious chapel choir (when not overtaxed) – as good as any we have heard in recent years, a great deal better than many schools that claim to be 'strong' in music.

Background and Atmosphere: Set in the Western margins of the Yorkshire Dales beneath an imposing limestone escarpment, 60 minutes' drive north of Manchester.

Giggleswick was founded in 1512, moved to present site in 1869. Attractive buildings overlooking Giggleswick village (for which it used to be the boys' grammar school) beneath an incongruous-looking mini-St Paul's (copper dome and all), gift of an inspired (but by what) benefactor. Large development plan recently completed: library, dining hall, girls' boarding house, floodlit all-weather pitch etc, funded principally from money in hand. Girls' quarters exuberantly decorated. A full boarding school: exeats only one weekend out of three. Happy atmosphere.

Pastoral Care and Discipline: Shot out for sex or drugs. Parents from abroad appear to be well satisfied on this front.

Pupils and Parents: 85 per cent board, the rest local children from a large catchment area, more boys than girls, mid-range academically. School fully co-ed since '83. Five per cent foreign, 40 per cent ex-pats, also Forces children and popular with all these. Parents in business and the professions. OG: James Agate; OG society well established on the internet.

Entrance: Not a great problem. At 3+ (pre-prep, Mill House); 7+ (junior department, Catteral Hall) via own test and reports; 13+ CE, tests, interview and previous school's report. Entrance into sixth form is by five GCSEs at C grade (about 20 a year).

Exit: Five plus to Oxbridge, others principally to a wide spread of universities. 20 per cent do a gap year.

Money Matters: Several scholarships, including general distinction, art and music, and locals. School in good shape financially owing to gift from OG Norman Sharpe.

Remarks: Traditional and character-building co-ed boarding school serving the locals

and the English business community abroad (who provide 40 per cent of the intake). Extremely strong links with business reflected in curriculum and attitudes through the school. Doing a good job for a broad intake in this relatively isolated area.

GLENALMOND COLLEGE
Perthshire, Scotland PH1 3RY
TEL: *01738 842 056* FAX: *01738 842 063*

E-MAIL: registrar@glenalmondcollege.co.uk

WEB: www.glenalmondcollege.co.uk

✦ PUPILS: 401 pupils (267 boys, 134 girls; all board except for 50 day pupils) ✦ Ages: 12-18 ✦ Size of sixth form: 156 ✦ Episcopalian ✦ Fee-paying

Head (Warden): Since 1992, Mr Ian Templeton, MA BA FRSA (fifties). Previously head of Oswestry, taught at Daniel Stewarts and Melville, and Robert Gordons. Educated at Gordonstoun, he read maths and logic at St Andrews, followed by a degree in philosophy in London. Cultivates prep schools assiduously, and every local prep school we visited gave Glenalmond as their number one choice. Head incredibly proud of the school; he was appointed following a disastrous period, and has directed a considerable recovery. Not everyone's cup of tea – parents can see him as cold.

Mr Templeton used to teach maths and hopes to be able to take PSE with the thirteen-year-olds and key skills with the lower sixth as from September 2000, in order 'to know the children better'. His wife, Aline, who writes crime fiction (six books to date), is said to 'be the power behind the throne' and invites all new pupils to breakfast six by six. Two grown up children. Not fans of this guide: 'Ian and Aline Templeton feel very strongly about some of the comments made in *The Good Schools Guide* in past years.'

Academic Matters: Not desperately academic. A proportion of good staff at all levels. Head has injected new young staff to counter-balance long-servers. (It's a community and a way of life,' said one who has been here well over 20 years'). Popular new head of geography led trips to Cevennes and Morocco; the chaplin led a much vaunted trip to Kenya in July 2000 – the pupils helped to build a new school outside Nairobi, but had to find '£2000 each by themselves, parental contributions not allowed'. Girls complain 'that there are too many chauvinists amongst the staff'.

Computers in place but not taken as seriously as they might be (Warden disagrees), fibre optic cabling and new hardware all over the school. Setting in the third year. School does both Highers and A levels, with the majority going for the English system – about a quarter take Highers over two years. Maths, English, geography, history are popular; economics, geology and theatre studies now on the menu. Some support for light dyslexia. Part time specialist EFL.

Games, Options, the Arts: This is a school which majors in outward bound activities and uses its fantastic site to good advantage – all sorts of activities (and active is the word) – conservation projects, Munro Club, terrific CCF (has strong army links), full bore shooting, Scottish Islands Peaks Race, skiing (own artificial ski slop and regular trips to freezing Glenshee – school boasts a number of past and current members of Scottish ski teams), own nine hole golf course and sailing. Rugby not the religion it was – team no longer sweeping all before it. Boys' hockey coming up fast, girls' hockey very strong with the appointment of hockey International as head of girls' games. Enough girls now to muster full strength sports teams who keep tennis/netball teams flying the Glenalmond flag. Sports are a key part of life here, and daily participation is compulsory, but the constitutionally disinclined can get by with a spot of umpiring. NB sports regularly interrupted by vile weather (now has a second all-weather hockey pitch).

Fishing (on the River Almond), sports hall, indoor heated pool. Pipe band – which is hot shot on the charity front. Design and technology now holding its own, Glenalmond Enterprise (their own YE) popular, art on the up. First XV matches timetabled to ensure that players can participate in music and art – which they do with enthusiasm.

Background and Atmosphere: Known to the pupils as 'Coll'. Founded in 1847 by Prime Minister Gladstone, this is Scotland's oldest most elegant school. Spectacular self-contained quadrangle of cloisters, centred round the chapel, and set in its own mini 300-acre estate, beautifully tended parkland, and surrounded by some of the smartest grouse shooting in Scotland. Several modern additions stuck round the back, including Basil Spence music block.

A proper boys' boarding school; admitted girls at sixth form in 1990 and went 'all the way' in '95. No thoughts of increasing girl boy ratio to more than one third/two thirds. Five boys' houses (refurbished) and two rather snazzy girls' houses. Sexes mix socially 'during the day and after prep, in school not in each others' houses,' plus sixth form bar on Saturdays. Rather set apart from the world and protective – you can't just wander round at will. 'Shopping bus' to Perth twice a week. Leave outs – one on either side of half term; parents have 'free and welcome access to their children at any time,' and can take them out on Saturdays and Sundays.

Staff all live on site (part of their contract). Beautiful prospectus which could be a Scottish Tourist Board guide to Perthshire and is remarkably low on actual information about the school. Parents too mutter about not getting enough information.

Pastoral Care and Discipline: Favourable 1999 HMI report (ask for a copy) on the care and welfare of boarding pupils nonetheless points out a few areas in need of improvement. No reported bullying. Anorexia said 'to be a problem' by girls. Vodka, gin and whisky trenches now no longer discussed ad nauseam on the Scottish cocktail circuit, though still apparently in use – 'not completely clean' admits the head. Very boisterous party on St Andrew's night resulted in an awful lot of drunken children and a very cross headmaster. Smoking fairly common still, with punishments of a lesser degree. Drugs – straight out, only one recent incident when a thirteen year old girl brought some cannabis to school, probably 'just showing off', but out all the same.

Pupils complain about lack of consistency in punishment (girls receiving harsher penalties than boys); school counters that the code of practice is used in all cases and applies equally to boys and girls. Some complaints too of lack of easy way to discuss matters of concern with the staff.

Pupils and Parents: Scotland's school for toffs. 'Jolly nice parents'. Traditionally Scottish upper middle and middle class, army, Highland families. About ten per cent locals and ten per cent foreigners from all over. Fair number of first time buyers. FPs (known as OGs) a generous bunch and include Sandy Gall, Robbie Coltrane, Miles Kington, Allan Massie, David Sole and Andrew MacDonald (Train Spotting fame).

Entrance: Own entrance exam at 12, most at 13+ via CE. Some at sixth form, six passes at Standard Grade or GCSE or entrance test and previous school's recommendation. Entrance not a difficult hurdle at the moment. School boasts 'waiting lists at all levels' for the next two years.

Exit: 90 per cent+ to university or some form of higher education. Three to ten per cent annually to Oxbridge.

Money Matters: Discounts for siblings, for children whose parents are in the Armed Forces, and Fil Cler Bursaries for offspring of the Clergy. Otherwise a clutch of bursaries (means-tested) plus help if circumstances change. Music, art and academic scholarships available.

Remarks: School popular and highly thought of, saved by the 'belles' after a period of falling numbers, but not very girl friendly 'really a boys' school at heart'. Not for retiring flowers, rebels or non-joiners in.

GODOLPHIN SCHOOL

Milford Hill, Salisbury, Wiltshire SP1 2RA

TEL: *01722 430 500* FAX: *01722 430 501*

E-MAIL: admissions@godolphin.wilts.sch.uk

WEB: www.godolphin.org

✦ PUPILS: 410 girls (half board, half day) (plus preparatory school with 110 day girls) ✦ Ages: 11-18, prep 31/2-11 ✦ Size of sixth form: 115 ✦ C of E ✦ Fee-paying

Head: Since 1996, Miss Jill Horsburgh MA Oxon. (forties). Previously deputy head at Benenden, where she was a housemistress, and before that taught at Downe House. Modern history is her subject, she also studied part-time at Sheffield Business School. Keen musician, traveller and horsewoman.

Academic Matters: Broad-ish intake and certainly not a hothouse, (though there are usually exceptionally clever girls here). Twenty-five subjects on offer, and school claims that any sensible combination is possible, and subjects are seldom precluded through timetable conflicts. Science teaching 'gives us lots of practicals and hands-on explanations – most of us need that'. Sixth form has grown dramatically in past years; steadier now.

All take nine GCSEs, with excellent results. At A level English, business studies, history and biology popular – philosophy now much less so; results are good. All take general studies at A level.

Higher education taken seriously, a long process that starts at GCSE course selection. Many of the teaching staff are male.

Games, Options, the Arts: Exceptionally strong on extra-curricular activities, 'the best thing about the school,' say many pupils. Unusual after-school course in babysitting (childcare/first aid) – 'so many of our girls babysit for extra pocket money'; jewellery making, sailing, fashion design, enthusiastic Duke of Edinburgh award take up, and CCF too. Strong music, with 85 per cent of pupils learning one or more instruments and several pupils usually holding places in national, county and regional orchestras and choirs. Recording studio. Lots of sport (the school usually hatches county players in lacrosse, hockey, athletics and tennis). Large five-studio multi-media art department – open at all hours. Commissions from local railway station etc for art work puts girls in 'real life' situations, considering suitability, practicality etc. 350-seat Performing Arts Centre opened in '96, dance studio in '99.

Background and Atmosphere: Distinctly uninstitutional cluster of purpose-built houses and classrooms atop chilly Milford Hill (fabulous view of Laverstock Down). School divided by unpavemented road (footbridge for juniors mandatory). School moved here in 1890, founded under the terms of Elizabeth Godolphin's Will of 1726. All girls to the sixth wear blue sleeveless cotton pinnies (popular) and boaters. Day/boarding girls well integrated (flexible exeat programme for boarders). Day girls (called 'Sarums') stay till 4.45, many stay much later (casual boarding as and when). Much needed sixth form centre opened in '97. Natty little blue prospectus.

Pastoral Care and Discipline: A caring school, emphasis on the individual. Pupils communicate often and easily with staff, and trust is paramount, very carefully nurtured especially among seniors. All house staff are married (lots of young families and men about the place, 'It's normal'). Smoking is the the main irritant (not drink) – this is regarded as a punishable offence that could end in expulsion.

Pupils and Parents: All sorts, from the landed to modest first-time buyers; a sprinkling of Forces' children. Parents are not (overtly) wealthy. Friendly, chatty girls, who enjoy life and 'have their priorities in the right place,' commented a parent. Famous Old Girl authors: Dorothy L Sayers, Jilly Cooper, Minette Walters, Antonia Fraser, Josephine Bell, Amanda Brookfield.

Entrance: 11+, 12+ and 13+, and at sixth form. As popularity has increased, so has pressure on places. Also from the school's own dear little preparatory school (= just down the road but still on site).

Exit: Universities old and new, (three or four high-fliers per year to Oxford or Cambridge), art and music colleges – and thereafter all manner of careers.

Money Matters: Six foundation scholarships (originally destined for orphans), awarded to girls who have lost one or both parents through death, separation or divorce ('Nice for single mums,' said one fervently). These are non-academic, based on a girl's potential and 'her likelihood to benefit from Godolphin' – and vice versa. There are variable number of academic and music scholarships at 11+, 12+; 13+ and sixth form (up to half fees), plus bursaries in addition in case of need).

Remarks: Flourishing and deservedly popular small boarding and day school for girls that offers an all-round education, runs a full programme, and has good facilities, in good shape.

*JUNIOR SCHOOL:*Tel: 01722 430 652; fax: 01722 430 651; e-mail: prep@godolphin.wilts.sch.uk. Head: since 1993 (when the preparatory school was founded) Mrs Christine J Leslie BA Cert Ed (fifties). Has full access to senior school facilities. About 70 per cent go on to the senior school, others to the St Marys and South Wiltshire Grammar.

GODOLPHIN AND LATYMER SCHOOL

Iffley Road, London W6 0PG

TEL: *020 8741 1936* FAX: *020 8746 3352*

E-MAIL: registrar@gandl.hammersmith.sch.uk

WEB: www.gandl.hammersmith.sch.uk

✦ PUPILS: around 700 girls; all day ✦ Ages: 11-18 ✦ Size of sixth form: 200 ✦ Non-denom ✦ Fee-paying

Head: Since 1986, Miss Margaret Rudland BSc (fifties), educated at Sweyne School in Essex and Bedford College, London. Read maths and physics. Previous post – deputy head of Norwich High, and has also taught at St Paul's Girls' School, and at a boys' school in Nigeria. Impressive – very fair, perceptive, warm. One of your approachable heads and an excellent administrator, she has gained the respect and liking of staff, pupils and parents. President of the Girls Schools Association '96-'97, very highly regarded by other heads.

Academic Matters: Outstanding results at both GCSE and A level. Almost all A★ to B at GCSE. Gentle start as school assimilates large numbers from different educational backgrounds. English teaching excellent right through. Strong science teaching (a pioneer in the Nuffield Science scheme), though dual award only at GCSE. The occasional Bengali, Punjabi, Persian, Portuguese GCSE reflects cosmopolitan intake of school (even one doing Serbo-Croat at A level in '97). Twenty-two subjects taught at A level, the most popular being English, chemistry, biology and maths. Girls will take four or five ASs and then three or four A2s.

Pupils are expected to be self-disciplined, and from the start are taught to be academically self-reliant (strong tradition of individual research). Teaching good, very thorough, with occasionally mutterings of 'worthy and dull teaching;' particularly good on individual attention, helping less able, and advice on revising for exams (and exam results are never far out of mind). Classes of 26 for first three years, far smaller thereafter. Non-competitive, no regular read-out markings. Staff often take courses, intellectual inquisitiveness a characteristic of the school – as school mag shows.

Games, Options, the Arts: Extra-curricular activities busy over lunchtime. Out-of-hours and out-of-term travel, field trips, social work, regular exchanges with schools in Hamburg, Paris, Moscow and New York. Compulsory gym twice-a-week, own playing fields adjacent and swimming available four evenings a week between 4–6pm at Latymer Upper School. Rowing at Latymer Upper School, coached by 'Rob, Superman of the River'. Good enthusiastic drama with weekly classes for all during first two years, with annual form play competitions and musicals (often written by pupils); takes shows up to the Edinburgh fringe. Good

careers department, discussions, plus really useful programme of work-shadowing.

Background and Atmosphere: 'Sister' school to Latymer Upper (qv), though they don't get together much. Stands in four-acre site, originally built (1861) as boys' boarding school, since when it has evolved through many stages (including LCC aided, voluntary aided status and during the mid-seventies fought hard not to become comprehensive). Good facilities for science, also good library. Place is warm, friendly and fairly untidy. Situated in slightly grotty area of London ('but improving', says head). Only two stones' throw away from the maelstrom of Hammersmith Broadway, and very handy for the tube but tucked in a peaceful leafy backwater. Sturdy redbrick original grammar school building with large numbers of buildings tacked on, some gruesome, some less so; girls bolt into a narrow side entrance like homing rabbits. Liberal progressive tradition. Old 'Dolphins' and parents dedicated and helpful. Sixth formers (uniform-free) may lunch out of school. A bit lacking in glamour (but it's not alone in that), which often appeals to the pressure-cooked potential pupil.

Pastoral Care and Discipline: Few complaints. Christian values subtly inculcated. Form teachers have a second colleague to help with pastoral matters, also heads of lower, middle, and sixth form. Small group of pupils gather together off the premises for a quick fag before the school day starts.

Pupils and Parents: Mixed, lively bunch, but less competitive than St Paul's. Complete social mix from all over London and outskirts – shopkeepers' daughters, nobs, down-at-heel middle class, lots of working mothers, heaps of first-time buyers, some who have failed to get into St

Paul's (but NB it can work the other way). Lots of foreigners (Indians, Middle Easterners and Americans etc).

Entrance: Consistently large numbers sit for 100 places from 136 schools, half state, half private, and are put through an enormous number of hoops. (NB this school interviews the girls, never the parents as so many do.) Not only interested in high fliers. According to the school, about 10-15 come in at sixth form to fill in for leavers – and even then, there are sometimes spaces. Occasional vacancies in other years.

Exit: The overwhelming majority to old established universities (London particularly popular at time of writing), a healthy dozen or more to Oxbridge (more Oxford than Cambridge), a handful to interesting art and art foundation courses. Medicine and biology courses popular.

Money Matters: Reasonable fees, with few extras. One music scholarship. The school had 176 assisted places at last count, and phasing them out will cause some agonies. Some school bursaries towards the cost of fees are available. £500 deposit required on acceptance of place.

Remarks: One of London's very strongest academic girls' day schools. Very lively, with excellent teaching and a good broad curriculum. Don't be put off by the look or location of the place.

GORDONSTOUN SCHOOL

Elgin, Moray, Scotland IV30 2RF

Tel: *01343 837829* Fax: *01343 837808*

E-mail: admin@gordonstoun.org.uk

Web: www.gordonstoun.org.uk

✦ Pupils: 390 boarders, 17 day; boys to girls ratio 55/45 ✦ Ages: 13-18
✦ Size of sixth form: 200 ✦ Inter-denom
✦ Fee-paying

Head: Since 1990, Mr Mark Pyper BA (fifties). Educated at Winchester, dropped out of Oxford and finished his degree externally at London. Father, grandfather and great-grandfather were all prep headmasters, and Mr Pyper started his teaching career in the prep school world. Came to Gordonstoun from Sevenoaks, where he was deputy head. 'Rather like it here', 'suits me'. His wife likes it too, 'she jogs, plays the guitar'.

In a world where headmasters are progressively a scruffy bunch, he is unique (in our experience) in wearing a natty three piece tweed suit (it was a steaming hot June day). Study (drawing room more like) of lairdly splendour full of the works of Eric Meissner, first warden of the school. 'Likes to give the impression of being laid back', but would like the world to know that he's 'quite switched on and can be quite tough as well'. Forging closer links with Aberlour, where he teaches Latin, and enjoys 'teaching tinies again'. HRH The Princess Royal is still a governor ('and very supportive').

Academic Matters: Academia is not what Gordonstoun is about. 'Pupils are here for the whole broad experience'. Huge range of ability from children 'at the lower end of the academic scale for whom two Ds at A level is a real achievement' to the really bright. Exam results are pretty uninspiring, with their sprinkling of Ds, Es, Ns and Us; perhaps no better or worse than one would expect, though we have heard complaints of low quality teaching (good staff hard to find up here, 'matrons, musicians and mathematics' the most difficult posts to fill says the head). Business studies, English literature, biology, history, the most popular A levels, with a wide range of interesting subjects close behind. German got 23 As and one B at A level in '00 – an extraordinary result for any school, let alone this one.

Excellent new networked computer set-up on stream. Classes set for maths and English from thirteen. Good remedial support, though parents have complained with reason that school doesn't pick up dyslexia early enough. Will scribe for exams. ESL (English as a second language) available at all levels.

Games, Options, the Arts: Community service is important at Gordonstoun, and many chose the school for just this reason. All children must take part, and do service training in fifth year, before opting for the fire brigade (the most popular), mountain rescue (MR), off-shore and in-shore rescue, ski patrol, granny bashing (in old folks and mental homes) etc. Lots of exchanges with other Round Square schools – Canada, Germany, Australia etc. Joint international expeditions to India, Tanzania, Thailand, Kenya to work on service 'projects' (expensive), popular and full of teenage japes.

School has its own sail training vessel and timetabled sailing weeks (when they can be 'pretty wild' according to the skippers), as well as expeds – outward bound expeditions. Tall ships a recent and popular addi-

tion. Mainstream games on course, but long distances to other schools for matches cause problems. Good sports facilities and trips all over – Europe, Australasia, points west.

Drama very popular. Two artists in residence. Magnificent art, lots of disciplines, graphic design impressive. Particularly strong DT with pupils learning not only to make lights, but to cost them effectively.

Background and Atmosphere: Founded in 1934 by the German educationalist Kurt Hahn, founder of Salem School in Switzerland and believer in educating and developing all aspects of children, not just the academic. Grounds and setting lovely, half a mile from the Moray Firth with cliffs and beaches nearby, and not as cold as one might think.

Gordonstoun House is a former residence of Gordon-Cumming of card-cheating fame. Beautiful circular stable block (hence the Round Square tag) houses the library and a boys' house. Cunning music rooms round exotic chapel (shaped like an open book – magnificent, but repairs to the pews are incredibly botched). Sixth form study area in attic – lots of nooks and crannies – very busy, with extra rather than curricular activities. (Why on earth choose the library?) A flurry of bustle and scurrying red faces greeted our arrival. Houses spread all over, the cedar-built Altyre House recently condemned by Health and Safety.

Minimal exeats, distances are huge, but pupils often do not want to go home. Prospectus lists nearby hotels, B&Bs (with prices) and ways of getting to school (a good four hours from Edinburgh). Non-stop social life which swings right through the holidays – caveat for Southerners. Excellent prospectus information booklet.

Pastoral Care and Discipline: The Betts parents (father and step-mother of Leah, who died after taking one ecstasy pill) give harrowing anti-drugs lectures. Occasional problems with smoking and boozing: 'not totally whiter than white'. Head tough on perpetual offenders – particularly bullies and 'children have eventually had to leave the school as a result'. Commendably clear rules. Girls and boys can visit each other's houses with a certain amount of freedom. Each pupil has an academic tutor; house parents and assistant house parents in each house. Recent 'problems' mean that Elgin is now out of bounds on Saturdays; regular bus service during the week though.

Pupils and Parents: A third English, a third Scottish and a third from the rest of the world. Can be cliquey; some parents deeply rich, some less so, with locals benefiting from serious scholarships. FPs include royals, William Boyd, Eddie Shah, the composer of The Flower of Scotland – Roy Williamson, Martin Shea, Alan Shiach.

Entrance: Not a hurdle. CE, with Aberlour the principal prep-school feeder, offering guaranteed entry to Gordonstoun (get there by 11). Assessment for those joining at fourth form (about ten each year) and influx to sixth form. Odd places usually available for pupils 'at any level of the school for short periods – although not normally less than one term'.

Exit: Some leave after GCSE 'because they believe they might get higher grades elsewhere', some to crammers, otherwise standard 80/90 per cent to universities. Newcastle and Edinburgh currently popular.

Money Matters: No set fee; parents can 'opt above'. If they 'opt below', then 'questions are asked' and they may be means-tested. Masses of scholarships and bursaries. Hardship fund. Vast sums accumulated via flourishing summer school for foreigners.

Remarks: Children and parents appear happy. Fashionable co-ed outward-boundish boarding school with vast range of pupil backgrounds. Probably not for mavericks, the academic or the highly imaginative.

GREENHEAD COLLEGE

(SIXTH FORM COLLEGE)

Greenhead Road, Huddersfield, HD1 4ES

TEL: *01484 422032* FAX: *01484 518025*

E-MAIL: college@greenhead.ac.uk

WEB: www.greenhead.ac.uk

✦ PUPILS: about 1,400; all in the sixth form ✦ Ages 16–18 ✦ Non-denom ✦ State

---

Head (Principal): Since 1987 Dr J K (Kevin) Conway (early fifties). A Tyrone-born physicist (first class honours from Queen's University), an upbeat, friendly, charismatic, white haired and open man; well organised, and much given to praising staff and students, and to measuring their performance. Believes that 'everyone is individual, everyone is valuable'. If you wish to be in his good books, do not call him 'Kev'.

Academic Matters: Excellent results overall, on a strongly improving trend and with the FEFC awarding all curriculum areas its prized grade 1. About 30 A level courses; with the sciences, maths, psychology, English and history notably popular. Most subjects have excellent results, but look before you leap. GNVQs in business and health. There is a reasonable range of extra-curricular offerings (known as 'enrichment') especially sport, D of E, music and drama, and a vibrant set of relationships with local companies, clearly appreciated by both sides, that allows for an outstanding system of work-shadowing and project work. A level general studies for almost all.

Games, Options, the Arts: Sport is restricted by the city centre site, but good hockey, rugby league and swimming; soccer, badminton, squash teams, and netball too. Art and drama are well supported at A level.

Background and Atmosphere: Greenhead differs from the general run of sixth form colleges in many ways; the tutorial system is based on specialist tutors, rather than every teacher playing a part (as happens elsewhere); every term the timetable is abandoned for a day so that every pupil can have a meeting with all their teachers to discuss results. New teachers are required (if they are not new to the profession) to demonstrate that the groups that they have taught over the past four years have achieved good results (not at all common elsewhere). The college runs a highly sophisticated and complete quality assessment and control system. Teachers are traditionally shy of measurement, but they have responded enthusiastically to a system which allows them to analyse the reasons for each student's performance, and take specific action to improve it, from half way through the first term. Staff and students enthusiastic and communicative, even in large groups, and clearly like the college and the way it is run.

Pastoral Care and Discipline: A sixth form college, so all the usual caveats, but the close monitoring of student's performance means that problems are picked up early and dealt with well. There are some whole-college assemblies (rare elsewhere).

Pupils and Parents: Locals, an open and chatty lot, half from the 'partner' schools,

others from a wide range of state and independent schools.

Entrance: Apply in January of the year you want to go: several open evenings are held towards the end of the month. First priority is given to students from 'partner' schools who have achieved five grade Cs, including maths and English, at GCSE; the remaining places (about 350 annually) are allocated competitively based on interview, school reports, mocks.

Exit: About 80 per cent to higher education, including 30 or so a year to Oxbridge.

Remarks: Outstanding state sixth-form college, with an ordinary lot of students in an ordinary town doing extraordinarily well. The brightest do succeed here, and all can expect to do markedly better than in the average state (or private) school.

GRESHAM'S SCHOOL

Holt, Norfolk NR25 6EA

Tel: *01263 713271* Fax: *01263 712028*

E-mail: Headmaster@greshams-bursar.demon.co.uk

Web: www.greshams.com

✦ Pupils: 305 boys, 220 girls (two-thirds board, one-third day) ✦ Ages: 13–18 ✦ Size of sixth form: 210 ✦ C of E ✦ Fee-paying

---

Head: Since 1991, Mr John Arkell MA (fifties), educated at Stowe and Selwyn College, Cambridge, where he read English (also rowed and acted). Served in the RN (as a submariner) post-school. Formerly head of Wrekin College, head of English at

Fettes and set up the junior school there (one of very few heads who manages to move effortlessly between prep and senior schools). Married with three grown-up children. Teaches English a third of timetable. An enthusiast, and fun with it, approachable, informal manner but decisive. Keeps a boat on the Mediterranean, keen on old cars, rides a motorbike. Tries to encourage pupils to be 'resourceful and energetic'. Commenting on the school's extraordinary and continuing success in producing winners, Mr Arkell says: 'I can't really explain it .... but from the start the school was quite forward-looking, there was almost no corporal punishment .... innovative in that maths and science were very strong, classics maybe less so .... there was a sense of freedom .... you could develop as an individual .... there was a certain magic.' Retiring July 2002.

Academic Matters: Exam results in general pleasing, particularly given intake. Outstanding maths department, with good results at both exam levels – and it's by far the most popular subject (more boys than girls studying it). Department headed by Mr Smithers, who gives potential staff a test ('some walk out'), never uses textbooks, insists that all six classes work in parallel which allows pupils to move up and down sets without affecting other subjects. 'Maths pinches a lot of prep time,' comment other staff. After maths, girls favour traditional girls' subjects such as English lit, French. Classics practically non-existent. A level choices not restricted to picking from columns (this is rare and wonderful) – only about three pupils per year have to forgo a first choice. Theatre studies on the menu, also Japanese. Head well aware that Norfolk has been called the graveyard for the ambitious and continues to inject new young staff. Nearly all pupils now take 10 GCSEs (and a few may take maths/French early). Good careers advice (former careers master developed the Oasis careers programme, now widely used in schools).

Games, Options, the Arts: Strong and keen sports. Very successful shooting (two Athelings currently), under Nigel Ball, England shooter; regular prize winners at Bisley. Sailing teams do well (fourth in the national dinghy finals two years ago). Traditionally strong cricket. Very strong rugby team coming up. Outward-boundish and outdoors pursuits generally 'easy to sell'. Some swim before breakfast daily. Tremendously well-supported D of E scheme – participants must also do CCF (army and RAF): an incredible 530 gold medals notched up in 25 years. New weights room/multigyms, rowing machines popular with both boys and girls. Sophisticated DT; computers widely used. A few do art at A level. Music is much encouraged, choral music especially, bumped up in recent years to a good standard. Theatre studies and drama gathering momentum – new theatre completed '98. The school also produces wonderful poetry.

Background and Atmosphere: Set in 170 acres of very beautiful Norfolk landscape, and most definitely out on a limb. Founded in 1555 by one Sir Thomas Gresham, turned into a public school at the turn of the century. Friendly, happy and fairly homely atmosphere, good relations between staff and pupils. 'They don't put us under any pressure', said a pupil. Lively social life within the school (a result of geographical isolation?) with sixth form club, lower and upper sixth divided (alcohol for the upper), and Dave's Diner, the tuck-shop bob-shop for the rest of the school, both open five nights a week, post-prep hot spots. Big School used for lunch time concerts, performances, assemblies etc with gold leaf Oxbridge honours boards (including Maclean of spy fame), and one recent addition, misspelt 'Oxen' (sadly now corrected). Very regular chapel (no complaints). Busy weekend programme (games, outdoor pursuits, including sailing). Boys' houses have maximum 8-bed dormitories, study bedrooms (shared at first) from 14/15 upwards. Three girls' houses (one with 84) extremely comfortably furnished. CFB = central feeding block, known as 'the trough', drearily functional. Twenties temporary thatched huts ('scruff shacks') are now listed buildings.

Pastoral Care and Discipline: One of the first public schools to appoint a counsellor. Well liked, well used. Sixth formers have sessions on stress. Gentle tightening up carries on (local pubs few and far between and can recognise Greshamite 'a mile off'). Laziness and non-participation frowned on (including by pupils).

Pupils and Parents: Delightful: open and friendly, easy, unpretentious, pleasantly self-confident, relatively unsophisticated boys and girls. By and large parents are farmers, solicitors, accountants etc. Mainly from East Anglia, some from London (especially those with Fishmonger connections), some from the Midlands. 25 ex-pats, 12 foreigners. Outstanding list of Old Boys includes Sir Stephen Spender, W H Auden, Benjamin Britten, Ben Nicholson, Sir Christopher Cockerell (inventor of the hovercraft), James Dyson (the bagless vacuum cleaner), Lord Reith, Hugh Johnson, Prof Alan Hodgkin – and lots more.

Entrance: From a large number of prep schools, especially Taverham Hall, Beeston, Town Close (Norwich), and fed by own prep school down the road (225 boys and girls, ages 7-13). Numbers swell at sixth form – approximately five leave post-GCSE, and 15 come in (increased interest at this level), via exam and interview.

Exit: 95 per cent take degree courses – all over the place, to universities new and old – Nottingham, Durham, Leeds, Cambridge, Bristol, not to mention the occasional one to Harper Adams, Loughborough, Bangor, UEA, UMIST etc. Business, economics and management currently favourite courses, followed by engineering (perennially popular here), medicine, and farming etc.

Money Matters: Generous scholarships from the Fishmongers' Company, with whom the school is associated (lots on the governing body), two specifically for children entering at 13+ from the state sector. Three art and music and one for drama, at both sixth and third forms. Internal scholarship to a pupil continuing into sixth form and showing most academic improvement. Sports scholarships at 13+ and 16+.

Remarks: Super new-style public school (now with girls and day pupils) still as always producing real winners in all walks of life. Well worth driving to the top of Norfolk to get to.

GUILDFORD HIGH SCHOOL

London Road, Guildford GU1 1SJ

TEL: *01483 561440* FAX *01483 306516*

E-MAIL: registrar@ghs.surrey.sch.uk

WEB: www.guildfordhigh.surrey.sch.uk

✦ PUPILS: 590 girls (plus 293 girls in Junior School) ✦ Ages: 11-18, junior school 4-11 ✦ Size of sixth form: 132 ✦ C of E ✦ Fee-paying

---

Head: Since 1991, Mrs Sue Singer, BA (fifties). GSA president elect, and co-chairs the GSA/HMC Education/Academic Policy Committee. An impressive profile – married young (abandoning plans for a medical career), studied for Open University maths degree while bringing up three children and running a play group. When youngest safely ensconced in school, she embarked on teaching career, with a short period at a comprehensive, followed by St Paul's Girls', where she became head of maths. Charming, undaunting, deservedly popular with girls and parents, she teaches a few periods a week as a means of getting to know the girls.

Academic Matters: Powerful academic school, with results to prove it. Head very keen to develop a European dimension: their lucky five-year-olds are taught German with their bilingual teacher, and, at the other end, sixth formers are strongly encouraged to maintain a language. Italian, French, German, Spanish, Russian, as well as Greek and Latin, on offer. Girls are very computer literate; CD-ROM facilities in the library include seven years' (indexed) *The Guardian* newspaper plus encyclopaedias: 'really useful,' commented one sixth former, 'we can research a lot here.' IT formally taught through junior school and senior school; RSA computer literacy and IT courses available in the senior school; extensive high speed network. Open access to all computers – before and after school, lunch time etc. Good range of software.

Excellent results on the whole – and so there should be, given intake. Maths, biology, chemistry, English and French are (in that order) most popular at A level – another witness to the astonishing rise of maths as a subject. Girls getting mostly As and Bs. One or two doing economics, history of art, theatre studies, and art and design, though this is not a school which revels in these subjects. GCSE – 99 per cent plus A*s -Cs – close to half of them A*s last year, good grief.

Games, Options, the Arts: Heated indoor pool, four acres of games fields two minutes from the school. Very successful lacrosse. Very strong music tradition, with bias towards contemporary music – regularly commissions professional composers. Ten large keyboards link up to computer software (for sequencing and editing) and lots of budding composers. Lots of drama and the occasional play/musical a co-operative effort with the Royal Grammar School. Debating taken very seriously. Girls very actively involved in running clubs – science popular. Highly qualified careers adviser.

Background and Atmosphere: Modest Victorian main building (walls no longer decorated pink though) reflecting general warmth and homeliness of the school. New buildings proliferate, including light and airy junior school, fine sixth form block, with other building works recently completed providing assembly and dining halls, music and drama studios, labs and a gym

Very happy atmosphere with strong feeling of everyone working at full stretch. School founded in 1888, among the eight schools governed by the Church Schools Company providing a 'sound education based on Christian principles'.

Pastoral Care and Discipline: Works well. Sixth formers assigned to each class – 'It's easier for them sometimes to talk to us about their problems'.

Pupils and Parents: Solidly upper-middle/middle class as might be expected in a city bursting with prosperity. Guildford, Cobham, Woking and Godalming the main catchment area. Celia Imrie and Julia Ormond are Old Girls.

Entrance: You need to be bright, although less pressure for places than equivalent London day schools. Nearly all junior school pupils go on to senior school. Around one-third of intake at 11+ from state sector. Excellent road access, and rail station opposite. A few girls enter at sixth form: via assessment, plus eight GCSEs including, 'normally', As in subjects chosen for A level.

Exit: Almost all to university with between 8 and 15 per cent to Oxbridge annually.

Money Matters: Had assisted places and potential parents will mourn their passing, but unlikely to rock this school. Academic and music scholarships, plus bursaries for the daughters of clergy. Limited number of Church Schools' assisted places at 11+.

Remarks: Successful, purposeful, well-resourced academic girls' day school in the heart of stockbroker belt. Hard to fault, but possibly too 'safe', with its remarkably homogeneous intake and many girls spending 13-14 years in the school. Onward and upward, at a fairly relentless pace.

HABERDASHERS' ASKE'S SCHOOL

Butterfly Lane, Elstree, Borehamwood, Hertfordshire WD6 3AF

Tel: *020 8266 1700* Fax: *020 8266 1800*

E-mail: office@habs.herts.sch.uk

Web: www.habs.herts.sch.uk/

✦ Pupils: 1,100 boys (plus prep school, with 209 boys); all day ✦ Ages: 11-18, Prep-School 7-11 ✦ Size of sixth form: 300 ✦ C of E ✦ Fee-paying

Head: Since 1996, Mr Jeremy Goulding MA (forties). Previously head of Prior Park, Bath; went to school in Nottinghamshire, then Magdalen College, Oxford, where he started to read classics, then switched to philosophy and theology. Keen sportsman, rowing in particular. Taught at Abingdon, and Shrewsbury. Married to Isobel, who also has a degree in philosophy and theology; four children.

Academic Matters: All pupils bright as beavers. Classes of around 20/25 at the youngest age, then 10/12 for A level. Remedial help on hand for mild dyslexia. Three separate sciences at GCSE (dual award not an option). The school is very computer literate and has £150k worth of Nimbus at last count: over 70 networked machines where each boy has his own space and can use it in his spare time. Increasing use of IT across the curriculum. CD-ROM machines in the library. Low turnover of staff, 'terrifically keen teaching', report many parents. Hugely successful in a wide range of national Brains Trust-type competitions. Consistent outstanding exam results, at GCSE and A level, particularly in maths. Huge bias to sciences – possibly not the most exciting place for arts people, though those that do it, do well; history, English and geography are popular, as is French.

Games, Options, the Arts: Beefy on the games field – rugby and hockey both strong (regular tours abroad), also some budding athletes and swimming. Water polo still very successful. Good games pitches, Astroturf, sports hall. Magnificent pottery and art department – though art and design hardly get a look in at exam level (one taking art at A level in '00). Lively drama – usually in conjunction with the Haberdashers' Girls', next door. See The Skylark magazine for an 'insight into a wealth of extra-curricular activities'. Masses of clubs and activities, thriving community service, CCF popular.

Background and Atmosphere: Founded in 1690 in Hoxton by the Worshipful Company of Haberdashers, who continue to play a powerful role in the governing body. Moved to the present site in 1961, a random selection of sixties flat-roofed class-rooms which cluster awkwardly round Lord Aldenham's pretty red-brick former home (which houses the admin offices and accommodation upstairs for young teach-ers). Charming grounds with rustic bridge leading towards the girls' school. Purposeful atmosphere pervades, with dreary uniform.

Pastoral Care and Discipline: Tight on disciplinary matters, a school where prefect power counts for something. Staff beady-eyed ('relaxed', says school) over to-ing and fro-ing with the girls' next door. Staff also watchful of bad language.

Pupils and Parents: Polyglot. Parents main-ly professionals (mothers as well as fathers); school busily fosters links with 'the home'.

School appeals to first-time buyers. Pupils come from an ever-increasing large catch-ment area: boys and girls are bussed in together (parking permits for the lucky few). Old Boys include Sir Leon Brittan, Nicholas Serota, Dennis Marks (English National Opera), Michael Green (Carlton TV), David Baddiel, Sacha Baron-Cohen (aka Ali-G), racing driver Damon Hill and the wonderful Brian Sewell.

Entrance: Tough, currently oversubscribed and highly selective. CE at 11+, many from Haberdashers' own prep school; about 25 at 13+. Some at sixth form – no specific entry requirements given.

Exit: Very small post-GCSE leakage (main-ly to sixth form colleges) – pupils expect and are expected to last the course. To uni-versity – with rare exceptions. Anything between 35 and 45 to Oxbridge annually.

Money Matters: Had 230 assisted places, but the Haberdashers are planning to replace these out of their own funds. Some small scholarships, plus 20-25 bursaries for those in financial need.

Remarks: Thorough and rock solid acade-mic day school for boys (but not for social climbers). Delivers the goods, and expects a great deal from its pupils.

JUNIOR SCHOOL: Haberdashers' Aske's Prep School. Tel: 020 8266 1700, Fax: 020 8266 1800. Head: Since 1997, Mrs Y M Mercer. A popular choice as a way in to the senior school, heavily oversubscribed, competitive entry exam plus report from previous school, and the (long) short-listed boys and their parents are called in for interview. Pleasant building, light, airy classrooms, lots of outdoor space. Very rare for boys at 11+ to be directed elsewhere.

HABERDASHERS' ASKE'S SCHOOL FOR GIRLS

Aldenham Road, Elstree, Hertfordshire
WD6 3BT

TEL: *020 8266 2300, Admissions 020 8266 2302*

FAX: *020 8266 2303*

E-MAIL: theschool@habsgirls.org.uk

WEB: www.habsgirls.org.uk

✦ PUPILS: 590 girls (plus own Junior School, with 300 girls); all day ✦ Ages: 11-18 ✦ Size of sixth form: 230 ✦ C of E ✦ Fee-paying

---

Head: Since 1991, Mrs Penelope Penney BA (fifties), educated at Chatelard, Switzerland, and Bristol University. Previously head at Putney High (five years) and head of Prendergast School, Catford (seven years). Head of English before that. Married to a 'management consultant cleric' (nice), three grown-up children. President GSA '94/'95, chairman GSA inspection committee. Believes learning should be fun and aims to produce 'confident not cocky girls, who are interesting and interested, with intellectual curiosity. People of integrity, who accept others' point of view'. Important to remember that 'we are educating future Europeans'. Very enthusiastic, 'has never been as happy'. A top-class head. Wants girls to have 'a go at things and be able to fail safely'. Has increased number of staff. 'It's a treat to teach girls like this in surroundings like these.'

Academic Matters: Very impressive, as you would expect of a highly selective academic school. Like its brother school, keen on maths and sciences (separate sciences at GCSE), also keen on English and languages. Set in maths and French from age twelve. Girls 'encouraged' to take two modern languages at GCSE, and can do Japanese and Modern Hebrew in sixth form. Two large computer labs with network and internet. CD-ROMs everywhere (two in library); computers in classrooms, and satellites in language labs; all girls have e-mail. Video conferencing and shared projects with partner schools in Europe via internet. No learning difficulties support.

Games, Options, the Arts: Lacrosse team 'strikes terror', loads of county and national players, regularly knocks the socks of schools far and wide. Otherwise netball, tennis, swimming, fencing, badminton, athletics, football, water polo. Some lovely art in smart music and art building opened '95 (but it still hardly exists at A level). Good sculpture and strong music. Girls can and do play everything, can have a go. No domestic activities – no domestic science, dressmaking or fabric design. D of E award. Masses of debating, regular champions. Several plays each year and some drama productions with the Haberdashers' boys next door. CDT good, with girls making serious model cars – for themselves.

Background and Atmosphere: Haberdashers' Company originally bequeathed money by Robert Aske in 1690, girls' school founded in 1901 and moved to present fifty-acre site adjoining Haberdashers' Boys' school in 1974. Two schools run separately joined by 'Passion Gates', much to-ing and fro-ing at lunch time for joint clubs (for everything). They also share the one hundred and nine buses which bring pupils from as far away as Luton, and all over Hertfordshire, North Finchley, Muswell

Hill, St John's Wood, Hampstead. Collection of somewhat stark airy redbrick buildings joined by upper and lower walkways; new buildings in '00, and more to come. Girls say they don't get lost; specialist classrooms in blocks. Fun drama workshop on top floor. Upper sixth can and do drive to school. Great feeling of peace and purposefulness. Lots of 'girl-inspired' charity involvement. Haberdashers' Company visit in robes on St Catherine's Day Deputation Day: lots of fun links with the Company.

Pastoral Care and Discipline: Form tutors take a tutorial lesson each week. 'Girls aim to please.' Not much naughtiness: 'two sets of really naughty girls since I arrived,' says the head. Massive leadership training: prefects are elected by peers, staff, and the years above and below; help with juniors and provide a 'listening ear'. Drugs policy commendably clear: 'any girl in possession of, or using any illegal substance whilst at school or under the school's jurisdiction or travelling to or from school must expect to be expelled'.

Pupils and Parents: Parents interested and very supportive – currently equipping music technology room, and provided seating in hall, organ in hall, second language lab etc. Strong ethnic mix – Jewish, Asian (and of those girls who take a 'gap' year, a large percentage of them go to Israel). A strong work ethic, parents regard education as a 'family commitment'.

Entrance: At 11 and 16. Seriously oversubscribed: five or six to one. Prospective pupils do a full-day exam in English, maths and verbal reasoning, the successful examinees are called back for interview and some are chosen. No priority for siblings. Everyone is looked at as an individual. Five GCSEs at A-C needed for entry to sixth form, and, for outside candidates (up to 20 per year), 'usually' As in their chosen A level subjects.

Exit: Tiny trickle leave after GCSE (logistic, financial, not many fail to make the grade), 99.9 per cent to university (eventually), with a record-breaking 34 Oxbridge offers for '00.

Money Matters: Haberdashers' Company provide generous special fund each year for real emergencies, and Aske Bursaries to replace some of the many assisted places. Entrance bursaries, and academic and music scholarships.

Remarks: V v good worthy academic girls' day school. An impressive oasis of excellence.

JUNIOR SCHOOL: Haberdashers' Aske's School for Girls, Lower School. Tel 020 8266 2400. Head: Mrs D Targett (who was previously deputy head here). 300 girls, ages 4-11, with fiercely competitive entry, via an hour-long playgroup, followed, for the successful, by an interview later. Attached to the main school building, and shares all the senior school facilities, but has its own science lab, computer lab, art room, music room and gym.

HABERDASHERS'
MONMOUTH SCHOOL FOR
GIRLS

Hereford Road, Monmouth

TEL: *01600 711100* FAX: *01600 711233*

E-MAIL: admissions@hmsg.gwent.sch.uk

WEB: www.habs-monmouth.org

✦ PUPILS: 574 girls; around 110 board (full and weekly), the rest day; plus own Junior School, with 108 girls ✦ Ages: 11-18, junior school 7-11 ✦ Size of sixth form: around 160 ✦ Christian foundation, non-denom ✦ Fee-paying

Head: Since 1997, Dr Brenda Despontin BA MA PhD (forties). Took over from Mrs Newman.

Academic Matters: Offers good range of subjects. English and languages traditionally strongest, science also popular. Latin from 12. Strong GCSE – nothing much below C, and good French. Excellent at A level – 70 per cent As and Bs, few stragglers. State of the art science building opened '94 – impressive labs and equipment. Extended sixth form provision by offering A level subjects at either Monmouth School or here. Boys come over for religious studies, Italian, classical studies; girls go to boys' school for Russian and history of art. Lots of male staff.

Games, Options, the Arts: School has keen drama and theatre studies A level. Strong on outward bound (with glorious Welsh hills on the doorstep), D of E, CCF (with Monmouth School.) School has five star sports hall, also gym and wonderful pool. Rowing introduced relatively recently, but already eights have won the Gold Medal at the National Championships and the Junior Eights at Henley. Keen lacrosse – UK under 15 champions, and South Wales and West of England champions in '00 – though sport shows no signs of dominating the place. Lots of jolly events – barbecues, fetes etc. School has excellent needlework department – imaginative and careful work in different areas (well, what would you expect from the Haberdashers?). Super art department and proper one-to-one teaching. School holds Eisteddfod, and has new music rehearsal rooms and recording equipment. Excellent careers department with own head of department.

Background and Atmosphere: School has the enormous strength of financial backing of the Haberdashers' Company. Founded in 1892, out of the bequest of a local merchant made good, William Jones, who had provided for foundation of the boys' school in 1614. Boys' school (Monmouth, with super head from St Paul's) has strong links – site is close by in the town, and lots of brother-sister links, as well as joining for academic and non-academic activities. May ball the social focal point. Recently redesigned maroon uniform. Healthy site with beautiful view over Monmouth, on hill, with some departments across the road (pedestrian flyover). Lots of walking about to get to different locations and good sense of space. Rather unexpected large panelled dining room. Boarding house just behind the main block – modern purpose-built and unremarkable, though rooms recently upgraded. Boarding numbers reduced with national trend/recession, though increasing numbers now flexi-boarding. Lots of weekend and evening activities for boarders. Sixth form have their own block with common room, and wear a different uniform.

Pastoral Care and Discipline: School tutors and heads of year; PSHE on the curriculum.

Pupils and Parents: Children of local business and professionals, one or two from Hong Kong. Broad social mix. Friendly. Very supportive parents.

Entrance: Mainly via the junior school. Also from local primaries and preps. Entry at 11+, 13+ and 16. Testing in March for entry to junior school in September.

Exit: To universities all over the UK, 10 per cent plus to Oxbridge, some to ex-polys, a few to art school, breadth of destinations a credit to careers department. Girls go on to professions, medicine, Services and the arts – even to Moscow Space School – and become engineers on oil tankers.

Money Matters: Owing to the strength of the Jones Foundation, school an absolute bargain (annual fees currently around £11,000 for boarding) and well worth considering. Academic scholarships of up to 50 per cent of fees at age 11 and into the sixth form. Some music scholarships. Had assisted places. Haberdashers very generous to parents in genuine need.

Remarks: Worth a look, particularly if money is tight.

HAILEYBURY

Hertford SG13 7NU

Tel: *01992 463353* Fax: *01992 407663*

E-mail: nickjg@haileybury.herts.sch.uk

Web: www.haileybury.herts.sch.uk

♦ Pupils: around 680. 100 in Lower School (50/50 boys/girls, 30 per cent board), 580 in main school (65/35 boys/girls – 'fully co-ed' says school) ♦ Ages: 11-13 lower school, 13–18 main school ♦ Size of sixth form: approx 250 ♦ C of E ♦ Fee-paying

---

Head (The Master): Since 1996, Mr Stuart Westley MA (Oxon), (fifties). Educated at Lancaster Royal Grammar School, and read law at Corpus Christi, Oxford; cricket blue, and a serious cricketer. Previously principal of King William's College, Isle of Man, and before that deputy head at Bristol Cathedral School, also taught at Framlingham. Married with one young daughter. Jolly looking. States that the key issue for him is the 'satisfaction and fulfilment of the individual in an environment he or she enjoys' – a nice emphasis. Keen that no single activity on the games and options front should be seen as more important or more valuable than another – but emphasises that the academic is more important than anything.

Academic Matters: Academically ambitious but not massively selective. Results very pleasing. Mathematics popular, well taught and produces good grades. Physics and German also currently strong, with good number of pupils taking history, economics, geography and politics. Sports studies available at A level, as are ancient history,

Arabic, Chinese, Japanese, Latin, religious studies, Russian, technology and theatre studies. Dual award science for all at GCSE – excellent results here.

Two members of staff provide assistance with EFL, one special needs specialist. IB on offer since 1999 – currently 25 participants, and rising.

Games, Options, the Arts: Art department continues to produce some stunning results and prizes – consistently good A level and GCSE results, with a good take up and altogether worth a detour. Successful public speakers and debaters and the school does well at The Hague Model United Nations. Other arts, including drama, also busy, and a small theatre, named after OH Alan Ayckbourn. A good range of musical activities, including concerts in London, and tours abroad. Famous for successful sportsmen (athletics, rackets, soccer, cricket). Indoor sports hall, CCF, D of E popular.

Background and Atmosphere: Amalgamated with Imperial Service College, housed in defunct East India College, the training ground for generations of boys destined to govern India. Fine and imposing William Wilkins architecture, college-style, laid out around vast quad – sympathetic additions hidden among trees. Houses are small – 50ish in each – and either new or refurbished. Very strong sense of community, partly, say pupils, because the whole school meets together four times a day (morning chapel and at meals in the domed dining hall which has an incredible echo). Cafeteria system – pupils eat at magnificent polished oak tables made by the Thompsons: Yorkshire carpenters who signed their work with a mouse. School shield is a crossed sword and anchor surmounting three flying hearts. School's wonderful windfall of £3 million (left in his will

by OH Russell Dore – good name for a rich OB, this – who made his money in the City) used to build lower school for 11-13 year olds (including mixed boarding house 'Highfields').

Pastoral Care and Discipline: At time of writing, few major disciplinary problems.

Pupils and Parents: About one-tenth children of OHs; some from overseas – including ex-pats; some parents in the Services (but fewer than previously). 20 or so Germans in the sixth form. New boys/girls decent sorts, conventional on the whole, mixed ability. Old Boys: Clement Attlee, most of the founding fathers of the Royal Air Force, including Sir John Slessor. Also Lord Oaksey, Neville Coghill x 2, Stirling Moss, Rex Whistler, Lord Allenby, Clive Martin, John McCarthy, 19 VCs and GCs.

Entrance: 48 per annum at 11+ into lower school, 70 or so into main school at 13+, 50ish at sixth form. Scholarship pupils come from an exotic selection of local schools and further afield (eg Craiglowan School, Perth, Dodderhill School, Droitwich). Entry at sixth form: six GCSEs at grade C or above, including four Bs and passes in English and maths.

Exit: Over 95 per cent to further education. Traditional careers now the Empire is no longer with us: banking, medicine, accountancy, estate management etc.

Money Matters: Academic scholarships, and for music, art, and 'all-rounders.' Bursaries for children of clergy, and others in need.

Remarks: On the up – most who look at it like what they see.

HALLIFORD SCHOOL

Russell Road, Shepperton, Middlesex TW17 9HX

TEL: *01932 223593* FAX: *01932 229781*

E-MAIL: registrar@halliford.ndirect.co.u

WEB: www.halliford.ndirect.co.uk

✦ PUPILS: 316 boys (10 of whom are girls in the sixth form), all day ✦ Ages: 11-18 ✦ Size of sixth form: 74 ✦ Non-denom ✦ Fee-paying

---

Head: Since 1984, John Crook BA (early sixties); wonderful, hands-on, charismatic head. Takes huge personal pride in the school, staff and pupils. Educated University College Cardiff (he's Welsh) and formerly in the state sector as deputy head, Heston Comprehensive. School has been turned around by him in terms of results, ethos and expectations. A real teacher who still takes his own classes, and regularly drops in on others. Four grown-up sons and daughters living away. Typically, grandchildren are listed on his CV as a hobby – he loves young people and it shows. Member of Richmond Shakespeare Society, oversees plenty of thespian activity in the school. Wife Mary teaches government and politics part-time, central figure; 'lovely person' says a parent, and goes on 'they are like a mother and father taking care of their children – what else could you want?'

Academic Matters: Nominally selective, remedial needs only turned away. Special needs catered for; dyslexia, Asperger's, ADHD. Peripatetic ESL teacher currently supports 5 boys. Optimum results from a mixed range of abilities: 86 per cent pass at A level – 60 per cent grades A-C. 85 per cent pass GCSE at grades A*-C.

First 2 years taught in 2 sets, maximum 25 per class. After this, put into three sets for all academic subjects, C sets have smallest size (12-14) and A and B sets are under 20 per teacher.

Staff on hand in lunch hours and after school to help strugglers prepared to put in extra effort. Latin compulsory till year 9, and popular Latin teachers – fair few boys go on to GCSE Latin, some to A level. Good number of academic and semi-vocational exam options. No one is ejected for GCSE results that don't measure up, retakes quite possible.

Majority of those in sixth form sat 3 A levels. Links with St David's (independent girls' school) for shared teaching of some A level subjects. Students bussed between the two sites in popular arrangement that allows each school to offer wider range of exam possibilities.

Games, Options, the Arts: Adequate but not overwhelming sports provision, although there is a flashy high tech gym to back up GCSE PE exam. Playing fields on site for rugby, football, cricket and athletics. Sport plays its part in ubiquitous emphasis on self-esteem and school morale. Plenty of passion for rugby at time of our visit. Unsporty pupils under no pressure; 'never forced to participate or made to feel that they're letting down their friends'. Reciprocal arrangement with Walton on Thames boat club (they get to use school gym) allows for rowing. School justly proud of Old Boy Steve Trapmore's Sydney Olympic Gold with the rowing eight.

Signs of a rich after-school life. Orchestra and solo music competition. Musical instruments taught on extra-curricular basis; trad flute, violin, piano etc rub alongside electric guitar and sax. Masses of drama, purpose-built 'theatre workshop' and new hall/theatre under construction. Head co-directs all year 8 pupils in annual excerpts from Shakespeare show; popular confidence building exercise. Plenty of other productions. Theatrical kids thrive; Perrier award winning comic Kim Noble is a venerated Old Boy. Loads of trips, field, recreational, theatre, music, museums etc.

Background and Atmosphere: Established 1921, the school moved to present 6-acre site in 1929. Listed semi-grand old house (now largely offices and staff rooms) and accompanying lodge (housing sixth form centre) make up the frontage. Behind this, outdoor access only to a cluster of modern classroom blocks, reasonably well equipped and maintained. Some IT and science labs are expensively kitted out with state of the art equipment. Difficult to comment further on the accommodation as, at time of visit, an ambitious building programme was well under way. A new hall/theatre/dining room and also sports hall and library supposed to be in place by September 2003.

Mutual respect in evidence and happy boys, good relationships with staff and each other; amazingly cosy/friendly vibe.

School prides itself on being both amenable and democratic as an institution. Boys get a school council for their ideas, annual guardian's meeting for parents to consult, elect and indeed become governors. Head just at the end of the phone and members of staff 'are easy to approach, they always have time' (commented a parent).

Pastoral Care and Discipline: A close eye is kept on the boys. There are three formal reports to parents each year and grade reviews (informal feedback) every half term. System of censures and merits enforces the rules and acknowledges effort and good behaviour. Disruption in the community is stamped on very quickly and, in worst cases, expulsion a reality not a threat. School will give pupils sacked from elsewhere a second chance and there have been some rewarding results. Uniformed until the sixth form, pupils are generally well presented.

Pupils and Parents: 'Nice mix of families, not all high living' cites a father. Good transport links (near Shepperton station) and a school bus ensure wide catchment area across Middlesex, Surrey and south west London. Fairly equal numbers arrive from state primaries and private preps. Growing tendency for boys to join mid-education, mid-term even; plenty of late joiners who were disappointed with things elsewhere.

Entrance: School's test and interview at any stage prior to GCSE ('no one needs to worry'). GCSE results speak for sixth form applicants; suggestion of C or above at GCSE to sit A level in given subject.

Exit: Careers classes across the curriculum and lots of help with further/higher education and employment decisions. Post GCSE, some leave for world of work and other further education institutions.

University in the main for A level leavers, recently 1 or even 2 to Oxbridge.

Money Matters: Scholarships (50 per cent of fees) 3 or 4 at 11+ for exceptional achievement in admissions exam. Two awards of £40 per term from year 9 until the end of school for academic excellence and ability in the creative arts. Sixth form bursary system rewards students for GCSE results, grades translate into points, points into pounds and discounts of up to £900 per term can be achieved. Innovative way of hanging on to the most able 16-year-olds.

Remarks: Hard not to like this lovely, inspirational, little school which seems to get the best out of the academic and the non-academic. Clearly not first choice for those after a hothouse academic environment, which is not to say that clever boys don't do well. Possible drawback – head's retirement some time in the next few years. His avowed intention is to run things awhile with the new buildings in place (they are due for completion September 2003). Let's hope that he is not as irreplaceable as he appears and that the school can find a successor in his mould.

HAMPTON SCHOOL

Hanworth Road, Hampton, Middlesex
TW12 3HD

TEL: *020 8979 5526* FAX: *020 8941 7368*

E-MAIL: admissions@hampton.richmond.sch.uk

WEB: www.hampton.richmond.sch.uk

✦ PUPILS: 1000 boys, all day ✦ Ages: 11-18
✦ Size of sixth form: 280 ✦ Inter-denom
✦ Fee-paying

Head: Since 1997, Mr Barry R Martin MA MBA FIMgt FRSA (forties). Educated at Kingston Grammar and St Catherine's College, Cambridge – read French, Russian and economics. Hockey blue and twelfth man for the Varsity cricket match. Previous post, principal of Liverpool College. Before that taught at Mill Hill, Repton, Caterham and Kingston, with three years out working for the Bank of England. Qualified ISC lead inspector and chief examiner in business

studies at A level to the Cambridge board. Competent, successful. Married with a young son and daughter. Took over from Mr Graham Able, who is now at Dulwich.

Academic Matters: Strong team of staff on the whole; many long-standing, mostly male. Most popular A level is maths, with results right across the scale – mostly A-Cs, but too many D–Us, and interestingly, some pupils confess to ALIS that doing maths was the wrong choice. Biology also popular with very successful results, and good number going on to biology courses at university. All boys study three sciences at GCSE. French and maths taken a year early by some – followed by AS level in the 5th year. Thirty or so pupils taking Latin at GCSE, but numbers dwindling to tiny handful at A level. General studies (examined) for all sixth formers. Computing much enlarged with second IT laboratory being built.

Games, Options, the Arts: Sports results wonderfully listed as though they were exam results, with flying colours for rowing – impressive array of victories (boat news and successes take up notably more space than any other sporting news in the school's annual report, a dry little booklet). New boathouse near the school, a joint project with Lady Eleanor Holles. Three times winners of the Triple since '85, and among top six rowing schools since early eighties. Rowing all the year round. Rugby and soccer both winter terms, and both do well. Saturday morning sports 'pretty keenly' attended. Long (one-and-a-half-hour) lunch break accommodates all sorts of extras, including music, drama etc, though some longer sessions are held after school for orchestra, CCF. Work experience taken seriously. Good (and early) careers advice.

Background and Atmosphere: Old grammar school foundation (1556), went fully private in 1975. Depressingly unaesthetic functional original buildings (1930s onwards) on what seemed to us like a main road, but the head describes as 'quiet, residential'. Multi-purpose building houses the sixth form common rooms, history department, lecture theatre and the cricket pavilion. Set on 27 acres of playing fields in comfortable suburbs, with Lady Eleanor Holles bang next door (qv). Well-equipped library; and all facilities – sports hall, technology department etc, in place, though some pupils have suggested that more quiet study space would help – atmosphere quite noisy. Senior students often use computers/word processors at home for project work. Purposeful get-on-with-it atmosphere. Some joint activities (drama, music, CCF and community service) with neighbouring girls' schools. Energetic programme of activities laid on by staff during the holidays.

Pastoral Care and Discipline: Beady eyes are kept on the boys. Lack of tolerance is considered the worst sin; persistent poor work etc, merits Saturday morning detentions (on average 5 a week, 'but more by the end of term').Year tutors run teams of form tutors, senior boys act as mentors to junior forms. Smoking: boys caught outside school get instant Saturday detention. Staff themselves are now limited to smoking in a 'fairly unattractive shack'. Four boys sacked for drugs three years ago. Long hair tolerated in sixth form, 'but a skinhead would be sent straight home.' Older pupil's main complaint is that 'the rules treat you like kids even though you're eighteen', and main wish is 'more freedom' – parents may find this reassuring.

Pupils and Parents: Courteous boys, solid and steady citizens from broadly differing social and economic backgrounds. School's insistence on boys' involvement in many aspects of education on offer produces balanced individuals. Pockets of energetically involved parents. Boys bus in (with Lady Eleanor Holles girls) from as far away as Woking, Windsor, Ascot. Old Boys: Olympic rowing gold medallists Jonathan and Greg Searle.

Entrance: Selective (top 20 per cent of ability band), and getting harder as more plump for day education, though results would suggest that it is well worth an average+ boy having a go at getting in. Head has firm policy of refusing to take boys at 11 from IAPS prep schools which run to 13. Between 250 and 300 sit for 100 places at 11+, approximately 130 for 50 places at 13+. Some (to fill leavers' places) come at sixth form – school hedges its bets slightly on entry requirements, but states 'grade A or B is virtually essential in any subject a boy intends to study at A level'.

Exit: Almost all to university (eventually, after gap or reapplication); one or two to the Forces; two or three to industry. Oxbridge entrants waver between 10 and 25. Southern/Midland universities preferred; followed by a wide variety of careers.

Money Matters: Surprisingly well-off foundation, though it doesn't look it (head says it is increasingly looking it). Various scholarships and bursaries at 11, 13 and 16.

Remarks: Solid powerful suburban boys' grammar school much sought after and appreciated in an area where there is not much choice.

HARROGATE LADIES'

COLLEGE (HLC)

Clarence Drive, Harrogate, North Yorkshire
HG1 2QG

TEL: *01423 504543* FAX: *01423 568893*

E-MAIL: enquire@hlc.org.uk

WEB: www.hlc.org.uk

✦ PUPILS: around 360 girls (200 board, 160 day) ✦ Ages: 10-18 ✦ Size of sixth form: around 120 ✦ C of E ✦ Fee-paying

---

Head (Principal): Since 1996, Dr Margaret Joan Hustler BSc PhD (forties), biochemist (her research degree was industry linked). Taught at Lady Eleanor Holles, Atherley School and comes here from being head at St Michael's, a missionary foundation in Surrey. Well liked by students and staff, accessible and interested. Set on continuing to improve the school; a good marketeer. Married, with eight children. Husband looks after the school's properties. Born and bred in Harrogate.

Academic Matters: Not an academic hothouse, but academic work is clearly taken seriously and examination results are solidly good, though perhaps not as consistent as they might be. Increasing emphasis on extras and non-mainstream subjects, such as design and drama; all girls follow a full general studies course (though few take the exam). Computer facilities excellent, and used by all; office skills (including touchtyping) taught to RSA 3 for all. Good and stimulating facilities, much celebration of pupils' work in the classrooms; good staff.

GCSE retakes offered as a matter of course; a serious business GNVQ course (aimed at achieving distinction and university entry) for those not suited to A level: you will not be chucked out to boost the league table position here.

Games, Options, the Arts: Sport is part of the essence of this school, keenly pursued by all, and lacrosse ('lackie') is queen of the sports: the girls have frequently been Northern champions. Golf course nearby, lots of tennis courts, 25-metre pool, riding, six badminton courts, enormous indoor general-purpose court (though outside sports would continue in a hailstorm) – good facilities and much used. Multigym, keen D of E (member of staff is head of northern scheme). Strong timetabled music, especially choir. Sensible use of local theatre, cinema, concerts and opera (Leeds). One or more of the LAMDA speech and drama examinations taken by most. Flourishing Ham Radio station (call sign GX0HCA), run by infectiously enthusiastic master; contact regularly made with 52 varieties of country; historic triumph was a hook-up with the Mir space station. Subaqua, windsurfing and ski trips now on the extra-curricular menu. Chocolate society (please lick your fingers before leaving). Two weeks' work experience for all. Art could do better.

Background and Atmosphere: School founded 1893 on a nearby site. One of the 'Allied Schools' (though this does not appear to mean very much today). Present premises akin to seaside hotel with mock Tudor beams and gables. Being in Harrogate, as opposed to isolated in the country, is one of the school's principal attractions to its inhabitants. Houses neat and well appointed (notably better than other schools locally), common rooms focused round the telly with easy chairs. Excellent new sixth form centre. Friendly comfortable feel, not smart or snobbish or overtly feminist, but you have to be a joiner-in. All ages mix freely, and great efforts are made to ensure that year-groups do not disintegrate into cliques. C of E (including the great hymns) in small doses for all without exception. Weekly boarding as well as 'day' and full boarding, but still very much a boarding school and the weekends are just packed.

Pastoral Care and Discipline: Manners strictly monitored. At 16+ girls are allowed out one night a week – 10 minutes' walk to town centre. There are limited links with Ashville and Leeds Grammar for controlled exposure to boys. Drugs and similar problems are rare and are treated with firmness, but head has discretion.

Pupils and Parents: Many from Harrogate and Leeds; number of boarders from overseas, including Hong Kong, Saudi Arabia. Buddhists, Jews and Muslims in the school. Solidly middle class. Strong OG network, including Anne McIntosh MP and Jenny Savill (author).

Entrance: Own entrance exam for the 10-year-olds and above, plus previous head's report and interview.

Exit: 95 per cent to degree courses. Two to five to Oxbridge, otherwise to a very widespread selection of universities including London, ex-polys, even some to universities overseas (eg Cornell, Johns Hopkins), and to Lucie Clayton.

Money Matters: Bursaries at 11 or 12 of up to one-third of fees (which are not unreasonable), plus two or three at sixth form. Discounts for siblings. Two music scholarships of up to one-third of fees. To judge from the recent spate of capital works, the school is not without financial resources.

Remarks: An altogether lovely school for unpretentious, bright and gamesy girls. Not currently a fashionable choice but could well be so again.

HARROW SCHOOL
Middlesex HA1 3HW

TEL: *020 8872 8007* FAX: *020 8872 8012*

E-MAIL: admissions@harrowschool.org.uk

WEB: www.harrowschool.org.uk

◆ PUPILS: 794 boys (all board) ◆ Ages: 12-18 ◆ Size of sixth form: 327 ◆ C of E (but over 100 RCs) ◆ Fee-paying

Head: Since 1999, Mr Barnaby Lenon BA PGCE (mid forties). Educated at Eltham College, Oxford (read geography), and Cambridge (PGCE). Taught at Sherborne, Eton (for thirteen years), Highgate (deputy head) and then Trinity Croydon, where he was head from '95 – 'meteoric rise' said another head. Super – a doer and a shaker, bouncy, articulate. Desert travel a keen interest. Succeeded Mr Nicholas Bomford, head since 1991.

Academic Matters: Takes a wide spectrum of boys and, as far as we can see, does well by all levels of ability. All boys now taking a minimum of 10 GCSEs, and all boys must take one science subject. Steady teaching, staff 90 per cent male. Staff all accommodated on the Hill – no wonder they like to work here. 'But the trouble is,' said a parent, whose sons' schooling spans two decades, 'they tend not to move, so there is dead wood.' 10 per cent have moved on, though, in the new head's first year. There are seven new heads of department, also some dynamic young right-on masters. Eight or nine sets per subject (generally), with larger numbers in top sets than lower sets; groups of up to 14 for A levels. Under the new system, all boys will take 4 ASs, some 5. Average points per A level at last count 7.9 (ie good, considering mixed intake), average total, 26.0 (ditto), good value-added scores. Popularity stakes: maths, English, chemistry, history, economics, biology.

Not historically the place for dyslexics or EFL, but full-time special needs co-ordinator from Jan '99. Harrow runs v popular summer schools for foreigners.

Games, Options, the Arts: Rugby no longer trouncing everyone for miles around – despite presence of former England coach Roger Uttley. Traditionally and actually very strong on all main games (including Harrow football) and keen, with a great deal of house competition and special ties for everything. 'Competitive to the eyeballs,' commented a visiting parent. One of the last two Lord's cricket schools. Smart indoor sports complex with magnificent 'ducker' (pool). 'Too much emphasis on sports,' from several boys (plus ça change). Popular CCF, with outstandingly successful Royal Marine section, the rifle corps winning the Pringle Competition in six out of the last seven years. Extremely lively drama – given a boost now by the new Ryan Theatre. All manner of productions constantly on the go, occasionally with girls from North London Collegiate. The Speech Room (Burgess in a restrained mode) is annually transformed into Globe Theatre replica for the Shakespeare production. Good art department (with an artist in residence). Music has 'transformed' over the last five or six years and is now producing notable work eg Purcell's Dido and Aeneas, the piano trio played in the final of the National Schools' Chamber Music Competition at St John's, Smith Square, and – a recent innovation – the competition for singing self-accompanied on the guitar. An enormous number of extras in other areas (this is a rich school), including the farm, now a dairy farm, but no longer providing milk for the school.

Background and Atmosphere: Founded in 1572 by John Lyon; on a site of more than 300 acres on the Hill. The chapel by Gilbert Scott is very fine. Altogether, this is an island of dignity and elegance in a sea of hideous suburbia. Oldest buildings date from 17th century, collegiate buildings spread along either side of the High Street, worlds away from nearby Betjeman-esque. Very fine collection of antiquities in the museum and fine watercolours (mostly 19th century). The quality of modern buildings is outstanding and should be seen by other schools for non-carbuncular possibilities. The older teaching blocks have been mostly redesigned inside to give spacious and light classrooms.

Magnificent uniform with 'bluers' (blue jackets), braid, straw hats, tail coats on Sundays, not to mention top hats and sticks for monitors – an inspiration for Coco Chanel, who had an Old Harrovian lover. Pecking order keenly felt by boys – the boarding houses themselves have an ancient order – smart, sporty etc. Some complaints that 'innovative thinking' – eg students' union, any mildly left-wing thinking – is 'deeply frowned on by the establishment'. Very male atmosphere often remarked on by visiting mothers; traditional and with a keen entrepreneurial streak. Exeats every three weeks, more earned by sixth formers for good work. Eleventh and last house finally refurbished at giant cost. Most boys share double rooms for the first two years, then single rooms – no dormitories.

NB The Clarendon Committee of the 19th century found the school was not sticking to its charter of educating 'the people of Harrow', so the school set up a whole new school for them, the John Lyon School, out of endowment funds – hence has a good right to call itself a charity. Today, the John Lyon School is a successful day school for boys aged 10-18 (515 of them, with 130+ in the sixth form) with steady if not startling results. Tel 020 8872 8400.

MARKETING NOTE: the school has set up an international school in Bangkok – object of much interest.

Pastoral Care and Discipline: Several boys sacked for drugs offences in '97 – harrowing, but comfortingly speedy action for parents not involved. Being off the Hill without written permission could mean instant dismissal (and usually accounts for the loss of one or two boys per year), 'but most of them don't take advantage of the temptation.' Stiff anti-drugs ruling: drug testing on pupils suspected of taking illegal substances recently introduced ('96). Sporadic reports of bullying continue to reach us – head says 'strong anti-bullying policy in place now.' Some antagonism between school and locals. One of those schools where housemasters have tremendous power (tenure of housemastering – 12 years). Outstandingly good 'way of life' course initiated by the previous head, who was an innovator in this field, run with girls from three local schools, with small groups discussing/reflecting on 'their experience of the environment, soci-

ety, ourselves and God' – under guidance of specially trained counsellors. School also has consultant psychiatrist on call. School suffered damaging publicity in '98 over a geography master (now ex-) pocketing expedition funds.

Pupils and Parents: One of the rare schools that can truthfully claim to be international. Long tradition of exotic foreigners, including maharajas and royalty. Lots from Scotland and Ireland. Loads of fiercely loyal Old Harrovian families. 12+ Jewish (rabbi comes in), 110+ RCs (full-time chaplain). Strong links with trade, old landed and aristocratic families, also social climbers and new money. Polite ('though the cad element lingers,' says a distressed mother.) Famous Old Boys: a very long and distinguished list, both old and new, including seven prime ministers (including Winston Churchill and Stanley Baldwin), Byron, Peel, Trollope, Palmerston, Galsworthy, Terence Rattigan, the wonderful King Hussein of Jordan, the Nizam of Hydrabad, the Duke of Westminster, Evelyn de Rothschild. Also the acting Fox brothers. Not to mention Julian Metcalfe (founder of Prét a Manger foodie joints), Bill Deedes, Robin Butler, Sir Charles Guthrie, Sir Peter de la Billiere, Alain de Botton, Julian Barrow, Richard Curtis.

Entrance: Names down early – at a particular house. 'Housemasters are kings of their castles in this area,' comments the head. 55 (formerly 50) per cent pass mark at CE. Currently full, and lists healthy.

Exit: A gap year is popular. All over the shop to universities Bristol, Edinburgh, Newcastle particularly popular, also Durham, Oxford Brookes, Southampton, Oxbridge (25-ish) and a dozen or so to American universities. Slight bias to arts.

Making money matters less in the nineties than in the previous decade, thinks the head.

Money Matters: 20 scholarships per year. 'Everyone thinks we're well endowed, but we're not well endowed,' emphasises the head. We would say: all is relative. The school does indeed appear to be rich (and has lots of very rich Old Boys) and definitely comfortable, sense of quality, extremely well kept (freshly painted and no ugly rubbish bins or lurking crisp packets). School had a huge unbreakable fund rolling up for the upkeep of the road between Harrow and London – a task now undertaken by others; the income now goes to local charities.

Remarks: One of the country's most famous public schools, which has never quite regained the top slot following a downslide some years back, but still very strong and consistently breeding an impressive roll call of winners in all sorts of fields. Has not (hurrah hurrah) chased league table success at the price of offering places to ordinary boys.

HEADINGTON SCHOOL
Oxford OX3 7TD

TEL: *01865 759 113* FAX: *01865 760268*

E-MAIL: admissions@headington.org

WEB: www.headington.org

✦ PUPILS: around 600 girls in Senior School. Plus 230 in Junior School. Mainly day, but 200 board, weekly and full, from age 11 (occasional sisters at 9)
✦ Ages: 11-18, junior school 3-11
✦ Size of sixth form: 180 ✦ C of E
✦ Fee-paying

Head: Since 1996, Mrs Hilary Fender BA (early fifties), educated at the Marist Convent, Devon and Exeter University, where she read history, followed by King's College, London. Married with one son. Previously head of Godolphin School, Salisbury – a great catch. Has a nice sense of humour. Very pro single-sex education, says she 'wants girls to have full lives, to realise they have choices – and to go for it.' Parents v keen on her, say she is putting zip into the place. Occasionally writes for *The Times*.

Academic Matters: Traditional teaching, and good results, though swings a bit from year to year. A level results back on form however, with Eng. lit. (perennially popular here) and theatre studies (less so) the only subjects showing more than one or two marks below C. Chemistry, biology, geography and maths are the four top favourites here at A level. The range of A level subjects on offer has been broadened recently with the introduction of politics, economics, history of art, environmental science and theatre studies, and with the advent of the new curriculum law, ethics and psychology (the latter a sell-out). Girls will take four or five ASs, followed by three A2s. Pupils doing 'Chinese' A level and GCSE – mostly getting A*s and As, which all helps with the league tables. Greek non-existent, alas. GNVQ in business studies – pupils pass with flying colours. Separate sciences or dual award science course at GCSE. IT taken by most girls at GCSE. Science very strong, very well taught and deservedly popular. Modern languages alive and well at GCSE, as is home economics, and almost everyone is doing Information Systems. Learning support from qualified visiting staff, provided as and when. ESL properly provided by specialist staff – lessons on rotation from certain timetabled lessons. In the two GCSE years, the normal English lessons are taught by specialist ESL teachers.

Games, Options, the Arts: Heavy on sporting opportunities, with high standards – county champions regularly in several sports, and girls often selected for county teams – sailing, judo, riding, hockey, fencing, rowing. The boat club goes from strength to strength – most years several girls row for England or GB (eight in 2000). New(ish) sports hall, lovely indoor swimming pool. Hundreds of girls do music – choir, chamber orchestra, chamber choir (tours abroad), groups galore, operatic production. Not ashamed of doing cookery (something to do with the scientific mind, perhaps) and does it well. Art, once the poor relation, is getting/has got a state of the art new building, an artist in residence, and a new head of art; numbers taking art exams have mushroomed as a result. Exceptionally strong D of E, though less so than two years ago when they were going for 30 gold, 68 silver and 120 bronze. Two Young Enterprise groups (have been county prizewinners) and a 'very active' BAYS (British Association of Young Scientists).

Background and Atmosphere: Founded 1915 (note the year – what a time to choose) by a group of Church of England members with faith in the future who 'saw that there was a need in Oxford for a combined day and boarding school where girls could grow up in a Christian atmosphere ... sense of service ... fulfil ...' Generous amount of space, given position, ie bang on (though set back from) the main road, opposite Oxford Brookes. Original Queen Anne style building quite mellow, some new buildings very functional, particularly some boarding houses, though teddies, posters etc, are much in evidence. Further new buildings in the offing for classrooms, theatre, music.

One particularly glorious boarding house – Davenport for girls up to 13 (there are now three houses in all) – looking on to mellow garden, run by dedicated staff, formerly a family home, with friendly feel, a loo called Everest, and cosy dormitories with names like Owl, Squirrel etc, and, when we visited, a real hedgehog hibernating in a cubbyhole in the basement (school reports that its current whereabouts is unknown). Also smart new(ish) kitchens (following Children Act). Separate sixth form boarding house (Celia Marsh House) in which girls can and do do their own thing – particularly in dress – pedal-pushers, flares and appliquéd cardigans. Weekly boarding – wistful looks as parents arrive to whisk off the lucky ones. A day school with boarders, rather than vice versa, though several day girls have converted to boarding since the new house opened. Lots of activities – car maintenance, aromatherapy, as well as socialising with local boys' schools.

Pastoral Care and Discipline: Good at TLC and works diligently to foster it. Second deputy head with specific responsibility for pastoral care. Mrs Fender operates an 'open door' policy – at specific times pupils can and do walk in to discuss problems (the head's study conveniently placed for this). School council, with members from each form, meet regularly. Lovely contract ensures that girls using the internet/e-mail must use it for work or for personal correspondence and the latter 'must remain decent' – shades of contracts to come.

Pupils and Parents: Bright daughters of Oxford academics and professionals, Hong Kong contingent all the way up, Brunei and Malaysian government scholars, Nigerians (one second-generation), Pacific Rim plus 'girls from Europe' in the sixth form. Most famous OG is Christina Onassis. Also Baroness Young; the moderator of the movement of the ordination of women, Olympic long jumper Yinka Idowu, and Julia Somerville (newscaster).

Entrance: Broader ability range than Oxford High, particularly on boarding front. Entry into senior school at 11+, 12+ and 13+ by spring CE; entry at 14+ and into sixth form by getting at least six GCSEs grades A-C, with As or Bs in proposed A level subjects, plus interview. (Overseas sixth form candidates take school's own exam in the A level subjects of their choice). Internal candidates are 'expected' to get five A-Cs, but would not be forced to leave if school satisfied they could cope with the courses. (Bravo.)

Exit: To wide range of practical university and other courses, including pharmacy, accountancy, biotechnology, business studies etc, as well as law, philosophy, veterinary science, equine studies, medicine etc.

Money Matters: Was left a cool £1.2 million in '98 by Celia Marsh, the wonderful old ex-senior mistress after whom the sixth form house was named – she died in '97 aged 95. RIP. The income from her legacy is to be used for awards at 11+ and sixth form, based broadly and mostly on the assisted place criteria of academic and financial need. Small proportion of fee income will still go on scholarships. Fees kept 'reasonable' on founders' wishes. School had just started assisted places, but will not notice their passing.

Remarks: One of Oxford's two academic girls' day schools. Broader based than Oxford High, extremely appealing and now looks set to match it in popularity.

JUNIOR SCHOOL: Tel: 01865 759 400 Fax: 01865 761 774. Head: Since 1998, Mrs Rachel Faulkner, who was previously head of E Block at The Dragon School. Took over after the long reign of Mrs Boon. Across the road from the main school in a Victorian house set in four acres (mature trees and Wendy house). Boarding for little girls is in the main school boarding houses. New nursery class opened '97.

HEATHFIELD SCHOOL

Ascot, Berkshire SL5 8BQ

TEL: *01344 898 342* FAX: *01344 890689*

E-MAIL: info@heathfield.ascot.sch.uk

WEB: www.heathfield.ascot.sch.uk

✦ PUPILS: 225 girls; all boarders ✦ Ages: 11-18 ✦ Size of sixth form: 65. NB this can fluctuate. ✦ C of E ✦ Fee-paying

Head: Since 1992, Mrs Julia Benammar BA M es Lettres (forties). Educated in Manchester and at Leeds University, followed by a masters degree in France. Her former post was housemistress at Wellington. A neat, self-contained, direct person, and a good organiser. Also appears to have a talent for finding good staff. Mrs Benammar teaches the top and bottom forms.

Academic Matters: Consistently good GCSE results. A levels looking excellent – far better than they did a few years ago – though with such tiny numbers taking each subject it is impossible to generalise and next year the profile may change again. English and history are consistently the most popular A level subjects; the sciences, maths, art and theatre studies can feature too. Rich mix of subjects however: the school – unusually – can offer almost any subject you want at A level in almost any combination, at no extra cost. This results in very small classes (often ones and twos – which some might consider too small) at A level, getting more or less individual attention, but not being limited in choice. Enthusiastic, competent and highly dedicated staff who, says Mrs Benammar, have to turn their hand to any number of different things in the school.

Computer lessons are timetabled – Apple Macs for eg word processing and design, PCs for scientific applications, e-mail, the web and key skills. Separate sciences at GCSE. General studies and key skills now part of the A level curriculum, lots are doing keyboarding applications at GCSE (with good results) and PSE is timetabled for all. Years are divided first into two forms – A and alpha (max 18 to a form here), then into three in some subjects. Some excellent language staff, and language students have, among other things, work experience organised for them – but surprisingly few taking French at A level. School claims 'very little in place' for dyslexia etc, and girls whose first language is not English must be able to join in ordinary lessons.

Games, Options, the Arts: This is not traditionally a gamesy school, but in a quiet way does rather well. The games pitches are in constant use, with periods timetabled throughout the day, which gives a nice feeling of variety. Head of PE is a former England lacrosse player – girls regularly make the county teams. Tennis courts in constant use, with coaches, and has a sports hall which would be the envy of many bigger schools.

Art is excellent – particularly impressive, and again, most unusual, is the art department's success in fostering totally different styles – from stylised draughtsmanship to embryonic post-modernism. Pottery is also good. The art room is constantly open – the school feels it is therapeutic to be able to come and potter (or artter) in spare moments (littles must have someone to supervise, usually there is someone about). Well patronised and good results at A level.

Background and Atmosphere: Founded

by educationalist Miss Eleanor Beatrice Wyatt in London (in what is now Queen's Gate School – note Heathfield house names 'Queen's' and 'Gate') in the 19th century, moved in 1899 to this elegant Georgian house in a most pleasant green site surrounded by rhododendrons. Behind the rhodies is a busy road, and not far off, Ascot race course. The original house now has any number of additions, but the whole is still pleasant, and the overall impression is one of light, with windows everywhere. Bedrooms are charming – with flower names (Buttercup etc) for the younger pupils, and literary giants for the older girls – sixth form decor a mile ahead of the average. It feels very uninstitutional. Younger children are in the Georgian house (above the library, where their leaps from bunk to floor can be heard by passing staff...) The school operates a system of making the first year sixth prefects responsible for 'running' the school, so that in the upper sixth they shed their community responsibilities along with their uniform and migrate to a modern brick self-contained sixth form house. Chapel is still very much at the centre of the school, as decreed by Miss Wyatt, and the school motto: 'the merit of one is the honour of all' with it, along with a slightly more dubious little motto attached to a particular school prize – 'Power through control' ('they meant self control, of course,' says Mrs Benammar). All the girls are boarders (no exceptions to this), and the difference in atmosphere between this and a day/boarding mix is very noticeable. Exeats are kept to one on each side of half term – from Friday afternoon to Sunday evenings, plus two Saturdays or Sundays out. Distinguishing mark of the Heathfield pupil is the huge number of badges for games etc pinned on their navy sweaters, until some end up looking like Chelsea pensioners on

Remembrance Sunday. The school mag has a nice section for hatches, matches and despatches, pride of place going to matches. Centenary in '99 with an indoor swimming pool opened in celebration.

Pastoral Care and Discipline: Has its moments of excitement, but behaviour generally is good and responsible. Each senior pupil has a tutor for both academic and personal matters.

Pupils and Parents: Well-mannered, charming, interesting girls, many from London and roundabout, also ex-pats and one or two bilinguals. As ever a nice place for making friends. A good place to become a big fish in a small pond – excellent for self-confidence. OGs energetic and enterprising.

Entrance: School does its own selective test in October for the following September. Also via CE at 11+ (most), 12+ and 13+. Girls come from London preps such as Garden House, also a clutch from Godstowe. Also entry at sixth form – 7 GCSEs grade C, including B grades in chosen subjects, plus interview etc. If GCSEs not taken, entry tests.

Exit: Large numbers to the current smart choices – Edinburgh, Bristol, Newcastle and Durham, with a clutch going to exciting places overseas, the occasional scientist to Oxbridge, and one or two to arts foundation courses – a very impressive list of destinations. The humanities predominate.

Money Matters: Fees are not small, but you get very good value (we cannot see how the sixth form can even break even). The school operates a flexible scholarship scheme – for academic, for music, and would-be scholars are also invited to bring art portfolios. Around 5 per cent of fee income goes on scholarships, and the school also has the capacity to 'carry' an existing parent in a case of hardship.

Remarks: Super little up-market establishment offering at sixth form the staff and flexibility of a crammer, with the pastoral care and sense of community of a school – a place where you get the best of both these worlds. Showing real spark.

THE HENRIETTA BARNETT SCHOOL

Central Square, Hampstead Garden Suburb, London NW11 7BN

TEL: *020 8458 8999* FAX: *020 8455 8900*

E-MAIL: hbs_school@btconnect.com

WEB: members.aol.com/hbsschool

✦ PUPILS: 700 girls; all day ✦ Ages: 11–18
✦ Size of sixth form: 230 ✦ Non-denom
✦ Voluntary-aided state grammar school

Head: Since 2000, Mrs Jacquelyn Paine MA MA MBA PGCE. Took over from Mrs Jane de Swiet.

Academic Matters: Excellent. Better GCSE results than the eight fee-paying schools in the area, and impressive A levels too – 'and so they jolly well should be', points out a parent. (Average 8.1 points per A level subject at last count, and 24.4 average in total) Dual award GCSE science for all, plus sprinkling of exotic languages, reflecting ethnic intake. Sciences currently popular A level choices, as are Eng lit and maths. Large classes, up to 31 pupils in key stage 3, up to 25 at GCSE, cramped into sardine-tin space. Budget extremely tight due to highly experienced (ie higher-income) staff – a Catch-22 situation – leaving the head without the financial leeway to appoint additional teachers to relieve pressure (the right decision in the light of recent research). Teaching remarkably strong right across the board. Pupils have commented there was 'not enough academic guidance'. One of the few state schools to offer Greek at GCSE and A level, and all pupils study French, German and Latin. Increased interest in science, perhaps because now taught as a double award to GCSE, and lots of girls head towards medicine.

Games, Options, the Arts: Though sporting options have much improved over recent years, sport is still relatively modest. Karate, canoeing, sailing, squash as well as the usual girls' options. Possibly not enough use is made of the capital's art galleries, theatres, debating forums etc – though the head queries this.

Background and Atmosphere: Founded by the redoubtable Henrietta Barnett as part of her overall vision for Hampstead Garden Suburb. Safe, secure, high expectations,' pressure from parents to do well'. Elegant exterior, building a fine example of Lutyens, with Bigwood House (which has a friendly feel) for the 11-13 year-olds, facing the main school across a pleasant green square. Main school is rather forbidding (but mercifully rescued from terminal gloom by light streaming through beautifully proportioned windows). Redecoration work inside – desperately needed – has taken place, 'at last.' Overstretched teachers work all hours under difficult conditions – short of space etc, and still manage to do an outstanding job. 'They are amazing,' said one former pupil, 'better than my university teachers.' Computers now much more in evidence than previously.

Pastoral Care and Discipline: Excellent pastoral care overseen by the pastoral team. Personal, social and health education for all now well established.

Pupils and Parents: The usual multi-cultural city mix with a fairly representative North London Jewish contingent. Only a minority of parents could have afforded to pay for a private academic education. 'Most would not have the opportunity of an academic education if they didn't come here,' said a father. Girls are modest, unassuming – and very aware of their good fortune.

Entrance: By exam and two entrance tests. Ferociously competitive. (One bright north London girl for example recently got offered places at St Paul's, North London Collegiate and South Hampstead High – but not Henrietta Barnet.) Up to 3,000 attend open days and applicants for admission not far short of the 1,000 mark. School is looking for innate intelligence, potential – 'sparky intelligence shines out,' according to the head. She is emphatic that parents do their children no favours in opting for cramming.

Exit: A few girls leave post GCSE – and some return again after discovering that the grass at sixth form colleges is not so green. Virtually all go on to higher education – to top universities, occasionally to ex-polys.

Money Matters: Voluntary aided state grammar. The Department of Education and the Borough of Barnet 'really have no excuse to starve the school – which doubles as an Evening Institute – of funds and over-pack the classrooms,' commented a parent. A field centre near Shaftesbury is maintained with parental help.

Remarks: Undoubtedly one of the top state schools in the country: tightly organised academic girls' school, though with little attention paid to expanding pupils' social horizons. Relentlessly hard work, increasingly high expectations.

HIGHGATE SCHOOL

North Road, Highgate, London N6 4AY

TEL: *020 8340 1524* FAX: *020 8340 7674*

E-MAIL: office@highgateschool.org.uk

WEB: www.highgateschool.org.uk

✦ PUPILS: 600 boys (in Senior School; Junior School – see separate entry); all day ✦ Ages: 13-18 ✦ Size of sixth form: 200 ✦ C of E ✦ Fee-paying

Head: Since 1989, Mr Richard Kennedy MA (forties). Educated at Charterhouse and read maths and philosophy at New College, Oxford; taught at Shrewsbury, Westminster and was deputy head of Bishop's Stortford. Enthusiastic, ambitious; represented GB at athletics, musician (sings with the Academy of St Martin-in-the-Fields), one of the few heads whose wife (a very high-powered civil engineer, awarded the OBE in 1995) has her separate entry in Who's Who. Two sons. Comments: 'We have come a long way in the last ten years and I'm pleased with the improved academic standards. There is still more that I want to do to develop the facilities.' Governor of Wycombe Abbey.

Academic Matters: Can attract top-quality staff by dint of offering super des. res. accommodation, eg 170 people applied for deputy head's post (sensitive subject this, though, as not all get the perk). Academically good all round, and results good given the broad intake. The school can – and does – cope with the bright ,who flourish here, 'though we would really prefer our son to have more competition,' said the ambitious father of one high-flyer. The average, the screwballs and the slower learners also feel at home. Some remedial help. 'Maximise potential,' is one of the head's favourite phrases.

Good GCSE results. A level results show a bias to A grades, and not too many Ds and Es given the intake. Maths and science (physics especially) are traditionally the most popular subjects, but economics has now overtaken all but maths. Dual award science at GCSE. Good general studies at sixth form. Average class size 22, lower end of school, dropping to around ten at A level.

Games, Options, the Arts: Strong games reputation; often national champions at Eton fives – 18 fives courts, is this a school record? Keen cricket, with masterclass. Successful athletics; splendid sports centre. Also strong music: Channing girls collaborate sometimes, also on the drama front, another lively area. Lunchtime activities include large number of societies (environmental, car mechanics, Jewish Circle), also urban survival course for older boys (how to fill in tax forms, use a launderette), CCF, D of E; field centre in Snowdonia. Interesting list of visiting speakers. Good track record of raising money for charities. The boys are very into computers and most have their own.

Background and Atmosphere: Founded 1565. Fine site between Highgate and Kenwood, buildings spread over generous acreage and covering many architectural dates and hotch-potch of styles – surprising and pleasing patches of greenery and space, main block on main thoroughfare and across the road (via subterranean passage), another teaching block with astonishing view over London. Lovely setting, up above the fumes – one of the school's trump cards. Feels almost like a country public school.

Pastoral Care and Discipline: House masters visit boys' homes before they come. House system arranged by geography, eg Westgate for boys whose families live west of the school. Houses vertically streamed like boarding schools, and the 'pastoral person' is the housemaster; almost all staff are 'house tutors'. The sixth form tutors know all there is to be known on getting on to the next stage. Has occasionally caused anguish among the locals due to rowdy behaviour in Highgate village.

Pupils and Parents: Strong on ethnic minorities – cheerful mix of class and culture – everything from sons of city gents to corner shop owners. Distinguished list of Old Boys includes John Tavener, John Rutter, Clive Sinclair, Patrick Procktor, Barry Norman, Murray Walker, the lovely Geoffrey Palmer, not to mention Gerard Manley Hopkins and Anthony Crosland.

Entrance: Via Pre-Prep and/or Junior School, thereby virtually gaining a guaranteed place, or by entry tests and CE – about 70 from each; the lowest hurdle at 13+. Minimum qualification for entry to sixth form (from inside and out) is grade B at GCSE in subjects to be studied 'although an A is desirable, especially for those joining from elsewhere'.

Exit: Most to higher education of some sort. Seventeen to Oxbridge in '97 and '98, fifteen in '99.

Money Matters: Had a reasonable number

of assisted places. New scholarships and bursaries to replace these at age 11 and in the sixth form – suggests the school is not short of a bob or two.

Remarks: London boys' day school with good facilities and plenty of 'buzz', in super surroundings, doing well and giving the other North London day schools a run for their money. Not perfect, but one of the relatively few London boys' schools that is not grindingly academic.

THE HIGH SCHOOL
OF GLASGOW

637 Crow Road, Glasgow G13 1PL

Tel: *0141 954 9628* Fax: *0141 959 0191*

E-mail: lmc@hsog.demon.co.uk

Web: www.hsog.demon.co.uk

✦ Pupils: 660 (boys and girls 50/50); plus own Junior School (see entry under junior schools); all day ✦ Age: 10-18 ✦ Size of sixth form: 190 ✦ Non-denom ✦ Fee-paying

---

Head (The Rector): Since 1983, Mr Robin Easton OBE MA (fifties), educated at Kelvinside Academy, Sedbergh, Christ's, Cambridge. A linguist, became head of modern languages at George Watson's. A quietly confident head, who wants to turn out 'all-rounders' who leave to become 'responsible well-adjusted citizens with a caring attitude to others'. The Rector thinks that the school is 'a happy school, where children feel at home, in a Christian (with not so small a 'c') background where they can learn concern for others'. Although pleased with the academic standards, he does not see the school as a 'hothouse'. Still teaches 'well, supply teaching in the modern languages department'; and has 'no thoughts on changing the size of the school'. Commented recently that running a school is rather like riding a bike – 'you cannot afford to stop and stand still'.

Academic Matters: Scottish system exclusively, and for bright children: Almost all achieve Grades 1 or 2 at Standard, 90 per cent plus grades A and B at Highers. 20 subjects on offer at Highers, 16 at Advanced Highers and Advanced Highers and many 'crash' and short course available in sixth form. English, maths, chemistry and physics particularly popular. Wide range of National Certificate modules available. Keyboarding skills popular. Has vied with Hutcheson's' Grammar School for first place in Scotland's league tables in recent years. Videos and computers everywhere. Max size class 26, with 20 for practical subjects. Limited learning support, first few years only and linked with junior school. One learning support teacher who co-ordinates the 'buddy system' – each dyslexic pupil in the first three years is teamed up with a senior pupil who encourages and befriends them and helps them with any organisational difficulties and with homework and so on.

Games, Options, the Arts: School surrounded by 23 acres of games fields and car parks; masses of district players (Alison Sheppard FP, Olympic swimmer), lots of representatives on West of Scotland rugby, girls shine at hockey – have been Scottish champions. Current Scottish caps at hockey, rugby, cricket, badminton, swimming and athletics – 10 medals at recent Scottish athletics championships and 76 at the Glasgow Schools championships. Four badminton court-sized games hall much used. PE module in great demand, also survival cooking! D of E awards, and excellent debating/public speaking: winners of the international final of the ESU Observer Mace debating competition in '98 and '99, and of numerous other competitions. Fantastic media studies. Art department flourishing, and dynamic director of music. Choirs sing at Glasgow Cathedral and Paisley Abbey. Stages ambitious drama productions. School makes much use of Glasgow cultural activities.

Background and Atmosphere: Founded as The Grammar School of Glasgow in 1124, the school was closely associated with Glasgow Cathedral but, despite (because of?) its high academic standing, was closed by Glasgow Corporation in 1976. An appeal launched by the High School Former Pupil Club funded the new purpose-built senior school on the sports ground at Anniesland Cross, already owned by the FPs, following a merger with Drewsteignton school in Bearsden three miles away, now the junior school. Purpose built from 1977 onwards, latest addition 2000, round courtyards, with buttercup yellow walkway: new drama studio, refectory and fitness studio. Square split-level assembly hall. New suite of music practice rooms and floodlit artificial grass pitch. Purposeful air about the school, with wide corridors (full of bags: lockers too narrow for pupils' clutter) whose walls are covered with notice boards. Each house has a designated area within the main building.

Pastoral Care and Discipline: Highly defined house system with colours (but not names) carrying on from junior school: siblings follow siblings into same house, with house tutors. 'Transitus' (10-year-olds) pupils are lovingly tended with lots of back-up from junior school (particularly with learning support). The Rector has enormous parental support, and says that he is 'not complacent, but no problems'. No recent drugs case (Glasgow not an easy city, from this point of view). Suspensions for 'major offences'. Otherwise punishments range through sanctions, lunchtime detentions, clearing up litter (Black Bags), to school detention after school on Fridays. Clear drugs education, child protection and anti-bullying programme in place.

Pupils and Parents: Ambitious; strong work ethos: almost half come from Bearsden and Milngavie and the remainder from different parts of Glasgow and outlying towns and villages within a radius of about 30 miles. High status amongst the upper middle class. Pupils can and do drive to school – large pupil car park. The geographic jump from the centre of Glasgow changed the bias of the school which now has few Asian or Jewish pupils (no synagogue in the West End), but still large element of first time buyers.

Entrance: 10 and 11. Automatic from junior school (qv), otherwise three times oversubscribed. 50-60 applicants for 22 places at Transitus and 75-90 applicants for 22 places at first year. One or two vacancies in most year groups. Own exam. Small quantity after Standard grades, 'not many, not really looking for customers' – would expect Fifth year entrants to have grade 1 passes in virtually all their Standard grade exams (or mainly A grades in GCSE if coming from England).

Exit: 98 per cent to degree courses, with around one fifth going to Glasgow University, large contingents also to

Strathclyde, Edinburgh and St Andrews. The rest are scattered widely, ten or so to Oxbridge. Pupils occasionally sponsored by a firm and may spend gap year (if any) working for that firm. Law and medicine favourite careers, followed by business studies and accountancy.

Money Matters: 'Always some bad debts', which school makes 'provisions for'; not a major worry, but there are a few chancers. School sympathetic to genuine problems. Three or four academic scholarships a year, and about 40 bursaries awarded on a financial need basis. Had around 50 assisted places and Rector comments that it will be a major challenge to build up the bursary fund to replace them.

Remarks: Going from strength to strength. A remarkable success story – a High School truly worthy of its name.

HILLS ROAD SIXTH FORM
COLLEGE

Cambridge CB2 2PE

TEL: *01223 247251 or 566741* FAX: *01223 416979*

E-MAIL: arc@hrsfc.dialnet.com

WEB: www.hrsfc.ac.uk

✦ PUPILS: 1,500; all in the sixth form
✦ Non-denom ✦ State

Head (Principal): Since 1984, Colin Greenhalgh OBE DL MA (pronounced Greenhalge, as in Algy (met a bear)) (fifties). Combines the looks and the charm of Clive James and Clive Anderson. The college as it is now is largely his creation, and it ranks as a most friendly and celebrated member of the grammar school tradition.

Academic Matters: Hills Road is an extraordinarily wonderful place to be an academically gifted child, or anyone who would flourish in such company. The college as a whole, staff and students, is friendly, protective and welcoming. The joy that the students take in their work informs a very special spirit, which seems to lift the exam performances of gifted and less able alike.

A vast range (fifty or so) of A levels on offer: maths, English, history, biology, followed by chemistry, physics, psychology, languages and geography; dance, electronics, geology and modern Greek among the exotics. The FEFC inspection report (so much more informative than Ofsted) is stuffed with grade 1s. Vocational A levels in business and art/design. Welcomes blind students and others whose special needs can be accommodated. General studies at A level for almost all.

Games, Options, the Arts: A good range of extra-curricular activities, with much participation in sports, arts, music and drama. There is a new theatre given by a millionaire former student, a new sports hall, an indoor and outdoor tennis centre, an indoor cricket school and a fitness centre. Art excellent. All do a wide-ranging 'enrichment' programme.

Background and Atmosphere: Formerly the Cambridgeshire High School for Boys. Very much a city-centre site. A collection of good buildings, old and recent (the product of the principal's fundraising prowess), crowded (but not yet overcrowded) onto a long rectangular site. Sports ground within easy reach.

Pastoral Care and Discipline: A good

tutor group system provides access to support and advice, but this is a sixth form college – you are expected to be responsible for yourself.

Pupils and Parents: As academically able as those in an average grammar school. Some from private schools. OK for nerds.

Entrance: Priority is given those who attended, or live within the catchment area of, a number of partner schools within 15 miles of Cambridge; a hundred or so gain entry from outside this area.

Formal entrance requirements are five Cs at GCSE with Bs in the subjects to be studied, but the college's reputation for being high powered and academic redirects many towards the neighbouring Long Road Sixth Form College, which has a less academic intake (and atmosphere), but also does exceptionally well by its students.

Exit: 90 per cent of students go on to university (60ish a year to Oxbridge).

Money Matters: The principal is a masterful fund raiser, squeezing money out of all sorts of people and companies – hence the splendid facilities.

Remarks: Superb state sixth form college. A match for any fee-paying school; it must send shivers down the spine of local bursars. Exam performances at A level are superb by any standard. There are no weak subjects.

HURTWOOD HOUSE

(Sixth Form College)

Holmbury St Mary, Dorking, Surrey
RH5 6NU

Tel: *01483 277416* Fax: *01483 267586*

E-mail: hurtwood2@aol.com

Web: www.hurtwood-house.co.uk

♦ Pupils: approx 280 students, half boys, half girls; almost all boarding ♦ Ages 15-18 ♦ Sixth form college ♦ Non-denom ♦ Fee-paying

---

Head: Since 1969, Mr K R B Jackson MA (late fifties). Educated at Cranleigh (just down the road) and Corpus Cambridge, where he read history. Avuncular and easy to communicate with – for both staff and students – and his jolly exterior (with beard and paunch) hides a sharp business brain. The school is his 'baby' (ie, he owns the buildings though the operations are now a not-for-profit company) and he runs it jointly with his wife, Linda (whom we did not meet). Mr Jackson says his aim is two-fold: to make sure that students feel they are 'in the most exciting place imaginable', and that parents feel their children are in the 'safest place'. Started working life very successfully in marketing (Crawford's).

Academic Matters: The school follows the A level syllabus, majoring on those subjects public schools have tended to pooh-pooh, but pupils are keen on, eg theatre studies, media studies, business studies (the school is particularly hot on these – see below). Outstanding facilities for media-related subject (eg television studio). Music technology is a recent addition to the A levels on offer. Consistently good maths results. Also offers GCSEs – all boards – for pupils who have come unstuck elsewhere. Results published in pie charts. Hurtwood comes out well in value-added data (which have some relevance here), indeed, says an educationalist, 'it does well whichever way you look at it'. Also does amazingly well in A level points averages, particularly considering its mixed intake.

Games, Options, the Arts: The popular place for theatre studies. Everyone is allowed to join in; rehearsals take place in what looks like a big room with a stage at one end (which allows pupils to concentrate on technique and not be distracted by fancy gadgetry) – but is 'actually extremely high-tech'. One of the most popular subjects here is drama – imagine 30 students packed into the auditorium, all attempting to get in touch with their emotions. Small art department. Games takes place every day. The school looks like one of those places where games does not feature at all, but in fact Hurtwood were South-East England Junior Netball Champions when we visited.

Background and Atmosphere: Founded in 1969 by Mr Jackson, building on his experiences in the now defunct prep school of Heatherdown. The school is tucked away in one of the prettier parts of Surrey, miles from the bright lights and good from the security point of view (it's near Sutton Place). Buildings are a mixture of National Trust and institutional, some stockbroker-belty looking, scattered on a steep leafy slope, with birds tweeting. Pupils appear thrilled to be here and the atmosphere is consequently electric. Houses mostly cosy, and the environment feels easy to work in.

All faiths are welcome – Muslims have the opportunity to pray the requisite five times a day, and halal meat, etc is provided.

Pastoral Care and Discipline: The school gives pupils an illusion of freedom, but in fact the pastoral care is all enveloping. The school holds random drugs tests, alcohol is not allowed; sex: 'no kissing and cuddling in public, though we're quite relaxed about it'. No uniform is worn, but pupils are expected to look neat and clean. Staff are called by their Christian names.

Pupils and Parents: Students who, for one reason or another, want out of their existing school – 'I wanted a change,' is the usual reason given. (Contact with the opposite sex could be part of a hidden agenda; outgrown public school another.) Many come from single-sex boarding schools, eg Benenden, Queen Anne's Caversham, Worth etc. Parents not short of a bob or two.

Entrance: Non-selective, but the place is popular, so apply early to be safe.

Exit: Most to university, one or two to jobs.

Money Matters: Fees are in line with major public schools.

Remarks: A cosy, expensive, very successful private sixth form college knocking spots off older, rival establishments; hugely popular with the pupils who don't want to be at a school. The rise of co-ed sixth forms and broad curricula elsewhere has reduced its uniqueness a bit.

HUTCHESONS' GRAMMAR

SCHOOL

Beaton Road, Glasgow G41 4NW

TEL: *0141 423 2933* FAX: *0141 424 0251*

E-MAIL: rector@hutchesons.org

WEB: www.hutchesons.org

✦ PUPILS: 1250 boys and girls (about 50/50)
✦ Ages: 11-18 ✦ Size of sixth form: 400
✦ Ecumenical ✦ Fee-paying

Head (Rector): Mr John Knowles BSc MSc FRSA PGCE (fifties), educated at St Bees School in Cumbria. Mr Knowles first studied physics at Manchester, followed by a PGCE at Worcester, Oxford, then an MSc in theoretical nuclear physics at London University. He was ordained in 1998 after taking a part-time course at Queen's Birmingham, whilst headmaster of King Edward VI Five Ways in Birmingham. Before that was vice master of Queen Elizabeth's Grammar School, Blackburn, having started his career at Mill Hill, followed by Wellington College, with an eight year spell as senior science master at Watford Grammar. Cor. He trails clouds of glory in the education world, (chairman of the Association Heads of Grant Maintained Schools, chief examiner for Nuffield physics at A level) as well as writing notes for CDs and playing the organ. Giggly, fun, he walks and talks as fast as any we have known, and dashed back from the HMC in Harrogate in time to show us round the junior school (at breakneck speed). Married, with three grown up daughters, his wife teaches children with special needs.

Despite the anomaly of having an ordained Anglican priest as head of what is basically a piece of Presbyterian history, both rector and school are on a high. The rector runs this hothouse of academic excellence with a gang of three depute rectors plus a bevy of assistant rectors.

Academic Matters: Depute rector, Mr Sandy Strang was at pains to dispel the myth that 'Hutchie's cream off the brightest'. 'It's the homework that counts', 12-15 hours a week from the first day in secondary school' and 'each child is issued with a homework policy book when they arrive in the school. Strong work ethos, the day often lasts from 7am to 7pm. Five Highers the norm, 15/20 per cent get six, with early morning classes and twilight classes (from 3.30–5pm) to top up to seven. This is very senior stuff. Mixture of SYS and A levels, though watch this space as the new Higher Stills are absorbed into the curriculum. Masses of languages, all the normal ones, plus Swedish and Russian, language labs, satellite TV. Vast classics department and Latin compulsory till third year. New double decker library stacked with as many videos (Shakespeare on film) as books and computers everywhere intranetted, internetted. Biology currently top of the pops, but children encouraged to take as wide a spread as possible. And they do. No particular bias, beyond the traditional Scottish 'feel' for engineering, but as many pupils now opt for careers in arts or media as follow the engineering, medicine, accountant route.

EFL on offer for non-English speaking foreigners – we are after all, on the edge of silicon glen.

Games, Options, the Arts: Small Astroturf, plus Clydesdale ground adjacent to the school, but mostly pupils are bussed to Auldhouse for the main games pitch. No swimming pool on site (problems with old coal minings underneath) but huge sports hall with fitness centre and gym. All the usual games, rugby (almost a religion as in so many schools in Scotland), hockey, etc, plus rowing and '25 sporting options'. School currently holds gold medal for takido!

Good and busy drama, new theatre and church coming on line soon; lots of external competitions, winners of recent Scottish drama and music festival and off South for the finals. Two big shows each year. Surprisingly, no pipe band or CCF; granny bashing and masses of charity work popular. Masses of music, several orchestras. Art fantastic, with kiln and fabric design options and thankfully, for an academic (and the strongest academic) school, home economics is a popular option. In sixth form, pupils can do advanced driving, archaeology, first aid, Italian plus a raft of other options. Lots of trips abroad and pupil exchanges. D of E.

Background and Atmosphere: Both Hutcheson's hospital and school were founded in Ingham Street in 1641 by the brothers, Thomas and George Hutcheson. In 1841 the school moved for the 'quietness of the situation, good air, roomy and open site' of Crown Street in Glasgow's Gorbals, moving to leafy Pollockshields in 1960, five minutes' from the M8 and easily accessible from both sides of the river. Good local buses, plus a fantastic train service. The school amalgamated with the girls' school in 1976 (with the junior school moving into the girl's school) and went independent in 1985, and the current board of governors is full of the great and the good of Glasgow: the Merchants House, Hutchesons' Hospital, the Trades House plus the Church of Scotland Presbytery.

Plans afoot to enlarge the dining area, and convert the local Congregational church (the school has bought the building) into a music and ICT centre. The congregation will still be able to use the church, but at the moment are using the school staff-room.

Think large, flat roof, wide open corridors, huge blocks of classrooms – think Hutchie. Super chunks of new build on what is basically a sixties flat roof horror, masses of photographs, good pupil inspired art. Subjects are grouped either horizontally or vertically, and there is a certain amount of moaning about more labs being needed NOW – they only have fifteen.

School runs on swipe cards, the original cashless economy, where pupils top up their cards at the beginning of term (or when needed) and use them to buy lunch, (v good, lots of veggies and salads), brekky, or whatever from the vending machines. Swipe cards also act as passes in the library.

Pastoral Care and Discipline: School divided into four houses for games, competitions and the like. Seniors 'buddy' littles when they join senior school. Strong emphasis on PSE, with fatigues or detention in place for minor wickedness, though individual teachers may set their own punishments, the ultimate deterrent is expulsion. Tutors for all over a two year period.

Pupils and Parents: A mixed bag. 'Social A-Z and economic A-Z'. Cosmopolitan collection of parents, about a third bus their children daily – over 20 miles – from Paisley, Renfrewshire, Lanarkshire, north of the river. Tranche of Australians, Koreans, pupils either stay with relatives or have surrogate mothers. Long tradition of having a significant (10 per cent) number of Jews – separate assemblies for them; Muslims may go to the mosque at lunchtime in Friday, have separate lessons for gym and no problems with scarves. Number of FPs' children. FPs include John Brown of the shipyard, plus John Buchan, Russell Hillhouse and Carol Smylie.

Entrance: Either from local prep or state. 100 a year more or less automatic up from the junior school, plus a 100 extra (and all pupils then get mixed up), otherwise by written test 'with interview for a number of candidates', pupils are actively encouraged to join the school at sixth form 'to top up Highers'. Admission usually in August, but if space available can join at any term and two pupils were being assessed (for the junior school) when we visited in October.

Exit: 95+ per cent to universities: 15/18 a year regularly to Oxbridge, and many leave with firsts; an impressive list of firsts (and double firsts) from all graduates. More gap years taken than previously, lots do work experience and then travel, most to Scottish universities, but a fair trickle down south.

Money Matters: School previously had 250 assisted places, their phasing out is a real problem. Currently discounts for siblings, some scholarships for sixth formers and more funds being sought. All scholarships are means tested.

Remarks: Awesome. Fiercely academic, but children achieve their impressive grades from a fairly unselective background. This is old fashioned teaching, with enormous breadth, at its very best. As the rector says: 'it's cool to succeed here'.

JUNIOR SCHOOL: Hutchesons' Junior School, 44 Kingarth Street, Glasgow G42 7RN. Tel: 0141 423 2700; Fax: 0141 424 1243. Rector Mr John Knowles as above, with acting depute rector Mrs Lorna Mackie DCE.

This is an enormous (800 boys and girls) junior school, in the most fabulous original Victorian academy, think green and cream tiles, think fabulous carved oak assembly hall, think huge sunlit classrooms (three of the old ones now converted into two), spacious, full of light, full of child inspired art with a super old fashioned gym. Exciting new build now houses the tinies, serious academic work here. One intake a year (but see above), all children assessed, 120/150 apply for 81 places.

French from age eight, serious little faces doing proper science, with a goodly collection of male as well as female staff and lots of specialist staff. Computers all over, good learning support.

Reduced playground means timetabled breaks, main gym at senior school (bussed) but ten minutes' walk away, and bussed to Auldhouse for games.

Sibling discounts, in line with main school and after school club till 5.45pm when pupils can do homework (costs extra in the evening, but early drop-off not a problem). Note, five-year-olds only do a half day for the first term.

Most children go on to senior school, having learnt how to work (with a vengeance). Super – only snag is the parking, but school have 'a working arrangement' with the local supermarket (who built on what was the girls' sports ground – if you follow) and a 'certain number' can park there.

JAMES ALLEN'S GIRLS' SCHOOL (JAGS)

East Dulwich Grove, London SE22 8TE

TEL: *020 8693 1181* FAX: *020 8693 7842*

E-MAIL: juliee@jags.demon.co.uk

WEB: www.jags.demon.co.uk

✦ PUPILS: 768, plus junior school (JAPS) qv; all day ✦ Ages: 11-18 ✦ Size of sixth form: 200 ✦ C of E Foundation but all are welcome ✦ Fee-paying

---

Head: Since 1994, Mrs Marion Gibbs, BA, MLitt (forties). Read classics at Bristol university, where she also did her PGCE and part time research. Previous post was as an HMI inspector – still inspects for ISI. Before that she taught in both private and state schools, including Burgess Hill, and at Haberdashers' Aske's School for Girls, Elstree. Very keen classicist, has been an examiner in the subject, and is the author of books and articles (under the name Baldock). Married for the second time, no children. Highly efficient, business like, fast talking, direct and lively. Teaches up to nine lessons per week – Greek mythology to year 7; Latin to year 9, current affairs from year 10. A hands-on head who knows all her girls – quite a feat in a school this size. 'Interested' in IB, but leaving it alone for the time being 'because we've found it's not yet acceptable to all medical schools'.

Academic Matters: Perennially very strong, and consistent. Maths the biggest taker, followed by English, biology, chemistry and history. GCSE results also impressive. Two girls in the National Biology Olympiads at the time of writing. Good teaching in modern languages, (including writing poetry) with provision for those in the fast track, and school/family exchanges for children learning Italian, Spanish and French; German, Russian and Japanese also on offer. Hard work ethos firmly in place. Notice boards bursting with information, courses, articles, and girls reading them. Some outstanding staff, reasonable turnover, 20 per cent men. Head keen on professional development, very proud when staff get promotion and a better job elsewhere.

Games, Options, the Arts: Outstandingly good art – demanding teaching with high expectations. Music is also outstanding, under Rupert Bond, founder of the Docklands Sinfonietta and conductor of London Blackheath Sinfonia. Drama intensely keen, in small but inspiring theatre, modelled on the Cottesloe. Good careers department, and design technology another strong department. Traditional games compulsory for the first three years, and a wide range of sports played in all years, with masses of games and matches at all times. Good playing fields and sense of space. PE an option at GCSE (unusual in an academic school). Impressive debating – they win competitions. JAGS girls always do well in the Youth Parliament, a seriously politically minded streak runs through the school. Broad outlook and general studies encouraged, good use made of the wonderful Dulwich Picture Gallery, occasional joint studies with Dulwich College at upper sixth level. Huge new swimming pool, linked to the sports hall, is due to open in 2001. Partnership with state schools keenly fostered; JAGS girls help in local primary schools – head dead keen on community work.

Background and Atmosphere: Founded in 1741 (claims to be the oldest independent girls' school in London, though Dulwich was not London in those days) in 'two hired rooms at the Bricklayer's Arms' – a nice symbolic beginning. One of the three schools of the Foundation of Alleyn's College of God's Gift to Dulwich, named after James Allen, warden in 1712 of Dulwich College and described as 'Six Feet high, skilful as a Skaiter; a Jumper; Athletic and Humane' – not a bad role model. School became girls only in 1842 and moved to present 22 acre site in leafy Dulwich in 1886 following Act of Parliament passed to reorganise the Foundation. Large rather dour purpose-built building plus lots of additions, including new very fine library. Huge development programme ('we're borrowing money from ourselves') well under way, to include a new dining room (in place of old swimming pool). Famous Botany Gardens planted by Lillian Clarke (pioneer ecologist at the beginning of the 20th century). As we have said before, the whole place bounces with energy and pride.

Pastoral Care and Discipline: Regular meetings between head and girls to discuss problems/complaints – girls are very articulate at these sessions. Prefects elected by girls, and they are 'pretty powerful' according to a non-prefect. Detention the usual punishment for misdemeanours (parents warned in advance). All staff act as shepherds. Sixth former expelled for drugs within the last year (reported in the press).

Pupils and Parents: Mostly from south of the river, as far away as Bromley. Also increasing numbers from north of the river – girls from the City and Islington (London Bridge to East Dulwich train takes twelve minutes), school bus from Victoria.

Unusually rich social and ethnic mix. Old Girls include Anita Brookner, Lisa St Aubin de Terain, Mary Francis.

Entrance: At 11+ by exam and interview: all 400 children trying for places are interviewed – mental liveliness an essential ingredient. About one quarter from their own excellent junior school (see separate entry), though all must pass the exam. (January, for places in September). Nearly 50 per cent from the state sector, altogether from nearly 100 'feeder' schools. Constantly oversubscribed and hot competition to get in. NB Overshot on applications for 2000 entry, and had to add on an extra form (five forms, each of 26 girls), 'but never again'. Sixth form entry: six A or B grades at GCSE, with a minimum C in English language and maths (for girls already in the school, as well as those coming in from outside). Variable numbers come in at 16+.

Exit: 95+ per cent to higher education, with at least 12-15 to Oxbridge, and sometimes around 25 offers. Wide variety of top universities, often reading tough subjects. Medicine popular, also history. Foundation art courses popular, also a gap year. Usually around twelve girls leave post GCSE. Recent appeal to Old Girls to offer work experience/work shadowing.

Money Matters: Almost 40 per cent of pupils on financial assistance of some sort. A well resourced school, with an annual grant from the Dulwich Estate, all of which goes towards scholarships, including bursary elements where necessary). Generous with the help they give. Up to 20 scholarships per year currently offered at 11+, including one for music and one for art – major scholarships of 30 per cent of fees, minor ones of 20 per cent (and occasionally more for those in dire need). Fifteen James Allen's

Assisted Places (means tested) each year, and ambitions to increase this. One or two scholarships offered at sixth form.

Remarks: Strong strong on all fronts – an exciting school that works and plays hard.

THE JUDD SCHOOL

Brook Street, Tonbridge, Kent TN9 2PN

TEL: *01732 770880* FAX: *01732 771661*

E-MAIL: Headmaster@juddschool.org.uk

WEB: atschool.eduWeb.co.uk/judd

✦ PUPILS: 856 boys; all day ✦ Ages: 11-18 ✦ Size of sixth form: 250 (including a few girls) ✦ C of E ✦ State (voluntary aided)

Head: Since 1986, Mr K A Starling MA (Cantab) (mid fifties). A geographer whose teaching experience includes high-profile private and state boarding schools. Considers this to be 'the happiest school I've been in. Boys naturally want to learn.' Relaxed, and at ease with running the establishment, in spite of crowding.

Academic Matters: Excellent GCSE results (a normal state of affairs), with no weak links. Maths still outstanding, with top two sets taking the subject at GCSE a year early, and some taking AS-level maths in Year 11. All pupils sit 10 GCSEs including three science subjects. Very strong results given the class size of 30. Excellent also at A level, and has been reducing the numbers falling below the D line in recent years. Mathematics the most popular A level subject, excellent physics, well taught and popular, with large majority getting As and Bs.

English also perennially popular and excellently taught, French, chemistry and history also popular. Altogether, very impressive. Minuscule sixth form fallout.

Games, Options, the Arts: Sporty and competitive; blessed with three rugby pitches literally on the doorstep (with tours of Canada, USA, South Africa), an open-air pool much used in summer, a cricket pitch (tour to Barbados) plus two all-weather pitches. Music is strong and vigorous, now inspired by recently opened music centre, with senior orchestra (one of three) interpreting ambitious works, Choral Union performing ambitiously. Jazz and brass groups active and bands with groovy names. Several pupils in regional youth orchestras and bands, and usually one in the National Youth Orchestra. In other areas, there is a fairly traditional mix of options. Duke of Edinburgh awards, CCF, voluntary service, debating, drama and plenty of outings and club activities. Good links across the sea (including regular group of students from Hiroshima visiting the school). School acknowledges that its design and technology facilities could be better.

Background and Atmosphere: Late Victorian building in a suburban setting on the edge of Tonbridge, bursting at the seams. Hard to disguise its institutional atmosphere, with cramped classrooms and brown-tiled corridors doing nothing to dispel the gloom, though fresh paint has lighted all this. But outside the main building all is redeemed by a splendid £2 million classroom and technology block, new(ish) science labs and airy art studio and music centre: two fine buildings that have helped greatly to reduce the claustrophobic (we think – but this is STILL hotly denied by the school) atmosphere and pressure on space.

Pastoral Care and Discipline: Well in place.

Pupils and Parents: Well-behaved motivated sons of Tonbridge, Tunbridge Wells and the Kent Weald.

Entrance: Always oversubscribed. Via Kent selection procedure, effectively the 11+. Normally limited to top 15-20 per cent of the ability range. Catchment area of west Kent includes Tunbridge Wells, Tonbridge, Sevenoaks and villages of the Weald of Kent. A few 'Governors' places' are reserved for some outside the catchment area, a few girls enter at sixth form. Not at all affected by the increase in day places at Tonbridge School: pressure, they say, is the other way round.

Exit: Well over 95 per cent to university, with the governors awarding one major scholarship and up to four leaving exhibitions. Around 10 per cent a year to Oxbridge (14 places in '00).

Money Matters: In the 19th century the sensible burghers of Tonbridge, finding the fees for Tonbridge School beyond their reach, requested that the Skinners' Company provide affordable academic schooling for their offspring. The Company obliged, opening The Judd in 1888. Doubtless the inhabitants of Tonbridge continue to be relieved that their children can enjoy state-funded academic education. They, and Old Juddians, show their gratitude by contributing most generously to the much-needed building funds required as a voluntary aided school.

Remarks: A highly successful, traditional boys' grammar school which deserves its strong reputation and the high regard in which it is held. An example to state school staff elsewhere of what can be done despite large classes and limited resources.

KELVINSIDE ACADEMY

33 Kirklee Road, Glasgow G12 0SW

TEL: *0141 357 3376* FAX: *0141 357 5401*

E-MAIL: Rector@kelvinsideacademy.gla.sch.uk

WEB: www.kelvinsideacademy.gla.sch.uk

✦ PUPILS: 550 pupils, including 100+ girls throughout ('it's still a new pioneering spirit') ✦ Ages: 3-18 ✦ Size of sixth form: 97 ✦ Inter-denom ✦ Fee-paying

Head (Rector): Since 1998, Mr John Broadfoot BA MEd (fifties), who arrived at the school 'along with the girls'. Educated at Merchiston, he then read English at Leeds and 'is delighted to be teaching English to the fifth year Highers set'. Comes to Kelvinside after ten years at Strathallan, having briefly dabbled in the state system 'very boring, no drama', and spent a short time teaching in the West Indies. Married with three children, two of whom are in the school. Keen for the children 'to have achieved not only their academic potential, but also to have realised their talents in other areas and to leave the school full of self confidence'. Interested and interesting.

Academic Matters: Mr Broadfoot is only too aware of the pitfalls of converting to co-education. His solution is to 'radically shake up the system', and divide the school into four faculties each with its own management structure – which should get round the problems of 'dyed in the wool' department heads and make the school more girl friendly. The faculties are: science, maths and computing; social studies including geography, history and RE; the expressive arts including music, art etc; and a language faculty embracing French, German, Spanish and Latin (and can 'pull on experts' to teach Russian and more esoteric languages), Italian on stream for the top end. 'The shake up is much bigger than originally anticipated, and has had a much speedier impact'.

Follows the Scottish system, with the odd A level in sixth form, as well as Sixth Form Studies and the new Advanced Highers, which can be combined with SQA modules. School traditionally strong on maths and sciences, 'science within the class' but strong across the board; with the advent of girls, the arts may get a better image. Max class size 20, parallel classes, upper school set for English, maths, and modern languages. Good work shadowing arrangements. Strong learning support with trained teachers in each faculty.

Games, Options, the Arts: Lots of music – masses of tinies carrying instruments bigger than themselves were struggling off to junior orchestra when we visited; a lovely sight. Drama timetabled and impressive. Masses of extras: liberal studies include a wide range of classes – philosophy, psychology, cooking.

Rugby and cricket powerful, girls play hockey. PE is mixed and can be taken by staff of either sex (to the distaste of some parents). Curling and Olympic wrestling on offer. Two serious gyms, school uses Glasgow University games fields ten minutes walk away. CCF compulsory for all for one year, thereafter voluntary. D of E, and camping at Rannoch (costed into fees).

Background and Atmosphere: Kelvinside school is technically The Kelvinside Academy War Memorial Trust, in a purpose built building in Kelvinside. The school has expanded down to nursery level, with parents dropping off early and collecting late (late waiting till 5.30pm). Certain amount of spreading across the road – the two houses here are destined to become a sixth form house, and plans are afoot to roof over part of the frankly disorganised area at the back of the school proper to form a social area. Super new computer complex which includes a multi-media lab 'that anyone can use', and a small lab for the web site, with conference and digital-enhancing facilities. Rather a fine double-decker library.

This traditional Glasgow boys' school held out against the tide of girls until 1998; but three years later one has no feeling that this is a boys' school with girls tacked on.

Pastoral Care and Discipline: House system, strong PSE. 'A certain amount of smoking', 'we flush the smokers out'. Only one recent drugs incident; will use random testing if suspected evidence of involvement; counselling on hand, but miscreants are probably out anyway. School boasts 'a strong partnership with parents'. Holiday club to help with baby sitting problems.

Pupils and Parents: Middle class, professional, a significant quantity of first time buyers, lots of travelling. From Gairlochead, the Trossachs, to Dunlop in Ayrshire. A Newton Mearns/Southside bus is shared with Laurel Park.

Entrance: Through the nursery, or wherever; traditionally at 5, 11, 12 or at sixth form level. Not academically selective; by interview and assessment.

Exit: Over 80 per cent to universities: usually Scotland; Glasgow and Strathclyde Business School popular. 'We're a parochial lot'. A trickle elsewhere and the occasional Oxbridge candidate. Lots of engineers.

Money Matters: Usual discounts for siblings, good collection of scholarships and a 'bursarial fund' is being put in place. Will help 'wherever possible' if financial difficulties occur.

Remarks: Strong traditional school subject to big changes; watch this space. The girls look as though they have always been there.

KILGRASTON

Bridge of Earn, Perthshire PH2 9BQ

TEL: *01738 812257* FAX: *01738 813410*

E-MAIL: ahughes@kilgraston.pkc.sch.uk

WEB: www.kilgraston.pkc.sch.uk

✦ PUPILS: 245 girls (110 board, the rest day) including junior school (The Grange) with 40 boys and girls, and nursery school with 30 ✦ Ages: 11-18, junior school 5-11, nursery 2.5-5 ✦ Size of sixth form: 50 ✦ RC but inter-denom as well ✦ Fee-paying

---

Head: Since 1993, Mrs Juliet L Austin BA (fifties); educated at Downe House and studied English language and lit, old Icelandic and medieval Latin at Birmingham. The first lay head of this famous convent school, and an RC convert, Mrs Austin previously taught at Birmingham primary schools and Downe House. Married with one daughter who is housemistress at Badminton; her 'retired' husband spends much time organising conferences, 'he knows more nuns than I do' said the head. Thoughtful, and obviously enjoying running this flourishing school.

Academic Matters: Not the sleepy place it used to be, though exam results are still not as bright as they could be. School runs primarily on the Scottish system, with Standard grades followed by Highers to university in lower sixth, and A levels or Sixth Form Studies in upper sixth. No particular strengths; English lit not strong; excellent science labs, less excellent results ('coming on' says head;) 'bright and encouraging results from lesser sparks.' Pupils can 'top up' Standard grades in sixth form and often take French, maths and Latin a year early. Tiny classes, 8/20.

Piloting Scotvec clusters, four modules equals one cluster. Only one or two do secretarial studies/keyboarding skills. Business studies. Computers everywhere plus two dedicated computer rooms. Really good IT and laptops for everyone on the way. E-mail for all. Good remedial unit, with specialist teacher for dyslexia and dyspraxia – one-to-one teaching and EFL on offer. Languages popular. Masses of exchanges, French, German and US (both pupils and staff) via Sacred Heart network.

Games, Options, the Arts: Magnificent sports hall faced in sandstone, with niches echoing those in the stable building (well converted into junior school with attached nursery); Historic Scotland at its best. Nine Astroturfs with floodlighting (good grief). Wide choice of other sports. Climbing wall. Strong drama, and inspired art ('going from strength to strength'); the art department overlooks the Rotunda and currently boasts an enormous computer-linked loom. D of E, debating, leadership courses. Music centre in the attics, with keyboards and individual study rooms; guitars and stringed instruments everywhere. Writers' group. Enthusiasts building sports car – the 'automobile association'. Cooking and brilliant needlework, the girls make their own ball gowns for the annual ball with Merchiston. Religion very much in evidence (saints on tap) and school mag has good big section on chapel.

Background and Atmosphere: Founded in 1920 and one of 200 networked schools and colleges of the Society of the Sacred Heart. Moved to the handsome red Adamesque sandstone house in 1930, masses of extensions including spectacular Barat wing, light and airy with huge wide passages. Common rooms for all, single rooms throughout senior school, tinies dorms now divided into attractive cabins for each.

School stops at 4.10 on Fridays for day and weekly boarders, but masses of alternative activities for those who stay back – though usual moans about 'not having enough to do'. Computers, games hall, courts, art, music and sewing rooms open throughout the weekend. Boyfriends can and do visit at weekends.

Pastoral Care and Discipline: Sacred Heart ethos prevails, staff enormously caring. Disciplinary committee, gatings, suspensions, fatigues round school for smoking. Will test areas, not girls, if drugs suspected. The girls here are not the dozy lot they used to be. Counsellor on hand, and bullying handled by BFG (Big Friendly Group). Charming little handbook for new pupils full of helpful advice.

Pupils and Parents: Day children from Fife and Perthshire, though bus no longer collects children from the school's front door – the main gate was damaged too often. Boarders from all over Scotland, and Old Girls' children. Toffs' daughters, including non-Catholics, and Muslims. Academically pushy parents may move their children elsewhere, but the school breeds loyalty among those who value 'other things'. Currently 21 foreigners ('the Internet is handy' says the head).

Entrance: Not that difficult. All sit the school's own exam in February in tandem with scholarship exam. Junior school entrants also do CE. Otherwise 11+ from primary schools, and 12+ from prep schools. Pupils can come whenever, half term if space available. Sixth form entry: 'good Standard grades/GCSEs' to follow A level course. Pupils steered to 'appropriate' levels of study. Has recently picked up three or four pupils from Glenalmond who weren't tough enough.

Exit: 80–90 per cent annually to universities. Occasional departure for sixth form in boys' schools; some leave after Highers.

Money Matters: A rich school. Up to ten academic, art and music scholarships available. Also riding, tennis and sporting scholarships. Almost one third receive assistance of some sort. School is 'good at finding Trust funding' for those who have fallen on hard times.

Remarks: The only all-girls boarding school left in Scotland and popular. Small, gentle not overtly Catholic, with terrific facilities. Scots parents see it as a viable alternative to St Leonards (recently gone not very successfully co-ed).

JUNIOR SCHOOL: (The Grange): Pupils from the age of 5, with boys to 8. School shares main school facilities and is based in the delightfully converted stable block, which also shares with the nursery. The nursery includes local children paid for by County Councils.

KING ALFRED SCHOOL

North End Road, London NW11 7HY

TEL: *020 8457 5200* FAX: *020 8457 5264*

E-MAIL: kingalfred@cwcom.net

WEB: www.kingalfred.barnet.sch.uk

✦ PUPILS: around 500, all day, roughly 50:50 boys and girls ✦ Ages: 4-18 ✦ Size of sixth form: 55 ✦ Non-denom ✦ Fee-paying

---

Head: Since 1999, Ms Lizzie Marsden (thirties). Educated at Mirfield High, West Yorkshire and Hertford College, Oxford. Was assistant head at Rugby for five years and before that 'under master' at St Paul's Boys'. Married to a barrister. Has one daughter at pre-prep school. Interests: cooking, Handel operas and Leeds United. Friendly, open, as befits the head of North London's more-or-less only 'progressive' school. Great things are expected of her in the way of sweeping out cobwebs from dark corners. 'She is on the ball,' commented a parent. 'She very soon worked out what areas need shaking up.' Teaches English A level, and throughout the school by rotation – 'but I'm not primary trained so in the lower school I'm really a classroom assistant.' Her greatest challenge? 'To identify really and truly the ethos of this school for the 21st century and then to follow it through.'

Academic Matters: Best A level results ever in 2000 – nearly 70 per cent As and Bs. GCSEs less startling; head points out that in a non-selective school (with about 30 per cent special needs children) the results will vary according to the quality of the intake.

As usual, all six who took photography A level got grade A – 'They are brilliantly taught,' says the head. The school has an arty bias (but the head says she's working to increase the profile of science), with the most popular A level subjects in 2000 being history and English (the only two in double figures), followed by politics, art, maths and photography. Its small size means the school can only offer 20 subjects at A level, but will 'meet pupils' needs wherever possible.'

The school is committed to mixed ability teaching, except in the sixth form, but streams for maths and French from Year 7. 'You don't get spoon-fed,' commented a pupil who moved there from a selective girls' school. 'It's less pressured, so you have to do a lot more thinking for yourself.' The head feels that parents' expectations have changed: 'They want their children to get as vigorous an education as anyone in North London.' She admits that while the less able have always been well-supported, the brightest may not have been stretched. Lower school parents in particular can get nervous about a seeming tolerance of sloppy work. Head will have no truck with theory that correcting work stifles creativity. 'I am not a very modern educationalist – I believe in being quite thorough.' Has introduced a much-needed staff appraisal system – parents comment that under-performing staff have previously been left to drift on regardless. 'There can be an amazing depth of study,' said a mother, 'but it's very dependent on the teacher.' Class size: maximum 24, but often smaller, especially higher up the school.

Games, Options, the Arts: As previously mentioned, very strong on photography. Strong artistic tradition too – several move on each year to art school. Musical bias towards jazz, because of the interest of the head of department ('classical music doesn't get so much of a look-in,' complained a parent). Jazz Works group has performed at the Albert Hall; recently formed chamber orchestra. Pupils often get together to put on their own performances rather than joining a school-initiated group. Offers music technology A level – an unusual opportunity. Plenty of upper school drama productions written and performed by students ('though the new drama syllabus is making it more difficult,' comments the head). No theatre, but a new floor being added to the arts/science block will create more space for drama. Recent performances include *The Diary of Anne Frank*.

Outdoor amphitheatre – 'Used occasionally'. Not a school passionate about games – murmurs from some lower school parents about its lack of importance on the curriculum though praise for its variety, including badminton and judo. 'The football team came back very shocked after playing a very competitive prep school and losing 11 nil,' said a mother. But an upper school parent commented: 'It's infinitely better now than it used to be. My daughters are fervent hockey and rounders players and have done really well.' Outdoor activities are, however, an integral part of school life: 8- and 9-year-olds build camps in the wooded area around the edge of the site, and there are various swings, aerial cableways and tree houses – including a large, intricate structure designed and built by middle school members. Year 5 and upwards go on one week camps – 'with plenty of time to play in the woods and have stories round the camp fire,' said a parent. The school has recently designed and built a boat, and plans to start a sailing club on a nearby reservoir (mutters about a general lack of after-school clubs). School animals include rabbits, guinea pigs and two goats.

Background and Atmosphere: Started by parents in 1897 in Hampstead to 'educate boys and girls together … and to draw out the self-activity of the child.' Moved in 1921 to present six-acre grassy site near the Hampstead Heath extension. 'Very calm, very quiet, very conducive to learning,' commented a parent. No uniform; staff and pupils on first-name terms. Small school with an intimate atmosphere and its own particular non-competitive ethos. Some parents become deeply involved in the school, and indeed elderly ex-Alfredians still maintain close connections. 'The school is very entrenched in its history. They're not good at listening to outsiders,' said a mother. But hopes for change with the new head.

The lower school classrooms, each with its own covered outdoor space, curve round one end of the site. The three infant classes have their own playground area with climbing frames, and reception has its own small garden. The collection of middle and upper school buildings varies in construction from mellow brick to glass and concrete, with several outdoor metal staircases ('which can become a waterfall when it rains,' commented a sixth-former). There is a general air of shabby homeliness ('one of my aims is to improve the general fabric of the place,' says the head). The tuck shop has recently been repainted by the sixth-form in a startling pink and blue colour scheme – 'A post-Barbie ironic experience,' says the head. A new floor is being added to the present science block, to make more room for art and drama and also for an Exploratorium, which is planned along the lines of the Launch Pad in the Science Museum, with plenty of hands-on apparatus. 'We would like this to become a community resource, with local primary schools coming to use it.'

Pastoral Care and Discipline: The relaxed relationship between staff and pupils tends not to provoke anti-authoritarian revolt, though one mother commented that her son had sometimes found it difficult to predict where teachers would draw the line between friendliness and over-familiarity. The school has recently rewritten its drugs policy, which involves automatic expulsion for dealing drugs, but some lee-way for more minor offences. 'It's hard to throw someone out for what might be a one-off event, particular if we think they are a worthwhile member of the school.' Head will try to find a place elsewhere for anyone expelled. Suspension for smoking in the school grounds.

No detentions as such, but pupils may be kept back to finish work. Anyone misbehaving in class will be sent to the head or deputy. The new anti-bullying policy document (drawn up with the help of children on the pupils' council) lists unacceptable behaviour (including 'leaving people out' and 'hurtful whispers about anyone') and the responsibilities of school and pupils to deal with it. The school succeeds in promoting a genuine family feel, with sixth formers encouraged to get involved with the lower school. Some parents have commented that the small class sizes and their mixed make-up provide only a small pool of potential friends.

Pupils and Parents: Children friendly, confident and undeferential. School popular with North London glitterati. Otherwise, parents seeking a green haven for their kids away from the frenzied competitiveness of most North London private schools. No ethnic mix to speak of.

Entrance: Mainly at 4, 7, 11 and sixth form. At 4, largely first-come-first-served, taking siblings and gender mix into account, though children spend a half day in the school – 'to assess the child's sociability' – and parents are also interviewed – 'we like to think that parents will work within the ethos of the school'. Another class-full enters at 7, selected along the same lines, with children spending two days at the school. At 11, as well as the two-day visit, around 60 candidates for at most 10 places sit maths and English exams similar to those set by other private schools. The highest scorers do not, however, necessarily get offered the places. 'We look very closely at the previous schools' reports and take the ones we think will fit in best.' At 16, 'we look at their ability, where they have been before, and why they want to come here.'

Exit: Around 20 leave after GCSEs, to other sixth forms and sixth form colleges in the area. At 18, nearly all to university. Sussex used to be a popular destination. Two or 3 a year to art foundation courses, 2 or 3 to Oxbridge.

Money Matters: No scholarships or bursaries.

Remarks: Genuine alternative to competitive North London private schools. Although some parents are unsure how much work gets done in lower school, all emphasise how much fun their children are having. 'You have to stay with it and be confident,' advised an upper school parent whose children have come through with flying colours.

KING EDWARD VI HIGH
SCHOOL FOR GIRLS

Edgbaston Park Road, Birmingham
B15 2UB

TEL: *0121 472 1834* FAX: *0121 471 3808*

✦ PUPILS: 545 girls; all day ✦ Ages: 11-18
✦ Size of sixth form: 160 ✦ Non-denom
✦ Fee-paying

Head: Since 1996, Miss Sarah H Evans BA MA educated at King James' Grammar School, Knaresborough and Sussex, Leicester and Leeds Universities. Previously head of the Friends' School, Saffron Walden, and before that taught at Leeds Girls' High School, also Fulneck Girls' School. A lovely, chirpy, calm Quaker, passionately committed to the children and their education. Wants to give her pupils 'wings to fly somewhere unexpected'. Focused on community – working with other schools, Birmingham University etc, and on breadth – building characters for life. Much liked and appreciated by pupils. Took over from Miss Ena Evans ('Old Miss Evans').

Academic Matters: Outstanding academically for decades, and undoubtedly one of the country's top academic schools, with outstanding teaching and an ethos of hard work (lunch is soon done). Excellent across the board – in '00 223 As, 57 Bs, 30 Cs, 6 Ds, and 5 Es. No weak subjects. Biology, chemistry, maths English and French are currently the most popular subjects. Brilliant teaching all round – staff of long standing but excellent, lovers of teaching who have decided not to move up to administration. GCSE results = nothing fancy on offer, but what it does comes out with astounding results – only Latin less than 90 per cent A/A*. Girls are achievers with high expectations who 'learn to want to excel'. Lots of individual attention given to the girls, help is available from all and any staff at all times; head says this accounts for girls who get Bs and Cs at GCSE getting Bs and Cs at A level.

Wide syllabus. Classes of 'mixed ability' (on a very narrow range, however), maximum class size 26. One-third of pupils take A level sciences (and must follow a non-A level English course), one-third take arts (and must follow a non-A level maths course) and one third mixed. General studies taken as fifth (in the new system) A level – and girls get mostly As in this too. Russian, Italian and Spanish on offer at sixth form. Classics department flourishing and innovative.

Nine science labs, two computer rooms (free access during day); equipment not of the finest but upgrading. Classrooms double as subject rooms, with old-fashioned desks in the main, but filled with pupils' work on display. Some classes taken with King Edward's School (qv). 'Outsiders sometimes think teaching here must be a soft option,' commented one member of staff, 'because all the girls are bright – but the fact is that a little doesn't go a long way: they lap it up and want more.' Girls are adept arguers and class discussion and debate is encouraged from the earliest forms.

Games, Options, the Arts: Formidable hockey teams, and lots of county representation, netball good, also tennis and athletics. Fencing, basketball, good, strong dance group, ballroom dancing, aerobics. Girls picked for county squads in several sports, 'They get madly keen'. Sports hall, two artificial hockey pitches. Swimming outstanding, own pool, boys have their own next door. Girls in sixth form must take some type of exercise but team games not mandatory, golf, archery on offer.

1983 Centenary Art and Design block filled with three-dimensional paper sculptures, textiles, and tie-dyeing; as well as trad painting and superb ceramics. Few doing art A level, however, and none doing design. Many concerts, plays and dance productions; girls took part in the Schools' Proms, in '97, as part of the Birmingham Schools' Symphony Orchestra which was given an 'outstanding performance award'. In '97 one girl got the highest mark in her associated-board piano exam in the country. Food technology (cooking) on offer and King Edward boys do it too. Careers advice and work experience all on offer. Masses of fund raising and community service. Theatre studies shared, and popular. Drama very good, and music outstanding – combined again. Girls bring out school newspaper, High Profile.

Background and Atmosphere: Part of the King Edward Foundation group of schools (all bursarial work carried out jointly), founded in 1883, and followed King Edward's School to present site in 1940. Share same architect and campus is a pleasing blend of redbrick plus usual later additions (not always totally in keeping); feeling of space and calm inside. Girls leave their stuff in piles all over the place in the certainty that it is safe anywhere. Direct Grant school until 1976. 'KEHS' girls wear uniform to sixth form, when free rein is given to fashion.

Pastoral Care and Discipline: Marked discipline. Staff hold a short weekly meeting to discuss concerns, but have 'been very lucky'. Girls follow a pastoral care and personal decision-making programme, and can discuss problems with any member of staff, but normally with form tutor, year co-ordinator, deputy or head. No prefect system, no head girl, no houses. No school drugs offence policy – 'any cases would be dealt with on an individual basis'. Good parental contact. In principle, parents can contact senior staff, head or her deputy, 'certainly within the hour' if it is clearly an urgent matter (other schools please note). There are clear rules on smoking: a 'letter home works wonders'.

Pupils and Parents: Seriously bright children of professional families, middle to lower middle class. Shares transport system with boys at King Edward's, girls come from as far away as Lichfield, Bromsgrove, Wolverhampton, Solihull. 'There's not a school in this league for miles, and precious few anywhere,' say parents. Approx 30 per cent ethnic minorities as you might expect – no problems here. Ecumenical outlook.

Entrance: School's own v selective test 'designed to test the children not their teachers' (nice one). School spends two weeks searching the completed tests 'for potential not raw marks'. About half come from state primaries. Tough entry post-GCSE (and girls are 'warmly welcomed' at this stage) – school's own exam in relevant subjects, plus interview and previous school's report.

Exit: Very few after GCSE (having the boys next door removes the urge to fly off to a co-ed); 10-20 to Oxbridge, and the rest to the top range of universities – Bristol, Leeds, Nottingham, London etc – almost always their first choice. After university to the professions, arts, media, industry, business; school records 'noticeably more and more high achievers – no glass ceiling.'

Money Matters: Had a very large number of assisted places and their loss is felt, though some have been replaced by an 'equivalent governors' means-related' scheme – up to 14 places a year. Academic scholarships up to the value of two full-fees at 11+ (not more than 50 per cent per pupil) plus the equivalent of half a full-fee scholarship at 16+. Now has some Ogden Trust bursaries for 'above-average children from a state primary school of limited or no parental means'. Parents' Association does the odd bit of fund-raising (though mostly used for social activities), second-hand shop in summer term.

Remarks: One of the country's top academic girls' city day schools, turning out a long line of academic high flyers, and an example to the grammar school tradition of how this can be combined with breadth and civilisation.

KING EDWARD'S SCHOOL

North Road, Bath BA2 6HU

TEL: *01225 464313* FAX: *01225 481363*

E-MAIL: headmaster@kesbath.biblio.net

WEB: www.kes.bath.sch.uk

✦ PUPILS: 710 pupils (128 girls, 582 boys). Plus 186 in junior school, (46 girls, 140 boys), 113 in pre-prep ✦ Ages: 11-18, junior school 7-11, pre-prep 3–7 ✦ Size of sixth form 227 (57 girls, 170 boys) ✦ Non denom ✦ Fee-paying

---

Head: Since 1993, Mr Peter J Winter MA (Oxon) (forties), educated at Trinity School, Croydon, and Wadham College, Oxford, where he read French and German. Taught at Latymer Upper and Magdalen College School (Oxford) before going to Sevenoaks School, where he was head of modern languages, then ran the International Centre, the sixth form boarding house for boys with his Ghanaian-born wife. Two children. Mr Winter is a keen all-round sportsman and Francophile. Keen IB supporter but economics and new AS/A2 curriculum give pause for thought. Live wire.

Entrance: At 3, 7 and 11 and also at sixth form. Academically selective but not vastly so, and also recognise other talents. Wide catchment area. Many children coming into Bath on buses from outlying areas. Roots are ex-direct grant. Had 130 assisted places and feels their loss. 9-10 entrance bursaries per annum (3-4 children pay very little). Bursary fund for those who fall on hard times. Scholarships.

Exit: Almost all to higher education. Thirteen places at Oxbridge in '00, good numbers to UCL and Birmingham, large numbers to new universities and ex-polys. A small but regular number of pupils go on to have Service careers; art foundation and drama courses also popular.

Remarks: Unpretentious, busy school. Started to go fully co-ed in 1997, after much discussion and planning to take four years over it. Day school with increasingly wide catchment area and a distinguished history. Founded as a grammar school in 1552 (Old Boys include Sir Sidney Smith, Arctic navigator and explorer, Sir Edward Parry, the founder of Sandhurst, Major General le Marchant). The school moved from the centre of Bath in 1961 (bringing in funds) to elegant large house on a hill near the edge the city – splendid view of Bath one way, cows in the field next door. Many additions, including sixties purpose-built block now converted into fine theatre. Took over (in 1999), for use as its pre-prep, The Park School, a prep school fallen on hard times based in a Victorian house on the other (west) side of the city. Theatre studies and sport studies recently introduced as A levels, and the school has a strong dramatic tradition. A level results good at the top end, but notable levels of Ds and Es. Popular subjects are biology, geography, maths, English, chemistry, physics and business studies. Work taken seriously – but there is also a sense of fun. Art is distinctly good, sports are keenly followed (though 'it is almost possible to get away without doing anything,' confided one pupil) – athletics, rugby (strong for boys, girls train enthusiastically – 'presence of NZ exchange teacher may have had some influence,' says head,) netball, cricket and soccer and school runs a hockey festival. Scruffy, piles of bags everywhere; new team of porters to tackle this. Pupils come from all walks of life, and are polite and lively. Fees kept purposely low.

New purpose-built junior school (behind the main school) is well designed with classrooms centred around the open-plan library – a hive of purposeful activity. Selective entry (children come from top twenty per cent of range). Children given lots of praise. Regular awards and commendation certificates. Part time special needs. Sets for French from year 3, maths year 4, and English year 6. Awarded four out of five scholarships to senior school. Emphasis on manners and courtesy. Prefects (aged 10) show parents around. Our escort rather sweetly pointed out the wide selection of Fun Fax books available in the school bookshop as we passed by the window.

KING EDWARD'S SCHOOL
Edgbaston Park Road, Birmingham
B15 2UA

TEL: *0121 472 1672* FAX: *0121 414 1897*

E-MAIL: office@admin.kes.bham.sch.uk

WEB: www.kes.bham.sch.uk

✦ PUPILS: around 880 boys; all day ✦ Ages: 11-18 ✦ Size of sixth form: 250 ✦ C of E ✦ Fee-paying

---

Head (Chief Master): Since 1998, Mr Roger Dancey MA (fifties), educated Lancing, Exeter University (read economics and government). Previously head of City of London School, where he reigned for three years before leaping at the chance to be head here; before City of London he was head of King Edward VI Camphill, and before that senior master at Royal Grammar School Worcester. Married with two children, both teachers. Outgoing and charming, extremely keen on the theatre (the play based on *Les Liaisons Dangereuses* was dedicated to him by the playwright), also cinema, cricket and golf. Took over from the popular Mr Hugh Wright.

Academic Matters: Outstanding academically and gets five star results. New staff appointed to cope with the increase in numbers (school now has five forms in each year block), including a head of computing, and a full time librarian (library has been updated and extended to include resources and career rooms). All departments strong. 25 to a class, fewer for specialist subjects and A levels. Streamed for maths after three years, but not otherwise streamed – difficult across such a narrow ability level. These are bright boys taking heaps of GCSEs and usually four A levels each, (but this includes general studies for all). High percentage of As across the board: physics, chemistry and maths the most popular subjects and results amazing in all three (eg 44 As, 20 Bs out of 69 taking chemistry at A in '00). Science school recently refurbished. Arts subjects have a lesser following at A level by and large. School 'does not teach to exams, but beyond them.' Satellite and e-mail used in language depts: dedicated staff, and wide and capable common room. Competitive note: school scores not quite so well at A level as its sister school.

Games, Options, the Arts: 'Music brilliant,' according to parents, huge number of people play instruments, and combine with King Edward VI High School for Girls on adjacent site; lots of ensembles etc. Drama strong, junior and senior workshops; boys join with girls to put on plays and concerts post A level. Runner up in World Schools' Debating Championships in '00. Good games: regular county and even international representation, former under 15 rugby champions, 'not often beaten in the hockey world', plus basketball (national U19 champions, 8 England school players in the last decade), cricket, tennis, water polo, swimming, athletics (have had England schools finalists at all levels) etc. 'Embarrassingly good,' said the former chief master. They use the hockey Astroturf of sister school, which shares the same campus. CCF gaining in popularity, Young Enterprise, masses of D of E and lots of community service. Upper school boys do food technology (cooking) at the High School, and sixth formers do the odd bit of 'guinea pigging' and research for the university opposite.

Background and Atmosphere: School founded in 1552 by King Edward VI; and is flagship for the famous King Edward Foundation, which was expanded in late 19th century to include a further six schools. The chief master is head of the foundation, though each school is autonomous, but often with shared governors. The foundation provides £2 million plus in grants per annum to its schools. King Edward's moved to present 32-acre site, which it shares with King Edward VI High in 1936, surrounded by botanic gardens, University of Birmingham, lakes and golf course. Feels like deep country, but only 10 minutes from Birmingham centre. Very thirties redbrick and oak buildings with modern additions for design and music. Impressive. Very committed to partnership with schools in the maintained sector, and are developing links wherever possible.

Pastoral Care and Discipline: Deputy appointed '97 with responsibility for this. Also form tutors, housemasters, the chaplain and heads of middle and lower school take up the slack. Chief master instigated a pastoral review, no overt problems, or bullying: 'the school does not suffer from big city syndrome'. Strict line on drugs. Personal and social education programme throughout the school.

Pupils and Parents: Complete social mix, around 40 per cent ethnic minorities, but 'absolutely no social frisson'. Parents' Association mainly social, but the odd fund raising. Lots of first-time buyers. Boys wear their uniforms with pride: loads of different ties and hair styles! Bus companies run a school bus service to the campus during term time.

Entrance: Highly competitive exam at 11+ or 13+, at least four for every place. For sixth form entry: school exam plus at least six GCSEs, with As in subjects to be studied at A level – difficult and very selective, but several come in at this stage.

Exit: Rare for a boy not to go on to university. Large numbers to Oxbridge, London, Birmingham, Durham, Leeds and all the civic unis popular, reading everything from medicine to classics and to oceanography. J R Tolkien, Viscount Slim, Enoch Powell, Bill Oddie and Kenneth Tynan were Old Boys.

Money Matters: Approximately 30 per cent of all boys on some form of assistance. Governors' scheme in place to replace most of the assisted places which the school had – remarkably good foot-work here. Also four fees-worth of academic scholarships awarded annually (can be spread), plus 3-4 named scholarships in particular subjects. Now has some Ogden Trust bursaries for 'above-average children from state primary schools of limited or no parental means'. Funds available for real hardship; no one need leave in exam years.

Remarks: One of the country's top academic boys' city day schools with consistently strong results year after year, churning out dozens of high-fliers. Fantastic.

KING'S COLLEGE
Taunton, Somerset TA1 3DX

Tel: *01823 328 200* Fax: *01823 328 202*

E-mail: kingscol@aol.com

Web: www.kings-taunton.co.uk/

✦ Pupils: approx 300 boys and 140 girls (250 boys board, 100 girls board – the rest day) ✦ Ages: 13-18 (also separate Junior School) ✦ Size of sixth form: approx 200 ✦ C of E ✦ Fee-paying

---

Head: Since 1988, Mr Simon Funnell MA (fifties). Read English at Cambridge, formerly a housemaster at Shrewsbury, keen on music. Married, three children, likes golf – seriously.

Academic Matters: Some excellent young and not so young staff, particularly in the history and languages department. Sound in mainstream subjects. A level results acceptable. Head comments that 'it is not our policy to withdraw borderline candidates in order to improve A level statistics'. Does not take general studies as exam. Biology department working with United Nations to conserve the giant marine turtle in the Mediterranean.

Games, Options, the Arts: Lots of jolly facilities, including wonderful, super, big, light, inspiring art centre made out of old day boys' house, spawning pictures all over the school. Purpose-built CDT centre and video studio. Plays rugby and cricket with enthusiasm and success. Cricket tour to Australia, one pupil recently in the MCC Schools England side. Girls under 16 West of England hockey champions. Under 17 national ladies sabre champion. Games are compulsory until age 15. Zestful drama – including large-scale musicals in new theatre. Music active – the choir sings evensong annually at St Paul's Cathedral and St George's Chapel, Windsor. Notable jazz band who play hither and thither and make CDs. Keen CCF (Navy, Marines and Army) – a long tradition of this. Good at good works – granny bashing etc. Some ambitious trips, including to Mount Sinai. Busy extra-curricular programme.

Background and Atmosphere: One of the Woodard Foundation schools (muscular Christianity). Pleasant 100-acre site on the edge of Taunton. Beautiful old Gothic chapel has been converted into a 'function room and study centre.' Present chapel a more humble white-washed affair and quite jolly (look at the portrait of Bishop Fox in the Lady Chapel). Boarding houses just across the road from the main buildings – like an advanced housing estate, looking on to Astroturf/hockey pitches/tennis courts. More than adequate facilities. Sixth formers have cosy study bedrooms done up with tender loving care by some (drapes etc). Recent upgrading and refurbishing of some boarding houses, approving noises from pupils and parents. Three girls' boarding houses.

Pastoral Care and Discipline: One or two hairy moments, but on the whole good. Prefects allowed into pubs – a cunning ploy, as 'what do we do when we encounter our illegally drinking non-prefect mates?' asks one. A school in which the word 'community' still means something.

Pupils and Parents: Easy option for West Country and Welsh families. Social mix – more to the middle side of middle class.

Strongish army and navy element. A number of non-nationals in school – the majority from Germany and the Far East – especially at sixth form. OBs: Geoffrey Rippon, cricketer Roger Twose, rugby international Matthew Robinson, historian John Keegan.

Entrance: Registration and CE. Also entry at sixth form for 'suitably qualified' pupils.

Exit: To universities old and new all over, a good handful to Oxbridge. 91 per cent to higher education at the latest count.

Money Matters: Generous percentage of fee income goes on scholarships and bursaries, including those for sons of clergy and school-masters. Academic, art, drama, technology, sport and music scholarships. Also one or two scholarships at sixth form.

Remarks: Useful second division public school, with girls.

KING'S COLLEGE SCHOOL (KCS)

Wimbledon Common, London SW19 4TT

TEL: *020 8255 5300* FAX: *020 8255 5359*

E-MAIL: admissions@kcs.org.uk

WEB: www.kcs.org.uk

✦ PUPILS: 710 boys; all day ✦ Ages: 13–18 ✦ Size of sixth form: 280 ✦ C of E (but other faiths welcome) ✦ Fee-paying

---

Head: Since 1997, Mr Tony Evans MA, MPhil (fifties). Educated at De la Salle School, London, followed by the French Lycèe in Kensington, then Paris University and St Peter's, Oxford, where he read modern languages, and University College, London. His mother was Jersey French and he married a French wife (widowed) and has two children. Previously head of Portsmouth Grammar, which he ran with great flair and espiéglerie for 15 years, helping pioneer, among other things, language courses in France in the hols. Also taught at Eastbourne College, Winchester and Dulwich. Keen (energetic!) committee man, including Admiralty Interview Board '84-'97, and Chairman of HMC in '96, where he made a very thoughtful inaugural speech on the problems of children today and the need not to sweep them under the carpet. A governor of Sevenoaks and of Winchester. Recreations 'soccer, France, theatre, avoiding dinner parties' (the later is a pity as he would make an erudite and interesting dining companion!) Forward thinking 'European' in his attitude. A fan of the International Baccalaureate. Took over from tall, handsome Mr Robin Reeve, who became head here in 1980 – a long innings.

Academic Matters: Strong, strong, strong. School committed to enriching the boys' academic diet, encouraging study of subjects 'because they are intrinsically interesting subjects to study rather than because they're going to lead to X'. Head wants boys to think creatively as he says there is a 'touch of autism in over stimulated and structured children'. Setting from the first year. Sciences taught separately towards dual award examination. Ten GCSEs the norm (some early), but several take as many as 13. English is an outstanding department, also maths and classics, 'but every department is good', commented a parent. Biology, chemistry, English, French, history and maths were popular A level choices last year. Two full-time librarians and existing (small) library being extended next year. Many distinguished members of staff – some of whom stay many decades. Will be offering the IB from 2001.

Games, Options, the Arts: Lots of everything – 'Boys aren't just eggheads,' said a pupil. Get a copy of the school mag – very glossy, black and white bar the fat section on art – and you will get the gist of the breadth of activities. Rugby, hockey fields etc, on site (plus 15 more acres at Motspur Park), cross-country on Wimbledon Common, good rowing from the school's boathouse on the Tideway at Putney. Renaissance of extra-curricular activities since Saturday school was abolished (though up to a third of the boys come in for sports or rehearsals on Saturdays). Ceramics must be among the best in any school. Music also very vigorous and so is drama with what one mother calls 'Surprisingly sophisticated productions'. Societies busy at lunchtime and after school, and the great and good drawn in to talk on all manner of topics – recently, for instance, Lord Saatchi, Lord (Robin) Butler, Bob Ayling, Anne Widdecombe and Lord Cranborne.

Background and Atmosphere: Situated on the edge of Wimbledon Common. Curious hotchpotch of buildings, including fine collegiate hall, elegant 18th-century house and sundry modern additions with plenty of elbow room, pleasant grounds, junior school (qv) on site. Sixth form block with good tidy common room. Originally founded in 1829 in the Strand, as the junior department of King's College, University of London. See the recent history published by James & James which, among other things, recounts the ghastly death by bullying of a boy in the 1880s. Back to the present: a sombre and busy seat of learning with bustle and purpose. Lively place with boys involved with all sorts of activities other than excelling at exams.

Pastoral Care and Discipline: Well disciplined school. Well organised looking boys. Alarming recent report of bullying has caused them to re-think. School have appointed a master in charge of pastoral care and hold open forums with parents, big emphasis on responsibility. School gives parents advice about pastoral issues. No long hair. Manners are OK but not polished. Prefects now sent off on leadership training courses (like many others), and regard themselves as junior managers. Copes with the occasional odd-ball.

Pupils and Parents: Middle class, professional parents, 'the parents and pupils are mostly life's natural hard workers,' joked one of them. Largely from South-West London, Kingston and Surrey, lots of ethnic minorities (mainly Asians). Sixth form allowed to drive to school. 'Boys not born with a silver spoon,' commented another, 'but often well aware that they are the intellectual elite.' Old Boys include vast numbers of university dons, Dante Gabriel Rossetti, Walter Sickert, Roy Plomley.

Entrance: Two-thirds from school's own wonderful prep (qv), the rest from a wide variety of schools, pre-tested at 11. CE pass mark is 65 per cent, 'but boys need spare capacity as well'. Head says they are not a hot-house and that they take boys who have something other to offer than academic excellence.

Exit: Virtually all to university (conservative in their choices), heaps to Oxbridge. Engineering, the law, the City and medicine continue to be likely careers. A few leave post-GCSE.

Money Matters: Up to 15 entrance scholarships at 13+ and several at 16+ of varying values from 10 per cent to a maximum of 50 per cent fees. Three awards for boys showing 'outstanding promise as scientists, classicists or modern linguists'.

Remarks: A hot shot boys' academic day school in South-West London, with less of the high-pressured atmosphere than some London establishments, helped in this by being situated in a desirable suburb (ie lots of space).

KING'S SCHOOL BRUTON

Somerset BA10 0ED

Tel: *01749 813326* Fax: *01749 813426*

E-mail: kingshm@kingsbruton.somerset.sch.uk

Web: www.kingsbruton.com

✦ Pupils: 300 boys, 70 girls (260 board, 110 day) ✦ Ages: 13-18 ✦ Size of sixth form: 170 ✦ C of E ✦ Fee-paying

---

Head: Since 1993, Mr Richard Smyth, MA PGCE (fifties), educated at Sedbergh and Emmanuel College, Cambridge, where he read law and history. Taught at Christ's Hospital, worked in the family business, taught at Gresham's, Housemaster at Wellington College. Keen cricketer (Cambridge blue), Swiss wife and three children.

Entrance: Via CE (not a high hurdle); five GCSEs at C or above for entry to sixth form, and Bs for subjects to be studied. Many come to King's Bruton through the school's own prep, Hazlegrove Tel: 01963

440 314, at Sparkford, Yeovil, with around 350 boys and girls, in glorious setting, housed in Mildmay's family home, surrounded by parkland. It is assumed that children will go on to King's Bruton, and almost all do.

Exit: After degree/higher education, careers often in estate management, farming, Services, architecture, the law, medicine.

Remarks: A small, traditional, competent and efficient school with a broad intake. Founded in 1519 by Bishop of London and a chancellor of St Paul's. Many staff of long standing, some thorough teaching, very good facilities, including computer department. GCSE results fine – almost all above C in the crucial subjects. Maths, English, business studies and thee sciences feature at A level; the average grade is C or a bit better, reflecting the intake, but almost all pass. Exceptional design centre (for art, technology and IT) producing some exciting work, and good art – with ten or so pupils taking art and design at A level (results spread A–E, not thrilling). New science building.

Pupils are kept busy, though the pace is fairly gentle, with three-weekly reports, record of achievement, regular church services and assemblies (proper provision is made for RCs and Muslims,) games three days a week, Saturdays included (major sports tours every few years). Serious sports (reports take up a huge chunk of the school magazine), notably successful at hockey, netball, rugby and tennis. Special Learning Unit with full-time specialist and helper (also qualified), plus EFL teacher. Policy is to 'support rather than withdraw our pupils from other classes'. Caring environment, with good pastoral set-up. Popular with Forces (38 MoD children at last count) and girls have doubled. Vast majority go on to degree courses, including a good number to Oxbridge. The school started to go fully co-ed in a small way in 1997 (has had girls in the sixth for many years) – with the opening of Arion (girls') House. Now has two girls' houses.

Certainly a school to consider if you are looking for a small rural school that does everything, isn't daunting, has the facilities, set in a charming ancient little town in a lovely part of the country. A good place to be a big fish in a small pond. Not smart, low profile, but does its stuff, giving the average boy confidence. Some recent reports from very happy parents – gentle approach and thorough teaching not easy to come by these days.

THE KING'S SCHOOL

Canterbury, Kent CT1 2ES

TEL: *01227 595501* FAX: *01227 595595*

E-MAIL: headmaster@kings-school.co.uk

WEB: www.kings-school.co.uk

◆ PUPILS: 425 boys, 335 girls (620 board, 151 day) ◆ Ages: 13-18 ◆ Size of sixth form: 344 ◆ C of E ◆ Fee-paying

---

Head: Since 1996, the Rev Canon Keith Wilkinson BA MA FRSA who comes here from being head of Berkhamsted, and previously taught at Eton etc. Went to Cambridge and Hull Universities; he has worked as a parish priest. Married (his wife is a teacher and a probation officer), with twin teenage daughters. Starting to get approving noises from pupils. Governors a daunting lot. One third have, or have had, their children or close relatives in the school.

Academic Matters: A level results mostly excellent. A wide choice of courses, with English, French, history and chemistry all popular. Good numbers taking art, geology, politics and Spanish. Under the new system pupils will take four ASs and an 'enrichment course' (eg Italian), a key skills course, or general studies. Japanese available. GCSE consistently excellent; the brightest can take maths, Latin and a modern language early. Separate sciences for half, double award for the others. The top set of Latinists take Greek with it – 'Gratin.'

Slightly dry talk-and-chalk approach to teaching – the aim is first and foremost to get those exam results, so no wandering off into gardens of bright images. Streaming and setting; 'work is taken seriously at King's,' says the prospectus (certainly true of mainstream subjects). Supervised evening prep (even at the top of the school). IT has not been brilliant, but computing facilities are now receiving major additional investment. Library by Butterfield – his first major building. School owns the personal libraries of both Sir Hugh Walpole and Somerset Maugham. Children are 'worked like dogs' according to a parent.

Games, Options, the Arts: Dynamic head of sport. County-standard sports centre, with pool, six squash courts, blue sports hall, fitness suite, snack bar etc, which members of the public can also use (at a price) when the school isn't. Two all-weather pitches. Rowing school – girls as well as boys – two FPs at Sydney Olympics. Choice of sport increases as pupils move up the school. Hockey, national-standard fencing.

Excellent CDT facilities, ditto art centre in converted 13th-century priory; small theatre. Several choirs, including one which sings for the school in the Cathedral (though NB this is not the Cathedral choir, which is a separate entity). Lots of drama and music generally. The 'climax of artistic endeavour' is the annual King's Week, spoken of lyrically by all as feast of soul and flow of reason in the last week of summer term. D of E, CCF, community service.

Background and Atmosphere: Romantic setting in the middle of Canterbury in the shadow of the Cathedral (son et lumiere), and using glorious ancient buildings and quad owned by the Dean and Chapter, as well as rich variety of architectural styles for different boarding houses, art school, former synagogue (this last a monument to Egyptomania). Beautiful at every turn (pretty gardens, flint walls), and, said a housemistress with glee, 'when parents see the place they are instantly won over'. Atmosphere of ancient customs and traditions in fact totally at odds with the truth, which is that a small school on the site was turned by Canon Shirley (head of King's from 1935-62 and one of the great pioneering entrepreneurial heads) almost overnight into a place with smart uniform, quaint customs, in a marketing exercise of which any captain of industry would be proud. Girls now 46 per cent of pupils and wear smart uniform, pinstripes and jacket and white shirts with wing collars – like little barristers, and pupils so taken with it apparently some go on wearing it when they leave school.

Pastoral Care and Discipline: Bullying problems now seem to be a thing of the past. Pupil-based anti-bullying committee set up; Shell (first year) pupils have acted out bullying incidents to raise awareness – bravo. Head has put a former sergeant-major on the lawn to enforce dress rules etc. 90 members of staff NON-SMOKING – how about this for a good example? Not enough female staff, but 'positively trying to get them'. Personal tutor assigned to each child, keeps same one throughout school. Fortnightly report for each pupil. Housemasters and housemistresses are all members of the academic staff. Discipline is strict – and pupils know what is expected. Alcohol a perennial temptation – pubs right on the doorstep, but supermarkets the worst offenders. No mercy for drug users.

Pupils and Parents: A rich mix, middle class, upper class, children of Kent shop-keepers, and they have recently fielded three minor foreign royals. Around 5 per cent ex-pats and 5 per cent foreigners – Germany, France, USA, Hong Kong, India, Russia, Japan and Nigeria. Parents often Foreign Office diplomats, lawyers or 'with the BBC.' Pupils outward-looking, confident and conformist – and very middle class.

Entrance: Parents and children choose which house they wish to go into. CE for most. Pupils here from 40 different prep schools. Pupils entering at sixth form expected to have eight GCSEs at B or above, As or Bs in A level subjects.

Exit: A good number to Oxbridge; the rest to 'other universities and colleges', and a clutch to medical schools and to ex-polys, the odd one to re-take. OBs: Somerset Maugham (who hated it, and is said to have based *Of Human Bondage* on it), Walpole, Marlowe, Patrick Leigh Fermor (expelled), William Harvey, David Gower, and the first Englishman in space, Michael Foale.

Money Matters: 'Up to 30' scholarships, including music and art. Bursaries for hard-ship cases 'when a child is on his/her way to a public examination'. No endowment.

Remarks: Popular co-ed boarding school which works well for the bright, bouncy extrovert in search of straight up-and-down academic education. Of late a kinder atmosphere is beginning to prevail, and the head avers that 'gentle imaginative children' can now blossom here. Cleverly marketed. Glorious setting.

THE KING'S SCHOOL

Wrexham Road, Chester CH4 7QL

TEL: *01244 680026* FAX: *01244 678008*

E-MAIL: admissions@kingschester.co.uk

WEB: www.kingschester.co.uk

✦ PUPILS: 500 boys and 30 girls (in the sixth form) (all day). Plus own junior school on site, with 170 boys ✦ Ages: 11-18, prep school 7-11 ✦ Size of sixth form: 155. Girls in the sixth form since 1998 ✦ C of E ✦ Fee-paying

---

Head: Since 2000, Mr T J Turvey (fifties). Educated at Monkton Combe, read botany and zoology at Cardiff. Taught at The Edinburgh Academy and then Monkton Combe, ending as deputy head. Moved to The Hulme Grammar School, Oldham as deputy head, becoming head there in 1995. Principal examiner for Nuffield A level biology. Married to Dr Janet Webster, one son (at Manchester Grammar School.) Churchgoer, musician. Took over from Mr A R D Wickson, who was here from 1981. School's patron: His Grace, the Duke of Westminster. Chairman of governors: the Very Rev the Dean of Chester.

Academic Matters: Strongly and unashamedly academic school. Outstanding GCSEs – as you would expect – little below

C, strong across the board, German and the sciences – all As and Bs. 'We do it because we are selective. The results are what they ought to be,' commented the former head. A level good, though it is hard to understand why there should be so many Ds and below – 17 per cent in '00. Maths is the most popular subject as usual, closely followed by physics and chemistry. Geography, economics, history are also popular. All take general studies as an A level, and a few take Latin (but nothing more exotic.) Much emphasis on intellectual challenge, critical thought, and general studies are taken well beyond the confines of the curriculum. Largely male staff, many long-standing.

Games, Options, the Arts: Very strong rowing, boys constantly in training for this and winning all kinds of trophies, sometimes beating university teams, and boys picked for World Junior Championships. Fine boathouse on the River Dee (in the town centre, two miles away), excellent coaching. Main games showing good number of wins. Drama is good, including outdoor Shakespeare. Good on visiting speakers/lecturers, mainly academics. Art the poor relation in terms of time/energy – grim results at GCSE and A level in '00. Flourishing and expanding CCF.

Background and Atmosphere: Founded in 1541 and linked to the Cathedral. Moved to its present site (32 flat, bare acres) on the outer edge of Chester in 1960, inconvenient for public transport though double-decker school buses pile up with pupils, parents sweep in and out on school runs. Main block, pleasant brick with dignified proportions incorporates some items from the original building in the city, but overall aspect (many later additions) is featureless. However, atmosphere within hums with activity, energy.

Pastoral Care and Discipline: Staff chivvy away at loutish behaviour. Poor work, untimely work, untidy appearance, smoking etc, merit detentions, but serious breaches of conduct non-existent, says Head. Newsletter helps keep parents in touch. Pupils face 'immediate expulsion' for drugs offences. Drugs awareness programme for removes through to 4/5th years.

Pupils and Parents: Decent, hard-working professional parents (some very rich in this area) who send their boys here from miles away. Elegant dark green/blue-striped blazer. Articulate, confident, unpretentious boys with a rich mix of accents.

Entrance: By examination; highly selective at 11+ and for later 'chance vacancies'. No automatic entry from the junior school. Entry there at 7 (down from 8) with queues for places and tests. Minimum qualification for sixth form entry is five GCSE passes at A or B (some require A) plus interview etc.

Exit: Wide variety of degree courses, London, Durham, Leeds fielding some, but for '97 no real marked favourites, except around 11 to Oxbridge. Huge breadth of careers afterwards – from assistant manager for Bass Taverns to singing as well as the usual solicitors etc. Quite a lot of gapping, before and after college.

Money Matters: Had 107 assisted places and school is aiming to replace them with its bursary fund, but it will not be easy. One full-fee academic scholarship for outstanding ability with financial need. Good value (£1,917 per term at time of writing).

Remarks: The top, flourishing, academic boys' day school in the area which crams a lot into its day and retains an agreeably personal touch.

THE KING'S SCHOOL

Worcester WR1 2LH

TEL: *01905 721 700* FAX: *01905 721 710*

E-MAIL: info@ksw.org.uk

WEB: www.ksw.org.uk

✦ PUPILS: 785: 455 boys, 330 girls (Plus two Junior Schools, one 7-11 with 176 boys and girls, the other 3-11 with 200). All day ✦ Ages: 11-18 ✦ Size of sixth form: 240 ✦ C of E ✦ Fee-paying

Head: Since 1998, Mr Timothy H Keyes, MA (forties). Educated at Christ's Hospital, Wadham College, Oxford and Exeter (PGCE). Classicist. Previously second master at the Royal Grammar School, Guildford, before that climbing the classical pole at the Perse, Whitgift and Tiffin. Active churchman, chorister, campanologist. Succeeded the friendly, likeable and long-running (fifteen years) John Moore.

Academic Matters: Work and homework taken seriously. Overall results at GCSE and A level seem good in the light of a moderately broad intake – good ALIS scores too.

Games, Options, the Arts: Music tradition (organ and choral scholarships to Oxbridge have been chalked up regularly). Sport is an important part of school life, success is valued and widely celebrated; a wide range on offer, including rowing. Art (under Mrs Liz Hand) flourishing, a bit un-celebrated and hidden away – it hardly features in the prospectus or magazine – but results outstanding. Large numbers of computers, good IT. Superb pupils' newspaper, The King's Herald, makes you wish that other tabloids were that good. High-quality concert/theatre programmes produced by pupils. Vigorous careers department, with industrial links. Unusually successful Young Enterprise, CCF (Army and RAF), D of E, climbing expeditions to the Himalayas (they do aid work there too). 'Full of get up and go staff with ideas,' said a parent.

Background and Atmosphere: Steady and solid performer, which has had girls in the sixth form for some years and started going fully co-ed in '91. Has closed its last boarding houses to go all day. Strong muscular Christianity. Ancient foundation (7th century), and refounded by Henry VIII after the suppression of the priory. Big expansion and building programme to meet the demands of day co-education all completed in '95; a further development programme now in progress. Set in the precincts of the Cathedral, the school sits compactly between the River Severn and the city. Buildings of many dates, including the 14th-century refectory, now the main hall, the ancient Edgar Tower which houses the library, and a maze of uninspiring but acceptable modern buildings all grouped around gardens and quadrangles. Pleasant and popular King's Junior School (also co-ed), stands in its own grounds next door (uses many of the senior school facilities), and provides choristers for the Cathedral choir. The other (recently acquired) junior school, King's Hawford, is in the country just north of the city.

Pastoral Care and Discipline: Drugs taken seriously, punishment at head's discretion.

Pupils and Parents: Parents mainly professionals. OVs (Old Vigornians) in business and the professions, include Geoffrey Mulcahy, Rick Mayall and Chris Tarrant.

Entrance: Register in good time, the school is oversubscribed and entrance is by exam (qualifying for those coming up from the Junior School, competitive for external candidates). Fifty or so places at 11+ (own exam), twenty five at 13+ (own exam or CE), about 20 at sixth form; selective but not outstandingly so. Junior schools entry by test.

Exit: University for 95 per cent, all over the place, around 10 per year to Oxbridge.

Money Matters: Not a well endowed school, but lots of scholarships and exhibitions. Bursaries, help for OVs, and special arrangements for choristers.

Remarks: Traditional, organised but pleasantly relaxed school; flourishing, and producing well-balanced boys and girls who do not end up thinking the world owes them a living. School very well considered locally.

KINGSTON GRAMMAR

SCHOOL

70-72 London Road, Kingston-Upon-Thames KT2 2PY

TEL: *020 8546 5875* FAX: *020 8547 1499*

E-MAIL: head@kingston-grammar.surrey.sch.uk

WEB: www.kingston-grammar.surrey.sch.uk

✦ PUPILS: 600 boys and girls✦ Ages: 10-18
✦ Non-denom✦ Fee-paying

Head: Duncan Baxter MA FRSA (late forties). Educated at Lord Williams School, Thame followed by Trinity College, Oxford where he read English. Wife Neredah 'a huge support' helps with PR and at school events. One son at Oxford the other in lower sixth at the school. Sharp minded and urbane, a powerful personality. He is not afraid of maverick decisions. Stood by Jeffrey Archer delivering prizes at speech day, just hours before his ousting from London Mayoral race. Prides himself on a range of personal celebrity contacts wheeled in to raise school's public profile.

Academic Matters: Very strong, plenty of pressure, good deal of homework. Despite girls, some bias in maths and sciences. Setting in maths and French, but largely taught in forms of no more than 25. Results thoroughly impressive, (99 per cent pass at A level – 79 per cent grades AB) (98 per cent pass at GCSE – 85 per cent grades A★–B). Majority pupils held to 10 GCSEs (head sees no need for more). Most common sixth form combination 3 A levels plus general studies (well-chosen range of externally delivered lectures provide light relief from academic workload). A few high-flyers sit 4 A levels. Strugglers might leave to less hothouse environments during the course of their schooling. One member of staff on hand for special needs support to mild dyslexics. Post GCSE some movement in and out before sixth form. Absolute requirement of B or above at GCSE to sit A level in any subject and minimum 5 GCSEs.

Games, Options, the Arts: Avowed emphasis on all round development. Well written and illustrated 'Kingstonian' mag talks up full extra-curricular programme. Active CCF and Christian Union. Success in debating and drama (plenty of school productions, pupil in National Youth Theatre). Expanding music department, quality orchestra, many recitals, 1 in 3 play an instrument.

Sports are ubiquitous despite their exile to leafy 22-acre grounds 15 minutes away by minibus. Winning matters. Much focus on areas of considerable past success: namely rowing and hockey: Numerous Olympic hockey players amongst the Old Boys. Much venerated coxless four Olympic hero James Cracknell heads the field of rowing alumni. Minority interests catered for with shooting team that does well nationally, real tennis and girls' cricket.

Background and Atmosphere: Established in the late middle ages. A long history as a boys' public school, grant maintained by the state from 1926 until the late '70's, when it reverted to full independence and took in girls. Ultra-urban location bounded by once gracious, now jaded 'Fairfield Park' (part owned by the school) and 4 lane A308 into Kingston. Head cites accessibility (nearness to main railway station/bus routes) as an asset; weigh that against the inner cityness of it all. Located opposite Tiffin School (state boys' grammar) – what barely passes as friendly rivalry is intense. The site is small, its Victorian frontage offering the best aspect, housing offices and refectory. To its rear the school hall and the junior and senior teaching blocks, recently much developed with mezzanines and extensions squeezed alongside, and, in cases, on top of, utilitarian '50's and '20's built lower floors.

Outdoor space at a premium. Wholesome insistence on outdoor breaktimes for all but the sixth formers – where do they all go? Despite the buildings' warren-like qualities, they are light, clean, perfectly decorated and maintained. Technology areas brimming with state of the art equipment. Notable new additions; multi media language lab and art gallery which is part corridor, part conservatory, displaying impressive range of pupils' art and technology projects. Walls throughout evidence pupils' endeavours. Restrictions of site geographical rather than financial.

Uniform compulsory until (suited) sixth form. School captains and senior prefects are gowned to denote rank. School lunches compulsory only in lower years, popular decision. Some parental comment that 'you are encouraged to stay at the gate'. Communication between school and home only stepped up if problems arise, otherwise organised feedback once a year at parents' evening. Head points out the three parent organisations, parent/staff social events, two written reports each year and two grade cards each term, as well as two newsletters and a head's letter each term.

Pastoral Care and Discipline: 'All valued and respected for who and what they are' asserts a parent. Borne out in head's own emphasis on the nurtured individual. Self-awareness, and self-belief are preached within a community described as 'pretty worldly-wise'. Saturday detention for three infringements of school rules, commendations for good work/behaviour. As regards major taboos; drugs, sex, bullying, smoking and alcohol, message is: 'can't get away with much on a site this size'. Pastoral care devolved to form teachers, form prefects pick up minor problems and a school counsellor attends weekly.

Pupils and Parents: Parents 'pretty down to earth' cites a mother. More than 50 per cent from Kingston and close environs, others commute in from SW London and Surrey. At entry 60 per cent from state maintained schools 40 per cent from private preps. Reasonably broad cultural mix.

Entrance: Schools' test and interview for 10s (25 enter at this stage), same for 11s (majority of year group joins at 11). Common entrance at 13 (15 boys join post-CE). Local reputation for difficult entrance standards – uniformly bright intake.

Exit: 99 per cent to university, up to 10 to Oxbridge, gap years increasingly popular after A levels.

Money Matters: Bursaries (25 per cent of fees): 10 at 11+ and 2 at 13+ based on achievement in entrance examinations. Scholarships (50 per cent of fees) at 11+, 13+, or 16+ for outstanding potential in music (2) art (2) and sport (5).

Remarks: Traditional academic co-ed school in a town setting. Well presented, confident, happy pupils. Inordinately well run institution, slightly masculine feel to it although plenty of girls in evidence (60:40 boy:girl mix). Twice as many male teaching staff as female. Not the first choice for shrinking violets (of either sex). Ideally suits the street-wise go-getters.

THE LADY ELEANOR HOLLES SCHOOL

Hanworth Road, Hampton, Middlesex TW12 3HF

Tel: *020 8979 1601* Fax: *020 8941 8291*

✦ Pupils: 710 girls in the senior school, 190 in the junior school; all day ✦ Ages: 7-18 ✦ Size of sixth form: 200 ✦ C of E foundation ✦ Fee-paying

---

Head: Since 1981, (and staying), Miss Elizabeth Candy BSc FRSA (fifties). Went to Merrywood Grammar School for Girls, Bristol, and read chemistry at Westfield College, London. Sees her role as an 'enabler' for both her girls and her staff, for former to emerge 'confident and assertive' in what she sees as a society 'still rife with sexist prejudice'. Dynamic, fit, perceptive, with a dry sense of humour (breezy, jokey), commands respect. 'She's tall and scary and gives evil looks at assembly,' says a lower school girl, while senior girls find her 'positive, encouraging, involved'. Ex-Putney High second-in-command, she still teaches PSHE and general studies and pitches into school activities.

Academic Matters: Good solid exam results achieved without undue pressure. Compulsory Latin for two years (strong but inevitably small classics department – 5 took Latin A level, 3 Greek in '99 – all got As, par for the course). LEH pioneered Russian in the '50s, very few taking it, sadly. Bias to traditionally female subjects fading: most popular A level subject is still English literature, with excellent teaching and results, but maths is hard on its heels now, and chemistry and biology have both overtaken French. Some less academic options at A level available including home economics, textile and design, theatre studies (joint with Hampton School), practical music. Also psychology on offer and ever more popular (23 taking it in '00). 24 girls in a class (pre A levels) under almost exclusively female staff – 'reflecting the well-qualified wives of established professional men in this fairly prosperous area,' comments head. General studies remains 'an examined course to keep them interested,' although 'league tables are absolutely rubbish,' she adds fiercely.

Games, Options, the Arts: Top girls' rowing school, listing among trophies Women's Henley, Schools Head of the River. Squad often includes both National and Junior World Championship rowers. New boathouse, owned jointly with Hampton School, at Sunbury. Indoor pool (keen scuba diving), 15 tennis courts, badminton courts in excellent gym, lacrosse etc, 'but you can choose to do whatever you want, or not,' approves an un-gamesy pupil. Recent innovation: girls' Army and RAF Cadet Corps. Keen music, good chess. Popular art under 'inspiring' head of department. Active fund-raising for charities.

Background and Atmosphere: Founded in the Cripplegate Ward of the City of London in 1711; two early 18th-century plaster figures from the original school bear incongruous witness to the transplant to the suburbs in 1936. The school (largely inaccessible by public transport) is a tranquil oasis on a suburban avenue. Main building is 'very unprepossessing' said a disappointed would-be parent – a cross between a '30s factory and an American high school – light, airy, wide corridors, spacious grounds. Recent sixth form library and classrooms. Cherry-red and grey uniform, ties optional. At sixth form anything goes.

Pastoral Care and Discipline: Small evidence of bucking the system here. 'There's a lot of space to move here and a lot going on to occupy physically and mentally,' comments the head, 'and there's room to make a noise if you need to.' Two pastoral tutors per class. Sixth formers can leave the premises at lunchtime or invite Hampton boys in: 'They sometimes hang around outside school for the middle years, but we can take them or leave them,' disparaged a sixth former.

Pupils and Parents: Daughters of stockbrokers or yuppies (with a light dusting of ethnic minorities) who bus themselves in via school-organised buses and coaches over a wide catchment from Weybridge and Windsor to Guildford; increasing numbers commute out from Richmond, Barnes, Kew and Twickenham. Parents are middle-class, comfortably-off, involved with the school. Girls are busy, capable, civilised and unpressurised who get on well with each other.

Entrance: Slightly under half from own junior school, via exam. 'We can afford to be fairly selective in looking for those who really want to be involved in all aspects of school life,' says the head, who gets five to six applicants for each place, about 20 per cent from state schools. £500 non-returnable deposit required on acceptance of place (refundable at end of final term). Restless girls leaving at 16+ are likely to go to boys' schools, such as Westminster, Richmond College, Ardingly, Stowe, Wellington. Automatic transfer to sixth form 'unless there is a particular problem'.

Exit: Most to the longer-established universities: Bristol, Birmingham, Nottingham etc; 15-20 average annually to Oxbridge.

Money Matters: A few academic and music scholarships on offer, plus an increased number of means-tested Cripplegate Schools Foundation entrance bursaries. Several sixth form scholarships of 30 per cent fees.

Remarks: Impressive premier league girls' day school, sound and popular, geographically advantaged, and excellent value, steered strongly but calmly by characterful, unpushy head. A local favourite for yonks, it has now caught the selector's eye. Doing well, producing enthusiastic live wires.

JUNIOR SCHOOL: Burlington House is in the grounds: some girls who have been on the same site since the age of seven are keen to 'bolt' post-GCSE.

LADY MARGARET SCHOOL

Parson's Green, London SW6 4UN

TEL: *020 7736 7138* FAX: *020 7384 2553*

E-MAIL: j.oliver@ladymargaret.hammersmith-

fulham.sch.uk

✦ PUPILS: 577 girls; all day ✦ Ages: 11–18
✦ Size of sixth form: 142 ✦ C of E
✦ Voluntary aided state

Head: Since 1984, Mrs Joan Olivier BA (fifties). Came from Camden Girls as deputy in '73. State educated, read history at London and did her postgraduate work at Cambridge. Splendidly vocal (gassy) lady, totally open-door policy, wedded to the school, though plenty have tried to poach her. 'I love it here, I say: why should I want to move?' Cheerful, positive, liberal with praise, also firm in rebuke where necessary. Husband worked in the City, own son at university. Insists on bright colours on the walls, flowers in the hall etc. 'People think it's rather odd, but I tell them that if you give children a bright environment, they'll be proud of it and won't wreck the place.'

Academic Matters: Rigorous teaching and expectations. Traditional approach. Several staff with both private and state school experience. Most are exceptionally committed. Study skills keenly taught. Homework from one hour per night from the start. Class sizes variable. French and Spanish options. The only state school in the borough to offer music at both GCSE and A level. Does excellently well at GCSEs and at A level (brilliant by inner London state school standards). Good and well-used library.

Games, Options, the Arts: Imaginative drama. Sixth form put on their own ambitious productions. Loads of outings and trips, sleep-overs in the school, special leavers breakfast. Netball/tennis courts on site, energetic sport matches programme. Good art (good uptake at A level); signs of embryonic fashion designers in evidence. Music another lively department.

Background and Atmosphere: School has its origins in Whitelands College School, founded in 1842, threatened with closure in 1917 and rescued by Miss Enid Moberly Bell and other staff to become Lady Margaret in 1917. Elegant Georgian bow-windowed mansion with common in front and gardens behind, plus modern gym, hall etc. Super design and technology building (for which the school energetically raised vast sums). Moral values and caring aspect breed deep loyalty and a distinctly happy atmosphere, much commented on by parents and staff. Feels like a private school, and very much run along those lines.

Pastoral Care and Discipline: High marks for discipline. 'This is a Church school,' says the head firmly. Truancy is negligible, but some condoned absences. Girls neat and tidy (and ticked off if they're not). Has never had a discipline case involving drugs (touch wood – how many schools can say that?) and head comments she would 'probably wait to see the nature of the offence before I decided what to do about it'.

Pupils and Parents: A big mix, including a handful of very keenly involved parents. Some brilliant fund raisers. Some refugees from the private sector, more middle-class professionals than many state schools. Girls are polite, articulate and fiercely supportive of each other.

Entrance: Incredibly difficult and no flexibility – parents wring their hands and ask what must they do to get children in. Accepts 45 Church-going girls (letters from vicars needed), 45 others: from eight boroughs – including Ealing, Barnes, Wandsworth. No preference to siblings. 600 children tested in December (maths, English, non-verbal reasoning) to ensure a mixed ability intake; all Church applicants are interviewed. 'I like girls who are going to do something, who have potential, who need a break, who will appreciate the value added here.' Five GCSEs at C or above usually required for entry at sixth form level (some departments require B).

Exit: Some always leave post-GCSE, but the majority stay on for A level, and are joined by pupils from other schools. Increasing numbers go on to further education, (training courses/qualifications/degrees) – and a few to Oxbridge annually.

Money Matters: State-funded. Parents regularly raise money for the school – currently looking for £150,000 for art, music and science. Head keen on boosting coffers by letting out the school for Weight Watchers, weddings etc.

Remarks: Super successful state girls' school, with a well-deserved reputation for being a nice, caring place under an exceptional head.

LANCING COLLEGE
Lancing, Sussex BN15 0RW

Tel: *01273 452 213 Admissions: 01273 454 599*

Fax: *01273 464 720*

E-mail: admissions@lancing.dialnet.com

Web: www.lancing.org.uk

✦ Pupils: around 410 – 330 boys and 80 girls – mostly in the sixth form, 20 or so at 13+ from '00 ✦ Ages: 13-18 ✦ Size of sixth form: around 250 ✦ C of E ✦ Fee-paying

---

Head: Since 1998, Mr Peter Tinniswood MA MBA (late forties), educated at Charterhouse and Magdalen College, Oxford where he read PPE. Previously head of Magdalen College School. Was also a housemaster at Marlborough, where he helped introduce business studies before leaving to do an MBA at INSEAD. Funny, unusual turn of phrase (makes the boys laugh), very much a manager. Altogether a good man, and one to watch. Has high-powered Swiss-French wife who works part-time in the fashion business as well as taking her role as head's wife seriously. Took over from Mr Christopher Saunders, who was here from '93.

Academic Matters: Good wide curriculum. Separate sciences offered for all at GCSE (some dual award). Good exam results given the relatively broad intake of pupils: 'My middling bright son has done better than we hoped,' commented a father, pleased with the commitment and high expectancy of staff here. No streaming, but setted for English, maths, sciences and languages. Fantastic electronics department. Lots of modern languages – exchanges with Spanish, Italians, Germans. Everyone does two languages in first year – French, Spanish, or German, and can pick up Italian. Classics particularly strong with some excellent teaching (three full-time staff) – everyone does either Latin or classical civilisation, and about 60 per cent go on to do one or the other at GCSE. Greek is timetabled for anyone to do – it's an 'official' option (not many choose it for A level, but younger boys are triumphant at inter-school classical reading competitions). Classes in lower school no more than 20 pupils; A level sets between 6-12, with upper limit of 15. Some good, dedicated staff, though parents caution that it is not all singing and dancing. Twelve female staff at last count.

Games, Options, the Arts: Huge art department in crypt of chapel, now expanded into a whole new building. Some excellent work being done. Good pottery department. Good drama. Very strong music – every corner alive to the sound of practising. Head of chapel music, Welshman Neil Cox, acknowledged to be a star. Choir tours Europe every year. Strong games: good soccer school (won the Independent Schools FA Cup in 1997), currently terrific tennis, sailing etc. Keen mountaineering club – off to cliffs and to Scotland. Traditional links and exchanges with Kamazu Academy, Malawi. Strong debating and public speaking – long tradition of success here, and have recently made it to the finals of the Cambridge Union Schools Debating competition, and to the semi-finals of The Observer Mace. On no account overlook the school's famous farm. Does wonders for boys and girls interested in veterinary science (steady little flow of these) but also, say

staff, all pupils like to go and commune with the animals.

Background and Atmosphere: Occupies one of best school sites in the country, 550 acres on hill above the A27 looking out to sea. Dwarfed by a monstrous school chapel of the upturned-pig school of architecture (opinions differ on this, however, and some find it glorious, awe-inspiring etc). Monument to the worldly ambition of the school's founder, Canon Nathaniel Woodard (of Woodard Schools – muscular Christianity – fame), whose tomb takes huge pride of place within the chapel. Made of sandstone. Acoustics bad – 'like singing in a sand dune', says head of chapel music. Beside this edifice, the largest school chapel in the world, the daily round of the school pales into insignificance, though pupils say they get used to it. (Maintenance bills paid for by the Friends of Lancing Chapel – and by heck it needs a few – by the Woodard Foundation and English Heritage.) Glorious flint-faced cloisters through which the wind whistles – freezing cold as charity (go in spring when blossoms out for best viewing). One of v few schools where boys' dorms are ritzier than girls'. Girls in two neat little houses, small and without character. Studies (in girls' case) formerly and aptly called 'pitts'. Boys in rooms worthy of Oxbridge colleges, much panelling, lots of individual studies: the 'refurbishment' programme has done away with the huge dormitory that vied with Loretto's for being the biggest, most gruesome in the land. (Five hundred sailors stationed here in the war.) Friendly atmosphere.

Pastoral Care and Discipline: Discipline tightened up ('it jolly well needed it,' warned a mother). Pupils' appearance has been 'improved'. Staff boldly claim the pupils now know where they stand and 'have responded very positively to the stricter, but in no way oppressive, regime.' This is, needless to say, not what the pupils say. Boys choose their own tutor after the first year (to give them time to look around). In theory each member of staff limited to 15 pupils, but popular ones take on more. Each new boy is issued with a copy of The Pupils' Charter. Other faiths welcome, but all must come to chapel. Achievers – in any field – are liberally praised and encouraged. Staff are ambitious for their pupils rather than for themselves.

Pupils and Parents: About half of pupils come from South-East. Popular with ex-pats, and a goodly number of pupils from Hong Kong, Korea, Malaysia, Germany, also US exchange. Around 10 children of clergymen at any one time. Girls from nearby schools, including one or two from Roedean, and occasionally from Benenden, also from St Swithun's. OBs: Tim Rice, Tom Sharpe, Trevor Huddleston, Peter Pears – who wowed them in the choir, Evelyn Waugh, and Tom Driberg, who was expelled; also playwrights Christopher Hampton and David Hare. Strong links with Korea – first bishop of Korea was here. Few second-generation.

Entrance: By CE. Pass mark 50 per cent. Pupils coming from state sector separately assessed. Girls need to register for entry into sixth form asap.

Exit: 10-15 to Oxbridge. Lots to Newcastle, Leeds, Durham, Edinburgh – the fashionable universities, also ex-polys. Some to art college, and eg organ scholarships to Oxbridge.

Money Matters: Twenty-five awards a year, including two exhibitions for families of clergymen, and others for music and art (music and art scholarships keenly sought after and make real difference to standard of pupil in school).

Remarks: Low profile public school now getting stronger; worth considering. Girls at 13+ from 2000.

LATYMER SCHOOL
Haselbury Road, Edmonton, London N9 9TN

Tel: *020 8807 4037* Fax: *020 8807 4125*

E-mail: latymer@aol.com

Web: www.latymer.co.uk

✦ Pupils: 1,344 girls and boys (in equal numbers); all day ✦ Ages: 11–18 ✦ Size of sixth form: 440 ✦ Non-denom ✦ State – voluntary aided

---

Head: Since 1999, Mr Michael Cooper OBE BA (fifties). Previously head of Hillcrest (in Hastings) and then, for nine years, principal of The British Schools in the Netherlands (where he earned his OBE). Says that 'school life should be valued for itself and not just as a preparation for adulthood'. Took over from Mr Geoffrey Mills BA (head here since 1983, widely respected and a 'brilliant manager').

Entrance: Hugely oversubscribed (1800 applications for 180 places), academically selective – by test to weed out some, then exam. 40-50 places usually available at sixth form – six GCSEs at A grade needed, plus interview.

Exit: Nearly all to university, 20+ a year to Oxbridge.

Remarks: Successful high-powered co-ed grammar school which gets super academic results with wonderfully devoted staff – they are often in at 7am, and don't leave till after 6pm and many have children in the school). Maths and science perennially popular here. A level subjects offered include Russian, sociology, theatre studies, PE.

School has special needs co-ordinator, plus a teacher appointed to co-ordinate provision for gifted children, and another monitoring individual pupils' progress. All twelve labs and tech areas refurbished, and ICT now hugely improved. Regular exchanges with schools in France, Russia and Germany. Outdoor pursuit weeks for years seven and nine at school's own field centre in North Wales. Music is a great strength – three full orchestras, four major choirs, chamber orchestra, madrigal group, wind band etc. Drama another strength: new performing arts centre opened '00. Keen sports too – this is a school which takes everything it does seriously. Strong house system. There are some super staff. Functional building stretching sideways (steamy canteen), large hall which can house the entire school for assemblies, drama, music. Playing fields behind, a pleasing girdle of green in a dreary area of outer London.

This is the school they're all talking about. If you live in this area, you need look no further.

LATYMER UPPER SCHOOL

King Street, Hammersmith, London W6 9LR

TEL: *020 8741 1851* FAX: *020 8748 5212*

E-MAIL: registrar@latymer-upper.org

WEB: www.latymer-upper.org

✦ PUPILS: 950 boys; co-ed at sixth form (Plus own preparatory school with 140 boys); all day ✦ Ages: 11-18, prep school 7-11 ✦ Size of sixth form: 330 including 80+ girls ✦ Non-denom ✦ Fee-paying

---

Head: Since 1991, Mr Colin Diggory BSc MA CMath FIMA FRSA (forties). Married with three school-age children. Educated at Redcar Grammar School and Durham, where he read mathematics. Energetic, dynamic, jolly, a total believer in the grammar school ethos. Started his teaching career at Manchester Grammar School, 'You can only go sideways after that,' moved to St Paul's, then Merchant Taylors' (head of maths), came to Latymer as second master, took over as acting head before becoming fully fledged head. Has had a happy time 'shaking up the curriculum' and 'consciously raising the academic profile'. Maintains 'We're very good at the top end,' and dead keen to 'protect and do very well for those pupils capable of three Cs'. Works with a very strong management team – and a useful set of governors.

Academic Matters: Sound and very thorough, with some high-powered teaching, with results sharpened up to produce excellent overall GCSE results in '97, with outstanding physics (46 candidates, nothing below A) – and chemistry. Maths the most popular A level subject (good results), followed by English literature; economics also popular but perhaps too many Ds and Es? Staff decreasingly male, increasingly young; head of English generally considered 'brilliant and fun'. Class sizes reduced to around 20, number of sets increased (but staff numbers kept the same). Sciences offered as three separate subjects and dual award GCSE. Strong IT and well-used computers all around the place.

Games, Options, the Arts: Rowing a special strength – impressive boathouse with Olympic oarsman as a coach. Saturday morning a busy time on the river here. One of the few schools that rows from home. Under 13s regularly produce winning teams. Good place for the sporty types, with lots of matches (864 fixtures of one sort or another during one academic year), 'though you can get away with doing very little,' said a non-sporting pupil. Strong rugby (have been Middlesex champions), also good at cricket and football (girls' team too). Art and drama both very popular (most recent production The Rivals), and there is a strong music tradition (joint orchestra with Godolphin and Latymer (qv), and exchange with The Johanneum in Hamburg)

Background and Atmosphere: School founded in 1624, present buildings (centenary celebrated in '95) are functional redbrick Gothic (now lit up at night), plus many additions – a tight squeeze, and every corner fully used. School divided into middle and upper for pastoral purposes. Bulging, functional, urban: no gracious lawns here. New arts centre with theatre, arts studio and music school, and the purchase of adjoining property, have relieved the former cramped feel in some areas. Sense of busyness pervades, pupils and staff going places. Unpretentious and stimulating. Visiting parents are hit by their first impression of the school bang on the main road, breathing in petrol fumes. Recent sixth form common room – and several other changes afoot, clever tampering with space, adapting to changes, (girls and deliberate policy of increased size of sixth form).

Pastoral Care and Discipline: By and large, not a problem. Tolerance really is the keynote of this school. Consultant psychologist recently taken on for one afternoon per week. Staff kept on their toes with training sessions on tutoring, pastoral care etc. Complaints from locals of boys loutishly loitering and smoking near the school gates and beyong are now 'a thing of the past' says school.

Pupils and Parents: Many races, many creeds, many colours. Streetwise, polite and (mostly) very hard-working sons (and now daughters too) of professional men and women. Boys not noted for their charm factor – girls may improve matters. Not the place for social climbers. Old Boys include Sir James Spicer, George Walden, Mel Smith, legions of MPs, Hugh Grant.

Entrance: At the ages of 11 and 13 from a wide variety of state and private schools (initial exam in January weeds out the non-starters) and boys from Latymer Prep. Not so easy now – plenty of competition. About 50 places at sixth form by interview and offer conditional on getting around five GCSE B grades (these grades also needed for pupils already in school).

Exit: To a wide variety of universities, old and new: anything between 10 and 20 to Oxbridge per year, Imperial College, Brunel, Manchester show up on the leavers list alongside Central Lancaster and John Moores, also art college, and an interestingly varied range of subjects – engineering (various), environmental sciences, medicine, business studies. Gap years are in vogue.

Money Matters: Good value for money, and parents – who are not rich – are conscious of getting their money's worth. Various academic, arts, drama, sports and musical scholarships and awards available, plus means tested 'Foundation Bursaries;' (governors are actively keen that gifted pupils are not denied places).

Remarks: Successful and worthy fee-paying grammar school, very thorough on all fronts: no-nonsense, slight A level factory feel, though broader than it first appears and pupils leave well prepared for the future. Efficiently run under extremely strong leadership. A first choice school (as opposed to the safety net it used to be).

JUNIOR SCHOOL: The Latymer Preparatory School, 38 Upper Mall, W6. Tel: 020 8748 0303 Fax: 020 8741 4916. Principal: Mr D Plummer BEd. Entry via interview and a competitive exam. This is an automatic stepping stone to the senior school. Super school, back on form after a wobble, quietly getting on with it.

LAUREL PARK SCHOOL
4 Lilybank Terrace, Glasgow G12 8RX

TEL: *0141 339 9127* FAX: *0141 357 5530*

E-MAIL: enquiries@laurel-park.gla.sch.uk

WEB: www.laurel-park.gla.sch.uk

✦ PUPILS: 407 girls, including 7 boys in nursery of 28; all day ✦ Ages: 2-18 ✦ Size of sixth form: 86 ✦ Inter-denom ✦ Fee-paying

---

Head: Since 1995, Mrs Elizabeth Surber MA PGCE (forties), whom we did not meet. Mrs Surber was educated at Tiffin Girls, read French at university, doing both her BA and MA at Exeter (with a spot of teaching in between) v keen on the West Country. She comes to Laurel Park with a husband and a cocker spaniel; previously taught at Tiffin, Cheltenham Ladies' College, and Bedford High School.

Academic Matters: The Scottish system. Good all round, English, maths, chemistry and biology the most popular; school also offers Spanish, French, German and Latin + Japanese. Science good and strong, physics lab particularly popular and on the up; 'no distractions' say the staff. Masses of new computers, including video conferencing, digital photography, scanning, voice recognition etc with a real enthusiast (male) teacher in charge. Keyboard skills taught in the 'qwerty club' at lunchtime. Impressive library with full-time fully trained librarian, William Morris fireplace with tiles to die for, and super ceilings. 'Problem busting' study nights, when staff presence is advertised and girls can get help on a formal basis. Well used. Library is open from 8.30-5pm. Max class size 20, girls set for maths at 10, English and French a year later. Pupils with suspected dyslexia problems are tested by the Dyslexia Institute, school can and will deal with 'minor' problems one to one or in small groups.

Games, Options, the Arts: Laurel Park Sports Club, funded partly by the sale of Park School buildings and the lottery fund, is open to the general public and for birthday parties, play schemes and the like. Hockey popular, and tennis; club itself is truly professional. No more gym in the old church hall, girls now troop a couple of miles down the road to Anniesland Cross instead – well worth the hike.

Drama option and timetabled in 10/14 year old module. Fabulous music and monthly concerts, quantities of choirs and almost any musical instrument possible; wind band, pipe band (in an all girls school!). Incredible number of extra-curricular activities – everything from gardening club to Greek. Home economics on line. Magical art room, with fancy Victorian ceilings and ornate mirrors, ceilings and fireplaces incongruously rubbing shoulders with some quite spectacular modern work. Parents can and do use the school facilities after school hours. Lots of expeditions.

Background and Atmosphere: The recent shake-up in Glasgow schools meant that the amalgamation of Laurel Bank and Park School was almost inevitable; surprisingly it does not appear to be the unwieldy elephant that it might have done. Mrs Surber masterminded the combination of these two great schools in 1996, 'the worst problem was the uniform' – they kept the utterly hideous Laurel Bank green in the form of jerseys but otherwise it's rather nice tartan trimmed blazers and skirts. School moved en masse to Laurel Bank's incredible wiggly-woggly conversion of four terraced houses in a cul de sac; a tunnel beneath the road connects with the disused church, where the ground floor houses assemblies, and the converted crypt a dining room. Nursery, junior and senior school all higgledy-piggledy round the place. All a bit cramped and pretty bleak. 'New build' underway, very little playground space, but apparently it is not 'cool for older girls to go outside, and doesn't feel cramped at all'. Competition for pupils sharpened recently by Kelvinside Academy (with whom they share a bus run) going co-ed. Enormously unwieldy rather soft focus prospectus.

Pastoral Care and Discipline: House system, lots of 'cosy' staff, very tough on drugs and good PSE. Formal warning for smoking (and Smoke Busters is an option); each case treated individually, but parents usually informed, with the odd exclusion for repeated offences.

Pupils and Parents: Parents a combination of medical, university and business; 'super PTA', very good fund raisers. Good number of Asian/black pupils – no variations in school uniform allowed.

Entrance: Through the school via nursery etc. Bums on seats rather than particularly selective.

Exit: 80 per cent plus to university; Scottish ones most popular, one or two to Oxbridge.

Money Matters: Collection of standard bursaries and scholarships. Park School Trust will pick up slack – but perhaps is not as rich as others may suspect.

Remarks: Super if you want single sex schooling, or fabulous sports facilities. Girls appear happy as do parents.

LEEDS GIRLS' HIGH SCHOOL

Headingley Lane, Leeds LS6 1BN

TEL: *0113 274 4000* FAX: *0113 275 2217*

E-MAIL: enquiries@lghs.demon.co.uk

WEB: www.lghs.demon.co.uk

✦ PUPILS: 590 girls. Plus own junior school (Ford House) with 205 girls, and prep school (Rose Court) with 170 girls. All day ✦ Ages: 11-18, junior school 7-11, prep school 3–7 ✦ Size of sixth form: 160 ✦ Non-denom ✦ Fee-paying

Head: Since 1997, Mrs Susan Fishburn BSc (early fifties). Educated at Dursley Grammar School and Birmingham University. Previous post deputy head, Stafford Grammar School. Has taught in both private and state sector schools. Enjoys sailing. Two children. States that she believes that 'education is much more than league tables. In a successful school the pupils are happy, confident and motivated.' Took over from Miss Randall who was here from '77.

Academic Matters: Excellent GCSE results – few below B – with outstanding modern languages. A levels also very good – slight sprinkling of Ds and Es, but no real bloops. General studies examined. Setting in maths, French, and science but no streaming. Good work in average class size – around 25. Long standing staff, some cosy figures plus an injection of new and young. Dual, separate and combined sciences all on offer at GCSE. Small handful of keen classicists under excellent teacher. School does not offer exotica.

Games, Options, the Arts: Show flair and imagination, and are pursued diligently. Excellent art department (though not many girls do art at A level). Five-star swimming pool, big sports hall, and floodlit tennis courts. Nice sewing work, super home economics department. Music excellent, and impressive music centre in old Methodist Chapel (two organs, and free tuition for two years). Energetic collection of activities, eg exchange programme with the Kamazu Academy in Malawi (the 'Eton of Africa', which seems to have links everywhere). French and German exchanges.

Some activities eg drama productions, music and 'insight into management' are joint with the boys at Leeds Grammar. Very successful Young Enterprise. Good careers advice.

Background and Atmosphere: Founded in 1876, ex-direct grant. Pleasant grounds. Buildings vary from original to sixties tat. Hall with organ and highly polished floor because pupils sit on it (no chairs). Compact and functional – all corners used, (and pretty battered in places). Some small teaching rooms for small groups, tutors etc, some windowless. Much rebuilding – four floored extension, with language labs, drama studios etc. Junior school with two storey extension (NB money for all this comes from fees, no appeals). Library used by sixth formers for study, and sixth have their own computer room and the inevitable common room. Atmosphere busy, purposeful and bouncy. Prominently displayed motto – 'age quod agis', which girls all know how to translate.

Pastoral Care and Discipline: Workmanlike – school functions competently without making a song and dance about it.

Pupils and Parents: All sorts of backgrounds. One-sixth Jewish. Brothers at Leeds Grammar. Fairly wide catchment area, and hordes of buses to and fro. Friendly and articulate girls. Many distinguished OGs including Catherine Pestell (Principal of Somerville, Oxford), and Pauline Neville-Jones, political director of the Foreign Office, also journalist Jill Parkin.

Entrance: Interview, written exams and report from current school except for those entering at 3+, who have an individual IQ-type test. Entry also at sixth form – exam and interview post-mock-GCSEs.

Exit: Small leakage post-GCSE. Around 8-14 to Oxbridge, others widespread, mostly to old established universities (Edinburgh, London etc) but also new (East London, Liverpool John Moores), a few re-takers, a few to art college, a few take a gap year.

Money Matters: Over 100 assisted places at last count, and school is in process of appealing for funds to replace them – eight bursaries per annum so far, plus some from the Ogden Trust. Unspecified number of music scholarships.

Remarks: Excellent city academic day school for girls, firmly traditional, even slightly old fashioned – and none the worse for that.

THE LEYS SCHOOL

Trumpington Road, Cambridge CB2 2AD

TEL: *01223 508904* FAX: *01223 505303*

E-MAIL: office@theleys.cambs.sch.uk

WEB: www.theleys.cambs.sch.uk

✦ PUPILS: 520; 333 boys; 187 girls. (270 boarders; 115 'home boarders'; 135 day). . ✦ Ages: 11-18 ✦ Size of sixth form: 185 ✦ Methodist/Inter-denom ✦ Fee-paying

Head: Since 1990, the Rev. John Barrett MA (fifties). Formerly Head of Kent College, Pembury. Educated at Culford School and Durham University, and Cambridge. Married with two children, and has one of the nicest headmaster's houses in the business. Methodist minister, tall, imposing, and generally thought to be well in control of the situation. 'I was brought in to put the school straight after a shaky period.' Has been steering the school into co-education and maintaining boarding numbers for the last three years – no mean feat.

Academic Matters: National curriculum plus. Traditional teaching plus some less formal; strong sciences as you would expect here (taught as three separate sciences but dual award GCSE), traditionally more science than arts subjects taken at A level, but this trend could be on the turn. Maths excellently taught and deservedly popular, also geography. Pupils set in each and every subject individually. Good English department, also theology. Theatre studies still popular. Special needs teacher – pupils taken out of second modern language lessons where necessary to learn 'strategies to cope'. Good solid results for middle-of-the-road pupils, lots of happy noises from parents. In the past we have expressed some doubts about sufficient challenge for the brightest pupils, but the strong improvement in results over the last few years leaves no room to doubt that the brightest can now do their best here.

Games, Options, the Arts: Keenly gamesy (overseas tours), holds its own against bigger schools. Good shooting. also squash and rowing, but unboastful about their successes. Good at judo and hockey too. Super £2 million sports complex, much in use. High-powered visiting speakers (somewhat taken for granted – but then, this is Cambridge). Much appreciated technology centre open all the time (except late at night), including weekends (rare), with a member of staff – and much used. Splendid little steam engine knocked up over several years chugs merrily by on high days and holidays ('We can't get hold of Welsh coal, it has to be Cumbrian,' moans master in charge, Mr George). Lively drama with nine plays a year. Head of chemistry runs the popular 'Challenge' whereby prep schools take part at the Leys ('a good way for us to get them in') in competitive projects. Increasing numbers go for D of E. Good trips for the art department. New sixth form club reported to be a rave success – selling 'limited' alcohol and soft drinks.

Background and Atmosphere: Founded 1875 by prominent Methodists. Undistinguished redbrick Gothic plus many additions, suffers from lack of cohesion, near the centre of Cambridge, on pleasant 50-acre site (seriously geographically advantaged). A great deal of refurbishing and reorganising has been undertaken recently, to allow for co-education. Went fully co-ed in '94 (smooth operation), and there are now girls in every year. Brighter looking – and confident with it.

General atmosphere is relaxed and friendly, marked sense of community – 'sixth formers smile and say "Hello" and don't make you feel like a squit', reported a new bug recently. Inspectors rightly reported on the thread of divinity teaching throughout (a strong feature) which contributes to the ethos. Less of a split personality school than some with boarding and day pupils, staying on until after prep ie 9pm-ish. 'Home boarders' (ie those staying for everything except sleep and breakfast) are based in boarding houses; day pupils have their own house.

Pastoral Care and Discipline: Pupils fairly carefully monitored. Illegal pub visiting has been a menace but 'I have no evidence that illegal pub visiting happens any less in other schools,' comments head. The city of Cambridge is a constant excitement on the doorstep.

Pupils and Parents: Popular with non-Brits, particularly for the boarding, including bright Europeans, 5 per cent Methodists. Pupils mostly local. Very friendly boys and girls, and mutually supportive. School prides itself on being able to 'adapt to the eccentricities of individuals,' and, says head, prep schools recommend it for oddballs, 'though we don't want too many!' Old Leysians include James Hilton, author of *Goodbye, Mr Chips*, Martin Bell, and Sir Alistair Burnet.

Entrance: From local prep schools including the Leys' own, St Faith's. Still a popular choice for girls at sixth form (fun, relaxed – 'and this is Cambridge'). Traditionally the choice for boys who 'aren't Perse material', but beginning to be chosen for its own self, in preference to the Perse.

Exit: Degrees – 95 per cent have gone to university 'somewhere'. London currently the most popular place, followed by Oxford, Cambridge and the field. Thereafter, professions of all sorts.

Money Matters: Had a fair number of assisted places. Assortment of academic, art, music, CDT and all-rounder scholarships; bursaries for the Forces. Day pupils pay £3080 per term, 'Home boarders' £3,580 and full boarders £4,835 – expensive compared with other local day schools, but the elongated day offers more.

Remarks: Per ardua ad better and better. Very friendly one-time boys' boarding school which is now accepting girls, day pupils etc. Taking over in popularity from the Perse (boys) School in Cambridge – numbers are well up again – and well worth serious consideration.

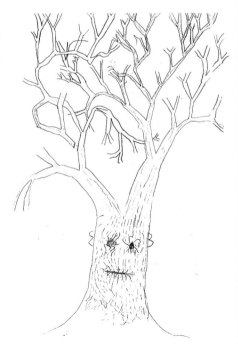

THE LONDON ORATORY
SCHOOL
Seagrave Road, London SW6 1RX
TEL: *020 7385 0102* FAX: *020 7381 7676*

E-MAIL: admin@london-oratory.org

WEB: www.london-oratory.org

✦ PUPILS: 1,270, all boys except for 80 girls in the sixth form; Junior House with specialist music training, for 80 boys. All day
✦ Ages: 11-18; Junior House ages 7-10.
✦ Size of sixth form: 350 plus
✦ RC ✦ State

Head: Since 1977, Mr John Charles McIntosh MA OBE FRSA (early fifties). Educated Ebury School, Shoreditch College, Sussex University. Determined, dedicated, a builder and creator. Married to the school.

Academic Matters: Takes a broad spread of ability. Classes are streamed on entry, with some setting in later years. Teaching styles are mostly formal; hard work is expected whatever your level of ability. A steady performer in the academic league tables for some years. A strong profile of GCSE results – a good number of A*s, not too many Ds and Es, few laggards; the brightest take 5 GCSEs a year early and go on to take English AS, Spanish GCSE from scratch, and maths A level modules as extras in the fifth form. Consistent results at A level, though in the last couple of years there have been more failures in some subjects than one might expect. Lots of computers, much used. Much appreciated general studies courses (whose A level results are no great shakes but which boost the points scores).

Games, Options, the Arts: Music immensely strong and popular (the good old hymns are sung here). Art OK, but we saw comparatively little display of it (or indeed any pupils' work) around the school. Sport is compulsory, and played with enthusiasm (but limited facilities); the CCF (Army and Air Force) is well supported. Every pupil will have had strong experience of IT and of public speaking by the time they leave – would that we could say this of more schools.

Background and Atmosphere: A very Catholic, very disciplined, hard-working all-ability school in pleasant modern buildings. The school's foundation derives from Saint Philip Neri (1515-95), a humorous and innovative preacher whose unorthodox views and behaviour (he was said to have shaved off half his beard for fun) would get him into considerable hot water here. Catholicism permeates everything, much more so than in many fee-paying Catholic schools. The discipline is exceptionally firm, more so than most private schools: the pupils daren't even visit the local McDonalds, let alone smoke within a mile of the school.

Pastoral Care and Discipline: It's clearly fun to teach here, and the teachers go out of their way to be helpful and friendly to pupils (but are called 'Sir' at all times). Pastoral problems are quickly passed on to one of the six housemasters. Operates the 3H rule – hair, homework and hard work. Pupils a happy and communicative lot nonetheless. Parents sign a written promise to monitor homework, ensure punctuality, and control absence. Uniform for all at all ages (parents not yet included).

Pupils and Parents: Committed Catholics from all walks of life from all over London.

Entrance: Apply a year in advance. You must be practising Roman Catholic, and prepared to accept the firm discipline, school regulations and parental commitment – none of which are to be sneezed at – involved. All applicants are interviewed, what counts is attitude: yours and your child's. Other factors taken into account include whether you have made the school your first choice, and family connections with the school. Girls (and some boys) come in at sixth form from Catholic schools all over London; five grade As, and Bs or better in the subjects to be studied, required; attitude to work and responsibility are additionally important at this age; those already in the school sometimes find that their sixth form place is made conditional on this. For entrance to the junior school you need an IQ of over 100 and a strong aptitude for music; juniors have a right of entry to the senior school at 11, and are expected to use it. Don't worry about where you live: pupils (such as young Blairs) get in from miles away.

Exit: Rapid and certain if you (or your child) kick consistently against the unbending pricks of the school's policies ('not quite the case' says the school.) A few leave at 16 for a change of air, but you should expect a strongly indignant reaction from the school if you are caught looking around while trying to keep your sixth form place open: you will have made a commitment to stay until 18 when applying. Of those who stay on for A levels, virtually all go to university, with ten or so per year to Oxbridge.

Remarks: Unique strong hard-working Catholic state school. Those the school suits, it suits well.

JUNIOR SCHOOL: (Junior House): Opened in 1996, specialising in musical training. All play two instruments and learn Italian, many sing as well in the Schola (for the top 25 per cent of voices) which performs every Saturday evening at the Brompton Oratory and performs in Rome and Paris. An hour and a half's homework each night, and an hour's music practice as well: surely a hard enough life without having to wear grey shorts too?

LORD WILLIAMS'S SCHOOL

Thame, Oxfordshire OX9 2AQ

TEL: *01844 210 510* FAX: *01844 261382*

E-MAIL: admin@lordwilliams.org

✦ PUPILS: 2,000 boys and girls; all day
✦ Ages: 11-18 ✦ Size of sixth form: 370
✦ Non-denom ✦ State

Head (Acting): Until September 2001 Mr Michael Spencer (fifties), formerly head of The Warriner School, Bloxham. Took over from Mrs Pat O'Shea, head from 1997, who left at short notice for personal reasons.

Academic Matters: Generally satisfactory, the pupils think very highly of their teachers. The school scores well at GCSE and has indeed come top of the Oxfordshire county schools in the past. Though only 3 per cent get A*, only 60 per cent get 5 A to Cs, and the boys do worse than that, very few exams are failed. A levels as you would expect with this profile, but again pleasantly few failures. English, maths, the sciences and art seem to earn the A grades. This is a 'proper' comprehensive school, entering children of all abilities for exams, including those with special needs (good provision here), who are integrated into the main school. The brighter kids seem to do as well here as they would in a grammar school. There is some setting, particularly higher up the school, so that able pupils may be well looked after. All take English language and literature, maths and dual award science at GCSE. All take at least one modern language (French or German), also design technology. Good range of subjects available at A level, and GNVQs (three levels) in the sixth form.

Games, Options, the Arts: Sports and arts centre offers some of the best facilities in Oxfordshire. All pupils try out all sports during the first three years, and most continue to take some sports seriously thereafter. Triple senior cup-holders in Oxfordshire rugby, cricket and soccer in '97 and '00, thriving girls' rugby too. Over 300 inter-school fixtures a year, going as far away as London and Stratford to find opponents; includes cricket vs MCC. Classical music is extremely strong. There are two orchestras and two choirs, and the school provides many members of the county youth orchestra. Keen art and drama – good take up at art A level and good results. Masses of extra-curricular activities including the Syson Competition, in which every pupil in the school competes at public speaking.

Background and Atmosphere: A large school formed in 1971 by the amalgamation of the ancient Lord Williams's Grammar School and the Wenman Secondary School. Now on two sites in pleasant setting with lots of space and feeling of room. Great mix of buildings. £3 million project to provide extensive new and remodelled buildings completed in '95. Former boarding house used for sixth form library and new business centre funded by local companies. Super friendly atmosphere – every classroom you go into you are greeted with a smile.

Pastoral Care and Discipline: Tradition of strong links with parents, and of teachers putting themselves out to help individual pupils. Pupils report that bullying is dealt with immediately and effectively and that there are no other major problems. Strong on community service.

Pupils and Parents: A complete cross-section – no creaming by any other school – from offspring of Oxford dons (a few) and chief executives to pupils whose families have lived here in rural Thame for generations. Also some refugees from the selective system in Buckinghamshire.

Entrance: Principally via primary schools in Thame, Chinnor and Tetsworth in Oxfordshire and Brill and Long Crendon in Buckinghamshire. Many pupils join from other schools at sixth form (at least five GCSEs at grade C or above needed for A levels – but you can opt for GNVQs – four GCSEs at C or an intermediate GNVQ.

Exit: About 60 per cent stay on to do A levels, of which 3-5 to Oxbridge each year, and over 100 to universities and colleges. Some do a gap year. The rest go to FE of some sort, or employment.

Money Matters: Very good links with local companies, who provide finance for expansion and work experience for pupils.

Remarks: Good broad state comprehensive school. Friendly, articulate pupils and enthusiastic teachers.

LORETTO SCHOOL

Musselburgh, East Lothian, EH21 7RE

TEL: *0131 653 4441 Admissions 4455*

FAX: *0131 653 4445 Admissions 4456*

E-MAIL: admissions@loretto.lothian.sch.uk

WEB: www.loretto.lothian.sch.uk

✦ PUPILS: 260 boys and girls in senior school, plus Junior school, The Nippers, with 120 boys and girls (150 girls in total). 10 per cent day in the Senior School (this number likely to increase to 20 per cent) and 50 per cent day in Junior school ✦ Ages: 13-18, Nippers 5-13 ✦ Size of sixth form: 115 ✦ Ecumenical ✦ Fee-paying

Head: From April 2001, Mr M B Mavor, CVO MA (Cantab) (early fifties), head of Rugby for the past ten years, and before that head of Gordonstoun. He got his gong for supervising the schooling of HRH The Duke of York and HRH Prince Edward. Educated at Loretto, where he was head boy and head of almost everything else, he read English at St Johns (trails of scholarships); worked in the States before being appointed head of Gordonstoun at the age of 31. Good at PR, and was Chairman HMC in 1997. Married to Elizabeth, he has a son at Oxford, and a daughter at Edinburgh University. A governor of Loretto from 1994 to 2000.

It is a strange career move to leave a school of 760 pupils for a school of barely 400, unless you are umbilically attached to the place (and this is possible). Certainly Loretto will be in a safe and experienced pair of hands which should do much to redress the yoyo effect of the past two heads. Rolls had been falling, but school reports rising registrations with the news of the new head.

DEPUTY HEAD Richard Selley: BEd (Exeter), (the Vicegerent – from *Paradise Lost*, means he who stands in place of God), who has been with the school for over 20 years, is acting headmaster until April after the somewhat abrupt departure of the last head Mr Keith Budge. For the second time in five years, Loretto watchers have seen a popular headmaster go in a 'did he jump or was he pushed' scenario. Edinburgh parents are expressing concern at this turn of events.

Academic Matters: School mainly plies the English system, GCSEs for all, followed by As (and of course AS from next year); traditionally strong on maths and sciences. Only French and Spanish on the language front; pupils still moan about 'the lack of choice in the sixth form.

Games, Options, the Arts: Music as ever good and keen, with drama on the up (girls have helped with this). Much jolly if sometimes off-key singing in the war-memorial chapel, a focal point for Lorettonians and FPs. Loretto used to be famed for its prowess on the rugby field; now less so, although FPs still contribute to the Scottish squad. Pupils complained bitterly that they had to play a low grade hockey match and miss the Calcutta Cup. Cricket XI unbeaten last year, and the girls did well at athletics and lacrosse. Popular pipe band, and CCF; skiing apparently 'out' which is surprising, considering that Europe's longest artificial ski slope is within ten miles. Young Enterprise, D of E etc.

Background and Atmosphere: Site in the middle of Musselburgh; the East Lothian ochre-coloured buildings straddle both sides of the A1 and are linked by tunnel giving much scope for naughtiness – last year's school leavers flooded the thing and spent the night rowing to and fro, an activity which put up the expulsion figures on the last week of term. Various outbuildings, including the Nippers, across the River Esk. Holm House (new girls' house), and Balcarres (the old San) being upgraded again. Spectacular new communication & resource centre (CRC) which houses trad library, the ICT Centre, the careers department and learning support all under one roof, complete with complex inter-house/classroom intranet. Sixth form can e-mail from their study bedrooms. Complicated arrangement of computers in CRC mean that they rest below a smoked glass screen giving a flat surface to use as a desk.

This is a chilly corner of East Lothian and the east wind whistling across the race course from the North Sea is an almost permanent feature. Linkfield, the sixth form social centre ('pupil led' with a bar and 'good lively Saturday evening events and disco theme parties') is known to be pretty wild on occasion, outgoing head described it as 'good high spirited fun'. Quite.

Famous haunted Pinkie House with its important painted ceiling in the gallery under the roof is home to the youngest pupils. Fifth form pupils oversee younger dorms, graduating to study bedrooms in the sixth. Both sexes wear tartan on Sundays (and we are miles short of the Highland line), with the famous red jackets and open necked shirts.

Day pupils and the occasional flexi-boarder now based at School House, with study bedrooms on hand for sixth formers if need be. The day starts early for day pupils, at ten past eight, but no longer are they expected to stay until after seven – now 'not obliged to stay for prep.' School bus does a daily collection and delivery run round East Lothian. Occasional grumbles from day parents about the compulsory monthly Sunday chapel.

Founded in 1827, and bought by Hely Hutchinson Almond in 1862 (a distinguished scholar of unconventional convictions, Scotland's answer to Dr Arnold), the school went fully co-ed in '95.

Pastoral Care and Discipline: Few problems. Parents and pupils concerned about the apparent lack of consistency in punishments. Recent HM Inspector's report (June 1999) – the first when inspectors turned up at any school without prior warning – highlighted a spot of gentle fagging, when senior boys would ask junior boys to clear the tables at the end of meals. All is now egalitarian, but not surprisingly, all are not happy about it.

Automatic expulsion for drugs; gating, fatigues and hours of school tasks for smoking etc. Good tutorial system with regular tutee reporting

Pupils and Parents: 'Very Scottish' is probably still an accurate description; less than 3 per cent from overseas. Popular with ex-pats, large number of OL's sons, daughters and grandchildren. Fair number of first-time buyers – not really a Sloane/Charlotte Ranger school. OLs: Headmasters Mavor and McMurray (the kingmakers), MPs the late Nicholas Fairbairn, Denis Forman, Norman Lamont, racing driver Jim Clark, journalist Andrew Marr, Alistair Darling and a good collection of industrialists, Lord (Hector) Laing, among them, plus of course the chairman of the governors, law Lord Alan Johnston.

Entrance: CE from Scottish and northern prep schools, and pupils come up from The Nippers en masse. Special exam and interview for pupils from the state sector. Five GCSEs at C for entrance to the sixth form – about 10 or 15 annually.

Exit: Most (85 per cent) to degree courses, tranches of industrialists, engineers etc. Fairly high leakage recently post GCSE, but ambitious plans for sixth form reshape should make this less of a regular occurrence.

Money Matters: Well endowed with scholarships and some means-tested bursaries, may pick up slack in case of hardship 'for gifted applicants, less and less common' and wonderful bursaries post school for those 'who have deserved well of Loretto'.

Remarks: Famous Scottish public school, now co-ed, good for gentle middling souls in need of nurturing, needs trenchant management and an inspirational head to kick it into the 21st century. Enter Michael Mavor.

JUNIOR SCHOOL: aka The Nippers Tel: 0131 653 4570. Head: Since 1999, Mr Andrew Lewin BA (Hons) PGCE. Super school, just across the River Esk, cosy carpeted dorms with sag bags (children forbidden real shoes in the house and it is bedroom slippers only outwith the classrooms – so good for growing feet). Generously staffed, six classrooms, science lab and French language listening posts. Like big brother school went co-ed in '95, linked via cable to CRC and share main school facilities – the Astroturf surface, swimming pool and theatre.

THE EARLY YEARS: Very new, from age five upwards. Head: Linda M Watson MEd, who trained at Edinburgh. Tiny classes, 'French and IT will also feature'. Flexible dropping off and collection times.

LYCÉE FRANÇAIS CHARLES DE GAULLE

35 Cromwell Road, London SW7 2DG

TEL: *020 7584 6322* FAX: *020 7823 7684*

E-MAIL: skalsakis@lyceefrancais.org.uk

✦ PUPILS: 2,770 (including primary and nursery school); all day (but see below)
✦ Ages: 3-18/19 ✦ Size of sixth form: 300 (100 in the English section; 200 in the French last two years)
✦ No religious affiliation ✦ Fee-paying

Head (Principal): Since 1997, M J M Fouquet. Took over from M Henri-Laurent Brusa.

Head of the English Stream: M Rashid Benammar, who was educated in France – at Lille – was a housemaster at Wellington and whose interest is linguistics.

Academic Matters: Faites attention, svp, parce que c'est assez complicated. There are in effect two streams – French and English – and classes run from the sixieme year (= the first year) to the Terminale (= last year). The French pupils follow the French syllabus in preparation for the Baccalaureate (and, by the way, they may have to redoubler – repeat a year – if they are not up to scratch). The Filiére Anglaise follows the French syllabus until the end of the Quatrieme year, at which point they choisissent whether to go on and do the Baccalaureate (series ES, L, S offered), or go down the GCSE/A level route. For the Fr system, pupils choose whether to go down the 'literary' or 'scientific' route, but whichever they choose, ha[...] jects for the Bac. Cl[...] but they could be 3[...] 25. Teaching is very n[...] French tradition (Pupils [...] rified not to work) and no[...] and no official remedial help. [...] dred and ten per cent pass[...] energy. Results are consistently excellent (and, examiners please note, the results come in weeks before the English): eg 62.5 per cent 'TBs' plus 'Bs' (Trés Bien, and Bien for the uninitiated) recently with 100 per cent reussite. GCSE get 100 per cent pass with 75 per cent-ish As and Bs, and 60 per cent As and Bs at A level. Vraiment, c'est sensass – particularly given the comprehensive intake.

Games, Options, the Arts: Not the object of the exercise as far as the French are concerned, and your average London-based Lycée product comes out pretty white and flubby. However, games do form part of the French syllabus and so there is no escape. Games master tears his hair at lack of facilities (but so do they all in central London), but volleyball, football, rugby and basketball, ski trips etc, are all on offer and interclass competitions, which are 'passionnement suivies par les élèves' (je m'en doute). Gym, plus hall which can be used as a gym. Some evenings and Samedi matin there are clubs educatifs such as music, travaux manuels etc, but the school day is long, and clubs relatively few.

Background and Atmosphere: The school is now on three sites – tinies in Wandsworth, an annexe in Ealing (nursery and primary), and the rest in a huge block on the Cromwell Road, stretching back as far as Harrington Road, and with lovely views over the Natural History Museum for some. The interior consists of a huge quad, lots of duck-egg blue corridors, soul-

(few are in the same room … Avoid whole area at delivery and …tion times. The history of the Lycèe is intimately linked with that of the Institut Francais, and in 1915, what with the influx of Belgian and French refugees, the school opened near Victoria Station with 120 élèves. Then, to cut a long histoire courte, a nouveau batiment was constructed and inaugurated in 1958, et voila. The atmosphere is very, well, French. Institutional even. Et cool. Tinies may be flattened. Do not be put off when they answer the telephone in French, however: if you speak loud enough they will give in in the end and speak English. NB sartorial note: the Lycée has an Old School Tie – the only Lycée in the world to have one. Not a lot of people know this. FOOD: You would expect, would you not, at least a Michelin star in this home from home for the French in London, and indeed the menus are little poems of delight: Couscous Mouton (the chef's speciality, explained the member of staff who very kindly showed us round), Boeuf Bourguignon, Jardiniéres des Lègumes Frais etc etc. However, we have to relate that the reality is somewhat different: about three-quarters of pupils were eating hamburgers and frites, and the rest, heaps of grated carrot. However marvellous patisseries have sprouted up all round the area, to cater for those who could kill for a baguette.

Pastoral Care and Discipline: The French system decrees that matters spiritual and pastoral are to be mainly the province of the parents and the Church (Wednesday afternoons are traditionally for catechism, thus many French schools let the children go home for this). However, the Catholic Church is just round the corner, and Protestants have their own church in Soho.

Where discipline breaks down there is an elaborate system, ending with a conseil de discipline – rather like a court martial, at which the miscreant can explain himself and be heard by staff and his peers. There are also parent-staff meetings. Some reports of bullying reach us, to which teachers turn a blind eye, but this could be the English being wet in the face of French sauve-qui-peut-erie. However, 'There is no drug culture,' reports a parent, who put her Lycée-educated child into a southern English public school at sixth form and was horrified by the difference. Pupils register for every lesson. Each pupil has a carnet de correspondance – for staff to send messages to parents, and vice versa. Parental involvement is de rigueur (a key to the school's success?). During the school day surveillants patrol the building, supervising meals, discipline etc, leaving the teachers free to teach.

Pupils and Parents: Sixty nationalities, from French-speaking world, plus mixed marriages, embassy children. Parents from all walks of life, gardeners, Polish dressmakers, dukes, ex-pats (former French colonies). Three ex-MPs are former pupils, including Olga Maitland. 1,600 French children, approx 600 Brits plus approx 400 'others'.

Entrance: Registration, preferably before Easter for the following September, plus interview, plus test. All welcome, providing they can cope with the exigencies of the French language – school now insists on at least two years of French education before starting at the senior school, and is quite helpful about informing you of the London possibilities for this. For entry at 14 – tests in French, English and maths; for entry at 16 – test in A level subjects chosen. NB best not telephone the school for information during the lunch hours.

Exit: To French universities and to English ones, particularly in South East, (Royal Holloway, UCL, a handful to Oxford), and reading subjects such as French with law, international business studies, European law and languages and other such serious matters. Some do gap – though French tend not to. NB the school does not prepare children for Common Entrance, so if you are thinking of being here as a junior and then swapping to the English system forget it.

Money Matters: A snip at around £786-£1250 a term – subsidised by the French Government. No scholarships or assisted places (applied for the latter, but were turned down).

Remarks: Que voulez-vous? Children are imbued with French educational ethos – they learn to work and their intellectual curiosity is aroused. This is a vachement brilliant place to get a first-class academic education at a fraction of the cost of anything comparable in the land. It makes one despair of England.

MAGDALEN COLLEGE SCHOOL

Cowley Place, Oxford OX4 1DZ

TEL: *01865 242191* FAX: *01865 240379*

E-MAIL: sms@magdalen.oxon.sch.uk

WEB: www.magdalen.oxon.sch.uk

✦ PUPILS: 575 boys, all day ✦ Ages: 7-18
✦ Size of sixth form: 150 ✦ C of E
✦ Fee-paying

Head (The Master): Since 1998, Mr Andrew Halls MA (very early forties). Read English at Gonville and Caius, Cambridge (double first). Previously deputy head of Trinity Croydon, and head of English, Bristol Grammar School – impressive stables. Believes 'considerateness, hard work and imagination' form the basis of a flourishing school. French wife, two young daughters. Took over from Mr Peter Tinniswood, who went to Lancing.

Academic Matters: Strong. More Ds and Es at A level than you might expect, 'but we have a fairly catholic intake'. Sciences taught as three separate subjects, and all boys do three for GCSE. Good maths and English – half take these for A level – maths '00 results not so hot, but subject to a steward's enquiry as we write. Setting in maths and French; very high standards of teaching. Few (eleven) female staff – more than there used to be. (Fashion note: bow ties and corduroy jackets, plus one or two sexy looking young 'assistants'.) Saturday morning school now replaced by music, sport and other activities. Good sixth form non-examined options, three per term each given two periods a week. Homework notebooks/ diaries all the way up the school; lower sixth study periods supervised. Lovely bright classrooms converted in '93 from choristers' dorms for the 9- and 10-year-old intake (before that, the tinies were choristers only). No special provision for dyslexia or EFL.

Games, Options, the Arts: Keen on games, though not necessarily winners. Junior hockey teams do well (school's own playground version goes back hundreds of years), main playing fields adjacent, others 3 miles off; enthusiastic rowing (of course). New sports hall and all-weather pitch. Distinguished music tradition (especially organists), and choral societies: madrigals memorably produced on the river. The choir sings from Magdalen Tower at dawn on May morning, one of the great Oxford traditions and worth getting/staying up for. The school is umbilically linked (governors etc) to Magdalen College, for whom the school produces choristers.

CCF; also well-run community service – not the usual 'granny bashing' but work in schools, hospitals, Oxfam etc. Chapel converts to drama hall. Extra-curricular activities (keen politics society, also new fun juggling club) and lecture programmes keep students busy (lunch breaks and after school). Art exam results well below par. Good debating (some with girls from Oxford High), provoking high passions. Chess v strong. Wonderful creative essays (eg on homelessness in Oxford) in the Lily Literata mag.

Background and Atmosphere: Founded in 15th century by William of Waynflete, original home is in the grounds of the college; Cardinal Wolsey was an early headmaster. School House (on the roundabout by Magdalen Bridge), the Victorian collegiate building, originally housed boarders and choristers – now houses the junior school and the master and family. Across the road the main school buildings were a mish-mash of flimsy-looking edifices (including the thirties pebble-dash block) with many additions – 'grotty,' said a pupil fondly – but new teaching blocks and sixth form centre in '98 (appeal). Facilities don't compare with well-endowed establishments – but it's all here and adequate, and the atmosphere is keen, and unpretentious. Good relations between staff and pupils. 'They encourage us to make decisions for ourselves,' said a sixth former.

Pastoral Care and Discipline: Definitely good, problems spotted early on. One and only school rule: all boys must at all times behave 'sensibly and well' – actually runs to many subsections. Pupils have daily contact with their tutor; houses organised on geographical basis to help parents. Food 'much improved', say the boys. Prefects must chide younger boys who arrive late for daily assembly in chapel. NB 7- to 10-year-olds wear uniform – the rest in non-uniform sober jackets and trousers plus school tie.

Pupils and Parents: A big mix of backgrounds (including inevitably dons' sons, large contingent of sons of professionals), not rich. Catchment area spreads 20 miles in all directions: much gnashing of teeth over Oxford traffic problems. Old Boys include many academics, also Ivor Novello (a chorister), a batch of 15th- and 16th-century grammarians, including Holt, Thomas More's teacher, and some 20th-century sportsmen and sports commentators (eg Jim Rosenthal of the BBC, John Parsons, the Wimbledon expert), also producers Sam Mendes and John Caird.

Entrance: At 7, 9 and 11 with tests to eliminate the crammed child, CE at 13 (minimum of 60 per cent). Also at sixth form – at least six to eight GCSE passes at B or above with As in their A level choices (existing pupils must jump this hurdle too). NB until '93, the only 9-year-olds were choristers. Now the doors are open to all, but all boys must pass entrance examination.

Exit: A few leave (for other schools, eg Cherwell). Virtually all go on to university (14 to Oxbridge in a bad year, 22 in a good one). Increasingly boys go for a gap year first.

Money Matters: An inexpensive school. Up to nine scholarships at 13, two or more music and sports scholarships. Bursaries available.

Remarks: An obvious choice for locals wanting a liberal academic day school, where boys are treated as individuals. Currently in v good shape.

MALVERN COLLEGE

Malvern, Worcestershire WR14 3DF
TEL: *01684 581 500* FAX: *01684 581 615*

E-MAIL: SRJ@malcol.org

WEB: www.malcol.org

✦ PUPILS: 460 boys and 288 girls; 466 board, 282 day; plus own co-ed prep and pre-prep, Hillstone ✦ Ages: 3-18 ✦ Size of sixth form: around 280 ✦ C of E, but all faiths welcome ✦ Fee-paying

---

Head: Since 1997, Mr Hugh Carson MA PGCE (fifties). Educated Tonbridge (head boy) and – after Sandhurst and a number of years in the army in the Royal Tank Regiment – London and Reading universities, where he read history, history of economics and politics. Previous post – head of Denstone College, a Woodard school whose ethos he valued. Married to Penny, who was an officer in the WRAC and then followed her husband's example and went back to academic studies (history, PhD), is now a JP and 'freelance historian'. They have a young English springer spaniel. Took over from Mr R de C Chapman, who had been here since 1983.

Academic Matters: Broadish intake. Average total A level points 20.7. Good value-added factor, particularly with pupils of average ability originally – parents would agree. Popular A levels are maths, English, chemistry, physics, French. Dual award science at GCSE, about a third take separate sciences. French, Spanish, German, Italian, Russian, Latin and Greek.

One of about 30 schools in the UK that offers International Baccalaureate – and does so successfully, under the trés popular et gentil et sexy Dr Rene Filho. School gaining a good reputation in this, and numbers of pupils choosing IB versus A levels increases gradually each year (around 60 per cent). Diploma of Achievement, a skill-based course pioneered by the school, is compulsory for all. Four part-time specialist teachers to cater for special educational needs, and the school currently has about 70 pupils receiving specialist support (only suitable for mild problems however). Caveat: the school operates a tough policy on 'weeding out the grossly idle'.

Games, Options, the Arts: Main games football and rugby. Enthusiastic team tours abroad. Also rackets, fives, canoeing on local rivers, climbing wall in smart sports centre, cottage in Brecon Beacons for adventure training (compulsory for all at some point). CCF now an option with Community Service, or D of E award. Lots on offer at all times/stages, including exotic sixth form summer expeditions, eg climbing in the Alps. After GCSE pupils have a week of sixth form experience in which A level choices are tested. Music (including 90 strong choir and Glen Miller style band) based in converted Victorian monastery with monks' cells as practice rooms. Former Catholic church converted '98 to make a concert hall, with sixth form centre underneath. Ritzy art block. Pioneers of work experience, co-ordinated by three-man careers team. Technology centre (opened in '92) won an architectural award. Swimming pool entirely re-vamped and re-opened '96.

Background and Atmosphere: Large Victorian pile on side of Malvern Hills with games fields sweeping out below it. Houses 'One' to 'Nine' plus school houses arranged in horseshoe interspersed with other buildings on the campus. There are three girls' houses on the campus (with capacity for 180). Enormous influx of girls over the last three years – now much more of a co-ed feel. Has its own prep and pre-prep nearby.

Pastoral Care and Discipline: Intricate house and tutor system picks up most problems, and there are good reports on pastoral care. In the lower school pupils are allocated tutor in groups of 12-15. In sixth form pupils select their own personal tutors. The school has had the occasional drugs problem, which results in expulsion.

Pupils and Parents: Sons and daughters of professionals, many within 2-hour drive; some non-nationals, including some from Europe, also Far East, and some Service families (15 per cent discount). Pupils don't suffer from city temptations or over sophis-

tication, 'it's a blessing it's a bit isolated,' reported parents of a frisky teenager. OBs include Denholm Elliott, Jeremy Paxman, Lord Weatherill, C S Lewis and Lord MacLaurin.

Entrance: Registration and CE or separate test for state school entrants. And of course via their own prep school. Sixth form entry by five GCSEs, including As or Bs in subjects to be studied, plus interview and tests.

Exit: 90 per cent go on to long-established universities or other higher education. A handful to art college, one or two to work/armed forces etc.

Money Matters: Had 137 assisted places, and is replacing some of these with its own scheme. Currently approx 23 academic scholarships (up to maximum of 50 per cent fees). Also scholarships/exhibitions for sports, music, drama, technology and art, and sixth form scholarships.

Remarks: Co-educational traditional rural public school with a trump card – International Baccalaureate.

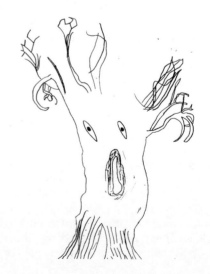

MALVERN GIRLS' COLLEGE

15 Avenue Road, Malvern, Worcestershire
WR14 3BA

TEL: *01684 892288* FAX: *01684 566204*

E-MAIL: registrar@mgc.worcs.sch.uk

WEB: www.mgc.worcs.sch.uk

✦ PUPILS: 420 girls (350 board, 70 day)
✦ Ages: 11-18 ✦ Size of sixth form: 170
✦ C of E ✦ Fee-paying

Head: Since 1997, Mrs Philippa (Pippa) Leggate BA MEd PGCE (fifties, but only just), educated at Royal School, Bath, read history at York, returned to Bath for masters. Impressive pedigree. First taught history in state system, moved to Middle East and was founding head of new international school in Oman. Last post: head of Overseas School in Colombo, Sri Lanka, from 1993-97. Very clued up, smart in mind and body, enjoys support of staff, pupils and parents. Passionate believer in single-sex education. 'Girls benefit from working alongside other girls because you can appeal to their particular interests.' High achiever ideally placed to nurture future generations of female high achievers. Intelligent, articulate (but chooses words carefully), efficient, means business. In many respects, more like chief executive than headmistress.

Academic Matters: Consistently high exam results with 7.9 average points per A level subject in 2000 and 27 total average. Good, solid teaching. Not as traditional as once was – now more challenging. But not so way-out as to risk damaging fine academic reputation. More to education than 'what takes place in the classroom,' says head. MGC is 'spring board into adult life.' Great choice of subjects at AS level include drama, Greek and philosophy. Very strong in sciences with over a third opting for science-related subjects at university. Award-winning three-storey science block (built on head's private garden), still only partly open for business, is testament to that. Chemistry and physics now in situ, biology due to leave ugly 60s home and take up residence with science bed-fellows shortly. Means more room now for other subjects to stretch legs. Extra help available for dyslexics.

Games, Options, the Arts: Art department is one to benefit from space freed up by sciences. Now has bags of room with three large light studios. A level arts students have own work area, can drop in whenever they like. Big lab too for cookery classes, still popular with 21st century MGC girls. 'Well they get to cook their own food and eat it, don't they. It's always preferable to school food,' I was told. Music a key ingredient in MGC life: 90 per cent study at least one instrument. Two orchestras, three choirs (girls only audition for chamber choir), and energetic new music head bursting with ideas. Sees chamber music as best way of bringing music to the masses. Double success in schools chamber music competition in consecutive years. 'Music here is very, very strong. These girls are bright conscientious kids,' he states with pride. Computers all over the place, internet access, girls free to surf in spare time. Loads of action on the sports field, big in hockey and lacrosse, but also keen on less mainstream girls' sports like football and rugby, also rowing, scuba diving, tennis, swimming, netball but no cricket. Large sports dome for badminton, squash and aerobics, much-used all-weather pitches and surely one of the few 'listed' indoor swimming pools. Lovely feature arched beams and changing cubicles (dating from previous life as Victorian hotel) but not much to inspire potential medal-winners. Much emphasis on community service work: locals can use pool, sixth formers teach pupils to read at nearby primary school and old folk helped with shopping etc. Head says: 'We see ourselves as a community but also a community within a community. We take our role in Malvern very seriously.' Success in Young Enterprise scheme, big following for D of E awards, many extra activities from needlepoint to white water rafting.

Background and Atmosphere: Set against breathtaking backdrop of the Malvern Hills. Formerly the Imperial Hotel, large redbrick imposing building with later additions, right by railway station (it was built to serve the hotel). School life revolves around the houses where girls eat as well as sleep. Six houses organised in age groups, so girl who goes right through the school will start in the junior house, move up to one of three middle houses and end in one of two sixth form houses. Comfortable accommodation ranges from multi-bed dorms to study bedrooms, plenty of opportunity for privacy as well as mixing in common rooms, girls encouraged to bring home comforts, laptops/mobile phones welcomed (mobiles banned from classrooms though). Weekend activities timetabled. Include riding, bowling, games coaching and the cinema. Pretty unexciting school uniform (no ties) compulsory until sixth form when 'suitable' home clothes can be worn. Very security conscious – all external doors have coded locks. C of E school where religion high on agenda, but other denominations well catered for. Long-

standing link with Muslim school in Gambia. Daily assembly with regular church/chapel for all. Glorious well-stocked library (21,000 volumes, multi media computers, CD-ROM etc) with one end devoted to careers information. Girls' work shown off in school corridors, notice boards display scale and range of non-curricula activity. Busy, fast-moving school which won't tolerate less than 100 per cent effort. One teacher said: 'This isn't a school for the shy retiring violet. Girls here tend to be rather outgoing.' MCG not an island – plenty of link-ups through sport, drama, debate and discos with other schools (independent and state) in Malvern and those further afield. Maintains contact with Malvern College since going fully co-ed. No bad feeling/competition. 'What we offer in a girls only school is something quite different.'

Pastoral Care and Discipline: Provided through housemistresses/parents and form tutors, as well as sixth formers. Successful 'peer mentoring' system in operation whereby younger pupils encouraged to talk problems through with an older girl. No school rules as such, but strong code of conduct. Girls taught to take responsibility for their actions, also made to see how actions effect others. Impressive PHSE skills course in middle school and learning for life programme in sixth form. 'We teach self worth and respect without arrogance,' says head. Discipline may be dealt with by head, housemistress or sixth form council (pupil/staff mix) depending on seriousness. Expulsion ('exclusion') for drugs 'at the head's discretion,' smoking only allowed off school premises by over 16s, and alcohol can extend to wine with a meal for over 18s. But no booze or cigarettes ever in study bedrooms. Girls allowed to walk into town (middle school pupils must go in groups), behaviour 'which brings school into disrepute' reported to council for possible disciplinary action. No evident problem with bullying. Pupils anonymously complete bullying questionnaire every year giving their views/experiences. Any problems dealt with swiftly.

Pupils and Parents: A large contingent from abroad (girls from more than 20 countries). Make up about a third of school. Lots from Far East in particular who excel in sciences but less so in sports. Cross section socially, academically and geographically. Some local, majority from Midlands and London. Increasingly dominated by professionals, especially lawyers, rather than 'the fabulously rich', some farming stock still but less since hard times, and the rest first-timers. Naturally attracts brains and much artistic talent in evidence. The late Dame Elizabeth Lane, first woman High Court judge, is old girl. Also novelist Barbara Cartland and Vogue editor Liz Tilberis. Not to mention, adds the head, numerous 'doctors, vets, lawyers, architects, scientists and good mothers.'

Entrance: At 11+, 12+, 13+ and sixth form. Common entrance and own entrance papers and scholarship exams. For sixth form, GCSE results must include Bs in chosen A level subjects.

Exit: Around 99 per cent to degree courses, up to 12 to Oxbridge. Careers taken very seriously. Top of the popularity charts are medicine, the City, Foreign Office, law and engineering.

Money Matters: Scholarships for academic, music, art and PE at Middle School and academic, expressive arts including music, art and drama, plus PE at sixth form level. Special scholarships for daughters and granddaughters of Old Girls, some bursaries and some assisted places.

Remarks: Much good work and modern thinking going on inside the old-world façade. Very sure of its single sex status, giving parents a choice as well as a first class education for their daughters. Girls come across as confident and content, those in their last year now impatient to get out there and get going. Not a school for the timid – not much hand-holding here. Would really suit robust types who can hold their own.

THE MANCHESTER GRAMMAR SCHOOL

Old Hall Lane, Rusholme, Manchester
M13 0XT

Tel: *0161 224 7201* Fax: *0161 257 2446*

E-mail: admissions@mgs.org

Web: www.mgs.org

✦ Pupils: 1,431 boys; all day ✦ Ages: 11–18 ✦ Size of sixth form: 410 ✦ C of E links, but basically non-denom ✦ Fee-paying

---

Head (High Master): Since 1994, Dr Martin Stephen BA PhD (forties), educated at Uppingham, and Leeds University, followed by PhD at Sheffield (poetry of the First World War). Read English and history for first degree. Prolific writer on English literature and naval history (15 books at last count, *The Price of Pity* about literature and history in the First World War is the latest). Taught at Uppingham, then housemaster at

Haileybury, deputy head of Sedbergh. Last post: head of The Perse, Cambridge, since 1987, where he detected a change in parents' expectations away from the 'driving, ruthless competition of the academic sweat shop – education from the neck up is no longer enough'. Married (wife is head of The Grange School, Hartford and in HMC – is this the first husband and wife HMC team?), with three sons. Likes drawing and painting as well as writing books. Doctor's son of Scottish extraction, early achiever, choc-full of the RIGHT STUFF – direct, very likeable, patient, energetic, fast-talker, thinks it is 'crucial' for a head 'to be about'. And witty with it. School has good 'management structure' in place: Mr Peter Laycock, the second master, and two 'surmasters', Mr Ian Thorpe and Mr Neil Sheldon.

Academic Matters: Academic power house, one of the best in the country. Outstanding common room: some young and enthusiastic, some old and enthusiastic, mostly top class and dedicated. An atmosphere of learning, a love of knowledge pervades the common room. Class sizes now reduced at lower end of the school to maximum 25/26, thinning down to 22/23 boys in middle school; 'creative subjects' taught in smaller groups. All must take separate sciences at GCSE, and most take (and pass) 9–11. Latin now becomes an option after two years. Greek, Spanish, Russian and German on offer. Boys setted for maths, mixed ability for all other subjects. Stunning exam results. Huge choice of A levels, plus choice of 120 'general studies' on offer, ranging from silver-smithing (MGS hall mark) to Arabic, Ukrainian, Welsh and Hungarian – 'going quite well at the moment'. Boys must take 12 'general studies' or games options, three in each half-year. Under the new system sixth formers will take four ASs in the first year and four A2s in the second; all pupils will take AEAs (advanced extension awards) and a short philosophy course.

The school has gone on record protesting at the unfairness of league tables which take no account of whether general studies are examined or not. Staff consider pupils 'often' more intelligent than they are themselves, but here this could be modesty. One member of staff commented, 'Let me put it like this – what we achieve together far exceeds the sum of our individual efforts.' One of the few places you will find staff discussing the tactics of getting into different Oxbridge colleges. Two busy libraries, with boys helping, security system and CD-ROM, and a vast bookshop. Careers room with everything you ever wanted to know.

'The good learning', as decreed by the founder, starts in the Lower School, under the head, Jim Mangnall, where boys study a broad general curriculum for four years before choosing GCSE subjects.

Games, Options, the Arts: Boys not 'press-ganged' to play in any team, but school still continues to knock the opposition for six. Rugby, football, and cricket popular, strong and successful – particularly the latter: Mike Atherton and the Crawley brothers are Old Mancunians. New super duper sports hall named after Mike Atherton. Astonishingly successful water polo, recent national finalists. 'I find it alarming that the boys in the team appear to be able to swim faster than I can run,' comments the high master. Music is very strong under enthusiastic head of department, with lots of individual instrumental teaching from the BBC Philharmonic or Halle Orchestra members amongst others; annual concert in the Royal Northern College of Music, James MacMillan composer in residence for 2000.

Drama course from second form and 'Dramsoc' popular – sent first production to the Edinburgh Festival in '97, second in '00 (Holly from the Bongs by Alan Garner OM). (School has dedicated theatre with wooden benches.) High master reports art and music staffing levels significantly increased in the last few years – these two subjects beginning to come in from the cold. Imaginative Parker Art Halls (named after previous head) encompass five storeys over main archway, and CDT compulsory for the first two years; Pied Piper in charge of pottery and ceramics. CDT thriving, but again not spectacular results by Manchester Grammar standards (though they would be quite acceptable anywhere else). CDT technology – related rather than craft – inspired keyboarding. Clubs for everything particularly chess and bridge, lots of debating, and masses of foreign trips, treks, camps – the younger boys start with weekends at the Owl's Nest at Disley before graduating to The Grasmere Barn. School newspaper The New Mancunian has huge circulation and wins awards.

Background and Atmosphere: Founded in 1515 by Hugh Oldham, Bishop of Exeter, a year before he founded Corpus Christi College, Oxford (with which the school has links), to educate able boys regardless of their parents' means, to go on to university and the professions, and open what the founder called the 'yate' of knowledge. Now the biggest private senior day school in the country. Moved in 1931 to present purpose-built site (28 acres) in the des. suburb of Fallowfield, down the road from the University, a huge redbrick-based building round central quad with heavy high portals, and brill green late art nouveau tiles to half-way up the walls. Enormously extended, with rabbit warrens through the

lab area, and senior biology at the rectory. Recently opened Marks & Spencer English Centre, not to mention a Marks lab area. New CDT centre means school has kissed goodbye to the Portakabins (party held for this). New tennis courts. Slightly depressing dining room, functional and noisy, to be refurbished. Lots of reshuffling going on. New boys are given a map to find their way about (even Mr Sheldon got lost, so take heart). Atmosphere dynamic and bursting with energy and happy with it. Slick southerners may find it rough at the edges. Sixth formers wear mufti, otherwise blue blazers. School now a litter free zone and much redecorated. High master comments: 'we are even willing to show journalists the famous west basement changing rooms, which until last year were the inspiration of several successful horror films, and which we have spent nearly sixty years leading important people away from'. Pupils still occasionally describe the school as a 'sausage machine' or 'conveyor belt'. Developing links with neighbouring city schools.

Pastoral Care and Discipline: Has recently pioneered a 'peer support scheme', in which sixth formers are trained in counselling skills. Also 'friends scheme' in which the existing arrangement of parents' association members visiting the homes of new boys has been extended to allocate a senior pupil as a friend to every new pupil. Easy access for parents. Discipline 'not too much of a problem'; punishments in the form of a communication slip, to be taken home and signed by parent, followed by detention – less used now. Serious punishments are referred to senior member of staff, who will talk to boys. Excellent drugs policy; drink 'not a problem', Saturday morning detention for smoking.

Pupils and Parents: Very wide catchment area, stretching far beyond Greater Manchester. Regular parental contact, evenings, meetings and regular discussions at 'crucial points' in boy's career. Cream of the intelligentsia, from a wide variety of ethnic and social backgrounds, many not rich. No earrings, no ponytails observed ('though when they were really in vogue, they had to be neat ponytails'). Bright boys, polite as you like at the bottom end, but fairly relaxed about visitors near the top, eg one chap was demonstrating a particularly fine line in 'Egyptian PT' (ie falling asleep – high master says he's dealt with him). Dozens and dozens of distinguished Old Boys (OMs – Old Mancunians), including 'rows' of FRSs, including Sir Michael Atiyah. Also Mike Atherton, the actors Ben Kingsley and Robert Powell, and RSC/ENO director Nicholas Hytner, as well as John Ogdon, Thomas de Quincey, plus several members of the Sieff family and Simon Marks.

Entrance: Not at all easy. The main entry is at 11, where 550/600 boys vie for 200/210 places. Entry exam in two parts, sheep from goats sussed out via questions like 'Four consecutive odd numbers add up to 96, write down the smallest of these numbers.' 50 per cent of pupils come in from state primaries. Entry at sixth form requires a minimum of five A grade GCSEs (this may be waived for deserving internal candidates).

Exit: Around 98 per cent to degree courses; around 50 a year to Oxbridge (58 offers in '98). Medicine and law still popular, also languages, engineering, natural sciences – 'lads don't look for soft option'. One or two go on to crammers and sixth form colleges, one or two to art college. OMs become civil servants, bankers, scientists, businessmen and teachers.

Money Matters: School had a gigantic number of assisted places which provided £800,000 a year income, and their phasing out had the potential to wipe out the school in its present form. However, huge MGS Foundation Bursary Appeal, with powerful support including Sir Alex Ferguson, has raised £6 million (£4 million to go, and a most worthy cause). Cheers, cheers, cheers. Now has some Ogden Trust bursaries for 'above-average children from a state primary school of limited or no parental means'. The bursar used to be known as 'the Receiver', but no longer. Bargain of the century: fees £1,800 a term for 2000/2001.

Remarks: Five star academic day school, one of the strongest and most famous in the country.

MANOR HOUSE SCHOOL

Manor House Lane, Little Bookham, Surrey
KT23 4EN

Tel: *01372 458538* Fax: *01372 450514*

+ Pupils: 350 girls, 170 in junior school; all day + Ages: 11-16, junior school 2-11 + Non-denom + Fee-paying

---

Head: Since September 2000, Mrs Alison Morris BSc (forties). Joined school in 1983 and 'loves the place to bits'. Was deputy head when she applied for headship – 'the thought of someone else coming in and changing the school was more than I could bear'. Educated at Sutton High and read maths and economics at University of Kent. Married with two grown up children and TV journalist husband. Positive, upbeat, outgoing, approachable, straightforward lady. Adamant that intelligence is not just academic. A hands-on head who knows her pupils. Takes the junior children away every year on an activities week and teaches maths in the senior school. Wants 'the pupils to discover all their talents and use them'. Keen to emphasise the confidence building, caring atmosphere of the school. Honest enough to admit that all this nurturing can 'sometimes mean that the big world can be a bit of a shock for the girls when they leave at 16, but if parents do not want this family atmosphere then they will send their children elsewhere.'

Academic Matters: Not an academic hothouse. A mix of academic and middle of the road girls. Used to be nicknamed 'the Bookham finishing school for naice young girls'. Head is 'very glad that label has now gone, we do not finish the girls we launch them into further education'. All girls seen as potential candidates for higher education. Pupils take GCSE exams in 9 or 10 subjects. Most popular optional subjects are geography, religious studies and art.

League tables do not show a realistic picture of such a mixed intake school. The academic girls get some impressive GCSE results. In 2000, they were awarded seven scholarships including two to Lancing College and one to Cheltenham Ladies' (1999 three scholarships and 1998 six including St Catherine's Bramley and City of London Freemen's). The less academic are equally well catered for, find their own niches and chalk up some impressive grades in subjects such as art and music. Classes are relatively small approx 18-20. Mild dyslexics and dyspraxics can receive one to one support from qualified special needs teachers on an extra-curricular basis. Not a school for computer and new technology

addicts, but the new head is on the case and the computer system is being upgraded.

Games, Options, the Arts: Games are compulsory and broad-based. Enthusiastic teaching. All sports facilities including games fields and athletic track are on site. Pupils who would be sidelined in a large school have the opportunity to get into the teams – a big plus for the less pushy. Teams are fielded for all ages and they do surprisingly well for a small school. Outdoor swimming pool. Tennis courts include two very smart, all-weather and floodlit courts paid for by a grateful parent.

Drama and music are a flourishing and integral part of the school. Many learn a musical instrument. There is a choir, jazz band and orchestra. New head of music is the only male teacher in the school. Very good music department built up under his predecessor Lyndsay Macaulay, who was hugely enthusiastic and will be a hard act to follow. Art and design department encourages work in a wide variety of media and exhibitions are staged.

Background and Atmosphere: Founded in 1920, moved to present site in 1937. Splendid Queen Anne manor house surrounded by 17 acres of beautiful grounds. Flower gardens are an absolute delight. School is frequently used for weddings at weekends. Additional redbrick buildings which house new sports hall etc built to blend with the original house.

Happy family atmosphere and pleasant environment much commented on by both parents and pupils. First time visitors struck by the friendliness of the place. Administration can sometimes be creaky.

Pastoral Care and Discipline: 'Excellent spiritual, moral and cultural ethos' (report of Independent Schools Inspectorate). Hard to find a more tranquil community. Drugs, drink or smoking problems are unheard of. Concerns are dealt with in a quick, diplomatic manner. With such small classes any difficulties are spotted early by form teachers. Some teachers are trained counsellors. Popular school nurse ready to mop fevered brows and deal with teenage traumas. School is keen charity fundraiser.

Pupils and Parents: A mix, although the location in the Surrey stockbroker belt means that a number of parents are not short of money. Quite a large percentage of first time buyers. School also attracts girls escaping from the more pressured academic schools. Escapees add to the broad academic mix and help bump up the results. Pupils are friendly, polite and very supportive of each other. Smartly dressed. No platform shoes or skirts half way up the backside here. Bus service to surrounding areas and free shuttle bus to Effingham station. Old Girls include Susan Howatch (author), Elinor Goodman (political editor Channel 4), Sarah de Carvalho (founder of the charity, Happy Children) and Rose Gray (co-owner of The River Café.)

Entrance: Many via the junior school (see below) but places available at 11+. Entrance not a huge hurdle. Depends upon a satisfactory day's assessment and own exam results. Happy to take girls who do not want the academic hothouses.

Exit: A levels not on offer, so all exit at 16. Leavers go everywhere from Cheltenham Ladies' to state sixth form colleges. Popular destinations include Lord Howard of Effingham, Godalming Sixth Form College, St John's Leatherhead and City of London Freemen's.

Money Matters: Scholarship may be offered at 11+. The Mason Scholarship

available for girls entering from the state system. Scholarships 10-50 per cent of the fees. Girls may be considered for art or music bursary at 11+. Drama, music and sports bursaries may also be awarded to girls in the senior department if their performance merits it.

Remarks: Super, traditional, small, caring, all-round girls' day school ideal for nurturing the more tender flowers of this world. Suits girls – both academic and middle of the road- who would be invisible in a larger school. Does not try to compete with the larger, more pressurised institutions, so may not have all the facilities and challenges that surface in a bigger more competitive academic community. New head brings abundant enthusiasm and will no doubt stamp her modernising mark on the school, which is no bad thing. School achieves a rare combination turning out happy, confident girls of all abilities with some excellent academic results from the bright pupils.

JUNIOR SCHOOL: (includes a nursery). All pupils (from 2-16) are on the same site so the friendliness and family atmosphere pervades the school from top to bottom. Separate buildings for nursery and prep departments, which are due to be rebuilt in the not too distant future. Classes are small, about 14-16. Automatic transfer from junior to senior school with very rare exceptions. Small leakage of bright girls to more academic schools, but most enjoy the place so much they stay on until they have to leave at 16.

MARLBOROUGH COLLEGE

Marlborough, Wiltshire SN8 1PA

TEL: *01672 892300* FAX: *01672 892307*

E-MAIL:admissions@marlboroughcollege.wilts.sch.uk

WEB: www.marlboroughcollege.org

✦ PUPILS: 835; two-thirds boys, the rest girls. A very few day, rest board
✦ Ages: 13-18 ✦ Size of sixth form: 360
✦ C of E ✦ Fee-paying

Head (Master): Since 1993, Mr E J H Gould MA (fifties). Previous post: head of Felsted, where he earned the nickname of 'Basher' – belies his sensitivity. Looks like a professional bouncer. Read geography at Teddy Hall, Oxford, collected four and a half blues (rugby and swimming), rowed for Great Britain. Before Felsted was housemaster at Harrow. Comments he is homing in on three things: 'confidence, morale and attitude – none of which you can pass rules on'. Wife v good on girl and parent fronts.

Academic Matters: Some excellent staff and teaching. Dual award science only at GCSE. Results now looking impressive – 7.4 average points score per A level subject, 31.0 average total. Classics, Arabic, Japanese, Mandarin Chinese, plus the usual languages are all possible (though NB exotics like Italian not offered as a matter of course). Good careers centre – school pioneered this. Twenty-three took A level theatre studies in '97, and double that number at GCSE – good results. EFL and help for dyslexics available and well used. The impressive old library has now been overhauled and is much less dusty.

Games, Options, the Arts: Famously strong on extras. Art still upholding the distinguished tradition built up by the previous head of art. Facilities up with the best, and current exam results outstanding – 53 taking it at GCSE in '97 with 40 As and nothing below C; 20 at A level. Every child has to do a 'creative project' in 'Shell' year (first year) as a 'counter-blast' to electronic gadgetry. Traditionally strong on mainstream games, and rugby results have been particularly good recently (one boy even won a rugby scholarship to university). Girls are now also more than holding their own against single sex schools – they do hockey, netball, lacrosse, athletics. There are dozens of societies, a beagle pack, a strong music department. The famous brass band, the 'brasser', which is still going strong.

Background and Atmosphere: Founded in 1843 for the 'sons of clergy of the Church of England', though you would not guess so to look at it. Buildings grouped round central Queen Anne building at head of court, contrasting with Memorial Hall built after World War I – good for concerts etc – and earthwork known as 'The Mound'. 'In' houses and 'out' houses (ie on and off the main campus which is spread about the town). Girls' quarters cosy and comfortable (four girls' houses, plus some girls still in boys' houses but 'well segregated now'). NB choose your house carefully. School has flogged off land from time to time to finance refurbishment, large grounds remain. 'Somewhat impersonal atmosphere', say some parents. Pupils' appearance is much less scruffy than before. That said, if you visit the school you will – as always – see a couple of characters slouching against columns like something out of the OK Corral, looking for trouble; bedrooms can be extremely untidy.

Victorian chapel, imposing and stuffy. Girl talk: do not send your daughter straight into the sixth form here unless she is a toughish egg on all fronts.

Pastoral Care and Discipline: Previous inadequacies have now more than melted into history, and the now not-so-new regime has brought forth fruit in such abundance that boys comment 'it isn't any fun any more – they've over-corrected'. Be that as it may: there is a male and female tutor 'team' in every house. The school tests for drugs. Everything is talked through, with written self-assessments – a system of continuous assessment for encouragement. Head is still pursuing a 'hands-on' approach – seeing pupils daily as necessary on a one-to-one basis, and on Saturday mornings – 'there is an academic rogues' queue at 8 am'.

Pupils and Parents: Middle and upper middle class – accountants, lawyers, dealers, army, one or two clergy. Also foreigners. Girls from wider background. One visiting parent reported that 'boys and girls were self possessed and showed little consideration to visiting parents; did not stand aside to let us pass, nor did they open doors, nor even a word of thanks when doors were held open for them'. OBs include William Morris, Anthony Blunt, John Betjeman, James Mason, Peter Medawar, Nicholas Goodison, Wilfrid Hyde White, James Robertson Justice, Lord Hunt (of Everest fame), Francis Chichester, Louis MacNeice, Siegfried Sassoon, Bruce Chatwyn.

Entrance: Getting selective once again. Registration and CE for boys and girls. Three GCSEs at C and three at B grade is a minimum for entry to sixth form – v popular with girls, and not easy to get in.

Exit: Twenty-two to Oxbridge in '97 (numbers are well up on when we last went to press), to art foundation courses; more than half do a gap year, one or two to foreign universities.

Money Matters: The school is still rich in floggable assets. A movable percentage of fee income goes to children of clergymen. Approximately 20 per cent of pupils are subsidised in some way. Large number of scholarships and bursaries, and 'limited' help for parents with children in the school whose income has gone down the tubes: 'We would do our level best to get them on to the next "break point".' Also music, sport and art scholarships.

Remarks: Famous designer-label co-ed boarding school, now back in fashion. Some reports of arrogance, and resting on recent laurels.

THE MCLAREN HIGH SCHOOL

Mollands Road, Callander FK17 8JH

TEL: *01877 330156* FAX: *01877 331601*

E-MAIL: mclaren@post.almac.co.uk

✦ PUPILS: 650 boys and girls; all day
✦ Ages: 11-18 ✦ Size of sixth form: 180
✦ Non-denom ✦ State

Head (Rector): Since 1996, Mr Daniel Murphy MA MEd. Read history at Edinburgh University and has taught in state system all his life. Previously rector, Crieff High School. Married with four children. School under Stirling Council since 1996.

Academic Matters: Follows Scottish exam system only. All mainstream subjects, including wonderful classics teacher – Latin on offer at senior school level. Gaelic also offered – about 10 take it – and new project being developed in primary schools associated with McLaren. Careful setting. Good results – though still a few too many low grades. Points system for good work. Excellent computing facilities and current development plan boosting IT. Fifty-four staff (full and part time), 18 subject departments.

Games, Options, the Arts: Given the time restrictions, the school manages to pack in a lot. Lots of clubs and activities in the lunch hour, and trips, skiing and abroad. Not much emphasis on competitive team games – to the relief of some – and the official line is that all must be catered for, 'not just the first eleven'. Very keen on music, with festivals and overseas trips every other year with school orchestra (and concerts after school). All manner of musical tuition offered, including the bagpipes. Art and design strong. Annual plays etc produced – recently 'Grease'. Activities week in June for all younger pupils, while seniors are on study leave for exams. A new community leisure centre opened '98 on the campus with the school getting 'priority access' during the school day.

Background and Atmosphere: Stunning setting by the river in Callander (some good fly-tiers among the pupils) in the Trossachs. Sixties buildings have received civic trust award – though they sit slightly bleakly among the spectacular scenery, and look pretty institution-y, especially inside. First-class library and resource centre. Room for wheelchairs through the school, including staircase, lift, ramps (school used for adult classes in evenings). Pupils wear uniform – recently the subject of much debate, ending in a re-designed one – though this is still not immediately apparent, as they are invariably swaddled up in the latest plush slinky anorak and white socks. There is a happy-go-lucky atmosphere about the place, tolerant of what pupils at another school called 'weirdos' (by which they meant 'individuals'). The Foundation dates back to 1844, endowed by Callander philanthropist Donald McLaren in 1850 with a view to providing a 'salary of sufficient amount to induce men of superior talents and acquirements to become and continue Teachers in the said School...' School 'dux' boards go back to 1909. Motto: ab origine fides.

Pastoral Care and Discipline: A brisk and realistic approach. Usually it's punishment 'exercise' and the occasional detention. New head has reviewed the whole subject and come up with new policy which includes emphasis on rewarding good behaviour more than punishing poor. (Previous head commented that parental control over children is not what it used to be and even in the comparative calm of Callander, 'we feel ripples'.) Anti-smoking crusade 'at all times'.

Pupils and Parents: All sorts, from catchment area of 400 square miles – which obviously makes organising extra-curricular activities difficult.

Entrance: By registration.

Exit: Farming, university, the arts – total cross-section. Of those going on to university, virtually all go to Scottish universities, of which Glasgow is the most popular.

Money Matters: State school with foundation endowment (see above). Well supported by local industries, manages to provide subsidies where necessary (eg for outings).

Remarks: Sound, much-admired Highland state school with lively friendly pupils.

MERCHANT TAYLORS' SCHOOL

Sandy Lodge, Northwood, Middlesex
HA6 2HT

TEL: *01923 820 644* FAX: *01923 835 110*

E-MAIL: admissions@mtsn.org.uk

WEB: www.mtsn.org.uk

✦ PUPILS: 777 boys all day
✦ Ages: 11-18 ✦ Size of sixth form: 260
✦ C of E ✦ Fee-paying

Head: Since 1991, Mr Jon Gabitass MA (fifties), educated at Plymouth College, followed by St John's, Oxford, where he read English. A rugby blue, he still coaches, and will turn his hand to anything: play soccer, fives, cricket, v keen on music and drama – 'exceptionally high (standards) here'. Previously taught at Clifton College, and was second master at Abingdon (no relation of the educational agency – observe the spelling). His wife teaches at a local primary. A wandering head, who reckons to know every boy in the school, but doesn't see it expanding much more. He still teaches (English law), and believes that it is important for boys to leave school at 18 'self-sufficient, with good A levels, good communication skills, languages, IT skills, a sense of purpose and above all, confidence in themselves'. Gives pupils lots of responsi-

bility to take the initiative. Very approachable – eats lunch with the pupils every day.

Academic Matters: Terrific teaching and thoroughly good examination results. Favourite subjects – economics and maths. No special provision for learning support, but, says head, 'teachers are very willing to help those with problems'. Lots taking general studies at A level. All pupils take nine plus GCSE subjects, with French and maths a year early. Bias to science subjects. Japanese, Chinese, ethics, law etc are available as modules in sixth form. Computers (IBM compatible) which were in the attic, are now in 'satellite areas' around the school (in keeping with progressive thought on the matter) and they are on the internet. School has been building: new library and information centre opened '96, and IT centre '97, more in '99 and '00 too. No Saturdays – school has a five-day week with slightly longer terms.

NB for inscrutable reasons, in government statistics you will find Merchant Taylors' listed under Hertfordshire.

Games, Options, the Arts: Superb facilities for everything. Boys take their games seriously: rugby pitches everywhere, play every school in sight. Cricket has amazing record – first XI very rarely beaten. New all-weather hockey pitch opened '98. Good big range of sports 'to accommodate everyone' – fives, fencing, sailing, golf, judo, even windsurfing. Parents' society, The Friends of Merchant Taylors', invited to regular lectures on educational topics, and self-subdivide into groups supporting drama, music, hockey, rugby etc. Art looks like a poor relation, hardly features at all at A level, but new facilities for '99.

Background and Atmosphere: Founded in 1561 by the Worshipful Company of

Merchant Taylors, the original building destroyed in the Great Fire. Moved from the City of London to deep suburbia in 1933 to purpose-built school (designed by Sir William Newton), dominated by Great Hall. Later additions include science and modern languages block (opened by Lord Coggan, OMT) which harmonises beautifully with slightly young music and the old science block. 250 acres of trees and playing fields, set in sunny suburbia. One of the original 'Clarendon Nine' schools which include Eton and Winchester. The Manor of the Rose, the boarding house, has been phased out – head feels the future lies in day pupils. General purposeful feel throughout the school.

Pastoral Care and Discipline: House system very strong, with house plays directed by senior boys and starring juniors to get them involved during their first term. Tutors throughout (and tutors stick with tutees throughout a boy's school career): but 'all staff have a pastoral role'. Mr Gabitass is 'prepared to sack if necessary'. Has sacked for a physical attack on another boy off campus, and for a drugs offence (seven years ago). He comments: 'boys need to know where the line is drawn...' School prepared to be 'upfront' about smoking, and believes that 'boys want rules applied consistently'. Punishment fits crime: forgotten homework, do twice plus a bit. Head believes that school's own 'air of tranquillity' produces confident but not brash streetwise children, certainly the ones we met bear this out.

Pupils and Parents: Pupils come from 'up and down' the Metropolitan Line, 20 mins from Baker Street. Meaty ethnic mix, all apparently living in harmony 'we're very proud of this' (school motto concordia parvae res crescunt). Parents v supportive, join the sports club and use school facilities in the evening and in the holidays. Fair number of first-time buyers. There is a regular coach service to Radlett, Beaconsfield, Edgware, Harrow and Ealing. Links with St Helen's Northwood, including drama, careers, charity fund-raising, combined orchestra, social events, CCF.

Entrance: Quite selective. About 40 each year at 11 from local state schools: competitive exam in January. The rest at 13 from local preps: St John's Northwood, Orley Farm, St Martin's, Northwood Prep, York House, Alpha and Quainton Hall. Head interviews candidates in Christmas term to suss them out; if thought to be a suitable candidate will be marked A and assured of a place by January for the following September, following entrance exam. Lots of telephoning between heads of preps and MT. Boys need six GCSEs at grade B to enter the sixth form – perhaps one pupil a year falls at this hurdle.

Exit: To a fascinatingly wide collection of higher education establishments – about 25 to Oxbridge, then in descending order, to LSE, Manchester, UCL, Bristol etc – the occasional one to Liverpool College of Performing Arts, Guildhall School of Acting, ditto of Music, St Martin's, South Bank etc.

Money Matters: Had over 90 assisted places at last count, but the Merchant Taylors' Educational Trust is set to provide bursary scheme to replace these, for 'academically suitable candidates who come from families of very limited means'. Otherwise, five scholarships at 11, five major and six minor awards at 13, and one major and one minor at 16+. Scholarships also for music at 11+, 13+ or lower sixth, and four internal exhibitions. Plus travel awards to sixth formers, outward bound and sail training as well as leaving scholarships to assist at university. A well-endowed school.

Remarks: A school which is definitely, if quietly, getting it right. It has re-emerged under the current head as an excellent public day school with superb facilities, well endowed, and producing charming pupils and impressive results.

MERCHISTON CASTLE SCHOOL

Colinton, Edinburgh EH13 OPU

TEL: *0131 312 2200* FAX: *0131 441 6060*

E-MAIL: AdSec@mcsch.org.uk

WEB: www.mcsch.org.uk

+ PUPILS: 366 boys (70 per cent board, 30 per cent day) + Ages: 8-18 (now 10-18, eight-year-olds from 2001 on) + Size of sixth form: 135 + Non-denom + Fee-paying

Head: Since 1998, Mr Andrew Hunter BA PGCE (forties), educated at Aldenham and Manchester University where he read combined studies: English, theology and religious studies. Comes to Merchiston from Bradfield, where he spent ten years, and was latterly housemaster of Army House. Trails of glory on games fields, ex-county hockey, squash and tennis players and international under-23 England squash cap 'but lazy these days, too busy to play'. Despite these protestations, he coaches tennis on occasions and is starting fitness training again.

Comes from an ex-pat family, and brought up on a Kenyan coffee farm, he started school at Kenton College, Nairobi. His wife, Barbara teaches art and design and they have three children, one son at Merchiston and a daughter at St Georges. Keen on the arts, theatre, wine tasting etc. Took over from the apparently everlasting David Spawforth after 'rather a long run in' (actually only a year, but rumours of Mr Spawforth's retiral had been much exaggerated over a number of years which did the school no good, and numbers had fallen nervously). The school is already showing signs of previously lacking dynamism and Mr Hunter and his wife have produced a forty-five page Further Information Booklet for the school that is undoubtedly the best guide to any school we have ever seen, plus a really comprehensive leaflet on exam results including a rather complicated value-added section – other schools please note. Occasionally teaches A level classes and presentation skills.

Academic Matters: A levels for the majority (less than a third do Highers, over two years); results excellent and rising strongly to 2000, when there was a bit of a dip. Science and the arts both strong; disappointing design results have been countered successfully by appointing a new head of department. New heads of physics, and English (a female no less in the bastion of maleness). Currently all boys must do a minimum of two separate sciences at GCSE, 18 A levels offered, plus top ups in sixth form. Classics about to undergo a revival, and Chinese Scotvec a popular choice in lower VI. Setting in most subjects, ratio of 1:8 staff to pupils.

New head of learning support and EFL. Strong learning support unit, all pupils 'screened on entry', with both individual and group help on hand plus fully staffed

EFL department, (approximately 10/12 per cent of pupils are non-nationals).

Games, Options, the Arts: Very sporty, particularly at rugby (comment from one opponent, no sylph himself: 'they're massive hunks who tower over teams from other schools, and terrify'). Also strong on cricket and athletics. School has own golf course (much in use when we visited), squash, sub aqua (pool popular in any case), full and small bore shooting ground, sports hall and 100 acres of playing field plus the use of all the facilities of Colinton Castle Sports Club. Drama enthusiastic, art inspired, with lots more facilities down at Pringle. CCF mandatory over two years, with much marching and drill. Over two-thirds of school making music of one sort or another.

Background and Atmosphere: Founded in 1833 by scientist Charles Chalmers, school moved from the now ruined Merchiston Castle to the rather gaunt purpose-built Colinton House in 1930. Set in 100 acres of park like playing fields, with the main buildings grouped quite close together. Pringle House, the junior school is cosily situated quite near. Exciting new computer room re-jigged and connected to music room – fabulous views. Charming small theatre good for parties. Stunning conversion of new Spawforth library, a double-decker affair; the sixth form are currently scheming to take over the top floor.

Acres of polished wooden floors, including the Memorial Hall, which doubles as chapel (service inter-denominational) and dance hall. Girls are regularly corralled in from (primarily) St George's, but also Kilgraston and St Leonards for reel parties, with lots of practice before the real thing. Merchiston boys are regularly voted the best dancing partners in Scotland.

Boys progress through the houses by year group, some dorms still pretty gruesome, though the dark wooden cattle pens of yesteryear have been modified – not entirely convincingly, and with a distinct lack of posters or even pin boards. First year sixth formers are billeted to each house for the year to act as monitors; and have pretty snazzy kitchens to make their tasks less onerous. Visiting girls 'not a problem', they come and go at weekends and can join the boys in the sixth form bar.

Pastoral Care and Discipline: Good rapport between pupils and staff. Excellent and detailed PSE programme in the info booklet. The horizontal house system is said to have made bullying 'non-existent' – humanly impossible, so perhaps they're just not looking hard enough. School was praised in the recent (May 2000) inspector's report: 'The high quality pastoral care and concern for pupils' welfare' was deemed one of the school's key strengths.

Head will and has asked pupils to leave, 'ton of bricks on drug dealing', otherwise treats ordinary misdemeanours (alcohol, smoking) on their own merits (or demerits). Discipline seminars.

Pupils and Parents: 'Not a flash school', (says the head) but currently in the somewhat unexpected position of being the only all boys boarding school in Scotland. Mainly middle class, mainly Scottish, some roughish diamonds, but this is changing as single-sex schools regain momentum, and parents and boys prefer to come here rather than make the long trek South. Good Asian contingent. Boys open, friendly and well-mannered, though they speak with many (regional) tongues.

Entrance: At 10+, also 11+, 12+ and 13+, always via exams, 55 per cent pass mark at CE, boys come from prep schools all over

Scotland and the North of England. Entry to sixth form automatic from inside school, others need a satisfactory report from previous school.

Exit: Refer again to the natty little booklet for details of the favoured unis: 75 per cent to England (Durham, Bristol, London etc, 10 per cent of which to Oxbridge), 25 per cent Scotland (Edinburgh, Glasgow, Aberdeen), biology, ecology, economics and engineering being the favoured subjects. Pupils go on to be fully paid up members of the Edinburgh mafia – law lords etc.

Money Matters: Myriads of scholarships for almost everything. Business partnership fund in sights, looking for £300,000 school fund; will in any case carry any boy 'on to next exam' in cases of hardship.

Remarks: No change. Still the top boys' school in Scotland, 'which extraordinary position has been achieved by defection to co-education by the rest – and it is on the way up anyway'. Quite. Charismatic head, leading a school which is tough, well run, middle of the road, preparing boys soundly for their future; where boys are encouraged to 'try their hardest, make the most of their talents and look after each other'.

MILLFIELD SENIOR SCHOOL

Street, Somerset BA16 OYD

TEL: *01458 442 291* FAX: *01458 841 270*

E-MAIL: admissions@millfield.somerset.sch.uk

WEB: www.millfield.somerset.sch.uk

✦ PUPILS: 1,220 boys and girls (about 75 per cent board, the rest day) ✦ Ages: 13-18 ✦ Size of sixth form: 550 ✦ Non-denom ✦ Fee-paying

---

Head: Since 1998, Mr Peter Johnson MA (Oxon) CertEd (fifties). Educated at Bec Grammar, read geography at Mansfield, Oxford (rugby and judo blue), Mr Johnson came to Millfield via a spectacular career in the Parachute Regiment. Previously taught at Radley (housemaster, director of lower school studies etc) followed by seven year stint as headmaster of Wrekin. Reckons that 'schoolmastering is the most professionally challenging job' he has ever done. Enormously keen on sports, rugby blue etc, and is sad not to be either playing or coaching, 'as a head you have to resign yourself to the glory of others'. Married to Chrissie, whom he met while still at school; they have two sons. Took over from Mr Christopher Martin.

School is run by senior management team: headmaster, two deputy heads, bursar, the heads of Millfield Prep and Pre-Prep Schools, plus other senior staff, and operates more like a serious business than many educational establishments.

Academic Matters: Quite difficult to assess, given the very broad intake and numbers of non-native English speakers (though there is a comprehensive initial language course – run by MELS, (Millfield English Language School), which operates within the core school on the basis of total immersion, booting pupils into the Millfield proper when their English is up to scratch).

Huge numbers of subjects on offer at GCSE, including ballet, travel & tourism, and inspirational design & technology (systems & control) for budding inventors, plus 40 different A levels and GNVQs. Famous and excellent language development department (dyslexia, dyspraxia et al to you and me – a few of the children are statemented), staff ratio of 1:7.5 allows for finely tuned setting, and classes are tiny. Statemented children occasionally sent here by their local LEA. Offers one year sixth form courses – useful for foreigners and some Brits.

NB This is still a school with a truly comprehensive intake – everything from A level at the age of 14 for the gifted, to children for whom five GCSE passes is a miracle.

Games, Options, the Arts: Famous for sporting prowess. Would-be internationalists are offered mega scholarships with facilities to match. Olympic sized swimming pool, four sports halls, plus fencing hall, judo dojo, weight rooms and a physio department. Squads win everything and regularly compete at county and national level. Rugby, cricket and hockey strong, also swimming and fencing.

The Lawn Tennis Association recommends school for would-be tennis stars – ritzy new facilities include three indoor tennis courts. Inspired equitation centre, school is renowned for polo (boarding fees for ponies 'is like having to pay for another child'). Pupils encouraged to have a go, and can do ballroom dancing or play golf in their compulsory three PE lessons a week.

Underwater hockey and corfball popular. The new library, though 'award-winning', seems rather a poor relation compared to the sports facilities and closes 'at sixish'. The school is fully intranetted, with one PC for every two pupils.

Music scholars produce results, but no great take-up at GCSE or A level. Impressive 600 seat Meyer theatre, and professional television studios. Art department one of the best equipped we have seen; the grounds are littered with fabulous metal and stone creations. Outstanding ceramics, 2D art less so. Lots of extras, though pressure on popular options can sometimes overwhelm the resources.

Background and Atmosphere: Founded in 1935 by 'Boss' Meyer, whose philosophy was to put the individual child's needs before those of the school, to adopt an aggressive marketing attitude, and to insist that all pupils were good at something, even if it was only tiddlywinks. The 120-acre campus is an educationalist's dream, manicured lawns dotted with pleasing limestone-clad classroom blocks and boarding houses (sports halls everywhere). Pupils keep their books in 'the bomb shelter'.

School owns 600 acres in all, and permission has just been given for a further eight boarding houses to be built in the grounds. Kingweston, with its polo ground, The Grange, and a couple of the older houses are being kept, but the rest will all be on site; a boarding village. 23 boarding houses in total, with houseparents and tutors in each. A gigantic dining hall was being erected when we visited.

School open for conferences and the like during holiday time, as well as hosting summer and Easter schools for their English Language School. The school is brilliant at marketing itself (and has been so long before other schools had heard of the word) – and never forgets that it is basically a business. Staff exude excitement even after showing the nth parent that day around the school. The prospectus is a masterpiece of fancy promotion.

Pastoral Care and Discipline: Excellent in parts at grass-root level, but problems arise owing to size of campus and the to-ing and fro-ing in buses between academic and boarding staff and resulting responsibility gaps; pupils complain of a lack of sense of community. School is tougher than most ('we have to be, it's the Dartington Hall image'). Pupils 'part company automatically' for drugs, and pupils are tested 'on suspicion'; repeated alcohol and smoking offences also equal expulsion. Counsellors on hand. Much reported fatal alcohol-related accident in '98. School is pioneer of the 'six-inch' rule, and 'boys and girls may not meet as solitary couples'. Bullying 'equals relationships gone wrong', PSE and group approach. Voice mail for parent/child messages: each pupil has their own pin number. Fair amount of traditional aggro with Street, 'only to be expected' says head, 'but as we employ some 900 people, we are probably quite important locally'.

Pupils and Parents: Lots of talent from humble backgrounds, eg the Welsh valleys, on scholarships. Large local contingent, many first-time buyers, fair amount of flash new money, about 20 per cent overseas students of 50 plus nationalities (Princes as well as paupers – Yeltsin's grandson was here for a bit) and the odd dyslexic Sloane. Duncan Goodhew was an OM, also John Sergeant, Chris Law, Gareth Edwards.

Entrance: Interview and previous head's report. CE for setting purposes. Large numbers from school's own Prep (see separate entry) and from all over. Some leave after GCSE, and rather more arrive (school has some leeway to pick and choose here – don't assume it's easy peasy). Pupils can join at any term or half term – very flexible.

Exit: All over, with around 200 to universities either in the UK or America, 20 or so to Oxbridge.

Money Matters: Generous scholarships for sports, academic, music and 'all round talent'. Up to 50 per cent get some financial assistance, but it is means-tested; the largest recent scholarship was 90 per cent of full fees. No quarter shown to parents in financial difficulties: commercial loan offered, and, 'if they don't pay up we take them to court' says the bursar. Contrary to endless reports in the press it is not the most expensive school in the country, and 'the textbooks are included in the basic fees'.

Remarks: Famous boarding and day, genuine co-ed school, genuinely comprehensive, offering all things to all people. This also could be your first choice of school if you have a dyslexic child, providing the child is reasonably robust and determined, or if you have a real winner but no money. Seriously contented noises from parents of day pupils. Definitely not a place for wets, nor for social climbers. Tightening up on discipline.

MILL HILL SCHOOL

The Ridgeway, London NW7 1QS

TEL: *020 8959 1176* FAX: *020 8201 0663*

E-MAIL: headmaster@millhill.org.uk

WEB: www.millhill.org.uk

✦ PUPILS: 595, 410 day, 185 board; boys and girls (25 per cent and rising) ✦ Ages: 13-18, plus separate junior and pre-prep ✦ Size of sixth form: 240 ✦ Non-denom ✦ Fee-paying

Head: Since 1996, Mr William Winfield MA (forties), educated at William Ellis School, Clare College Cambridge (where he read French, German and Norwegian) and the Royal Academy of Music. Previous post (from '95) was acting head here, following unscheduled departure of last head. Has been in the school for 25 years, and set up the much admired Section Bilingue at Mill Hill in the '70s and '80s. His wife, Margaret, is a professional musician – with the Apollo Consort. Governors: some changes but still some tough eggs. Head of governors (since 1995) is Dame Angela Rumbold.

Academic Matters: Extremely enthusiastic business studies department – just the place for budding R Bransons. Keen computing, good Design Technology, generally stronger at practical subjects, reflecting preferences of pupils. That said, staff common room was in need of a shake-up. The EFL form, recently disbanded, has now been resurrected – too early to comment – ask for glossy booklet called The European Initiative.

Good network of exchanges with Institution Join-Lambert in Normandy (25th anniversary of these exchanges in '93), Goslar in Germany and in Salamanca. Brand new library. Next to library is the Murray Scriptorum – James Murray of OED fame was master and worked on dictionary here.

95 per cent get A★ to C at GCSE, with almost nothing below D – a good performance. Chinese, Persian, Urdu, Russian, Gujarati and other exotics on offer. A level results a broad spread from A to E – pleasantly few failures, and a good number of bright kids doing well (average points score for the top 25 per cent was 30); lack of As reflects breadth of intake: popular subjects maths, physics, business studies, chemistry.

Games, Options, the Arts: Formerly famous rugby school which used to have blood matches with Harrow. Has links with the Saracens, and recently provided the under 19 captain for Ireland. Splendid Sports/Social Club which raises around £15k a year for sporting tours. Other main games hockey and cricket – school was County champion in this last recently (has ex-county cricketer as coach). Girls play hockey and netball (Astroturf just arrived). Jolly golf and croquet. Art school has no-nonsense approach to basic technique (boy – clothed in school uniform – posing on podium for fellow pupils to draw when we visited). New theatre complex. School has its own Field Study Centre in village of Dent in Cumbria for the pupils to observe wildlife etc.

Background and Atmosphere: Founded as grammar school in 1807 by Non-conformists (United Reform Church, though links minimal/non-existent) and has vestigial traces of the past in rows of headmasters' portraits plastered (we use the word advisedly) on the dining-room walls, and much bigger portrait of school treasurer. Built as a school – grandiose main buildings with giant Doric columns, bristling with war memorials and marble on gorgeous site in 120 acres on pretty draughty hill-air so clean lichens grow on school walls, and on a clear day you can see Windsor. Despite imposing design (dwarfs the pretty surrounding village) the atmosphere is wonderfully informal, with pupils punching each other playfully as we passed. Dining room bang in middle of school. Atmosphere tolerant and friendly, bouncy, scruffy. Despite boarding history, feels very much like a day school. Recently opened girls' boarding house.

Pastoral Care and Discipline: Cannabis smokers (but not dealers) readmitted on condition they have regular drug tests. Head comments 'If you expel a pupil you don't solve the problem. You simply pass it to the next station along the line.' First rate chaplain, and every pupil has a tutor for academic and pastoral matters. Hot on bullying.

Pupils and Parents: Sons of local businessmen – lots of self-made first-generation parents, also strong contingent of long-established Millhillian families. Almost equal numbers of Protestants and Jewish boys; of the remaining third, half are Hindu and half Muslim. Interesting OBs (and OG) = Richard Dimbleby, Francis Crick, Nigel Wray, Denis Thatcher, Simon Jenkins, Katherine Whitehorn and several members of the Wills family.

Entrance: A broad intake. New 'own entry assessment exams'. Parents liable to be looking also at North London Consortium schools, Haberdashers' Aske's, Highgate, Merchant Taylors', Aldenham. Name down a year in advance. Sixty per cent of pupils come from school's own junior school.

Exit: 90 per cent to universities everywhere.

Money Matters: Scholarships and bursaries and 'we try and bail them out if possible'.

Remarks: One-time traditional boys' boarding school which has recently gone co-ed and is recovering well from the wobble of a few years ago.

JUNIOR SCHOOL: Belmont. Tel: 020 8959 1431 Fax: 020 8906 3519. Head Mr J R Hawkins. Ages 7-13, (plus pre-prep, Tel: 020 7959 6884. Started in '94 in a redundant boarding house, suitably tarted up thanks to donation from an OB). Pupils are tested on entry at 7, and test plus interview at 9, 10 and 11. The great majority go on to the senior school. Popular prep, one of the few in the area, which does very well for most of its pupils.

MILTON ABBEY SCHOOL
Blandford Forum, Dorset DT11 0BZ
TEL: *01258 880484* FAX: *01258 881194*

E-MAIL: info@miltonabbey.co.uk

WEB: www.miltonabbey.co.uk

✦ PUPILS: 220 boys (a handful of day boys, the rest board) ✦ Ages: 13-18 ✦ Size of sixth form: 75 ✦ C of E ✦ Fee-paying

---

Head: Since 1995, Mr W J Hughes-D'Aeth (pronounced daith) BA (forties), educated at Haileybury and Liverpool. Previously a housemaster at Rugby. Read geography, is still teaching geography – to the juniors. Formerly a 'keen Territorial Army officer' and still occasionally dons uniform to help with the CCF. Married with four young children. Charming. Says of the pupils here that he immediately 'perceived they are gentle men'.

Academic Matters: A key school for helping boys with a learning difficulty. Dyslexics are integrated with the rest (lots of remedial help where needed). 20/30 per cent of pupils come with an educational psychologist's report (a summary of which stays in staffroom, and tutors and staff have instant access). In the light of this, most results are a credit to the school – with a sprinkling of A*s at GCSE, and a good wodge of As. Some of the A level results perhaps show over-ambition, with too many E-Us for comfort, particularly in communication studies, funnily enough. Art and design results continue disappointing – few pupils taking either subject, and no As or Bs. Also some 'very bright' boys – the occasional genius (including one 14-year old who got a place at Peterhouse, Cambridge). Most classes are under 12, with individual attention and tutorials often instantly available at any time on any subject. Ratio of staff to pupils 1:7.5. Low staff turnover, much emphasis on staff training.

Academic tutors do study skills and monitor progress; teaching staff set aside two periods each week for official tutorials or help with problems. IT popular and computers everywhere (most boys have them for private study) as well as computer rooms. Business studies linked to economics department. GNVQ in advanced land and environment; NVQ cookery.

Games, Options, the Arts: Compulsory activities on Tuesday and Thursday afternoons, huge choice: art, v active theatre, boat maintenance, clay-pigeon shooting, fencing, model making etc. Natural history still strong with moth trap shining through the summer months. Boys do regular head counts of birds. Ferrets. CDT dept expanded, and CCF popular. The school has strong links with Royal Armoured Corps at Bovington, also with the Royal Navy. Excellent sports facilities: rugby is the main game. Peter Alliss-inspired golf course (his son was a pupil) and new indoor heated swimming pool – which can be used at weekends. Sailing, good and popular, and particularly successful, recently won the southern area and south-west area regattas, D of E awards.

Background and Atmosphere: Enormously friendly and truly kind atmosphere here – all are cared for and appreciated, weirdos are not picked on (the head takes us to task for using this word) and (almost) without exception (recent) old boys report that they 'loved it' at the school. Approving noises also from prep school heads. Immensely beautiful listed Grade 1 building (begun by Sir William Chambers and taken over by James Wyatt), set in fold of valleys and Dorset hills. Abbot's Hall and King's Room breathtaking. Magical. School founded in mid-'50s. Modern blocks cleverly hidden, stable block converted into light classrooms plus art, music and CDT, with stunning theatre (and CDT below). Daily worship in ravishing Abbey (also occasionally used by local community). Houses in main building, each with its own territory. All housemasters (one of whom is a woman, Jane Emerson) are married, family atmosphere pervades, boys know each other well, graduating from dormitory/ common-rooms (ie with working spaces round the beds) to single study bedrooms. The head has instigated a major programme of refurbishment here to bring the school 'somewhere towards the 20th century', aiming for the 'faded country house look', and commenting that 'buildings and the whole environment is so important...' Boys are kept occupied in this isolated school: Lovat trousers and jerseys (suits on Sunday). Not a girl in sight – boys tend to get slightly restless as they go up the school – but increasing contact with local girls' schools has been reported.

Pastoral Care and Discipline: Housemasters (who are normally also academic tutors) plus assistant house tutors. Chaplain's wife is a counsellor. The school is small enough to pick up any worrying vibes via the bush telegraph. It's no longer automatically out for drugs –rehabilitation is now a possibility. 'Constructive restrictions' for smoking in building, plus rustications. Good prefectorial system: prefects are called 'pilots', atmosphere is structured and disciplined, good manners and consideration for others noticeable. Almost OTT in its marketing of the 'caring' image.

Pupils and Parents: Upmarket ('for gents', commented a parent). Not so very many first-time buyers, but more than there used to be. Some Services children. Boys are courteous, relaxed and friendly, and responsible, 'have an outstanding sense of belonging,' and 'really miss it when they leave'. Geographically widespread. Monthly rendezvous for Old Boys at the Duke of Wellington pub, Eaton Terrace.

Entrance: Via CE, flexible. From everywhere, including all the top preps, over 100 feeders plus state system. Entry post-GCSE if chap has the right qualifications (currently five Cs at GCSE) and is 'good enough'.

Exit: Around 70 per cent on to some form of further education, with 50 per cent to degree courses. Ex-polys particularly patronised – including Oxford Brookes and Manchester Metropolitan, also such colleges of higher education as Cheltenham and Gloucester, plus Harper Adams etc. Boys tend to opt for careers where 'they have to sell themselves' – v entrepreneurial. Practical subjects such as business studies and hotel and catering are popular.

Money Matters: Some scholarships, including music, art, sailing even and drama. Will carry pupils through exam year in cases of financial hardship.

Remarks: Boys' boarding school which resolutely continues to give good experienced professional help to those with learning difficulties. A great confidence-building place which runs on kindness and encouragement. Don't take our word for it, read Dr Rae's *Letters to Parents* (Harper Collins).

MORE HOUSE

22-24 Pont Street, London SW1X 0AA

Tel: *020 7235 2855* Fax: *020 7259 6782*

E-mail: office@morehouse.org.uk

Web: www.morehouse.org.uk

✦ Pupils: around 215 girls, all day ✦ Ages: 11-18 ✦ Size of sixth form: around 35 ✦ RC ✦ Fee-paying

Head: Since 1999, Mrs Lesley Falconer MA. Studied microbiology at London, then combined research with teaching at a sixth form college. Teaches some biology and science herself. Early reports from parents uncertain. Took over from Miss Margaret Connell, who was head from 1991.

Academic Matters: OK. Science, maths and languages are consistent hot spots at GCSE; English and geography and some other subjects less so. Some head off for be-boyed pastures at A level, so some of the remaining students find themselves receiving individual tuition. Too few in each subject to judge subject performance at A level, but overall it is average. The aim is to teach the girls to work with others and do well for themselves, hence there is little notice taken of who does best in the class, but much pleasure gained from the maths team beating other schools.

Games, Options, the Arts: Games are restricted by the location and an un-gamesy past, but are gradually being taken more seriously – there is a large entry for the London mini marathon. Refurbished gym. Arts OK, if not particularly celebrated. Music, most notably the choir, good. Drama and photography groups, D of E.

Background and Atmosphere: Pont Street Dutch architectural rabbit-warren in prime location (two minutes to Harrods), but the rooms are well proportioned and the whole effect quite comfortable. Founded by RC parents in 1953, the school retains a strong RC ethos which, nonetheless, doesn't hit you in the face as you go round – 'all faiths are welcomed,' says the school. Food cooked on the premises (and smells good); no packed lunches allowed, though some of the senior girls run a flourishing trade in alternative breakfasts, undercutting the caterer's prices. The girls most hoped-for development – 'build a boys' school next door.'

Pastoral Care and Discipline: Solid, supportive, small-scale cosy set-up with lots of personal attention from caring staff ('who bother about us, take us out for coffee' approves a sixth former). Partly for this reason, and partly because of the lack of bike sheds to smoke behind, the problems of the world seem to be left behind at the door.

Pupils and Parents: After a long history of anything goes for clothes (which left some parents bothered about the Fast Set), the new dark blue corduroy and gingham uniform came as something of a relief. Lots of bi- and tri-linguals among the pupils who, though mostly London residents, are notably diverse in their national origins. RC status steady at around half, a draw for diplomats etc. Quite a sheltered environment, produces nice unspoilt girls. Not a Sloane school, and proud of it.

Entrance: From prep schools across London, but particularly from nearby Hill House.

Exit: Some to co-ed schools at 16. After A level to wide spread of courses at a spread of universities, with an emphasis on London, and the odd Oxbridge.

Money Matters: The mid-range fees include items which most others would charge as extras. Academic scholarships, and bursaries for established pupils in financial need. Had a few assisted places.

Remarks: Small, somewhat limited, Inner London girls' day school at smart address. All the girls that we talked to said that they themselves had made the choice to come here, and potential pupils have reported they 'much preferred' More House to other private schools in the vicinity. Should do well by those that it suits.

MORETON HALL

Weston Rhyn, Oswestry, Shropshire
SY11 3EW

TEL: *01691 773671* FAX: *01691 778552*

E-MAIL: jfmhall@aol.com

WEB: www.moretonhall.org.uk

✦ PUPILS: 260 girls (around 30 day, the rest board) ✦ Ages: 11-18 ✦ Size of sixth form: 85 ✦ C of E ✦ Fee-paying

---

Head (Principal): Since 1992, Mr Jonathan Forster BA (forties), formerly housemaster in charge of girls and head of English at Strathallan School. Educated at Shrewsbury and Leeds University. Teaches English to A level students. Very hands-on, and giving the school a much needed shake-up. Married (his wife is a teacher, English is her subject), two daughters (one still at the school). Madly keen on 'everyone using all facilities as often as possible'.

Governors almost all Old Moretonians or related to them.

Academic Matters: Has been producing more-than-commendable results recently, though this is a school with a broad intake, a place you choose for personality more than anything else, with emphasis on sound middle-of-the-road education. GCSE results good – plenty of A*s and hardly a D in sight. A level results well weighted to As and B, a few Ds, but almost nothing below that. Biology, English, art and business studies the most popular subjects, theatre studies and home economics on the menu, though

not well patronised. Interesting life-skills course for sixth formers. IBM-sponsored IT centre; school networked, and sixth-formers have internet access in their bedrooms. Full-time qualified special needs teacher – private tuition, but no mainstream lessons missed (though French is sometimes dropped). EFL also catered for, plus 'acclimatisation courses' for overseas students.

Games, Options, the Arts: Gamesy (despite small size) with a traditionally strong lax record. Keen tennis (indoor court). Design technology and art both good, and keen drama, 'Lots of it,' enthuse pupils. Music is good (some done with Shrewsbury boys), also social activities, lectures etc, with the boys, and careers department/work-experience record is far stronger than many bigger grander schools. The sixth form is renowned nationally for Moreton Enterprises, the latest of which is a commercial recording studio and radio station (and there have been some pretty spectacular ones in the past). 'Excellent practical hands-on work-experience,' commented a parent. Good links building up (music, drama, careers conference etc) with Shrewsbury School (NB head is OB).

Background and Atmosphere: Founded in 1913 by Mrs Lloyd-Williams ('Aunt Lil') of Oswestry as a school for the daughters of the family. Very friendly and uninstitutional, rather a hotchpotch of buildings in lovely country. Flexible exeats. NB a ceiling of 270 in number has now been decided upon following considerable improvements (cosying up) to dormitories and common rooms.

Pastoral Care and Discipline: Much changed, much improved from being centrally run to house system with housemaster/mistresses being given considerable powers. Tutor system instigated and tutors visit tutees twice weekly – 'General feeling of staff working harder and girls have someone to turn to now,' from a parent. Workshops and widening-horizons weekend programmes in good shape (compulsory until sixth). Clear line on drug offences – it's out.

Pupils and Parents: Truly mixed bunch, socially and geographically. Some ex-pats; mostly from Cheshire and Shropshire and Wales (parents might also consider Malvern Girls and Cheltenham Ladies'). Open and chatty girls, jolly. Composer Thea Musgrove is an Old Girl.

Entrance: 11+; 13+ via CE or own entry test and interview at other ages/stages. Also around six-ten come in at sixth form – six GCSEs at A–C needed (as is the case for pupils already in the school).

Exit: Most leavers go to university , expolys popular, often after a gap year.

Money Matters: Three scholarships at 11+, three scholarships at 13+; one tennis scholarship at 13+; also award at 16+. Had 20+ assisted places.

Remarks: Unstuffy small boarding school in a rural area that teaches girls to stand firmly on their own feet and does not produce stereotypes. Doing fine.

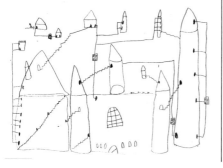

MORRISONS ACADEMY
Crieff, Perthshire PH7 3AN

TEL: *01764 653 885* FAX: *01764 655 411*

E-MAIL: principal@morrisons.pkc.sch.uk

WEB: www.morrisons.pkc.sch.uk

✦ PUPILS: 178 boys, 150 girls (85 per cent day, 15 per cent board); plus junior school: 80 boys, 80 girls; plus nursery: 25 boys and girls ✦ Ages: 11-18; junior school 5-11, nursery 3-5 ✦ Size of sixth form: 120 ✦ Inter-demon ✦ Fee-paying

---

Head (Rector and Principal): Since 1996, Mr Gareth Edwards MA (forties). Born in Wales and has a 'keen affinity with the Celts.' Educated at Tudor Grange Grammar, Solihull; read classics at Exeter, Oxford. Taught at King Edward's Edgbaston, was a head of department at Bolton Boys, and then vice principal of Newcastle-under-Lyme School. Married, with one daughter in the school, he has just been appointed to take over from Frank Gerstenberg at George Watson's in Edinburgh from August 2001.

A slow speaking, deep thinking head, he has all the Welsh charm and a quiet charisma. He is also very giggly. Morrisons will have done well out of him. Mr Edwards has overseen a considerable turnaround at Morrisons; boarding numbers had fallen considerably for years, and are now recovering; the outlying boarding houses have been sold with the resulting cash poured into revamping the seriously old fashioned school buildings. Junior school numbers have doubled over the past four years.

New rector from 2000: Mr J B Bendall, deputy head of Queen Elizabeth's Hospital School, Bristol.

Academic Matters: School follows a 'mixed economy', with pupils ultimately taking Sixth Year Studies and A levels in their final year, but 'not highly academic'. The traditional tremendous bias towards science is rapidly fading in favour of arts-based courses. Masses of computers on site and the staff have to take their European Computer Driving Licence (as do the pupils.) The head of the computer department often builds his own. Goodish results, particularly in the trad subjects, not really much language take up though geography and history good, as are the English results. Can cope with special needs: dyslexia, dyspraxia and mild Asperger's not a problem.

Games, Options, the Arts: Masses of pitches on site, and school plays all the standard games. Swimming pool (a veritable relic – still labelled Baths) popular.

Strong pipe band and v popular – with Chinese students forming a large part, which makes for interesting photographs.

CCF, D of E strong, almost all get bronze, lots of silver and gold. Enthusiastic art, but no CAD. Music and drama good with a stunning girls' chamber choir which plays regularly to lots of local acclaim.

Background and Atmosphere: Built in 1859, it was then said of this Scottish baronial styled building with its crow stepped gables that 'Its healthful locality and commanding view of extensive and beautifully romantic scenery cannot be surpassed, if at all equalled, by any such public building in Scotland.'

The gift of Thomas Mor(r)ison, who lived in the neighbouring village of Muthill and made his fortune as a master builder in Edinburgh, he instructed his trustees to erect an institution carrying his name 'to promote the interests of mankind, having a particular regard to the education of youth and the diffusion of useful knowledge.'

Previously an authority-aided school, with a large boarding ethos, the school dropped in numbers once it became fully independent, and boarding numbers fell dramatically: only two houses are now in use. Some of the current boarders are indeed Scots, but many come from overseas, and add an exotic flavour to what is otherwise a fairly pedestrian environment – almost all religious festivals are celebrated. Fabulous if somewhat underused buildings, recently revamped.

The original school building is fantastic with large open corridors and a terrific hall which doubles for daily assemblies and socials, the head is keen to remove the overpowering sixties 'lowered ceiling'. The Beatrice Mason building is home to the junior school: charming, and decorated with littles' art work.

Pastoral Care and Discipline: Excellent pastoral care and guardianship for boarders and the same applies across the school. Head quite tough on sin, though pupils on the whole 'quite docile': 'tobacco could get you suspended and Chinese pupils do like smoking.' Drugs = 'you should expect to be expelled', but no problems for the past two years. This is not really a street-wise school.

Pupils and Parents: Day pupils from all over the middle belt, Falkirk, Stirling, Comrie, Perth, Auchterarder and Stirling are bussed to school. Most of the boarders from abroad: not a lot of 'trawling', 'though the ex-head does a bit', but Russia, the Far East, the Middle East plus ex-pats on the boarding side. The Scots are mainly middle middle class.

Entrance: Children can and do arrive at any time, during the term and at the start of any term − particularly for boarding from abroad, if space available. Not desperately academic. Interview for nursery and junior school and more or less automatic entrance into senior school from the junior school. Some join the senior school at 11 from the state sector or from local prep schools such as Ardvreck, interview and assessment again. Sixth form entrants (for Highers or SYS) are assessed 'on their potential, taking into account their grades at Standard level, GCSE or whatever.'

Exit: Three or four off to (usually) Scottish independent schools at either 11 or 13. Otherwise a dribble occasionally to Oxbridge, most go to Scottish universities. One or two to Imperial London, or Manchester, Newcastle, Leeds. Many study computing of some sort or another, otherwise the usual: law, medicine and engineering.

Money Matters: The loss of assisted places has hit hard. Discounts for siblings, one or two means tested bursaries, scholarships for the final year.

Remarks: This is a good proud school that had fallen on hard times, but is now on the up. Does well by its pupils and is a real (but less fashionable) alternative to the big independent Scottish boarding schools.

THE MOUNT SCHOOL
Dalton Terrace, York YO2 4DD

TEL: *01904 667 507* FAX: *01904 667 524*

E-MAIL: registrar@mount.n-yorks.sch.uk

WEB: www.mount.n-yorks.sch.uk

✦ PUPILS: 255 girls (90 full board − 25 weekly, 165 day), plus co-ed prep and nursery department (see below) ✦ Ages: 11-18 ✦ Size of sixth form: 75 ✦ Quaker ✦ Fee-paying

Head: From 2001, Mrs Diana Gant BD PGCE (fifties). Studied theology at King's London, has taught RE and careers guidance. Formerly head of RE at King's Worcester, head of careers at Tonbridge Grammar, and deputy head of Norwich High. Married to Brian, an Anglican priest; two grown-up daughters. Enjoys walking and gardening. Took over from Miss Barbara J Windle, head from 1986, a serene Quaker.

Academic Matters: Good overall examination results − 7.5 average points per exam at A level, about 70 per cent A★/A at GCSE. Detailed examination results not usually available − ask for them. Set maths and French but no streaming; computers widespread but not worshipped; technology taught to A level. Dyslexia support in tandem with the Dyslexia Institute in the city.

Games, Options, the Arts: Marvellously maintained 16-acre oasis in the middle of York, with tennis courts everywhere, impressive indoor pool, gymnasium and integrated PE block, new sports hall, standard collection of all-weather pitches (hockey or tennis). Games played primarily for enjoyment – but teams do well at tennis and athletics, and individually at other sports. Two-thirds of all girls learn at least one musical instrument; steady stream of success in speech and drama field. Lots of co-productions with brother school, Bootham. D of E award v popular, and lots of minor sports: fencing and orienteering (girls compete at national level), basketball, riding etc. There is a strong tradition of community service, as you would expect. Clubs for everything from bee-keeping to conservation. Ceramics, dressmaking, fabric painting etc, in Art and Design Centre, open at weekends. Art more high-class illustration than exuberant experimentation. Sixth form girls have joint general studies with Bootham.

Background and Atmosphere: School started in 1831, but foundations for 'a good liberal education for the daughters of Friends' laid in 1785; moved to present site in 1857: a fine building with added warrens (though mercifully Portakabin free). Facilities on the basic side, though improving steadily. Girls graduate from Laura Ashleyfied mixed-age dorms in School House to study bedrooms in separate sixth form house 'College', post-GCSE. New girls are allocated a 'nutcracker' to show them round and help them settle in. 'College' have considerable freedom to sample the delights of York, which they appear to do with discretion, and with the result that they seem at home in the world when they leave.

This is a Quaker school (the only all-girl one in the country) through and through, though only about 10 per cent of school are from a practising Quaker background, and ditto staff. Quaker values: community, tolerance and critical enquiry; 'answering that of God in everyone' translates as looking for each individual's particular talent (academic or otherwise) and fostering it. Morning Meeting based on silent worship and consideration of a text for the day; ethos purposeful, friendly and caring. Active Friends of the Mount School (FOMS) who lay on excellent extras such as summer balls and fireworks displays. There are exchanges with Quaker schools internationally, eg USA, Australia.

Pastoral Care and Discipline: Weekly tutorial systems, and whole staff and 'College' meet annually as a 'Policy Review Committee to consider general matters of school life'. Each 'College' girl has her own personal tutor to discuss academic and personal issues. Positive self-image encouraged. Asked to leave for 'extremely serious' offences, otherwise withdrawal of privileges ('on report'). Masses of parental contact.

Pupils and Parents: Local parents and Quaker-related pupils from all over, with over 50 boarders from abroad (including ex-pats). A wide range of religions, some Army parents even: there's Quaker tolerance for you. Parents can camp on school grounds during leave weekends. Pupils wear white blouse, tartan (Gordon Dress) skirt and blue sweater, mufti in 'College'. Not a county set school, and glad of it.

Entrance: Own entrance exam at 11+, 12+, 13+. Sample exam papers available; and emphasis on motivation and 'the potential, not the results we are examining'. Sixth form entry on GCSE results (five A to Cs) and interview: 10 or 12 each year.

Exit: Ten or twelve post-GCSE (to boys' schools etc). Virtually all girls go to university – a mix of older universities (notably Newcastle) and ex-polys, three or four a year to Oxbridge. The professions, both caring and uncaring (eg the media) are common careers thereafter.

Money Matters: One full academic scholarship at sixth form, and academic awards at 11 and 13. Music, drama and art scholarships available, the latter mainly to help with the wherewithal to visit art galleries and buy specialist books etc; bursaries available too. 'Sympathetic' in event of emergency. Had a fair number of assisted places, which will be missed.

Remarks: Famous Quaker girls' school strong and still on the up. Pupils referred to as 'Mounties'.

JUNIOR SCHOOL: Tregelles. Tel: 01904 667513. Head: Since 1995 Miss Jan Wilson (thirties); immediately impressive. Ages 3-11, boys and girls. Founded in '91. Entrance by observation (looking for potential), supplemented at 6+ by examination. You need to book when considering conception to be certain of a place in the queue for this exceptional school. Has the benefit of the facilities and involvement of the senior school, from academic staff (three foreign languages are offered), music and food to mentoring by older girls. Most girls go on to the senior school, boys go on to St Peter's, Bootham etc.

NORTH BRIDGE HOUSE

SCHOOL

1 Gloucester Avenue, London NW1 7AB

TEL: *020 7267 2542* FAX: *020 7267 0071*

✦ PUPILS: around 859 boys and girls, all day
✦ Ages: 2¹/₂ − 16 ✦ Non-denom
✦ Fee-paying

Head: (Principal): Since 1972, Mr Wilcox. Truly amazing seventy-something-year-old owner who keeps a low profile and still requests not to be in this guide. (Founder of school was Mr Warwick James.) Also owns Akeley Wood School in Buckinghamshire, and popular nursery Stepping Stone in Hampstead. Wheeler dealer. Sits like a large spider in his web, watching. Comments he is 'traditional and old-fashioned'. Two of Mr Wilcox's sons are working in the school on the administrative side.

Head of Upper School: Mr J Lovelock BA MSc PGCE (whom we have not met). Head of Prep (and Senior) School: Mrs Mary Anderson BA CertEd. Took over from Mr R Shaw CertEd, one time publicity officer for Simpsons. Likeable.

Head of Lower School: Ms J Battye CertEd. (early forties). Acknowledged by one and all to be the secret of the school's success. Dynamic. Works tirelessly and through the holidays. A head who, according to the head of a top London senior day school, has 'really got her act together'. NB boys switch to Upper School at 10+, girls stay in Lower School if leaving at 11+.

Entrance: Name down at bottom of school and all are welcome − wide ability intake.

Take the 'tour' before registration seriously – it's an interview in disguise. Testette at 11+, 12 and 13 for 'outsiders'. Large deposit to keep your place open.

Exit: Mostly to London day schools: at 11+ to South Hampstead High, Channing, City of London Girls, St Paul's Girls, Queen's College, the Francis Hollands; at 13+ to City of London, St Paul's, Highgate, Westminster, University College School.

Remarks: Housed in what was the Japanese School (and before that a convent) – just over the road from Regent's Park Zoo. Success partly due to catchment area for NW intellectuals – average intelligence high, and partly to the school's understanding of the needs of bright, easily bored, children. Not for wilted flowers. Large Jewish contingent and kosher meals on offer. Strong cabbagey smell in the school dining room in the basement when we visited. Formerly a co-ed prep school, started taking pupils to GCSE (first batch through in '91) and now has around 30 pupils taking GCSE – numbers growing. Doesn't perform too hotly at GCSE by hot swot North London senior school standards (very few A*s, 85-90 per cent get five A*-Cs,) but remember the school has a mixed intake.

The school believes in streaming and setting – 'the children have got to be taught' – and Mr Wilcox has no time for staff who think otherwise. Lots of good old-fashioned virtues aspired to, and no apologies for this. 'Undesirable vicious habits,' will result in expulsion, as will even the 'smell' of drink or drugs. Main pastoral role falls to form teacher, with time set aside at the end of each week for sessions on overall progress. School 50/50 boys and girls in prep, fluctuates higher up, with some classes entirely of boys. Maximum class size 24, much lower in the upper school. Small and useful English

as Foreign Language unit so overseas students can be trained up from scratch. School plays soccer and rugby, rounders, hockey, netball 'in various places' with permanent buses on tap. Teeny weeny playground and pupils constantly barging into each other in corridors. The Lower School has a long tradition of being outstanding at chess, owing to member of staff, Russell Fell, who is crackers about it, and excited chess games spill over into corridors after school hours in the 'Juniorate'. Music keen and sophisticated, with seven-year-olds doing what one termed 'abstracts' from A Masked Ball, Aida etc. Some excellent art. Altogether, a school which, in our opinion, is seriously strong at prep school level, tails off further up.

NORTH LONDON

COLLEGIATE SCHOOL

Canons, Edgware, Middlesex HA8 7RJ

Tel: 020 8952 0912 Fax: 020 8951 1391

E-mail: office@nlcs.harrow.sch.uk

Web: www.nlcs.harrow.sch.uk

✦ Pupils: 1014 girls in all, including 254 in the junior and first school; all day ✦ Ages: 11-18 (plus junior school and first school ages 4-7 and 7-11) ✦ Size of sixth form: 230 ✦ C of E – all faiths welcomed ✦ Fee-paying

---

Head: Since 1997, Mrs Bernice McCabe BA MA FRSA (forties). Educated at Clifton High School and Bristol University (English followed by a PGCE). Previous post was head of Chelmsford County High School, and before that extensive experience in big state comprehensives. Simply won't discuss her personal circumstances (though points out that she styles herself 'Mrs') but admits to doing a 'bit of swimming and theatre-going' in her spare moments. Glamorous-looking, dynamic, immensely articulate – ideas and concepts and plans for the school roll out with almost American zeal. Her philosophy is 'to give floors rather than ceilings'. She comments that 'this school has everything – academic ability, beautiful surroundings'. She is lyrical about these last – which 'contribute a sense of repose ... with space to roam and places to sit'. Vocal and ambitious, she feels the school should 'trumpet their strengths' – in a modest sort of way. Top class head.

Academic Matters: Gets the fabulous results you would expect from a highly selective over-subscribed school drawing on the intelligentsia of a huge North London catchment area. One or two Ds and Es knocking about and Mrs McCabe showed no concern about them: 'it's a good profile' she says. She is more interested in emphasising that the school does not put undue pressure on the pupils. This was also emphasised by her former deputy, who retired in 1999 after being at the school for 33 years, and by other members of the staff. The fact is there is an immense feeling of academic pressure, and complaints continue to reach us of a 'desperate sense of pressure to do well all the time.' Mrs McCabe points out that the pupils 'put pressure on themselves' – and we would agree with this.

Immensely strong mathematics department with consistently large numbers. Modern languages has four native 'assistants'. The school sticks to the straight up and down academic subjects – no media or

business studies etc. General studies are not examined (two lessons a week – philosophy, psychology etc). Double award science at GCSE – separate sciences 'cramp the other options'.

Excellent careers advice. Not the place for a dyslexic, but the school has recently appointed a part-time special needs teacher to help those who are 'very able but have learning difficulties'.

Games, Options, the Arts: Excellent facilities, but poor relations compared with academic matters, and a senior pupil commented that the worst thing about the school was 'the frustration of so many things to do and we don't have the time to do them'. Mrs McCabe comments that she does not wish pupils to feel pressured to perform.

School confident of its excellence in music and has pool of talent; however, it's difficult to assess this. The school regularly gets groups to the finals of the National Chamber Music competition (and have held the founder's trophy for nine consecutive years), and the admissions secretary points to three orchestras, five choirs, numerous instrumental groups and successful OG musicians; however, there is little other evidence of music in action – little in the school magazine about music, no music exam results available (said to be a private matter, though we are told that about 40 reach grade 8 annually), a handful take music at GCSE. There are no cassette recordings of musical performances.

Not a cutting edge on the games field, which said, the school does pretty well at its matches (lots of lacrosse). Splendid indoor pool. New sports centre has replaced rather mangy gyms; Astroturf and multi-gym exercise hall. Trampoline teacher, Miss Spring, has sadly bounded off for kangaroo country.

Small design technology department (v small take up at A level). Keen on drama – and does some productions with 'Habs', John Lyons and Harrow, though: 'boys tend to get the best parts, we prefer to do it all on our own.' Main assembly hall doubles as theatre, studio theatre won prizes, now used for drama workshops. Art shows flashes of excitement, and those who take exams do very well. New library on three floors replaces teeny-weeny but wonderful old library that bulged in all directions with excitement, computers, and girls.

Background and Atmosphere: A lovely peaceful spacious oasis on an ugly outer edge of London. Founded by Frances Mary Buss (pioneer in the field of women's education) in 1850 in Camden, and moved here in 1929 to the site of the former house of Lord Chandos. Main old building beautiful, with wrought iron gracious staircase and intricate mouldings; modern additions less lovely, though could be worse, Glorious grounds, 30 acres, with huge cedar trees, rose gardens, lime tree avenue, ponds. Hic amoena delectent is carved on a wooden bench in the grounds 'and that sums it up,' says Mrs McCabe. Girls in dark brown uniform (woolly tights, or cord trousers up to sixth form) – playing everywhere, including rowdy traditional games in 'Budge Square' right outside Mrs McCabe's window (good news). Atmosphere electric – girls bounce along the corridors – much letting off of steam which staff tolerate – visitors flattened by excitement and giggling. Unrepressed is the word. However, once lessons start – concentration is good. Catchment area is defined by large number of coaches which go as far afield as Radlett, Golders Green, Pinner, Islington, Hampstead etc, and the pupils are totally used to long bus journeys.

Pastoral Care and Discipline: Discipline not an area which causes the head worries. She has not expelled anyone in her years of headship and doesn't intend to: 'if there is a problem, it needs sorting'. 'The most I have to do is slightly frown at the girls if they don't open the door for you', she says, and: 'it's based on self-discipline'. Total silent concentration in the classroom, but girls can be insolent and 'give lip'. Fierce anti-smoking campaign (posters everywhere) – not heeded by some. Anorexia not unknown.

Pupils and Parents: Approximately a third of the school is Jewish (Jewish assemblies on Wednesdays), and 20 per cent other ethnic minorities (mainly Asian). Broad range from families who are financially very comfortable to those on very generous bursaries. North London accents around. Old girls include Stevie Smith, Marie Stopes, Helen Gardner, Judith Weir, Esther Rantzen, Eleanor Bron, Barbara Amiel, not to mention Susie (Fat is a feminist issue) Orbach, who was expelled.

Entrance: From the junior school (via exam). Strongly competitive exam at 11+. Children are likely to be choosing between NLCS, Haberdashers' Aske's, South Hampstead High, and maybe St Paul's and Henrietta Barnet. At sixth form approximately five leave (for boys' schools or sixth form college), but 25 come in – and at last count 85 applied. One-hour paper for each proposed A level. School fed by huge number of north London pre-preps and primary schools, eg Radlett Preparatory, St Christopher's (NW3), NW London Jewish Day School, Pinner Park Middle, Broadfields Junior etc.

Exit: All to university, and around 25 per cent to Oxbridge. Medicine, law, engineering are popular options.

Money Matters: Pays out £250,000 plus in scholarships and bursaries – appeal to raise funds for more. The school had a very large number of assisted places.

Remarks: Top outer London academic school in glorious setting that brings in pupils from a very wide area and has an almost boarding school community feel to it. Consistently brilliant exam results in academic subjects. Main criticism is still – 'over-pressurised'. The school is terribly aware of this and sensitive to it, but don't even think of sending an academically borderline child here.

JUNIOR SCHOOL: Tel: 020 8952 1276, Fax: 020 8951 1293. Head: Since '95, Mrs Dee Francken BA MA, a wonderful steady lady from Chicago who was previously teaching in the senior school. Ages 7+-11, also recently added infants' school (now called 'first school') for children aged 4-7. Tests and assessment to get into first school thereafter automatic entry into junior school. Tests for 7+ entry. 99.9 per cent of pupils go on to the senior school. The junior and first schools are in a nice light friendly separate building in the grounds. Two parallel classes of 24. Strong chess. Some wonderful art here, and exciting teaching, and altogether a place worth bustling about to get into.

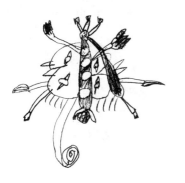

NORWICH HIGH SCHOOL
FOR GIRLS

95 Newmarket Road, Norwich NR2 2HU

TEL: *01603 453265* FAX: *01603 259891*

E-MAIL: enquire@nor.gdst.net

WEB: www.gdst.net/norwich/

✦ PUPILS: 650 girls, plus 250 in the junior school ✦ Ages: 11-18, junior school 4+ – 11 ✦ Size of sixth form: 160 ✦ Non-denom ✦ Fee-paying

---

Head: Since 1985, Mrs Valerie Bidwell BA PGCE (very early fifties). Read French and German at Newcastle. Previous post at Framlingham College. Brisk, businesslike and hot on discipline.

Academic Matters: The one and only serious girls' academic day school in Norfolk – huge catchment area and pressure on places means girls are from fairly narrow ability band and standards remain consistent. Traditional grammar school teaching, French and German results good at both exam levels. Art and design and technology increasing (at A level) from a low base. Five Old Girls are on the staff, many have connections (husbands/wives) with the University of East Anglia. Fine well-stocked library. Four classes of approximately 25 girls per year group, limited streaming.

In a normal year you might expect 60 per cent plus of students to get A or B at A level, and almost all to get A to C in general studies (which is well taught, and usually contributes substantially to average pupil performance). In '00, however, one third of the girls got D or below in general studies, and (partly as a result of this) only 45 per cent overall got A or B grades. The school has been unable to discover the reason for the general studies collapse, but the head attributes most of the remaining disappointment to some girls doing too many A levels.

Games, Options, the Arts: Good music (performances in the glorious Norwich Cathedral) and high expectations in musicianship and impressive Associated Board exams. Keen swimmers (good indoor pool), successful lacrosse, tennis popular ('I wish we had more courts'), rowing and fencing available. Sports hall, but games space on the tight side; grounds contain listed trees. Good Duke of Edinburgh and Young Enterprise take-up rate. Long lunch hour for extra-curricular and some musical activities, school tries hard to produce visiting speakers for senior girls. School-wide computer network.

Background and Atmosphere: School founded in 1875 (the first GDST outside London). The main building is an attractive Regency house (fine conservatory for staffroom 'very cold in winter'), plus later additions. Sixth form centre previously private Victorian house (as was the music house), with large common rooms, girls prefer to eat here. Girls fit a lot into a busy day, with some long journeys either end (parents organise buses and spend hours ferrying about girls who have friends at opposite ends of the county). School feels small and low key. Uniform dark green and navy.

Pupils and Parents: Hard-working daughters of doctors, accountants, farmers etc, middle class, and a few clever working class. Ethnic minorities a rarity – as indeed they are in East Anglia in general. Substantial numbers of parents connected with UEA, also several second and even third generation. Girls cheerful, pleasant, unsophisticated and unspoilt.

Entrance: At 11+ by exam (oversubscribed) and some at sixth form (minimum six GCSEs A-C grades and As or Bs in A level subjects).

Exit: Most to university (enormous spread up and down the country of both old and some ex-polys).

Money Matters: School had nearly 200 assisted places, and the GDST fund to replace these is not, as we write, nearly big enough to replace them all yet.

Remarks: Useful, worthy city high school, with very strong junior school, in an area not noted for academic ambition. Appears unaffected by Norwich (boys') School's taking in of girls at sixth form.

JUNIOR SCHOOL: A junior 'department', not a separate school. Head: Mrs J Marchant, but apply to the main school for information on entry. This is the power house of Norwich High – lively, jolly, buzzing with excitement. In a separate house in the grounds. Well, well worth making an effort to get into. Maximum class size is 20-25, depending on age. Entrance is via tests and interview, virtually everyone goes on to the senior school.

NOTRE DAME SCHOOL

Burwood House, Cobham, Surrey KT11 1HA

TEL: *01932 869 990* FAX: *01932 860 992*

E-MAIL: hm@notredamesenior.surrey.sch.uk

WEB: www.notredamesenior.surrey.sch.uk

✦ PUPILS: 700 girls in total (372 prep, 338 senior); all day ✦ Ages: 10/11-18 senior, 4-10 prep ✦ Size of sixth form: 45 ✦ RC ✦ Fee-paying

---

Head: Since 1999, Mrs Margaret McSwiggan MA (forties). First lay head appointment at the senior school, she is now into her second year and seems to be well regarded by both parents and pupils. 'Didn't want to make too many waves at first' commented one parent 'so was hard to get to know'. Grew up in Australia and moved to England ten years ago. Previous appointment, nine years at King Edward, Witley (head of junior boarding and housemistress to junior school). Gained an MA in educational management from University of Surrey and is married with an eight-year old daughter who attends Notre Dame Prep School. Loves skiing and walking and spends any spare time in Alps. Believes strongly in encouraging each girl to achieve her potential, not only academically, but also through playing a part in the life of the school.

Academic Matters: Mixed-ability school which nevertheless achieved good results last year both at GCSE (80 percent at A★-B grades) and A level (87 percent at A-C grades). One of the best performing Catholic girls' day schools in the league tables. Girls are offered a wide variety of subjects, English, Spanish, French and German being popular choices (Latin available, Italian at 6th form), but the sciences and maths feature strongly as well. Art department is popular and results are good despite pupils wishing for better facilities (more light, more space). Pupils are set for subjects whenever there is more than one class. It is a flexible arrangement. Average class sizes are less than 20, going right down to 4 or 5 in the sixth form. Looking to encourage entrants to sixth form with building of new study facilities (current facilities a little cramped).

Offers part-time support for pupils with SEN (mild dyslexia etc) and has a part-time EFL tutor for foreign students (5 percent). Close academic links with Reed's School in Cobham (boys' senior school) for certain sixth form subjects.

Games, Options, the Arts: Major sports include netball, swimming, tennis, rounders, athletics and cross-country. Outdoor sports facilities could be improved upon as Notre Dame has the acreage. This seems to be the primary parental gripe, but the head says that the upgrading of these facilities (field hockey for instance) is part of the planning for the school. Full-sized, heated indoor swimming pool and the senior school currently shares the use of a very modern indoor sports hall with the prep school. New appointment to head up the music department is starting to pay dividends with keen choral performances and pupils raving about the choice of material and instruction. Drama department also gets a thumbs-up from the pupils and parents for putting on 'wonderful, inspirational productions every year.' Plenty of educational visits abroad, and activity holidays in Britain and on the continent.

Background and Atmosphere: The school is part of a world-wide educational order, The Company of Mary Our Lady. Founded by St Jeanne de Lestonnac, the order came to England in 1892 and the school was opened on its present site in Cobham in 1937. The core of the school is the wisteria-strewn and rather beautiful Burwood House, though large modern blocks attached to the house have overshadowed it completely. Classrooms generally could do with some updating, but apparently there are grand plans to do all this and more. Prep school is attached to the senior school (Burwood House being in the middle), so many of the girls who start here at 4 must feel at 18 that they know the school really well. School has easy access to the A3 although the actual road to the school is a bit narrow and potholey. Six coach routes laid on from surrounding areas.

40 full time staff and 7/8 part-timers teach here and traditionally the staff turnover has been low. However with any new change of head there is bound to be some turnover and this has already happened (to parental approval, as far as we know). New head believes that staff should aim high and be encouraged to move up the ranks even if it means a move to another school. 'Keeps the teaching fresh and ideas fluid.'

Pastoral Care and Discipline: A small caring school that offers a secure environment for its pupils. Quite a few of the sisters of The Company of Mary Our Lady still live on site and provide a strong support network for the pupils. Full time school nurse and a counsellor (assistant deputy head). Sixth-formers are a useful resource and to keep them in touch with the rest of the school, they are called on to act as 'Big Sisters' whereby they are responsible for the settling in of 3 new girls.

Sex education has not moved far beyond the purely biological, according to one pupil, but things are slowly changing. School has a clear and unambiguous policy on drugs. Alcohol and smoking are suspendable offences and bullying is taken very seriously with the head commenting that bullying is a fact of life at any school, it's how you deal with it that matters. There is an anti-bullying committee made up of staff and pupils and an attitude of zero tolerance.

Pupils and Parents: Many families dual-income professional in and around Cobham, Walton, Weybridge, and Esher areas. Majority are British, but strong multi-cultural feel which parents regard as a plus. Five per cent foreign students. Girls are polite, neat (hair tied back and the colour they were born with) friendly and self-assured.

School has a long history of charitable involvement in the community and all girls are encouraged to take part. Although strongly Roman Catholic with attendance at Mass and assemblies compulsory, it does not discourage pupils from other denominations applying. In fact, less than half the pupils are Roman Catholic.

Entrance: Entrance exam at 11+ (maths, English and verbal reasoning) but the school is not particularly selective. Preference is given to pupils from the junior school. Most go on to sixth form, and even where the pupil seems to be struggling academically the school would rather reduce her work load (number of subjects) than encourage her to leave.

Exit: More pupils than would be expected from a mixed intake school go to the traditional universities (medicine, law, and maths). Most opt for higher education in some form. Last year, all bar one of the sixth form got into their first-choice university.

Money Matters: School offers a number of short-term bursaries based on personal hardship. Limited number of scholarships available, these vary up to 50 per cent of fees.

Remarks: Notre Dame is not a flashy school (Burwood House notwithstanding) but it does what small schools do best – providing a quiet, structured and caring environment for the girl who likes to feel secure. It is the only all-girls Catholic day school in the immediate area, and with its good academic results is growing in popularity. Parents feel that the new head will go a long way in making the school more high profile because of her warm, engaging manner and expanded vision for the school.

JUNIOR SCHOOL: Notre Dame Preparatory School. Tel: 01932 869 991 Fax: 01932 868042. Head: Mrs Brooke. Early Years Dept: boys and girls from 21/2 to 4. Infant and Junior Departments for girls 4 – 11. No entrance exam as such and most pupils go onto senior school. Larger than the senior school – register early.

NOTTING HILL & EALING HIGH SCHOOL

2 Cleveland Road, London W13 8AX

TEL: *020 8799 8400, Admissions 020 8991 2165*

FAX: *020 8810 6891*

E-MAIL: enquiries@nhehs.gdst.net

WEB: www.gdst.net/nhehs

✦ PUPILS: 560 girls, plus own junior school 270 girls, all day ✦ Ages: 11-18, juniors 5-11 ✦ Size of sixth form: 150 ✦ Non-denom ✦ Fee-paying

---

Head: Since 1991, Mrs S M Whitfield BSc (early fifties). Read natural sciences at Cambridge. Previously taught biology at St Paul's Girls' School. Married with five children. Charming, with a sparkle in the eye. Determined that the school should be 'fun to be at' – a wonderful, uncommon aim.

Entrance: Junior school by professional interview at four (an hour in a 'play' situation aimed at evaluating potential); all who apply are interviewed: no advantage in applying at birth. Competitive consortium examination and interview for entry to the senior school. Candidates to join at sixth form sit entrance exams in the subjects to be studied, and a general paper (which all in the school take, as a basis for awarding scholarships). Internal candidates for the senior school/sixth form usually get in automatically; those few who are felt to be falling too far behind are told of this at least a year in advance.

Exit: Almost without exception, girls go on to university – Manchester and Bristol popular, eight or so to Oxbridge. Medicine and drama feature notably among the courses chosen; Pupils go on into the professions and the media

Remarks: Extremely popular (heavily oversubscribed) and successful GDST day school: the low-key prospectus bears witness to their not needing to shout about their virtues. Strong on the academic side (early pupils were among the first women in the country to get degrees). GCSE and A level results excellent all round. Plenty of subject-related activities to back up – foreign exchange trips, lectures, conferences etc. All pupils leave with computer skills (to RSA 2 or 3). Support for mild dyslexia. Art good, drama all pervasive, music taken seriously for everyone (the string quartets have been so excellent in the past that they now have an un-viva'd entry to the Cambridge Symposium) and PE/games varied and universal. Clubs/activities better attended than at many other day schools. Confined city site, but nice buildings and spaces pleasantly situated at the top of the hill: lots of sky and light. Equipment a mix: ancient desks and modern computers. Pupils work on display everywhere. Self-confident, happy and motivated girls, parents often unusually involved with the school. Broad social and cultural mix – many Eastern Europeans as well as Asians and some Afro-Caribbean descendants etc. Out first time for drugs, and suspension for smoking, if either is done 'in the context of the school': eg in the company of a girl in uniform. Clear rules consistently enforced. Had 127 assisted places – GDST bursaries (up to full fees) are replacing these to the tune of a dozen or so a year. Super junior department. Altogether a cheering school; fun and

relaxed within its academic mission. Popular choice for bright locals. Good reports.

OAKHAM SCHOOL

Chapel Close, Oakham, Rutland

LE15 6DT

TEL: *01572 722487* FAX: *01572 755786*

E-MAIL: admissions@oakham.rutland.sch.uk

WEB: www.oakham.org.uk

✦ PUPILS: 500 boys, 500 girls. Approx 500 board, 500 day ✦ Ages: 10-18 ✦ Size of sixth form: 350 ✦ C of E ✦ Fee-paying

---

Head: Since 1996, Mr Tony Little, ARM MA (forties). Educated at Eton and Corpus, taught at Tonbridge, Brentwood and was head of Chigwell School before coming here. Married, and has daughter in the school. Has two golden retrievers, is an accomplished musician and produces plays.

Academic Matters: Performance appears stable, and good, given ability intake and large numbers and school's policy of not weeding out weaker candidates. Most popular subject maths, followed by English, history, chemistry French, business studies. Maths, the sciences and modern languages have notably good results, geography consistently disappointing over past three years. School has special separate Oxbridge swot house started by Christopher Dixon, so potential candidates get suitably hotted up. Oxbridge house is a special ghetto-blaster-free area. School says that comments from parents that 'social life has greater priority than work' now out of date. IB on offer from 2001.

Known for its learning support department; to quote a parent 'very very good'; two dedicated full-time teachers, plus two part-time, (some tuition instead of foreign languages.) Also EAL – one full-time, one part-time.

Games, Options, the Arts: Keen chess school, with chess coach and chess scholarships (including one recently launched by Kasparov) – the idea is the game promotes a 'disciplined and methodical mind'. Also keen on music, and regularly contributes players to the National Youth Orchestra. NB gives free music lessons if you pass Grade VI with merit. Works with Loughborough university on art and design; lots of theatre. Strong on games of all kinds. Good on, squash and shooting, regularly reaches finals of Squash National School Championships. Lots of D of E gold awards. Enormous range of extras on offer, so much so that pupils commented that there was a danger of flying off in too many directions at once. Shooting range and Astroturf pitch. Amazingly glossy A3 size school magazine – The Oakhamian – looks very much like a PR production 'but designed by the students and staff'. Computers everywhere and much used.

Background and Atmosphere: Founded 1584, by Robert Johnson, Archdeacon of Leicester. Small local boys' school until 1970s, when changed from direct grant to full-blown co-ed almost overnight with loads of money given by a grateful old boy (the Jerwood Foundation). High-tech £2 million library, Resource and Study Centre (complete with CD-ROM and computerised library). Cosy stone buildings. Boarders mainly housed in twin bedrooms, comfy. Atmosphere v difficult to pin down

as school large and widely spread – feels a bit like an American high school campus; fun, say pupils. Co-ed activities: 'we encourage them, after all we are co-ed'. Exeats every three weeks.

Pastoral Care and Discipline: Self-discipline vital. Competitive house system. Expulsions for 'serious anti-social behaviour', persistent bullying, drugs and sex. £10 fine to Cancer Research for first offence smoking.

Pupils and Parents: 30 per cent of parents are local, 20 per cent overseas (ex-pats and foreign). Rest scattered, pupils come from 'up and down the A1' and Norfolk; hotchpotch of backgrounds, a fair number from London, and contingent from Scotland. Less spotty than many co-eds but some on the wild side. Smart checked kilts for girls up to 'seventh' form (ie upper sixth – Oakham has a rudimentary language of its own). Famous Old Boys and Girls: Thomas Merton the Trappist monk, plus Matthew Manning the Faith Healer, Dr Charlotte Uhlenbroek, Sir Peter North, Julia Carling.

Entrance: 10, 11+, 12+, 13+ and sixth form. School sets its own exam for pupils from state sector, CE for the others – not too difficult. Sixth form entrants have own exam in November for following September – or you're expected to have seven respectable GCSEs (including B or better in 'principal subjects'.)

Exit: A few leave after GCSE, otherwise 97 per cent to higher education; practical courses (eg marketing, hotel management, computing, urban planning, accounting, speech therapy, business studies) popular. Lots to middle England unis.

Money Matters: £1 million handouts annually: approx ten academic for sixth form (one for IB), approx ten academic at each of 11+ and 13+, and about twenty assorted other scholarships (music, drama, chess – including one of full fees for up to seven years, to be given probably in the first instance to a Russian – also art and design, computer science, DT) awarded each year. 'Some internal, some upgrades, and some external.' Plus bursaries. Help considered for those in exam years who fall on hard times. Had some assisted places, but not much affected by their loss.

Remarks: Large and lively proper co-ed boarding school for independently-minded good average children. Not a cosy environment: 'I wouldn't contemplate sending a child here,' said a prep school head, 'who was not very highly motivated ... it is possible to sink without trace'.

OBAN HIGH SCHOOL

Soroba Road, Argyll PA34 4JB

TEL: *01631 564231* FAX: *01631 565916*

E-MAIL: paulinem@obanhs.demon.co.uk

✦ PUPILS: 1,100 boys and girls. Mainly day, but boarding available ✦ Ages: 11–18.
✦ Size of sixth form: Around 100
✦ Non-denom ✦ State

Head (Rector): Since 1998 Miss Linda Kirkwood, formerly head of Dalbeattie High.

Entrance: Takes all sorts.

Exit: About 60 per cent to Scottish universities, the rest to further education courses and employment.

Remarks: State school with very large catchment area and pupils coming from 26 associated primary schools covering North Argyll and the Islands. Pupils (approx 55) from large distances board in the school hostel, which has four staff on evening duty and academic staff actively help with studies. Seven class intake, staff of about 75 – good staff/pupil ratio. Staff a 'good blend of youth and experience'. A great deal of fine spacious and well-designed new building: only the administration block remains to be done, and at the end of the project all trace of the old buildings will be gone. Full range of Highers Still subjects and Advanced Highers; historically achieved results in line with national averages, now well above. Extra-curricular activities in lunch hour, after school and weekends – difficulties because of large distances and buses generally overcome. Pupils generally well behaved in lessons and out.

OLD PALACE SCHOOL

(OF JOHN WHITGIFT)

Old Palace Road, Croydon, Surrey

CR0 1AX

TEL: *020 8688 2027* FAX: *020 8680 5877*

E-MAIL: opalace@rmplc.co.uk

WEB: www.oldpalace.croydon.sch.uk

✦ PUPILS: 545 girls in the Senior School, 305 in the Preparatory Department, including 100+ in the Pre-Prep Department; all day ✦ Ages: 4-18 ✦ Size of sixth form: 140 ✦ C of E ✦ Fee-paying

---

Head: Since 2000 Mrs E J Hancock BA (early fifties). Read history at Nottingham University. Previous post head of Bromley High (for 11 years); before that at Brighton and Hove. Warm, cosy-looking, energetic and enthusiastic. We met her at Bromley, and recorded of her there that 'she breathes life and heart into her staff and school and is fondly regarded by them. Sees herself as "an enabler", believes paperwork should be kept in its place and 'that I should have time to say to pupils "Have you read this poem, that play?"'. Behind her desk is a bright display of cards (good luck, thank-yous etc) – 'I had up timetables, schedules and then thought no, this is what it's all about, and I add to the collection every year'.

Took over from Miss Kathleen L Hilton, head since 1974. The school has some super kind and friendly staff.

Academic Matters: School continues steady and strong right across the board and comes high in any GCSE league tables you care to look at; all take nine or more subjects. Broad choice of subjects. Strong languages and good take-up – French (their prep pupils start at seven), Italian, Spanish, Greek, German, Russian as well as Latin. A handful of students take exams in their mother tongue – ranging from Polish and Afrikaans to Gujerati and Hindu. Maths very popular, from prep school upwards. Science still strong (separate sciences or dual award at GCSE). Sixteen A★ grades in physics here out of sixteen taking it – though numbers taking it have halved from two years ago. Chemistry lab with bright yellow tables, and lecture/demonstration area with raised seating provides a most attractive environment to work in. School prides itself on 'choice' – letting sixth formers opt for any combination of subjects – an indication of the staff's energy and willingness to tailor timetable to individual need. Design technology, headed by former Goldsmith College lecturer on the teaching of technology. 11- to 13-year-olds produce wonderfully designed moulded plastic clocks, design and build their own radios, devise travelling games etc. Computers used as a tool right across the curriculum – PC network. Infants have 70 minutes a week IT age five, and 35 minutes a week age four. All pupils take general studies as an A level exam (and lots get A in it).

Games, Options, the Arts: No room on this medieval site for field sports, therefore pupils are bussed to eg Trinity for hockey; swimming pool on site from '99. D of E. Young Enterprise strong – as you might expect in this thriving commercial centre; winners of the Croydon Young Achiever of the Year in '93, '94/5 and '96/'97. High-profile drama, theatre workshops, emphasis on speech in drama lessons. Dance popular also. Debating vigorous, via Rotary Club, United Nations Association. Music thriving, with two orchestras and choirs which have performed at eg St Mark's Venice.

Background and Atmosphere: Rose-decked oasis in the middle of grotty part of Croydon. Former residence of the Archbishops of Canterbury, full of atmosphere and architectural interest. Thoughtfully designed new buildings next to Grade 1 14th- and 15th-century buildings. The latter include a Great Hall where Henry VIII and Catherine of Aragon were entertained, an outstandingly beautiful Chapel, a Guard Room where the young James I of Scotland was held prisoner (now the library), Queen Elizabeth's Room (she visited a number of times), Laud's bedroom (part of the staffroom), and small courtyards joined by low arched passages. Can't call that nothing, though the downside of the wonderful buildings is that space is severely limited (and upkeep expensive). Not a school in which God is forgotten.

Pastoral Care and Discipline: Welcoming 'open door' policy, particularly at pre-prep end – where parents can talk to staff from 7.45am, before start of school day, or after school. Genuine feel of a 'family' school built on Christian ethos of the founding Sisters of the Church, with a notable emphasis on parental participation. Strict monitoring of homework diaries can reveal 'a surprising amount; we can often tell if there are difficulties'. Pupils raise large sums of money for charity.

Pupils and Parents: Lively, social mix with offspring of professional high-fliers and also inner city estates. One recent year's head girls were Muslim and Chinese. At the infant end it is Asian and Afro-Caribbean parents who seem most willing to commit themselves to financial sacrifice so their children can be taught in small classes.

Entrance: At 4+ (32 children) into over-subscribed pre-prep department, or at 7, 8, 9 via exam to prep department (virtually all go on to senior school) and via 11+ entrance (oversubscribed 3:1). All applicants interviewed with parents.

Exit: To strong universities such as Exeter, Imperial College, Manchester, St Andrews, Oxbridge. Some do exciting courses at ex-polys. Medicine, business studies and engineering popular. Well-known OGs reflect wide range of career choice – from BBC weather girl Helen Young, to first BA woman pilot, Wendy Barnes, heart surgeon Farah Raines, and harpist Rachel Harris.

Money Matters: School became part of the famously rich Whitgift Foundation in '93 – a foundation formerly for the two local boys' schools, Whitgift and Trinity, but finally the feeling that 'something must be done for the girls' won through to action. This means more money for bursaries, altogether more financial muscle, and the Foundation have already provided the dosh to replace the school's assisted places. Basic fees are kept at the lower end of the scale.

Remarks: Outstanding girls' day school with lively, open and friendly atmosphere. 'The best,' 'the happiest,' 'the clever choice in Croydon,' are typical remarks from parents. Good new head. All this and now lots of loot to boot.

THE ORATORY SCHOOL

Woodcote, Nr Reading, Berkshire RG8 OPJ

TEL: *01491 680207* FAX: *01491 680020*

E-MAIL: enquiries@oratory.co.uk

WEB: www.oratory.co.uk

✦ PUPILS: 388 boys; 264 board, 124 day; 60 in Junior House ✦ Ages: 11-18 ✦ Size of sixth form: 120 ✦ RC ✦ Fee-paying

Head: Since 2000, Mr Clive Dytor MC MA (forties). Born and bred in Wales, read oriental studies at Trinity, Cambridge (played rugby and rowed.) Joined the Royal Marines, serving in Belfast and the Falklands (where he earned the MC.) Read theology at Oxford in 1986, worked in the Church for a while and then taught at Tonbridge. Converted to RC and joined St Edward's, Oxford as housemaster; thence to here. Married to Sarah, a professional musician; two children (11 and 5.) Took over from Mr Simon Barrow, here from 1992.

Entrance: Presents no particular problem. Regular intake from own prep school.

Exit: Around two-thirds to universities old and new; also to US colleges, business studies, art school. Some post-GCSE leakage to sixth form colleges.

Remarks: Smallish, worthy, caring, Catholic boys' boarding school, taking trouble over a broad ability range; produces solid, responsible middle-class citizens. Language links with Caversham Park BBC external monitoring service. Nearly all boys do three separate sciences, and IT is compulsory until GCSE – about eight the norm. Good staff/boy ratio, though 'some teachers are not high enough calibre,' according to high-flier's mother. Overall exam results respectable at GCSE given intake; A level, too many Ds-Ns for comfort. There is a superb cricket pitch with views right across Berkshire, fourteen tennis courts, golf course, a good indoor swimming pool, squash courts. Own indoor rifle range, rowing and sailing take place at nearby Goring and Theale. Under 14 rugby XV recently unbeaten. Popular CCF, especially the navy, where boys can spend a night on a warship (affiliated HMS Invincible). Founded in 1859 by Cardinal Newman at the time of the Oxford Movement, to provide an intentionally lay Catholic public-school education for the sons of upper-crust converts. 'Married housemasters, lay staff with mortgages, and our own chaplain give it the feeling of a parish.' Imposing Georgian stone-faced house on remote spur of the Chilterns with cluster of newish buildings – still being added to – politely described as functional. Regular retreat and daily Mass for those who want it. 'Religion is not too obvious but it is taken seriously,' says a parent. Fairly relaxed ethos. Weekly boarding a draw for Londoners, but takes the edge off commitment. Boys have 'chores' and are expected to wash their own clothes (ie Mummy does them). Pupils mostly from Thames Valley and London, around 10 per cent from overseas, including some from Ireland. By and large from the Catholic middle class, though the RC percentage is now down to 60. Popular with parents of mixed marriages, less suspicious in the lay environment of 'monkey business', to quote one. Old Boys include Hilaire Belloc, Lennox Berkeley, Michael Berkeley. Gerald Manley Hopkins taught here. Fine, but lacks excitement.

OUNDLE SCHOOL

Oundle, Peterborough PE8 4EN

TEL: *01832 277 125* FAX: *01832 277 128*

E-MAIL: registrar@oundle.co.uk

WEB: www.oundleschool.org.uk

✦ PUPILS: 657 boys, 372 girls; 814 board, 215 day ✦ Ages: 11-18 ✦ Size of sixth form: 409 ✦ C of E ✦ Fee-paying

---

Head: Since 1999, Dr Ralph (pronounced Rafe) Townsend (mid forties). A star. Recently head of Sydney Grammar School, Australia; previously head of English at Eton. Took over from Mr D B McMurray, who had been head here since 1984 and whose style (illustrated by such comments as 'if Oundle produces a 'type' then I will have failed' and 'to try to inculcate sensible attitudes and expectations of the opposite sex, while keeping those sexes separate, is like teaching people to swim without allowing them to get wet' (Parental comment: 'Lots of to-ing and fro-ing, but they'd have to do a lot of work to sleep together')) made a large mark on the school. Governors are Grocers' (Company).

Academic Matters: CDT outstanding but not many taking it at exam level (see Games etc below). Wide variety of languages offered – school even has two Mandarin Chinese teachers seconded by their government each year. Three out of eight sets take French GCSE early 'and they don't get Bs'. Latest addition is the Anglian Water Board Building which has been turned into the modern language block – hi-tech lab style (press button everything), also housed here is the music school, and the terrifically impressive IT labs. GCSE – rarely anything below C (and not many Cs either). A level consistently good. Maths the most popular subject, then chemistry, physics, history, English. Some impressive staff -the thoroughness of teaching 'makes the pupils think', according to one parent.

Games, Options, the Arts: School pioneered CDT and idea of learning through doing at the turn of the century – the subject is still very much in the fabric of the school, and pupils all come out with a proper and very useful grounding in this, way above the standard of most schools. Thirteen-year-olds spend an afternoon each week in the school's magnificent workshops to design and construct something – the atmosphere here is more like industry than a school – with foundry, lasers, wind tunnels, microelectronics and lots of computers. Thirty-two sports cars built over last four years, and there's an aeroplane under construction, not to mention a science and technology 'park' in the pipeline.

Other matters: 50-yard swimming pool. Three climbing walls, sports centre, running track, two rifle ranges (and regular successes), grounds stretching as far as the eye can see. Strong rowing – club founded 1886. Rugger coach John Olver (ex England international) – two unbeaten domestic seasons since his appointment, with lots of trips abroad (Canada, South Africa) and national squad players. Good hockey for girls. Average Oundelian considered 'a pretty competitive animal' – even the girls. Pupils 'can't escape Oundle without some music,' as it is compulsory for the first year. Major exchange programmes with France, Germany, China and Spain.

Stahl Theatre in converted church in Oundle High Street puts on both professional and pupil productions, good and popular and gives pupils a feel for 'the real thing'. Artists in residence and huge variety of arts on offer. Massive Frobenius organ in school chapel and marvellous John Piper window. CCF, and adventure training. Long-running community scheme in association with MENCAP. Exchange programmes with schools in China and Europe. School's newspaper *Off the Cuff* recently had a world scoop in the form of a survey which found that the headmaster was the most 'significant or influential individual at Oundle'.

Background and Atmosphere: Possibly a bit dozy – 'not a very exciting place', said a parent wistfully. But beautiful mellow buildings – see Pevsner – scattered throughout the pretty medieval town of Oundle, with pupils scurrying to and fro like university students. Furthest boarding house a good ten minutes' hike to central quad (the head says six minutes – but he has very long legs). The official tour of the school for potential parents takes a record one and three-quarter hours – wear comfortable shoes for this one. (Look out for the 'Oundle walk', by which OOs recognise each other in later life.) Wonderful avenue of trees, games fields etc. Massively built boarding houses, most recently revamped with smaller dorms and lots of bed-sits. Girls' houses look more like an American Hilton ('nuts', said one American parent, 'girls' houses look more lived-in now'). Lots of chaps in striped shirts, looking keen and purposeful (girls have red or blue option). Large 18,000-volume library in converted gym plus Muniments Room, that includes 1626 school register. Lots of Oundle traditions continue after school, with strong

clubs, including Masonic Lodge.

Oundle has now, at long last, re-merged with Laxton School (and hence the arrival of day pupils throughout). The Master of the Worshipful Company of Grocers and Lord Mayor of London, Sir William Laxton, left provision in his will for the re-endowment of the grammar school he attended, that dated back to 1485. In 1876 the schools divided into Laxton Grammar School, for inhabitants of the town who did not want classical studies, and Oundle, for sons of gents who did. Now one school again.

Pastoral Care and Discipline: Large percentage of Old Boys' children, many Oundle families, with fathers, uncles, cousins etc, all here. 'Fair number from overseas' (approx 10 per cent), with Hong Kong Chinese and Malays predominant. Good staff/parent contact. Lots of solid steady East Anglians. Old Boys: Arthur Marshall, Peter Scott, Cecil Lewis the aviator, A Alvarez, Anthony Holden, Richard Dawkins.

Pupils and Parents: Pastoral care very much on the house tutorial system, and each pupil has his/her own tutor throughout his/her time at school. 'Pupils need to have clear-cut boundaries,' says the head, 'but we push those boundaries out as far as we dare.' 'Instant out' for drugs, drink: 'a can of beer is different from being blotto'. For alcoholic offenders it's the 'one, two, three out system'; ie 1 – gated, 2 – rusticated, 3 – expelled. School has a few lively offenders. Head stands firm on exeats – few and far between. Newcomers from cosy-ish preps find the going 'tough'.

Entrance: Own exam at 11+ or CE at 13. Assessment day for borderline cases – Head comments he would like to see 140 pupils sit for 140 places and not have pupils sitting who will not get in. IQ wide fluctuations, but a 'switched on' IQ of 110 would probably get in, depending on demand' (though school now says 'we keep standards as consistent as we possibly can'). Six GCSE passes at B or above for sixth form entry (even within the school). School has been known to reject a pupil and change its mind later.

Exit: Large percentage to degree courses, 20-30 each year to Oxbridge. Pupils thereafter go on to be captains of industry, entrepreneurs and engineers.

Money Matters: Not as well endowed as perceived. However, masses of scholarships, including music and art. Only two scholarships for 11-year-olds, plus Continuation Scholarships for eight pupils to 'remain at their Preparatory School with an award of 15 per cent of Oundle's Junior House fees per annum' before joining Oundle at 13, when the scholarship is worth from 20 per cent to 50 per cent (depending on circumstances).

Remarks: Strong solid traditional public school with girls in it. Not an easy option and not noted for setting the world alight – but good, all the same. One of the top choices in co-ed for girls. Parents keen on new head.

OXFORD HIGH SCHOOL
FOR GIRLS

Belbroughton Road, Oxford OX2 6XA

TEL: *01865 559888* FAX: *01865 552343*

E-MAIL: oxfordhigh@oxf.gdst.net

WEB: www.gdst.net/oxfordhigh

◆ PUPILS: Senior Department 550 girls; Junior dept (Greycotes) 230 girls. Prep-prep dept (The Squirrel) 140 pupils including 40 boys. All day ◆ Ages: 3-18 ◆ Size of sixth form: 150 ◆ Non-denom ◆ Fee-paying

Head: Since 1997, Miss O Felicity S Lusk, BMus DipEd DipTchg CertMusEd (forties). Educated Marsden Collegiate School, New Zealand, Victoria University New Zealand and other establishments. Trained as organist and pianist. Started teaching career in New Zealand, then came to the Hasmonean High School in London in '90 (and became a Councillor for the Borough of Enfield while she was about it). Recently appointed a governor of Guildhall School of Music and Drama. Comments to the fun, informative OHS school mag that in her spare moments she 'likes to do things with her son'. Glamorous-looking, with purple nail varnish. Took over from, Mrs Joan Townsend, who was here from '81.

Academic Matters: Strongly academic – the Oxford environment. 'The brains are hanging off the wall,' said a visiting parent. The school has some outstanding staff – and no problem recruiting here. Streaming in maths, languages (French, German, Russian, Spanish, Latin, Greek, Italian). Compulsory to take English, a foreign language, maths, double award science at GCSE. Girls take GCSE 'in their stride' – a stunning 85-ish per cent A★/A grades, Cs in art and science only. Maths popular at A level, as are biology and chemistry (does well in UK Senior Maths Challenge and Science Olympiads). English, French, geography and history the humanities in fashion – hard to say that they are particularly 'strong' because so few grades below A in any subject. Computers everywhere and in subject rooms, internet etc. A levels timetabled around the sixth form. Special needs teacher on tap where needed, but not the place for dyslexics (though 'peripatetic help' is available for them.)

Games, Options, the Arts: Games up to year 11; music magical, head of music is particularly keen on choirs, good orchestra; also very strong drama; lively art (murals everywhere). Trad games, sports hall, swimming pool, rowing, weight training, trampolining etc. Lots of county players. Parents can use facilities in the holidays. Regularly winners/runners up of various Oxfordshire Schools Championships. CCF, D of E, Young Enterprise.

Background and Atmosphere: Started in 1875 by the Girls' (Public) Day School Trust in St Giles', with a view to educating dons' daughters. The school expanded at a great rate, and a series of moves brought it to its present site, which is mostly pretty grizzly boxes surrounded by garden and games pitches. School says 'endearingly quaint, refurbishment is going on but will never be beautiful, but WE DON'T MIND.' Ecumenical and sparky assemblies. Stimulating, and intellectually vibrant, combined with laid-back underlying discipline, and a good sense of humour throughout. Girls required to do regular self-assessment. School uniform includes navy cord trousers and polo shirts

– no uniform in sixth form.

Pastoral Care and Discipline: Tutorial system. Picks up problems early, good parental vibes, and regular class parent meetings so that parents can suss out exactly what their little darlings are up to 'when every-one will be there'. School council. Girls consulted on recent sex education policy review, uniform review and statement of school purpose. Lots of staff time spent talking to pupils.

Pupils and Parents: 50 per cent from Oxford, masses of dons' daughters, local schools pride themselves on the number of girls who get places here. Pupils are bussed from all over the shop. Occasional problem 'with over-articulate donnish parents' who like arguing for arguing's sake. But on the whole parents are very supportive. OGs: Miriam Margoyles, Josephine Barnes, Maggie Smith, Martha Lane-Fox, Sian Edwards, plus dons, lecturers and other high-powered academics.

Entrance: Queues of keen local (and not so local) applicants; apply one year before the September term of entry. Serious multi-assessment day at 7+, 9+, 11+ – written English, maths, science; verbal, numerical and perceptual reasoning. Children encouraged to bring in hobbies or examples of art. Considerably oversubscribed. Entry at sixth form requires As in GCSEs to be studied at A level, and five B (+) grades in core subjects. Internal candidates don't have a problem with this, as a glance at the results shows.

Exit: A handful leave after GCSE – boys. Otherwise to degree courses, almost 30 per cent to Oxbridge, then to city universities eg Bristol, Edinburgh, Warwick, Exeter, Manchester, Leeds. 'Girls are becoming very picky about which courses and universities to go to.'

Money Matters: Had 70 assisted places, GDST scheme replaces some of these. 64 currently hold scholarships at present – academic, music, sport and art.

Remarks: Oxford's number one girls' academic day school. 'Has maintained its place in the premier division of the ghastly league tables for four years, not that we enjoyed it.'

JUNIOR SCHOOL: School has recently merged with two popular local schools within walking distance – Greycotes (Tel 018655 515647) and the Squirrel (Tel: 018655 558279), which now house juniors and pre-prep respectively. The Squirrel has boys as well as girls. Moving the juniors has freed up space in main school.

THE PERSE SCHOOL

Hills Road, Cambridge CB2 QF

TEL: *01223 568300* FAX: *01223 568293*

E-MAIL: office@perse.co.uk

WEB: www.perse.co.uk

✦ PUPILS: 570 boys; around 30 girls in the sixth form. All day. ✦ Ages: 11-18 plus junior school ages 7-11 and co-educational Pelican pre-prep ages 3-7 ✦ Size of sixth form: 180 ✦ Non-denom ✦ Fee-paying

---

Head: Since 1994, Mr Nigel Richardson (early fifties), educated at Highgate School and Trinity Hall, Cambridge. Previous post – deputy head of King's School, Macclesfield ('92-'94), and before that he had a couple of years as head of The Dragon (prep) School. An enthusiast, author of six history books for children, and does freelance writing for the TES etc. Wife Joy is high powered, confident and also an author – with over 50 information books for children under her belt plus children's guides to museums – not to mention an Ofsted Registered Inspector. Two sons.

Academic Matters: Rigorous and traditional in classes of around 20-24, with two thirds male teachers though around sixteen women (including cheery youthful science mistresses). Distinct bias to sciences (NB no GCSE combined science) and consistently excellent maths and physics results. Spanish (from 13) and Russian (in the sixth form) are options. Very little take up of art etc at A level, classics more or less non-existent at A level though flourishing at GCSE. 25 per cent taking more than five AS levels under the new system. Interesting tradition of teaching younger boys English through acting and mime (the 'Play Way') in the 'Mummery', small theatre equipped with lights, music, costumes where boys cast and direct their own productions from traditional ballads to Shakespeare, with minimal intervention from calmly presiding master. Little formal special needs teaching, or EFL.

Games, Options, the Arts: Twenty-eight acres of prime Cambridge greenbelt for compulsory rugby (twelve rugby teams, first XV to South Africa). Hockey inspired by new all-weather pitch. Thriving chess and bridge. CCF or community service (good works include boys helping at neighbouring Addenbrooke's Hospital), D of E awards and Scouts. Head of music has done much to raise standards (a 'colours' music tie sports a treble clef) and introduced a music technology course. 100+ learn an instrument at the school, and head says 150+ learn at home; 60 per cent of Persean hearts do not appear to be in music. Art and ceramics in brick studio block (GCSE Art taken a year early), all do GCSE architectural project with much to inspire them a few minutes walk from the doorstep. Annual art show and sale of boys' and local artists' works in school's Pelican Art Gallery (the school emblem recalling Sir Francis Drake's ship), encouraged by Friends of the Pelican Gallery. Stunning ceramics.

Background and Atmosphere: 400-year historic background – founded 1615 by Stephen Perse, a Fellow of Gonville and Caius, though the endowment has sadly long since been embezzled. The school feels somewhat lost in '60s purpose-built ecclesiastical-cum-chalet style red-brick premises (with later additions) in the Cambridge margins. Direct grant until '76. Non-exclusive small friendly ethos with scions of the middle classes (sprinkling of ethnic minorities) in grey herring-bone tweed jackets and purple ties; 'dress code' only for the sixth form with fairly staid results. Airy high-ceilinged dining hall. Immaculate corridors, manicured grounds (NB no crisp packets); slightly soulless feeling of under-used space.

Pastoral Care and Discipline: Tutorial system and safety-net of prefect appointed as 'minder' to individual younger classes as a method of detecting bullying. Lots of staff time spent boosting weaker academic end (with results apparent). New posts of head of sixth form, middle and lower schools have been put in place to strengthen pastoral structure. Clear detailed anti-drugs policy, which parents note thankfully, given all the temptations of Cambridge on the doorstep. Drugs sackings '97.

Pupils and Parents: Across the economic and social divide, and until 1995, provided the last bastion of all-boy secondary education in Cambridge. 20-25 per cent sons of Cambridge-associated professionals, otherwise teachers, farmers, employees of the Science Park and 'parents who ten years ago would have boarded their sons'. Catchment area of around 35 miles' radius reflects migration of families from housing-starved Cambridge. Old Boys include two (scientific) Nobel Prize winners, F R Leavis, Sir Peter Hall, Marius Goring, Mel Calman, David Tang.

Entrance: Seventy-two boys at age 11 (two-thirds from associated prep, rest from local primaries) two applicants for each place judged on IQ, maths, English and interview; a couple of dozen places at 13. Those added on at sixth form need a minimum of twenty points at GCSE (A* or A = 3, B = 2, C = 1), and A grades in chosen AS subjects are strongly recommended. Home grown candidates have no formal hurdle to entering the sixth.

Exit: Virtually all to universities. Most to Oxbridge, then other medical schools, then Bristol, Durham, London.

Money Matters: Fees kept to around £7,000 per annum (ie cheaper than most Cambridge preps). Scholarships are understandably not an item here, though there are 'some', generally of 10 per cent of the total. Had fifty-five assisted places, which will be missed. Now has some Ogden Trust bursaries for 'above-average children from a state primary school of limited or no parental means', and Harvey Awards for science and technology.

Remarks: Academic boys' day school with a few girls in the sixth form. Holding its own, catering for the able sons of the Cambridge middle class. Serious competition on the doorstep in the shape of Hills Road Sixth Form College (qv).

JUNIOR SCHOOL: Tel: 01223 355377, Fax: 01223 568273. Head (The Master): Mr P C S Izzett. On separate site in Trumpington Road, about one and a half miles from the senior school. Entrance by exam – this is the sure way into the senior school. Also now co-ed pre-prep – The Pelican – head Mrs P Oates, Tel 01223 568315, Fax 01223 568316.

THE PERSE SCHOOL
FOR GIRLS

Union Road, Cambridge CB2 1HF

TEL: *01223 359589* FAX: *01223 467420*

E-MAIL: PerseGirls@aol.com

WEB: www.perse.cambs.sch.uk

✦ PUPILS: 711 girls, including junior school; all day ✦ Ages: 7-18 ✦ Size of sixth form: 115 ✦ C of E ✦ Fee-paying

Head: Since 1989, Miss H S Smith, MA (late fifties), educated at King Edward's Birmingham and St Hilda's, Oxford, where she read mathematics. Previously head of maths, and before that taught at Cheltenham Ladies', also at the International School in Brussels. Old fashioned, no-nonsense head.

Academic Matters: Superb results. Topped league tables in 1999. Very strong modern languages, with all girls doing two at GCSE (French plus either German, Italian, Russian or Spanish). Hot on exchanges and visits abroad, including European work experience. All girls take three sciences at GCSE. Classes large (up to 28), 'but this isn't a problem here, the girls apply themselves' and there is setting in maths and French from year 7, and science from year 9. Popular modular course in creative subjects for girls in their third year. Good facilities for IT. Extremely high calibre of staff, as you might expect in Cambridge.

Games, Options, the Arts: Main playing fields 10 minutes away and new Leys sports hall used for 8 hours a week. Several girls in county squads for both hockey and netball, but not really a gamesy school, though there is an element of compulsion. Girls swim in The Leys pool. Drama is popular (lots of speech and drama exams passed with distinction); high standards in music, some charming poetry in The Persean – worth a look. Fairly busy lunch-time programme for extra-curricular activities – debating, chess, bridge, music etc, though by comparison with some other schools, these are relatively thin on the ground, and the head makes no bones about the fact that 'we are an academic school' (though she points out that 'we also value recreational activities'). Sixth formers help Junior School drama and also coach younger girls.

Background and Atmosphere: Cosy, squashed, rather sedate institution with carpets, polish, wallpaper and good pictures on the walls. Some parts reminiscent of the worst of St Trinian's, said to have been modelled on The Perse, with new buildings helping to diminish the sense of cramp. School started in 1881, looks like students' digs, overlooked by the university chemistry lab. Sixth form centre (converted from a parish institute) near the school's back gate, with an art studio, quiet study rooms, common room, teaching rooms etc. Very cost conscious. Notice in staff loos reminding staff of high charges in recent water bills.

Pastoral Care and Discipline: Prefect system. Potential problems are likely to get spotted at an early stage via form teachers plus head of year.

Pupils and Parents: Wide catchment area. One girl travels up from London daily. A fairly broad social mix. Dons' daughters and distinguished academic names litter the school list. Some from Hong Kong and Singapore. Europeans, Russians. Self-confident and hard-working girls who know where they're going. Old Girls include Bridget Kendall, BBC Moscow correspondent as well as Jean Rhys, Philippa Pearce and Lady Wootton, considered a particularly good example: 'High-powered, sceptical, detached, non-conformist.'

Entrance: Examinations (The Perse's own) and interview all on the same day. Also via the Junior School. Very selective at 11 (60 children for 25 places). 60 per cent at 11+ come from local state primaries. Almost always some from private sector post GCSEs: numbers in sixth form vary from year to year, and they only offer places to girls who would benefit.

Exit: A few at 16 to Perse Boys and Hills Road Sixth Form College. After A levels to all manner of universities, including, at last count, a fair number of ex-polys including Sheffield Hallam, Leeds Met, Greenwich, and one or two to arts foundation courses, even has had one to an acting school. A good number to Oxbridge (more Ox than Bridge) and a gap year is popular.

Money Matters: Bursaries available (currently 36), and sixth form scholarships.

Remarks: Academically strong and highly sought-after city girls' day school that continues to be very successful. Not a school for girls who need constant reassurance.

JUNIOR SCHOOL: Tel: 01223 357322, Fax: 01223 467420. Head: Mrs D N Clements. Ages 7-11. Around 170 girls, in class sizes 15-24. Entrance is by tests at the beginning of the year.

PIMLICO SCHOOL
Lupus Street, London SW1V 3AT

TEL: *020 7828 0881* FAX: *020 7931 0549*

✦ PUPILS: 1,350, all day ✦ Ages: 11-18
✦ Size of sixth form: 180 ✦ Non-denom
✦ State

Head: Since 1995, Mr Philip Barnard (late forties). Educated in Singapore, Darlington and UMIST. Joined Pimlico in '73 to teach maths; has risen through the ranks. Acting head before the disastrous '92 appointment, turned to again in '95. Has not lost the charisma that we saw in him years ago as head of maths, though now longer on experience and grey hairs. Liked and respected by pupils for his keen interest in them and their doings. Pragmatic.

Entrance: Complicated. Don't apply to the school direct. If you live in Westminster and your child attends a Westminster Junior School, apply through that school. Otherwise contact the Westminster Council School Admissions and Benefits Section (Tel. 020 7828 8070) and ask for advice and/or a Westminster application form. Priority for siblings, medical and social need; thereafter judged on the basis of walking distance from the school to your home: someone at Westminster City Hall spends their days working this out, and worrying about their job being contracted out to the Ramblers Association. Twice over-subscribed but you can succeed (notably for the music course) from as far away as Dulwich or Camden.

Exit: Half move on to College after GCSE; of those who stay for A level about 80 per cent go on to a wide range of universities old and new, including some to Oxbridge.

Remarks: Popular oversubscribed inner London state day school that has recovered well from the trauma of a head who did not work out. Street clothed, streetwise, bouncy and thoroughly pleasant pupils (though they can alarm locals and shopkeepers). A committed staff who seem to manage to make all-ability teaching and even the ghastly ILEA maths system work. Though new educational techniques (and perhaps even – shock horror – a teachers' dress code) are starting to appear, this is one school where the virtues of the '60s will not be thrown out with the bathwater.

Improving academically; could do better. Bright kids can succeed here if they have sufficient determination to work, concentration and maturity. All-ability, probably lower than average levels of achievement at 11, and some with behavioural problems, but the staff are alert and on top of things Exam results above local and national averages, good in relation to the intake, and NB Pimlico's exam policy is to enter every pupil who completes the course – no weeding out of the weaker candidates. Watch out for disappointing results and over-large classes in individual subjects, and for strong subjects that may be dependent on one particular teacher. Art and music have quality in depth with results to match. The home of the Pimlico Special Music Course; 10 per cent of the school's annual intake selected by interview: innate ability

and attitude are what count. Vocational qualifications in science, art and design, and performing arts produce good results.

Housed in award-winning 1970 building which feels like a concrete car ferry – huge glass windows set at an angle – light, with staircases running up the middle of the school. Glorious architecture: impractical though, badly thought out, inflexible and falling apart. The are plans for a complete rebuild, so maintenance is not a priority.

Pupils from surrounding primary schools regularly opt for Pimlico rather than what they see as the dozier local alternatives. School hit headlines in '98 following Mr Straw's 17-year-old son's spot of trouble over drugs.

THE PORTSMOUTH GRAMMAR SCHOOL

High Street, Portsmouth PO1 21N

Tel: *023 92 819125* Fax: *023 92 870184*

E-mail: ahh@pompeygs.demon.co.uk

Web: www.pgs.org.uk

✦ Pupils: 820 (450 boys, 370 girls); plus 210 in Lower School and 150 in pre-prep. All day ✦ Ages: 11-18, Lower School 8-11, pre-prep 4-8 ✦ Size of sixth form: 230 (about a third girls) ✦ Non-denom ✦ Fee-paying

---

Head: Since 1997, Dr Tim Hands BA AKC (theological diploma) D Phil (early forties). Read English at King's London, then on to St Catherine's Oxford, followed by Oriel, followed by King's Canterbury, where he became a housemaster. Post before coming here was second master at Whitgift School. Comes from a long line of teachers, including both parents and an ancestor who was schoolmaster on HMS Victory. Likes rugby, cricket, music, and writes books, articles etc. Married, two children. Comments (which very few heads do) that he attempts 'always to consider what a pupil might be when he or she is 25'. Took over from Mr Tony Evans, here from '83 – not an easy act to follow, and the post itself has been described as 'the toughest job on the circuit'.

The buck stops with Dr Hands for all three schools, but he is totally responsible for the senior school.

Academic Matters: Maths the most popular subject at A level and regularly in Olympiad, physics also popular – results good in both subjects. Sciences strong (environmental jobs) and majority take three separate sciences at GCSE. New A and AS level curriculum and general studies programme from '99: much broadened, with 'a focus on life and employment to match the head's ideas'. Most pupils do 10 subjects at GCSE, including two or three options and 'AO maths'. Classes now only set for maths (one term in) and thereafter sets are decided by option choice.

Games, Options, the Arts: Pupils bussed to games fields at Hilsea, with swimming either in the pool at the Lower School or in Victoria Baths. Cross-country very strong, regular finalists, also successful athletics – 'a whole range of international athletes here'. Sea-rowing (clinker rowing), also sailing, as you might expect, plus rugby, hockey. Choice after GCSE. Girls play netball, with aerobics, modern dance. Girls also more enthusiastic at CCF, and there is often a whole girls' team competing in the Ten Tors Long Endurance race. Art and music very

much part of the curriculum, and the whole of the lower school must play some instrument. Pottery and ceramics exciting. New-ish sports hall on the site of the headmaster's house, plus music hall. Glossy brochure produced for school's cricket/netball/hockey tour to Barbados, complete with palm trees and blue skies.

Background and Atmosphere: School founded in 1732, formerly direct grant, becoming 'independent' in '76 at which point girls were first admitted to the sixth form. School went co-ed from the bottom in '89 and became fully co-ed in '95. The main school is Listed throughout (and so nothing can be done to buildings, not even the verandahs removed); campus in the centre of Portsmouth. The school is still hoping to buy an about-to-be-redundant naval building on adjacent site (they already have half of it). Space at an very high premium.

Pastoral Care and Discipline: Like his predecessor, new head is deeply concerned about matters pastoral. V v strong pastoral structure, now house-based rather than form-based. Two trained counsellors plus chaplain, and part-time chaplain as well, not to mention five staff acting as counsellors.

Pupils and Parents: See above. Pupils come from as far afield as Southampton, Lancing, Winchester and the Isle of Wight. Not the middle-class dream. Ethnic mix 'matches that of the area,' comments head.

Entrance: Competitive exam at 11 recently abandoned in favour of interviews and creative writing. Approx 50 per cent from Lower School – 'virtually all do, but three or four might not make it'. Some from traditional preps at 13 – Prebendal, Boundary Oak, Great Ballard, Westbourne Park, West Hill Park, Twyford (all local). Interview and GCSE results for entry at sixth form (seven needed, 'preferably' As and Bs).

Exit: 'All but one or two a year' go to university – London, Leeds, Birmingham, some to Oxbridge.

Money Matters: Locality (Navy, IBM, Marconi etc) is now relatively buoyant. Not a well-endowed school, and one with lowish fees. Some scholarships available, recently enhanced by four (from Peter Ogden) for state school pupils. The school had nearly 200 assisted places, and though the rolls are rising despite their loss the school will lose some of its social breadth.

Remarks: Seriously strong grammar school offering the best possible academic facilities, left in good heart by previous head.

PORTSMOUTH HIGH SCHOOL

Kent Road, Southsea, Hampshire PO5 3EQ

TEL: *023 92 826 714* FAX: *023 92 814 814*

E-MAIL: admissions@por.gdst.net

WEB: members.aol.com/portsmthhs

✦ PUPILS: 605 girls, (398 seniors, 207 juniors) all day ✦ Ages: 4-18 ✦ Size of sixth form: 98 ✦ Non-denom ✦ Fee-paying

---

Head: Since 2000, Miss Peggy Hulse BA (forties). Started as a teacher in 1974, and while working took her degree at The Open University. Taught English and drama for thirteeen years at Newcastle-under-Lyme School, then deputy head at Northampton High. A Quaker. Interests include poetry (which she writes), theatre, cinema. A governor of Sibford School

(which specialises in teaching severe dyslexics). Took over from Mrs J M Dawtrey, who was here from 1984.

Entrance: Name down in Autumn for school's own tests the following February for entry in September for ten/eleven-year-olds. V modest registration fee. No advantage in putting down name early – the school is academically selective only. Separate sixth form prospectus.

Exit: Remarkably few to Oxbridge (about four a year, if that, at last count), given performance in A levels. Otherwise – rich wide net from nearby universities (Bristol and Southampton popular), ex-polys, gap year, one or two to higher education colleges and to Project 2000 (nursing). A number leave after GCSE to go to local sixth form colleges, and to the now co-ed Portsmouth Grammar.

Remarks: Useful GDST school, which follows narrow-ish academic curriculum and gets good steady results in what it does. Numbers again down on previous edition, including sixth form – losing out to Portsmouth Grammar now that it is co-ed, perhaps? Excellent music department, housed in rather seedy-looking converted Victorian building. Numbers taking music exams at high levels has exceeded that of many of the traditional music schools. All manner of different instruments – oboe, flute, viola, treble recorder, singing, trumpet etc. Has been known to wipe the floor with other schools in the Portsmouth annual music festival. Little in the way of games facilities – school rents Southsea Common from the council – 'freezing,' say pupils. Games mostly thankfully abandoned at sixth form, though some exercise (aerobics v popular) required. Art department looks like a giant greenhouse, exciting though.

Founded 1882. Dreary site (though efforts have been made to brighten up the outside areas. Housed in red-brick building (shiny brass plate) tucked behind seafront at Southsea (bracing). Behind the red brick, which looks as though it was designed to accommodate about a hundred girls, the school now has any number of bolt-on extras. Not very inspiring library when we visited. No fields and minimal grass/garden – very urban feel, despite the sea. Pupils look you straight in the eye and smile. Parents work in IBM, some Service families, professionals. On the middle side of middle, with some humble backgrounds in on bursaries etc. OGs include Dillie Keane, Debbie Davies (synchronised swimmer), Denise Black (soap star), city whizz, Anne McMeehan, Mrs Justice Ebsworth. Had 133 assisted places – the Trust is busy raising money to replace them.

PUTNEY HIGH SCHOOL

35 Putney Hill, London SW15 6BH

TEL: *020 8788 4886* FAX: *020 8789 8068*

E-MAIL: putneyhigh@put.gdst.net

WEB: www.gdst.net/putneyhigh

✦ PUPILS: 540 girls; all day ✦ Ages: 11-18 (junior department 4–11) ✦ Size of sixth form: 145 ✦ Non-denom ✦ Fee-paying

---

Head: Since 1991, Mrs Eileen Merchant BSc (fifties), educated at a Convent School in East London, studied chemistry at Sheffield. Previously deputy head of Latymer School. Teaches maths, visits classrooms regularly and sees girls when they 'sign the excellent book'. Keen supporter of all extra-curricular activities. Described by parents as 'impressive, cool and detached; very clever and terribly honest'. Strict: 'the girls know where they are with her.' 'Highly dedicated'.

Academic Matters: Very good results, much improved in recent years. Less formal than some GDST schools. Twenty-three subjects offered at A level, including history of art, theatre studies and economics. Excellent language results at GCSE as usual (French, Spanish, Latin, German) and not to be sneezed at at A level either. Maths the most popular A level subject – brilliant GCSE and excellent A level results. Biology also perennially popular (dual award science at GCSE), so are English and geography. Needs more young teachers.

Games, Options, the Arts: Broader than some – lots of good, enthusiastic extra-curricular activities. DT popular; textiles to A level, but possibly slight lack of imagination. Ditto art, competent rather than inspired, but good results and gets the pupils on to where they want to go. Music good, has players in The National Youth and Stoneleigh Orchestras. Have been in finals of Music For Youth at Royal Festival Hall etc. Gym in new sports hall, plus Barn Elms and Putney Leisure Centre. Special link for athletics with Belgrave harriers. Tennis (championship grade) and netball teams successful (particularly so in '98), but much emphasis on individual exercise: aerobics (v popular), fencing, trampolining etc. Rowing from Thames Rowing Club, girls surprisingly successful at regattas.

Background and Atmosphere: Leafy suburban site half-way up Putney Hill, three large Victorian villas (one for Junior Department) plus sundry modern revamped and recently upgraded purpose-built additions. Has abandoned plans to sell up and move to Menrosa House (a Palladian mansion variously reported as being 'in the middle of Alton council estate in Roehampton' and 'in 14 acres of grounds with views over Richmond Park.') Octagonal hall for junior music and drama. Girls wear purple (no uniform for sixth form) with rather jolly sweat shirts, and any combination of purple and white for summer dresses. Well organised and effective communications with parents.

Pastoral Care and Discipline: Parents report pastoral care is excellent: 'people feel they can take problems to teachers', and the school takes pains to look after each girl. Mrs Merchant perceived as very strict, cross the line and you're out. Excellent anti-bullying and behaviour policy drawn up by pupils, parents and staff. Only sixth form allowed in street during day. 'Girls very co-operative and keen to do well,' says Mrs Merchant.

Pupils and Parents: Predominantly Putney locals and those from surrounding areas of Richmond, Twickenham, Fulham and Barnes. City money – parents from professions with fair amount of law, banking, medicine, media. Amanda Waring, Baroness Symons and Virginia Bottomley are Old Girls (the latter was head girl).

Entrance: 40 per cent via Junior School, fair number from state schools. At 11+, very stiff entrance exam – approx 360 girls sitting for 84 places, plus interview. Vacancies in other years, however. Sixth form entry: six GCSE passes at A or B with A grades for A level subjects, plus interview (about 12 a year). Competitive. No sibling concessions.

Exit: Up to 10 leave after GCSE either to Westminster and the like or to sixth form colleges. Six or so to art foundation courses (including the much oversubscribed Wimbledon). 'Fair number do gap year before taking up university place.' Southern and south-west universities are currently favoured (eg Bristol, Oxbridge). Some medics.

Money Matters: Had 109 assisted places; now offers GDST bursaries (means tested, but can cover the full fees). Some academic and music scholarships.

Remarks: Good popular local school under good head. Happy reports from (most) parents and pupils. 'Slightly tunnel-visioned but good as far as it goes,' said one, perhaps rather too severely.

JUNIOR SCHOOL: Lytton House. Head: Miss C J Attfield. Teaching cert. Approx 270 girls ages 4-11, all day. Entrance by assessment and interview. Name down by mid-November for following September. Very popular – this is the bit of the school they fight to get into. Plans for two-stream entry at 4 will mean it's harder to get in later. Has won serious silverware for netball and tennis. Regularly Music for Youth finalists: recently produced a cassette of pupils' favourite hymns. Gave a spirited rendering of The Wombling Song in '98 music concert. Winner of Parker and Osmiroid handwriting competitions.

QUEEN ANNE'S SCHOOL

6 Henley Road, Caversham, Reading,
Berkshire RG6 0DX

TEL: *0118 918 7300* FAX: *0118 918 7310*

E-MAIL: admis@queenannes.reading.sch.uk

WEB: www.qas.org.uk

✦ PUPILS: 325 girls. 200 board (full and flexible), 120 day ✦ Ages: 11-18 ✦ Size of sixth form: 105 ✦ C of E ✦ Fee-paying

---

Head: Since 1993, Mrs D Forbes MA (fifties), educated at Bath High School, and read English at Somerville. Previous post for ten years taught English at Cheltenham, ending as head of English. Married to a writer; two grown-up children. Mrs Forbes has been quietly rebuilding confidence in the school with a minimum of fuss and a maximum of humour and consultation – 'with everyone'. 'It is difficult to know what traditions are sacred and what they are longing for you to change.' But doesn't 'want to tamper with the ethos of the school, the changes are more superficial.' Instituted a school council to consider the changes. Looks to produce 'good all-rounders with good academic education and plenty of other things besides'. Head was very committed to full boarding, now embraces 'flexible' boarding as well.

Academic Matters: Does quietly and not at all badly for your average to average plus mortal. Results average 7.5 A level points in '00, 23.5 average total. Traditionally keen science, and some become medics. Both double award and separate sciences at GCSE.

No sign of computers yet linking to CDT, or geography – still in the pipeline. No specialist dyslexia unit or teacher, but will take children with mild dyslexia. Three libraries, including one super octagonal double-decker showpiece; the old library is now a lecture hall. General studies no longer examined at A level.

Games, Options, the Arts: Lacrosse still strong, they are once again the under-15 (joint) county champions, and an Old Girl is captain of the England Under 21s. Serious tennis coaching throughout the winter (with ball thrower). All-weather tennis courts much in demand. Swimming pool with underwater lighting and 'music facility' equally popular. Statutory brand new sports hall. Masses of music; drama good, lots of external activities, particularly at weekends – skating, dry-skiing, sailing. Girls good at rowing. Strong art department, super 3D textiles, with girls making own clothes including ball gowns: sewing machines available at weekends, and computer rooms. Keyboard skills and RSA qualifications. Good careers advice. Young Enterprise and D of E Award.

Background and Atmosphere: The history of the school reaches back to 1698 and the opening of the Grey Coat Hospital in Westminster. In 1706 Queen Anne granted a charter to Grey Coats, and in due course part of the endowment was used to found a boarding school in the country. Grey Coat Hospital is now in the state sector and links with its 'country arm' are somewhat tenuous, though relationships were strengthened for QA's centenary in 1994. Purpose built in 1894, the charming redbrick complex sprawls round two sides of the 40-acre grounds less than five minutes from the centre of Reading. Magical combined performing arts centre and 250-seater theatre.

Massive games fields. Girls are based in one of four boarding houses. Sixth formers have own houses and wear mufti (not jeans for lessons), give dinner parties and stay out later than rest of school. Boys welcome for tea in house; most girls have own rooms (head girls have either private shower or bath). Visits to Reading allowed on basis of seniority. School does an enormous amount of girl-inspired charity work.

Pastoral Care and Discipline: Not often much of a problem. Pastoral care under chain of command via 'pastoral deputy head', house mistress and tutor to head; strong Christian ethos. School counsellor. Sensible rules: sacking for drugs; smoking: letter home, suspension for repeated offences; booze, not without permission, but OK at school parties – in moderation.

Pupils and Parents: From within 50-mile radius. Home Counties. Delightful, not particularly streetwise, mainly 'the unmentionable middle class, good solid citizens whose values are straight' (still). 40/50 non-Brits, (stiff English exam) and similar number of ex-pats, plus fair number of first time buyers and OGs' daughters. Still quite WASP-y. Famous Old Girls: cartoonist Posy Simmonds, Jenny Seagrove.

Entrance: Quite gentle. Mainly 11+, rest 12, or 13+. CE and interview. Pupils come from local schools, and prep schools such as Godstowe, Maltman's Green, Rupert House, St Mary's Henley. Places 'usually' available at sixth form level: entrance examination, five GCSE passes A-C, and interview.

Exit: 95 per cent + go to university (particularly the popular ones – Nottingham, Edinburgh, Exeter, Manchester etc). Traditionally a small number to Oxbridge.

Money Matters: Well funded (by girls' schools standards). All funding from Foundation Office in London, who also deal with bad payers. Help always available for genuine hardship, particularly in exam years. Otherwise two open scholarships for the sixth form, and four internal ones based on GCSE results. 'Several good' scholarships at 11, 12 or 13.

Remarks: Nice low-key girls' boarding school which delivers the goods – both sporting and academic – in a quiet sort of way. Worth a look. Grows on you.

QUEEN ELIZABETH'S GRAMMAR SCHOOL

Blackburn, Lancashire BB2 6DF

TEL: *01254 686 300* FAX: *01254 692 314*

E-MAIL: headmaster@qegs.blackburn.sch.uk

WEB: www.qegs.blackburn.sch.uk

✦ PUPILS: 800 pupils, all boys except for 20 girls in sixth form. All day ✦ Ages: 7-19 ✦ Size of sixth form: 200 ✦ Inter-denom on C of E Foundation ✦ Fee-paying

---

Head: Since 1995, Dr Hempsall MA PhD (early fifties). Read history at Cambridge. Previously head of Scarborough College.

Academic Matters: Strong science bias still, (lots of serious manufacturing businesses around – ICI, Philips, BAe Systems etc). General studies at A level help to produce a high overall A level points score. Maximum class size 25, fewer for GCSE, and average 10 for A levels. Language labs (French, Spanish and German on offer). Latin and Greek possible to A level. Lots of computers, all networked. Good hard-working ethos prevails. High powered staff. No remedial help, but less able taught in smaller sets.

Games, Options, the Arts: Regular major music and drama productions, but auditorium too small to hold whole school. A soccer school, ISFA cup winners in '96 (note to fans: close links with Blackburn Rovers) and county representation in cricket, swimming, cross-country and athletics. Superb swimming pool – which locals have been using in the evenings for some time. Regular trips abroad, lots of foreign exchanges. Young Enterprise, and D of E Awards. Much extra-curricular involvement, especially debating and public speaking.

Background and Atmosphere: School founded in 1509 by the second Earl of Derby and incorporated by Royal Charter from Queen Elizabeth I in 1567. Went direct grant in 1944 and returned to private sector in 1976. Moved to present site in 1882, much of this building remains, with elegant stained glass and serious 'boy-proof banisters' (with knobs on). Portraits of previous heads, and school silver proudly displayed. Recent extensions and acquisition of neighbouring buildings makes campus somewhat crowded. Games fields and sports hall 20 minutes' walk away, pupils are bussed. Grounds immaculate, with Junior School sharing premises and facilities. Light airy library at top of Queen's Wing, good feeling of quiet purposeful study. Bespoke sixth form centre.

Pastoral Care and Discipline: Problems are relayed via form tutors, heads of year to deputy head (pastoral) and head. Chaplain part of informal counselling service, and staff get in-service training five times a year.

Punishments range from detentions, to temporary or permanent removal from school. Hot policy on bullying and verbal abuse, seminars on drugs.

Pupils and Parents: 'Genuinely sociologically much more representative than many in Lancashire'; un-WASP background, one-sixth Asian. Open to 'anyone with ability', pupils wear school uniform with pride. Parents expected to turn up for PT meetings. PTA hot on fund-raising. Catchment area all over NE Lancs, from Preston to Colne and Bolton to Clitheroe, school bus service covering thirteen routes. Old Boys include Russell Harty, the former bishops of Woolwich and Chester, Sir Kenneth Durham (former chairman of Unilever), Gary Smith (film producer), Peter Holloway (flamenco guitarist), Nick Dougherty (golfer).

Entrance: At 11, school test in English, maths and verbal reasoning, plus school report and interview with the head; strict academic cut-off, but preference given to siblings, OBs' children, and those with the 'X factor'. At sixth form, via interview and five Bs minimum at GCSE recommended.

Exit: Most to universities, 10 to Oxbridge, sometimes sponsored by local industries (Shell, BP).

Money Matters: Had huge numbers of assisted places and was over-dependent on these. Tough on those who 'refuse to pay when we know they could'. Can support 'in proven need and academic worthiness'. 20 bursaries a year at 11+ now on offer.

Remarks: Good, tough, boys' grammar school, achieving the academic ambitions and aspirations as set out by its original Foundation, despite hot competition from the local state sector. Numbers again down on last edition, both overall and in sixth form – move to co-ed in response to this? Hard to know how the school will change.

QUEEN ELIZABETH GRAMMAR SCHOOL, WAKEFIELD

Northgate, Wakefield, West Yorkshire
WF1 3QX

TEL: *01924 373 943* FAX: *01924 231 603*

E-MAIL: admissions@qegs-Wakefield.net

WEB: www.qegs-Wakefield.net

✦ PUPILS: 690 boys, (plus Junior School of around 260 boys.); all day ✦ Ages: junior school 7-11, senior 11-18 ✦ Size of sixth form: 190 ✦ Inter-denom ✦ Fee-paying

Head: Since 1985, Mr R P Mardling MA FRSA (fifties), educated at Nottingham High School, read languages (German and French) at St Edmund Hall, Oxford and teaches German in sixth form. A teacher manqué, he 'fits in'. Chairman, HMC Professional Sub-Committee. Previously deputy head of Arnold School in Blackpool and before that at Nottingham High. Aims to produce 'self-confident, caring, modest, open-minded children who will have a go at things' and encourages 'good organisational skills and respect for others'.

Academic Matters: Science and maths strong and school bursting with mathematicians. Some languages studied with the Girls' High; boys can opt for extra language in sixth form: Russian, Italian, business French or German. Head of English depart-

ment has 'added impetus'. All the sixth form do general studies at A level – caveat league tables. Remedial help on hand for mild dyslexia, children are screened, and additional help can be organised, usually at lunch time. Laptops allowed.

Games, Options, the Arts: Art blossomed and is a good and popular A level subject, v energetic, screen printing, photography, dark room popular. Enthusiastic head of music, with over 200 individual players, and swing bands, junior swing bands (hired out for weddings and things – money earned goes to funding trips abroad). Concerts often held in Wakefield Cathedral, for which school is choir school. Drama is popular, with regular blockbusters, My Fair Lady, Amadeus, Macbeth etc. Superb stage which doubles as assembly hall. Rugby (keen), hockey, cross-country, cricket, tennis and athletics, plus ancillary badminton, basketball – rugby team to Australia and NZ, and cricket team to Holland recently. School 'has use of' over twenty-seven acres of playing fields, the senior boys play 'up the road' (which is also used by the nearby Police Academy as a helicopter landing pad – great excitement). Marvellous CDT development, super new labs, IT moving into its own slot, out of DT. Library expanded with false floor (brill Victorian roof still visible through mezzanine) and CD-ROM.

Background and Atmosphere: School founded by Royal Charter in 1591, and moved to present site in 1854. From 1944-76 it was a direct grant school, and reverted to fee-paying in '76. Marvellous Victorian Gothic facade hides multitude of extensions and make-overs; some very imaginative, some less so. Junior School also on site, small learning pool is used by juniors and those learning to swim, plus Junior Girls' School.

No real swimming pool or sports hall.

Pastoral Care and Discipline: All boys carry record book at all times which can be inspected by staff at any time, and must be signed by parents at pre-ordained intervals. If a boy misbehaves in public, the line is to remove the record book and send it back to school, which will then reprimand the owner. Brilliant. Works well, other schools could do well to copy. School will tail boys if they complain about being bullied; limited problems with drugs but speaks to Drugs Squad. Head says drink is the biggest problem of the middle classes. Tuesday pm 'staff detention' for minor sin, Saturday morning detentions for serious infringements – two lessons in two of pupil's weakest subjects (as determined by him and confirmed by master). Suspensions and exclusions; vandalism, bullying and aggressive behaviour are stamped on hard AND IT WORKS.

Pupils and Parents: Fair number of first-time buyers (ie at least 50 per cent), school regarded as local option for boarding or disaffection with state system. Strong middle-class ethic about getting value for money evident: boys work hard, fair ethnic mix. 50 per cent have Wakefield postcode, rest from as far as Doncaster, Sheffield and Wetherby. Parents organise school buses.

Entrance: 11+, 13+ CE paper (CE paper now used by both boys and girls at sister school of Wakefield High). 12+ own exam, plus head's report plus head's judgement. About 50/55 per cent of boys come from own Junior School, but no automatic entry, and from local preps – Westbourne, Sheffield, plus state primaries. Sixth form entry: good GCSEs – B or over required for A level subjects. Boys can and do move into the school at all other times, subject to academic OK and space available.

Exit: Some post-GCSE, of the rest, one or two drop out, one or two to art foundation courses, one or two to employment, a handful to Oxbridge, some to retakes or improved offers but the majority to degree courses all over Britain (Sheffield, Durham and Newcastle popular).

Money Matters: Numbers steady. 'Special arrangements in place' for some, but lots of parental commitment and a very efficient clerk to the governors. Lots of encouragement to opt for direct debit. Four or five being kept through exam year. Had 141 much needed assisted places – governors' own system to replace 12 of them. 25 per cent of school was on some sort of fees assistance, and the fees are reasonable. Twelve sixth form scholarships, and music scholarships, plus bursaries in Junior School for choristers, one-third paid by Cathedral and one-third by school.

Remarks: The best boys' city day school in this area. Serious, unpretentious grammar. In need of a benefactor to help replace those assisted places.

QUEEN ETHELBURGA'S

COLLEGE

Thorpe Underwood Hall, York YO26 9SS

TEL: *0870 742 3330* FAX: *0870 742 3310*

E-MAIL: remember@compuserve.com

WEB: www.queenethelburgas.edu

✦ PUPILS:: 200 girls, 11 boys, of whom 173 board, 38 day; plus prep school 'Chapter House': 72 girls, 40 boys, of whom 17 board; plus Queen's Kindergarten of 31 tinies (open all year) ✦ Ages: main school 11-18, prep 3-11, kindergarten 3 months to 3 years ✦ Size of sixth form: 76 ✦ Inter-denom ✦ Fee-paying

---

Head: Since 1997, Mrs Erica Taylor BSc MA PGCE (late forties) who was educated at St Anne's Convent, Southampton followed by University of East Anglia where she majored in mathematical physics, then PGCE at Southampton and MA in education management at the Open University. She came to Queen Ethelburga's from York College for Girls where she was headmistress, having previously been housemistress at Bootham School and Lancing. She teaches six periods of physics a week. Married to an RAF officer stationed at Brize Norton, she has three stepchildren and a large black labrador. Gassy and highly efficient, she has kicked QE up the academic ladder.

Academic Matters: On the up, but results will never set the world alight, though having said that, pupils have gained five A levels (taken as modules wherever possible) plus the general paper. French from six and German from ten (which means that pupils arriving at the senior school form a different class for these subjects). Spanish for all at 14, dual science (v popular – and fab modern labs with spectacular views) plus the usual trad subjects. Plus an unusual spread of alternative A levels embracing psychology, photography, performing arts, as well as business and leisure & tourism vocational A levels. Other vocational sixth form courses include NNEB. Dyslexia help available and free in the Junior School, EFL free throughout the school.

No apparent problems getting appropriate staff: 'no term has started without the right number of staff required,' the full staff list is on the web site.

Games, Options, the Arts: Horses are an important part of QE. The Royal Court Equestrian Centre (which cost three million quid) has an impressive indoor riding school, outdoor manege and masses of pony paddocks plus three serious cross country courses. Pupils may (and do) bring their own animals, all living in a vast double-decker American-style barn capable of holding 185. Pupils get up to muck out at 6.45am, and generally do their own horses, but full livery is available at £1600 per term, indulgent fathers please note. £750 a term to use a QE horse, (the school has seven) but there are a variety of options available if you are prepared to share your own. BHSAI on offer in the sixth form and riding is timetabled. Cor. Plus ten acres of floodlit all-weather courts for hockey rather than lacrosse, football, high jump, volleyball etc. Ballet popular, and clubs for yoga, pets – which are kept in a poly-tunnel ('redesigned greenhouse' says school), dance and sugar craft. Magical fitness rooms (one in senior house plus sauna and suntan beds).

Music on the up, masses of keyboards and regular musical either performed in York or in house. The lecture theatre converts into seating for the stage in the sports hall (if you follow), all very cunning. Small swimming pool (the Martin's original one) now roofed over in slightly strange juxtaposition with the refectory. Art good and strong, though not much take up at A level, and a proposed fashion design course failed to get off the ground – though relaunch planned for 2001 ('our parents prefer the more academic subjects'). Enthusiastic home economics and Leith's food and wine course for sixth formers (no more than two sets of eight per year group) with the smashing new kitchen used for grown up classes in the holidays. D of E with masses of gold participants.

Background and Atmosphere: Founded in 1912, QE was the intellectual doyenne of the Northern Circuit, rivalled only by St Leonard's in Scotland. However, falling numbers and threatened closure precipitated the move to Thorpe Underwood, conveniently situated 15 minutes from York and Harrogate and ten minutes' drive from the A1. Surrounded by 100 acres of beautifully manicured grounds, Thorpe Underwood dates back to the Domesday Book when it is described as Chirchie, Usebrana and Useburn, before becoming part of the Monastery of Fountains Abbey in 1292 (the stew pond used by the monks to supply food for the passing travellers has been meticulously restored.) The hall itself was rebuilt in 1902 in best Edwardian Tudor style and the extensions have been sympathetically carried out with leaded paned windows to match the original, though some of the blue wallpapered classrooms are a bit surprising (not to mentioned the rather grand Sanderson curtains).

Previously home to the Martin family, the front hall is filled with stuffed leopards and hung with odd guns, halberds and the trappings of posh country house living. Impressive new-build dormitory blocks – dorms would be a misnomer for these elegant little bedrooms, some with private bathrooms, all with tellies (on a timer) and telephones with voice mail. The school recently bought the next door nursing home to convert into extra dorms to cope with the increase in boarders. Boys and girls accommodation separated by locked doors. Charming little chapel due to be expanded this year, and a Moslem prayer room (the first we have encountered on the GSG).

Leased for a peppercorn from a charitable foundation (originally the brain child of Brian Martin, whose younger daughter and two grandchildren are in the school) QE has benefited from seventeen million quid's worth of investment. Good, if not lavishly stocked, libraries, banks of computers, teletext business info displayed in series of fours around the school, free availability to the internet (though not all computers networked, and houses not intranetted.) Regular formal dinner parties with silver service and speaker for sixth form 'to give them practice in the real world'. Excellent NNEB suite in the ground floor (and open all the year round), immaculate parking facilities, just like the army.

Pastoral Care and Discipline: Tutorial system which changes yearly, no more than a dozen tutees to each. Pupils are not streetwise, and the house system, though a bit wobbly, seems to pick up any real problems. Bullies are confronted head on, and the bully box where notes either signed or not can be deposited for scrutiny by the head or her deputy is rarely used. Mrs Taylor has only ever asked two girls to leave: one for bullying and one for staying away without permission twice during the first two weeks she was at school.

Regular socials with Welbeck College and Barnard Castle, the sixth formers have a bar twice a week, with a non-alcoholic bar for younger members of the school and lots of inter school beanos like karaoke and the like. The sixth form also has a smoking room where pupils may smoke 'with parental permission' – another first for the GSG.

Twice a week the head hosts a discretely separated lunch table where sixth formers can let their hair down; if the matter raised is contentious then the pupil concerned is 'invited to see me in my office later'.

Charming 'leaver's letter' inviting any former pupil (until they 'leave university, or their 21st birthday, whichever is the later') to contact the College or Mr Martin – reverse charge – at any time – if they have got into a scrape and need help or (free) legal advice. (Another GSG first.)

Pupils and Parents: Fiercely middle class, pupils come to board from all over – Scotland, Wales as well as East Anglia and locally on daily basis; horses come too. Expect a mass of regional accents, some 16 per cent 'real foreigners' from abroad – Germans, Russians, Scandinavians et al, most of whom come via the internet, with quite a lot just coming for the sixth form. Eight buses collect day pupils from all over Yorkshire (not cheap).

Entrance: Either via Chapter House, or schools internal exam which 'few fail', As and Bs at GCSE for potential A level candidates at sixth form. External candidates tend to come from the local state schools or out of the area. Pupils accepted at any time during the school year 'if places available'.

Exit: Most, who want to go to university, go to the university of their choice – these tend to be Liverpool, London , Nottingham and the newer universities, with a couple to Oxbridge.

Money Matters: Well underpinned financially, but seriously expensive. Masses of scholarships, rebate if you move to QE from another independent school; 20 per cent discount for Forces, diplomats and professional bodies. Sports, art and music scholarships plus a discount for the first year for boys entering the senior school and many many more – including a Karen Dixon scholarship for equestrians. 'You can also pay by Barclaycard or Amex' at no extra charge; but it costs extra to spread the payment over several months.

Remarks: This is a mind-boggling transmogrification from a moribund institution to something more like an American campus. Gentle and not aggressively academic or street wise, this is a nurturing school, which in view of the amount of cash thrown at it, is as good as it looks. Boarders are on the up and boys are gradually creeping their way up the school. Mrs Taylor would like to see the school become properly co-ed, with two parallel classes throughout and five hundred on the roll. Given the dramatic increase both in pupils and boarders over the past eight years this may not be so far off the mark.

QUEEN MARGARET'S SCHOOL

Escrick Park, York Y19 6EU

TEL:*01904 728261* FAX: *01904 728150*

E-MAIL: enquiries@qmyork.force9.co.uk

WEB: www.queenmargarets.org.uk

✦ PUPILS: 367 girls, all board except for 37
✦ Ages: 11-18 ✦ Size of sixth form: 124
✦ C of E ✦ Fee-paying

Head: Since 1993, Dr Geoffrey Chapman, MA (fifties), educated at St Bartholomew's Grammar School, Newbury; read classics at Trinity College, Oxford. Teaches some Greek and Latin (to one or two). Previously head of classics at Christ's Hospital, Horsham, and before that was professor of classics at University of Natal. Known for serious research on Aristophanes, keen on golf. Wife (a popular lady) teaches drama, two grown-up children. Keen on breadth and choice. 'No one can excel at everything, but everybody can excel at something.' A listener.

Academic Matters: Academic success is what matters here; on the edge of grammarschooldom, with relatively little open celebration of pupils work or art (outside the art department), though it manages to avoid too much of a hothouse atmosphere. Superb GCSE results: English sets the overall pattern of 50 per cent plus A/A★, the rest B or C; art and modern languages do well too. Sciences every which way with strong individual subjects, but too many stragglers in dual award (and indeed in maths) in each of the last three years, and (perhaps as a result) few take these subjects on to A level. At A level government and politics, English, art and French especially popular, otherwise there's a bit of everything – history of art, business studies, economics, classical civilisation. The overall performance is good, but some of the individual subjects (eg art, chemistry, English and maths) do better than others. Special needs department (two part-timers), two members of staff for EFL.

Games, Options, the Arts: Lots of healthy outdoor life – games are keenly played, 9-hole golf course, lacrosse, hockey, squash, tennis etc, and masses of girls ride (riding school on the campus, some box their ponies over for the term, but have to look after them if they do). Good art, but not an arty school. Home economics for all. Strong choral music, and lots of drama. Mass for the Catholics in the adorable tiny Lady Chapel.

Background and Atmosphere: Founded in Scarborough in 1901, moved to this fine Palladian house (by John Carr, with later Portakabins) in 1949, lovely setting in 65 acres of parkland; Victorian additions, clever conversions and recent additions. Splendid library (panelling, wood, open fire, huge windows looking out on to lawns); shame about the contents. Circular dining hall (once an indoor lunging school) with dreadful acoustics. The school was originally part of the Woodard Foundation, and was taken over by parents in a 1986 drama. Now not at all what it was then (a fearsome finishing school for farmers' daughters), which is an unequivocally good thing. Feels much more traditional, structured, protective and uptight than its Yorkshire rivals. Nice separate boarding house for the 11-year-olds. Food nothing special – features corned beef pie and spam – but girls can take in tuck. Uniform raspberry and grey – but tartan on the way; home clothes ('mufti') worn after tea – don't provide anything that you would object to being boil-washed. Girls live in year groups ('prevents them growing up too fast,' observes a pleased parent, though this has obvious disadvantages). Girls are kept 'pretty busy' all the time.

Pastoral Care and Discipline: Girls are in the slow lane – this is a rural boarding school, and very protective of its inmates. 'There are no silly rules,' say parents and girls, though it is more rule-bound than its immediate neighbours. Sixth formers are given a fair amount of freedom (eg can go into York during free time on Wednesdays and Saturdays), which they are keen not to abuse, and a fair amount of responsibility.

Pupils and Parents: Friendly pupils, less touched by the world than many of their contemporaries. The county set are clearly in evidence here. Parents mainly upper and upper middle class, landowners, farmers, a small Hong Kong contingent, lots from Scotland ('it's the first real school you hit driving south,' commented a parent), Cumbria, the East coast and, of course, Yorkshire. The teacher who put up the 'Ban Hunting' poster provoked a strong reaction. OG Eleanor Mennim (author), Winifred Holtby (author), Ann Jellicoe (playwright).

Entrance: Own examination at 11+; CE at 12+ and 13+ (a far tougher hurdle at 13 than 11), and at sixth form (minimum eight GCSEs, with at least three B and two C grades including Eng lang, maths, a modern language and a science). Not particularly selective at entry, though less able are probably put off by reputation and atmosphere.

Exit: Virtually everyone goes on to further education (a preponderance in the North). Some leave at sixth form to go to co-ed schools.

Money Matters: Scholarships at 11, 12, 13 and sixth form; music scholarships; some bursaries.

Remarks: Posh rural girls' boarding school that would like to be top rank, academically and socially. It earns many approving noises from parents.

QUEEN MARY'S SCHOOL

Baldersby Park, Topcliffe, Nr Thirsk, North Yorkshire YO7 3BZ

TEL: *01845 575 000* FAX: *01845 575 001*

E-MAIL: admin@queenmarys.org

WEB: www.queenmarys.org

✦ PUPILS: 265 girls, 60 boarders (mostly weekly), the rest day ✦ Ages: 3-16 ✦ Size of sixth form: not applicable ✦ C of E (Woodard school) ✦ Fee-paying

---

Heads: Since 1997, Mr and Mrs (Ian and Margaret) Angus – both have masters degrees, (fifties). Previous post: joint heads of Windlesham House – resigning when the governors decided that the Angus' 'did not share their philosophy for the future development of the school.' Before that, Mr Angus was head of Orwell Park School, Suffolk, which worked out very well. Runs the 3-11s and the school fabric. Educated at Harrow (now a governor) and Trinity College, Dublin. Voluble, full of ideas, can get on the wrong side of people. Mrs Angus the more relaxed and relaxing of the two (though steely with it). Educated at Colchester County High, Dartford and

University of London. Before Windlesham was head of St Felix, Southwold – briefly, after which time she married Mr Angus. Runs the 12-16s and the paperwork. An energetic and experienced pair with clear ideas of where they want the school to go. Took over from the Belwards, who were here for many years, much loved (and their dog even more so).

Academic Matters: Very mixed-ability intake: how it manages to cope with this huge range, given small size of school, is a mystery. Still, the GCSE results are noticeably good, French and German particularly so; maths relatively disappointing. Streaming and setting. Special educational needs co-ordinator: good provision generally.

Games, Options, the Arts: Music seems to be the defining force here: wide participation and great enjoyment. There are a range of other usual activities: drama, sports are played, horses hop over poles, girls camp and debate, but all for fun. New outdoor manege has increased riding facilities. Art on the up.

Background and Atmosphere: Baldersby Park is a grand Palladian mansion (Colen Campbell 1721, Jacobethanised following a fire in 1902) – a good selling point – and girls live in converted flats, with somewhat homely but good-sized dormitories, also conversions of the farm buildings and out-houses. The Angus' set out to upgrade facilities generally, starting with IT – there are now two computer rooms, a school network, and good internet access. Much other refurbishment.

The staff bring their pets to school, girls feel able to run around in bathing dresses. A friendly place with a strong family feel; all ages mix. There are many day girls and some full boarders, but the core of this school is weekly boarding. The early assumption of seniority (at 16 rather than 18) gives pupils confidence and maturity. All senior girls participate in keeping the place clean, and seem to appreciate the experience. Uniform based on Hunting Stewart tartan.

Good nursery and pre-prep, now with two new classrooms.

Pastoral Care and Discipline: Like home. No petty rules, and others which are bendable, but there is an underlying sense of organisation. Parents' requests granted when reasonable.

Pupils and Parents: Traditionally looked after the children of local gents who were not overly worried about how their daughters fared academically at school, but now has greater senses off purpose, and pupils of all sorts from all walks of life. Yorkshire county set, local professional, business and army families.

Entrance: At all ages. Testette, but only those with special needs beyond the school's scope are likely to be turned away.

Exit: At all ages, but principally at the top of the school to sixth forms country wide: Ampleforth, Ripon Grammar, King's Canterbury, Stowe, Uppingham, Rugby and Queen Margaret's all feature in recent lists. The Angus' have visited and assessed most schools of interest to their pupils.

Money Matters: A few scholarships, and bursaries for clergy daughters.

Remarks: Useful small girls' weekly boarding school without a sixth form for the Yorkshire county set. A home from home, and a good education too.

QUEEN'S COLLEGE

43-49 Harley Street, London W1G 8BT

TEL: *020 7291 7000* FAX: *020 7291 7099*

E-MAIL: queens@qcl.org.uk

WEB: www.qcl.org.uk

✦ PUPILS: just under 400 girls, all day
✦ Ages: 11-18 ✦ Size of sixth form: 80 ✦ C
of E ✦ Fee-paying

Head: Since 1999, Miss Margaret Connell (fifties), MA (Oxon). Previously head at More House for eight years, and before that deputy head of Bromley High. Was educated at a direct-grant school in Leeds before taking a degree in physics at Oxford. Unmarried: 'I have a career; no way could I have coped with a family too.' Interests include music (she is an accomplished pianist), theatre and travel: 'Central London is so cosmopolitan it gives me a great yen to see the world.' A parent commented: 'She is plainly a lover of education, and is genuinely interested in all the girls.'

Academic Matters: Strong tradition of computer studies to A level. New glass-sided computer room ('the goldfish bowl') where girls can do internet research ('rather than just sending e-mails to friends'); a mile of cabling went in during the summer of 2000 to link all the school's computers and telephones (staff and girls each have their own email address.) Also strong on languages. All first years study ancient Greek, as well as French, before moving on to Latin. 'The Greeks are inherently much more interesting than the Romans,' says deputy head Jim Hutchinson. In the second year they are given a taster of a variety of foreign languages ranging from Italian to Russian before choosing one in the third year. Plenty of trips abroad. Most girls do 9 GCSEs, including dual science. About a third of parents work in the media, tending to give their daughters a bias towards arts subjects, but science has improved significantly, says the head.

About 45 per cent get A and B grades at A level, the most popular subjects being English and history of art. Girls not bumped off courses but may be able to drop a subject if they feel overloaded. 'But we don't want to reduce their workload too much, particularly if they're not likely to make good use of the extra free time.' Not at the top of the academic league tables – 'They give girls of all abilities a fair chance,' said a mother. But Head emphasises, 'People are worried that we won't do for the brightest, but we will. Girls are just as capable of getting an A here as anywhere.' Four of the leavers in 2000 were bound for Oxbridge, awash with A grades.

Fine, book-lined junior and senior libraries with over 17,000 volumes; six science labs, including one named after ex-student Sophia Jex-Blake, who paved the way for women to enter the medical profession; two computerised modern language laboratories equipped with a great many headphones. Class size: 20 at the bottom of the school, getting smaller higher up as streaming comes into play. 'And the streaming is discreet,' said a parent. 'Your daughter doesn't feel an idiot if she's in a less able class.' One dyslexia specialist and one to help those with English as a second language. Unpressured environment. 'We pick up quite a number of girls who got stressed out at very academic schools,' says the head. 'We have more patience with them. We take a long term view, and let them grow at their own rate. The girls are very supportive of each other rather than being competitive.

Games, Options, the Arts: Despite its central London location, Queen's takes sport seriously, with matches three or four nights a week. 'We can't afford not to,' says the head. 'Girls come in from the prep schools very keen on sport.' The head of games is a former Olympic rower, so although rowing is not a Queen's College sport, 'She knows what competition is about.' Fencing taught (very successfully) by the No. 1 British Women's Fencing Champion. Aerobics, gym and dance in the basement gym, netball, hockey and rounders in nearby Regents Park and swimming at the Seymour Baths.

Strong art department – 'It fits in with the background of our parents' – with three teachers across art and history of art, and many textile designs in evidence in the airy, vaulted art room. Music booms from a sound-proof basement. Lively jazz concerts and musicals such as Grease; music technology A level – 'It is more practical than music A level and you don't have to perform to such a high level, so it is more inclusive.' About 80 per cent of the present first years have individual music lessons at school. Good drama. 'It has given my daughter a great love of performance,' said a parent.

Background and Atmosphere: A green flag and white columns mark the entrance amidst a sea of upmarket doctors' consulting rooms. It was founded in 1848 by F D Maurice, professor of History at King's College London, as 'the first institution to provide a sound academic education and proper qualifications for women'. Former Queen's pupils who have founded other schools include Frances Mary Buss (North London Collegiate and Camden School for Girls) and Frances Dove (Wycombe Abbey). The school occupies four Harley Street houses, all on different levels, which involves much climbing and descending of stairs (with wrought iron banisters), and windows looking onto brick walls and fire escapes, as well as high ceilings and William Morris wallpapers. The buildings are 'a bit of a blessing and a bit of a curse,' says the head. 'In a building that's not designed to be a school you have to work harder to achieve the same.' Large school hall with uncomfortable wooden chairs engraved with the names of Old Girls ('either they go or I do,' says the head). Cafeteria in cheerful, glassed-over ex-courtyard in a basement. No outdoor space to speak of.

Pastoral Care and Discipline: Three section heads have plenty of time to devote to pastoral care, a very strong point of the school. 'People survive here who wouldn't survive elsewhere,' says the deputy head, and parents agree. One commented that with some media families' tendency towards disorganisation, 'It's a good thing their daughters have such a sane, kind and sheltered environment to come to.' No uniform – girls mostly in jeans and sweatshirts. 'We have more important things to do than worry about uniform; it just leads to conflict,' says the deputy head. The head, who introduced a uniform at More House, says, 'They were terrified that I would do it here. But I don't think it matters in the slightest.' Smoking is: 'What they go out for at lunchtime. We hope they do it far enough away not to annoy the neighbours.' Drug-taking has not so far been an issue, 'But I think I would be fairly drastic about it.' She is not in favour of fixed sanctions for offences, because circumstances vary, but might send girls home for extreme rudeness: 'The parents don't like being inconvenienced, so it's quite effective.' Only sixth formers (who can sign in and out as their timetable permits) are allowed out at lunchtime, 'But now we've improved the lunches they tend to stay in.'

Attendance can get wobbly at the higher end of the school, which accounts for some disappointing exam results. 'It is not a huge problem, but one over which we do not have much control,' says the head. Much liasing with parents, including a weekly newsletter, often by e-mail.

Pupils and Parents: 'It's like a posh comprehensive,' said one mother, and head agrees. Huge variety of backgrounds and professions, though with strong bias towards the media. 'Some come with a chauffeur and body-guard, while others, like my daughter, have struggled in on assisted places,' said a parent. Used to take about two-thirds from state schools, but with the abolition of assisted places this has gone down to one-third. OGs include Katherine Mansfield, Emma Freud, Emma Soames, Sophie Ward and Jennifer Ehle.

Entrance: At 11+ by exam (part of group one of the North London Independent Girls' Schools Consortium). But head interviews all applicants before the exam. 'The children are much more nervous afterwards. They are afraid you are going to ask them about the maths questions they got wrong.' She tries to circumvent the standard answers in which many prep school pupils are coached. 'Sometimes I can get them to tell the truth.' Worth trying for spaces higher up the school, too.

Exit: Some after GCSEs, particularly to Camden School for Girls; one or two to boarding school. After A levels, nearly all to higher education, including several a year to Oxbridge.

Money Matters: No bursaries at 11+; a few at 16+.

Remarks: Lively, laid-back central London school in unlikely setting. 'It is an open, unsnobbish and unterrifying place,' said a parent. 'I can't think of anywhere that would have suited my daughter better.'

QUEEN'S GATE SCHOOL
133 Queen's Gate, London SW7 5LE
TEL: *020 7589 3587* FAX: *020 7584 7691*

E-MAIL: principal@queensgate.org

WEB: www.queensgate.org

✦ PUPILS: 258 girls; all day ✦ Ages: 11-18 ✦
Size of sixth form: around 50
✦ Non-denom ✦ Fee-paying

Head (Principal): Since 1987, Mrs Angela Holyoak Cert Ed (age not revealed). Elegant, efficient, enthusiastic. Generous with praise, enormously positive and humorous. Runs the whole school with panache and terrific attention to details. Cares passionately about the individual, 'Which is why we never put pressure on parents or children at any stage to stay here if they think their talents might be better suited elsewhere.' Well aware of the difficulties of shedding the image of the past. Pupils admire and like her. Headmistress: Miss Skone-Roberts, BSc, PGCE, previously head of science at Heathfield, Queen's Gate's sister school.

Academic Matters: Relatively small number of subjects studied at A level (nineteen) but what it does it does well, and the results are superb. Heavy bias to arts – popular subjects change from year to year, but art, history of art, classical civilisation usually feature. Not a place you would choose for a straight up-and-down academic, but this school does extremely well for gentler folk ('those with an IQ below 105 really won't fit in') and has enough competition for the above average. X and Y streams (flexible). Very good history of art (under Miss de Leeuw), who lives on the premises, and is also careers adviser, cleverly bouncing the ball in straight at the girls: 'If they want to read English at university, I tell them to do the research on courses and come back to present it to the whole class.' Science labs in basement (along with sixth form sitting rooms and coffee bar). Good computer room on the fourth floor since we last went to press, with Apple Macs,PCs, even laser printers; there are also computers in the (small but well equipped) DT department for graphic design. All pupils learn word processing. Large art room on the new fifth floor with fine views over London. Very small sixth form (though now back up to pre-recession size), with several leaving after GCSE (some have been here since the age of 4). Interesting and not unusual cases of girls returning, having tried somewhere else for a short spell.

Games, Options, the Arts: Excellent art in large light art room on the fifth floor with inspiring views over London. (NB nearby museum resources constantly drawn upon). All seven pupils taking A level art in '00 got As. Battersea Park and Kensington sports centre for sports, keen music and drama (enhanced by hall built across two of the houses, much fund-raising). Good on trips and outings. 'They're always doing things and going away,' said a parent.

Background and Atmosphere: Three large mansions in South Kensington house the school. 'We've more space than you first imagine,' points out the head, as former broom cupboards in erstwhile mansions of this size provide useful dark rooms/tutorial rooms etc. Well kept; walls full of noticeboards, photographs, work. Children amazingly quiet during classes ('Some visiting parents ask if all the children are out'), the silence broken excitedly at break times.Very friendly atmosphere, a big family where the littles know the big ones – and aren't scared. Particularly good teacher/pupil relationships. Black glossy dining room for seniors, used by staff at break. Good food (children may bring packed lunches). No uniform. Civilised atmosphere.

Pastoral Care and Discipline: Something Mrs Holyoak cares passionately about. Lots of links with parents.Tutor system throughout the school. Sixth formers are allowed out at lunch time: 'I'm not terribly keen on them hanging around South Ken, but they are 17 or 18.'

Pupils and Parents: Pretty upper class. Street-wise in a sophisticated way, articulate and poised girls. A good number of foreigners, encouraged by the Principal, as long as their English is up to it, 'This is London and we're a cosmopolitan city.' And, observes Mrs. Holyoak, it also sets up a useful worldwide network. School breeds fierce loyalty. OGs Redgraves, Sieffs, Guinnesses, Amanda de Souza, Camilla Parker-Bowles, Lucy Lambton, Jane Martineau, Nigella Lawson, Liz da Costa, Tracey Boyd.

Entrance: From Junior School (qv) three quarters of junior girls come on to the senior school, and a huge variety of other schools. Potential parents have recently reported off-hand behaviour by school.

Exit: All to university. Keen on a gap year, and all nowadays keen on degrees; art college popular. 'Our girls are ambitious and getting more ambitious all the time,' says the principal, 'but we don't talk about it as loudly as some schools.'

Money Matters: Two internal scholarships for upper sixth.

Remarks: Charming cosy, friendly, lively, small, unpressurized girls' day school in central London. Is currently one of the two most popular of the less 'academic' London schools (its results would grace many that make greater claims to academic status) – does what it claims to, satisfied parents and happy girls.

THE QUEEN'S SCHOOL

City Walls Road, Chester CH1 2NN

TEL: *01244 312078* FAX: *01244 321507*

E-MAIL: secretary@queens.cheshire.sch.uk

WEB: www.queens.cheshire.sch.uk

✦ PUPILS: 635 girls; all day ✦ Ages: 11-18 (and junior school) ✦ Size of sixth form: 130 ✦ C of E ✦ Fee-paying

---

Head: Since 1989, Miss Diana Skilbeck, BA (fifties), splendidly forthright, delightful, down-to-earth, doesn't stand upon ceremony, stocky, modest, humorous. Warmly appreciated by children (who are not afraid of her), also by staff and parents. Has worked in both state and private schools (previously head of Sheffield High). Read geography at London University. Determined to 'edu-

cate the whole person and help every pupil live up to their potential – I know it's what everyone says, but it really IS what matters'.

Academic Matters: Traditionally and actually a power house, scoring high A level averages. Biology, maths, English, French, history popular. Fairly competitive with the boys at King's (schools are unrelated, though many brothers/sisters at both). Traditional teaching (some Old Girls on the staff), classes of 24. Broad-based general studies programme for all sixth formers. Good careers/university advice, with a real advisor, who visits universities regularly etc. Incredibly hard-working staff: girls lie in wait for them outside the staff room.

Games, Options, the Arts: Wedge-shaped playing fields over the road produces some good lacrosse (some girls chosen to play for Cheshire), 'we even beat some of the boarding schools'. Good art. Keen on charity fund-raising, successful YE, D of E popular; several music groups, including the operatic society with King's. The girls share the swimming pool with Nedham House, Queen's Junior School, five minutes away by car ('Slightly annoying having different sites to fetch and carry on different days,' commented a mother). Cooking and textiles, with good standards in both. Some powerful art.

Background and Atmosphere: Original Victorian building is redbrick Gothic (many sepia photographs of Queen Victoria dotted about the school), on the edge of the city, backing out to the Cathedral, looking out over the city walls and river, a pleasant site, donated by the first Duke of Westminster. Heaps of additions tacked on for new essentials (IT, science labs, language block, sixth form centre), playground area endlessly encroached on. 'Every time you dig foundations to build here,' explains the head, a keen archaeologist, 'you come across Roman remains.' Cheery red sweaters. Unpressurised, friendly atmosphere. The school magazine – called *Have Mynde* – has a quote from its 1897 issue: 'in these days of much reading, much hearing, much doing, and much talking, there is some danger lest the noble industry of thought should be neglected. HAVE MYNDE, my dear girls...'

Pastoral Care and Discipline: Firm emphasis on consideration for others.

Pupils and Parents: Solidly middle class, mainly from professional and business backgrounds, also farming, and traditionally the popular choice for Welsh parents (easy by train). Enthusiastic and hard-working girls. Huge catchment area: long journeys for some (train plus bus).

Entrance: By own entrance exam at 11. Pre-prep and prep entry by assessment.

Exit: Almost all to universities. Both the (nearby) Sheffield and Leeds universities are popular. A good wide variety of subjects chosen. School has produced a huge number of doctors. Old Girls include Anne Clwyd MP, Anne Mynors (architect).

Money Matters: Fees extremely reasonable. Had some assisted places.

Remarks: Successful girls' city day school, the automatic choice for parents with academic daughters in the area.

QUEENSWOOD

Shepherd's Way, Brookmans Park, Hatfield, Hertfordshire AL9 6NS

TEL: *01707 602 500* FAX: *01707 602 597*

E-MAIL: registry@queenswood.herts.sch.uk

WEB: www.queenswood.herts.sch.uk

✦ PUPILS: 380 girls (boarders and 40 per cent 'day boarders') ✦ Ages: 11-18 ✦ Size of sixth form: 100 ✦ Christian non-denom ✦ Fee-paying

Head (Principal): Since 1996, Ms Clarissa Farr BA MA PGCE (early forties), read English at Exeter, followed by a Masters in modern literature, and previously taught in a sixth form college, a comprehensive school, a grammar school and abroad before coming to Queenswood as deputy head (academic) in '92. Married to the sports news correspondent of The Times; they have two small children. She teaches English and theatre studies. Fun and outgoing, Ms Farr's hobby is running marathons; she was wearing a natty trouser suit when we visited, and is much approved of by her pupils. Aims not to produce a 'typical girl', but to turn out 'charming, confident and kind' pupils who will be efficient and have a sense of values without being 'shrinking violets'. She passionately believes in producing 'whole girls', whose range is broader than pure academia.

Academic Matters: Exam results on track and rising. Geography and English strong, girls usually do two modern languages at GCSE and continue with at least one in sixth form. 'Business' options in German, French, Spanish and Italian; girls encouraged to continue studies in their own native languages. No longer the case that no child is refused 'a go' at GCSE. Set in maths, French, English and science, no class larger than 24. Theatre studies and drama strong. Girls follow a general studies course of their choice alongside their A levels. Lap-tops for all from year 8. Internet on tap all over, and computers in classrooms. Younger pupils work at carrells, with plug below each for laptop (and ghetto blasters etc). Enormous, rather remote library with CD-ROMs, and swipe cards for books. Careers advice and learning support throughout.

Games, Options, the Arts: Sports are 'high on the agenda'. School is a national LTA clay court centre and hosts the annual National Schools Championships. The Lawn Tennis Association suggests it for would-be tennis stars. With twenty-six courts in all, including twelve clay, thirteen all-weather and two indoors 'You can play tennis at any level', and at (almost) any time. There is a community-based letting programme. Masses of inter-school competitions. Astroturf hockey pitch, indoor swimming pool plus weights room, aerobics room and huge sports hall. This is a school for budding internationalists. Keen on music, impressive music centre, and re-vamped organ in the chapel, regular lunchtime recitals, as well as lots of community use. Strong choral, and masses of orchestras, loads of inter-house competitions. Good drama, with workshops. Fabulous art, and spectacular ceramics. Textiles important, with dress design and sewing skills. Regular art history trips to Europe. Model United Nations Association for debating, plus charity works, and the Queenswood Raven Exploration Society: the place hums.

Background and Atmosphere: Only just out of suburbia. Founded in Clapham in 1884, school moved to purpose-built neo-Tudor building in 1925 with masses of later additions. Spectacular Audrey Butler Centre (aka the ABC) houses lecture theatre, language labs and masses of class rooms; science labs opposite functional and uninspired. 120 acres of sports fields and woodland two miles out from the M25, a 'short hour' out of London. Houses divided by year for youngest (Trew), with some resident lower sixth on hand to help. Upper sixth have own houses, with single or double study bedrooms. Rest of school live in mixed age houses, with each house having a com (common room) where other houses can visit. Sixth form common room known as the Pizza Hut, tellies everywhere, but viewing restricted. Boarding breaks on hand for 'day boarders', who are anyway at the school from early till very late. Fixed 'activity' and 'home weekends', otherwise boarders can spend Saturday night at home, as long as they are back in time for evening chapel on Sunday. Daily chapel, Sixth formers line the cloister 'to make sure socks are pulled up', school wear purple and grey, but mufti in sixth (the school prefers the term 'smart own clothes', and indeed they were).

Pastoral Care and Discipline: Each house of 40/60 girls is run by teaching house mistresses with assistants and a team of academic tutors. Each tutor has around ten tutees, and sixth formers choose their own tutor. Deputy principal in charge of boarding. Parents informed, plus fines (out of pocket money) and community service for smokers and boozers – fines and time spent on community service increase for second offence: immediate suspension for smoking indoors or third offence. Girls taking drugs 'lose their right to be a member of the school'. There has been the occasional report of bullying.

Pupils and Parents: Lots of first time buyers, with both partners working, masses from London, very strong parent supported Queenswood Fellowship much involved with social activities throughout the year. 25 per cent from abroad, with half of these ex-pats. Not a snob school, 'no social over-tones' – 'this is a school for real people,' said a visiting educationalist.

Entrance: Registration advised three years before entry date, either by CE at 11, 12 and 13 or by own entrance exam. Strong sixth form intake, candidates must get six GCSEs at B or over, with A in the subjects they want to study at A level.

Exit: Most to university, ten to Oxbridge in '98. Lots do gap years, organised by the school. Few now leave post GCSE to do A levels elsewhere.

Money Matters: Came late to assisted places, so not noticeably affected by current government change. Academic scholarships throughout, two at sixth form. Art, music (including organ scholarship), tennis, hockey and PE scholarships. All scholarships renewed annually while the holders are at Queenswood provided they prove themselves worthy'. Occasional bursaries. School will pick up any financial disasters as long as parents are upfront about the problem.

Remarks: Refreshing, zappy, highly-structured girls' boarding school, extremely handy for busy London parents. An all round education, where sport and the community are as important as academic results. Announced in March, 2000 that it was raising day boarders' fees by 35 per cent from September, 2000 – just a few days after the new intake had committed to the school.

Resulting rumpus has now died down, with chastened governors agreeing that the fee rise should be phased in over four years. Parents seem to accept the need for it and remain strongly supportive of the school.

RADLEY COLLEGE

Abingdon, Oxfordshire OX14 2HR

TEL: *01235 543000* FAX: *01235 543106*

(but phone rather than Fax if possible)

E-MAIL: warden@radley.org.uk

(but route enquiries through the Web site)

WEB: www.radley.org.uk

✦ PUPILS: Around 620 boys; all board ✦
Ages: 13-18 ✦ Size of sixth form: 240
✦ C of E ✦ Fee-paying

Head (Warden): Since 2000, Mr Angus McPhail MA (early forties), educated at Abingdon School, read PPE at University College, Oxford. Came from being head of Strathallan, and before that at Sedbergh, where he was a housemaster. Started his career as a banker, switched to teaching ('far more satisfying') and first taught at Glenalmond. A delightful man with ease of manner, many talents and interests (keen cricketer, all-round sportsman, very musical, sings, plays the violin and guitar). Ravishing wife and three young children. Fond of children: 'You can't be a good teacher unless you like children – and I've met lots of people in the profession who don't like them.' Cites resilience and adaptability as being key qualities the young will take away when they leave here. Took over from Mr Richard Morgan, a top class head with a genius for gathering a good common room round him.

Academic Matters: Results still very very good given intake (see Entrance) – 80 per cent A/B grades at A level. Maths most popular subject still, and good results; other popular subjects physics (amazing results), history, chemistry, English, Economics and French. GCSE a walkover in all subjects – not a weak link. Dynamic, excellent young staff in top-class common room. Smart new futuristic circular building – Queen's Court – houses six departments, plus a new arts building.

Games, Options, the Arts: Twinned with seven schools in Europe, links with European Youth Parliament. All boys expected to take part in community action programme IN THE SCHOOL HOLIDAYS eg for the seniors running a camp in Romania for Romanian students or building a house in India. Very keen games school, both traditionally and currently. Rowing is hot stuff with cups everywhere, Henley win in '98. Rugby in Michaelmas term – Wellington are the oldest rivals. Hockey in spring term for 'dry-bobs' and strong in cricket, tennis etc, in summer. Own beagle pack. Stunning swimming pool with probably best diving facilities in private sector in the country. (School in general has a slight aura of a country club at times with tip-top facilities all round including two Astroturfs, plus 'tartan' athletics track.) Arts department – the Sewell Centre – continues to produce some amazing work, and art is taken seriously at exam level. CCF compulsory at 14 until proficiency test is taken.

Background and Atmosphere: Green and pleasant site – even Turner was moved to paint it in his youth – lots of mellow red brick (1720) and Victorian Gothic, overlooks the school's golf course, lake, games fields and pavilion. 800 acres of prime Oxfordshire, totally self-contained and away from the rest of the world. School founded 1847 on Oxford college model – with cloisters, quads, 'dons' (masters), shortish black gowns. Idea of founders (the Revs William Sewell, don at Exeter College, and Robert Corbet Singleton) was to give boys an aesthetic education (some may laugh hollowly) and school is blessed with wonderful collection of furniture. Warden's house listed (NB Warden and Common Room tucked away from the coal face). Old-fashioned dining hall though school has succumbed to canteen feeding (institutional fare). New library – a converted medieval barn – great improvement. Clock tower a meeting point. Sixth formers have much pride in 'JCR' (bar, but rhyming unintentional) in basement – in what was a cosy black hole, but now sadly refurbished. Brilliant tuck-shop at which all boys have what is aptly called a 'jam account' – bacon butties at all hours. Jolly red theme to school and uniform, though pupils allowed to wear any sensible dark jacket and shirt – status marked by type of tie. The school still feels slightly inward-looking and its strength and current status is a source of amazement to some other schools, not to mention some ORs. John Murray has recently published a history of Radley College by OB Christopher Hibbert – worth a browse, though not cheap.

Pastoral Care and Discipline: Complicated hierarchy of 'stigs' (new boys) – each with a 'nanny' – to 'pups' (prefects – from stat pup?- warden not sure). Housemasters ('tutors') preside over 'Socials' – houses, eg Social A, Social B (traditionally the gamesy houses); Social E has been popular. Warden says 'houses now equally popular with no particular bias towards games etc in any.' Staff lean on 'pups', who have intricate privileges in exchange for their responsibilities. There is compulsory evensong four nights a week. 95 per cent of staff live on the campus in school accommodation – brilliant for packing in the talent. Staff, young, new and old, have annual 'MOT', one-to-one meetings with head at which they can air grievances/produce ideas etc.

Pupils and Parents: Pupils a very homogenised British middle-class lot. Very English – not much room for anyone else, given intake policy and success. Still few foreign pupils here (they tend to turn up too late). ORs include Andrew Motion, Sir Richard Wilson (Cabinet Secretary), Ted Dexter, former world rackets champion James Male.

Entrance: Still largely on a first come, first served principle, which explains why lists have been consistently full for years ahead. So – name down asap still. However, the warden has introduced a 'Warden's List' here of up to 10 places nominated by prep school headmasters which he can dole out to deserving late arrivals. Note the weedy little pictureless prospectus – status symbol.

Exit: On to the usual universities. ORs then go on to be headmasters, Servicemen, one or two barristers, one or two art dealers, 'general management'.

Money Matters: One 'Silk' bursary at sixth form (named after a previous warden) on money raised. Five instrumental music scholarships and several exhibitions, also bursaries for needy. Two art scholarships, up to 12 academic scholarships and exhibitions, and three Thompson scholarships for

all-rounders. Two sports scholarships. Sold art works bequeathed by the Vestey family to produce money for a contemporary collection.

Remarks: Outstanding public school which has had a long innings as one of the most popular boarding schools in the country. Now very much in the first division though 'I can't understand it,' said a (very) Old Boy, 'in my day it was very much a second division affair'. Old boys report that there is still a slight pressure to conform. Continuing satisfied reports from parents.

RANNOCH SCHOOL

Rannoch, Perthshire PH17 2QQ

Tel: *01882 632332* Fax: *01882 632443*

E-mail: headmaster@rannoch.co.uk

Web: www.rannoch.co.uk

✦ Pupils: Around 113 boys, 68 girls. Plus Junior School with 12 boys and 12 girls
✦ Ages: 13-18, juniors 10-13 ✦ Size of sixth form: 60 ✦ Non-denom
✦ Fee-paying

Head: Since 1997, Dr John Halliday BA, PhD (forties). Educated at Abingdon School, followed by Exeter and Cambridge where he read German and Linguistics. Previously housemaster at Sedbergh and before that he taught at Merchiston. A linguist, he currently teaches five lessons a week in German. Elusive, lots of meetings all over, but sympathetic and utterly charming when you do eventually get together.

Academic Matters: Very small classes, and occasionally reaps spectacular results with even the most unpromising of its pupils. Pass rate in maths good, but otherwise fairly mediocre, 34 As, 41Bs and 50 Cs against 50 failures at Higher last year, 39 candidates, 175 exams. Retakes the norm, no shame here, have as many attempts as you like. Recent appointments include a new head of chemistry and extra maths staff.

The school has a reputation for employing gifted if unorthodox teachers, most of whom have serious outdoor skills. Parents have commented recently that some staff are not 'challenged enough' and inclined to be too cosy in this isolated spot, and school did admit that it could be 'rather insular down the valley, which is why we maintain so many international links'. School still stresses 'the outdoor image'. Holistic approach to education, with excellent professional learning support and extra staff for English and maths; scribes and dictating machines for exams. Up to 75 SEN children, many of whom are statemented and many of whom are paid for by their local LEAs. Two qualified EFL teachers plus several part timers. Majority of school follow the Scottish system, but A levels 'on demand'. Lap tops on the ascendancy, good computer rooms and whole school communicates via e-mail.

Half or whole term exchanges with France, Germany, Australia, Canada, and India, you name it – a Round Square school.

Games, Options, the Arts: Tends to be wild and woolly – the kit list includes a rucksack as well as a winter-weight sleeping bag; Lots of 'teenult' activity, high ropes, water sports plus mainstream games, also skiing and 9 hole golf course. D of E award scheme plays a prominent part in school activities with oodles of pupils getting gold, and D of E award winners listed on smart honours board in main dining room, ie where other schools might put academic honours. The six hundredth gold D of E award achieved in May 2000 – the five hundredth was only five years ago; that's twenty a year and no mean feat. Head very proud of the High Ropes Course, 'an extraordinary construction some forty feet off the ground incorporating ladders and walkways'. Rannoch is the second school in the UK and the first in Scotland to be awarded an Adventurous Activity Licence, which allows the school to lease the facility to other schools (Kelvinside Academy and Blundell's to name but two). Rannoch mini-marathon is run each year.

True to Kurt Hahn's principles, community service plays an integral part of school life; fire fighting, mountain rescue, ambulance service, loch patrol as well as granny bashing and helping the Forestry Commission with their Blackwood Conservation project. There is also a building service, with pupils helping to renovate the beautiful chapel and music complex converted from outbuildings. Recent service projects (expensive for the pupil) include building work in India, Kenya and Tanzania and ecological projects in Hungary. Enthusiastic art and magical music, with almost half the pupils learning an instrument – broad church, everything from trad to bagpipes. Choir justly famous, regular tours and telly appearances. Ceilidh on Saturday evenings, but really just Scottish 'lip service'. No debating society.

Background and Atmosphere: Founded in 1959 by A J S Greig and two teaching colleagues from Gordonstoun. Wonderful Highland setting, but lousy wiggly roads with passing places make Rannoch quite a hike from civilisation, and the roads on the loch side from Kinloch Rannoch are even worse. Rannoch folklore stories of hand-to-hand chains to get bread to school in bad snow conditions are not that far fetched. The midges in summer are vile, but the views fantastic. Magical turreted castle in 120 acre estate, recently refurbished with massive grant from Historic Scotland, now water tight and inside up to scratch with a refurbished dining hall, boys' house, new careers department, new classrooms, fitness centre and staffroom. The staff themselves have been kicked into line, and no longer float around the school in trad hiking gear. School turns into an Adventure Centre in the holidays.

Pastoral Care and Discipline: All staff as shepherds, plus tutors as academic watchdogs. Recent double expulsion for drugs, otherwise main problems booze and fags: 'but you must never be complacent'. 'Less binge drinking' 'always concerned,' 'we have to sit up with them, and matron is not very sympathetic' – suspension nonetheless. Fags = fine and gating and letters to parents plus PD (punishment drill) which includes working in the grounds, alternatively physical exercise and wearing uniform, not home clothes at weekends is found to be effective.

Pupils and Parents: Sixty per cent from Scotland, but an increasing number from Europe, particularly Germany, sometimes they come for a term or two, but often for a couple of years, and integrate properly. One or two from Africa. One or two on Ritalin, one or two refugees from the state system and the snobbier end of the private school system – children who have failed to thrive elsewhere for all sorts of reasons. Around 80 per cent first time buyers. Popular with hoteliers, farmers, and busi-

ness people alike. Happy self confident children, relaxed, robust and energetic.

Entrance: To Junior School by interview and report from primary schools, at 13 via CE 'where appropriate', otherwise 'satisfactory school report and interview'. Children with very low IQs not accepted.

Exit: About 80 per cent to some form of university or further education. Certain number go straight into business, farming or further retakes.

Money Matters: Very good value. Fees well below equivalent of southern schools, several academic awards of 50 per cent, sympathetic in cases of job losses; and help can be given through Schiehallion Trust.

Remarks: Very good at what it does well, not really for your academic high flyers but perfect for the non-academic and those needing learning support – but go easy on your wilting urban flower. Popular with parents and children, and no longer regarded as the place for daft Scots.

REPTON SCHOOL

Repton, Derbyshire DE6 6FH

Tel: *01283 559222* Fax: *01283 559223*

E-mail: boss@repton.org.uk

Web: www.repton.org.uk

✦ Pupils: 530: 335 boys, 195 girls; 360 board, 170 day. Plus prep school 'Foremarke Hall' ✦ Ages: 13-18 ✦ Size of sixth form: 254 ✦ C of E (other faiths welcome) ✦ Fee-paying

Head: Since 1987, Mr Graham Jones, MA (mid fifties), educated at Birkenhead and Fitzwilliam, Cambridge, where he read economics. Teaches a third timetable (more than most), 'that's what it's all about'. Former pupil of his recently described him on radio as 'an inspirational economics teacher'. A good manager, enthusiastic, humorous. Married, no children. Previously taught and was housemaster at Charterhouse.

Academic Matters: Broad intake, with five sets for most subjects. Classics has had a bit of a 'renaissance' led by bright young staff. Traditional teaching. IT centre; all pupils have their own E-mail address and free access to the Internet. Very fine library in the Old Priory building, though the most ancient and valuable tomes are kept locked away. Modern languages are taught almost entirely in the native tongue. Sciences examined singly or as dual award at GCSE. All will take four or more ASs, and general studies on top. Fairly broad programme of options available to sixth form; those on

PSHE, relationships and study skills are the only ones which are compulsory. Recent additions to curriculum: business studies, PE, theatre studies and Spanish – these are designed to provide 'more accessible options to the less able pupil'. One qualified member of staff helps pupils with dyslexia; school also draws on the Derby Dyslexia Institute as necessary. All dyslexics study French at GCSE.

Games, Options, the Arts: Outstanding tennis school (recommended to tennis-mad parents by the LTA). Tennis is played all the year round outdoors and indoors (two indoor courts). Regularly wins inter-school tennis championships. Fine cricket record, (has produced astonishing numbers of test cricketers), strong football and hockey; girls sports well established and successful. Daily games. Huge indoor sports hall, and Astroturf pitch (three in all – one floodlit). Vast indoor swimming pool. CCF compulsory for all for a time; big Duke of Edinburgh take-up. Unusual and good art (with artists in residence). Good music tradition – ambitious chorally and orchestrally, always one or two outstanding players in the school, generous with scholarships. House drama is enthusiastic and ambitious. IT being beefed up.

Background and Atmosphere: On the banks of the River Trent. Very much a part of the village and proud of it, with houses, art department etc, spread hither and thither. 'We feel part of life,' commented a boy. 'Less of an ivory tower atmosphere,' said a master. Founded under the will of Sir John Port, who died in 1557. A Bloody Mary Foundation, with a long and interesting history dating back to the medieval monastery, still at the heart of the buildings. Attractive rugged pinkish stone, and mellow. Repton went fully co-ed in '91, but 'of course,' said head, 'there have been girls in the sixth form since the late '70s: we ran training days for staff, but they didn't really need it' – a view not necessarily shared. Boy/girl ratio now around its targeted 2:1. 'But we're happy to settle where the market demands it,' says the head realistically. Girls' boarding houses extremely well designed (have won prizes), centred around a courtyard, a walk-through common room (prevents cliques, good for the shy). Girls' bedrooms 'where they can make nests', as suggested by Miss Lancaster, ex-head of Wycombe and an ex-governor of the school. Boys' houses vary in their sleeping and working arrangements; most boarders in study bedrooms, but some small dormitories. Some houses have mixed-aged studies (can span the entire age range, a fairly unusual arrangement – 'It's good,' confirmed a boy, 'you don't muck about so much, olders can help youngers with work and you get to know people outside your own age'). A very house-ori-entated school, and one of the few where pupils still eat in their houses.

Pastoral Care and Discipline: Strong lines laid down, by and large adhered to. Gating for two weeks for smoking (on second/third offence). Instant out and no quarter shown for drugs. Good staff-pupil also staff-parent links. 'We're treated as human beings,' commented a boy. Three exeats (chosen by parents) and half term each term. Many local pupils go home reg-ularly on Sundays, but sixth formers often stay in school.

Pupils and Parents: Largely middle-of-the-road, middle class (lots of muck and brass, according to a member of staff), from the big industrial conurbations of Sheffield, Leeds, Bradford, Doncaster and Manchester. Day pupils stay till 9 pm most nights. Unspoilt, conservative and pleasant

pupils, relatively unsophisticated. 56 over-seas pupils (most Hong Kong and other Chinese, also Korean, German, Thai and Russian).

Entrance: 40 per cent from own prep, Foremarke Hall (nearby, co-ed since early '70s, and NB pupils go on to a diversity of schools). The rest from a large number of prep schools. Current qualifications to enter sixth: five GCSEs at grade C plus and Bs in A level subjects (about 97 per cent of Reptonians already in the school qualify); external candidates – entrance test.

Exit: 95 per cent to higher education. Mainly to northern universities, old and new. A steady 10 per cent to Oxbridge. Several to art foundation courses. Conservative choice of subjects and ulti-mately professions.

Money Matters: Unspecified number of academic scholarships, worth between 50 per cent and 20 per cent of the fees; some exhibitions worth 10 per cent of the fees.

Remarks: Pleasant low-profile boarding school with a lot going for it. Still feels like a boys' school with some girls – free from the ivory-tower syndrome.

ROBERT GORDON'S

COLLEGE

Schoolhill, Aberdeen AB10 1FE

TEL: *01224 646 346* FAX: *01224 630 301*

E-MAIL: b.lockhart@rgc.aberdeen.sch.uk

WEB: www.rgc.aberdeen.sch.uk

✦ PUPILS: 1423 boys and girls (63/37 split), also nursery 39 boys and girls ✦ Ages: 5-18, nursery 3-5 ✦ Size of sixth form: 300 ✦ Inter-denom ✦ Fee-paying

---

Head: Since 1996, Mr Brian R W Lockhart MA DipEd (fifties) who was educated at Leith Academy and George Heriots in Edinburgh, followed by Aberdeen University and previously taught history at Heriots. Married, he comes to Robert Gordons after 14 years as depute head of Glasgow High School, and talks faster than any headmaster we have ever interviewed.

Strong supporter of the girls, who came in 1989, he has prettied up this fairly bleak site (rose beds, benches, 'made the playground a more pleasant place' and about to revamp the entrance foyer of the Auld Hoose – automatic glass doors within the William Adam exterior (can't do too much because of Historic Scotland). Appointed lots of new young staff (not too much paying-off, turn-over and retirement) but demands 'a lot of them', though not in the first year or so, then 'they are expected to pull their weight extracurricularly'. Obviously enjoys the job, enjoys the school. Very competent and efficient.

Academic Matters: Refuses to publish its detailed examination results, claiming that they are all wonderful so there's nothing worth seeing – a rare attitude these days, and not parent friendly. Unashamedly academic, with over 90 per cent consistently getting A-C for Highers over the last five years which also produced standard grade results 1-3 of anything between 98/99.7 per cent and credits in the nineties. Follows the Scottish system, traditionally v strong on maths and sciences, but drama now timetabled and gentler feel all round. Head vocal about the new Standard/Higher/ Higher Still invasion, looks forward to pupils with Higher Stills escaping the first year of (Scottish) universities and going straight into second year. Five Highers the norm after fifth year (lower sixth) and masses of add-ons in sixth form: philosophy, psychology, entrepreneurship (in conjunction with Robert Gordon's University which shares the campus) plus pre-med courses, Scots law course. An educational triumvirate with Aberdeen University.

ICT strong and internet connection sourced through the University (ie = free), computers throughout, from nursery up, with banks of PCs on hand for sixth form in their free time. E-mail for all. Eight parallel classes throughout, max 22, two classes of mixed ability in each of the four houses, French for all, Latin for all, Greek for the bright. Set at 12 for English, but otherwise 'continuous assessment'. German a popular option with Italian on hand. Spectacular biology room groaning under the weight of various heads and skulls of horned beasties.

Learning support in primary with follow up to secondary level, can and do provide help at all times.

Games, Options, the Arts: Fairly pedestrian art school at the top of one of the many wings; variety of disciplines, but nothing to make your heart stop. Drama now timetabled and a standard grade subject, good and thriving.

Magnificent 45 acre sports ground at Countesswells with artificial pitches for tennis/hockey, cricket and rugby strong, plus hockey, golf. Internationalists in all disciplines. Well used swimming pool (water polo, canoeing) on site under the aegis of former European and Commonwealth FP Ian Black, who is head of the Junior School. Two gyms.

Music department recently refurbished, masses of instruments on offer, seriously impressive recent concert to celebrate school's 250th birthday, with specially composed music, featured the Robert Gordon's College Anniversary Choir and Orchestra. Enormous (brass) oompah band of over 200, plus pipe band, part of the CCF (army and RAF sections only). Hugely popular D of E, with 138 basic and 28 gold in 2000 – a credit by any standards. Impressive 30 page paper – complete with ads – regularly professionally produced and printed in school. Zillions of clubs and societies.

Background and Atmosphere: 'Robert Gordon was born in Aberdeen in 1688, he spent most of his life as a merchant in the Baltic ports, building a significant fortune in the process. He had always had the idea of building a Hospital for maintenance, aliment, entertainment and education of young boys, and when he died in 1731, that was his legacy'. Magnificent William Adam quadrangle in the centre of Aberdeen, now shared with Robert Gordon's University. The school occupies the northern side, with masses of modern add-ons behind a fabulous front, with the Governors' Room and the head's suite occupying visibly W Adam areas (with two somewhat neglected Ramsay portraits at the top of the stairs). The first incumbents however, were not local boys, but Hanoverian troops under the Duke of Cumberland on their way to Culloden; the first 14 boys did not take up residence until 1750. The Hospital became Robert Gordon's College in 1881, went co-ed in 1989, and added a nursery unit in 1993 (popular after school club for nursery and junior pupils until 5.30 each day, where they can either play or do supervised homework). Masses of rather uninspired and totally familiar education add-ons behind the spectacular facade, with dedicated (and rather complicated) floors for each discipline. New library under construction when we visited.

Sixth former who help with school meals are spared paying for lunch, though from 16 onwards they can (and most do) go into the town for food., Girls wear rather jolly Dress Gordon kilted skirts.

Pastoral Care and Discipline: House system recently reinforced, with monitors at all levels plus sixth form assistants at 11 to help those newly arrived in the senior school feel more at home. Guidance system in operation = tutors, as well as good PSE. Sin 'par for the course'; 'very little bullying, and come down on them like a ton of bricks', expelled for drugs (one or two instances, but 'not a problem'), suspended for booze, 'not a lot of smoking', campus too small and 'it's a bit obvious out of school'.

Pupils and Parents: This is the school in Aberdeen. Lots of university parents (easy to drop off), oodles of professional and oil-related ditto, plus farmers etc. Day starts early at 8.30 and children often come from as far away as Montrose ie 35/40 miles away. Parking at drop off and collection times hideous. Good PT newsletter and parental involvement.

Entrance: Interview for nursery and five year olds entering Junior School; test for those over nine and exam for senior school. Pupils either come up from primary school, or from local state schools, hugely oversubscribed. Rather jolly in-house instruction manual for S1s (ie first year senior school).

Exit: Coming and going with relocation, otherwise (93 per cent) to universities all over, the odd gap year, 'few don't go to university'. Edinburgh popular also RGU, Aberdeen, Glasgow '12 or so' down south and a trickle to Oxbridge.

Money Matters: Huge number of endowments – Robert Gordon's expectation that 'those who came to the Hospital and did well in later life would plough back some of their gains'. In 1816 'a generous bequest by Alexander Simpson of Collyhill made it possible to extend the accommodation' and Gordonians and FPs have continued to do so ever since. 250 children on some form of bursary, with 100 per cent help available to those in real need with bright kids. Plus The Aberdeen Educational Endowment which takes up slack left by the demolition of the Assisted Places scheme.

Remarks: Very strong co-ed day school. Some of the fabric of the building needs more than a little help, but if you want to keep the little darlings at home, and you live near enough, you couldn't do better. Not a school for social climbers and probably rather intimidating for shrinking violets.

ROEDEAN SCHOOL

Roedean Way, Brighton, East Sussex
BN2 5RQ

TEL: *01273 603181, Registry 01273 667626*

FAX: *01273 676722, Registry 01273 680791*

E-MAIL: admissions@roedean.co.uk

WEB: www.roedean.co.uk

♦ PUPILS: 430 girls, all board except for 40
♦ Ages: 11-18 ♦ Size of sixth form: 190
♦ C of E, but other faiths also ♦ Fee-paying

Head: Since 1997, Mrs Patricia Metham, (fifties), BA JP. Educated at Upper Chine School, Isle of Wight and Bristol University where she read English and drama. Has taught all over the country. Previous post was as head of Ashford School. Likes theatre (and has written plays), singing, travel (to places of cultural and archaeological interest), good food, good wine. Teaches some drama. Direct, hugely energetic. Loves the zany approach and projects e.g. writing an Agatha Christie spoof Murder Mystery to educate and entertain potential new girls, in practice a hands-on science project in disguise (girls mix chemicals to diagnose blood types for suspects etc). Busy involving the school with the local community eg running courses for specially gifted children – pupils, parents and staff from 8 schools have been engaged in a range of activities linked to the life and works of Galileo. Called 'Madam' by the girls, as are all the female staff. Married to Dr Tim Metham, arts and science development officer at Sussex University.

Academic Matters: Best ever A level results in '00, super results – 77 per cent A and B grades (by the way with 81 candidates); 24 girls notched up 3, 4 or 5 A grades. Maths the favourite subject, with 28 out of 41 getting A grades. Eng. Lit. and all the sciences produce pleasing results. Sciences are finely taught, terrific facilities). David Fisher, head of physics, is a new appointment (ex state system), who re-organised the curriculum for 13 year olds (out went sound and waves, in came stress, strains, the mathematics of friction, the chemistry of batteries etc) so that girls could take up the Green Car Challenge, held at Goodwood, where they took part as drivers and mechanics in the electrically powered racing car they had built (maximum speed: 20 mph, single motor, rechargeable battery), a Formula One look. Careers department building up impressively. Lively French and Spanish reading competitions. Maths (and soon classics) courses at the university for those that can cope.

Games, Options, the Arts: Stunning art – exceptionally well taught, sophisticated, accomplished, thought through. Games as beefy and strong as ever, with everyone taking part. Masses of pitches and courts. Famous for cricket, lacrosse recently mooted for the chop but the girls wrote in protest producing formidably strong arguments for keeping it (stating, amongst other things, that it teaches discipline) so it has been re-instated, and the girls knock the opposition for six. Music hotted up under the inspiring Paul Brough (ex lecturer King's College, London, organist at Tewkesbury Abbey). Keen D of E (14 golds a the last count, and this has been far higher). Fabulously professional Design Technology, some with a Young Enterprise approach i.e. pupils decide what to make and market, so maths and company business also come in to play. Keen drama and dance, both flourishing.

Background and Atmosphere: Bracing sea air blows up the cliffs to forbidding pebble-dashed buildings, set in 40 acres, 3 miles from the centre of Brighton. Founded in 1885 by the Misses Lawrence, modelled on a boys' public school – functional, structured, traditional – though definitely more user-friendly since our last visit. Inspiration of many a popular ditty, eg 'We are good girls, good girls are we. We take pride in our virginity...' Good facilities for everything, large numbers of computers, an impressive arts complex. Sixth Form now in Keswick House – a separate building, previously home to the youngest year, and a huge success for the top end of the school who have a new sense of self contained independence (long mirrors on landings – unique?). The youngest are now in the main body of the school, which, said a housemistress, 'means they are part of the family, and it's far easier for them to fit in.' Four dining rooms, four main houses, (each year group has its own common room per house), deeply competitive, food good. Houses being upgraded (again), but do not necessarily expect a basin in a bedroom. Good number of male staff (including the deputy head, Mr Farmer, who has been here 29 years and is still enthusiastic). No Saturday morning school, compulsory 'options' instead. Ambitious reading scheme – a book a week, managed by most.

Pastoral Care and Discipline: Firmly in place – very much undertaken on the basis of team work, with good individual care. Watchful staff. Flexible weekend arrangements, with families often scooping up children on Saturday afternoons (post match) and coming back some time on Sunday.

Older girls taxi to Brighton, and the marina is near enough to walk, with cinema, restaurants, a pub. School officers recently introduced – powerful young women (ie pupils) involved in school management.

Pupils and Parents: Remarkably confident, outward-looking, articulate girls. Very much an English boarding school – though there are now 38 per cent of pupils from overseas, including some ex-pats (Roedean fostered links with the wide world from its inception). Particularly popular with girls from Thailand, Nigeria, Russia – but no concentration of any one nationality in any one house and no places awarded to non-nationals without an interview first. Old Girls include Baroness Chalker, Sally Oppenheimer MP, Verity Lambert, Dame Cecily Saunders, founder of the Hospice movement, and a budding actress or two.

Entrance: The brightest – also the not so bright, though these girls may have to leave after GCSEs for a lesser establishment. At 11+, 12+ and 13+. Big (at least 30) new intake at 16 – the school is intentionally top heavy, must have six GCSEs in grades A*-B.

Exit: To all the top universities – UCL, Imperial College, King's particularly popular. Some to Oxbridge, a few to drama or art school. Medical studies are particularly popular. High powered careers follow.

Money Matters: About 6 per cent of fee income goes towards scholarships; about 35 per cent scholars/exhibitioners (up to 50 per cent of fees) in the school at one time, including music scholars. Plus bursaries – good at lending a hand in hard times.

Remarks: Powerful girls' public school under strong leadership, fosters intellectual curiosity and is fun. More user friendly than before, but not a school for the faint hearted.

ROSSALL SCHOOL
Fleetwood, Lancashire, FY7 8JW

Tel: *01253 774247* Fax: *01253 774247*

E-mail: rrhodeshmrossall@compuserve.com

Web: www.rossall.co.uk

♦ Pupils: 415: 175 boarding, 240 day; about 40:60 girls:boys. Plus 140 in prep school (a few board), 130 in pre-prep, and 55 in the Lugard International Study Centre ♦ Ages: 11-18, 7-11 in prep, 2-7 in pre-prep, 10-18 LISS ♦ Size of sixth form: 125 ♦ C of E ♦ Fee-paying

Head: Principal of Rossall Schools: Since 1987, Mr Richard D W Rhodes (fifties) BA JP. Educated at Rossall, and Durham. A historian; taught at St John's Leatherhead, and was head of Arnold School, Blackpool before coming here. Photographer, lake-district gardener, JP (juvenile and youth court). Tall, down-to-earth, comfortable to be with, married with two daughters.
Headmaster of the Senior School: Since 2000, Mr Simon Pengelley (forties). Educated at Repton and Bristol; a historian. Deputy head of Rossall from 1992, and before that at Abingdon and Strathallan. Married, with three sons at the school.

Academic Matters: Hard work. Acceptable results overall at GCSE and A level given the unselective nature of the intake, but improvements have taken place and more seem possible. Inspiring English. Some good language teaching. From '98 the IB has been offered as an alternative to A levels: about 50 pupils take it. Special needs support taken seriously, but not equipped to deal with very difficult cases. All take CITC.

Successfully set up ('93) The Lugard International Study Centre, for overseas students from Hong Kong and elsewhere, who come in often with only a few words of English and are given intensive English language courses followed in many cases by IGCSE or transfer to the main school. Good news, and the accommodation, though not exactly ritzy, is reasonably comfortable.

Games, Options, the Arts: Beefy games, and famous for Rossall hockey – played on the beach and extremely popular (only possible thrice a fortnight, owing to tides). Impressive, enthusiastic head of CDT (who doubles up as head of maintenance) – CDT rooms being thoroughly overhauled when we visited. Art energetically taught and exciting. Keen CCF (Army and Navy) – including girls. Strong music with professional and school concerts. Careers room locked at lunch when we visited. School has its own outward-bound award – the Rossall Award – which all pupils do.

Background and Atmosphere: Founded in 1844 on the windswept muddy coast of the Fylde, an easy tram-ride away from Blackpool. Looks like a hotel at first sight – low lights along a winding tarmac drive – then opens up into Oxford-type quad, with a mound in the middle and chapel to one side. Very fresh, very healthy sea air. Mellow redbrick buildings grouped on large site now circumscribed by housing development; pleasant enough. Boarding houses (flexi-boarding) were horrendous – wind whistled in, bosomy pictures peeling from the walls, in need of painting etc – even the pupils noticed it, a bit – -but it's all being refurbished now. Time-honoured names, though – Pelican, Rose, Mitre Fleur de Lys

etc. Sixth form centre with bar popular with boarders and day pupils alike. Religion of no great importance (according to pupils): many find chapel a bore. Food traditional stodge (but salad option).

Pastoral Care and Discipline: Strong anti-bullying. Not a druggy school. Head has commented that the foreign pupils 'often set our boys and girls very fine examples...'

Pupils and Parents: Now principally a local school. Parents are farmers, businessmen. A few Services' children. Over 50 per cent first-time buyers – a long tradition here. 20 per cent ex-pats. Chirpy children. School awash with inscrutable faces – the overseas contingent (from Germany, Central and Eastern Europe, Asia, the Gulf and South America) mix well. OBs seem to gravitate to business, the services and the professions; (Very) OBs include Leslie Charteris (creator of 'The Saint'), Patrick Campbell, David Brown (of Aston Martin fame), Sir Thomas Beecham.

Entrance: 'Flexible': not a problem. All pupils assessed on entrance for dyslexia.

Exit: 95 per cent to a wide spread of universities.

Money Matters: Had 34 assisted places at last count, and these will be missed. Currently half a dozen or so half-fees academic scholarships, and a couple (one academic, one all-rounder) whose terms require that the holders receive the full Monty.

Remarks: A once traditional public school that had a difficult few years in the '90s but re-emerged as a day school plus boarding and an outstandingly successful international study centre. Pupil numbers (day and boarding) rising steadily; growing signs of prosperity and success.

THE ROYAL GRAMMAR SCHOOL

High Street, Guildford GU1 3BB

TEL: *01483 880 600*

FAX: *01483 800 602 or 306 127*

E-MAIL: bwright@mail.rgs-guildford.co.uk

WEB: www.rgs-guildford.co.uk

✦ PUPILS: 840 boys; all day ✦ Ages: 11-18
✦ Size of sixth form: 250 ✦ Non-denom
✦ Fee-paying

Head: Since 1992, Mr Tim Young, MA (late forties). Educated at Eton and Cambridge, where he read history. Previously a housemaster at Eton; has taught in California and New Zealand. Charming. High-powered wife (consultant radiologist), two children.

Academic Matters: Outstanding teaching, and good results, as you would expect from the high calibre of pupil. Rigorous standards, many staff of long standing, and high expectations all round, with boys buckling down to hard work: the grammar school ethos in action. Maths and sciences are traditionally the strongest subjects, and substantially more boys take science rather than arts at A level. Maths the most popular subject at A level currently, followed by physics. Economics also keen and well taught. One member of staff trained in special needs, and all new boys given diagnostic test in their first month; 'We only admit dyslexics if we are confident they will thrive.'

Games, Options, the Arts: Sports also taken seriously (playing fields are two miles away), and this is Bob Willis's old school. Current cricketing coach – Monte Lynch (played for Surrey). Sailing club is still very successful, and shooting is, currently, even better. Nice little drama studio. Car maintenance, drama productions, not to mention ballroom dancing (with local girls' school) and bachelor cooking on offer. Two thirds of the boys do CCF and/or D of E

Background and Atmosphere: School founded in 1509 in the centre of Guildford. Main teaching block is bang on the main road, a faceless and dreary '60s hulk, to which a science and technology block, among other things, have been added. Across the road is the delightful tall white ancient original building now used by the sixth form, music and careers. Breakfast service for early beavers – sausage rolls etc.

Pastoral Care and Discipline: Boys' development well taken care of. Head gives parents guidelines (not so easy; Guildford is not un-druggy), and keen on good citizenship. On the whole, boys make 'active and purposeful use of their time'.

Pupils and Parents: The brightest and best, academically speaking, in the area. Parents are middle class and stockbroker belt-ish. Ambitious, and 'take their children's education and upbringing seriously'.

Entrance: CE: a tough 65 per cent required. Hot hot competition. Many come in from the prep department, and from the state sector. For entrance to sixth form: As at GCSE in A level subjects, plus some 'respectable supporting grades'.

Exit: 20-30 a year to Oxbridge – and this is a genuine figure.

Remarks: Strong straight up and down boys' grammar school, which happily whips in the brightest 10 per cent from its juicy catchment area and, on the whole, does them proud.

JUNIOR SCHOOL: Prep Department: Lanesborough School. Tel: 01483 880 650, Fax: 01483 880 651. Head: Mr Keith Crombie. Around 350 boys, all day. Ages 4-13. No automatic entry to the senior school. Edwardian house plus many extensions set on the green north east edge of Guildford. Lively and traditional; also acts as choir school for the Cathedral − v good choir, and music excellent.

ROYAL GRAMMAR SCHOOL

High Wycombe, Buckinghamshire

HP13 6QT

TEL: *01494 524955* FAX: *01494 551 410*

E-MAIL: admin.staff@royalgrammar.bucks.sch.uk

WEB: www.royalgrammar.bucks.sch.uk

✦ PUPILS: 1365 boys, all day except for 70 boarders ✦ Ages: 11-18 ✦ Size of sixth form: 450 ✦ Christian foundation ✦ State

Head: Since April, 1999 Mr Tim Dingle BSc MBA PGCE (early forties). A chorister at King's Cambridge, then The Perse and read biology at East Anglia. Taught biology at Mill Hill, rising to become deputy head in 1995. While at Mill Hill he undertook research into rheumatism, a study of European schools, and an MBA in education (from Westminster); he helped run the CCF, taught climbing, sailing and windsurfing, and was in charge of rugby (he is an England selector). Hobbies include art, jazz and motorbikes. One of those who fills the unforgiving minute with ninety seconds worth of distance run. Took over from Mr D R Levin, a fine head and a good manager, who was here from 1993.

Academic Matters: Excellent, without question, particularly given its size; steadily maintaining its position as one of the strongest academic state schools in the country. In '00, three candidates got five As at A level, fifteen got four, and twenty-five got three − by no means an exceptional year. Overall 60 per cent A-Bs. Weakest subjects the less traditional ones − business studies, communication studies etc (possibly being taken by weaker candidates). Maths most popular subject at A level by a very long way − fair number of Ds-Us in this. Wide (30+) choice of AS levels and A2s (25) to choose from. All take eleven plus GCSEs. First batch of lessons stop at 11.40 am for break, 'The last lesson before break can seem very long,' warn the boys. Staff are prepared to give extra tuition where necessary (high praise from parents). Parents comment that the teaching tends to be 'challenging' and 'high standards and high expectations are there from the start.' 'Rigour' and 'attention to detail' are words you often hear within this school. Language notes: designated Language College by the DfEE in '96 and '99 as part of the government's specialist school scheme (sponsoring companies − HSBC Holdings, British Aerospace, Vickers, Rolls Royce). Establishing further links with SE Asia and Europe. Believed to be the first school in Europe to offer Bahasa Malay in the sixth form. Lots of work experience opportunities abroad. Excellent language results, as you would expect.

Games, Options, the Arts: Rugby, hockey,

cricket, golf, rowing, basketball and fencing all especially strong, providing international players, not to mention big turn outs for Saturday afternoon matches. The competitive element reigns, many more wins than losses. Strong drama tradition (several OBs have gone on to become professionals, usually after a spell with the National Youth Theatre), with regular productions with Wycombe High School. Boys keen on managing computerised stage lighting, sound etc. Good music, with loads of concerts and recitals, sometimes linking up with the girls at Wycombe High. Splendid jazz group, which performs professionally and is much in demand locally. Unusual among state schools is the CCF, with all three services. 'It's a good place to find army chaps,' say the professionals who visit schools looking for future soldiers. Debating, chess, photography and wide variety of clubs which boys 'get very keen about'. Regular lunch-time talks from prominent personalities – eg Jeremy Paxman, Andy McNab.

Background and Atmosphere: Twenty-two acre site north of High Wycombe (which it has occupied since 1914). The main block is pleasant purpose-built red-brick Queen Anne style, plus many plain later additions built around the quadrangle. Most recent additions are the library (on the small side?), the sports hall, some teaching blocks and the boarding house. Highly organised, orderly atmosphere, notice boards everywhere, spick and span (bar the odd crisp bag/carton), positive sense of keen competition but certainly not unpleasantly so: chaps have time to enjoy life too and are friendly.

Pastoral Care and Discipline: Manners and courtesies taught and expected. Very strong emphasis on self-discipline and self-

sufficiency, and not much infringement. Parents comment on quick access to staff when necessary.

Pupils and Parents: Mainly sons of middle class professionals, a great many of whom have moved to be close to the school (and expensive housing area, so parents are often 'paying mortgages, not school fees,' said the head). Boys are polite, tidy and civilised. Old Wycombiensians include Professors Roger Scruton, Michael Zander, Denis Stevens; Richard Hickox, Howard Jones, Sir Peter Fry, Lord McIntosh of Haringay, judges, MPs, Concorde pilots.

Entrance: At 11+, admission carried out in conjunction with Bucks County Council (182 day places each year, Tel 01296 395000 for further inf; and 10 boarding places, contact school), and heavily oversubscribed, with priority going to boys living within the 'reserved' area. Very selective: takes the top 30 per cent of the ability range. Tests, interviews, report/letter from previous school. 40 per cent come here from fee-paying prep schools. Around 25-30 pupils come in at sixth form, qualifications – interview, previous school reference, and 'achievement' in GCSE in relevant subjects.

Exit: 98 per cent of boys go on to university (a gap year is popular beforehand), around 23-25 to Oxbridge each year, 12-ish to medical schools.

Money Matters: Head works extremely hard, pressing 'all sorts of organisations to secure backing for our various new ideas'. Cost of boarding realistically related to food and accommodation (family feel, renewed in '99 to include ensuite bathing, IT and telephones in every room) – £2400 per term.

Remarks: Outstanding state school (don't

just take our word for it – Ofsted awarded the school 'outstanding' status in '96), strong in all it undertakes, under a five star head. Feels just like a public school, and run along similar lines.

ROYAL GRAMMAR SCHOOL

Eskdale Terrace, Newcastle upon Tyne
NE2 4DX

TEL: *0191 281 5711* FAX: *0191 212 0392*

E-MAIL: admissions@rgs.newcastle.sch.uk

WEB: www.rgs.newcastle.sch.uk

✦ PUPILS: 925 boys. Plus junior school with 140 boys. All day. ✦ Ages: 11-18, juniors 8-10 ✦ Size of sixth form: 270 ✦ Non-denominational ✦ Fee-paying

Head: Since 1994, Mr James Miller MA (fifties), educated at Douai and Merton College, Oxford, where he read classical mods followed by PPE. Previously head of Framlingham and before that a housemaster at Winchester. Economist. Very positive, friendly, infectiously enthusiastic and confident. Sat on HMC academic policy committee. Married (his wife Ruth works with dyslexic children at a local prep school), with two sons who attended the school. Mr Miller's out-going manner is in marked contrast to his predecessor, and one sixth former reflected in mock-nostalgia 'heads should be seen and not heard'. Energetic governors.

Academic Matters: Hard to fault, with sciences particularly popular, especially chemistry, maths and biology; highly successful results. GCSE results a pleasure to see. Boys clock up impressive achievements and prizes nationally in a variety of subjects, at different levels (see the neat little handbook). Sciences have been given a huge boost with the fabulous new science and technology department, with state-of-the-art labs and facilities in a light, bright, really well designed block (cost: £4 million), opened in '97 by Professor Richard Dawkins. Staff to go with it, ie bright and bushy tailed (all ages), 'My teaching hasn't changed' commented one, showing us around the labs, 'but the boys seem to be ten times more interested in their work now. Single subject science for the vast majority. The usual story on classics – small department, very strong, and very well taught. Many staff of very long standing makes for occasional parental grousing and some accusations of the school having a complacent attitude, 'Does complacency matter?' queried a master. Good general studies – non-examinable – programme for sixth formers: breadth matters here. Brand new re-jigging of class sizes to make them smaller – down from 30 to 24 with five/six classes per year group (which accounts, perhaps, for the general trend downwards in overall numbers in recent years?), and time table changed to make shorter lessons with short breaks in between, to take some of the pressure off (in theory). IT overhauled – three new computer rooms, network etc.

Games, Options, the Arts: Keenly sporting, with a large number and variety of sports on offer and well subscribed: strong rugby, and several individuals in national teams, including cricket, rowing, gymnastics, fencing and basketball, though which sports are in the ascendant varies from year to year. Football – for the sixth form only, introduced in '97/8, instigated by boy demand, set up by a new master, and already proving powerful in its matches. Some sport is done on the school's own grounds, and extra sports grounds at the nearby school for the deaf are used, boys run on Town Moor, play squash at the local tennis club. Busy on the extra curricular front with more emphasis on drama (some with Central Newcastle High and Newcastle Church High girls), CCF (also with the girls), thriving debating, Greek play every other year, keen chess club (meets three times a week), bridge club, bee-keeping etc. Flourishing and enthusiastic art department (six-day trip to New York in '97 and '99), music reviving following the departure of some particularly musical boys.

Background and Atmosphere: Busy, noisy, purposeful – the place is thronging with activity at all times. A new management team is now in place, 'It makes a big differ-ence ' commented a father, 'there is now a sense of modern efficiency.' Overall, things are happening here, and the school is more open and outward looking, and works hard at having good relations with the city (eg Saturday science for children at local schools.) £6 million has been spent in the last few years, part of a ten year re-building and re-furbishing plan/spending spree. For the boys, the big excitement, in the pipeline, will be the innovation of the sixth form centre, 'We need it urgently!'. Proud of being an ancient foundation (the school cel-ebrated its 450th anniversary in '95), it is housed in handsome Queen Anne style 1906 redbrick buildings, with some func-tional later additions, spread around the rec-tangle of sports grounds at the back, a cohe-sive whole, against a backdrop of flyovers and the ceaseless gentle hum of traffic. Fine old school hall with pews, organ and honour boards. Lively notice boards everywhere. The Junior School is a pebble's throw away in Lambton Road: boys come over for com-puter studies, science and games.

Pastoral Care and Discipline: Overhauled under Mr Miller's headship, 'and it certainly needed it', growled a father. Closer relations with parents than under the previous long reign, and, to quote one mother, 'It's alto-gether softer, gentler, kinder on the human side.' Vigorous new anti-bullying policy in place, with staff, aware that boys can be 'insensitive and careless', gradually breaking the sub-culture whereby boys never report a problem.

Pupils and Parents: First choice for clever boys from every corner (inner and outer) of Newcastle and Sunderland, Durham and County Durham, and also from far-flung rural corners eg Berwick, Wooler, Alnwick. Broad social mix, rich assortment of dialects, a fairly scruffy bunch who don't always observe the school's dress code. Popular with local bigwigs in industry, the professions, academics from the universities, the Asian community. Closer relations with parents now actively fostered – some like it, some don't. Boys are well aware of being at the strongest school in the area, in the main hard working, keen to succeed and 'don't feel life owes them a living,' observed a master with memories of working in a famous public school further south. Old boys include England winger David Rees, Lord Taylor, Brian Redhead.

Entrance: Tough and competitive, via the school's own entrance exam at 11 and 13. Drop in entry numbers for '98 due to loss of assisted places. Fifty plus from the Junior School (via the year's work, ie if suitable). Around 10-15 extra boys come in at sixth form, almost always from local state schools; very few – if any – leave post GCSE.

Exit: 20+ a year to Oxbridge, and to Newcastle, Leeds, Edinburgh, Manchester, Nottingham and London. Science (especially medicine) and social sciences are popular subjects.

Money Matters: Good value. Some bursaries available (in case of need, up to 100 per cent), though more money desperately needed now that the assisted places have gone (there were 220): old boys and businesses are being tackled on this issue. Now has some Ogden Trust bursaries for 'above-average children from a state primary school of limited or no parental means'.

Remarks: Powerful traditional grammar school, with currently high morale under dynamic headship, and an obvious choice for ambitious locals.

THE ROYAL HIGH SCHOOL

Lansdown Road, Bath, Avon BA1 5SZ

Tel: *01225 313877, 01225 313873*

Fax: *01225 420338, 01225 465446*

E-mail: royalhigh@bat.gdst.net

✦ Pupils: 900, day and boarding, girls only ✦ Ages: 3-18 ✦ C of E ✦ Fee-paying

Head: Since 2000, Mr James Graham-Brown BA MPhil. Read English at Kent and Bristol. Took over from the charismatic Miss Margaret Anne Winfield, much admired and loved former head of Bath High.

Entrance: As selective as poss. At 11 or 13 by school's own exam etc. Also entry at 3/4 into nursery.

Exit: Too soon to tell.

Remarks: Long and painful amalgamation process now complete, to provide what the PR bumph describes as a 'vision becomes reality'. In reality, however, this is the joining of two very different schools – the old Bath High, and The Royal School, founded originally for the orphaned daughters of army officers, and renowned more for its Angela Brazil-type boarding than for its brains. Exam results looking OK so far, with four top-five places at A level – one at biology and three at philosophy. Junior School now located in the old Bath High premises (wonderful mellow old town houses), and the seniors in the old Royal School (altogether much grander, more spacious, lovely old buildings). Too early to comment on new entity, but it is likely to turn into good standard GDST fodder – straight up and down, day academic education.

RUGBY SCHOOL

Rugby, Warwickshire CV22 5EH

Tel: *01788 556 274* Fax: *01788 556 277*

E-mail: registry@rugby-school.warwks.sch.uk

Web: www.rugby-school.warwks.sch.uk

✦ Pupils: 760 in all: 390 boys boarding, 100 day; 190 girls boarding; 80 day ✦ Ages: 11-18 (day pupils only at 11 and 12) ✦ Size of sixth form: 340 ✦ C of E ✦ Fee-paying

Head: Since 1990, Mr M B Mavor CVO MA (v early fifties). Educated at Loretto and Cambridge. Previously head of Gordonstoun (got his gong for supervising the schooling of HRH The Duke of York and HRH Prince Edward – no mean task).

Quite quiet, but beady. Keen fisherman. Wife brought up in Peru, graduate of London University, two children. Outstanding head. Particularly good at public relations. Comments that he has 'encouraged everyone to make Rugby a happy as well as a hard-working school'. Leaving April 2001 to go to Loretto – so there may be a certain lack of momentum for a while.

Academic Matters: Getting better and better, with very good results in many areas – particularly impressive, given mixed-ish intake. The occasional dropped catch at A level – business studies one year, maths the next – may reflect a lack of close monitoring. Three separate sciences at GCSE for the top sets, dual award for the lowest only. GCSE drama and A level theatre studies offered – the curriculum now has a good number of 'new' subjects. Every subject is setted. Huge design and technology centre, and pupils can get real, solid, hands-on experience of a practical subject (see art below). Fantastic multi-media language lab, with computer programmes in different languages – wouldn't disgrace a university. Every pupil and every teacher now has a lap-top – way out ahead of the field in this. Japanese and Italian offered as non-examined 'options'. Popularity stakes: maths, physics, chemistry, history, English, business studies, economics, politics.

The common room has young energetic and often inspirational staff, including increasing number of female ones (twenty-five at last count). Two full-time specialists in school to help with dyslexia and with dyspraxia. One full-time EFL teacher plus one part-time.

Games, Options, the Arts: Smart sports centre, also used by the town. Keen, voluntary CCF. Strong drama and a great deal of it, with at least three school plays a year, plus house plays and visiting professional productions in school's own Macready Theatre, and good enthusiastic staff. Professional standard photographic studio (which is indeed used by professionals as well as by pupils); lots take it at A level and do brilliantly. Design and art is now outstanding, hugely popular, and incredibly successful at A level.

Fantastic media studio with all the gear for pupils to practise making tapes, videos etc. Well thought out 'life skills' programme teaches pupils stuff they really benefit from knowing. Super careers department (the excellent head of the sixth form house, Mrs Phelps, is also head of careers).

Notable for the enthusiasm with which pupils cram their evenings and weekends with activity.

Background and Atmosphere: Founded in 1567 but metamorphosed as a Victorian 'railway' school in the 19th century. Home of the famous Dr Arnold of *Tom Brown's Schooldays*. Head still uses study in a corner of which is a door leading to a staircase built by Dr Arnold through which the boys could slide in without having to run the gauntlet of the school secretary. Imposing buildings very much in the middle of and dotted about the town – heavy traffic on one side of the campus. Feels rather like North Oxford. Sixth form 'Social Centre' has a bar. House prefects allowed out into Rugby on a Saturday night.

School went fully co-ed in 1993. Now has five houses for girls and nine for boys. All pupils eat in their own boarding houses (one of the last large public schools in the country to do this). 'Social' eating in each others' houses by invitation. Girls houses very civilised, particularly the sixth form one, Stanley (the food is reasonable here too). Boys' houses have been less ritzy (to put it mildly), but recently money has been thrown into upgrading them, particularly School House, right in the middle of the school, which was Dickensian, and is now beautifully thought out, state of the art, but retaining the old panelling and structure. Girls' uniform elegant long skirts, now redesigned so that it is possible to run in them.

Pastoral Care and Discipline: Head has single-handedly eradicated, as far as it is possible, a long tradition of bullying in the school and deserves a medal for it. Some housemasters are still said to turn a blind eye to bullying (choose house with care), and relationships remain strongly hierarchical making it a difficult place for sensitive boys in their first year. Geographical layout and position of temptingly nearby pubs etc, in town make this a difficult school for staff to police. Disciplinary matters centralised (boarding houses used to be run, very largely, by boys on traditional lines, with some horrendous results). Responsibility is now being 'handed back' to the pupils, but 'in a controlled manner'. Girls v v well looked after. On drugs, the head comments: 'the school has set in place a drugs policy to include increased education, counselling, urine testing which in most circumstances would not result in expulsion...' – a pioneer in this approach.

Pupils and Parents: From the Midlands, a sprinkling from overseas, still some from Scotland, the North of England, and London. Wide social range, but school is 'not snobby' – not (or rather, no longer) impressed by social credentials. OBs Rupert Brooke (a girls' house is named after him), Hugh Montefiore, Ian (Lord) Lang, Robert Hardy, Tom King, Tom Brown. 12 per cent of pupils are sons and daughters of OBs – who usually regard the place with nostalgia.

Entrance: Interview first, 'then weed' and entrance exam. Not stiff, but stiffening. For sixth form entry: six GCSEs with two Bs for pupils already in the school; for those coming in from outside (around 30 girls and 15 boys each year, and oversubscribed) a day-long programme of exams and interviews, and six GCSEs including Bs in A level subjects. School comments that an IQ below 110 would be struggling. School has grown by over 100 in past eight years, and lists looking 'healthy'. Choice of house may be deferred until nearer time of entry. Fed by Midland and East Anglian preps, such as Bilton Grange and Beeston Hall, and by wide mix of schools from Arnold Lodge to Llandaff Cathedral School and Yarlet Hall.

Exit: 100 per cent to university. Edinburgh and London are particularly popular at time of writing, which is strange, given the excellence of the art. Around 10 per cent go to Oxbridge.

Money Matters: No problems. Around 15 scholarships at 13; 10 at 16, four music scholarships at 13, two music scholarships at 16 – all up to 50 per cent of fees, but can be augmented by bursary in case of need. Six all-round bursaries, two major 'foundation' scholarships and four minor ones to entice bright day pupils (major scholarships are 100 per cent of fees and pupils must live within 10 miles of the school). Head points out that the original foundation was for 'local boys' to be educated. Also help for the needy and for sons of Old Rugbeians etc. Overall percentage of income devoted to scholarships etc = a creditable 11 per cent (and plans for more). School owns London estate including Great Ormond Street.

Remarks: Famous public school going from strength to strength. Has undergone huge changes in the last few years and is now one of the most popular, and deservedly so, choices among all co-ed boarding schools. Friendly, hard working and, say pupils (particularly the girls), 'fun'.

ST ALBAN'S HIGH SCHOOL

Townsend Avenue, St Albans, Hertfordshire
AL1 3SJ

TEL: *01727 853800* FAX: *01727 792516*

E-MAIL: info@stalbans-high.herts.sch.uk

WEB: www.sahs.org.uk

✦ PUPILS: 861 girls, all day ✦ Ages: 11-18 ✦
Size of sixth form: 150 ✦ C of E
✦ Fee-paying

Head: Since 1994, Mrs Carol Daly BSc (fifties), graduate of chemistry and geology at Nottingham University, previously head of Forest Girls' School in Snaresbrook E1, has taught in state and private sectors. The Dean of St Albans is chairman of governors.

Entrance: By entrance exam, plus interview etc. At four and seven into the junior house, eleven for the senior school. Worth a try at other times. Places in sixth form depend on getting six A-C passes, including A-Bs in A level subjects. Many girls come in from school's own super lively junior school over the road, the rest from a large number of private and primary schools.

Exit: Post-GCSE leavers numbers have dropped (Haileybury or local sixth form college). Northern universities currently popular; good handful to Oxbridge.

Remarks: Strong traditional girls' day school serving local needs and also popular with families in furthest reaches of Hertfordshire and increasingly north-west London. Perhaps a bit dull. High morale, partly due to school's league table results, 'And the parents do take notice.' Twelve school buses ferry girls to and fro daily (up to one hour away). School founded in 1889 (as a boarding school) by the Church Schools Company (retains strong links with the Abbey), and moved here later to purpose-built Queen Anne-style block with many later brick additions, not far from the centre of St Albans. The setting, once rural, is now suburban. Large tarmac playground, outdoor swimming pool, big, much-used sports hall, one grass half-size pitch, games fields five minutes' walk away. Thorough teaching on all fronts in functional classrooms (walls on the bare side when we visited). Latin for all for three years, choice of German (most popular) or Spanish, plus French (sensible exchanges). Girls are worked hard 'but we're not pressurised'. Separate or dual award science at GCSE. Circus rota for music, home economics (one or two doing A level in this) and art (excellent art results at both levels); sports, IT, design technology, are all fitted in to a tightly packed day.

GCSE results virtually all A-C, A levels well biased to A grades, though some Ds and Es. English Literature continues to do well and is popular; history ditto. Both now overtaken in popularity by maths, biology and chemistry – though Ds and Es aplenty in these subjects. Examined general studies. Class sizes sometimes up to 28, balanced by a small-school feel. 'You can't get lost here,' said a pupil. Sixth formers are all encouraged to share responsibilities: they run the houses, organise fund-raising etc. Polite and enthusiastic. Keen music department (briefly headed by Barry Rose). Though the school is very firmly Christian, there is a strong Jewish contingent, and a few Muslims. 'On the whole our girls emerge happy from the tunnel of adolescence,' to quote the head.

ST ANTONY'S-LEWESTON SCHOOL

Sherborne, Dorset DT9 6EN

TEL: *01963 210691* FAX: *01963 210786*

E-MAIL: st.antony@virgin.net

WEB: www.leweston.co.uk

✦ PUPILS: 250 girls; two-thirds board, one-third day ✦ Ages: 11-18. (Plus pre-prep and prep of around 120, with boys and girls, ages 2.5-11) ✦ Size of sixth form: 70 ✦ RC – but the majority are other denominations ✦ Fee-paying

Head: Since Mr Henry J MacDonald MA, head of classics, and latterly deputy head, here. Took over from Miss B A King, who took over from Miss C Denley Lloyd, each of whom lasted only three years as head.

Entrance: Not a problem. Waiting lists for the later years of the prep. CE at 11+, some later. Also at sixth form.

Exit: A wide range of degrees and further education courses (town planning, nursing, event management), often after a year out.

Remarks: Originally a boarding school for nice Catholic girls run by a Belgian order of nuns, now caters for girls of widely varying abilities, of varying religions and varying degrees of day/boarding (and very flexible on exeats as well). All things to all people. Housed in a fine park and imposing house with many additions and extras, not least the science block. Arts and crafts well taught in very well-equipped block (which NB is open on Sunday afternoons). Popular biology department. Small sixth form and statistics mean little here. Good record of associated board exam results, also drama taken seriously. Currently winning or coming close to top of all sorts of sporting events in the area, including hockey and riding (hunting gals warmly welcomed). Joint orchestra with nearby Sherborne Boys' School, and other links with them and the Girls. Good 'individual needs support' department, also EFL for foreign girls. Good prep and pre-prep. A small caring school.

ST BEES SCHOOL

St Bees, Cumbria CA27 0DU

TEL: *01946 822263* FAX: *01946 823657*

E-MAIL: mailbox@st-bees-school.co.uk

WEB: www.st-bees-school.co.uk

✦ PUPILS: 180 boys, 120 girls. 110 board (half weekly), the rest day ✦ Ages: 11-18 ✦ Size of sixth form: 95 ✦ C of E ✦ Fee-paying

Head: Since 2000. Mr Philip Capes, deputy head of Warminster School (similar size boarding/day co-ed), previously taught at Forest School; engineering degree from

Exeter, married to junior school teacher, three teenage children. His first job, according to Chairman of Governors, is to produce a 5-year development plan. Took over from Mrs Janet Pickering BSc, who was only here for a couple of years before leaving for the more academic shores of Withington Girls' School.

Academic Matters: Broad range, from special learning unit to top scores at A level. Not a hot-house, and doesn't claim to be. Much satisfaction over Es turned into Ds and Cs. 'We're getting there academically', says Mrs Pickering. 'Everyone is stretched', says one satisfied parent, whose two sons' indifferent junior school achievements were turned into 3 x A at A level; attributed to confidence arising from being valued as an individual. Usual small school constraints on A level choices, but Latin, Greek and further maths available. Science very popular. GCSE results: over 40 per cent at A and A★. IT and French, Spanish taught using satellite reception in innovative and successful Management Centre (see below). Very committed staff, who insist on hard work and high standards; according to one parent, 'competent but a bit set in their ways – could do with some new blood'.

Games, Options, the Arts: Games fields everywhere in stunning 150 acre site. Rugby strong (tough fixture list), girls' sport also very good. Large sports hall, squash and fives courts. Much PE teaching mixed. 60 acre 9-hole golf course on headland, shared with locals. Proximity to unspoiled part of Lake District and sea means the school has developed a distinctive and highly successful tradition of outdoor activities: adventure training in curriculum for youngest, St Bees Award Challenge ('home-grown, more testing version of D of E Awards') taken in Sixth by 40 per cent. Expeditions in holidays, mainly organized by pupils (a recurrent theme; much stress on self-reliance and responsibility). CCF for all ages 13-16. All this staffed from within. Art improving, drama lively, music very good; new music school opening 2000 – many instrumental groups, choir sings in chapel and village priory, tours Germany with chamber orchestra every other year.

Background and Atmosphere: Founded as a grammar school in 1583; original schoolroom now a dining hall, with past pupils' names carved on wall panels. Handsome Victorian additions in local sandstone spread over splendid site 'between the sea and the sheep', and well integrated with 2,000 pop. St Bees village. Girls admitted since 1976, so a proper coeducational school – a process possibly advanced during Mrs Pickering's short stay. Girls' houses in attractive terrace on the other side of useful local railway (footbridge), senior boys in same building as HM. International Centre opened in large house to provide specialist TEFL plus general courses for one year for up to 20 overseas students aged 11-16. Some join St Bees thereafter, some return home; from 2000, international pupils will be integrated with existing boarding houses.

Management Centre, opened in 1992, is an unusual and successful joint venture: used commercially as a conference centre in the week, by the school in evenings and at weekends. 'We are still discovering ways of using this unique partnership' (Mrs Pickering). Very plush, stuffed with high-tech IT equipment and its own catering.

A general air about the whole school of unhurried but purposeful activity. Working day ends for all pupils at 5.45pm. Various efforts to overcome inescapable sense of isolation, eg visits to Stratford and visiting lecture programme. Leavers' ball (with parents) is the high point of the social calendar.

Pastoral Care and Discipline: Housemaster (and now one housemistress) and spouse, plus tutorial system. Staff 70 per cent male. Claim that in a small 'family' school no one slips through the net seems reasonable, eg kitchen staff notice if someone isn't eating properly. 'Centralised matrons', husband-and-wife GP team, counsellor on call. Not much real naughtiness in this quiet backwater; pupils seem content with traditional discipline. Drug supplying and sex mean the sack.

Pupils and Parents: Many local, though an increasing number from the north east (parents seeking a secure environment?); 10 per cent foreign nationals. Extensive private bus system ferries day pupils to and fro, boarders picked up at nearest airports. Pupils refreshingly old-fashioned: neatly dressed in formal uniform, frank and unaffected.

Parents very supportive (some allow their names to be used in prospectus for potential parents to telephone); Cumbrian farmers and professionals, local industrialists (Sellafield a huge local employer). Efficient marketing team (deputy head and registrar) go on frequent recruiting trips abroad.

Entrance: Not very competitive – though International Centre students have to show realistic level of competence. 2-form entry, mainly from state schools, topped up at 13 and 16.

Exit: Nearly all to higher education (very little fall-out at GCSE), from Oxbridge (a sprinkling) to newest universities and ex-polys (quite a lot). 1999 leavers' list shows good cover of engineering, law, medicine, straight arts under-represented.

Money Matters: Bursaries for children of clergy, HM Forces, and former pupils, and a few for deserving cases. Up to 50 per cent fee academic and music scholarships; art and sport awards post-16.

Remarks: Good local school, strong reputation, palpable atmosphere of security in beautiful surroundings. Endless care taken over individuals.

ST CATHERINE'S SCHOOL

Bramley, Guildford Surrey GU5 0DF

TEL: *01483 893 363* FAX: *01483 899 608*

E-MAIL: schooloffice@st-catherines.surrey.sch.uk

♦ PUPILS: 500 girls; 113 boarders, rest day. Plus junior school of 200 girls, all day ♦ Ages: 10/11-18, junior school 4-11 ♦ Size of sixth form: 104 ♦ C of E ♦ Fee-paying

---

Head: Mrs Alice Phillips M.A. Cantab (40) appointed in July 1999, and took up her post in April 2000 after the birth of her daughter (now 17 months). Former deputy head at Tormead, she is smart, capable and matter of fact. Girls say she is 'strict but fair'. Passionate about music, she met her solicitor husband, Simon when they sang together in the chapel choir at Queens' College Cambridge. Teaching is another of her passions (teaches in the sixth form general studies programme, and makes guest appearances teaching English in the lower school) and she says ' I'd walk out of this job tomorrow if I couldn't teach.' Sees herself as a facilitator and maintains that all that separates her from her pupils is experience.

Academic Matters: Excellent academic results, particularly so in 2000 with St Catherine's gaining a place in the top 20 in the League Tables. 99.1 percent of girls gained grades A★-C at GCSE level, and at A-level 83.3 per cent percent achieved grades A★-B. All departments seem equally strong with modern languages in particular gaining 100 percent A★-B grades (French, Spanish and German). Maths and the sciences are also strong (9As for maths and 12 for biology) and one of the most popular subject choices. Not surprising when one sees the new science labs and modern language facilities. 'Bright, white and sort-of American' comments one pupil. Economics and business studies also get great results. Impressive IT facilities throughout the school with every girl having her own e-mail address and IT being a compulsory subject all the way through the school. Library is modern and well stocked.

Art department is in its own block and produces some amazing work. Every year a fashion show is put on by the Art students – unbelievable designs! Fifth form also won a prestigious award at the Tate Modern. Excellent DT department.

Mrs Phillips, like any good head, wants her pupils to feel challenged and develop a lifelong love of learning. Whether this translates into academic pressure is a moot point. Some sixth form pupils agree that there is pressure but argue that much of it is of their own making. Many parents feel that their girls are kept firmly up to the mark. In the past, the school has been a bit pushy, 'said one parent, ' quite concerned with its league table position.' ' Maybe this will change with the new head' said another.

Games, Options, the Arts: St Catherine's has a strong sporting tradition and extensive grounds. Netball, lacrosse, tennis, swimming, rounders, athletics, and gymnastics form the core sports. St Catherine's girls have played lacrosse and netball for England. Additional sports offered include basketball, volleyball, hockey, badminton and squash.

Excellent new music block. At any one time about 400 girls are receiving individual tuition. There are a number of choirs, orchestras and ensembles. The senior chamber choir sang with Russell Watson on his CD, which made No. 1 in the classical music charts. Enthusiastic drama department which puts on a number of productions each year and excellent dance studio offering ballet, tap, jazz and modern dance. Plenty of clubs and societies cater for any spare hours in the pupil's already busy day.

Background and Atmosphere: Main school building is quite an attractive red brick and tile building that has not been fiddled with too much. Adjoining the main school building is the extremely beautiful St Catherine's Chapel, which on its own is worth a visit to the school. The rest of the school is laid out in a logical way with a mixture of old and modern buildings. Quite a walk from class to class especially in bad weather but the pupils soon learn the shortcuts through buildings.

Sixth form centre is well planned offering quiet study areas, common room complete with sofas, stereo, kitchenette and television. Sixth form boarders are also housed in this centre. Two to a room with posters up on the walls – typical teenage bedrooms. They love it. ' We get a lot of freedom they don't seem to have at other boarding schools' said one pupil, 'but if we break their trust, they'll come down really hard on us'. Lots of organised outings for boarders and food has improved dramatically – they even get tapas and faijitas, according to one.

Other boarders are housed in two sections Junior House (11-12) and Main School (12-16). Rooms are comfortable, freshly painted and carpeted and girls allowed to put up posters and knick-knacks. Great common rooms with squashy sofas, TV, VCR, Stereos, vending machines and pool tables. Full and weekly boarding is offered as well as flexible boarding for day scholars (space permitting) if parents are going to be away for any reason.

Uniform has had a bit of a blitzing by the new head recently. Lengths of skirts, height of heels – popular with parents, not so with pupils. Sixth form wear what they like (within reason of course).

Pastoral Care and Discipline: A strength of the school is the house system, which offers the pupils a support structure all the way through the school. Along with her form tutors, the same school housemistress will be available throughout a girl's life at the school and so by the time she reaches sixth form; they know her really well. There is also a resident school nurse as well as matrons, boarding housemistresses and resident tutors.

School is aware of anorexia and keeps an eye on the girls, especially boarders. Additional information and counselling offered through PSE classes. Good career counselling.

Discipline is firm but fair. Long hair tied back and no evidence of make-up or bizarre hairstyles. Clear alcohol, drug and smoking policy. Busy and challenged pupils are generally self-disciplined argues the head.

School is Church of England and a local chaplain leads the spiritual life of the school. Everyone attends chapel once a week. RE is a strong and important part of the school curriculum.

Pupils and Parents: Most of the pupils come from professional families. The wealthy (and obviously clever) Surrey set is represented, but also girls whose parents have made big sacrifices. Pupils used to come from local areas in and around Guildford, but the school is becoming increasingly fashionable and high profile and girls are coming from Wimbledon, Richmond and London. Some foreign students. Parents are greatly supportive and involved in organising social and fundraising events.

Entrance: At 11+ and the entrance exam consists of English, maths, science and verbal reasoning. Most of the junior schoolgirls carry on to the senior school but they too have to do the exam. Admission is not automatic.

Only the top layer is offered places. The school will also make provision for bright children who may have dyslexia and offer them the relevant support..

Most go on to do sixth form, and there are increasing requests from outsiders to join the sixth form. Their entrance requirements are the same as the school's own- at least six GCSE passes at grade C or above.

Exit: Most go on to the traditional universities –Durham, Leeds, Cardiff, Bristol, Oxford, and Cambridge.

Money Matters: The school offers two academic scholarships at 11+, and one music scholarship. In the sixth form, there are also ten internal academic scholarships, one sport, one music, one art, and three external academic scholarships. These amounts vary from one-sixth to one-third of the fees.

Remarks: A leading academic and sporting girls school. A wonderful place for your clever and confident daughter. We feel that it is not the right school for a shy violet even if she is very bright, but the head says the school enjoys a reputation for giving girls confidence as they progress through the school.

JUNIOR SCHOOL: Tel: 01483 899 665 Fax: 01483 899 669. Head: Mrs S. Fellows BA PGCE. Around 200 girls. Ages 4-11. All day pupils as junior boarding house is not taking any new pupils. Academically selective entry at 4+ and at 7+ and at other times if places are available. Own facilities and grounds across the road from the senior school. Admission to senior school is by passing senior school entrance exam.

ST CHRISTOPHER SCHOOL

Letchworth, Hertfordshire SG6 3JZ

TEL: *01462 679301* FAX: *01462 481578*

E-MAIL: stchris.admissions@rmplc.co.uk

WEB: www.stchris.co.uk

✦ PUPILS: 380 boys and girls (225 boys, 155 girls), 105 board, rest day. Plus own on-site junior school with 95 boys, 75 girls, (all day except for four boarders) and Montessori nursery with 40 children ✦ Ages: 11-19, juniors 5+-11, Montessori 2-4 ✦ Size of sixth form: 85 ✦ Non-denom ✦ Fee-paying

---

Head: Since 1981, Mr Colin Reid MA (fifties), educated at Brentwood School, read history at Cambridge. Came here from Atlantic College, and before that taught at

Tonbridge. His wife, Betsy, teaches English and history at this school. Their three children have all been in the school. A charming, confident, unassuming and capable Head – incidentally, only the third in seventy-five years.

Entrance: By interview at 11 (lots come up from the junior school), 13 and 16. Always a contingent from abroad (parents working overseas, diplomats, British Council etc), sons/daughters of Old Boys/Girls, not to mention over 30 staff children. Extremely broad social and ability intake. Help for (mild) learning difficulties, a few 'special needs' places available.

Exit: Most stay till sixth form. Almost all to further education, (anything from Oxbridge to ex-polys) also art, music and drama colleges in substantial numbers.

Remarks: Successful gentle alternative school, founded (with Theosophical links) as a co-educational progressive school in the twenties, and is true to its original aims, ie that of developing the whole child, mind, body, and spirit.

Results creditable, given intake: pupils of very varied abilities but are all required to be 'average plus' (ie IQ of over 100), and there are occasional scholar refugees from highly pressured establishments. Quaker aspects alive, with moments of silence (before meals, at some meetings/assemblies). Boarding numbers down – but day numbers up.

Keen and good drama, well above average art exam results at both levels, emphasis on craft. Very Third World conscious – notice boards alive with posters, talks, fundraising events for Save the Children, Green Peace etc.

Strong emphasis on challenge, adventure and outdoor pursuits – all the usual games, some on the premises, others – squash, riding, golf – within easy reach. Rock-climbing, canoeing, orienteering etc, and famously busy end of summer term expeditions for all years.

Pupils extremely supportive and friendly, tolerant. Informal atmosphere, no uniform (or rather, the unofficial uniform is T shirts and track suits), all staff are called by their Christian names, pupils play vital role in running the school, 'We are teaching freedom and that means responsibility,' said a member of staff. 'And we are all – pupils, parents, staff – involved in the same way of life here.' (School claims the oldest parent-teacher association in the country).

Parents on the whole caring types, looking for something different. Reports still continue to reach us from parents who are 'very happy' with their children's development here – though as ever some suffer niggling worries that 'the caring aspect may need stronger academic underpinnings'.

Now housed in Edwardian mansions (one was Laurence Olivier's childhood home). NB Letchworth was the first of the garden cities. Many additional and varied buildings (including new technology, sixth form centre, and pool) in a well worn-patchwork. Some of the original arts-and-crafts aspects (settle, big bow window seats, plain wooden floors etc) intact in boarding houses (all are mixed age, mixed sex), underpinning pleasantly homely atmosphere. NB vegetarian food only; excellent and varied – school is extremely health – and diet-conscious. Cookery lessons for all in the 'well-equipped vegetarian centre' (v popular). Famous OB Paul (Lord) Hamlyn.

ST COLUMBA'S SCHOOL

Duchal Road, Kilmacolm, Renfrewshire
PA13 4AU

TEL: *01505 872238* FAX: *01505 873995*

E-MAIL: stcolumba@rmplc.co.uk

WEB: www.stcolumbas.renfrew.sch.uk

◆ PUPILS: 178 boys, 188 girls; plus junior school of 280. All day ◆ Ages: 11-18, juniors 4-11 ◆ Size of sixth form: 97 ◆ Non-denom ◆ Fee-paying

Head (Rector): Since 1987, Mr Andrew Livingstone BSc (Aberdeen), Dip Ed (Glasgow) (fifties), educated at Campbeltown Grammar School, previously deputy rector of Paisley Grammar School. An educationalist (he served on the Scottish Exam Board), he is the first Rector of this previously traditional girls' school which went co-ed in 1978. Teaches maths and occasional computing. .

Academic Matters: Structured learning, with masses of parental encouragement and strong work ethos. Recently results have been consistently excellent – very very few failures at either level. Pupils take Scottish Standard Grades, with Highers the following year and then Sixth Year Studies. Learning support for registered dyslexics, either from part-time staff and extracted from lessons, or tutors after school.

Games, Options, the Arts: Tennis courts and Astroturf a couple of hundred yards away, and main games field near junior school, along with massive games hall. Orchestra popular, masses of choral work, good drama, art. Exchange with Canadian school. Public speaking encouraged. Heart-rending wee poems in the '97 school mag: '... Oh God, please will you lend, Lend me a friend, I pray! ...' and one worthy of McGonagall: 'I didna' mean tae squash ye flat – I did the same once tae a bat...'

Background and Atmosphere: Original school was founded for girls in 1897, red brick. Very tidy and rather cramped surroundings. Centenary project for '97/'98 set out to improve art, music, technical, business studies and computing departments in the main school ('98 the school's centenary year). More new building on the way. The junior school went co-ed in '78, and the senior school in '81 – one of v v few girls' schools to have achieved this successfully. Imaginative new sixth year common room with microwave.

Pastoral Care and Discipline: Four houses, and inter-house everything. Discipline done through house system, order marks for 'not covering books [in brown paper] or non-attendance at hockey club'. 'We don't really have problems,' says the rector. Theft or drugs would be out automatically.

Pupils and Parents: Local professional families, bussed in from all over Renfrewshire and North Ayrshire (to the detriment of traditional Glasgow schools, which are still losing boys). Approx 2-3 per cent ethnic minorities. Massive parental support. Very middle-class and trad values, including first-time buyers who like the same.

Entrance: Automatic from junior school, waiting lists at most ages. Own test and interview. Priority to siblings, FPs' children.

Exit: V occasionally to trad public schools. Occasional one after Standard Grade, otherwise 90+ per cent to university, almost all to Scottish ones, everywhere from Aberdeen to Paisley, Glasgow, Moray etc, with one or two to agricultural college.

Money Matters: Scholarships and bursaries for 'hard times rather than academic'. Had a few assisted places – not enough to worry.

Remarks: Good flourishing local school. Gone a bit quiet.

JUNIOR SCHOOL: Tel: 01505 872768. Head: Mrs Davina Grant. Just over 280 boys and girls, ages 4-11, plus nursery school. Entrance by assessment and interview at primary 1 stage 'or at any time throughout primary'. Automatic transfer to senior school.

ST DAVID'S SCHOOL
Church Road, Ashford, Middlesex
TW15 3DZ

TEL: *01784 252494* FAX: *01784 248652*

E-MAIL: office@st-davids.demon.co.uk

WEB: www.st-davids.demon.co.uk

✦ PUPILS: 253 girls (28 board 225 day); plus on site junior school of 147 ✦ Ages: 11-18, junior school 3-11 ✦ Size of sixth form: 40 ✦ C of E, but others welcome ✦ Fee-paying

---

Head: Since 1999, Ms Penny Bristow BSc (early fifties). Educated at Newbury Grammar followed by University College London where she read chemistry. Three grown up sons not at home, she lives on site in the charming creeper clad schoolhouse.

Relatively new to the post, previously head at St Hilary's (girls' independent day school, Cheshire). Strong personality, something of a reformer, installing academic tracking and new pastoral hierarchy. Takes her turn in the boarding staff rota. School in process of change to head's way of doing things. Parent describes her as 'inspirational'.

Academic Matters: Emphasis on the ethos that 'the girls are not under enormous academic pressure'. Average IQ gains entrance, and school works stolidly to obtain the best from the pupils. Some special needs supported, dyslexia, dyspraxia, ADHD. Also EFL extra-curricular language tuition offered (one free lesson per week, more than that at cost).

Some clever girls and creditable results all round. (90 per cent pass at A level – 33 per cent grade As) (94 per cent pass GCSE at grades A-C). Not much setting except, maths (three streams) and science. Largely taught in form groups of 20 -25, but smaller for GCSE. Minority language GCSEs, taught peripatetically, boost results of some of the foreign students.

Good number of options at GCSE and A level, including combined science and semi-vocational subjects. Range of A levels guaranteed through link with nearby Halliford (independent boys') School. Students bussed between the two sites. Popular shared teaching arrangements for some subjects.

Year groups of up to 20 at sixth form stage. Requirement of B or above at GCSE to sit A level in given subject, and minimum 5 GCSEs. Some flexibility in this if a girl really wants to stay on, although for some the exam criteria may provide 'a good excuse to let them go'.

Games, Options, the Arts: Gymnastics team (with longstanding teacher/coach) performs well nationally. Scholarships offered to promising gymnasts. Senior gymnasium due for refurbishment. Cross-country running at time of visit; plenty of competitiveness and encouraging staff. On-site lake allows for kayaking club. Teams do well in hockey, rounders and athletics.

Drama popular curriculum option. Ongoing redevelopment programme to provide modernised shared space for drama and indoor games. Up to a third of pupils play a musical instrument; lunchtime lessons, plenty of pianos, music block with practice rooms, school orchestra. D of E awards scheme very strong. Fair number of school trips, outward bound, skiing etc.

Background and Atmosphere: Established in Clerkenwell in 1716 as a charitable institution educating children of Welsh parentage living in London. Relocated to Ashford in 1857. In 1881 it became an independent girls' boarding school. Originally named 'The Welsh Girls School', it changed its name to St David's in 1967 by which time pupils came more from the locality and non-Welsh backgrounds. Still owned by 'The Most Honourable and Loyal Society of Ancient Britons' who set it up. There is compulsory learning and singing of the Welsh national anthem, Welsh names for all the classrooms and dormitories and a prevailing red dragon logo throughout the school and its literature.

The main building is a splendid gothic edifice facing magnificent playing fields and gardens, bounded by its own lake and the nearby Thames. Convenient for Ashford town and railway station, although neither make their presence felt within the tree-lined 30-acre site.

Wonderful building and grounds from the outside, but the practicalities of maintaining an ageing, listed building such as this are more obvious once behind the massive oak doors. The interior, beyond the grand entrance foyer, is less imposing. Refectory takes up the central body of the ground floor and at the time of our visit the adjacent kitchen made its presence felt with a smell of school dinners completely pervading the air. Hopefully, this was just a one-day fault in the venting system.

A pretty wood-lined chapel fits everyone for assembly, and the library is light, attractive and internet linked, if not exactly crammed with stock. Many of the classrooms are housed in newer blocks behind the main building; there is a schedule for refurbishment here. Juniors and seniors share many parts of the school.

Pupils appear good humoured, self-aware, and on occasions keen to assert their personalities. The school mag highlights the camaraderie built up among them. Wonderful uniforms, sweaters and kilts, until 'smart casual' sixth formers.

Boarding house situated on the top two floors of the main building, barely separated from the classrooms. Boarding facilities are not luxurious. There is plenty of privacy and cubicle style sleeping accommodation. Homely communal areas, bathrooms pretty basic. Boarders have the free run of school facilities evenings and weekends. Three staff, including one full-time housemistress sleep on floor below the girls (youngest is 9 although it is unusual for juniors to board). Majority of boarders from overseas, Hong Kong, Africa and Eastern European bloc.

A few Brits use weekly board facility. 'As required' boarding on offer to day girls. They may also opt for breakfast, for early birds, supervised prep and supper, and the chance to overnight – great for working mothers.

Pastoral Care and Discipline: Pastoral care devolved to form tutors then year heads,

head will get involved with serious concerns and parents are readily called in. System of fines for smoking in uniform, drugs may see expulsion; any bullying confronted and discussed, if proven to continue suspension results. 'Silent reading' in the very public foyer at break times for breaches of rules. Discipline is firm. Co-ed sixth form (link with Halliford) 'no (close) contact' rule between the sexes on the premises.

Pupils and Parents: Many pupils come from the on-site junior school. Of those joining at 11, 60 per cent from state maintained schools, 40 per cent from private preps. Good transport links and school bus service mean they come from a wide radius – into Middlesex, Surrey and SW London. Multi-cultural bunch, particularly the boarders (14 nationalities in the school). Nominally C of E but plenty of other religions accepted and valued. Parents very involved in the life of the school. 'A real community' states a mother.

Entrance: Written assessment at 11. Not a huge hurdle.

Exit: At 16 to vocational courses elsewhere. At 18 most to degree courses at university, some headed for HNDs.

Money Matters: Scholarships (mainly 25 per cent of fees) at 11+ based on performance in entrance exam. Also for exceptional talent at gymnastics, art and music. Means-tested bursaries for those in financial difficulties with priority going to girls of Welsh parentage.

Remarks: Small school with strong identity (keeps the Welsh flag flying in the heart of English suburbia). School engenders lots of loyalty from staff, parents and pupils. Will be interesting to see the effect of strong new head and planned refurbishments.

ST DAVID'S COLLEGE

Gloddaeth Hall, Llandudno, Gwynedd, North Wales LL30 1RD

TEL: *01492 875974* FAX: *01492 870383*

E-MAIL: headmaster@stdavidscollege.co.uk

WEB: www.stdavidscollege.co.uk

✦ PUPILS: 220 boys, 155 board, 65 day, plus growing number of girls (50 at last count)
✦ Ages: 11-18 ✦ Size of sixth form: 60
✦ Non-denom ✦ Fee paying

Head: Since 1991, Mr William Seymour MA (forties). Educated at Aldenham School and Christ's College, Cambridge. Wife, Shirley, helps in the school. Two children (one educated at St David's).

Entrance: Usually at 11 or 13, but other times possible, including at sixth form. Visit the school, plus school report. Register early for the dyslexia unit.

Exit: Each year a handful of pupils go on to university, the majority to ex-polys and technical colleges. Thereafter to all sorts of practical careers – designers, doctors, businessmen etc.

Remarks: Founded in 1965, initially with 37 boys, pretty site on the edge of Snowdonia. School a mish-mash of architectural styles, including beautiful old hall and a thankfully reducing number of Portakabin classrooms. Also minuscule departments in old cottage – all making a friendly whole. Muscular Christianity. Operates house system – including new sixth form boarding house, Chelsea House (named after ex-governor). Pupils come from all parts of the UK. There is much emphasis on building up self-confidence and self-reliance, initiative and individualism. The school has a deservedly high reputation for helping with difficulties – including dyslexia, late developers etc. Two-thirds of the school are dyslexics, and the dyslexic unit much in demand and very good. The school has pioneered a multi-sensory teaching policy for dyslexic pupils, evolving a 'whole school' approach, with much cross-referencing between main stream and individual lessons. Much care and understanding, a good place to gain maturity through outward-bound activities, hill walking, tough outdoor pursuits, eg sailing 3,000 miles to the Azores, climbing the fourteen 3000ft peaks of Snowdonia in twenty-four hours. Falconry on offer, with two buzzards now fully trained, and two Harris hawks. Travel scholarship for a 'holiday which involves a purpose'. Young Enterprise projects. Gap year students come to the school to help. 'Outdoor education' very strong overall – breeds athletic champions, not to mention mountain-bikers and board sailors, skiers and climbers who regularly represent Wales. All sorts of outdoor qualifications can be obtained here eg day skipper, artificial ski slope instructor, British Expedition Training Award, Sports Leader Award. Small groups (18-20 is large, average 10-12) for academic work. Separate sciences offered at GCSE, A levels include philosophy and theatre studies. Keen art, strong design, technology. IT at AS level on offer, new IT centre opened with sixteen networked Pentiums. New CAD and CAE laboratory offering range of City & Guilds qualifications. Business studies strong – in '96 one boy achieved top marks in the country for this subject at A level (AEB). GCSE results good, considering the learning difficulties. Good reports.

ST DUNSTAN'S ABBEY

SCHOOL

The Millfields, Plymouth, Devon PL1 3JL

TEL: *01752 201350* FAX: *01752 201351*

E-MAIL: info@sda.org.uk

WEB: www.sda.org.uk

✦ PUPILS: 290 (115 prep and 175 senior) girls including 42 boarders ✦ Ages: Three months – 18 years ✦ Size of sixth form: 62 ✦ C of E ✦ Fee-paying

Head: Since 1998, Mrs Barbara Brown BA (sixties); deputy-head for eight years having joined school in 1986 as head of English. She was prompted by the governors to take the helm after her affinity with the school as second in command proved her to be second to none. Previously worked as English teacher and brought up family of four children. English graduate of Liverpool University.

A strict disciplinarian, the head is tough on rare rule-breakers. Otherwise her open door, approachable manner and motherly demeanour have made her a popular head, whose reign compliments school's traditional teaching style. Well respected by parents. Could be hard to replace.

Academic Matters: Outstanding results due to small class numbers, allowing pupil's confidence to grow. Group sizes depend on popularity of subject ranging from two to 15; one to five in most sixth form subjects. Pupils seem hard to find among the maze of 47 rooms including nine music rooms.

Quality study space provided for A level students with six rooms shared amongst 20 students. Recognition is given on special board to Oxbridge students – 13 in 15 years. Usual subjects offered at GCSE, all continued at A level as well as business and general studies. Most students take nine GCSEs and (under the new system) a minimum of four AS levels.

Games, Options, the Arts: One of few Plymouth schools to offer A level drama, and school is renowned for its theatrical productions. Drama is taught to all girls, instilling self-confidence, and good interview and public speaking technique. St Dunstan's is also a part-time associate school of the Italia Conti Academy – Britain's oldest established theatre arts training school originally founded in London's Great Portland Street. Weekend classes in singing, dancing and acting are provided to pupils aged 3 to 18+ years – for fun or as part of a long-term career plan. Pupils participate in workshop productions and public performances. Provides an alternative route into St Dunstan's for proven scholarship-winning talent. Choirs also achieve considerable success in local festivals.

Adequate sports facilities include large field, tennis/squash courts, indoor gymnasium. Not a hockey school – loses to bigger schools who have more choice of players. Associated clubs and societies, supported by members of staff, include Rainbows, Brownies, Guides, gymnastics and games, music, country dancing, American line dancing and aerobics. Mini-bus takes students horse-riding, rock 'n roll, dry-skiing lessons or other pastime popular among students like D of E.

Background and Atmosphere: Hidden within the granite-walled compound of a former Royal Navy Hospital site with a security-guarded entrance; a Plymouthian would be forgiven for being ignorant of its existence. A few minutes from the city centre, surrounded by beautiful countryside. Fine architecture dates back to 18th century, including magnificent clock tower and chapel. Recently refurbished prep. Secondhand uniform shop.

Boarders taken from age seven, girls have option of a single study bedroom, most share. Cared for by three resident staff, house-mistress and two matrons. Additional bedrooms available for short stays or for friends to visit.

Pastoral Care and Discipline: Morning assemblies (three a week) and Communion services held in magnificent school chapel. Although strict C of E foundation when run formerly by nuns, 'the chaplain's sermon has been modified for congregation of today's mixed faiths' stated Barbara Brown. All boarders, under 18 must have a guardian or parent in the UK – the school holds a list of suitable people. Girls from overseas met at airport by guardians and escorted to school, or can make their own arrangements. Mini-buses transport pupils to and from train station.

Head abhors smoking and girls chewing gum. No known alcohol or drug-related incidents. Skirts below the knees please.

Awareness of others encouraged, with good manners, respect and courtesy expected at all times, although occasional shouting still heard around the school.

Pupils and Parents: Pupils have reputation locally for being responsible individuals with mature attitudes – helpful when seeking jobs.

Our impression is that the school, with its small classes, allows every variety of personality to develop, though none turn out to be shrinking violets. Pupils are public

spirited – supporting causes like The Children's Hospice.

Former students of St Dunstan's include actress Dawn French, Debenhams chief executive Belinda Earl. Actor Edward Woodward and wife Michelle Dotrice are patrons of St Dunstan's Italia Conti School and visit often.

Flourishing Parents' Association supports school by fund-raising and social events. Parents encouraged to join – perhaps as a sign that the school is talking to them at last. Parents are doctors, lawyers and successful small business owners; many move to area for the school. 'We chose St Dunstan's over other independent schools, it was recommended to us by parents'.

Entrance: Accepts 11+ failures if a pupil is particularly talented – the school's teaching strengths will push them through GCSE and beyond. At sixth form, entrance considered on personal and performance records (and on examination results). Open scholarship examination for senior school entry held in February. Pupils do not necessarily progress through school from nursery stage, though most leave due to parental circumstances rather than being pushed.

Exit: Undergraduates – 99 per cent; Royal Navy 1 per cent. All girls become members of St Dunstan's Abbey Association on leaving, and members return regularly for reunions. Every pupil is entitled to a sprig of myrtle from the Abbey's bush for inclusion in her wedding bouquet.

Money Matters: A registration deposit of £1,000 is required for overseas students, refunded during final term of attendance. Reduction of 10 per cent for siblings.

Two academic scholarships for prep pupils and two external scholarships available. Awards (50 per cent) for music, art, drama and sport. Bursary for one internal and one external pupil at 50 per cent, up to 100 per cent if pupil is particularly talented and parent has limited means.

Remarks: Strong all-round girls' school with good work ethos, clinging on to old traditional teaching styles but keeping students up with the times. Reputation for superb results, family atmosphere and happy pupils. If your theatrical daughter shines on stage or aspires to film or television this could be for her.

JUNIOR SCHOOL: The Flying Start Nursery: Three months to five years – 50 pupils (22 boys/28girls). Teaching techniques and some equipment Montessori in essence. Regular parent/staff meetings.

ST EDWARD'S SCHOOL

Woodstock Road, Oxford OX2 7NN

TEL: *01865 319200* FAX: *01865 319202*

E-MAIL: mrsannebrooks@stedwards.oxon.sch.uk

WEB: www.stedward.oxon.sch.uk

✦ PUPILS: 610 in all, 412 boys, 198 girls. 419 board, 191 day ✦ Ages: 13-18 ✦ Size of sixth form: 270 ✦ C of E ✦ Fee-paying

---

Head (Warden): Since 1988, Mr David Christie BSc Econ (London), BA (Strathclyde) (late fifties), educated at Dollar Academy and came here via George Watson's College, Edinburgh, Moray House, European School in Luxembourg and Winchester – where he taught economics while researching the 'economics of education'. A delightful man, whose kindly inquisitive and gentle manner is backed by razor sharp perception. Several hobby horses, for instance, breadth; also that there are many different kinds of intelligence, 'too often we only recognise the logical linguistic intelligence.' He believes it is important that we understand and recognise how we learn ('it's not the same for everybody'), and, to this effect, tries to match the teaching with the pupil. Describes himself firmly as a 'one school head' – which is not to say that others have not tried to poach him. Married with three children, and active member of HMC, publishes books, articles on literature and plays golf with zest.

Academic Matters: A school that is happy to accept 50 per cent at CE and proud with what its pupils achieve: intake is very broad, and results reflect this. Modern languages are very strong. Aiming for 4 or 5 AS, plus 3 (4 for the brainy) A2s, often adding a 'trendy' AS level in second year sixth form, subjects such as philosophy, sports studies, archaeology. Just moving to dual award sciences at GCSE, Latin for all in first year, Greek, German, Spanish available. Economics is popular, also sciences, 'and we get plenty of hands-on'. English another much liked subject. Pupils roughly streamed, setted for maths. Some help for mild dyslexia. Good vibrant mix of varied teaching methods (as per head's hobby horse), in line with aim to individualise learning. Pupils negotiate targets (with themselves), carry ARC (academic record cards), and discuss academic matters once a week with tutors. Pupils view their effort grades with huge interest. Some interesting and impressive staff. The head is given to arriving, un-announced, in lessons.

Games, Options, the Arts: As we have said

before, in line with the brawn/brainy upheaval, Teddy's has now taken to losing the occasional match – however, sports are extremely well served, with 90 acres of pitches, hockey notably strong, and recently unbeaten at rugby. Tim Henman's brother is a tennis coach. Rowing is powerful – they won Henley in '99, first eight won Schools' Head of the River in both '98 and '97. Big sports hall, indoor swimming pool, fabulous fitness centre, the Esporta (sixth formers only) complete with restaurants, hairdressers etc., which cost the school, who provide the site, not a penny, and also serves the citizens of north Oxford. Art flourishing; high powered music (several pupils National youth orchestra members); terrifically enthusiastic and ambitious drama. Marvellous library. Heaps of activities on offer from archery to the engineering society. Active D of E. Some mutterings from boarding pupils at the junior end that 'there's not enough laid on at week ends'.

Background and Atmosphere: School founded in 1863 and moved to its present site ten years later. Imposing red brick turreted building round busy squad with masses of unobtrusive additions, a mile from the dreaming spires, tucked into homely North Oxford. Playing fields run down to the canal on the other side of the busy Woodstock Road, connected by an underpass. Boarding houses are still a mixture of the comfy old and state of the arts new. Carpeted dining room, with roving staff to oversee. Common Room for sixth formers, with drinks and snacks, a popular social centre.

Pastoral Care and Discipline: Exceptionally well taken care of, with a lively network of tutors, parents, pupils, housemasters, and a trained counsellor on tap. Fierce anti-bullying policy with early signs picked up by prefects (sixth formers).

Very tough on under-age drinking; out for drugs and sex, and school continues to wage its 'ceaseless war' against cigarettes.

Pupils and Parents: Mainly professional classes, largely from Berkshire, Buckinghamshire, Oxfordshire and London. Several offspring of Oxford dons. Very friendly, easy to talk to, look you in the eye, this is one of those rare schools where pupils mix happily and easily vertically. Old boys include Sir Douglas Bader, Lord Olivier, Kenneth Grahame, Judge Stephen Tumim, George Fenton (Shadowlands musack).

Entrance: at 13 via CE from 54 schools. Down-payment of £500 at 11 guarantees place on successful CE; some from state schools (tests and assessments). Sixth form entry via school's own test and interview, with five GCSEs at B or above.

Exit: Around 10 leave post GCSEs, and more come in. 90 per cent go on to higher education (70/75 per cent to traditional universities), and a number to Oxbridge each year. Forces a popular alternative.

Money Matters: Up to 13 scholarships and exhibitions, two Service exhibitions, 30 per cent bursaries for sons of clergy, music and art scholarships (variable numbers), four continuation scholarships offered with a group of prep schools, plus Dragon/St Edward's School scholarship for a 9 year old at state school. Arkwright design scholarship for 16 year old, plus Rotherfield and Bader awards for 'bright all rounders'.

Remarks: The old Teddy's adage – more brawn than brain – no longer holds and has given way to something far more civilised: a traditional public school, with increasing girl numbers, which does more than most to look after the whole person, and treats each as an individual.

ST ELPHIN'S SCHOOL

Darley Dale, Matlock, Derbyshire DE4 2HA

TEL: *01629 733263* FAX: *01629 733956*

E-MAIL: admin@st-elphins.co.uk

WEB: www.st-elphins.co.uk

✦ PUPILS: 215 girls and 5 wee lads; 50 board, 170 day ✦ Ages: 2-18 (boys aged 2-7) ✦ Size of sixth form: 45 ✦ C of E ✦ Fee-paying

Head: Acting head Dr D Mouat, deputy head since 1999.

Entrance: Not a problem. No exam for pupils joining pre-prep and infants. 8-13-year-olds by school's own entrance exams. Entry at sixth form – relevant GCSEs, interview and school report.

Exit: To a strange and wonderful mix – Bath, Leicester, several Hong Kong Universities, one to Oxford, to London, Leeds, Bristol etc, some to art foundation courses and art and design degree courses.

Remarks: School was founded in Warrington in 1844 (and named after a little-known saint who perished in battle in the 7th century). Moved to a former hydro in Darley Dale in the Derbyshire countryside in 1904, now on A6, has a huge chimney stack in the background. (NB head says this is an unfair description as the chimney does not dominate, and the school is a very fine Victorian building with modern classrooms etc.) Small classes, wide range of ability intake. No streaming to start with, but streamed for GCSE according to ability. All girls take French, and Latin and German are on offer. Strong links with the Far East: Chinese girls take Chinese GCSE, most get A*s, and A level (grades A to C) – all on their own and without tuition. Textiles popular at A level, good results. Very small sixth makes results difficult to report on, but they still look healthy. Special help available for dyslexia, EFL. OG Richmal Crompton, creator of Just William, and Penelope Mortimer. Recently built junior school block – v popular. Swimming for all at the nearby Matlock Lido, good range of playing fields, including all-weather games pitch. Keen charity workers and fund-raisers. School is represented at the annual Buxton Festival of Speech, Drama and Music. Girls wear smart kilts. Friendly, with good pastoral care. Low key. Fees reasonable (discounts for clergy and Forces children). School fulfils a need in an area not noted for private schools.

ST FELIX SCHOOL

Southwold, Suffolk IPI8 6SD

TEL: *01502 722175* FAX: *01502 722641*

E-MAIL: mfeilden@stfelix.suffolk.sch.uk

WEB: www.stfelix.co.uk

✦ PUPILS: 155 girls (75 board, 80 day) Plus own nursery 'Little Dragons', pre-prep and prep school, St. George's, with 120 boys and girls ✦ Ages: 11-18 prep/pre-prep ages 2-11) ✦ Size of sixth form: 40 ✦ Non-denominational ✦ Fee-paying

Head: Since January 1998, Mr Richard (Rick) Williams BSc (fifties) educated at Rutlish Comprehensive in South London, also attended by John Major. Read mathematics at Westfield College, London University. Keen on golf, cricket and tennis, and he is an enthusiastic musician (jazz and classical) plays the double bass. His wife trained as an accountant and also as a teacher. Three children (two at university, one at Uppingham). Soft spoken, efficient and determined. The first head master in the school, and as such creating shock waves. Previously deputy head at Queen Margaret's York, and before that taught in state schools. Absolutely focused on getting the boarding ethos back in the place, 'I'm a late convert, and zealous'. Took over from Mrs Campion, who was here since '91 and left unexpectedly.

Academic Matters: Broad intake is reflected in results; fine GCSE results, and A levels looking excellent – more than half the results are As in the last two years. Small numbers mean that some teaching groups are minute (two, even one pupil per subject, though whether the school can afford this much longer is another question). Very small and distinctly strong classics, both Latin and Greek. Sciences taught as three subjects, with equal numbers of girls taking single and double awards. Excellent laboratories – far better than at many girls' schools. Setting for maths. Head is tinkering with the timetable, making the day longer, more work, more play, more activities. Enthusiastic language teaching. Help on hand for children with learning difficulties. Good work ethic, and sense of girls doing their best.

Games, Options, the Arts: Good art, (three-D under Mrs Viv Burns, fine art under Mrs Roberts-Rossi), with remarkable sculpture – metalwork, wood carving, stone, and breeze-blocks used by youngest girls – but it doesn't show through in the exam results. Super photography. Dramatist-in-residence. Strong netball, hockey and tennis, and keen riding (girls use the local riding centre), the best compete in inter-school events. Squash courts on site, local golf course, and much is made of water sports in the summer. Good on the individual music teaching front. Keen D of E take up, also Young Enterprise, which is paired with schools in Denmark and Germany.

Background and Atmosphere: Lovely secluded site not far from the North Sea, with seventy-five acres of finely kept grounds. redbrick purpose built 1897 Queen Anne design, plus some later additions, including the new super indoor heated swimming pool, built to celebrate the school's centenary, and 1999 sports hall / theatre. Currently there is a somewhat desolate sense of small numbers rattling round in huge buildings – numbers in the senior school have close-to halved. However, staff and girls all agree there's a new buzz and vibrancy about the place since Mr Williams arrived on the scene. Good staff/ pupil relations, friendly and unpressured atmosphere pervades. House system now changing to moving girls horizontally. Weekend programme being beefed up, 'It needed it,' commented a recent old girl.

Pastoral Care and Discipline: Good shepherds care well for the flock, and individuals can be themselves; discipline is not a problem. Female chaplain.

Pupils and Parents: From Suffolk, Norfolk and the A12 corridor, and a handful of children from overseas (Hong Kong, Taiwan, Russia, Germany). Gentle and unspoilt girls. Old Girls good at marrying winners – include Lady Prior, Lady Waley-Cohen, Olga Detterding, Daphne Pagnamenta, pioneer of riding for the disabled.

Entrance: Via exam at 11+, 12+, 13+ and 16+.

Exit: Wide variety of universities, usually one or two to Oxbridge, some to art college. Interesting careers and achievements clocked up by old girls – champion golfers, writers, travellers, museum curators, a very early campaigner for birth control.

Money Matters: Flexible number of scholarships – art, music, drama, sport – for variable amounts, also bursaries. Funds are now given a boost by dint of Easter and summer lets to language schools etc. Used to have income from gravel pits which it owned; these, alas, now sold.

Remarks: A small, gentle girls' boarding/day school, in need of more pupils but with no clear idea of where they will come from, in a gloriously unspoilt isolated area, with extremely good facilities, where daughters can grow up without any undue pressure.

ST GEORGE'S SCHOOL

Ascot, Berkshire SL5 7DZ

TEL: *01344 62900* FAX: *01344 629 901*

E-MAIL: office@stgeorges-ascot.org.uk

✦ PUPILS: 285 girls; 137 board, 148 day
✦ Ages: 11-18 ✦ Size of sixth form: 79
✦ C of E ✦ Fee-paying

Head: Since 1999, Mrs Joanna Grant Peterkin BA. Educated at Downe House, Wycombe High School and Durham University (read history) then PGCE at Oxford. Previously 'ran her own business advising students and their parents on university entrance', and was head of sixth form at St Paul's Girls. Teaches current affairs to sixth formers. Took over from Mrs Anthea Griggs, who was here from 1989.

Entrance: Not difficult for boarders (more demanding for day places). CE at 11+, 12+ and 13+, mixed ability, girls who have something to offer, assessed by time spent at the school the year before entrry. Foreigners on interview and comprehension exam, ditto for sixth form entrants plus previous head's report and six GCSEs at A*-C.

Exit: Some leakage post-GCSE, but most will stay on to do four or five ASs and three A2s, and on to university etc.

Remarks: Small pine and rhodie girls' boarding school, useful for the less academic. Refuses to publish detailed examination results – ask for them nonetheless. Keen design technology (incorporating textiles and art rather than wood and plastics) and good art and ceramics. Computers everywhere, email address and voicemail for every girl. Games in four-badminton-court-size sports hall and surrounding 30-acre campus. Sports hall has enviable weight training and ballet/aerobics (ballet taught or catered for to a good standard), fencing, exercise area on top floor, but swimming pool is outside (heated) across St George's Lane. Games important here, especially lacrosse and tennis. Drama and public speaking are popular, with regular awards for the former (LAMDA exams). Photography strong and own dark room very much used, and at GCSE. D of E, Young Enterprise and lots of charity work. Founded in 1877 as a boys' prep school and converted to girls at the turn of the century. Tucked down St George's Lane on edge of Ascot High Street, with purpose-built dorms and interlocking classrooms (incredibly narrow claustrophobic staircases and passages everywhere). Recent buildings funded by sale of Queen's Hill. No timetabled lessons on Saturdays, day girls stay to complete prep; all boarders are full boarders. Girls complain there is 'nothing to do at weekends' in the school – fair number of complaints on this front. Boarders move from small five-bed dorms to study bedrooms, with common rooms and kitchens for each year group. Sixth formers can take driving lessons and entertain boys in common room. Girls 'graduate' via a set of increasing privileges; great feeling of being in the social whirl still pervades. No uniform in sixth, girls ambivalent about marvellous Red Riding Hood cloaks. Automatic expulsion for drugs. Pupils mostly come from the south rather than London, with tranches of social parents from further afield, some brash, some rich, many first time buyers. Popular with foreigners and Fergie.

ST GEORGE'S SCHOOL FOR GIRLS

Garscube Terrace, Edinburgh EH12 6BG

TEL: *0131 332 4575* FAX: *0131 315 2035*

E-MAIL: office@stgeorges.edin.sch.uk

WEB: www.stgeorges.edin.sch.uk/

✦ PUPILS: 945 girls; 900 day, 50 board. Nursery 50 including 5 boys ✦ Ages: 2-18 ✦ Size of sixth form: 150 ✦ Non-denom ✦ Fee-paying

Head: Since 1994, Dr Judith McClure MA DPhil FRSA. Scot (early fifties), educated Newlands Grammar School, Middlesborough (was briefly a nun), studied law, later got a first in history at Oxford, lectured at Liverpool and Oxford Universities. Previously at St Helen and St Katharine, assistant head at Kingswood School and head of (what was) the Royal School Bath. Super, enthusiastic head, larger than life, though some would say OTT, and 'not to everyone's taste' says a parent. Dr McClure believes that girls do better in single-sex environment, and looks forward to 'building characters, and running a happy school with capable, confident and committed teachers'. She puts pupils, parents and staff in that order of importance. Refreshingly honest. An educationalist, who recognises that there is no time for a head to teach in a large school, but 'tries to keep in touch', giving philosophy seminars to the upper sixth. Married to 'portable' historian husband, Dr Roger Collins, who specialises in 7th–9th-century Spain. No children. Mrs Davis, capable deputy head, is very much the hands–on executive here.

Academic Matters: Very much a grammar school feel to the place – straight academic performance with not many frills (though NB head disagrees about the frills). Three distinct departments, Primary, Lower School and Upper School (plus nursery). Girls take Highers in one year and A levels (if they wish) the following year – or do the complete A level course. Excellent results. Most popular subjects maths, English, biology, French and chemistry – a good mix of sciences and arts. Marvellous French with interesting computer courses. Good general studies course and careers advice. Support learning throughout (two half-time staff), both for those with learning difficulties and for the gifted child. One full-time EFL teacher – there are about twenty-two students in the school whose native language is not English.

NB league tables are meaningless in this school, given that two systems are followed.

Games, Options, the Arts: Fabulous Centenary Sports Hall with good viewing area over hall and squash courts, marvellous lacrosse, including flood-lit 'synthetic' pitch. Playing fields recently upgraded. Robertson Music Centre home of three orchestras etc, with choirs, wind groups, chamber music – over 600 musicians. Art popular (new-ish art and design dept), as is drama. D of E Award. CCF with Merchiston. Any number of lunch-time and after school clubs, which operate more as tasters than anything else. Sixth formers go to Edinburgh Academy for sports, arts, music and boys.

Background and Atmosphere: Cluttered collection of modern extensions round purpose-built 1912 complex in Murrayfield (including boarding house), surrounded by sports grounds and excellent selection of wilderness areas. Schools' inspectors found boarding well organised and comfy (with one or two dark comments about the loos etc in Lansdowne House). Pupils have a purposeful air. Mufti in sixth form. Does things (play and dance) with Merchiston, though traditionally linked with Edinburgh Academy.

Pastoral Care and Discipline: Problems dealt with on an 'individual basis' with much parental involvement, under aegis of a 'head of guidance'. Occasional sackings. School very proud of its 'Working Together' document setting out policies on drugs etc and including a catechism on student rights and responsibilities.

Pupils and Parents: Unashamedly elitist and hard-working. Mixture of Charlotte Rangers, incomers and first-time buyers. Parent Teacher Forum for curriculum debate, The Friends of St George's for social events. Popular with foreigners.

Entrance: Serious test from four and a half. Selective. Parents have been known to cram their tinies for entrance to the junior school (and to weep copious tears when their darlings are refused entry), otherwise exam. Entry to sixth form is automatic for home-grown pupils; external pupils need five A/1 – C/3 passes at GCSE/Standard grade.

Exit: A good 10 per cent leave after GCSE, to boys' schools or (after Highers) with university places already in the bag. The rest go on to gap, degrees and higher education of all sorts – Scottish law popular, as are the sciences and medicine. Around 50 per cent of university entrants go to Scottish universities – Aberdeen and Edinburgh are particularly popular – 50 per cent head south.

Money Matters: Had a good number of assisted places, and must miss these. Selection of scholarships and bursaries, discounts for siblings, and brothers at Edinburgh Academy.

Remarks: A straight-up-and down academic girls' day school, now back on track as the number one Edinburgh girls' day school. Still regarded as a bit 'narrow' by some Edinburgh parents, and occasional comments that 'you need to be in the St George's mould to succeed'. But good, however, and making efforts to broaden out a bit.

ST LEONARDS SCHOOL

St Andrews, Fife KY16 9QU

Tel: *01334 472126* Fax: *01334 476152*

E-mail: info@stleonards-fife.org

Web: www.stleonards-fife.org

✦ Pupils: 235 girls and boys, 155 board 80 day. Plus junior school of 66 girls, a few boarding. ✦ Ages: 12-18, juniors 3-12 ✦ Size of sixth form: about 100 ✦ Non-denom ✦ Fee-paying

---

Head: (Principal): Interregnum: acting head Pat Harris. From 2001, Mrs Wendy Bellars (late thirties). Educated at Hillhead School, Glasgow and Glasgow University (read English). Taught at Renfrew High School, then at Gordonstoun, King's Chester (head of English), and deputy head of Bishop's Stortford College. An ISC inspector, and has been involved with the army regular commission board and the admiralty interviewing board. Married to Brian, an officer in the RAF. Takes over from Mrs Mary James, who was here from 1988.

Academic Matters: Uneasy reports. School has now dropped the Scottish exam system in favour of GCSE/A levels only – against the (Scottish) national trend. Some staff have links with the University of St Andrews, and the school uses some of their facilities. Careers advice from 13. Complaints from parents on lack of flexibility of subjects on offer – but on the other hand, one pupil did A level chemistry in '97. Difficult to comment on results given sixth form and other changes.

Games, Options, the Arts: Strong games for Scotland, with international (Scottish) players at lacrosse, and three county hockey players. Judo, trampoline, badminton, all-year tennis, swimming. Good art department, but few taking it at A level. D of E Award. Music much improved (Bob Steedman, husband of a previous head, designed the centre). All the pupils are taught self-defence.

Background and Atmosphere: Founded in 1877, known as 'Smellie Lennies', now a conglomerate of St Katharines School (prep), St Leonards School and St Leonards Sixth Form College. 'Mother' school of Wycombe Abbey , purpose-built (and slightly awesome) with many additions, very near the sea – bracing air (track suits popular for games), in bustling university town. Golf, riding and the beach as well as trips up town and forays to the surrounding countryside. Mega library and selection of maryana in Queen Mary's House. Civilised houses – NB pupils do own laundry and ironing – and Chris Clyne-designed uniforms (skirts not cheap, but second-hand stuff now available), including Barbours and cloaks. Marvellous (Bob Steedman-designed) popular sixth form house with study bedrooms and glitzy bathrooms – second such now opened.

Pastoral Care and Discipline: School rules feature punctuality, security and civilised behaviour: sackings for OTT. Also two sackings for untruthfulness – saying going to friend for weekend and turning up at all-night party in Edinburgh. Principal makes an issue of every suspension (drinking and smoking) and brings in police where theft is involved. Full boarding – two weekend exeats a term plus half term. Recent complaints that pupils can get away with doing very little work, bunking off to town etc, with parents not informed 'till late on.

Pupils and Parents: Strong Scots contingent. Around 13 per cent of pupils from England, less foreigners and ex-pats. Lots of daughters of 'Seniors' (famous Seniors Betty Harvey Anderson, Dame Kathleen Ollerenshaw).

Entrance: CE at 11, 12, or 13 – not difficult. Own exam for state school entrants (own Junior School, take 12+ CE). Sixth form entry: six GCSEs or equivalent at C+, plus A-Bs in A level subjects 'preferred'.

Exit: 85 per cent to university (fewer than when we last went to press). Newcastle, Bristol, Exeter, Durham and Scottish universities popular – particularly Edinburgh and Aberdeen. Some to art or drama courses. Slight leakage post-GCSE.

Money Matters: Academic, music, art, drama and sport (including golf) scholarships; 25-50 per cent of fees.

Remarks: Famous traditional girls' boarding school where changes are afoot. In mid metamorphosis – can't yet tell whether it will become a butterfly or a moth.

JUNIOR SCHOOL: St Katharines (St Kays), The Pends, St Andrews, Fife KY16 9RB. Tel: 01334 460 470. Head: Since '96, Ms Joan Gibson. Entrance is via interview and previous head's report. Most pupils go on to senior school. Junior school uses senior school facilities. Pleasant atmosphere in boarding house. Satisfied reports from parents, who don't always continue sounding quite so enthusiastic when their children hit the senior school.

ST LEONARDS-MAYFIELD SCHOOL

The Old Palace, Mayfield, East Sussex
TN20 6PH

TEL: *01435 874 614* FAX: *01435 872 627*

E-MAIL: enquiry@stlm.e-sussex.sch.uk

WEB: www.stlm.e-sussex.sch.uk

✦ PUPILS: 400 girls, around 200 board ✦
Ages: 11-18 ✦ Size of sixth form: 126 ✦
RC (but non-RCs welcome)
✦ Fee-paying

Head: Since 2000, Mrs Julia Dalton (fifties). Educated at Bedales, then read English at York. Taught at Wakefield Girls' High, and a number of other schools. Married with two sons and a daughter. Returned to teaching when the children reached school age, rising to deputy head at St George's School, Harpenden before coming here. Husband is director of education planning for Hertfordshire. Took over from Sister Jean Sinclair, who was a wise, humorous, gentle and popular head from 1980.

Academic Matters: Good GCSE results generally, given the broadly based entry; science a little disappointing. A levels good too. Maximum class size 18, for first two years, then 16/18. Offers many languages – French, Spanish, Italian, Russian, German, Chinese, Greek and Latin. Hot on religious studies – as one might expect. Five girls a year regularly go into engineering, as well as medics, biochemists etc. The school believes in adapting itself to the needs of its pupils (as far as staffing and the physical facilities allow): the A level timetable, for instance, is fixed after the girls have made their subject choices, and is said to accommodate all without alteration. EFL in demand. Peripatetic staff to help with learning difficulties.

Games, Options, the Arts: Hits-you-between-the-eyes ceramics (with GCSE and A level results to match), excellent art too (including life drawing, female only – chiz!). Pupils of all ages are prepared for the City & Guilds professional cookery exams. Games of all kinds strong, and an important part of school life; one team or another usually in their national finals; pitches stunningly situated. Sixth formers can opt out of team games and plump for fencing, judo etc, covered swimming pool designed by nun-architect, and used by local villagers, inter-schools cross-country riding course, Young Enterprise and D of E Awards. Five choirs now. Some parents voice disappointment that more is not done in the way of educational trips etc.

Background and Atmosphere: Cornelia Connelly founded the Society of the Holy Child Jesus in 1846, and Mayfield School in 1872; amalgamated with an earlier foundation at St Leonards-on-Sea in 1954. Fine old buildings in the grounds of The Old Palace of the Archbishops of Canterbury (magnificent 13th-century Chapel was restored by Pugin and is used for worship by the whole school daily), with sympathetic additions on a lovely site. Dormitories and classrooms scattered throughout; two junior years in separate Aylwins House; otherwise, houses in clusters, with communal lunching (excellent food) in dining hall and own individual refectories for supper. OK dormitories; sixth formers have study bedrooms. Blue uniform for all but sixth. Lots of contact with the local community; much enjoyed Christmas procession with the village featuring inter alia a donkey, a female Joseph and a host of angels. Excellent school magazine 'The Cornelian'. A friendly and open place generally. Pupils are expected to be self-motivated, 'but we lean on them pretty hard'.

Pastoral Care and Discipline: Strong religion, underlying rather than overwhelming, with regular prayer groups and retreats plus lots of advice on where to go if worried. Discipline – 'not many problems'. Not a strict or regimented school; individuals valued in all their variety 'find the good in each and help them to use it as God intended'; complaints by some parents that the girls are allowed 'too much freedom' probably the reverse side of this coin. Some contact with boys from Worth and Tonbridge.

Pupils and Parents: Mainly from South-East England, diplomatic and army families. Around forty non-Brits, including Hong Kong Chinese, Nigerians and Europeans (particularly Spanish). Europeans often come for one year only. Pupils charming and articulate, work hard and play hard. Local parents are very supportive.

Entrance: 11+, 12+, 13+, occasionally 14+ and sixth form entry. By CE at 13+ and 11+; 14+ by interview and previous school report, and sixth form ditto. Five Cs at GCSE (A or B in the subjects to be studied) for A level attempts, but exceptions can be made (eg for overseas qualifications).

Exit: Some leakage after GCSE, but most stay. Wide spread of universities; three or so to Oxbridge.

Money Matters: Will carry exam-year crisis. Means-tested scholarships awarded to Roman Catholic girls at 11+ or 13+ for academic ability, art, and music.

Remarks: Wide-ability (but not all-ability) Catholic girls' boarding school with large social and ethnic mix, works well. Offers a good strong range of non-academic subjects as well as the usual. Numbers well down on previous edition.

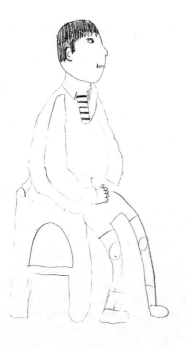

ST MARGARET'S SCHOOL,

EDINBURGH

East Suffolk Road, Edinburgh EH16 5PJ

TEL: *0131 668 1986* FAX: *0131 662 0957*

E-MAIL: contact@stmargaretsschool.net

WEB: www.stmargaretsschool.net

✦ PUPILS: around 600 girls, 20 boys; 25 board; 575 day ✦ Ages: Girls 3-18, boys 3-8, plus Teviot Playcare 3 months – 3 years ✦ Size of sixth form: 150/160 ✦ Non-denom ✦ Fee-paying.

Principal: Since 1998 at the merged school, and since 1994 at St Margaret's, Miss Anne Mitchell, MA (forties). Educated at Lossiemouth High, Elgin Academy and Aberdeen University, where she read English. Previously deputy head of Dunbar Grammar and head of English at North Berwick High. Articulate – a good communicator. Miss Mitchell's aim was 'to provide a period of stability and consolidation' at St Margaret's and she is enjoying the challenge of this new conglomerate. 'Standards of excellence remain a priority; it is what happens in the classroom that counts'. Looks to her senior pupils to uphold standards ('would Miss Mitchell approve of what you are wearing?'). Mrs Sally Duncanson MA, previously head of St Denis & Cranley, is deputy principal (guidance).

Academic Matters: Results not relevant as yet, but not expected to set the Forth alight. ESL and excellent learning support on hand throughout, also support for gifted pupils. It's Standard Grades followed by Highers then Advanced Highers. French, Spanish, Latin and German are available; Greek is extra-curricular, but with the current super-abundance of staff, extra languages may yet be timetabled. Classes normally around 20. Set for maths and English from 'Transition', languages from five. Computers everywhere. Careers advice from age 13.

Games, Options, the Arts: Girls are bussed to Edinburgh University's Peffermill sports grounds. The gym is above the music studios (still) in a converted church. Music good, with a thriving choir, plus plainsong, masses of orchestral, jazz, strings etc. Home economics, and 'survival skills in cookery' , also strong ceramics, photography, jewellery.

Background and Atmosphere: In '98, St Margaret's amalgamated somewhat precipitously with St Denis & Cranley school, whose Colinton Road site has now been sold. There is accommodation for some 810 pupils at this site, following an earlier merger between St Margaret's and St Hilary's school. Nursery and pre-nursery available, and after school care – highly popular. Amalgamated school based in a cluster of Victorian villas in bedsit land of South Newington, including a dead cushy boarding house (ex-Oratava hotel, with private bathrooms everywhere (excellent letting prospect). Flexi-boarding on offer. No thought of changing uniform for change's sake: girls will continue to wear 'any listed or recognised tartan kilt'.

Pastoral Care and Discipline: Miss M sacked one pupil on her first day, no complacency here, but 'seeing the principal is usually enough'. Anti-bullying is given high priority by all staff: four guidance staff, plus form teachers on hand to advise.

Pupils and Parents: School subsidises daily buses from North Berwick, Lauder and the Gyle. A thorough mixture, with gentrified children departing for their country estates on the one hand, and solid Edinbourgeoisie, plus children whose parents work at the local supermarket on the other. Head keen on 'diversity of backgrounds'.

Entrance: Throughout the school, any term. Whenever, very flexible, but primarily at 5, 11, and 16. Boys up to 8 only. Most difficult to get into the school's sixth form college: good GCSE or Standard Grades needed, plus satisfactory prelims.

Exit: Some leave to go to trad prep schools, or to public schools, otherwise some after Standard Grades, but 'most' stay for sixth form. Fair tranche to tertiary education, Scottish universities preferred.

Money Matters: St Margaret's had 69 assisted places – should be able to replace them when the land at Colinton is sold. Currently few debts or bad payers but 'the school is always happy to help with financial problems'.

Remarks: Amalgamation of two famous Edinburgh girls' schools, both cosy, and not for pushy career people. Too early to judge, but might work very well when the dust has settled.

ST MARY'S SCHOOL

Ascot, Berkshire SL5 9JF

TEL: *01344 23721* FAX: *01344 873281*

E-MAIL: admissions@st-marys-ascot.co.uk

WEB: www.st-marys-ascot.co.uk

✦ PUPILS: 350 girls; 330 board, 20 day ✦
Ages: 11-18 ✦ Size of sixth form: 89 ✦ RC
✦ Fee-paying

Head: Since 1999, Mrs Mary Breen MSc, the school' first lay head and an impressive one. Took over from Sister Frances Orchard, head from 1982.

Academic Matters: The school has a strong bias to the humanities, and produces outstanding GCSE results in most of these subjects, eg 100 per cent A★s/A in art and design, Greek, Italian, music and Spanish. No grades below C in any subject. A level also superb, averaging 8.1 points a subject. All pupils take religious studies at GCSE and, at time of writing, do very well in it. Languages are the school's biggest academic strength – new purpose-built language faculty and long tradition of foreign pupils in the school. Dual or triple award science for all at GCSE (80 per cent A★s/A in '00). Good range of traditional subjects on offer. Some dedicated wonderful staff. A place where nothing much distracts pupils from academic work, but you get the idea that work might be fun. Full-time teacher for those with mild dyslexia/dyspraxia – all pupils screened in first year. No EFL.

Games, Options, the Arts: Good art – taken at exam level by about 20 per cent at GCSE and has got nothing but A★s and As in the last decade. Drama (including house plays), community service and D of E award, not to mention dressmaking, computers, fencing etc. Tennis the top game, and keen coach is at the nets morning, noon and night. Music very popular – the majority of girls learn one instrument, several learn two 'or more' and size of music school recently doubled to accommodate them all.

Background and Atmosphere: Commuter-belt rhododendron country – impeccably kept. Head's house bang in the middle of the school grounds, as are all senior staff houses. Purpose-built in 1885 and extended since in similar red brick. The school was founded by the Institute of the Blessed Virgin Mary in the 17th century under Mary Ward, one of the great English educationalists. Civilised bedrooms for older girls, and even dorms are more like rooms, with much privacy. Houses, run by the lower sixth, are given the responsibility of running the school in rota, and this system helps break school age barriers vertically. No uniform for sixth form. Sheltered. Soothing chapel and slightly cloistered feel, a wonderful sanctuary from the world outside.

Pastoral Care and Discipline: No alcohol – the place for a smoke and drink is down in the woods. Regular larks with Eton boys (school keen on links with Eton) get into national press, and do school's image no harm at all. Strong tradition of pastoral care. The school could be a bit short of weekend activities ('plenty if they want them,' says school, 'the school spends a great deal of time and money on them including socials with boys' schools').

Pupils and Parents: Top Catholics. Conventional. Seven per cent non-Brits: a few smart (royal) foreigners, diplomats' daughters, OGs' daughters etc. OGs include Caroline of Monaco, the Spanish infantas, Sarah Hogg, Marina Warner, Antonia Pinter.

Entrance: Registration, plus day-long assessment exam at the school (11+, 13+). Five GCSEs at C including maths and English; Bs in A level subjects for entrance to sixth form (plus interview etc).

Exit: A few leave after GCSE, otherwise the majority to universities – Oxbridge (seven in '99), Edinburgh, Manchester, Bristol the most popular. A few to art courses (and some doing history of art degrees). Careers in the City, law, medicine and teaching. Secretarial and cookery skills often acquired in the gap year.

Money Matters: OG scholarship for sixth form entry and one for science. General, art and music scholarships at 11+ and 13+. Fees 'as high as the market place will allow'.

Remarks: Still excellent establishment with a quiet sense of community and purpose, and contented reports from parents. An oasis of tranquillity which has changed remarkably little over the decades, despite all. OGs still complain that the school does not prepare pupils for the hurly burly of 'life' today – we query that however.

ST MARY'S SCHOOL
Calne, Wiltshire SN11 10DF

Tel: *01249 857200 Fax: 01249 857207*

E-mail: registrar@stmaryscalne.wilts.sch.uk

Web: www.stmaryscalne.wilts.sch.uk

✦ Pupils: 306 girls; the majority board, about 45 day ✦ Ages: 11-18 ✦ Size of sixth form: 87 ✦ C of E ✦ Fee-paying

---

Head: Since 1996 Mrs Carolyn J Shaw BA PGCE (early fifties). Educated West Kirby Grammar school for Girls and University of London, where she read English. Married, two children at university. Previous post – university adviser at Cheltenham Ladies'. Started teaching career with VSO in the British Solomon Islands, did a stint in Bermuda, not to mention four years out of teaching (as marketing manager, Eastern Europe for Insta-Pro International Export Company – useful experience guiding pupils to the outside world). Took over from Miss Delscey Burns – a hard act to follow. After a quiet start all is now well. Mrs Shaw very different in style from Miss Burns, but 'she is making small but worthwhile changes,' comments a parent – and is holding her own, no mean feat. Interesting collection of governors; 'Visitor' the Lord Bishop of Salisbury.

Academic Matters: GCSEs good, and A levels almost all A-C, leaning heavily to English (consistently superb results), history and geography with other no-frills mainstream subjects. Pupils devoted to their teachers, and so tend to follow their subjects from GCSE to A level. Latin compulsory up to 14; school is 'too small for esoteric subjects,' as a parent put it, with theatre studies the only one featuring in results – 6 As in '00, and 'popular with Oxbridge candidates' says head. Others (eg classical civilisation, politics, sports science now on the list of available subjects.) Nine-ten GCSE subjects the aim. Keen peer pressure to work – and they do, in chalk-and-talk regime. Sciences taught for combined award only – 'over-taught but still not the ideal base for A level', was a comment. Some strong teachers, including a fair sprinkling of men. First fortnight in July post-GCSE set aside for general studies. Italian offered in sixth form, also Cambridge Computer Course leading to diploma.

Games, Options, the Arts: Take second place to academe (not true says head), though several girls currently represent Wiltshire for lacrosse, and county players also in netball, hockey, tennis etc. Fairly old-fashioned gym, but indoor pool on the way; keen tennis – 'the best time to grab a court is during Neighbours,' confided a player. Very well-subscribed D of E (currently thirty pupils going for gold). Purpose-built theatre for recent rousing successes and alternate-year form Shakespeare competitions, plus LAMDA. Music active – several groups, choirs etc. Weekends trips to Bath and London for plays. Keen riding, says one eventer who chose Calne 'so I can stable my pony and keep in with one-day eventing'. Upper sixth 'Unfashion Show' produces glossy pics of budding socialites heading for Tatler pages. Life drawing classes in Calne for sixth form; driving lessons. Weekends a bit empty; gap filled in the sixth form by outings to eg Oxford. Effective fund-raising, for eg school in East Africa.

Background and Atmosphere: Not a school you would choose for its facilities. Functional, practical, purpose-built building, founded 1873 by Canon Duncan (Vicar of St Mary's Church, Calne) in 25 acres of central Calne, an unglamorous little Wiltshire town once best known as home of now defunct Harris' sausage factory. Houses divided horizontally; pupils move each year while remaining throughout in 'companies', accumulating 'red points' for good deeds, and each with annual black-tie dinner. Junior house for new girls. Fairly rigid boarding system with fixed exeats. Slightly grammar school-y functional feel, but cosy at the same time.

Pastoral Care and Discipline: Quietly supportive tutorial system, staff keep a careful watch – 'We are well aware of social pressures,' – monitors for anorexia. Fine and letter home for smoking and suspensions (occasional) for alcohol ('No, they are not plaster saints'), straight out for drugs. Each new girl gets met at the door by 'school mother' from year above. Nice touch – making individual named cakes for each of a large class of pupils being confirmed.

Pupils and Parents: Largely establishment intelligentsia, in strongly C of E ethos with light dusting of RCs, Jews etc but little special provision for them. A few Forces' children, otherwise London and local with Yorkshire and Scottish additions. Bright-eyed, unhearty upper-crust girls whose parents tend to know each other. 'Confident, friendly all-rounders,' said a satisfied parent, 'full of initiative and well poised to partake in normal life' while remaining 'feminine and full of fun'. By reputation a little wild.

Entrance: Fairly selective. Many pupils from the cream of London preps. No one takes the exam, or even registers, till parents and child have visited the school. Close liaison with prep to ensure girls likely to thrive when they get here. 'We are looking for academic competence and signs of potential; we can always get the mechanics right later,' says head. Girls spend a day in the school before taking CE at 11+, 12+ or 13+. Younger sisters are no longer specially encouraged.

Exit: A few leave post-GCSE, 'we are certainly not losing our 'brightest and best,'' comments head. Post A level, the majority go on to strong universities (Bristol, Edinburgh, Durham etc) including a handful to Oxbridge in a typical year; otherwise teacher training, art foundation. A gap year is popular.

Money Matters: Two academic scholarships (and an exhibition for a day girl) at 11+ or 12+, and one at 13+; one at 11+ or 12+ for a daughter of the clergy or of an Old Girl; two music scholarships at 11+, 12+ or 13+. Three sixth form academic, one art, one drama, one music scholarships. Scholarships worth one third fees. No endowments.

Remarks: Academic girls' boarding school which enjoyed an astonishing period of being the fashionable choice in the south. Now settling into a lower key, more in keeping with the reality of the place. Still however a good place for well-bred brains to mix with their own kind in somewhat socially limiting atmosphere (though 'this is not what we are trying to provide' says the head, and perhaps it is becoming less so).

ST MARY'S SCHOOL
Shaftesbury, Dorset SP7 9LP

TEL: *01747 854005* FAX *01747 851557*

E-MAIL: admin@st-marys-shaftesbury.co.uk

WEB: www.st-marys-shaftesbury.co.uk

✦ PUPILS: 324 girls; 224 board, rest day ✦
✦ Ages: 9-18 ✦ Size of sixth form: 75 ✦
RC ✦ Fee-paying

Head: Since 1997, Mrs Sue Pennington MA (late forties). The first lay head of an IBVM school. Educated at the Convent of Jesus and Mary in Suffolk, read maths at Liverpool University – and then joined the army. Widow with two children, both at university. Previous post was as deputy head and housemistress here; has taught in the state sector. Plays bridge and golf, keen on music, reading and making soft furnishings. Sensible, approachable, with a good understanding of teenagers. 'I try not to over react'. Took over from Sister M Campion Livesey, who was here from '85.

Academic Matters: Results are excellent for mixed intake. Theology (taught by Mrs McGovern) especially strong, English and modern languages also very good. 20 or so subjects at A level, Mrs Pennington keen on choices; not a school that offers the 'fashionable' ones – eg economics but not business studies here, theatre studies, not media studies. Separate sciences now on offer for brighter girls. Girls being pushed more and harder these days, to stretch the able. Four sets for most subjects. Good calibre of staff, and increasing numbers of them. 'We won't give in over little things' – homework must not be late, poor work is not accepted.

Games, Options, the Arts: Strong on netball and hockey – and well kept grounds with lots of pitches; music on the up, keen drama, good art. Strong on extra curricular activities – self defence, modern dance, song writing competitions, D of E. Pitman's touch typing in French ('why not English?' asks a petulant mother). Retreats, pilgrimage to Lourdes etc. EFL, help for dyslexics.

Background and Atmosphere: Large converted Edwardian country house set in rolling acres (slight feeling of impending doom as you go up the drive). Heaps of room, wonderful views and – for the boarders – rather a sense of 'being out in the sticks': Shaftesbury (the nearest town) does not swing. Girls allowed cars in the sixth form, offsets the isolation a bit. Weekend activities considerably boosted in the last two years, 'though there will always be some dedicated sloths' sighs the head. Recent building includes new junior school, infirmary and library. Strong community happy-family feel.

Pastoral Care and Discipline: Improved and improving with increased numbers of staff per house; pupils meet with their tutor each morning. Spiritual life important – quite a number of C of E girls, and Anglican priest comes once a week: RCs and C of E girls share confirmation classes until the last moment. Fierce anti-smoking policy – fine and letter; suspended; expelled.

Pupils and Parents: Wide variety, including some from overseas (but not more than 10 per cent non-nationals) – Mexico, Spain, Germany, Hong Kong. Unspoilt, uninhibited girls – and relatively unsophisticated. Day girls go home at 6 p.m. Parents largely enthusiastic about their choice.

Entrance: Over-subscribed in '99 and again in '00 – clearly getting more popular.

Exit: Almost all to university.

Money Matters: Not a rich school, but does its housekeeping well.

Remarks: Girls' Catholic boarding school, with the same foundation as St Mary's Ascot, but with less social cachet, unpretentious and good at bringing out the best.

ST MARY'S SCHOOL

Wantage, Oxfordshire OX12 8BZ

TEL: *01235 763571* FAX: *01235 760467*

E-MAIL: stmarysw@rmplc.co.uk

WEB: www.stmarys.oxon.sch.uk

✦ PUPILS: 200 girls; all board, except for 15 girls✦ Ages: 11-18 ✦ Size of sixth form: 73 ✦ High Anglican ✦ Fee-paying

---

Head: Since 1994, Mrs Susan Sowden, BSc PGCE (forties), educated at Clarendon House Grammar School in Kent and read geography at King's College, London. Previously deputy head at Headington School, where she has two daughters; also has one son. Divorced and recently remarried. Also has a theological qualification, AKC, and an advanced diploma in educational management. Super lady, extremely popular with staff, pupils and parents, energetic and jolly with it. Operates totally open-door policy. 'She knows us all!' say girls appreciatively. Teaches geography.

Academic Matters: Improving exam

results (average A level point 5.5 in '97, 6.9 in '00) but takes girls of a genuinely wide ability range. and: 'It's OK if you're not clever,' said a pupil soothingly, 'they take time out and help you with essays. Value added data (ALIS and YELLIS – the real thing) extremely good – and they publish it too. History of art regularly does well at A level, and, with English, is perennially popular, also art, good results. Theatre studies has been an option for years; business studies also on offer.

Games, Options, the Arts: Extremely good art (on show all over the place), no less than five syllabuses on offer at A level (photography, textiles, pottery, sculpture, set design, general painting/printing in various combinations). Keen drama, described as 'inspiring' by one and all. Good music. Traditionally strong at lacrosse and tennis.

Background and Atmosphere: Founded by the Vicar of Wantage in 1873 to be run by Anglican nuns (they withdrew in 1972) and Christian ethos firmly underpins. Cosy and domestic redbrick buildings, very uninstitutional, in the town, some houses dotted about, and main road (with bridge across) whistles past. Very noisy dining room with good food. Dorms and older girls' bedroom walls plastered with pictures, pin-ups and posters. 'Rec rooms' pleasantly lived in. School committee allows girls to have a voice in admin. Saturday morning school, swimming pool reported to be closed at weekends, and the usual complaints of 'nothing to do' at weekends except mooch around town. Endless social life – boys ferried over for parties etc, and 'partying, snobbing and going about in gangs,' said a pupil from a rival establishment 'is where it's at,' adding in wonderment: 'They regard Radley as their private property.'

Pastoral Care and Discipline: Worst punishment, says an old girl, is 'being forbidden to join SMOGS' (the Old Girls association). Fierce anti-smoking campaign. High jinks post GCSEs a traditional feature and the school hits headlines from time to time giving good St Trinian's-type publicity, eg girls painted sperm patterns up the school drive. Girls report occasional anorexia outbursts – 'well below national boarding average' says the school.

Pupils and Parents: Upper class parents, who tend to know each other. Scottish contingent ditto. Some seriously rich parents. Change afoot, though – now has 25 per cent first time buyers, 15 per cent from overseas (17 nationalities), and 'some seriously poor parents as well'. Breeds terrific loyalty, with unusually large numbers of second and third generation pupils. OGs include Olivia Channon, Rosie Johnson, Lady Helen Windsor, Emma Nicholson, Lucinda Green. Girls are frisky, relaxed, full of smiles.

Entrance: By CE (not a great hurdle) and interview, at 11, 12 and 13. Day girls (twenty places only) introduced in 1996.

Exit: As many as seven per year to art college, occasionally to the Royal College of Music, and widespread universities, old and new, green wellie ones preferred.

Money Matters: One academic, two music/art/sport scholarships at 13+; one senior music scholarship; two sixth form scholarships.

Remarks: A small social famous girls' boarding school for toff-ettes that knows its market and serves it well.

ST PAUL'S SCHOOL

Lonsdale Road, London SW13 9JT

TEL: *020 8748 9162* FAX: *020 8748 9557*

E-MAIL: hmsec@stpaulsschool.org.uk

WEB: www.stpaulsschool.org.uk

✦ PUPILS: 770 boys, majority day: two boarding houses (around 60) ✦ Ages: 13-18 Size of sixth form: 310 ✦ C of E ✦ Fee-paying

Head (High Master): Since 1992, Mr Stephen Baldock MA (early fifties). Educated St Paul's (where he captained the cricket) then read classics (part one) and theology (part two) at King's College Cambridge. Came back to St Paul's to teach classics, headed the boarding house, was Surmaster (= deputy head in St Paul's-speak) for eight years before being appointed to present job. Married to GP, lives just across the road, has four children, likes sports and plays in staff teams. Teaches PSHE to first-year classes. Thoughtful, easy to talk to, and – that much overused word – is approachable. Lapsed recently into verse of Virgilian proportions on the school's winning the Princess Elizabeth cup at Henley in '97: '... hortanturque patres matresque et turba faventum Exclamantque parem spemque metumque suis; Nec frustra Paulina manus...'

Academic Matters: Brilliant, as always. Stimulating teaching, staff on top of the job. Lively debating and Socratic style of teaching. Notably narrow choice of subjects at A level – maths, biology and chemistry the popular subjects, extraordinarily few taking modern languages; economics – which was a weak relation – now excels with the rest. All boys have to take an option in a practical subject from second year. Most boys take GCSE French and maths at end of second year, and carry on with modular A level French and maths syllabus, which gives them extra strength in these subjects. Outstanding modern languages, with French, Italian and German assistants. Japanese and Spanish also available. Very strong science (separate sciences and Nuffield Co-ordinated Sciences – dual award). Some outstanding English and history teaching and generally very strong common room (sabbaticals and exchanges encouraged to gee up flagging enthusiasms). Maximum 24 per class, A level classes average nine or ten. Impressively long detailed reports each term can reduce non-brilliant to despair. Under the new system, boys will do 4 or 5 AS subjects followed by 3 or 4 A2s, plus non-examinable general studies.

Games, Options, the Arts: Two-hour lunch break daily during which boys are involved in a non-academic activity – eg rowing (impressive), music, swimming. Games traditionally and actually strong, though 'it's OK', said a pupil, 'if you're no good at them.' Cricket and rugby particularly lively – first XI unbeaten in '00. School recommended by Lawn Tennis Association for keen would-be tennis players. Good indoor pool, excellent fencing salle, rackets court; fives a major game here. Technology flourishes – super modern facilities, drama keen (nine productions a year.) Saturday mornings are taken up with games, rehearsals, extras (though not compulsory). Director of music since '96 – Mr Mark Tatlow, whose previous post was chorus master at the Swedish Court Opera, no less. A new music building opened in '99. There are some outstanding musicians in the school, and one or two top class staff. Some concerts given with St Paul's Girls'. Stunning palatial art department, with space for exhibitions and every resource and facility known to man – probably best school art centre in the country – though almost no-one takes art at A level. The school' newspaper, Black and White, produced a penetrating report on Teletubbies, and consumer report on Nintendo 64 versus Playstation. School also produced wonderful recipe book full of fattening boy-friendly recipes. Hunk note: OP Tristan Boxford the youngest person ever to reach the surfing World Cup finals in '96.

Background and Atmosphere: Super site, with 45 grassy acres (formerly reservoirs) sweeping straight down to the River Thames, the view of which has been much spoilt by ghastly boarding-house buildings (one just demolished to make new music school) and other purpose-built grimbo monstrosities – aesthetic considerations very low on St Paul's agenda. Entrance hall/atrium in main block is the central gathering place – like Grand Central Station – where messages are relayed out and boys to be seen congregating at all hours. School founded in 1509 by Dean Colet, friend of Erasmus and Thomas More, whose humanitarian principles still stand firm. Trustees of the Foundation are the Worshipful Company of Mercers, who provide much (too much?) of the governing body. School moved to its present site in 1968. New boys coming from London preps may find Pauline life a bit unstructured. To participate in 'Apposition' is every boy's aim (four or five outstanding pupils speak/make music etc, to assembled distinguished visitors, governors and parents). Boys bus in from all corners of the metropolis – can be difficult when clubs, societies demand their presence after bus leaving hours. Boarding houses are very useful for short-term stays either through demands of school, or when parents away.

School has very down-to-earth, slightly scruffy, grammar-school feel, with academic work the overriding priority. Very male atmosphere, without being macho (currently nine female tutors plus ten part-time). Boys complain that the school is 'not really a community' – little groups and cliques, people doing their own thing and 'you need a tough skin to survive'.

Pastoral Care and Discipline: Tutor system, which high master is keen to use as 'springboard' to promote feeling of school as community and to 'teach them that people matter' (ie, not just academic priorities). High master sees 1993 school photo (the first time whole school photographed since 1959) as 'big moment'. Parents are asked to invite tutor home for a meal on a regular basis: communication is intended to be frequent and open. PSHE courses (relationships with girls, drugs etc), and pre-university course on life with a capital F. High master agrees, somewhat uncertainly, that any boy 'in possession of illegal substances should expect to be expelled', but adds rider that 'you can't do a belt and braces on school rules'. School has weekly visit from psychologist/counsellor. Lively place, not easy to keep the lid on – endless excuses for being anywhere but in the right place.

Pupils and Parents: Drawn from all around London and from as far away as Guildford and Windsor. Some from state schools. All sorts, no types, though qualities which come up over and over again in OBs are doggedness, head-down approach to life, street smart. Very articulate – always winning public speaking competitions (two '98 members of the English Schools World Debating team). Old Boys include John Milton, Edmund Halley, Jonathan Miller, Peter Shaffer, Viscount Montgomery of Alamein, G K Chesterton, Michael Marks, Oliver Sacks, Lord McColl, Isaiah Berlin, Lord Winston, Helly Nahmad (wave-making Cork Street dealer).

Entrance: Tough: all but the brightest and best weeded out at 10/11; intake is 150/160 per year – 75 from Colet Court (see separate entry), the rest from prep schools all round London – current tops, Durston House, Hill House, Tower House, The Hall. At 10 or 11, all prospective pupils and parents come to the school: high master interviews parents, the surmaster sees the boys and afterwards they compare notes. Main lists close then and CE follows on as qualifying exam. Boys must perform well in every subject. For sixth form entry – A grades 'at least' in proposed A level subjects, and 'at least' eight good GCSEs altogether.

Exit: Oxbridge (50-60 a year), with still more bridge than Ox. Four or five a year to art college. Otherwise, the older, popular universities (Newcastle, Nottingham etc). Pupils go on to be lawyers, doctors, civil servants, one or two to the Church.

Money Matters: There are 153 scholars (as many as the miraculous draft of fishes – scholars wear a silver fish badge): scholarships are mainly awarded on entrance, some develop in the 'Eighth', ie sixth form. Music scholarships available. No art scholarships on entry, but yes at sixth form (assuming two other subjects up to scratch as well). Scholars integrated with the rest of the school. Has established bursary fund to replace assisted places (but the Mercers may have to dig deeper into their funds to replace these if necessary).

Remarks: One of the top two (if not the top) London boys' schools.

ST PAUL'S GIRLS' SCHOOL
Brook Green, London W6 7BS

TEL: *020 7603 2288* FAX: *020 7602 9932*

E-MAIL: lhayward@spgs.mhs.compuserve.com

WEB: www.spgs.demon.co.uk

✦ PUPILS: 675 girls, all day ✦ Ages: 11-18 ✦ Size of sixth form: (known as seventh and eighth forms): 200 ✦ Anglican foundation ✦ Fee-paying

---

Head (High Mistress): Since 1998, Miss Elizabeth Diggory (early fifties), read history at London. Previously head of Manchester High (for four years) and before that head of St Alban's, a school she built up into a very popular, successful place. Forthright, articulate, low profile – some worries surfacing about how well she's doing. Took over from the wonderful Miss Janet Gough – not easy.

Academic Matters: Outstandingly strong and consistently so. 75 per cent A grades at A level. Maths now far and away the most popular subject, but with the largest number of low (for St Paul's) grades too. History – 'if you take history you can't fail,' said a pupil, 'it's so good'. English also very strong indeed (and much patronised). Languages – Russian, French, Spanish, Italian, classics and German all offered and taken up. Otherwise fairly narrow range of exam subjects to choose from at both levels. 95 per cent plus A*/A at GCSE – girls take an average of nine GCSEs, – the idea being to leave time to pursue a broader curriculum than the rather constrained demands of the GCSE syllabus. This causes no problems, says high mistress – universities know St Paul's is strong. Setting in maths after first term. No setting in languages. Non-examinable general studies. Dual award science for all at GCSE. Useful IT building.

Very strong common room (some housing for staff available). Always comes at or near top of A level league tables, which is no surprise, but still deserves all credit for sustained effort.

Games, Options, the Arts: Very strong music. Music director since '94 Dr Derek Bourgeois MA MusD – ex-Director of National Youth Orchestra, composer, did stint at Bristol University. School lucky to have him, though given tradition of musical stars at St Paul's (Gustav Holst was director of music here, and wrote wonderful things for 'SPGS') filling this post is never a problem. Art results superb at A level – and it's reasonably popular too. Swimming pool, two lacrosse pitches, sports hall, tennis courts, etc, but not a school that worships team games. School much keener on intellectual matters such as debating, language exchanges, exchanges with the US, etc. Work experience for all after GCSE, and job shadowing.

Background and Atmosphere: School opened in 1904 with money hived off from John Colet's Foundation, run by the Mercers' Company (Mercers abound on the governing body). Large red-brick purpose-built but mellow building nestling in Brook Green, surrounded by houses occupied by parents of (would-be) Paulinas. Calm but dynamic atmosphere: school does not stand still, but neither does it strive to change. Good big imposing hall, plus music hall, new science classrooms. No uniform.

Pastoral Care and Discipline: Has a slightly I'm-All-Right-Jack approach to discipline and care ('relaxed but not casual', comments school), both within and outside the school, but does produce a helpful leaflet full of telephone numbers for eg the Eating Disorder Association, and British Pregnancy Advisory Service etc. Anna Ford's glamorous brother is (still) chaplain here and is one of the people who interviews candidates.

Pupils and Parents: Solid professional classes, with a sprinkling of barristers, cabinet ministers, etc. Has the most impressive array of old girls in the country, including Rosalind Franklin, Evelyn Sharp, Celia Johnson, Harriet Harman, Brigid Brophy, Joan Robinson, Shirley Summerskill, Shirley Conran, Jessica Rawson (Warden of Merton), Dr Onora O'Neill (head of Newnham), not to mention Carol Thatcher. Large Jewish contingent a feature of the school.

Pupils are incredibly articulate, with views on everything (no easy ride for parents) and a teeny tendency to intellectual arrogance, but not toff-y. Pupils mentally very tough indeed. Robustness on all fronts essential for survival. 'Fine if your face fits,' said a pupil who was unhappy here.

Entrance: Regarded by most prep school heads as the equivalent of finding the Holy Grail. Potential Paulinas are treated like Derby winners by their prep schools. School sets its own exam papers in January for following September, with a fine disregard for would-be pupils sitting other London girls' schools exams. Tries to choose pupils for their potential as much as their performance. Entry at 11+ and 16+, with occasional vacancies in other years. A number from Bute House, otherwise one here and one there from London preps all over, including Hill House and Glendower. Draws a good number from state primaries (always on the look-out for intellectual fodder). Entry at sixth form: five GCSEs at C or above (including Eng, maths etc) for external and internal candidates; externals also sit St Paul's own exam

Exit: Look at the school honours board in the entrance hall – packed with Oxbridge. Medicine still very popular.

Money Matters: Academic and music scholarships and bursaries at 11 and 16, plus art at 16; bursary named in honour of ex-High Mistress Baroness Brigstocke. 76 assisted places at the peak, which were a real strength – school has appeal to replace these that (to date) offers 5 bursaries a year. Now has some Ogden Trust bursaries for 'above-average children from a state primary school of limited or no parental means'.

Remarks: St Paul's continues to reign confidently as the utterly wonderful top girls' academic day school in London, much sought after, and deservedly so. New high mistress will be watched closely however.

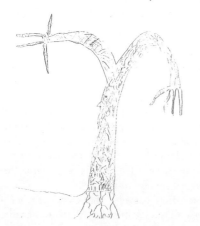

ST SWITHUN'S SCHOOL

Winchester, Hampshire SO21 1HA

TEL: *01962 835 700* FAX: *01962 835 779*

E-MAIL: office@st-swithuns.hants.sch.uk

✦ PUPILS: 470 girls, 220 board, 250 day, plus Junior School including boys up to the age of 8 ✦ Ages: 11-18, junior school 3-11 ✦ Size of sixth form: 120 ✦ C of E ✦ Fee-paying

Head: Since 1995, Dr Helen Harvey BSc PhD (forties), was at school at Lordswood School, Birmingham, Bedford College, did her PhD in cancer research at the Royal Marsden in Surrey. Dr Harvey was previously head of Upper Chine School on the Isle of Wight, has two children. Keen on sailing (crews for a boat moored at Cowes) and on music. Has an easy authority, competent, and we feel the school is in safe hands. She says that she has 'no plans for going co-ed'. Nice deputy head.

Governing note: The visitor is the Bishop of Winchester, council members include the Dean of Winchester, the Mayor of Winchester, not to mention the head of Winchester College. A Winchester production, in fact.

Academic Matters: 'Girls go in here,' said an observer, slightly bemused, 'and with no particular song and dance seem to come out with incredible A level results'. Exam results excellent as usual. Strong on general studies in general 'we feel there are many things – to do with politics and philosophy for example – which no girl should leave without knowing'.

Streaming for maths and modern languages, all take nine GCSEs, – no blocks, you can choose what (within reason) you wish. Three separate sciences for the majority. Some very pleasant classrooms, particularly in the English department – most conducive to study. NB most teachers are women – and one or two complaints that one or two can be a bit beastly in class.

Games, Options, the Arts: Modern sports hall opened by Princess Anne; newish swimming pool in which girls have buried a time-capsule. Also netball, riding, karate, cross-country, tennis, archery, rowing. Duke of Edinburgh award candidates spotted camping on the grass in front of the school (school spokesperson confirmed). Food technology is compulsory in first and third years – all part of the quest for a useful education – in gleaming kitchens.

Technology outstanding. Technology Centre under five star male head, Mr Vaughan Clarke, where goggled girls operate industrial robots and develop the most amazing ideas including, for example, a shuttlecock which makes a hum as it whizzes through the air – for partially sighted people, and a wonderful Heath Robinson device to separate clean hay from dirty in a rabbit hutch. St Swithun's girls regularly win heaps of awards in this field, including the Hampshire Technology Competition three years running, second and third in British Steel Construction Challenge for Schools, and recently won the Money Spinner Challenge with a design for a collecting box with mice emerging from a block of cheese (now being manufactured). School's engineering club recently chosen as one of top five such clubs in the UK.

Popular 16+ pre-driving course in Winchester. Music reputed to be good – there are lots of orchestral groups, etc, and 'you can have a bash at anything, including the harp,' says a pupil. Art has been the poor relation – few take it at A level, but those who do do well). Good crop of Guildhall music and drama exam results plus associated board.

Background and Atmosphere: Founded by the Dean of Winchester in 1884 for the Christian education of the daughters of Winchester dons and clergy, now housed in a huge '30s red brick Queen Anne-style purpose-built building, which looks like an elegant army barracks, with lots of space, set a bit bleakly between motorway escarpment and main road in green belt 20 minutes' walk into Winchester, with several additions and extensions plus adjacent brick junior school. Wonderful flower arrangements inside though, lots of polish, lots of light – good big windows – and a statue meant to be St Swithun. Separate day and boarding houses – latter cosy and warm. Lots of weekly boarders (very successful). Half and half breakdown of day/boarding 'makes for split in friendships', comments a pupil – except in upper sixth who have their own mixed day and boarding house. There is also the familiar baleful feeling of girls stuck in boarding houses while the day pupils – as they perceive it – are larking about in Winchester. No Saturday school but head volunteers that there is a 'degree of compulsion' about weekend activities (what joy to a mother's ears) – 'otherwise it is so easy for them to loll in front of the television all day'. Compulsory chapel. Rather uninviting looking libraries. The atmosphere is generally one of 'good work ethic' and purposefulness plus sensible discipline. Occasional activities with 'or against' Winchester College, including dances, but despite St Swithunites putting up notices in town 'for God's sake communicate!' Wykehamists are largely unaroused and viewed by some girls as 'off this planet'.

Uniform has a 'violently disliked' (by some) daisy on the front, legacy of the school's wonderful ample-bosomed Victorian benefactress, Charlotte M Yonge, author of *The Daisy Chain*.

Pastoral Care and Discipline: House-mistresses said to be 'caring and bothering,' and individual teachers are largely well thought of – parents' rumblings, however, of 'failures of communication,' though Dr Harvey comments that pupils hands are held every inch of the way and she cannot see what more could be done (and some parents corroborate this). 'It's out for drugs,' approves a parent living in Winchester, which manages to combine a cosy safe middle class environment while at the same time being drugs capital of Wessex (NB only one school drugs incident in recent years). Pretty strict on permission to go out or have visitors, fines for smoking and drinking of 'around £15'.

Pupils and Parents: 'Middle of the road' 'grammar school', pupils with IQs of 115+. Mostly from within a 50-100-mile radius. Children of middle-class professionals and business people, sisters of Wykehamists, fairly large contingent of ex-pats, eg Forces' children, a handful of Chinese and ethnics, otherwise Londoners, many with weekend cottages off the M3. Old Girls: Baroness Warnock, Professor Joscelyn Toynbee, Vivienne Parry.

Entrance: Over-subscribed for CE at 11, 12 13. Between a fifth and a quarter come up from the junior school. A handful of girls join at sixth form – no hard and fast qualifications for entry here – each pupil judged on her particular merits.

Exit: Almost all to universities, mostly the strong ones, including a good number to Oxbridge (eg quarter of the upper sixth has been offered Oxbridge places as we write). A fair number leave after GCSE – to Peter Symonds sixth form College in Winchester, and to boys' sixth forms.

Money Matters: An unspecified number of scholarships are available (exams late January). Music scholarships give free music tuition.

Remarks: The academic girls' school in the Winchester area. Suffers slightly from the 'split-personality' of a school with day and boarding in almost equal numbers. Much in demand, but somehow doesn't seem to inspire enthusiasm in potential parents or pupils (except for technology). Outdone by the good local state schools in some respects – though not in funding or social cachet.

JUNIOR SCHOOL: Tel: 01962 835 750. Fax: 01962 835 781. Head: Mrs V A Lewis MA MSc DipEd. Nursery, pre-prep and prep (boys go on at eight to local prep schools eg the Pilgrim's School, Farleigh). In the grounds of the main school, but autonomous. A fair number go on to the senior school, also to (other) girls' boarding schools, Downe House, St Mary's Calne etc. No automatic entry to senior school.

SEDBERGH SCHOOL

(Pronounced 'Sedber')

Sedbergh, Cumbria LA10 5HG

Tel:01539 620 535 Fax: *01539 621 301*

E-mail: sedsch@rmplc.co.uk

Web: www.sedbergh.sch.uk

✦ Pupils: 340 boys, around 320 board. Girls from 2001✦ Ages: 11-18 ✦ Size of sixth form: 140 ✦ C of E ✦ Fee-paying

Head: Since 1995, Mr Christopher Hirst MA (forties), educated at Merchant Taylors' and Trinity Hall Cambridge. Previously senior housemaster at Radley under Dennis Silk, before that head of Kelly College. Historian and Cambridge cricketer. Currently chairman of HMC sports committee. Described by a teacher in a nearby school as 'good and energetic', and by himself as a 'genuine enthusiast for full boarding'.

Academic Matters: Some sloppy teaching noticed. 'There's a sense of "getting boys through"', commented a parent. Fairly broad spectrum of IQs, and good support groups for the less able. Single science for majority at GCSE. GCSE results fine, A levels improved but scoring too heavily on the Es-Us. Biology, Geography and maths most popular departments. General studies taken at A level. Full-time member of staff for special needs.

Games, Options, the Arts: Lots and lots and lots of beefy games, playing morning, noon and night ('simply not true,' says head). Famed for its rugger (regularly beats Ampleforth, Stonyhurst and other strong rugger schools). Also famous for the Wilson Run – a 10-mile fell race open to ages 16+. Regular trips abroad with games. Good very keen cricket school. Sports hall, 25-metre indoor pool. CCF, National Champions Shooting '96 and '97, strong naval links. D of E. Good careers advice and interview experience (with Old Boys and parents). Good CDT and workshops, interesting art and pottery. Magnificent music school and good drama. 'Not bad' (said a father) on visiting speakers, and most societies well supported, CCF military band much recommended.

Background and Atmosphere: Founded in 1525 by Roger Lupton, a Provost of Eton. Traditional dorms for juniors (large) now converted and updated. School in centre of dear little town-ette surrounded by glorious high hills, real tourist territory – hill walkers milling about pavements, sheep baaing. Limestone boarding houses throughout the tiny town: music in former Bursar's House, Guldrey, on Main Street. Impressive conversion of Georgian building on site of Lupton's original school into Churchill Library; some buildings showing signs of dilapidation. Boys fiercely loyal to houses. Planning to go co-ed from 2001.

Pastoral Care and Discipline: Well-thought-out punishment system, with points/endorsements, driving-licence style, pink cards for minor offences (a boy is 'pinked'), green for major. Good house system, with some 'super housemasters', according to pupils, parents and prep schools. Caring staff; positive atmosphere, with older boys and staff on good footing. Programme kept fairly busy at all times – possibly to lessen sense of isolation: miles from anywhere. The head points out that the school is in fact 5 minutes from the M6,

15 mins from a main line station and 70 mins from an international airport.

Pupils and Parents: Suffers from snobby attitudes: 'It's for farmer's sons,' said one local toff firmly, rejecting it out of hand for his son. Mainly local, some from Scotland. Professional and country parents. Variety of regional accents. 20 ex-pats and 20 non-Brits helping fill the coffers. OBs: Brendan Bracken, Will Carling, Sir Christopher Bland, Robert Swan, James Wilby, Sir Jock Slater (First Sea Lord), Lord Bingham (Lord Chief Justice), Simon Beaufoy (of Full Monty fame).

Entrance: CE, or to the Junior House via 11+ and interview.

Exit: 2 per cent post-GCSE; around 90 per cent to degree courses – reading subjects right across the board.

Money Matters: Had 65 assisted places, and their loss was a blow, but has since received a £4 million legacy for bursaries.

Remarks: Traditional, all-male, games-orientated boarding school in an isolated area, which has been through a difficult time, but is showing signs of cheering up. Now with girls in the offing.

SEVENOAKS SCHOOL

Sevenoaks, Kent TN13 1HU

TEL: *01732 455 133, Admissions 01732 467703*

FAX: *01732 456 143*

E-MAIL: regist@cs.soaks.org

WEB: www.cs.soaks.org

✦ PUPILS: 515 boys, 450 girls; 170 boys board, 345 day boys; 170 girls board, 280 day girls ✦ Ages: 11-18; ✦ Size of sixth form: 420 ✦ Non-denom ✦ Fee-paying

Head: Since 1996, Mr T R (Tommy) Cookson MA (mid fifties), previously head of King Edward VI Southampton where he made waves (metaphorically speaking). Pleasant company, with a strong vision of the school's future. Comments, a propos the school's IB programme, that 'it is a matter of some interest and even perhaps concern that the IB has not been adopted by more British schools than is at present the case.' – an interesting thought. Took over from the highly successful Mr Richard Barker, who was here from '81. Top class head's secretary, Mrs McMillan.

Academic Matters: Offers (and has offered for some long time) the International Baccalaureate (three main and three subsidiary subjects are studied, including a science, maths, a language and a national literature) – the course 'open to anyone who wishes to take it'; is considered a little harder than A level, the results are very good – in '99 four pupils gained maximum points (only 22 did so world-wide). The school has taken the decision to phase out A level –

pupils who entered the school in 2000 will only be offered IB when they reach sixth form. Strong languages, with exchange visits during term to/from France, Germany, Spain, Russia. GCSE results superb – about 75 per cent A and A★ – as are the combined A level/IB results. NB owing to large intake at sixth form, plus the sixth form doing two different exam systems, plus projected changes, etc, league table are even more meaningless here than elsewhere.

Games, Options, the Arts: Strong all round. Plenty of scope for budding musicians – over 800 individual lessons timetabled each week. Thriving drama department (own theatre), a public arts festival every year with 30 major productions, including an annual performance of a play in a foreign language. Most children do a creative subject (specialist craftsmen employed for this). School has a studio for budding TV reporters. National pioneers of Voluntary Service in the '60s: boys and girls are still much encouraged to be community-minded. Model United Nations debates. Flourishing D o E programme. CCF is voluntary and popular and includes many girls.

Several claims to fame on games field: two members of England under 18 rugby team in '97; girls' teams have represented the south-east in netball, tennis and squash. Shooting, tennis and sailing (particularly sailing) all strong – victories include the Glanvill and Youll cups. School has – among other things – three covered tennis courts. Recommended by the LTA for budding tennis players. You have to 'make the cut' to play some sports in later years.

Background and Atmosphere: Founded in 1432 (it is now thought) by William Sennocke, Mayor of London and a friend of Henry V, as a thank-you for his share in the victory at Agincourt. Purposeful air of efficiency pervades. Right in the main town of Sevenoaks. Its position and cramped buildings (new and old) give an almost claustrophobic feel to the place, but the school actually has 100 acres and opens up on to the gracious acres of Knole House.

Two boarding houses built recently, but the school is predominantly day and the nightly exodus can be disruptive, and causes some resentment on the part of boarders ('not apparent', comments head) who see themselves locked up while their day pupil peers lark about in town (not so, says head, senior boarders are allowed into town, and have their own 'boarders' bar' in the school). Separate boys' and girls' sixth form houses. NB the school feels like two different animals – a strong international sixth form (mainly boarding), and a town day school. The two co-exist a bit uneasily.

Pastoral Care and Discipline: Emphasis on the 'planned development of personal and social skills'. School counsellor works alongside the house staff. Strong house system. School 'reserves the right' to test pupils for drug abuse. 'Atmosphere socially very tough, children insecure, bullying results' reports one parent.

Pupils and Parents: Largely local (until you get to sixth form, that is), favoured by professional and media parents, some diplomatic. Many bilingual hybrids and budding linguists, attracted by the school's reputation for languages. Large numbers of foreigners at sixth form from 30 to 40 different countries. (20 per cent non-nationals in all.) 'And it's so fashionable to be foreign,' said an English parent. 'Your child comes back speaking with ze foreign accent.' Don't expect them to want to settle down in this country afterwards. Old boys and girls: Professor Simon Donaldson, Oliver Taplin; Lord Prout, Jeremy Harris, Paul Adams,

Chris Tavare, Paul Downton, Emma Hope.

Entrance: At 11 and 13 via school's own exam or CE for pupils at schools in the UK. Contrary to our report in the last edition, based on reports from parents, the school says it does 'not have a policy of weeding out weak pupils [post-GCSE] ... very occasionally an A level course will be considered unsuitable' – 'typically' about two pupils a year. £1,000 deposit required on offering of place. Large numbers come in at sixth form.

Exit: To a wide variety of universities (including overseas). About 40 to Oxbridge; Bristol, London, Nottingham, Durham too. Ex-polys popular for business-type courses. Medicine and engineering favoured careers. Some do gap year.

Money Matters: Offers 55 academic scholarships a year. Had a few assisted places – won't notice their passing.

Remarks: Co-ed day and boarding school which, with the help of the IB programme, grew into a very popular, much sought after establishment. Innovations in IT no longer so exceptional now that other schools have caught up; the lower school seems rather ordinary, but the sixth form is unique.

SHEFFIELD HIGH SCHOOL

10 Rutland Park, Sheffield S10 2PE

TEL: *01142 660 324* FAX: *01142 678 520*

E-MAIL: lfroggatt@she.gdst.net

✦ PUPILS: 940 girls, including 270 in Junior Department; all day ✦ Ages: 4-18
✦ Size of sixth form: 150 ✦ Non-denom
✦ Fee-paying

Head: Since 1989, Mrs Margaret Houston, BA (early fifties). Educated at St Hilda's, Whitby, and read English at Leeds University. Has been teaching all her life in grammar and comprehensives. Previous post: Deputy Head of Harrogate Grammar School. Married with two children.

Entrance: Tests in English, maths, verbal reasoning for entry to senior school from elsewhere: selective but not exceptionally so.

Exit: A few post GCSE; the majority to go on to higher education; Bristol, Chesterfield College (art foundation), Leeds, Manchester, Newcastle, London currently favoured, though this pattern changes a bit; about ten per cent to Oxbridge. A broad choice of courses.

Remarks: Useful GDST girls' day school. Solid and worthy. Excellent GCSE results, reflecting a selective but not super-selective intake. Creditable and consistent A level results. Examined drama. Buildings in quiet backwater tucked away in smarter area of Sheffield. Victorian main building with bits and bobs added on. No frills and not much space – but adequate, and £8.5 million development plan nearing completion producing all manner of smart new things, including dining hall, sports hall, more IT, new junior building etc. Information technology labs (IT for all) with Nimbus Network and computerised careers and library areas (pleasant library). Dance popular, also cross-country and trampolining. Music includes a swing band. Sports boasts international players and the occasional international tour (netball and hockey) – South Africa in '97 and Australia in '00. Had one hundred and twenty-six assisted places at last count, and the GDST will need incredible success with its appeal fund to replace all of them.

JUNIOR SCHOOL: 5 Melbourne Avenue, Sheffield S10 2QH. Tel: 01142 66 1435. Junior School on same site has cheered up numbers, and there is a generally more optimistic mood.

SHERBORNE SCHOOL

Sherborne, Dorset DT9 3AP

TEL: *01935 812 249* FAX: *01935 816 628*

E-MAIL: enquiries@sherborne.org

WEB: www.sherborne.org

✦ PUPILS: 510 boys, all board except for 35
✦ Ages: 13-18 ✦ Size of sixth form: 220
✦ C of E ✦ Fee-paying

Head: Since 2000, Mr Simon Eliot MA (late forties). Educated at Radley, read history at Queen's Cambridge. Taught at Winchester from 1976, and was a house-master (and a very popular one too) for 11 years. Wife Olivia read English and history of art at Cambridge and was a history of art examiner. Two children, 15 and 10. Interests include drama, music and sport.

Academic Matters: Results good and steady, with a handful of lively staff in among many traditional practitioners. Maths the most popular A level subject, followed by the sciences, ancient history, geography, economics and business studies. Small numbers doing exotic languages – not always with A grades. Quite a few taking design and technology at A level, and a fair number taking art and design. Six sets, varying ability. Classics department still waving the flag – no Greek at A level though. All boys now take nine GCSEs. French no longer compulsory, but one modern language (well-designed teaching block) is essential. All boys now take three separate science exams. Prep ('Hall') on Sunday evenings. Doing far more with Sherborne Girls on the academic front – full brother and sister schools now.

Games, Options, the Arts: Games record still extremely strong (lots of county players) and playing fields cover 50 acres. Compulsory 'sporting activities' till 16, and many continue thereafter. Very strong CCF (army, navy, marines). Successful art department under the enthusiastic, flamboyant Trevor Boyd, runs excellent inexpensive art tours to eg Paris, Amsterdam, New York. Very good drama, and plenty of it, at various levels (Powell Theatre used by visiting theatre groups). Lively and thought-provoking programme of talks by visitors (and sometimes boys). New structured minority studies programme with Sherborne Girls' to ensure breadth and continuation of more non-examinable subjects, excellent modern languages continuation courses pioneered by heads of department of the two schools. Lots of discussion and debate – boys do well in public speaking. Good music – ambitious programmes, two orchestras (with girls), jazz groups, swing band, chamber groups etc, just under half the boys learn an instrument. The school has a well-stocked, well-used 'open all day' careers department under Mr Philip Rogerson, assisted by the great and good Mr Rob Lloyd, who has visited every university in the UK.

Background and Atmosphere: Glorious setting, with rich honey-coloured ancient buildings around a huge gravelled courtyard, in the shadow of the Abbey. Many later additions. Founded by Edward VI as grammar school in 1550 (though origins go back to 8th century and subsequent arrival of the Benedictines in 998, who were removed by King Henry VIII), splendid library with famous hammer-beam roof. (Loveliness of setting and collegiate atmosphere brings in nice little income from visiting film companies.) Eight houses (choose with care), some scattered around the town, boys in dark blue guernseys with files/books scurrying everywhere (townspeople speak well of boys on the whole). All but one boarding houses refurbished and more study bedrooms introduced (bedsits, usually shared, from second/third year onwards). Abbey House' outsize dorm has been kept and now carpeted – by popular request (the boys love it), despite inspectorate's recommendations. Strong sense of tradition and moral fibre pervades. Lively social life with both Sherborne and Leweston girls. 'The Stick' (pretty grizzly sixth form common room – though pupils don't think so) is open to Sherborne boys and girls on Saturday nights. Food is plentiful. Supper at 6 pm – boys' pantries in full swing after prep at 9.15 pm

Pastoral Care and Discipline: Head not afraid to sack for drugs (about one a year) and occasional OTT behaviour (ditto). Resident tutor in most houses, plus housemaster (and family); chaplain. Firm rules, slacking frowned on. Well-thought-out programme of personal development, health education, etc, for third and fourth formers, parents called in en masse to co-opt for potential difficult times. School operates policy of (non-random) testing for drug abuse. Emphasis on responsibility (care and concern) not power/privilege of authority: clever initiation course for new prefects – mini managerial teach-in with outwardboundish session with staff in Exmoor, boys must run everything, including budgeting, role play, etc, to give them confidence with their peer group. Firm policy on alcohol.

Pupils and Parents: Sensible, self-confident, civilised, relatively unsophisticated. – applies to both age groups. Appeals to parents in professions and Services. Old Boys include David (now Lord) Sheppard, Nigel Dempster, Jeremy Irons, John le Carre (also, appropriately enough, the former head of MI6, Sir David Spedding), A N Whitehead, Sir Christopher Chataway, Sir Richard Eyre, Sir Michael Hopkins (the architect), the King of Swaziland, Dr Colin Lucas (Master of Balliol, vice-chancellor Oxford University), Alan Turing (Enigma code breaker), A N Whitehead, Cecil Day-Lewis – and lots more, from all walks of life.

Entrance: At 13 via CE, or by scholarship exam or school's own papers as appropriate. Reasonably selective.

Exit: Broad spread of universities (99 per cent), usually 15-20 to Oxbridge each year. Also London, Newcastle, Birmingham, Durham, Edinburgh and Bristol. Medicine, law and other conservative careers popular.

Money Matters: Unusual fiscal move: all departments in the school are now responsible for their own budgets. The Bursar shows them the annual figures. The school also owns the well-established International College, a school for foreign boys (and now girls), from all over the world, teaching English, preparing them for other schools/public examinations; this tidy little earner provides a scholarship fund for Sherborne Boys' School.

Scholarships of all sorts on offer at ten per cent to half fees (plus means-tested top-ups). Eight exhibitions worth one-fifth fees (one for those with proficiency in science); music awards each year, plus up to three full-fees worth of scholarships.

Remarks: An excellent traditional public school charging on, and doing a thorough job in a glorious setting, away from it all.

SHERBORNE SCHOOL FOR GIRLS

Sherborne, Dorset DT9 3QN

TEL: *01935 818 287* FAX: *01935 389 445*

E-MAIL: enquiry@sherborne.com

WEB: www.sherborne.com

PUPILS: 360 girls; the majority board
✦ Ages: 11-18 ✦ Size of sixth form: 168 ✦
C of E ✦ Fee-paying

Head: Since 1999, Mrs Geraldine Kerton-Johnson (fifties). Read chemistry and botany at the university of Natal, South Africa; taught in various SA schools ending as principal of Epworth High School, Petermaritzburg from 1992-99. Married to Anglican priest; four grown-up children. Well spoken of, but has much do. Took over from Miss June Taylor, head since 1985.

Academic Matters: Strong results at GCSE – not much below B; 40 per cent plus A grades at A level, with a tail of lower grades. Religious studies well patronised and successful at both levels; English, French, history of art, maths and Italian all popular. Thorough and solid teaching all round, and facilities are exceptionally good. However, there has been some dead wood among the staff – girls (particularly at sixth form) find lack of inspiration in some areas and parents feel their daughters deserve better. Occasional beefs from parents and pupils about not mixing subjects at A level despite claims of flexibility. As one parent commented, 'It seems strange in a big strong school.' Careers and university advice could be improved. Class sizes vary from 20 to far fewer; girls streamed early on into four bands (and can be shifted). Good modern language teaching in general, and it shows in the results (the satellite reception for foreign broadcasts well used).

Games, Options, the Arts: Fine music department, especially on the choral side (notable madrigal group – Emma Kirkby is an OG). Some orchestral playing with Sherborne Boys. Strong games school (with large numbers of sixth formers in teams), hockey and lacrosse, good tennis teams, squash, etc. Splendid sports hall. Splendid art block, jewellery making, design technology. Home economics, textiles, dressmaking, etc, all available. Some criticism that the school could/should coerce the girls to participate more in extra-curricular activities.

Background and Atmosphere: Founded

in 1899, large, architecturally dreary pur-pose-built conglomeration on a 40-acre site on the edge of the town, looking out over open country, with many later additions (particularly depressing compared to the boys' school). Close links with the (glori-ous) Abbey, daily prayers at school (some services in the Abbey). Good food and all meals eaten in houses (with accompanying emphasis on table talk and table manners). Recommended house: Aylmar.

Upper sixth house (Mulliner) known as the Sherborne Hilton, opened '93, spacious, lift, etc, though bare white walls have also earned it the nickname of the lunatic asy-lum. Girls kept busy and occupied most of the time, purposeful atmosphere pervades, though the usual girls' school complaints of not enough happening at weekends persists, and visitors comment on kilted girls 'wan-dering aimlessly about the town at week-ends'. (Head says 'not ours − from the International College') Social life with Sherborne Boys available (and occasionally distracting), sometimes officially (dinner parties, discos, etc). There is an underlying ethos of working hard and playing hard.

Pastoral Care and Discipline: Eight hous-es (competitive), mixed ages: choose care-fully. House staff vary in fierceness or other-wise, many have dogs (useful for night walking/checking). Tutor system more in principle than in practice. Which said, girls are well cared for. Sensible outlook on dis-cipline, though some parents critical of the amount of television watched. Number of exeats increased (and exceptions can be made), suits overseas and far-flung parents.

Pupils and Parents: Homogenised. Sizeable numbers of daughters of Old Girls, popular with army families, diplomats, Londoners with south-west connections. Girls are friendly, supportive, high-spirited.

Occasional public school tendency of the privileged to think the world owes them a living. Among the OGs are Maria Aitken, Dame Diana Reader-Harris, Emma Kirkby, and the first woman to make the board of M & S − Clara Freeman.

Entrance: 11+, 12+, 13+; by CE. Very def-initely selective. Also at sixth form.

Exit: Practically all go on to university (usually a good number to Oxbridge), the fashionable choices − Edinburgh, Manchester, St Andrews, Nottingham, Durham, Bristol − are all popular. Substantial numbers do medicine and lan-guages. Also to art and music colleges. Gap year favoured.

Money Matters: Five major academic scholarships, two exhibitions. One art, two music scholarships,

Remarks: Strong traditional all-round girls' boarding school, but needs to shake up its act; being watched with interest − can new head take it into the 21st century? Very much a girls' only school despite loads of social life and joint undertakings with Sherborne Boys'.

SHIPLAKE COLLEGE

Henley-on-Thames, Oxfordshire RG9 4BW

TEL: *0118 940 2455* FAX: *0118 940 5204*

E-MAIL: info@shiplake.org.uk

WEB: WWW.SHIPLAKE.ORG.UK

✦ PUPILS: 300 pupils, mostly boys (a few girls in sixth form). 230 board, 75 day
✦ Ages: 13-18 ✦ Size of sixth form: 116
✦ C of E ✦ Fee-paying

Head: Since 1988, Mr Nicholas Bevan, MA (fifties), educated Shrewsbury and Balliol College, Oxford. Soldiered for five years before deciding to become a teacher (trained at St John's College, Cambridge). Taught at Westminster, then Shrewsbury, where parents latterly considered him one of the best housemasters. Charming, approachable, dead honest (not all are) married with four children. Knows boys, and is to be found 'everywhere' – he will cover for most emergencies. Very proud of Shiplake (he insisted on showing us the view himself, despite the boy-guide standing in the background) and almost boyish in his enthusiasm. Very go-ahead, and very good at public relations. Keen on local involvement. Historical note: Mr Peter Carter-Ruck was chairman of governors here in the '60s.

Academic Matters: Copes well with less able boys; excellent learning support unit for those with dyslexia and other specific learning difficulties (one of the first in country), 16-24 boys admitted each year, 'English Plus' or 'Enrichment Studies' timetabled instead of French. Learning support offered throughout – new head, who has two part-time teachers to help. No pupils removed from other activities for Learning Support classes. Well spoken of by many preps, who use it as a standby for those who might struggle in a larger, more academic school. The less able shine here and numbers are viable. Small classes, maximum 16. Career planning starts early, timetabled from fifth year, and sensible advice given on appropriate GCSE and A level options. Boys are not academically submerged, policy being 'to obtain the maximum results with the minimum of fuss'. 17 A level subjects offered. Pik 'n' Mix A level boards – depending which suits best. Exam results consistent – around grade C at GCSE, grade D at A level, though a few get top grades each year. Business studies and art perennially popular. New academic tutor system. Computers everywhere, and used in GCSE by a few. Well-organised GCSE retakes (most useful) – mainly for own pupils, but pupils from outside may in special circumstances also re-take – and no shame attached.

Games, Options, the Arts: Boys much encouraged to participate – lots of opportunities, and lots of cups, pats on back. CDT very strong, with good workshop and draughting facilities. Brilliant ceramics teacher, very strong art. Enthusiastic public speaking. Music and drama particularly inspired – with regular plays in the tithe barn and fabulous spectaculars round the main house in the summer term organised by Malcolm Woodcock. Compulsory CCF, adventure training (trips to Kenya and South Wales) and Young Enterprise; as well as work experience. Games thriving – particularly rugby, hockey, tennis and cricket. Astroturf. Huge and much used sports hall;

rowing seriously popular and doing very well at it, plus regular tours abroad: Amsterdam, Ukraine, Switzerland and the States. Tradition of Olympic rowers.

Background and Atmosphere: Established 1959, stunning setting overlooking River Thames. Great Hall in main school for assembly and dining room (all beautifully lit and floored). Big building programme – pavilion/day boy house complex which includes a conference centre, flats for staff, ritzy rooms for day boys, many new classrooms. There are strong house bonds, v traditional with an emphasis on developing self-discipline. Boarding houses restructured: Welsh for weekly boarders, Burr for full boarders, Skipwith for flexible arrangements veering to weekly boarding, Everett for flexible arrangements veering towards full boarding. Boys graduate from largish dorms to study bedrooms. Houses have common rooms with kitchen, and senior boys run 'Junior Common Room' with bar.

Pastoral Care and Discipline: Boys fiercely caring of each other, small school, so 'no real problems'. Good housemaster/tutorial system run on old-fashioned lines. Very good handling of bullying (not much anyway), smoking equals fine, drink no problem (own bar), drugs automatic expulsion. Head will sack and has, three cases in five years – mainly bullying. Perceived as a 'tough' school (head prefers 'with clear and well understood codes of behaviour').

Pupils and Parents: From all over, trad parents and lots of first-time buyers, (close to London – lots of Londoners), not for socially competitive parents. Polite and gentlemanly breed of chaps. About 30 'from abroad', with 10 'real' foreigners. Regular parent/staff consultations.

Entrance: Mostly from prep schools: CE at 13+ plus school's own English paper. School's own English, maths and IQ paper from state schools, plus head's report in both cases. Boys with difficulties in English need to book early: they are assessed by Learning Support Department nine months before entry and 25 per cent turned away at interview. 60+ boys from over 50 prep schools. sixth form entrants come on basis of five GCSEs with Bs in A level subjects and head's report (but see Academic Matters above). In all cases, head's report rules supreme.

Exit: Some leakage after GCSE (often financially based), otherwise around 30+ to universities – Bristol, West of England, Loughborough, currently popular, several to diploma courses, and an excellent group to art foundation courses. Gap popular.

Money Matters: Despite strength of learning support unit, no extra charge is made for this – a bargain. Will 'try to help with financial crisis during exam years' – but parents report bursar can be very tough. Scholarships for art, music and sport. Discount for Services and sons of prep school masters. 10 per cent reduction in sixth form for pupil with best GCSE results.

Remarks: Super confidence-building establishment in the public school mould; many pleased reports from parents. Particularly sought after for the remedial department: under-achievers elsewhere can come up trumps here, and boys of quite mediocre ability achieve degree courses previously considered unthinkable. Girls now official at sixth form.

SHREWSBURY SCHOOL

The Schools, Shrewsbury, Shropshire
SY3 7BA

Tel: *01743 344537* Fax: *01743 340048*

E-mail: enquiry@shrewsbury.org.uk

Web: www.shrewsbury.org.uk

✦ Pupils: 695 boys. 558 board, 137 day
✦ Ages: 13-18 ✦ Size of sixth form: 280
✦ C of E ✦ Fee-paying

Head: Since 1988, Mr Edward Maidment, MA (fifties) ('Ted'), educated at Pocklington School, Scholar and choral scholar at Jesus College, Cambridge. Read history. Previously headmaster of Ellesmere College. Bachelor, jovial, keen singer, larger-than-life, refreshing (though some find his tongue a wee bit sharp). Definitely good at selling the school, and witty. Widely considered one of the best heads in the business. Knows the boys remarkably well, convinced that 'the heart of a good and successful education is not quantifiable'.

Fosters strong links with prep schools – 'important at a time when curriculum developments do not favour the 13+ entry'. Most interesting and articulate on the subject of boarding, adding to familiar arguments 'the deep and detailed knowledge of the individual' by housemasters, tutors and academic staff, plus strong resources means far more is possible in terms of achievement for the individual'. Enjoys quoting Cecil Day-Lewis, 'Selfhood begins with a walking away/And love is proved in the letting go.'

Retiring September 2001. Powerful collection of governors.

Academic Matters: Does very well indeed for boys of all levels (a fair number of scholars, the majority are average, some below average). Some excellent staff – Mr Maidment believes in waiting till he gets the right person and is encouraged by governors to cast far afield. Sciences still very popular. Noteworthy biology department under Ian Lacey. Electronic microscope, amazing collection of pickled organs. New chemistry and IT building in '96. Wonderful ancient library, one of the most important scholarly public-school libraries. Maths and English currently the most popular subjects – both strong, with excellent results; physics also very good. General studies at A level, business studies and religious studies were also very popular. Some pupils take AS levels (mainly French). Six full-time, eight part-time women on the staff at last count (compared with nil in '87). Three specialists for one to one tuition for dyslexics (outside the timetable). Good at keeping parents informed of a boy's academic progress (or lack of it).

Games, Options, the Arts: Famous for rowing, and strong on most games, aware 'of our superior fitness', as one Salopian commented. New all-weather playing surface and tennis courts. Music is very vigorous, 'talent brought out and developed' according to parents, and two 'major successes' at the Edinburgh Fringe. New music school opened 2000. Art taken seriously (pottery notable) with excellent results at A level and drama highly thought of by locals as well as the school. Art and history departments combine for trips (Italy – Rome and Urbino; Paris and Versailles) – hugely successful, adding extra dimensions for all. Renowned reputation for outward-boundish activities (basic camping, fell walking – tough leadership skills and all that), and serious community work (head dead keen). Lots of visiting speakers ('No, we don't feel isolated'). Boys encouraged to be outward-looking, especially towards Europe. Highly successful annual conference on European Affairs (requiring considerable stamina from lower sixth), brought officials from their London embassies for debates following pupils' strenuous efforts to recruit their help. Strong careers department and solid industrial links. School workshops flourishing.

Background and Atmosphere: Founded in 1552 (at one time reckoned to be the largest school in England), revived by Samuel Butler at the end of the 18th century and moved from the town to its present splendid position, fortress-like, across the river. Lovely campus: buildings on 'the site' are spread out, boys seen scudding about everywhere. Grounds superbly kept. Terrific refurbishment programme to all houses now complete (cost £4 million). Day boys have own houses. NB all meals now cafeteria-style, alas – bang go the table manners and checks on who's there/ok/not (good food though). Chapel three times a week – much admired chaplain, Gavin Williams. Moreton Hall girls and Shrewsbury High girls combine with boys for some music, drama, etc, not to mention socialising. Archive note: the school's private slang words -now dying out alas – are being gathered together for posterity; old boys requested to write in what they remember.

Pastoral Care and Discipline: 'Know your boys' is still the head's motto on discipline. Houses for 55, with well-used/structured tutor system. Boys choose their own tutors. Housemasters encouraged to contact boys' parents. All staff trained up to be watchful shepherds: Head forever watching the boys, 'but caringly, not critically,' said one.

Pupils and Parents: Steady civilised chaps with ease of manner. Catchment area is vast – Norfolk, Scotland, the north of England. Having said this, many are local. Lots of sons of Old Boys (loyalty a strong point). Fascinating list of Old Salopians, including Sir Philip Sidney, Sir Martin Rees (Astronomer Royal), Charles Darwin (statue installed '00,) Richard Hillary (author of The Last Enemy), Michael Heseltine, Michael Palin, Richard Ingrams, Willie Rushton, Paul Foot, Michael Abrahams, John Peel (the dj, that is).

Entrance: By CE, but early registration is recommended. Boys come via top prep schools for miles around, Abberley and Prestfelde especially, also Malsis, Bramcote, Locker's Park, Yarlet, Moor Park and Packwood Haugh. sixth form entry: via school's exam and minimum six B grade GCSEs.

Exit: A good number to Oxbridge (23 in '00), and it is rare for the rest not to take a degree. Many take a year off 'which is a state of mind' the head tells them. 'You can go to just as distant places within yourselves working among the handicapped at home as travelling exotically.'

Money Matters: Seventeen academic, four music scholarships at age 13, two at sixth form. Two hundred boys supported by the school (Foundation set up along American lines to provide extra funds).

Remarks: Still one of the strongest public schools in the country, and one about which we hear virtually nothing but good. Has a good blend of tradition and forward-looking attitudes, and produces self-confident boys. A few comments from educationalists that the school could be in danger of becoming complacent, but this could be competitive grapes. A connoisseur's choice, and well worth the journey to get to.

SHREWSBURY HIGH SCHOOL

32 Town Walls, Shrewsbury, Shropshire SY1 1TN

TEL: *01743 362 872* FAX: *01743 364 942*

E-MAIL: m.scott@shr.gdst.net

✦ PUPILS: 559 girls in total: Junior School has around 202 girls. All day ✦ Ages: 11–18, juniors 4–11, nursery (boys too) 2.75–4 ✦ Size of sixth form: 68 ✦ Non-denom ✦ Fee-paying

Head: Since 2000, Mrs Marilyn Cass (forties). Educated at Folkestone Grammar and the Royal School, Bath. Joined the army, married a naval officer and travelled the world with him, he retired (and trained as a teacher) while she went back to university to read Geography (1st class honours), do a PGCE (Exeter) and an MA in educational management (Bath). Taught at the Royal School, Bath, then deputy head at Redland High in Bristol, then here. A keen skier and traveller. Took over from Miss Susan Gardner, who was here from 1990.

Academic Matters: The one and only academic girls' private day school for miles around: huge catchment area. GCSEs very strong– – Cs a rarity – and a good profile at A level too. English, economics, biology, sociology, history, art and classical civilisation the popular subjects. Second modern language (German) introduced at the age of 12, along with Latin. Greek no longer automatically on offer. Single and double sciences. Good university advice is provided and involves both parents and daughters.

Games, Options, the Arts: Keen on drama ('But I wish we could do more,' from a pupil) and music. 30 plus county athletes, hockey, netball and tennis players, tennis probably their strongest sport. Use of six local tennis courts and swimming pool, to supplement school's own games pitches: sport is relatively low profile. Rowing available at sixth form, thanks to Shrewsbury School, and some girls go on to row for their universities. Nice art. Some careers talks, drama, etc, with Shrewsbury (lots of girls with brothers over the river).

Background and Atmosphere: Lovely setting (away from the town centre), south-facing, with grounds sloping down to the River Severn, directly opposite Shrewsbury School (where boys seen jogging in the snow on the day of our visit). Buildings a mixture of old and new, including separate sixth form house, music block, etc. Thriving junior school nearby with all its own facilities (including technology) on site (entry at 4, 7 and 9). School founded in 1885 (GDST). Lively and stimulating ambience.

Pastoral Care and Discipline: Mrs Cass keen on working closely with parents and on being involved in the community.

Pupils and Parents: Very broad social mix of backgrounds, including lawyers, doctors, farmers, landowners, etc, and variety of accents. Girls from Staffordshire, Wales, Cheshire as well as more locally. Bright and bushy-tailed girls, with pleasant manners and not afraid to state their own views, relatively unsophisticated compared with metropolitan pupils.

Entrance: Many from the Junior School; 11+ selective exams. Three form entry. Some leave pre-sixth form, these places are quickly filled.

Exit: Gap year for some, the bulk straight on to a big cross-section of old and new universities – some to Welsh unis, 5-6 to Oxbridge in a good year, to read anything from marine biology to business studies to fashion with technology, from American Studies to medicine.

Money Matters: Had over a hundred assisted places at last count, and the Trust is busy raising money to replace them. Fees currently very reasonable.

Remarks: No frills day school with a good local reputation that gets girls the exam results they need to go on to the next step.

SIR WILLIAM PERKINS'S

SCHOOL

Guildford Road, Chertsey, Surrey KT16 9BN

TEL: *01932 562161* FAX: *01932 570841*

E-MAIL: reg@swps.org.uk

WEB: www.swps.org.uk

✦ PUPILS: 580 girls all day ✦ Ages: 11-18
✦ Size of sixth form: 140 ✦ Non-denom
✦ Fee-paying

Head: Since 1994 Miss Susan Ross BSc (forties), read physics at Manchester University. Previously taught physics at Putney High and at Godolphin and Latymer. Very approachable head. Really knows her girls. Teaches all new entrants in Year 7. Parents say that she is very much on the ball. ' She is willing to take on a problem, gets on with it straight way and comes back to you with the outcome' comments one enthusiastic parent. Strongly involved with pupils and staff. She is well liked and much respected.

Academic Matters: One of the best performing girls' schools in Surrey. Very good solid exam results achieved without undue pressure. In 1999, there was a 100 per cent pass at A level with particularly impressive results in maths, physics, economics and art. 11 of the 64 A level students got three or more A grades. 99 per cent achieved A★-C at GCSE level. Strong showing for pupils in French, German and history.

Attracts top quality staff. Friendliness and commitment of the staff is much commented on. Size of class max 24 but frequently smaller. Well-stocked library and IT resources which are in constant use. All girls are computer-literate and each has their own e-mail address. IT is incorporated into other lessons. 'A very good strong IT teacher' says one parent.

Games, Options, the Arts: Good sports fields and wide variety of facilities on site, but no swimming pool. 'They have a very good swimming squad, so they must practice somewhere' comments a parent. Games are compulsory for the first four years. Emphasis on skills, enjoyment and development of active leisure pursuits. Opportunity to join in a wide range of team and solo sporting activities. Fitness room available for older girls.

'Drama and music is really big here' says a recent leaver. Drama teaching praised. Drama is taught as an extension to English, in theatre workshops and as a sixth form course. Acting, stage skills, design and music involve as many girls as possible. Thumbs up also for art and music teaching. Many opportunities to join in musical activities at all levels. School has orchestras, a swing band and choirs galore. Definite encouragement for girls to get involved in extra curricular activities and to develop individual talents. Excellent careers resources centre.

Background and Atmosphere: Founded in 1725 by Sir William Perkins, a wealthy Chertsey merchant. Originally started with 25 boys but a decade later extended education to 25 girls. Moved to present site in 1819. Situated on green belt land on 12 acres of gardens and playing fields. Original red brick building has been imaginatively extended and there is a continuing building programme to improve facilities. Pleasant courtyards are a tranquil oasis among the red brick. School buzzes with energy and enthusiasm. Friendly atmosphere much commented on by pupils and parents. 'Our whole year was like a family' says a past pupil. Teacher/pupil relationship is also praised.

Pastoral Care and Discipline: 'Very strong on pastoral care which starts from the head' comments a parent. Pastoral heads of sections, so problems are spotted early. A mentor system can be put in practice if necessary. Difficulties are dealt with firmly and fast. Anti-bullying policy, which has been worked out by pupils and staff. Exceptional care is taken of the new 11+entrants.

Pupils and Parents: Pupils are drawn from a v wide catchment area with a large school bus network. They come from the independent and state sector. Good cross-section of girls that many parents regard as a plus. Not a snobby school: wealthwise, parents are right across the board, so don't expect school gate gossip about second homes and swimming pools. Strong parents' association.

Entrance: Exam in January for year 7 entrants for the following September.

Academically selective and pupils need to be of a good standard. Full marks to the school for its bad day – the cat died or I had the flu – policy: if a girl's exam performance does not match up to what her junior school says about her, she can go back for an interview. A big plus compared to some other senior schools with their do or die on the day attitude. Joiners also into the sixth form.

Exit: A few want to escape after GCSEs but most stay on to do A levels.

'The sixth form is very different, the teachers treat you like adults and give you so much more freedom' says one pupil. Exit from sixth form to top range of universities, some take a gap year.

Money Matters: School policy is to keep fees 'as low as is consistent with the high quality of education that is offered'. Academic and music scholarships for Year 7 entrance according to performance. Four sixth form scholarships. Bursary sometimes possible if a family falls on hard times.

Remarks: A local favourite (for yonks) that deserves a higher profile. Very successful, well-run, school. Strong academic reputation without undue pressure. A nice, caring, place that turns out very good all-rounders. Does not have the snob appeal of some of the other academic girls schools in the county. Equally, it tends not to fall in and out of fashion for no good academic reason.

SOUTH HAMPSTEAD HIGH SCHOOL

3 Maresfield Gardens, London NW3 5SS

Tel: *020 7435 2899* Fax: *020 7431 8022*

E-MAIL: senior@shhs.gdst.net – OR

junior@shhs.gdst.net

WEB: www.gdst.net/shhs

✦ PUPILS: 660 girls, plus junior school of 260 girls, all day ✦ Ages: 4-18 ✦ Size of sixth form: 170 ✦ Non-denominational ✦ Fee-paying

---

Head: Since 1993, Mrs Jean Scott BSc (late fifties), educated at Wellington School, Ayr, and Glasgow University; read zoology, teaches biology; widowed with two grown-up children. Previously head of St George's School, Edinburgh, and before that senior teacher of Ipswich High. Precise, spruce, straightforward, sensible, with a fine sense of humour. Keen on music, jazz included.

Academic Matters: Strong results at both levels. Maths now outranks chemistry as the most popular A level; biology and English also feature in a fairly narrow range of options History results notably strong even in this company. However, expectations, as we said before, are extremely high here, and teaching of a high calibre and challenging: staff desperately committed.

No grading internally to avoid competition, 'They've got to be bright to be here anyway – but they all know precisely who is best.' Girls are kept on their toes in all subjects. Good programme of non-examinable general studies in the lower sixth.

Rigorous teaching; sloppy thinking is not allowed. All will take 4 Ass at the start of the sixth form. IT well established; a sprouting of computers, both in the senior and junior schools – senior school networked '96, second computer room '97.

Games, Options, the Arts: Amazing to relate – the school bought the Hampstead Cricket Club in '97, and now has its own four-acre sports ground. 'This has revolutionised sport in the school!' comments the head. To date, however, not a gamesy school though girls always do well in netball (some play for Middlesex), strong tennis team and one or two notably talented gymnasts and judo practitioners. Swimming pool planned for the sports ground – at present girls walk to Swiss Cottage for swimming and sports centre.

Lots going on, 'a real buzz'. Girls organise speakers regularly. Music department strong and has thirty-five visiting teachers. Art very good – A level results always superb. Programme of exchanges with France, Germany and Spain, culminating in work experience placements for sixth form students in 'their' countries. Some drama with University College London (qv) boys.

Background and Atmosphere: Unprepossessing red brick north London buildings tucked conveniently behind Swiss Cottage. The school was founded in 1876 – the ninth of the G(P)DST schools – and moved to its present site in 1882, and has been added to and adapted ever since. Dining area has circular tables (much friendlier than traditional school refectory tables) and there is a swipe card system for paying for school lunches.

Intake has been increased to four classes per year and the size cut from 26/28 to 24 – this overall increase made possible by the acquisition of Oakwood Hall next door, which is now a sixth form centre, plus creche for staff babies in the basement ('very trendy,' comments head). Some areas of the school are still down at heel, and there are some austere and traditional old-fashioned classrooms, though Mrs Scott has been addressing this, adding carpets etc. No prefect system, but all sixth formers submit a CV and have an interview for the post of head girl and (three) deputies. Sensible uniform allows trousers or skirt.

Pastoral Care and Discipline: Hard working, some would say pressure-cooked (though the pressure often comes from home as much as school). 'This place breeds survivors,' comments a parent. Structured personal social and health education syllabus for the senior school. Hot on PSHE.

Pupils and Parents: Large numbers from bright, bright, Jewish and Asian families ('very strongly family minded they are too,' comments the head, who thinks this may be what restrains over-sophistication). Wide social mix from far corners of north and north-west London as well as many locals. Among parents are Hampstead media, actors, psychotherapists. 'Pretty pushy,' commented a recent parent. Girls are competitive, ambitious, hard working, self-confident, notably articulate and totally unfazed to put forward their own opinions with adults, however distinguished. OGs include Rabbi Julia Neuberger, Helena Bonham-Carter, Dilys Powell, Fay Weldon.

Entrance: Highly selective. Searching entry tests and interviews. Oversubscribed. Increasingly via the school's own (enlarged) junior school. Many from state schools. Ten-ish places at sixth form – to fill leavers' places and new places available to clever girls (entrance exams in proposed A level subjects, plus you need three As at GCSE in your A level subjects).

Exit: Practically all to university – destinations swing considerably from year to year; medicine popular; ditto gap year. Some to Oxbridge, one or two to art foundation courses.

Money Matters: One or two scholarships of half fees for girls who top entrance exams. One (or two) sixth form scholarships (available internally and externally). Had 82 assisted places at last count – relying on the Trust to raise money to replace them all. Music scholarship at 11+.

Remarks: Excellent no nonsense academic day school with narrow-ish syllabus, getting good exam results for bright girls. Getting more sought after now, after a time in the fashion doldrums.

JUNIOR SCHOOL: South Hampstead H S Junior Department Numbers 5 and 12 Netherhall Gardens, NW3 5TG. Tel: 020 7794 7198, Fax: 020 7431 2750. Head: Miss K M Stayt BEd London. Entrance at 4+ and 7+ via telling testettes (no longer at 5+). NB if you flunk first time you can now resit at 7+. Register two years before date of entry. All go on to senior school. Very pressured indeed. Bright and busy and very active. In a cul de sac, with plenty of space – good selling point for London, and it now starts at four.

STEWART'S MELVILLE COLLEGE

Queensferry Road, Edinburgh EH4 3EZ

TEL: *0131 332 7925* FAX: *0131 343 2432*

E-MAIL:
<schoolsecretary@stewartsmelville.edin.sch.uk>

WEB: www.stewartsmelville.edin.sch.uk

&

THE MARY ERSKINE SCHOOL

Ravelston, Edinburgh EH4 3NT

TEL: *0131 337 2391* FAX: *0131 346 1137*

E-MAIL: schoolsecretary@maryerskine.edin.sch.uk

(The two schools operate under one banner)

✦ STEWART'S MELVILLE PUPILS: 775 boys (almost all day) ✦ Ages: 11-18 ✦ Size of sixth form: 110 ✦ Non-denom ✦ Fee-paying

✦ THE MARY ERSKINE PUPILS: 660 girls (33 board, the rest day) ✦ Ages: 11-18 ✦ Size of sixth form: 85 ✦ Non-denom ✦ Fee-paying

---

Head (Principal): Since 2000, Mr David Gray BA (forties). Educated at Fettes, read English at Bristol. Come here from being head of Polkington School, York (from 1992), and before that Leeds Grammar, Dulwich College, and EFL in Athens. Married to Lynda, twin daughters and a son. Recreations: sport, music and 'Balkan current affairs' – the mind boggles. Took over from Mr Patrick F J Tobin, head from 1989 and a superb HMC chairman.

Schools have devolved from Merchant Company's umbrella (as have the other linked schools). Mr Gray runs the twin senior schools with two deputy heads, and the co-ed junior school whose head is also the vice-principal. Stewart's Melville Deputy Head: Neal Clark (forties), read English at Oxford; two daughters. The Mary Erskine Deputy Head: Mrs Norma Rolls BSc (forties). Educated at Hutcheson's Grammar School, Glasgow University and Jordanhill. Two children in school, husband took early retirement, and she teaches 'a little, so much else to do,' and previously head of maths and deputy head of Bishop's Hatfield Girls' School. Expert on IT.

Academic Matters: 'Not a selective school,' however, described by an educationalist as a 'grade one academic machine'. Classes of up to 25 setted, groups sub-divided in an attempt to extend the most able. Standard Grades followed by Highers and Advanced Highers. Computers everywhere, schools are particularly strong in mathematics and the sciences. New-ish technology centres in both sites – conversion of existing building at Stewart's Melville, and infill at Mary Erskine. Languages (least strong, says Mr T), French, German, Latin and some Greek on offer.

Schools combine for sixth-form, most extras, and pastoral structure, but are essentially single sex. Five Highers are the norm, and some excellent results with 'new records being broken annually – girls work too hard' (says Mr Tobin). School has its own educational psychologist, and support for learning throughout: 'can cope with almost all learning difficulties' – good at this.

Games, Options, the Arts: Girls are still better at shooting than boys and both sexes join the voluntary CCF (over 100 girls).

Twenty-seven rugby teams; new swimming pool and cricket centre – but even so could do with better sports facilities. Masses of music, drama, orchestra. Pupils can learn to fly, ski (Hillend and the real thing); brilliant debating team (usually the Scottish Debating Champions, European Youth Parliament finalists and SMC has represented Great Britain at the Reichstag in Berlin in '94, MES in Thessalonika in '97). Masses of music, orchestras, drama. Fine joint musical productions eg 600-pupil *Noye's Fludde.*

Background and Atmosphere: Stewart's Melville campus is based round the magnificent David Rhind-designed Daniel Stewart's Hospital, that opened in 1855 and merged with Melville College in 1972. Fabulous Victorian Gothic with cluster of modern additions, surrounded by games pitches and car parks.

The Mary Erskine School was founded in 1694 (originally the Maiden Hospital) and moved to Ravelston in 1966, and changed its name to The Mary Erskine School, amalgamating with the boys' school in 1978. The school clusters in decidedly '60s architecture round the charming (1791) Ravelston House: swimming pool, tennis courts, etc.

Regular buses to eg East Lothian and Fife service the two schools, now under the auspices of Erskine Stewart's Melville Governing Council. Schools operate as one, but each is fiercely proud of its individual heritage. Girls wear specially commissioned Mary Erskine kilts.

Pastoral Care and Discipline: Both schools operate a tutorial system for the first year, followed by house system in Upper School. Good links with parents. .Two sackings since '89, no known drug problem, occasional temporary suspensions. Clampdown on bullying.

Pupils and Parents: Edinburgh hotchpotch of New Town and suburbs, with many first-time buyers and lots from England. Siblings and FP's children. Less elitist (and perhaps less dusty) than some Edinburgh schools. Children living far out can spend the night when doing evening activities. Pupils 'relaxed and happy, friendly and responsible', to quote school inspector.

Entrance: At 11, 12, 13 or sixth form – otherwise 'by default'. Entrance assessment held in January (but can be arranged for other times). Waiting lists for some stages, but just go on trying. Entrance to upper school by interview, plus school report plus GCSEs/Standard grades (five credit passes for fifth form entry).

Exit: Some leakage after Standard Grades, most sixth year go on to university (mostly Scottish), art college is a popular alternative.

Money Matters: Bursar deals with £14 million annual budget. 16 per cent of all secondary income from assisted places – had a massive 367 of them at last count, and feels their loss (though school remains full). Sibling discounts, and scholarships and good bursaries available.

Remarks: An enormous conglomerate which, amazingly, works well.

JUNIOR SCHOOL: Stewart's Melville and The Mary Erskine Junior School, Queensferry Road, Edinburgh EH4 3ZE. Tel: 0131 332 088, Fax: 0131 332 2432. Head: Since 1989, Mr Bryan Lewis MA. Huge and thriving junior school under remarkable head with around 1,122 boys and girls ages 3-12. Libraries in classrooms (also carpets and fresh paint), computers everywhere, good learning support department for languages and maths, and learning resources area for gifted children. French from five;

inspired art, ceramics. Provided all the children for recent Edinburgh Festival production of Joseph and the Amazing Technicolor Dreamcoat – caused lots of excitement, though some people heard to mutter darkly 'what about bedtime?'.

Around 200 children are learning to play 18 different instruments and make up an orchestra of 80. Most go on to senior school; a few to trad public schools in Scotland.

STONAR SCHOOL

Cottles Park, Atworth, Melksham, Wiltshire SN12 8NT

Tel: *01225 702309* Fax:*01225 790830*

E-mail: office@stonar.wilts.sch.uk

Web: www.stonar.wilts.sch.uk/

✦ Pupils: 450 girls; approx 190 board, 260 day. Plus own prep schools with 80 day girls ✦ Ages: 11-18. Prep 5-11; plus nursery for boys and girls ✦ Size of sixth form: 80 ✦ Christian, non-denom ✦ Fee-paying

---

Head: Since September 2000, and from 1985 to 1997, Mrs Susan Hopkinson (sixties). Educated at Howell's School, Llandaff, and St Hugh's Oxford (history). We remember her as a very enthusiastic and bubbly hard nosed business lady; she says 'now that I am longer in the tooth I would prefer to be described as a very enthusiastic forward-looking educationist.' Says 'The experience of being at school should prepare you realistically for a career, I don't want to produce little misfits who can't get a job' and 'Stonar has always had a strong sense of the possibilities of life for those with the will to grasp them.' After three years ascending Scottish peaks, Mrs Hopkinson has come to the rescue on the departure of her successor, Mrs Caroline Homan, who has agreed with the governors that she should seek a change of career. Mrs Hopkinson will stay for two years while the governors have another try at finding someone of equal calibre. Deputy head making a good strong impression.

Academic Matters: GCSE results are sound and steady. A levels much better in '00 than in earlier years, consistent, good in the context of the broad intake – from girls taking HND to Cambridge entrants. 20 A level subjects on offer, biology, geology (superb results), photography, geography, psychology the most popular. Teaching, needs tightening up,' according to a parent. New appointment is the academic deputy head, Claire Kelly, former director of studies at a sixth form college. Traditional teaching, staff mainly female but with some senior men. Reports every half term. Encouragement liberally given.

Games, Options, the Arts: Super stabling for over sixty horses ('better than the dorms' according to a mother), good sized covered indoor riding school and a mini Badminton cross-country course. (Local pony clubs rent the facilities for camps etc). Famous for holding British Inter-schools One Day Event each year – and, not surprisingly, Stonar girls do extremely well in this. Currently about 150 riders in the school. Top level riders do BHSI (horsey qualification). Sports are taken seriously, – one or two stars currently in the school (a swimmer, a trampoline high flyer, an ice-skater – who goes to Swindon), several county hockey and netball players. Fitness centre, sports hall, swimming pool. Lively art, and music does well: more play instruments than ride. Dead keen drama, with lots of productions. Imaginative on outings and trips – going as far as New Zealand in 1999.

Background and Atmosphere: Elegant Strawberry-Hill Gothic house (once the home of the Fuller family), at odds with a motley collection of modern out buildings; prep school on site (most girls move on to the senior school); separate sixth form house (Prince William the pin up here). Good new sixth form study centre. No five star accommodation here, but comfortable enough. Dining hall where each girl must wipe her place clean. Lots of computers – and lots of games being played on them: could do with more vigilance on this front? Parental grouses reach us that there is not enough emphasis on reading. Not overly tidy – relaxed, gentle, cosy. Horse boxes fill the drive at start and end of term.

Pastoral Care and Discipline: Not a problem. Lively school council consisting of girls of all ages, and staff. All staff are watchful, a key part of school policy. Non-teaching house staff, 'so they are fresh at the end of the day'.

Pupils and Parents: Mutually supportive friendly girls at ease with themselves and their teachers. Around 30 children from overseas, Europeans and Far Easterners. Londoners, locals and Home Counties girls. 180 weekly boarders. New green and white tartan uniform popular with girls.

Entrance: Not a problem.

Exit: About 80 per cent go on to take degrees – London, Nottingham, lesser lights. Several follow equine careers, some to art college.

Money Matters: Scholarships at 11+, 13+ and 16+, including for music, art, drama, sport and riding. Some scholarships up to 50 per cent.

Remarks: Just the place to send your pony mad daughter, where she will emerge pleasantly confident, and probably with some decent exam results as well. Being watched with interest following the former head's return.

STONYHURST COLLEGE

Stonyhurst, Clitheroe, Lancashire BB7 9PZ

TEL: *01254 826345* FAX: *01254 826370*

E-MAIL: admissions@stonyhurst.ac.uk

WEB: www.stonyhurst.ac.uk

✦ PUPILS: 340 boys, 60 girls; 320 board, 80 day ✦ Ages: 13-18 (plus co-ed junior school ages 5-13) ✦ Size of sixth form: 150 boys, 25 girls ✦ RC but enquiries welcome from other Christian denominations
✦ Fee-paying

Head: Since 1996, Mr Adrian Aylward MA (early forties). Married with three young children. Educated Worth School and Oxford, where he read Greats. Spent ten years in City and industry, latterly as MD of a plc before entering education. Smashing, young, friendly and cool in a crisis. Took over from Dr Giles Mercer, here since '85.

Academic Matters: Thorough teaching continually commented on by parents. Small groups, setting for languages and maths, questioning and probing so that sixth formers learn to think for themselves.

Results reflect the very wide ability intake, 'in which we take pride'. Maths, chemistry, biology, English, business studies and French the most popular subjects. School says that they do well in value-added data.

Broad curriculum (including, for instance, astronomy – own observatory for this and newly acquired remarkable telescope), strong languages (plus full-time teacher with EFL qualification for boys whose mother tongue is not English). Recent strengthening of international Jesuit links aims to broaden everyone's outlook, with gap year placements in Jesuit communities and some staff secondments. Study habits acquired via daily prep periods, plus prep on Saturdays and Sundays. Every pupil has a personal academic tutor.

Full-time special needs teacher for one to one and small groups (maximum four); computers available, sometimes English substituted for French. Thorough support for learning difficulties, and a fair number of children with difficulties in the school.

Games, Options, the Arts: Strong outdoor-pursuits tradition, with fell walking, canoeing, sailing, fishing on the Hodder for trout and salmon, successful shooting teams, and strong sport all round (rugby the main sport – beating Stonyhurst is a matter of pride for schools round about), with good facilities and lots on offer. Fairly strong take-up of D of E, and emphasis on community service (more meaningful than at many schools, annual trip to Lourdes, holiday for deprived children at Stonyhurst etc). Newish theatre at St Mary's Hall, the on-campus junior school (ages 7-13). Good music (free instrumental lessons). Large investment in IT – all upper sixth have computers in their rooms, and all pupils have an email address.

Background and Atmosphere: Imposing (and vast) building, previously property of the Weld family – reputedly the largest boarding school under one roof. Inside, acres of polish, worn stone, panelled wood, huge staircases, altogether, grand. Set in fine parkland. Somewhat isolated, definitely dignified if daunting. Chapel large-ish, but not overwhelming. School founded in France in 1593 (for RCs forced to be educated out of England). Full of treasures – paintings, ethnographica, largely donated by OBs – Thomas More relics on loan to British Museum recently; sense of history at every turn. Religion taken very seriously. School centrally run, with everyone sleeping under one roof. Boarding accommodation cosied up a bit recently, large study bedrooms for sixth formers. Boys divided into year groups called 'Playrooms'. Sleeping-out exeats policy continues to soften up. Ritzy prospectus in wallet looks like a company report.

Pastoral Care and Discipline: A caring school – all the staff are shepherds. Consciences carefully developed. Jolly yellow leaflet on AIDS distributed to all. Prefects have far more clout than at many schools (though staff most certainly run the place). Alcohol and smoking occasionally pop up, but head reassures us these are not now 'troublesome'. Bar for upper sixth. Monk ('should be Jesuit if true,' says the school) spotted coming out of local pub at 9 on a Saturday night adds a nice human touch here.

Pupils and Parents: Broad social and geographical mix, but mainly from middle-class professional backgrounds, 10 per cent not RC. 20 per cent from abroad, including Ireland, Germany, Benelux, Singapore, the Spanish-speaking world and Africa (pupils must speak good English). The international dimension 'goes back a long way and is something we nurture and cherish'.

Pleasant, articulate and mature boys. 'Alumni' include twelve martyrs (including three canonised saints), seven VCs, also Arthur Conan Doyle, Charles Laughton, General Walters, Paul Johnson, Peter Moorhouse, Bishop Hollis, Charles Sturridge, Hugh Woolridge, Jonathan Plowright, Bruce Kent, Mark Thompson, lords Chitnis and Talbot, Kyran Bracken, Sir Tim Chessels, Iain Balshaw.

Entrance: Via the school's own prep – St Mary's Hall, and St John's, Beaumont Windsor (this latter, incidentally, has been well recommended to us), also from a wide variety of other prep schools. Six GCSE passes at C or above (plus interview etc) required for entry at sixth form by all.

Exit: All over – no real trend, though London University is consistently popular. choice. Business degrees looking popular. Some to art college. 10 to Oxbridge in '00.

Money Matters: Not short of a bob or two: endowment money is entirely for bursaries, but, of course, this frees up money for other things. Up to twelve academic scholarships (depending on the quality of applicants), plus sixth form music, art, and art and design scholarships. Had 88 assisted places.

Remarks: Distinguished Jesuit boys' boarding school which started to go fully co-ed in '99 (though girl numbers have yet to build up,) a change that boggles the imagination, and means breaking up a strong and rather special all-male community. Change going v smoothly, says the school.

STOWE SCHOOL
Stowe, Buckinghamshire MK18 5EH
TEL: *01280 818 000* FAX: *01280 818 181*

E-MAIL: enquiries@stowe.co.uk

WEB: www.stowe.co.uk

✦ PUPILS: 480 boys plus 100 girls in the sixth form only; around 50 day pupils, the rest boarding ✦ Ages: 13-18 ✦ Size of sixth form: 307 ✦ C of E ✦ Fee-paying

Head: Since 1989, Mr Jeremy Nichols, MA (fifties). Educated at Lancing (captain of everything) and Cambridge, where he read English. Previous post – Eton housemaster. Has laboured like Hercules to bring the school up to its present successful state. Good teacher. Good-looking. Good at bowling over potential parents with his charm. Can appear slightly distracted ('!' comments Mr N). Married with four children. Keen on Dickens and has springer spaniel called Mr Boffin. Mr Nichols is quoted on the front cover of the new prospectus as saying: 'A Stowe education teaches young people to think deeply, to think for themselves and to think about others'. Also says the school is 'not afraid to be known as "gentle" and kind'. So there you have it.

Academic Matters: Separate sciences or dual award at GCSE. Pupils streamed, and some setting. Timetabled computing – keen. History of art on offer. Maximum class size 20 below sixth form, 14 higher up. Good wide variety of A level subjects including Urdu, religious studies, theatre studies, Japanese, music, photography etc. Visual education now part of the lower school curriculum, and much appreciated by pupils. EFL provided. Head has worked hard to get fresh blood in common room (average age of common room now under 40 – a triumph). Support, including one-to-one tuition, available for mild dyslexics – not a specialist school. Perennial worries about 'whether our son might have done better elsewhere' – head point to excellent value-added results, so ask him to show them to you.

Games, Options, the Arts: Excellent art results continue, lots of singing, deservedly famous for its drama and opera. See the most boring school magazine in the business, The Stoic, for reports on everything else, eg basketball: 'The game continues to grow in popularity for the girls...' pic of first XV beating the pants off Oundle in 1938, etc. For school's real thoughts, see pupils' own racy little newspaper, The Voice, full of exciting little snippets, eg grouses about why the tuck-shop isn't open on Wednesday, and 'overheard' quotes, eg 'A good journalist never relieves his sources.' Both boys and girls do community service. Own beagle pack, of which they are proud once more; school organised a bus-load to the countryside rally. CCF, D of E and all that. Fishing (own hatchery).

Background and Atmosphere: Architecturally outstanding – Grade I former ducal palace in stunning setting, gardens once tended by Capability Brown. Garden follies alone are worth a detour and now, luckily for the school, their upkeep is in the hands of the National Trust (kiosk sitting in grounds), with injections of cash from English Heritage. National Trust now owns all the 700-acre park, including the games fields. This has made a vast difference to the look of the place – now once more gracious and utterly wows potential parents. Acres of roof still belong to the school – it's a never-ending task looking after it all, and school has a slightly down-at-heel look. This is not helped by the truly awful modern classrooms run up in the grounds that provide a constant eyesore. Some of boys' houses are also pretty gruesome, heavy with old wooden honours boards and the smell of suffering (long past, of course). £6 million grant for restoration work begun spring 2000, and school now shrouded in scaffolding – plenty of scope for it to make a difference.

The school was founded in 1923 by, among others, Montauban (cf the school library, which is good and mellow), under famous first Head – J F Roxburgh. Original aim of school was to break away from traditional public-school tradition, and, my goodness, it has succeeded. Commercial Notes: The school, with its National Trust connection, is in forefront of trend to turn an honest penny in school holidays etc, eg renting out the place for civil marriage ceremonies (going like hot cakes). Gardens open – family tickets available – also 'refreshments and light lunches' and 'powered wheelchairs'. Allow two hours, or you can rent a temple (via the Landmark Trust), and should this pall, there is always the Silverstone circuit just down the road – throaty roars on summer days.

Pastoral Care and Discipline: Despite the school's comments that 'enterprising antics with the "unacceptable" are swiftly dealt with!', this is a sparky place, harbouring all manner of live wires as is its time-honoured tradition. 'Huge space to do your own thing in' said a member of staff. Tutorial system in the lower and middle part of the school. Might field your little black sheep when kicked out elsewhere.

Pupils and Parents: All sorts, socially, geographically, racially and academically. Particularly popular with toffs. Lots of Londoners. Some parents are bemused by the school's grandeur. OBs a very impressive collection, and say volumes for the way the school nurtures its little late developers. Among them: Richard Branson, Nigel Broakes, Nicholas Henderson, Leonard Cheshire, David Shepherd, Lord Ampthill, Lord Stevens of Ludgate, Christopher Wates, Sir Peregrine Worsthorne, Billy Butlin's offspring, George Melly (who has written lyrically about who seduced whom in his day), Lord Sainsbury, David Niven, Gavin Maxwell (GM literary prize, once won by R Branson).

Entrance: Common Entrance. 'Rigid 45 per cent pass mark' – ie they no longer take the very bottom of the spectrum. From 'all the best prep schools'. Once more the acceptable choice when you fail to get into Eton, though due to increasing popularity no longer has places for last-minute applicants. For entry at sixth form: five GCSEs at C or above. More difficult for girls than boys – smart girls fighting to get in.

Exit: 90 per cent to universities, including a dozen to Oxbridge; a few to agricultural college, one or two to art school, and drama courses. Lots of gap year. Look in the school's sixth form courses guide for detailed destinations of recent leavers.

Money Matters: A bursar's nightmare – the most expensive school buildings to keep up in the country, and endowment not nearly up to the constant drain on resources (not to mention energy). Has help from English Heritage, however, not to mention the Getty Foundation, and the National Trust (see above). However, 'Enhanced range of scholarships and bursaries, art, music and academic'. School no longer has a 'Marketing/Commercial Director', but not surprisingly there is still a 'finance director'.

Remarks: Famous designer-label public school which is once more seen as the fashionable alternative if you don't get into Eton. Approving reports, both from parents and pupils. As one school-leaver put it: 'I may not get very good grades, but I made some jolly good friends here'. A school that over the years has consistently produced high flyers, often after wobbly beginnings.

STRATHALLAN SCHOOL

Forgandenny, Perthshire PH2 9EG

TEL: *01738 812546* FAX: *01738 812549*

E-MAIL: admissions@strathallan.pkc.sch.uk

WEB: www.strathallan.co.uk

✦ PUPILS: 270 boys, 165 girls, all board except for 80 ✦ Ages: 10-18 ✦ Size of sixth form: 170 ✦ Non-denom ✦ Fee-paying

---

Head: Since April 2000, Mr Bruce Thompson MA (Oxon) (forties) educated at Newcastle High, thence New College where he read literae humaniores (classics to the rest of us) and comes to Strathallan via Cheltenham College, where he was head of classics, and Dollar Academy (he wanted to 'try the Scottish system'). 'Loves Scotland, and loves Strathallan', as does his wife Fabienne (French, teaches at a local prep school, worked in tourism, expert skier, teaches skiing). The Thompsons have two young daughters and are delighted to find a young staff with similar-aged young.

We visited Strathallan within three weeks of Mr Thompson's arrival, and he hoped he might 'do some teaching' definitely wants to coach rugby and the pupils are delighted to find him practising weights and generally mucking in. He already has a reputation for 'popping into houses unannounced for the odd chat with a pupil on their ground, and has lots of informal brain-storming sessions in the evenings. ('Great fun, got to kick 'em out'). He 'needs pupil stimulation' and finds himself 'whizzing up the road on a bike' to meet more young on an informal basis. Took over from Mr Angus McPhail, who has gone to Radley.

Academic Matters: Not tremendously academic – but you can reach the heights from here. School plays the system, both Scottish and A levels. 60/70 per cent take A levels, the rest do Highers (over two years). School tries to please parents, but the choice between A level and Highers is always a contentious one (will possibly ease off with the new Advanced Highers and AS exams). All pupils must opt for at least one science at GCSE, and most do all three. No subject particularly much stronger than others, but science, maths and English results not bad. CDT continues to be excellent. Sophisticated computer design equipment, and pupils work here in spare time. Intranet access all over. Four separate computer rooms and computers everywhere. Laptops about to become the norm for all. Smallish effective learning support system. Three week assessment orders for all – ie reports (these are becoming more commonplace).

Games, Options, the Arts: Fantastic new state-of-the-art art school over three floors with marvellous light and inspired work. Art/history combined field trips (to Venice etc) graphics camera and screen printing. Good music (Copeman Hart manual organ) including keen traditional Scottish music group. Popular pipe band. Lots of drama, and small theatre, a clever conversion of a former boys' house, the insides nattily scooped out (theatre doubles as an examination hall). Swimming pool curiously juxtaposed to the theatre, Houses allocated 'free swimming' times, 7-730 am. Sport taken seriously (hideous pale green Astroturf), rugby, cricket, own golf course, skiing, CCF (boys and girls, voluntary), flying, sailing, fishing in own loch plus 12 permits on the river Earn. Masses of charity work. NB head keen on rowing, expect rowing machines shortly.

Background and Atmosphere: School was founded in 1912, based in 18th century castle with masses of additions, set in 150 acres. Two fantastic double deck libraries, one with the (obviously commissioned) carpet reflecting the plaster work in the ceiling. Nice chapel, hideous dining room, the plaster flaking off round the school motto when we visited. Main classrooms 150 yards away beside the old stable building which has been converted into a splendidly cosy junior house, Riley. Riley now boasts a most amazing atrium plus library and music practice rooms etc.

Class rooms blocks quite tatty on the whole, but refurbishment in the pipeline.

Houses new and newish, boys and girls have own study bedrooms, lots of kitchens, and common room area on each floor. Much general to-ing and fro-ing, but co-ed works v well here; girls' houses out of bounds to boys on Sunday mornings so that girls 'can laze around in their dressing gowns if they want '. School facilities much used by groups during holiday period. Ladies (visitors) loo in main block a fifty year old disaster area – head please note (bet he never goes there). Staff live on site in school houses, lots of young and good family feel.

Pastoral Care and Discipline: House parents live on site with two staff on duty in each house every night, Tutors often using the time available for informal chats. Mr Thompson 'aware that things happen' and talks of rustication and drugs testing 'in case of suspicion'. Punishment system for misdemeanours of 'fatigues' – jobs around the buildings and grounds ('no shortage of them').

Pupils and Parents: A few from the Eastern Block via the HMC placement scheme, plus Hong Kong, Germany etc. A third in all live overseas, mostly expats. School is popular with Scots (regional accents of all kinds) well placed, an hour from either Edinburgh and Glasgow, plus a small contingent from south of the border. FPs Domenic Diamond (computer games whizzo), Colin Montgomerie (golfer), Sir Jack Shaw,(Bank of Scotland), John Gray (former chairman of the Hong Kong and Shanghai Bank). Not a toffs' school, despite brief showing in the fashion stakes when David Pighills took the school co-ed.

Entrance: At 10 or 11 for the junior house (interview and test) then automatic entry, otherwise by CE – more than one attempt OK. Not a high hurdle, but popular. Later entry if space available.

Exit: More than 95 per cent to universities, mainly Scotland (Aberdeen popular). Five Cambridge places in 2000 (which is spectacular when you look at the intake), usually 'a few' to Oxbridge.

Money Matters: School financially strong. Junior scholarships, open scholarships and sixth form scholarship plus academic, music and art scholarships. Parents can also apply to the Ochil Trust for means-tested help with fees.

Remarks: David Pighills (the last head but one who was all that was wonderful for Strathallan) is back as chairman of the governors and, with a dynamic new head, school should be on the up again.

STREATHAM HILL AND CLAPHAM HIGH SCHOOL

Abbotswood Road, London SW16 1AW

Tel: *020 8677 8400* Fax: *020 8677 2001*

E-mail: enquiry@shc.gdst.net

✦ Pupils: 460 girls, plus Junior School at with 325 girls. All day ✦ Ages: 11-18, Junior School 3–11 ✦ Size of sixth form: 95 ✦ Non-denom ✦ Fee paying

---

Head: Since 1979, Miss G M Ellis BSc (fifties). Read chemistry at Glasgow University, taught at comprehensive school outside Glasgow, then senior mistress of Croydon High. Forceful, direct, energetic, 'not afraid to come down hard if she needs to', has turned what was something of a sinking ship into an establishment to be reckoned with. 'Education isn't for life, it is life,' she says, and knows every girl. Unmarried. 'The school is her life,' comments parent.

Academic Matters: 'I sit in on a lesson taught by shortlisted staff candidates (in the senior school) – qualifications don't tell me all I need', says head. Traditional academic curriculum. Pioneering distance learning A levels via the internet in law, psychology, sociology and electronics. Head comments: 'There are girls here for whom a grade C at A level represents a tremendous achievement.' Good results at GCSE. A level results averaged 7.8 points per A level subject in '00, 24 total average – a continuing improvement. English, classical civilisation and history popular.

Games, Options, the Arts: Improved facilities at the Tooting site have eased pressure on space. £1.2 million sports complex opened '97. Key skills for lower sixth. Hall/theatre for regular school plays with girls playing male roles – 'Yes, it is a drawback that we have no links with local boys' schools,' sighs a pupil. Won first prize for Institution of Civil Engineers' Challenge to stabilise the Tower of Pisa. Sixth formers have been selected to play rounders for England, or perform with the National Youth Theatre. Has 'Investor in Careers' kite mark.

Background and Atmosphere: Functional if rather uninviting brick building (rebuilt after 1944 direct hit by flying bomb) in South London suburban hinterland near Streatham bus garage is now home to Junior School only, while senior school has moved to premises by Tooting Bec common. No frills, suburban environment, purposeful and hard-working.

Slightly startling and deeply unflattering lettuce-green uniform thankfully replaced with an 'updated' green uniform (with black fleeces and black tights in winter,) giving way to own clothes in the sixth – with a notable absence of front-line sophisticate dressers.

Pastoral Care and Discipline: Evident warmth and protection from day one include a personal tutor for every GCSE girl, who acts as a trouble-shooter. The school has a strict drugs policy and a fierce anti-bullying policy.

Pupils and Parents: Social and racial melting pot from sizeable chunk of South London, taking in Brixton, Dulwich, Streatham but, says head, 'since the move our girls are ever more local'. Most girls are from state sector as well as lots of first-time buyers. Daughters of teachers, solicitors, architects, the medical world. OGs = Angela Carter, June Whitfield, Hannah Waddingham and – from the days of the occasional boy pupil – Norman Hartnell.

Entrance: Via exam at 11. Head and deputy now interview children in groups.

Exit: 70-90 per cent to universities for medicine, law, humanities, arts.

Money Matters: Had 189 assisted places, and the Trust is currently raising money to replace them. Some sixth form scholarships are available.

Remarks: Unflash GDST girls' day school, increasingly for locals, enjoying increasing numbers. A possible South London solution.

JUNIOR SCHOOL: Wavertree Road, London SW2 3SR, Tel: 020 8674 6912.

TAUNTON SCHOOL

Staplegrove Road,
Taunton, Somerset TA2 6AD

TEL: *01823 349 200* FAX:*01823 349 201*

E-MAIL: enquiries@tauntonschool.co.uk

WEB: www.tauntonschool.co.uk

✦ PUPILS: 900 boys and girls; approx 180 board in the senior school and 50 in the prep school ✦ Ages: 2½-18 ✦ Size of sixth form: 200 ✦ Inter-denom ✦ Fee-paying

Head: Since 1997, Mr Julian Whiteley BSc MBA (early forties). educated at Sherborne and the Royal Naval Engineering College, served as a naval officer before taking a PGCE at Cambridge. Holds an MBA from Nottingham. Previous post was head of St Paul's in Sao Paolo, Brazil, before that taught at Rugby, and at Sherborne. Married, with three daughters. Took over from Mr Barry Sutton, head here since '87. Appears to be breathing a bit of fire into the place.

Entrance: Not a problem. CE or school's own exam, plus interview (on which much emphasis is placed). Most popular years of entry 7+, 11+, 13+, 16+.

Exit: 10/15 per cent leave after GCSE, otherwise steady stream to university. Some to Oxbridge. OB: Lord Hill-Norton, Nick Prettejohn.

Remarks: Useful local school in which you can put your child age three and leave it there for the next fifteen years. To all intents and purposes a day school: 'local and regional', comments the development director Graham Reid, who also comments that he is too busy to comment on our copy, and that in any case potential Taunton School parents 'don't read guides'. School founded in 1847 as school for children of dissenters – Baptists and Congregationalists – of which many in the south-west (Queen's, Taunton, was for Methodists). Co-ed throughout since 1971. All games fields are within walking distance, railway runs at bottom of cricket pitch in front of main school (grotty Gothic). School full of middle-class children from similar backgrounds (parents are teachers, farmers, doctors, dentists, accountants, businessmen). Boarding pupils tend to head for more upmarket King's Taunton down the road.

Bursaries for Services' parents, of which there were 22 at last count. School's secret weapon in the money-making stakes (started '96 on campus): International Study Centre, providing EFL etc for foreign children. Currently has about 45-50 pupils, and we hear good reports of it.

TIFFIN SCHOOL

Queen Elizabeth Road, Kingston upon Thames, Surrey KT2 6RL

TEL: *020 8546 4638* FAX: *020 8546 6365*

E-MAIL: office@tiffin.kingston.sch.uk

WEB: www.tiffin.kingston.sch.uk

✦ PUPILS: 1035 boys, all day ✦ Ages: 11-18 ✦ Size of sixth form: 330 ✦ Non-denom – but designated 'a school with religious character' ✦ State

Head: Since 1988, Dr A M (Tony) Dempsey BSc PhD (fifties). Educated at Tiffin and Bristol University where he read chemistry. Previously deputy head of Feltham Community School (has also taught in the private sector). Married with one son, keen walker and industrial archaeologist.

Dr Dempsey 'covers' lessons, says it is 'unrealistic to expect a head to teach and know all the boys' (apart from which his time costs three times more than most staff), but expects to know the 'goodies and the baddies,' and those who naturally come to the fore. Parents can (and do) have free access to him.

Academic Matters: An academic school. Boys take ten and eleven GCSEs and do very well in them – 98 per cent of pupils get five plus A⋆-C grade GCSEs. A levels good too; quite extraordinary numbers taking maths at A level and this subject still accounts for around a third of the Es-Us – perhaps weaker candidates might be steered to an easier option? All take four ASs and three A2s however. Latin popular and strong at GCSE. All pupils take three separate sciences. A certain amount of dead staff wood at the top has been pruned , and the school feels better for it: Pupils are expected to cover their 'home' language at GCSE, hence the occasional exotic language results. Homework one and a half to two hours a night.

Games, Options, the Arts: Fabulous Chester Centre, with dramatic art and really good ICT, also mega ritzy sports centre (sports studies on offer at A level). Art, design and music results very good (increasing numbers taking them). Games pitch on slightly cramped 1.5 acre site, with main rugby (Tiffin Parents Rugby Association organises events to support the game), cricket facilities at Grists by Hampton Court, and a boat house on the Thames. Masses of music and drama, with serious representation at many of the London venues – Festival Hall, the Royal Opera House, Albert Hall and Covent Garden as well as regular school performances in house. Have been chess club Zone Champions.

Background and Atmosphere: School founded in 1638 and moved to present site in middle of leafy desirable Kingston upon Thames in 1929, incorporating Elmfield House (circa 1770 – much watched by English Heritage, but fairly scruffy inside). Hotchpotch of handsome red brick (with later additions) and current head's brilliant extensions, school is amazingly tidy considering the numbers operating in the space.

Sixth form centre refurbished in '98 (not before time) in Elmfield and very nooky library. Uniform fairly strictly adhered to, including sixth form, and pupils occasionally feel the urge to express their personalities. School motto – faire sans dire – not much heeded. A purposeful atmosphere. Active Old Tiffinians' Association. NB excellent local transport.

Pastoral Care and Discipline: Head of year, form tutors, plus subject tutors as child progresses through the school. Strong house system, and everyone has someone with whom they can talk. Good PSHE programme, with drugs lectures from Customs and Excise. The sight of addicts gravitating towards the Kaleidoscope Centre next door for daily methadone fixes is a grim warning.

Pupils and Parents: Kingston is essentially middle class, so lots of those, with about 25 per cent ethnic minorities (strong on Koreans). 95 per cent of pupils come from within six miles – including Richmond, Merton etc, plus a 'sprinkling' from further afield. Very supportive parents – lots of car boot sales and associations.

Entrance: Very very selective. By verbal and non-verbal reasoning tests for entry into year 7 (marks 'age-weighted'). Apply before October (exam taken in November) for the following September. Seriously oversubscribed – 140 pupils accepted out of a staggering 1250 applying at last count, though here, as elsewhere, the figures are misleading as parents 'play the system,' and some potential Tiffinians will be offered places by St Paul's and Westminster. Indeed, the private sector has been known to troll almost at the gates of the school, enticing bright pupils away with lures of scholarships. Around 30 per cent new intake to the sixth form (you need at least six GCSE A or B grades, including maths and English and proposed A level subjects).

Exit: Lost one to Eton at sixth form in '98 (got a scholarship). 90 per cent to higher education, mostly to universities in the south – Bristol, London, Essex, Sussex, Surrey, Exeter, City, LSE etc. About ten per cent to Oxbridge. Engineering and medicine still the most popular subjects.

Money Matters: State funded – manages very well. Masses of parental input, only 11 pupils currently receive free lunches, and these are helped (discreetly) to do essential field trips.

Remarks: A beacon in the state system and indeed in the area – a strong traditional academic school in the old grammar school tradition.

TIFFIN GIRLS' SCHOOL

Richmond Road,
Kingston upon Thames, Surrey KT2 5PL

Tel: 020 8546 0773 Fax: *020 8547 0191*

E-mail: tiffin.girls@rbksch.org

Web: www.tiffingirls.kingston.sch.uk

✦ Pupils: 855 girls, all day ✦ Ages: 11-18
✦ Size of sixth form: 250 ✦ Non-denom
✦ State

Head: Since 1994, Mrs Pauline Cox BA MA (fifties). Educated at High Storrs Girls' Grammar School in Sheffield, followed by geography at Birmingham and an MA in education at the London Institute of Education. Comes to Tiffin from Cranford Community School in Hounslow, and previously worked in the British Embassy in Poland before spending three years teaching in Accra and thereafter in the 'plusher parts of London'. Teaches year 7 (ie the bottom of the school) English and study skills for one lesson a week 'you get to know them quicker'. Described by Ofsted has having 'a very clear vision, drive and high expectations for all' she is also charming, friendly and great fun. Fairly single minded, with the ability to switch between subjects and people at will – she runs the school with a couple of deputy heads. Husband is executive secretary with the Royal Society, one daughter. Mrs Cox is keen on sport including skiing ('avid but hopeless').

Academic Matters: The recent Ofsted Report (April 2000) says it all. 'Standards are very high. The overall quality of teaching and learning is excellent. The breadth of curriculum offered is very good with an extensive range of extra-curricular opportunities. Leadership by the head teacher is excellent. The school promotes excellent standards of behaviour; the personal development of the pupils is excellent. The school provides excellent value for money'. Bit difficult to cap that really, particularly as the word excellent recurs in almost every paragraph (and sometimes twice in a paragraph) throughout the whole report – over 90 times in all.

This is a first class academic school, the results are outstanding, with trails of As and AS at GCSE and an impressive collection of As at A level; results fairly evenly spread, with English and the sciences both featuring in the ribbons; maths popular. With the advent of the new syllabus girls will choose four (or five if they are real goers) subjects for AS at the end of lower sixth and can choose their A level subjects at the beginning of upper sixth when they have had the results of their ASs. 'Girls are fickle and their most favourite subject at the beginning of lower sixth may not be their favourite at the end, give them as much choice as possible'.

A dozen children currently getting learning support ('but they have to be bright to come to us in the first place'), and several getting English 'as an additional language'. 'Big staff turnover', usually they last 'two or three years, but they're good'. The school regarded as a jumping off point on the promotional ladder: recently lost head of history to Bedales. Lack of cash always a problem, and the 'staff have a much higher teaching load than in the private sector', bigger classes, more lessons per week and more homework to mark. 'Dynamic improving staff, no weaknesses at all' says the head.

Super friendly library, jolly librarian, who collects all those tokens you get in supermarkets – crisp packs whatever, and girls have 'bonding sessions' taking out the vouchers and deciding what to 'buy' with their haul. Trains girls to be 'librarians' so they can get Saturday jobs in bookshops and the like.

Games, Options, the Arts: Impressive community sports centre used by local community after hours at weekends, Astroturf, tennis courts, two gyms with adjoining doors, and sports area outside main building. Girls doing athletics when we visited on a very hot day in June, the Muslim contingent performing in tracksuit bottoms and their trad head scarves. Trails of glory on the sports field with regular finalists and championships (and masses of silver in the front hall).

'Proper' ICT, jewellery making, graphics and drama strong with annual musical; masses of music – regular concerts in all disciplines, with girls studying music after school. Keyboards computer linked. Art very exciting, with fabulous textile department (girls make their own costumes for their productions. Masses of trips, skiing in the States, trips to the High Atlas. Trips germane to course work (ie classical civilisation to Greece) and all other jollies must be funded by parents.

Background and Atmosphere: We nearly didn't find the place when we visited as the Tiffin boys had replaced the sign for Tiffin Girls with their own and vice versa. But by the time we arrived there were no signs, only one for the community sports ground shared with the school which moved to their rather dreary present building in 1987. Depressing former secondary modern has been radically transformed with passages and reduced kitchens to form workable warren of classrooms. Very hot on top floor. Separate sixth form room, masses of computers, a lot of revamping, but more paint would not come amiss. Number 65 bus stops outside the school.

Historically the school evolved courtesy of the brothers Thomas and John Tiffin who in 1638 and 1639 left £150 in trust for the education of 'some poor men's sons'. Elizabeth Brown left dwelling houses in St Brides to her son to be conveyed to the town of Kingston and a small yearly income to be paid to 'some honest industrious woman'. Edward Belitha had needlework in his sights for 'honest respectable women' and the consequence was the foundation of the Tiffin Schools in 1880.

Recent innovations have included the setting up of a house system, called after the second, third, fourth and fifth headmistresses. The first, a Miss Fysh, resigned after a spot of financial disagreement with the board over a matter of a gas bill and promptly set up a rival establishment with her deputy. But Bebbington, Flavell, Watson and Schofield are now part of Tiffin life; girls not entirely sure that 'they were that competitive', but seem more adjusted to the new concept which also gives scope for more girl responsibility.

Pastoral Care and Discipline: No exclusions, occasional 'falling by the wayside' means 'putting on report,' and signing in after every lesson, bullying no problem. Girls have masses of responsibility, with positions running from Easter to Easter so that the summer, exam term is free. Head girls, assistants, house captains, and assistants, form captains and assistants, and heads of art, ICT, music etc, all with assistants and sixth form volunteers do extra coaching for tinies. Good bonding. Counsellor on hand from Magic Roundabout 'down the road'. Tutorial system and strong PSE in place. School council – a girl inspired forum – advises the staff on changes they would like to see put in place, like the new (not particularly thrilling) summer dresses and (ultimately) the decision not to have trousers as part of the school uniform.

Pupils and Parents: Caring ambitious collection, mainly middle class, lots of ethnic minorities, with clever and hard working parents as role models.

Entrance: Difficult, 120 out of every thousand applicants, some leave after GCSE and rather more arrive. Competitive testing. Any one 'who can access the school' can come here (if they pass for which they probably need to be in the top 7 per cent of the ability range). A few places available after GCSE, must have As in A level subjects.

Exit: Almost all to higher education, but the occasional surprising choice, eg diploma in aromatherapy/massage. Masses to medicine, but also a high art take up. More girls now take a gap year before university. A dozen or so annually to Oxbridge, but the medics prefer London.

Money Matters: Kingston ('leafy green Kingston') is apparently the richest borough in London, but funds still a problem, parents good at fund raising, and regularly pay £15 a month for ten months a year by direct debit to boost finances. Last year they raised £80,000 for computers and the like. Local industry also tips in with donations.

Remarks: Super vibrant state girls' grammar school with an excellent record, remains delightfully unassuming and lacking in intellectual arrogance. Humming, and dare we say it, excellent.

TONBRIDGE GRAMMAR
SCHOOL FOR GIRLS

Deakin Leas, Tonbridge, Kent TN9 2JR

TEL: *01732 365125* FAX: *01732 359417*

WEB: www.tgsg.kent.sch.uk

✦ PUPILS: 1033 girls, all day ✦ Ages: 11-19
✦ Size of sixth form: 275 ✦ Non-denom
✦ State – 'foundation school'

Head: Since 1990, Mrs Wendy Carey BA (early fifties). Previously deputy head of King Edward VI Camphill (girls) in Birmingham. Born in Australia, grew up in Africa, moving between South Africa and Zimbabwe (where she took an external London BA in English) – came to England when civil war broke out, bringing her four children with her. Articulate, dynamic and perceptive. Her experience includes fee-paying, state, co-ed and single-sex schools. Is a firm believer in the advantages of single-sex education for girls. 'They don't have to

hold back, can take risks, question things, push themselves, be innovative,' she argues. Married to the school's bursar – v handy.

Academic Matters: Outstanding GCSE results; A level excellent. Large numbers take general studies at A level. Wide-ranging choice of subjects includes Latin (compulsory in the first year), textiles, government and politics. Strengths extend right across the curriculum. School also at the cutting edge of technological development. Unusual in a girls' school to encounter such serious commitment to planning and resourcing of technical options: the school's dynamic policy deservedly generates much enthusiasm. Large investment, too, in Apple Macs. Imaginative university/careers advice. Has a supportive partnership with the Eden Valley School.

Games, Options, the Arts: All the normal options available on their spacious and airy site with popular open-air pool recently refurbished and equipped with changing rooms. Local sports centre also put to good use. County players in hockey, tennis, rugby (and successful teams); national swimming and orienteering representatives. Plenty of opportunities for drama and music, with head commenting that many choose the school for its commitment to music. Some joint debating, drama and music with The Judd School, and some joint activities with Tonbridge School, including a Model United Nations day. D of E. Community service through the West Kent Voluntary Service Unit.

Background and Atmosphere: Main school bright, cheerful, though with signs of wear and tear. A few temporary classrooms dotted around a fine 19-acre hillside site overlooking the Weald of Kent (far fewer than when we last went to press). Facilities vastly improved by £1.25 million science and technology teaching block opened in '96. Sixth form now has its own self-contained common room and study room. There is remarkably little post-GCSE dropout – a testament to the school's ethos, teaching, the breadth of subjects and extracurricular options.

Pastoral Care and Discipline: Excellent.

Pupils and Parents: The majority are middle-class offspring of fairly well-to-do Weald of Kent parents, with brothers at The Judd, or at Tonbridge School. Large numbers come from Sevenoaks (the town). Friendly, unassuming. Uniform particularly nice. sixth form – very casual, no uniform. Strong links with OGs. OG of the moment: Rebecca Stephens, first British woman to climb Everest.

Entrance: 140 places via Kent selection procedure; 11+ exam; essential to pass exam, but not necessary to live in Kent (Tel 01892 523342 for details if you are coming from outside area). The school is oversubscribed. Its main criterion, after sibling preference, is placing in the exam. Sixth form entrants are 'welcomed where ability is appropriate'.

Exit: Almost all to university. Pupils display a dazzling diversity of choice, ranging from dance, fashion, marketing, aeronautical engineering and business information technology, to the more traditional career areas, including veterinary science, medicine and law. A good handful to Oxbridge.

Money Matters: State-funded. Music scholarships available at sixth form (including one for bassoon). Good financial management by governors.

Remarks: One of the country's top state grammar schools, getting special mention by Ofsted ('96/'97) for 'good quality education and achieving high standards' ('92 inspection also glowing). A lively place.

TONBRIDGE SCHOOL
Tonbridge, Kent TN9 1JP

TEL: *01732 365555* FAX: *01732 363424*

E-MAIL: admissions@tonbridge-school.org

WEB: www.tonbridge-school.co.uk

✦ PUPILS: around 720 boys. 420 board, 300 day ✦ Ages: 13-18 ✦ Size of sixth form: 293 ✦ C of E ✦ Fee-paying

Head: Since 1990, Mr J M Martin Hammond, MA (mid fifties), educated at Winchester and Balliol College, Oxford, a scholar at both. Previously Headmaster of City of London School, and before that taught at St Paul's, Harrow, also Eton, where he was Head of Classics, then Master in College. Classicist, he has published translations of the Iliad (Penguin) and the Odyssey (Duckworth) – 'it fills in the holidays'. Married (his wife teaches part-time in a local school) with two children. Described by former colleagues as a man of 'iron determination' and 'creative ruthlessness'. Pipe-smoking, positive, affable, confident and with a nice sense of humour. Teaches every boy in his first year for half a term 'but there is always a "real" teacher in the common room in case I am called away'. Still declares he is 'most interested in the ordinary guy and what he gets out of it all'. A builder – has been presiding over possibly the biggest school development project in the country. Excellent organiser – even the boys acknowledge they learn 'organisational skills' from the example set by the school.

Academic Matters: Has the most wonderful collection of enthusiastic, inspired staff we have encountered anywhere. You just go into most departments (particularly biology and chemistry) and immediately want to sit down and start learning. Staff put in many over-and-above hours including A level reading and revision groups in the holidays in Cornwall, and reading parties for Oxbridge students, 'brilliant,' said a boy. NB a staggering sixteen new heads of department have been appointed in the last eight years (is this a record?). Ratio of academic staff to pupils 1:8. Streaming from the start, and some setting (maths and languages). Latin compulsory in the first year, the top two sets combine it with Greek. Maths and French GCSE taken one year early by a substantial number of boys (most pupils take ten in all). 'Boys are really taught how to work, and have to work hard,' commented a parent. 'There's no let-up.' Lessons organised on a ten-day cycle. GCSE teaching groups of about 17 boys, down to eight at A level. Firm emphasis on the critical and analytical approach to study – how to think, reason and argue – starts well before the sixth form. Each department housed in its own area, with offices and (usually) own library. Wonderful warm main library, full of life and with an impressive budget. Exam results very impressive – hard to pick out any particular star in such a galaxy. Of the odd isolated D and E grade, the head says he 'doesn't know why that should be – probably means they weren't working.' Under the new system almost all will tale four ASs and four A2s. Learning support co-ordinator for able boys with some degree of dyslexia.

Games, Options, the Arts: A very sporty school, games still compulsory even for sixth form, huge numbers of squads and teams at all levels. Proud of their sporting reputation: powerful cricket, hockey and rugger sides, with 100 acres of pitches. Sports on offer (20+) include rackets, fives, sailing, golf (results in matches up and down but still good overall). Marvellous all-weather athletics track with discus, shot putting, high and long jumps; two all-weather pitches. Rowing, alas, being phased out. Keen and increasingly impressive music. Head of music is an outstanding teacher – Mr Hilary Davan Wetton – who arrived via St Paul's Girls' and is chief conductor of the Wren Orchestra, the City of London Choir, etc. Fine Chapel Choir with chorister scholarships for trebles from local prep schools. Excellent crop of grade VII and VIII associated board exams.

Drama is keen, and has ritzy new theatre and new head of drama from Bedales. Duke of Edinburgh awards, CCF 'encouraged'. Good language exchanges, and foreign expeditions are 'particularly well thought out and organised,' commented a parent.

Art 'booming' under new head of art James Cockburn (ex-Canford).

Background and Atmosphere: Founded in 1553 as the 'Free Grammar School of Tonbridge', which misnomer is still registered with the charity commission. (Re)built in the 19th century (Gothic style) along the bottle neck which winds into the pretty old part of Tonbridge – non-stop traffic. Boarding and day houses (five of the latter – numbers have been growing) scattered along the road, some in mellow brick, some not so mellow. A copious amount of new building – witness of the current £20 million development plan – including a school uniform boutique which would not look out of place in Knightsbridge, and a tuck shop like a trendy trattoria, with chairs and tables outside on a terrace at which to eat your bacon butties. Also brilliant development of existing buildings, with acres and acres of carpet, beautiful wood panelling and no expense spared.

And as for the chapel! It was gutted by fire in 1988, while a Mr Burn (yes) was preaching to the school on 'Tongues of fire'. Restored amidst unbelievable brouhaha in a modern style – highly successful, acres of glorious English oak, roof in Canadian hemlock, granite and Italian marble-patterned floor – the very best materials, creating a monument to the twentieth century. Cost – £7 million, including £0.8m for a new sweet-sounding organ built by Marcussen of Denmark, with four manuals, sixty-six stops, which stop people in their tracks. Well worth a detour.

Day boys and boarders keep to separate houses, new day house recently acquired as part of the school's expansion schemes. Slight element of 'we/they' split personality. 'Marvellous for day pupils,' commented a parent. 'They get all the advantages of a big, strong, round-the-clock boarding school.' Flexible weekend leave now allows weekly boarding. Boarding houses are 'twinned' with Benenden houses for occasional social life. The school is perceived as tough, ruggy-buggy, but this is no longer the case. There is a benign and friendly atmosphere, kind, tolerant and safe (albeit bouncy). Enthusiasm extends right through the school – not just the academic staff, but the gardeners, groundsmen and maintenance men in their smart uniforms (spotless loos).

Pastoral Care and Discipline: Both in very good shape. Tutors' brief is 'get to know the boys' and they do their best; first year groups of three or four visit the tutor at home. Small group pupil/tutor meetings for sixth formers to discuss/explore intellectual matters. Head fiercely anti-smoking (jacked up first-time fine to £10; detention, letter home, rustication). 'But you never entirely get rid of it.' Alcohol reported to be 'under control' and (appropriately aged) upper sixth boys are allowed to local pubs on Saturday evenings. Head comments that, 'Boys nowadays appear to be law-abiding, docile and well behaved.' Brave comment. Boys still eat in their own house – a significant pastoral factor. Few (12 per cent) female staff.

Pupils and Parents: A fairly broad cross-section, especially in view of the generous scholarships. Mostly within one and a half hours' drive (including the 'Eastern corridor' now that this is easily accessible), and not socially upper crust. Many sons of the solid middle middle class, not flashy. Few non-English. Boys are open, well informed, look-you-in-the-eye. Old Boys include Lord Cowdrey, E M Forster, Sidney Keyes, Lord Mayhew, Vikram Seth, Frederick Forsyth (note the literary strength – still much in evidence).

Entrance: Reasonably tough. Main feeds are Holmewood House and New Beacon, Yardley Court, Hilden Grange, also Dulwich College Prep School. Otherwise from over 50 prep schools round about, including music scholars from choir schools. Very much at the sharp end of competition with extremely good grammar schools on the doorstep. Two-thirds via CE at 13+, one-third through the scholarship exam (but not all with awards). Head notes (as others do) parents leaving the choice until later. For entry from outside at sixth form (very few): minimum six GCSEs with A grades in subjects relating most closely to A level choices. Internal hurdle – six GCSE passes, at least three at grade B.

Exit: All to university, including 20 per cent to Oxbridge. Medicine, law, engineering continue to be popular. NB the school does not weed out boys post-GCSE – 'a miserable idea', says the head.

Money Matters: Rich, rich – fat fees (£16,767 boarding '00/01), and large endowment by Sir Andrew Judd administered by the Skinners' Company (who also provide the governors). Over £1 million was shelled out in scholarships and bursaries last year (including top-ups to 100 per cent if necessary). 21 academic scholarships, 11/12 music scholarships, and five or so art or technology. Also junior scholarships for boys 'who would otherwise leave for the maintained sector at eleven'. Extensive resources for the unexpectedly needy.

Remarks: One of the very best, outstanding in everything that really counts. Good reports; happy parents – ditto pupils. Parents who need social status might not choose it, but otherwise, go and look.

TORMEAD SCHOOL

Cranley Road, Guildford, Surrey GU1 2JD

Tel: *01483 575 101* Fax: *01483 450 592*

E-mail: admissions@tormeadschool.org.uk

Web: www.tormeadschool.org.uk

✦ Pupils: 670 girls (160 junior, 510 senior); all day ✦ Ages: 4-10 (junior) 10/11 – 18 (senior) ✦ Size of sixth form: 106 ✦ Non-denom ✦ Fee-paying

Head: Since 1992, Mrs Honor Alleyne BA DipEd (sixty), retiring in August 2001. Educated at Queens Belfast, married to Anglican clergyman and has two adult children. Forthright and charming, she commands a great deal of respect from both parents and pupils. Can be quite daunting but, as comments one parent, 'this is offset by her wonderful sense of humour'. Reads voraciously and describes herself as' demanding', expecting the best from staff, pupils and parents.

Academic Matters: Academic school achieving very impressive results without too much pressure A wide range of subjects on offer with emphasis on each girl achieving her full potential. Excellent results in 2000 both at GCSE and A level. Outstanding art department (fine examples adorn the school), which is reflected in both the popularity of Art as an A level choice and the excellent results achieved (12 As). Other popular subjects include Eng Lit, French and Spanish. Maths is a strong area (mostly As and Bs) and the sciences feature well: the pupils enjoy the benefits of a brand new, well-equipped science block. Not many doing economics in '00 (more in other years), and other areas such as textiles, home economics and theatre studies have very few takers, which is to be expected in a traditionally academic school. Impressive computer room with scanners, printers and every computer connected to the internet. School encourages active IT participation from an early age and is in the process of constructing its own Website.

Games, Options, the Arts: Tormead has a reputation as the school for gymnasts, with many pupils competing at national level. Superb indoor facilities with a complex that includes spacious locker rooms, large sports hall, adjacent gymnasts' training hall (with special flooring) and numerous staff offices leading off a central meeting / strategy area complete with televisions and white boards. There are also two all-weather tennis courts and a long-jump pit. However most of the outdoor sport is played offsite due to Tormead's limited space (4.5acres). Pupils are bussed to the Spectrum Leisure Centre in Guildford for swimming and/or track training, and hockey is played at another offsite venue.

Some parents see the lack of outdoor facilities as a minus but despite this, the hockey and netball teams, athletes and swimmers have won quite a number of regional and county championships and taken part in national events. Sport is compulsory at Tormead until pupils reach GCSE and A-level when they are given a degree of choice. However, some pupils (and parents) feel there aren't enough games sessions and if you don't make the top teams (2 per age group), sport becomes less and less a feature of school life.

Strong musical tradition at Tormead with 50-60 per cent of the pupils receiving individual instrument tuition (many playing two or more instruments). Three choirs, two orchestras, various chamber groups and ensembles and, most popular, a large jazz band, which regularly performs to the general public. Even so, 'music facilities could be better' muttered a parent. A sentiment echoed by the head who feels that there are always areas of a school that need improving, even if they are achieving great results. Enthusiastic drama department which puts on a number of productions each year.

All the usual school clubs on offer and girls are encouraged to take part in as much as possible. But being a day school which ends at 4pm many pupils feel that they don't have enough time to partake of all that is on offer. Half a dozen girls a year selected by the British Schools Exploring Society, which takes part in six-week adventures throughout the summer in far-flung places. Other outdoorsy stuff includes team-bonding adventure challenges, which include rock-climbing, abseiling, and canoeing.

Background and Atmosphere: The school was founded in 1905, and the original Victorian building has been extended and adapted over the years. As often happens in these situations, the end result is quite confusing with stairs and corridors in all sorts of unexpected places. Pupils agree that you can get lost initially, but the early intake into senior school from the Junior School (at 10 – see paragraph entitled entrance) means that when the new girls arrive at 11+, at least half of their class mates already know their way around. The sixth form centre is a new addition, which offers pupils quiet study areas, small classrooms and common room complete with sofas, stereo and kitchenette. No television for R&R though.

Tormead is within walking distance of Guildford town centre, which is served by two railway stations. Several coaches are also laid on to bus pupils from outlying areas.

Pastoral Care and Discipline: A strength of the school is the nurturing environment it offers. There are various problem-solving options open to pupils that start with the form tutor. Two trained counsellors are also on hand to help girls (appointments made through school nurse). System of 'Aunts' put in place, whereby every new girl has another girl assigned to them to help them through the first few weeks. Good career counselling and advice.

A disciplined lot here with uniform being just that. Long hair tied back and no evidence of make-up or bizarre hairstyles. Firm and unambiguous policy on alcohol and drugs. Smokers are fined the first time, then suspended then expelled. Anti-bullying policy in place (numerous posters) which involves all parties and an arbitrator. Pupils encouraged to find solutions. A day's grace given for the 'dog ate my homework,' ' I left it on the bus' excuses. Detention follows if the work does not then arrive, and for minor transgressions. Persistent offenders put 'on report' and monitored closely.

School has a Christian foundation, but is non-denominational. Everyone attends assemblies and RE is a strong and important part of the school curriculum.

Pupils and Parents: Daughters of predominantly professional families with all professions represented. Come from local areas in and around Guildford, with quite a few coming from Esher, Walton, and Weybridge areas too. Some foreign students and for those whose home-language is not English, the school will accept them at 11+ (and offer EFL support), if they are deemed bright enough. Parents are greatly supportive and are involved in organising social and fundraising events. Girls are friendly, bright, self-assured and unpressurised.

Entrance: The 11+ year is made up of girls (50 per cent) who come across from the Junior School at 9/10, and are joined at 11+ by girls who have applied from outside and passed the entrance exam (English, maths, verbal reasoning). The head explains that they are looking for potential and each candidate spends half a day in the school as well as meeting the head. Only the top layer is offered places. The school will also make provision for bright children who may have dyslexia and offers the relevant support.

Most go on to do sixth form, although there are a few who want to experience different things and move on to other schools. There are also imports into the sixth form.

Exit: Most go on to the traditional universities – York, Durham, Leeds, Oxford, and Cambridge.

Money Matters: The school offers a number of bursaries based on financial need and these vary up to 50 per cent of fees. A number of academic scholarships on offer (33 to 50 per cent) and some music and art awards (can be made for a specific year 11+, 16+, A levels).

Remarks: A good, traditional academic girls school (one of the best in Surrey) that takes pride in turning out well-educated, confident and articulate young women. It is a safe and nurturing environment and well suited to the girl who needs security to spread her wings. Not the ideal school for the non-conformist or rebellious girl.

TRURO SCHOOL

Trennick Lane, Truro, Cornwall TR1 1TH

TEL: *01872 272 763* FAX: *01872 223 431*

E-MAIL: enquiries@truro-school.cornwall.sch.uk

WEB: www.truro-school.cornwall.sch.uk

✦ PUPILS: 480 boys, 276 girls, including 106 boarders (42 girls, 64 boys) plus separate prep (Treliske) 88 boys, 55 girls; nursery and pre-prep (35 boys, 24 girls) ✦ Ages: 10/11-18; prep 7-11, nursery and pre-prep 3-7 ✦ Size of sixth form: 245 ✦ Methodist foundation ✦ Fee-paying

---

Head: Due to change in 2001. Current head Mr Guy Dodd MA, 60, retiring after eight years. Read history at Cambridge;

taught in New Zealand, then Cheltenham College and for 11 years was head at Lord Wandsworth College. His door was always open even at his nearby home where students were known to share the occasional meal. Well-liked by staff and pupils, will be a tough act to follow.

Academic Matters: Consistently good results – the school is doing its not so selective intake proud. Once a weakness, French results have now improved. Traditional teaching in some subjects especially at A Level where maths, physics, biology and chemistry are popular. Sixteen science labs and dedicated teachers ensure budding scientists or doctors can excel here. Excellent technology, and IT although not routed to every classroom. A pupil may be encouraged to switch from an A to an AS if struggling but there is no policy of weeding out weak candidates to bump up league table results.

Special needs: a part-time expert comes in to help every week but pupils 'must be able to cope with ordinary lessons'.

Games, Options, the Arts: Creativity adorns the corridors. Chess no longer a strong point since master retired. Participation in Duke of Edinburgh Award encouraged. Head believes it instils discipline and enhances character as pupils recognise and work with one another's strengths and weaknesses. Still firmly into Young Enterprise (the first school to create a real aeroplane, which was flown across the channel). Varied sports including water polo, golf ('97 'independent schools' golf champions'), climbing, squash, trampolining, rugby and hockey. Lots of swimming and sailing going on. Many pupils reach county, South West or national standard. Girls and boys are currently in British sailing squad and national women's hockey team. Good on organising expeditions, keen on the great outdoors.

60-piece orchestra performs to 900-strong audience annually at The Hall for Cornwall; a jazz band tours West Cornwall. Cultural visits to London art galleries, frequent opera, ballet and drama productions.

Background and Atmosphere: Glorious site 'on the ridge' overlooking the River Truro and the Cathedral. Grounds overlook splendid old trees and picturesque views. The school, founded in 1880, is slightly older than Pearson's fine Victorian Gothic Cathedral, which can also be seen from its vantage point high on the hill to the south of the City. Rather scattered school buildings (need an umbrella if raining between lessons), with higgledy-piggledy annexes and extra science labs etc.

Truro School is outstanding academically, complimented by a huge amount of extra-curricular activity. Perhaps it is its large pupil numbers that make it reminiscent of a good state school. The Wednesday surf club is popular with many surfboards seen rushing towards the beaches after school. Fully co-ed from 1990, which school believes 'promotes equality in the workplace, understanding and respect between the sexes'.

Pastoral Care and Discipline: Appear to be firmly in place. Christian and spiritual values positively instilled and much goes into the safety nets, which catch bullying and other anti-social behaviour. Prefects, who represent each form, meet weekly to discuss 'their responsibilities' (peers). Woebetide anyone who falls below school's strict bottom line. Stragglers or troublemakers will be told to look elsewhere. Drugs: 'you lose the right to be here, but offenders may be re-admitted on condition that they submit to a regime of random testing'.

A 'getting-to-know-each-other' programme organised for first years in autumn term includes inter-form bowling competition and a visit to nearby amusement park.

Christian ethic is encouraged through teaching practices and supported by the ministry of the school chaplain and services. Joint confirmation and church membership services are organised with nearby Methodist and Anglican churches. A small Christian Union room exists for private prayer and contemplation.

Ex-pupils and teaching staff use chapel for marriages and baptisms. Parents also welcomed as congregational members.

Pupils and Parents: Pupils involved in variety of charitable projects, from local care for the elderly to organising sponsored events for charity. These help instil maturity and community spirit. Pupils have raised money to buy a house for Romanian orphans and return visits are planned to support it. OBs include Michael Adams (chess), Olympic sailors Ben Ainslie and Barry Parkin.

Parents come from across Cornwall: the Scilly Isles to Saltash and of course many from Truro itself. Their professions are varied from solicitors, engineers and geologists to doctors, carers and teachers.

Entrance: Admission to nursery via application. External admissions into prep (Treliske) by examination at age seven, automatic admission from nursery. Entrance into senior by 11+ exam in January on English, maths and general reasoning – Treliske pupils make up about 40 per cent of the entry. Mature 10-year-olds sometimes accepted. Grammar school ability is required, although this is pretty marginal in some cases, particularly if pupil is already in Treliske. About 10 per cent of the sixth form come from nearby state schools – via GCSE examination and school report.

Exit: About 60 per cent of Treliske's pupils go elsewhere. After A level, six pupils went to Oxbridge in 1999, more were due to apply after gap year; 20 pupils pursued medical courses at university. Falmouth College of Art is also popular. Final occupations are diverse: civil engineers, lecturers, stockbrokers, solicitors, businessmen, management consultants, not to mention a scuba diving instructor and shark feeder in Nassau. A number go into teaching – there are eight former pupils on the staff.

Money Matters: The Methodist church technically owns the school. 'The school has virtually no endowment for scholarships or bursaries, money has to come from general income'. Good value for money though. Loss of Assisted Places Scheme in 1997 has affected level of selectivity. A similar school scheme provides a small number of means tested bursaries up to the value of full fees.

Remarks: A phase of changes possible with a new head taking the helm in 2001.

JUNIOR SCHOOL: Treliske Prep School, Highertown, Truro, Cornwall TR1 3QN. Tel: 01872 272616, Fax: 01872 223431. Head: Mr Russell Hollins BA etc. Entry is by registration at pre-prep, assessment and report at 7+ plus interview and day spent in the school. Almost all go on to the senior school, but school has recently won scholarships to other schools eg Bristol Cathedral and Bath High (as was). Pleasant light building, good pastoral care. Super enthusiastic place (even had a witty poem dedicated to the 'Toilets in Dinan' in the school magazine). Boarding and day (draws from a wide area). One of the v few prep schools in the area. Two miles away from the senior school, and has 10 acres of its own plus good facilities. Scholarships and bursaries available. Remedial help available.

TRURO HIGH SCHOOL FOR

GIRLS

Falmouth Road, Truro, Cornwall TR1 2HU

TEL: *01872 272 830* FAX: *01872 279 393*

E-MAIL: admin@truro-hs.cornwall.sch.uk

WEB: www.truro-hs.cornwall.sch.uk

✦ Pupils: 460, including 55 boarders. 342 senior pupils, plus separate prep with 118 pupils and nursery with 15 girls and 4 boys ✦ Ages: three months – 18 years ✦ Size of sixth form: 62 ✦ C of E ✦ Fee-paying

Head: Since 2000, Dr Michael McDowell BA Hons M.Litt. (mid-forties). Joined the school following a successful eight-year head-ship by James Graham-Brown. Previously at University College Swansea and University of Edinburgh. After graduating in English language and literature, studied PhD through Columbus University, Louisiana. Loves classical music.

Appears to have fitted into predecessor's shoes quickly – already well-liked by pupils and parents alike. Perhaps his 'approachable' caring and genuine demeanour has earned him brownie points. He's even been known to adopt the role of lollypop lady, when necessary. If it means seeing his girls safe, he's the type of chap who easily bends to the task. Married with one daughter.

Academic Matters: As an ex-direct grant school it has a strong academic tradition and an enviable record of examination success and university entrance. Consistently excel-lent results in recent years suggest strength within the school. Now a 25-hour week with one hour per lesson. Traditional Latin tuition is a strong point, one of few Cornish schools still teaching the subject. Latin and classical civilisation are popular choices at sixth form. A recent tendency has been towards maths and sciences, over the previously popular history and literature.

Consistently good marks in French, German & Spanish. Traditional 'seventies' teaching style of listening booths with headphones and tape recorder proving fruitful. Foreign trip organised every year to compliment studies and enrich experience.

Games, Options, the Arts: Music, art and drama expressed loud and strong. Scholarship pupils are reminded of the privilege through compulsory music concerts. For girls showing music talent at audition, free lessons provided on one instrument if lack of funds would render their talent dormant.

New department of drama and theatre studies block named after and opened by actress Jenny Agutter in October, 2000, an inspiration to aspiring actresses. New art block also opened by art historian Anthony Slinn.

Rain never stops play on the extensive all-weather hard surface sports area. Four grass courts and three hard courts also available. Heated indoor pool and large gym. D of E encouraged.

Background and Atmosphere: School was founded in 1880 by Bishop Benson before he became Archbishop of Canterbury. It has retained its commitment to providing girls with an academic education in a purposeful, Christian community. Since moving to its present site on Falmouth Road in 1896 the school has seen much investment and improvement. The school is looking at expanding boarding facilities because of increasing transport problems to allow day girls to stay the odd night when they miss the bus or train home.

Achievement is stimulated through membership of one of four competitive house groups. Student guides appointed to help some 22 foreign students feel at home. A 'get-to-know you' weekend arranged every year at youth hostel in Fowey for Year 7 pupils and staff, helps to build foundations for strong family-like atmosphere. Many girls belong to Falmouth Sea Cadets, so boarding complements this popular interest.

Pastoral Care and Discipline: The whole school meets daily for an act of worship and boarders attend a local church on Sundays.

School known for recognising and nurturing pupils' talent, thus generating confidence. Learning difficulties/dyslexia well catered for.

All girls take part in work experience and have individual career interviews and aptitude tests. As part of PSE, 'issues relating to motherhood and a woman's role in modern society are addressed.'

Any breach of rules is acted upon quickly. Possession of drugs is punishable through expulsion. Mr McDowell would, however, look at each case individually and 'try to' avoid ruining a student's career for the sake of a few remaining weeks. He is renowned for his 'fairness'.

Pupils and Parents: Most parents live locally to Cornwall. Varied professions including doctors, solicitors, accountants. Now very few farming parents.

Entrance: Entry into nursery and the prep (40 per cent come from nursery) is via application. The senior school receives children from 36 Cornish feeders (about 60 per cent from own prep) via its compulsory 11+ entrance exams, based on maths, English and verbal reasoning. Those entering sixth form (about 11 per cent of own students) required to have at least 5 GCSE passes at grades A-C.

Exit: More than 85 per cent go to university. Classics and law undergraduates are common, other students choose a subject where there's an analytical bias; some end up in merchant banking. Veterinary science and medicine are popular career paths and Falmouth College of Art is an option for the more creative. London Academy of Music and Dramatic Art have also taken students. A small element on the other hand think life's a beach, want to have fun and prefer the Cornish surf.

Money Matters: Number of scholarships and governors' bursary places available for students entering sixth form – awarded on basis of academic merit, although with governors' bursary places parental income is also taken into account. Music scholarships provide up to 50 per cent of fees, available at 11+. Siblings: 5 per cent discount.

Remarks: Strong traditional all-round girls school with sense of family values and respect between staff and pupils. Pleasantly caring headmaster whose goal is to strengthen the school and further develop its excellent academic and recreational facilities.

TUDOR HALL SCHOOL

Wykham Park, Banbury, Oxfordshire
OX16 9UR

TEL: *01295 263434* FAX: *01295 253264*

E-MAIL: tudorhall@rmplc.co.uk

WEB: atschool.eduWeb.co.uk/tudorsch/

✦ PUPILS: 263 girls. 235 boarding, 28 day
✦ Ages: 11-18 ✦ Size of sixth form: 70
✦ C of E ✦ Fee-paying

Head: Since 1983, Miss Nanette Godfrey BA (fifties), educated at Northampton School for Girls and London University (read English). Taught at the Royal Ballet School, Abbots Bromley, and Ancaster House (deputy head). Magistrate; keen traveller (has lectured to teachers in Kiev), and keen theatre-goer. Professional and highly respected, purposeful, shrewd and immensely likeable – top class head. Girls comment, 'We can talk to her.' Teaches all ages: 'If you're going to discuss pupils with your staff, you must know them.' Believes that school should be a 'means to life after school'. Enormously positive about the benefits of a small school. Took a sabbatical term in '95 tracing Edward Lear's journey across Albania. Has a big blond retriever, Daisy, who has been known to disrupt the even tenor of life here with her exploits.

Super deputy head – Harriet Granville – who provides vital back up in Miss Godfrey's absences.

Academic Matters: Not a school where learning hangs heavily on the growing girl. Bubbly classes, jolly attitude to work and an apparently laid-back approach which has moved parents to comment that 'they could notch up the grades a bit' – but not so: GCSE generally 100 per cent grades A-C, with an average of 9.6 subjects per girl. Average points score per subject at A level around 7.5 – which given intake, and the school's policy of letting girls have a bash, should make parents delighted. Comes out well in value added data.

No great choice of A levels – a small school; History of art still one of the most popular A level subjects, with good results. Good language teaching, with Russian, Greek, Japanese and Italian crash courses available. The school offers an exchanged scheme with Le Caousou near Toulouse and those who go on it are 'plunged effectively into French life and education' – plus a similar one in Germany. About one third of pupils take three separate sciences at GCSE, dual award for the rest. Setting in maths, science and languages. Some complaints of 'patchy teaching', though the head acts swiftly and decisively when necessary. Girls given loads of encouragement by staff.

Games, Options, the Arts: Well organised to provide exercise (including the sixth form), and to give pupils skills that may be of use to them in later life. Good professional games staff; lacrosse and hockey, tennis courts in the old walled garden, and new covered tennis court for year round playing, plus resident tennis coach. Two squash courts, large sports hall, outdoor swimming pool (complete with slide; if girls need to use a covered pool, they go to Bloxham, which is just up the road). Disadvantage is that the nearest comparable games school is about an hour away. Smart bottle green sweat shirts with red Tudor rose on front awarded for games.

Needlework and big home economics

department (not offered for examination), and all fourth formers do a useful hostess cookery course. Riding, polo, clay pigeon shooting too. Lively art department, energetic art club, but exam results disappointing. GCSE dance and A level theatre studies on offer. Girls learn to type, as well as use word processors. sixth form community-service scheme for all girls. CDT block. IT under Squadron Leader Jones.

Strong debating and public speaking ('they'll need it') tradition, plus participation in European Youth Parliament. Geographically conveniently placed for cultural outings, which are given a high priority. School trek to Madagascar in '00 – all carefully thought out by the girls. Youth Enterprise also enthusiastically (and successfully) pursued – most recent company imported rugs from Portugal. Work experience is compulsory for every pupil.

Background and Atmosphere: Main building a large charming country house in mellow stone, much extended, in pretty grounds, with a heap of little conversions and low blocks built on and round it, rabbit-warren style. A bit too far from bright lights for pupil-comfort. Founded in 1850, has moved more than once to land up here at Wykham Park after World War 2. Friendly atmosphere. Quite a lot of weekend activities. Good food, well prepared. Girls live in very well-furbished houses/rooms (very cosy renovated 11+ house), and live by year groups, which very much contributes to the atmosphere of the place. Five-star sixth form accommodation, loads of space and light, and no uniform. A proper ('full') boarding school – with organised exeats.

Pastoral Care and Discipline: Good on both fronts, with positive pupil/staff relations. Firm rules, no major problems. 'Biddable girls,' commented a parent. Head

resolutely refuses to take in any girls who have been 'asked to leave' other establishments. She writes astute letters to parents, encourages parents to get together to discuss their stand on booze, boys, etc. Most recently gave parents guidelines on detecting early signs of anorexia. All staff know all the pupils, and have regular staff meetings to discuss progress.

Pupils and Parents: Pretty and pleasant girls with good manners, unspoilt, friendly, conventional capable and practical – like their parents, many of whom are county or City Sloanes, from far and near. Almost all British. Very cohesive lot. Pupils comment that one of the great strengths of the school is the opportunity to make good friends (and OGs endorse this). School motto: Habeo ut dem – I have that I may give.

Entrance: Getting in not difficult as such, but school continues to be very popular , so register early. Entry at 11+, 12+ and 13+; 'occasional' vacancy at sixth form.

Exit: 98 per cent to university – green welly and fashionable variety favoured – Edinburgh, Newcastle, Durham etc if poss, failing that. Northumbria, Bristol West of England. Art, design and fashion training also popular, as is the gap year.

Money Matters: Not a rich school, but manages an impressive building programme out of income – no appeals. Fees deliberately kept reasonable so that all may benefit: 'If you offer a lot of scholarships and bursaries,' says the head, 'someone's got to pay – usually the parents'. The school estate was bought for £10k during the American air force occupation – a snip. Travel scholarships for sixth formers.

Remarks: Famous small rural girls' boarding school. Formerly for toffs' daughters without academic pretensions, now for a good broad range of pupils who choose it because it really does feel like one big family – a true community, with each little member of it lovingly tended and polished. Gets good results. Rare to hear complaints from parents or pupils.

UNIVERSITY COLLEGE SCHOOL (UCS)

Frognal, Hampstead, London NW3 6XH

TEL: *020 7435 2215* FAX: *020 7431 4385*

E-MAIL: seniorschool@ucsonline.demon.co.uk

WEB: www.ucs.org.uk

✦ PUPILS: 730 boys in senior school, 220 in Junior School; all day ✦ Ages: 11-18, Junior School 7-11 ✦ Size of sixth form: 200 ✦ Non-denom ✦ Fee-paying

---

Head: Since 1996, Mr Kenneth Durham BA (forties), read PPE at Oxford. Previously director of studies at King's College Wimbledon (before Wimbledon he was at St Alban's). Has written some natty books on economics, including resource packs for primary, GCSE and A level studies. Keen on acting, film, books, music etc. Commented in his '97 report that moving in as a new headmaster is 'rather like taking over as the father in somebody else's family'. Married to a teacher. Took over from Mr G D Slaughter.

Academic Matters: Good sound teaching, and very professional assessments, though sometimes lacking in imagination, say par-

ents. Traditionally renowned for excellence in classics, maths and sciences – some feel to the detriment of other subjects, eg modern languages (surprisingly, in so cosmopolitan an environment, only French and German were on offer until recently, though Spanish has now been grafted on. English, history, economics and politics all doing vv well at the moment. Good economics staff. Theatre studies now offered. Average number of GCSE subjects taken = nine. Technology department good. Truly amazing exam results in '97. Comes out well in value-added data.

School 'not equipped' to deal with children with learning difficulties, but specialist part-time teacher in the school to help with assessments and assistance where necessary. Good help from tutors for Oxbridge boys.

Games, Options, the Arts: Good games facilities, especially given that this is expensive, built-up Hampstead; tennis and fives courts, sports hall and an indoor pool all on the premises; own playing field and all-weather pitch nearby. Soccer now looking stronger than rugger, both winning most matches over the last two years. Excellent well-equipped school theatre, regularly borrowed by professional theatre companies. Jazz still very strong – David Lund, the well-known jazz buff, retired as head of English here in '95. Choral and orchestral concerts. Visiting speakers – particularly from the media (eg Melvyn (Lord) Bragg) – a regular feature. Hosts literary festivals, has musicians and a writer 'in residence.' Art 'surprisingly good', according to visiting parent.

Background and Atmosphere: Very Hampstead. Founded in Gower Street in 1830 as part of University College London for non-Christians at a time when Oxford and Cambridge required membership of C of E as condition of entry. Arson attack in

1978 gutted the great hall – splendidly restored and rebuilt – and twenty-two classrooms. Religion is still not taught and a liberal outlook is still true of the school's educational policy. Emphasis on self-discipline, boys are given a good measure of responsibility for running activities outside the classroom. No bells. Masculine atmosphere. School has had a giant squillion pound development plan, including the new sports hall, a new library, a 'medical suite', etc etc. Partner school in Botswana.

Pastoral Care and Discipline: Non-authoritarian regime. No complaints at time of writing.

Pupils and Parents: Solidly middle class, often rich (though mothers more intellectual and less designer dressed than other Hampstead schools). Strong Jewish element, who do their own thing on the Sabbath and indeed, say one or two parents, do their own thing altogether, to the possible detriment of the social life of the school (though NB there are some who would disagree with this comment). OBs Professor Sir Roger Penrose, Sir Roger Bannister, Sir Chris Bonnington, Sir Dirk Bogarde, Alex Garland (novelist), Thomas Ades (composer), Thom Gunn (poet).

A fair number of media brats – parents in journalism, publishing, show business, etc. Pupils accused of being 'cynical, self-assured and worldly wise'.

Entrance: Two-thirds at age 11+ come from UCS's own excellent prep in Holly Hill (qv). The others from preps and primaries all over North London. Entry at sixth form from outside: – six or seven GCSEs at grade B or above, with As in A level subjects. No 'strict hurdle' for internal candidates – discussions with boy and parents if there is any doubt about suitability for sixth form.

Exit: The majority of leavers go on to higher education, large numbers to do social sciences-orientated subjects. A great many lawyers, doctors, accountants and civil servants result. Also successful businessmen (often third and fourth generation at the school). About 3 per cent to art colleges etc.

Money Matters: Had 84 assisted places at last count. Exhibitions, bursaries at 11+ and 16+, tend now to be rather more than 'honorary'. School very quick to respond to parental financial crisis where appropriate.

Remarks: Top North London boys' day school, very strong, but low profile. 'Unexciting,' said a parent a few years ago, 'and it shouldn't be' – seems to be perking up now.

JUNIOR SCHOOL: 11 Holly Hill, London NW3 6QN. Tel: 020 7435 3068, Fax: 020 7435 7332. Head: Mr J F Hubbard, previously head of science and housemaster at the senior school. Over 200 pupils, ages 7-11, which means NB that pupils cannot easily work towards senior schools starting at 13. Competitive entry at 7 and 8 – around 160 children sitting for 40 places. All children are interviewed before taking the exam. Automatic entry to senior school. A further 20 places at 8. Good and thorough grounding, teaching independent thought at an early age. Good facilities, plus use of some of the senior school's. Tremendously sought after.

UPPINGHAM SCHOOL

Rutland LE15 9QE

TEL: *01572 822216* FAX: *01572 822332*

E-MAIL: admissions@uppingham.co.uk

Web: www.uppingham.co.uk

✦ PUPILS: 650 pupils, 130 girls (currently all in sixth form, but going fully co-ed from 2001). Mainly boarding, but some day pupils ✦ Ages: 13-18 ✦ Size of sixth form: 350 ✦ C of E ✦ Fee-paying

---

Head: Since 1991, Dr S C Winkley MA (fifties). Educated at St Edward's Oxford, read Classics at Brasenose, doctorate in mediaeval Greek poetry. Was second master at Winchester, in charge of scholars there. Married with two young children, the elder to start at the school next year. Ebullient, thoughtful, impressive intellectual sophisticate who likes to pose philosophical teasers to the new boys. Popular, 'he goes around looking as if he doesn't know what's going on, but he knows everything,' said one pupil respectfully. He believes the school offers 'a proper childhood' in a fast-moving world. 'There are very few children here with whom I can't do business, we think we're all on the same side, with no Them and Us.'

Academic Matters: Confident they deliver the best for the individual, whether less academic or a real high flier. Good results in both arts and sciences. For a major public school, refreshingly unhung-up about league tables and Oxbridge results, but get impressive number in every year, and give good preparation for entry. Good A level results (40 per cent A grades in '00) – notably in economics, art & design, chemistry, physics, English, German and French. Information technology and life skills classes for all. GCSE retakes possible. Dyslexic pupils accepted, and EFL available.

Games, Options, the Arts: Very strong. Music is superb – currently 51 music scholars (many ex-cathedral choristers), and in the last five years have gained over 50 organ, choral and instrumental awards, mainly at Oxbridge. About 400 pupils learn an instrument (an Uppingham pupil has twice in the last six years won the highest marks for Grade 8 piano), and play in ensembles ranging from jazz groups to full symphony orchestra. Choir is famous, with demanding repertoire, has been invited to the Chapel Royal, Westminster Abbey, Canterbury Cathedral, Cologne Cathedral. Has been recorded. Neil Page is director, previous distinguished director was Douglas Guest, 1945-1950. Some resident teachers, and visiting staff include professional musicians.

Wonderful, envy-making art block – building designed by Old Boy Piers Gough. Immediate impression of exciting and diverse activity. Walls hung with accomplished drawings, paintings, sculptures. There is a film studio and photo lab which everyone can use to develop own photos. New master, architect Simon Sharp, has been brought in to combine art, architecture, design and technology. 12 out of 19 got A grades at A level last year.

Very well-equipped, newly refurbished computer department. The whole school is comprehensively wired up – 1450 points. Also computers in each house, and a computer in every pupil's study, their own or hired. Has long-standing relationship with Microsoft (UK) to keep right up-to-date.

Drama is very popular, as are dynamic

husband-and-wife team Mr and Mrs Freeman, 'She's been in a film, but won't tell us what it is, in case we go and get the video,' said one impressed pupil. 300-seat theatre, for polished productions of classics (the School for Scandal), musicals (Guys and Dolls) and recently a play written by a pupil. Biennual production taken to Middlesex School, Massachusetts.

Very strong on sport, but not obsessive. 'You don't have to be brilliant,' according to pupils. Sixty acres of playing field (the largest playing field in England), Astro-turf hockey pitch, reams of tennis courts, swimming pool and a diving pool. Rugby excellent, currently one boy is in England under-18's, and links with Leicester Tigers RFC. Great range of sports on offer, water-polo, shooting (Uppinghamians recently represented Great Britain), canoeing, fencing etc. Sailing and windsurfing on nearby Rutland Water. D of E popular. CCF or community service in the lower sixth. Gap year increasingly popular, useful international network of Old Boys.

Background and Atmosphere: Founded in 1584, the school with its splendid buildings dominates the pretty stone market town of Uppingham. Pupils are allowed a reasonable run in the small genteel town, but some places out of bounds, such as Safeway's 'because they sell alcohol' and tearooms which are the privilege of prefects. Relaxed attitude to comings and goings from their own house. 'We trust them to be sensible about where they go.'

There are thirteen boarding-houses in Georgian and Victorian houses around the main school, each with their own flavour. Fourth formers are in dormitories, with own studies, sixth formers have bedsits. Parents and prospective pupils are encouraged to look around and make their own choice. Furthest out is ten minutes walk from the main buildings. Pupils eat within their house – 'not the most economic way to do it, but it encourages friendship within a family setting.' 'Vertical' friendships encouraged ie. young boys will chat confidently to older boys and girls, not just with peers. Also have daily chapel service for the whole school. Girls well integrated – have been here since 1975. There is a tuck shop and buttery for all, and a bar for upper sixth formers (tightly restricted hours/consumption). Uniform is dark and undistinguished.

Atmosphere strikingly happy, lots of cheerful, lively faces.

Pastoral Care and Discipline: Good pastoral care deriving from small houses run by husband-and-wife teams (often with own children), and tutor system. Pupils have allocated tutor, who also lunches in the house once a week. Chaplain, Revd. Dr Megahey, is popular, and house just by the main gate is open to all comers. Wide choice of possible confidantes for pupils: housemaster/housemistress, matron, tutor etc.

Dr Winkley takes a firm line on drugs (expulsion), drink and smoking. No exeats but parents welcome to visit, and by arrangement take child out for a meal. But delivering child back to the school 'tanked up with drink' absolutely not acceptable. Passionately anti-bullying. 'I was bullied at school, and it's something I will not tolerate.'

Pupils and Parents: Not a grand school – solidly middle-class. Well-off professionals, farmers, business people. Mainly from Middle England counties. Some offspring of Brits working for multinationals overseas. And 'metropolitan refugees,' says Dr Winkley, who leave London and want their children to grow up more slowly. A very British school, with about 8 percent foreign nationals.

Very friendly, well-mannered pupils, confident talking to adults. 'It's really friendly,' say new boys. Accepting of each other – 'Girls don't have to be pretty to get on here!' About 10 per cent children of Old Boys. Old boys quite diverse – Rick Stein, Stephen Fry, Stephen Dorrell, Tim Melville-Ross (DG of the Institute of Directors), even Boris Karloff.

Entrance: Much emphasis on broadness of entry requirements – 'we only ask for 50 per cent at Common Entrance'– and ability to give 'added value'. Boys (and girls from 2001) at 13 take CE or Uppingham scholarship exam, but school will arrange entrance tests and interviews for children from state sector. Plus reference from existing school. Girls entrance to sixth form on basis of reports from present school, tests and interviews, then satisfactory GCSE results.

Excellent information pack for prospective parents, stuffed with detail, and also contact numbers of parents happy to talk about the school. Impressive parent contentment rating.

Exit: 12 to Oxbridge this year – Classics, economics, English, law, maths and computer science, modern languages, theology, engineering, geography, PPE, music. Present and next organ scholar at King's Cambridge. First girl ever to get organ scholarship at Oxbridge at Christ Church, Oxford. Loads to Bristol, Durham, Reading, Newcastle, St Andrews.

Money Matters: A dozen or so academic scholarships, 20 music, plus art and design, and an all-round scholarship. Dr Winkley hoping to set a up a scholarship scheme to provide places for children who could not otherwise afford it.

Remarks: A wholesome, positive, happy school. You feel a child of any ability range would be safe and happy there, and the best be brought out of them. Despite increasing nationally-set demands on the curriculum, loads of extra-curricular fun to stimulate and give ideas of the world beyond. From wine tastings and debates to Burns Night with haggis and reeling.

'Children aren't sent to boarding school any more, they come because they wish to, says Dr Winkley.' It shows.

WELLINGTON COLLEGE

Crowthorne, Berkshire RG11 7PU

TEL: *01344 44 4012* FAX: *01344 44 4004*

E-MAIL: registrar@wellington-college.berks.sch.uk

WEB: www.wellington-college.berks.sch.uk

✦ PUPILS: 734 boys, 54 girls (all in sixth form). 145 day boys, the rest board; virtually all the girls board (4 day) ✦ Ages: 13+-18 boys; 16-18 girls ✦ Size of sixth form: 346 ✦ C of E ✦ Fee-paying

---

Head (Master): Since 2000, Mr Hugh Monro MA (forties), educated at Rugby and Pembroke College, Cambridge. Married, with two teenage children. Historian, rugby blue. Previously head of Clifton College (from 1990) and before that Worksop, has also taught in America and worked in industry. A very popular fellow (and widely admired by other heads), bluff, open, forward-looking, humorous. When at Clifton we said of him 'a good ambassador for the school'. Still keen to get everyone here – staff and pupils – 'talking more'.

Considers his main job 'to develop the width of talents'. Took over from Mr C J Driver, head since 1989, poet, prisoner and philosopher. There are a sprinkling of important pongos etc among the governors. HM The Queen is the official 'visitor' and any alteration to the Statutes have to be approved by Buckingham Palace.

Academic Matters: Traditionally stronger on science side, but in recent years the most popular subjects have changed, from English and history, to maths and biology. Separate sciences offered at GCSE, and all must do English, maths, French, and two sciences. School has 20 laboratories, plus new physics lab opened '97. Maximum class size for GCSE year ('block 1') is 24 (large, by public school standards – but most classes much smaller). All pupils must take three A levels (some take more, indeed, one boy in '97 got seven As). A level results good, considering intake.

Games, Options, the Arts: Compulsory CCF, as you would expect of a school with such strong army links, but only for 'a year'. Girls play hockey and lacrosse 'girls pile in, have to join in'. Excellent CDT facilities. Keen drama, and art strong (new art school recently built). All must do games – even the weakest would be expected to don rugger boots and turn out for the house if needed. Seriously keen on games (80 acres of playing fields, giant sports hall, etc), and particularly strong rugby, cricket, hockey – almost taken for granted that school will be among the winners. Master keen on the school's 'leadership programme', which has been run now for eight years – housemasters and others get trained, then they train the pupils. After GCSE boys go on a 'team building' course run by Wilderness Expertise – 'the idea is to make kids work better with each other'.

School orchestra toured South Africa in '98 and Malaysia in '00.

Background and Atmosphere: Imposing John Shaw red-and-white brick building designed in 1854, plus lots of well-blended additions and glorious avenue of oaks, Wellingtonias and Andean pines. College founded in 1853 in memory of the Iron Duke. Main quad has porters in peaked caps at the entrance (no longer dispensing tuck). Shades of Empire fading fast – heavy whiskered portraits remain, but bleak cloisters beautified, and the school yearbook records that school slang (bims, tishes, ushers, etc) is disappearing, and fagging is now no more. Atmosphere still male, military and tough – though an official spokesman for the school disagrees with this. Girls very much honorary boys here. Definitely not cosy. Wonderful report by boy in school's alternative prospectus states that 'the best thing at Wellington (after the school holidays) are probably Saturday nights'.

Most boys' houses are in the main buildings, some out in the grounds – some houses definitely more fun than others. All dorms now refurbished (boys live in 'tishes' – derived from Partitions). The girls' house, Apsley, is jolly and popular. Dr Newsome, a previous Master, had a wonderful crypt chapel for quiet thought constructed below the main, very handsome chapel by Sir Giles Scott.

Pastoral Care and Discipline: Past master felt one of his main contributions to school's welfare had been the overhauling of the prefect system so that there was a proper chain of command. A parent picked up by school in time of distress says 'cannot speak too highly of the place'. All pupils have 'quiet time' on a Saturday evening between 6.45 and 8 pm – clever way of blunting the edge of Saturday night rave-ups. Girls reported to be 'very happy'; slightly less lyrical reports from boys lower down the school. Occasional reports of bullying still reach us. Good track record of community links.

Pupils and Parents: Services children (forty-four at last count) – but their numbers have been dwindling. Army families, and OWs heavy with decorations (including 15 VCs). OBs include Harold Nicolson, Robert Morley, Rory Bremner, James Hunt (who apparently didn't hate it), Gavin Ewart, Sebastian Faulks. Approx 25 per cent of parents are OWs.

Entrance: One hundred and fifty-five boys a year at 13+ from 60/70 different preps, plus 10 to 15 per cent from Wellington's own prep, Eagle House. CE or scholarship exams for boys. Entry into sixth form, from in or out of the school: at least six GCSEs at grade C or above (plus interview, test etc).

Exit: One or two post-GCSE to sixth form colleges, etc. The gap organisation was founded here, and a gap year is still popular. Otherwise on and up – Edinburgh, Oxbridge, London, Newcastle, Durham. Some on to the army – including a number of army scholarships.

Money Matters: Reckons to 'get child on to next stage' when parents have fallen on hard times, though this is not always possible. Nineteen scholarships, plus bursaries. Had some assisted places, but will not be affected much by their loss. Brilliantly run endowment fund, according to Master, set up by Frank Fisher in the '70s. Has also set up a Heritage Fund, to plough in land sales (400 acres in all belonging to the school) – now stands at £3.5 million after eight years. College's charter allows for children of deceased Army officers (and, latterly, other Services) to be educated here on a means-tested basis – currently a dozen of these, though numbers fluctuate.

Remarks: Distinguished army-linked public school, very traditional, old fashioned, with girls grafted on at sixth form. Best for the 'all-round enthusiast,' said past master. Not a place to send your little weed to be made a man. Should be five star, but somehow at the moment is not; though parents with children in the school are reasonably content. New head quite a mover and shaker – expect developments.

WELLS CATHEDRAL SCHOOL
Wells, Somerset BA5 2ST

TEL: *01749 672117* FAX: *01749 673 639*

E-MAIL: mainoffice@wells-cathedral-school.com

WEB:www. mainoffice@wells-cathedral-school.com

+ PUPILS: 550; 235 boarders, 315 day. 280 boys, 270 girls
+ Ages: 11-18, plus junior school ages 3-11
+ Size of sixth form: 175 + C of E
+ Fee-paying

Head: Since 2000, Mrs Elizabeth Cairncross, formerly deputy head of Christ's Hospital.

Academic Matters: Very hard-working, devoted staff – for whom the school is a way of life. Musicians timetabled separately, and take far fewer exams (typically seven GCSEs, two As) to allow for music practice.

Games, Options, the Arts: Music is, of course, outstanding: the music school (patron HRH the Prince of Wales) is highly selective in its choice of pupils, looking for talent, motivation and potential. (One of four schools in England designated by DfEE to provide specialist tuition for gifted young musicians. Huge amounts of time (from 7.45 am) devoted to music-making each day, though pupils mingle with the rest in houses. Plus 50-60 'special provision' music pupils, plus 40 choristers, all able musicians who follow the full academic programme and spend more time than mainstream mortals on music – though some of these, as in any school, also play instruments. 10-12 full-time music teachers, 50 visiting teachers. Director of Music – Roger Durston, chairman of the Music Education Council and of the European String Teachers' Association. Ex-pupil of School. Energetic.

Not a particularly sporty school, but it's all happening, without much pressure to take part. Plus all the usual extra-curricular public-school activities. Enthusiastic drama – school has been invited to take its '98 production of The Boyfriend to Edinburgh Fringe. Keen environmental projects – including sixth formers working on a pilot scheme to find a commercially viable alternative to a wastestream produced at ICI Polyurethanes. Good record of involvement with local community, including annual performance involving over 4000 children from primary schools in the area.

Background and Atmosphere: Ancient foundation – note the list of headmasters going back to 1188. Ravishing medieval and 18th-century buildings, as well as grotty new additions, spread about this glorious small city which is like a little island (John Betjeman called it 'the most beautiful square mile of Britain') and in the shadow of the Cathedral (pupils in and out constantly). Vicars' Close often recalled by students in later years as one of the delights, 'It gets through by osmosis,' say staff. One or two hideous teaching huts and Portakabins still sprout incongruously and untidily in warren-like complex behind the main school buildings (but new building programme is in the pipeline). The distinctly scruffy classrooms and dorms are now a thing of the past, indicates school spokesperson. Music a permanent presence that pervades absolutely everywhere. Split between boarders and day pupils. The middle years – 12 and 13 – are the low ones: not uncommon for parents to be casting about elsewhere at this period (especially if children are very bright), but many come back to roost. Smart prospectus with cut outs, like an advent calendar.

Pastoral Care and Discipline: Not without incident. Has been laissez-faire in the past, considerably tightened up by this head, who comments he feels he has been 'working closely with parents'. Deputy head also a force here. Pupils have fair amount of freedom: no sense of rigorous discipline, tight rules. Town locals observe pupils slightly 'woolly about the edges'. Good pupil/staff relations. Holds boarder/parent weekends. (Ex)-parents' allegations of sexual abuse of their children by member of staff in '97 caused headlines and great kerfuffle, but school bravely stuck by its staff. Then in 1999 married 33 year old games master and assistant house parent resigned after admitting affair with 17 yr old girl pupil. The school decided that the girl 'should not return to the school', and described the master as 'at the forefront of extra-curricular activities'!!!!

Pupils and Parents: All sorts – including, eg, three children from Soweto – not to mention from Albania, Romania, Russia,

America (American head chorister at time of writing. Also several children whose parents move to Wells to send them here for the music; more Services' children proportionately than any other HMC school (94 at last count; children can stay put during exeats). Otherwise, locals. Increasing number of first-time buyers. Friendly and happy and laid-back: 'an attitude some of us,' said a parent, 'see as a criticism'.

Entrance: Many from own Junior School. Some at sixth form. Not a high hurdle academically, but all manner of auditions for musicians.

Exit: Musicians to music colleges, and conservatoires for graduate courses, and distinguished record of music scholarships to Oxbridge. Of the rest, two or three go straight into employment, a regular few retake A levels, others to read wide variety of subjects (11 per cent opt for vocational subjects) at universities and ex-polys.

Money Matters: Not a rich school, no endowments. Beady bursar and an astute financial director discuss finances regularly. Generous music scholarships: 70 'specialists' are funded by the Department for Education and Employment. Had nearly 100 assisted places, and misses these considerably.

Remarks: An orderly, steady co-ed school, ordinary on the academic front, but flavoured throughout by the extraordinary music dimension, in a stunning setting. The only one of the four music schools (Chetham's, Purcell, Menuhin the other three) that operates in the context of a 'normal' school: hard for the aesthetics not to rub off on a pupil.

JUNIOR SCHOOL: Tel & Fax: 01749 672291. Head: Since 1995, Mr Nicholas Wilson, BA, formerly head of Berkhamsted Prep. Ages 3-11 (nursery set up '96). Some boarders, but mostly day. No tests into pre-prep, but 'friendly' tests into prep for all. The majority of pupils go on to the Wells' middle school, and thence to the senior school. Very lively school, particularly at the pre-prep stage and indeed there are many who think the Junior School is Wells' greatest strength. Violin tuition offered to 4-5 year-olds as part of the curriculum. Library staffed by parents. Has taken girl choristers from September '94 and issues a very nice pamphlet saying 'Could your daughter be a chorister at Wells?' (scholarships for them now available). Went to the States in '98.

WESTMINSTER SCHOOL
17 Dean's Yard, London SW1P 3PB

Tel: _020 7963 1000_ Fax: _020 7963 1006_

E-mail: REGISTRAR@WESTMINSTER.ORG.UK

Web: www.westminster.org.uk

✦ Pupils: 560 boys, 105 girls (all in sixth form). 411 day boys, 151 weekly boarders; 78 day girls, 27 weekly boarder ✦ Ages: 13-18 (but a few Westminster Assisted Places from 11, see below) ✦ Size of sixth form: 354 ✦ C of E ✦ Fee-paying

---

Head: Since 1998, Mr Tristram Jones-Parry MA (fifties), educated at Westminster and Christ Church, Oxford, where he read maths. Went into the National Coal Board for two years (research/computers) before teaching at Dulwich, then Westminster – where he was Under Master for seven years, followed by headship of Emanuel. Bachelor. Widely claimed as 'brilliant maths teacher'. Appears relaxed, open, knows his boys, goes round straightening their ties. We have previously described him as a 'stickler for discipline', not a comment he cared for, but he obviously cares about children and how they do, and likes clear guidelines – good news for the school. Busy opening the place up, involving Westminster with local schools. Knows the place inside out, from years of being an insider here – again, this is good for the school. Busy on three main fronts: the pastoral, IT development, and raising money for 'the middle classes caught in the poverty trap.' Personal note: he enjoys reading, travel, walking, cycling and watching sport. Teaches eight or nine periods of maths each week, to first year GCSE and upper sixth. Took over from David Summerscale, who strode the blast here from '86.

Academic Matters: Stunning results (and so they should be). Huge amount of academic pressure at all times, and pressure escalates as A levels heave into sight, though head strenuously denies pressure, and is dead against it – pupils and parents think otherwise, however – and says 'they work hard and are intelligent enough to know when they need to start: then they pull it off.' He reckons results are 'partly expectations'. Hard to pick out individual subjects for special praise, so many get gleaming results. Surprising amount of use of videos as teaching aid noted on our visit. Saturday morning school, with weekly boarders bent over their books on the train home. Fabulous science laboratories, round the corner in former Imperial Tobacco h.q. Wacky intellectuals among the staff, with 32 per cent females. Several new young staff. Entire school being wired up and fully networked, and laptop experiment in progress, whereby all 13 year olds use them, 'but I'm not convinced' says the head, 'good teachers are far better than any machine'.

The librarian is a new appointment (library previously run by a master). Glorious library – a series of rooms, where the atmosphere has been transformed from gentleman's club to meaningful library.

Games, Options, the Arts: Good art, also music (which has not always been the case). Terrific drama – 17 productions last year, an average of one every two weeks of the term. Latest acquisition is the Millicent Fawcett Hall nearby, now being revamped, to open September 2001. Debating, chess and other intellectual sports perennially popular. Tuesday and Thursday afternoons for sports: water sports and fencing both successful (fencing unbeaten in six years); cricket and football, however, inconsistent. Big on trips abroad – India, Mexico, Russia, Paris amongst them.

Background and Atmosphere: Glorious and historic buildings, something of a rabbit warren in parts. Umbilically tied to Westminster Abbey, where school services are held thrice a week, and Latin prayers once a week (Wednesdays). Founded in 1560 by Queen Elizabeth I, following her father's provision for forty King's Scholars at the Abbey (whose privileges still include queue-jumping Commons debates). Under the patronage of the Abbey, the Dean is the chairman of the governors, and the school is very much in the glare of the world. Beyond the calm of Dean's Yard lies a warren of buildings, some very ancient, often anything but calm – noisy, scruffy, seething with pupils and staff coming and going, not to mention goggling tourists. Dormitories in boys' houses being refurbished. Liberal tradition alive and well, without much structure beyond the classroom for boarders (staff disagree). Day pupils leave at 5, 6 or 9 p.m.- but this feels like a boarding school, which it is. No bells. Lunch with shortened grace is a ten minute affair. Library now an inspirational place to work in.

Pastoral Care and Discipline: Head has made determined efforts to organise more on the pastoral care front, with tutors meeting tutees every week, over lunch. Bullying given high profile, head hears of every case – 6 or 7 when he arrived, now down to two, creating a culture where boys can talk to housemasters and say 'I don't like what's going on'. School counsellor on hand.

Pupils and Parents: Some things don't change: boys are street smart; they are highly articulate, often nervously brilliant, with a reputation of being difficult to teach (also to have at home), they can be mocking and irreverent. Also, they can be charming and sophisticated. Large numbers with one or more parents from abroad; bilinguals in profusion; rich Middle Easterners; heavy middle-class intelligentsia and the offspring of ambitious yuppies, broken homes, also two-income, suburban, plus computer and chess geniuses. Day boys need (but don't always have) supportive solid family. Robustness an absolute essential ingredient to survive here – girls as well as boys. Recently instigated social evenings, class by class, at parents' demand – highly successful and popular. OWs include six prime ministers, the original William Hickey, Warren Hastings, Sir John Gielgud, Peter Brook, David Attenborough, Angus Wilson, Stephen Poliakoff, Tony Benn, Ben Jonson, John Locke, AA Milne.

Entrance: Still one of the most sought after schools in London. Put the name down at 10, boys weeded out at 11; interview and CE (highly competitive, minimum of 65 per cent). Large numbers of bright boys are encouraged to sit for scholarship (the Challenge) even if they don't have a real chance, thereby giving the school a more finely tuned exam to test able boys. 25 per cent come in from the Westminster Under School (same entry requirements apply). Entry at sixth form (for all candidates) – minimum four A grades at GCSE and a pass in at least six subjects, preferably A grades in A level subjects to be studied.

Exit: One and all to university, with around 30 – or more – going to Oxbridge. London, Edinburgh, Bristol, Newcastle. All manner of subjects and careers. Gap year popular.

Money Matters: Money newly acquired – £1 million from old boy Michael Zilkha – for the benefit of the teaching staff – a terrific fillip. Ogden Trust bursaries for 'above the average children of limited or no parental means from a state primary school.' At 11+ 5 Westminster Assisted Places tenable at the Under School from 11 and at the senior school to 18. At 13+ 8 Queen's scholarships per year – 50 per cent of fees, scholars must board – plus 5 music scholarships of up to half fees. Plus some means-tested bursaries at 13+.

Remarks: High profile famous central London public school for the brightest that is moving with the times and being shaken up on the pastoral front at last.

WESTONBIRT SCHOOL

Tetbury, Gloucestershire GS8 8QG

TEL: 01666 880333 FAX: 01666 880364

E-MAIL: office@westonbirt.gloucs.sch.uk

WEB: www.westonbirt.gloucs.sch.uk

✦ PUPILS: 200 girls. 120 board, 80 day
✦ Size of sixth form: 60 ✦ Ages: 11-18
✦ C of E ✦ Fee-paying

Head: Since 1999, Mrs Mary Henderson MA (forties), educated at St Andrews University where she played lacrosse for Scotland. Married to a lecturer at Bath University, no children. Previously was head of modern languages for three years, before that Warminster (co-ed) and Cheltenham Ladies' College. Sings with the Paragon Singers in Bath. Strong religious conviction. Following her predecessor at working hard to keep Westonbirt on the map. A defender of single-sex female education. Enjoys her relationships with the girls. A modern head; approachable, unshockable, kind.

Entrance: CE at 11-13+, or school's own exam thereafter. Not a hurdle. Some bursaries available. All girls within the school may go on to sixth form; those coming from outside need at least five GCSEs with As or Bs in their A level subjects.

Exit: Most girls go on to a degree, one or two to art foundation courses. Very few leave at 16.

Remarks: Small girls' boarding school which has gained, and rightly so, a reputation for helping gentle folk to shine and gain confidence. Stupendous large mellow neo-Renaissance pile (built for the Holford family), listed Grade I. Wonderful grounds and gardens, own golf course subsidises upkeep of grounds, glorious arboretum now in the hands of the Forestry Commission. 'Doesn't feel like a school at all,' said a visiting educationalist. Beautiful library, and some dorms in splendid bedrooms with old painted furniture – also study bedrooms for sixth formers are now tarted up, some with help from Laura Ashley (Cowslip range), Dorma and Mulberry.

Committedly Christian (Low Church). A rich mix socially, including Sloanes, first-time buyers, Londoners, Forces' daughters. Girls are good mixers, happy, articulate, fresh-faced, shiny hair, nice smiles. Not a 'bitchy' school. Small teaching groups throughout. Timetable is not set until after subjects are chosen. No horrors in exam results, on the contrary, very good indeed, given the broad academic intake. Biology, English and art particularly well taught. Strong DT. One girl had designed an amazing tent. Prep is now compulsory after supper – and evenings are not so free for friends and clubs. New satellite system installed to speed up delivery of Internet communications – Internet now used live in class as a teaching aid.

Good music tradition, and strong art. Almost all do Leith's Certificate in Food and Wine alongside A levels – a really useful extra. Sixth formers hold dinner parties for local boys schools, Radley, Downside and Cheltenham being recent favourites. Boys can also stay the night in guest rooms. Full-time dyslexia teacher and full-time EFL specialist. Very feminine atmosphere. Lots of things going on eg cookery demonstration, autumn bazaar, antiques fair, concerts. Lots of music; summer opera from

Bampton Classical Opera. Lacrosse, plus riding locally (including polo), tennis, golf etc etc. Successful Young Enterprise, also Duke of Edinburgh gets a good take-up.

A happy school, a lot of fun – a much rarer commodity than you might think. 'There's plenty on offer for girls to get their teeth into,' commented a parent, though some are concerned that their daughters may not be doing enough work.

WILLIAM ELLIS SCHOOL

Highgate Road, London NW5 1RN

TEL: *020 7267 9346* FAX:*020 7284 1274*

E-MAIL: willellis@aol.com

WEB: www.wellis.camden.sch.uk/

✦ PUPILS: 872 boys: 632 boys 11-16, sixth form 240. All day ✦ Ages: 11-18
✦ Size of sixth form: 1000 in a consortium of four schools, 'La Swap'
✦ Non-denom ✦ State, Voluntary Aided

Head: Since 1988, Mr Michael Wheale (forties), BA in politics and government from Kent, MA from King's College, London. Enthusiastic, open-minded and friendly. Relishes the liberating effects of running his own budget and organises it with flair. Travels in daily from North Oxford – but is usually in the school shortly after 7 am, as are the majority of the staff. Plays down the effects of the maelstrom that has hit schools for the best part of a decade, but nevertheless does not underestimate the effects on staff. Married to another head.

Academic Matters: Stimulating environment; dedicated and energetic teachers. Over the past few years efforts have been focused on the comprehensive nature of the intake, with an emphasis on motivating boys to succeed. Over 50 per cent (and increasing) achieving 5+ GCSEs grades A-C (eventually), which is very creditable given wide wide intake (forty-four mother tongues among the pupils). Also creditable are the lack of any obviously bad subjects (a notable improvement over the last three years), the 96 per cent A to G pass rate (so very few kids fail here, a great boost to the work ethic), and consistently positive value-added results. It would be nice to see more As and A*s though.

The giant combined sixth form 'consortium', called La Swap, created from William Ellis, Acland Burghley, La Sainte Union and Parliament Hill sixth forms, provides the numbers/funding for a huge range of subjects (all four schools are used for classes). Classes and staff totally intermingled, so difficult to comment on A level results, which seem average.

School became a specialist school in '97 with Language College status – this gave more funding, for eg dedicated suite of modern language rooms, and money has also been raised through commercial sponsorship (eg British Airways). French, Spanish, German the 'main' languages taught, but Mandarin recently started in the sixth form.

Assiduous use of value-added data and other monitoring systems to keep watchful eye on children's performance. Wide range of A level subjects, including Bengali, Portuguese, philosophy, sociology, theatre studies, economics, as well as the main stream subjects. One of the few local schools offering three separate sciences at GCSE, also music and German as a second language now on offer. GNVQs – wide range and at all levels and 'very popular'.

Huge ability range and classes currently running at 30+, with IQs ranging from 160+ down to 85+.Intelligent, long-sighted options, including offering geography GCSE in Spanish (studying the Madrid ring road system, rather than the socio-geographic considerations of the local leisure centre). Computer and technical programmes also well thought out, encouraging questioning, challenging minds, and a practical attitude to problem-solving. Highly qualified teachers for specific learning difficulties; quota of two statemented children per form of entry; oversubscribed for SEN applications also. New computer networks, and 'Success Maker' is proving popular with boys and raises reading ages 'quite quickly'.

Games, Options, the Arts: Rugby, soccer, basketball, cross-country running, Tennis and athletics mainly using Hampstead Heath (by arrangement with City of London authorities) but also playing fields at Edgware.There is also a cricket enclosure next to the school. More sporty than the normal inner-city comprehensive, although sport is not an obsession for most. School owns a very pleasant semi-rural residential centre – a converted water mill – which is much used by the first year, who spend a week under canvas, and for biology and geography field studies, for adventure activities and for sixth form revision.

Music considered a strength of the school; debating robust and there is a fully-equipped media studio (media studies popular). Computers interspersed with potted plants to humanise most impressively resourced computer rooms (PCs and Apple Macs – with more to come – not surprisingly there is a queue to join lunch time computer clubs).

Background and Atmosphere: Full to breaking point and spilling over into every square millimetre of space – land on the edge of Hampstead Heath is obviously at a premium.Tremendous feeling of a community at full stretch. Local Authority has at last funded some redevelopment and ICT expansion, so no longer reliant on decoration carried out by OBs, and teachers rewiring and decorating the staffroom. A third of staff are women, including the deputy head and head of English. On a rainy day the degree of co-operation and comradeship between the boys was noticeable – no sign of bored teenagers slouching around the vicinity of the school.

Pastoral Care and Discipline: A non-judgmental, purposeful, happy and confident community, with reward rather than punishment a central part of the ethos.

Pupils and Parents: Multi-racial intake, and pupils come from a staggering 76 different countries at time of writing, from Afghanistan to Zimbabwe, not to mention Venezuela, Ecuador, Sierra Leone, Mauritius, Slovakia, Somalia, Kosovo. Mainly from families of neighbouring manual workers, with a smattering of Hampstead liberal middle classes. Lively, open, friendly and street-wise. Motto: 'Rather use than Fame': Old Elysians become diplomats, lawyers, scientists (Toby Young an exception here).

Entrance: Around 120 a year from local primary schools – mainly Hampstead, Camden Town and Kentish Town; also twelve musical children, some from further afield. Admission criteria: (i) brother in school, (ii) musical ability, (iii) family connection, (iv) location. For admission to sixth form to study A level: minimum five Cs at GCSE, with B or better 'preferred' in A level subjects (apply early). (Lesser requirements for GNVQs.) Sixth form oversubscribed. 'The school has no interest in drug offenders thrown out of public schools!'

Exit: About 75 per cent stay on to do A levels at La Swap or elsewhere; of those, about 75 per cent them move on to higher or further education.

Money Matters: State-funded. Voluntary aided by the William Ellis and Birkbeck Schools Trust, but not rich, and constantly fund raising and 'always able to spend more money,' says head.

Remarks: Super strong broad North London state school with a tremendously hard-working, innovative staff, providing a real sense of community. Does an incredible job in unbelievably complicated circumstances. Exudes energy.

WIMBLEDON HIGH SCHOOL

Mansel Road, London SW19 4AB

TEL: *020 8971 0900* FAX: *020 8971 0901*

E-MAIL: info@wim.gdst.net

WEB: www.gdst.net/wimbledon/

✦ PUPILS: 586 girls; plus own Junior School with 276 girls. All day
✦ Ages: 11-18, Junior School 4-10
✦ Size of sixth form: 152 ✦ Non-denom
✦ Fee-paying

Head: Since 1995, Dr J L Clough (pronounced Cluff) BA PhD (Hull). Educated at Colston's Girls' School, Bristol and Queen Mary College, London, read English. Previous post was head of the Royal Naval School for Girls in Haslemere. Dr Clough is a FRSA, and has three daughters.

Academic Matters: Rigorous and largely traditional 'blend of old and new' teaching styles with largish teaching groups (25-28). 'It works because they're all high ability: they stimulate each other.' Long-serving mostly female staff ('only because fewer men apply'). National Curriculum plus with an initial choice of French, German or Spanish. Latin in the second year, virtually the entire group get As at GCSE. Three separate sciences at GCSE (combined award phased out) in modern airy block teeming with busy goggle-wearing girls in lettuce-green overalls. GCSE results are division one: A levels, one or two failures, but overall, very good. One or two AS levels taken.

Games, Options, the Arts: Netball, tennis, athletics track within walking distance at own Nursery Road playing field. Also golf and self-defence. Twenty-five-metre swimming-pool, sports hall. Plays, debates, music and liberal studies all in collaboration with nearby boys' King's Wimbledon. Duke of Edinburgh awards. Lots of keen community service, eg handicapped playgroup helpers, visitors for the lonely, old, etc. Exchange art trip, and also classics trip (to eg Sorrento and Pompeii). Conscientious careers advice. Committed work experience: hospitals, vets, business. Jazz is popular (keen saxophonists) plus numerous instrumental groups, madrigals and choir

Background and Atmosphere: Functional Victorian gabled red-brick buildings front tree-lined suburban street in the heart of prosperous SW19 (near tube and BR, just off the Village). Fairly cramped for space, steep staircases open off a galleried main hall ('too small for all of us') in cream and brown. Adjacent fairly faceless addition for science and sixth form – 'villa-style' house for very much the inner city teenage girl with regulation uncombed tresses, hooded tops, jeans, DMs, ethnic knapsacks, clearly relieved to cast off the rather austere navy pinafore and sweater of her juniors. Multicultural community creates an easy blend – a recent Hindu-style assembly featured Hindu readings, music and prayers and Indian religious dance.

Pastoral Care and Discipline: Strong pastoral and tutorial system. Counselling for 'social problems, divorce, abuse' can be arranged outside the school. PSHE classes cover health, sex, 'personal presentation' and how to write a business letter.

Pupils and Parents: Big, big mix of people. Multi-cultural and multi-ethnic. The pupils come from a wide catchment area south of the river and from as far as Surrey. This brings in all girls from all backgrounds 'from daughters of office-cleaners to publishing magnates'. 'They're kind, caring girls and good listeners,' comments a parent, 'I particularly like the tradition of older girls involved in teaching and helping the younger ones – they both benefit.'

Entrance: Selective at 11: girls come from own Junior School (not all of them make it), almost equal numbers from other schools, with tests involving English, maths, non-verbal reasoning. 'We're looking for academic calibre and interests.' 16+ intake hinges on minimum grade Cs in six subjects with A or B in prospective A levels.

Exit: Most to higher education, predominance of scientists, engineers, medics. London medical schools, and London University popular. Seven to Oxbridge in '97, ten in '98. Also the liberal arts, teaching training, arts foundation, and one or two more exotic choices such as equine studies at Writtle, HND in beauty, English National Opera foundation course.

Money Matters: Had 57 assisted places – not a lot by GDST standards. Now has approximately six bursaries a year. Academic scholarships at 11+ and 16+, also music scholarship at 13+ and sixth form science scholarship from OG's endowment.

Remarks: Strategically placed no-nonsense no-frills girls' day school producing good exam results for reasonably bright, unpampered city girls with a trace of sophistication as well as kindness. Good reports.

JUNIOR SCHOOL: Tel: 020 8971 0902, Fax: 020 8971 090. Head: Mrs Jacqueline Compton-Howlett (formerly deputy head here). Entrance via playgroup and interview at 4, tests at 7; register names one term early – the school is selective and oversubscribed. Brand new building. Same site as the senior school and uses some of their facilities. French in years 4, 5 and 6; philosophy course from '99. The school is popular and flourishing.

WINCHESTER COLLEGE

Winchester, Hampshire, SO23 9NA

TEL: *01962 621100* FAX: *01962 621106*

E-MAIL: information@wincoll.ac.uk

WEB: www.wincoll.ac.uk

✦ PUPILS: 675 boys: 640 board, 35 day
✦ Ages: 13-18 ✦ Size of sixth form: 265
✦ C of E ✦ Fee-paying

Head: Since 2000: Dr Nicholas Tate MA PGCE PhD (fifties). Educated Huddersfield New College; Balliol, Oxford; Universities of Bristol and Liverpool; a historian. Taught in colleges of education for fifteen years, published many textbooks; has worked in national curriculum organisations since 1989 ending as chief executive of SEAC and now of QCA (the Qualifications and Curriculum Authority). Recreations reading and music. Quite a catch, and we hear v g early reports – listens, and what's more gives you answers to questions (not a universal trait in headmasters). Took over from Mr James Sabben-Clare.

Academic Matters: Outstanding academic education coupled with outstanding teaching. A hundred and fifty options to choose from. GCSE taken on the wing at different moments – fewer than most schools, and results good rather than outstanding – endless shadow of exams might daunt lesser mortals. Surprising lack of A*s in English at GCSE – the same story year after year. Good take-up of Greek for GCSE (fewer for A level, but they all get As). Head has started a school for Oriental Studies, with Mandarin and Japanese language, plus Oriental culture and civilisation. Enormous numbers take maths at A level (far and away the most popular subject), often in strange combinations; '00 results include a highly unusual clutch of Ds-Us – head says that this illustrates school's policy of not preventing any boy from taking an A level if they want to. Physics and chemistry well patronised and successful. Modern languages is 'no longer the poor relation', and indeed large numbers take French, German, Russian or Spanish at GCSE, almost all getting A*/As, with good numbers for French and Spanish at A level. A little learning is imparted by 'div' = unexamined general studies (the school doesn't do general studies at A level). Each boy has one period a day at this with the same master ('don'), covering aspects of European history in whichever way the don sees fit, eg he might look at Zola's novels in the context of social upheaval in France, etc. More general knowledge also sucked in in the 'transition period' created by taking GCSE early. Library budget £20,000 a year – excellent collections, both old and new. Main library housed in old brewery and still smells faintly of this.

Several members of staff trained in special needs, share responsibility for looking after such boys. Trained part-time EFL teacher.

Games, Options, the Arts: The perfect place for a boy who is shaping up to be bolshie about team games. Individuals allowed to do their own thing here, and there are a huge number of things on offer. The 'main' games: soccer, the school's own variety of football (Winchester football) and cricket, are not compulsory after first year. Joy for some. Glorious grounds with one of the most beautiful cricket pitches in the country, stretching down to the River Itchen, where the school's famous fishing club (founder member: Lord Grey of Falloden) still flourishes under eye of keeper Mr McCarthy and his black labrador. Water polo – bolstered by the school's Hong Kong contingent, for whom swimming is number-one sport – virtually unbeaten. Basketball also good – 'not many schools do it,' says head modestly. And the school has been national cross-country champions for two years running. School very lucky to have one of the earliest sports centres, built large and well enough by vision of former head, Sir Desmond Lee – still in use a punishing 85 hours a week, not only by boys but also by outsiders. No big all-weather surface – city planners won't allow it. More tennis courts recently laid down. Keen CDT centre. Carpentry room much patronised not only by boys but also by staff. IT was the only area in which the recent ISC Inspection was less than ecstatic. Large light art department which has a fabulous collection of water colours – Cotmans, Rowlandsons, etc. Art and design does not appear to be an important part of school life, however.

Music outstanding. School has maintained the 14th-century tradition of having sixteen quiristers selected from all over the country and trained up by the director of chapel music to sing in chapel (CD of songs by former Master of Music recently published). A*/As for all at GCSE in music, As and Bs at A level, four to six (out of six) Oxbridge organ/choral awards. On non-classical front, has won schools jazz competition. Has magnificent 1960 concert hall, decorated with panelling by pupil of Grinling Gibbons (taken from elsewhere in the school). Two-thirds of the pupils learn an instrument.

Drama also considered strong – keen, and good theatre to work in.

Impossible to list everything – but NB, the idea is that pupils make a choice and stick with it – commitment is expected. CCF compulsory for one year. Some granny bashing, but in our opinion the school does not feel part of the local community.

Background and Atmosphere: Centre of school still the 14th-century quad built by William of Wykeham, Bishop of Winchester and chancellor to Richard II, and other buildings have been bolted on at regular intervals, giving a glorious but slightly rabbit-warreny feel to the place, where every other stone has a history. Chapel has christening robe of Henry VII's son Arthur, embroidered with red and white roses symbolically linked, some original stained glass.

Outstanding grounds – on one side the town, on the other the cathedral close, long acres of playing fields stretching lushly down to water meadows.

Architectural gems dotted all over the place, including a 17th-century Sick House beside which a 17th-century-style herb garden has been planted. Everywhere, a feast for the eyes and soul.

Boarding houses dotted around the town, cosy, in narrow ancient lanes and backstreets (difficult to park). Meals still eaten in house – one of the last schools to retain this civilised custom (NB some complaints by boys that supper can leave you hungry). Sign seen in one dining room: 'No Mandarin to be spoken at mealtimes'.

The school operates like a sixth form college from age 13 – lots of free time, not much structure. This can faze some boys. Scholars live in separate 14th-century house 'College', where, they report, they are worked like stink. Several buildings still used for purpose for which originally built – strong sense of continuity and purpose. Good reports of housemasters – Dr. David Ceiriog-Hughes (modern linguist) of Fearon's, Mr. Eric Billington (physicist) newly of Kingsgate House.

Pastoral Care and Discipline: House-masters reign here, but there are no unhappy reports of any particular house at time of writing. System of pupils working side by side in 'toys' for the first two years (study cubicles – NB Winchester has well-developed language, as befits its old age). Generally a Good Thing, as new boys kept in sight, and pupils of different ages mix; more like a family than many schools. Pupils seem for most part happy and well cared for. School does not go in for fleets of counsellors: 'If there is a problem,' says head, 'we expect to deal with it.' Parents confirm that this is so, and that the head in particular is brilliant at it. Alcohol is generally regarded as the menace – lots of pubs within stone's throw and reports by locals of noisy carousing by Wykehamists on Saturday nights. Occasional cannabis sackings (the City of Winchester reeks with the stuff). Interesting interview with a former cannabis smuggler recently in the school magazine.

Given the strong collegiate system, there is a slight sense of several entities beavering away in separate corners rather than working as a community: the head is still talking of 'drawing more threads into the middle'.

Pupils and Parents: Bright to brilliant. Largely from intellectual (upper) middle class, also contingent of bright Hong Kong Chinese. Overwhelmingly reports are of charming pupils, with good manners. Slightly inward-looking. Pupils from more down to earth backgrounds still comment that Wykehamists are a 'touch out of touch with the real world' (and see comment of local girls' school, St Swithun's). A selection of OBs: Willie Whitelaw, Hugh Gaitskell, Richard Crossman, Geoffrey Howe, the great Prof. Dyson, and Montague John Druitt (possibly Jack the Ripper). Also Sir Jeremy Morse, George Younger (now Warden of the College), Tim Brooke-Taylor, the Nawab of Pataudi, Richard Noble, David Cairns (Whitbread prize), Ian Fountain (pianist), Peter Jay, Sir Humphrey Appleby.

Entrance: Full to bursting. Register after child's eighth birthday. Interview at 11, with IQ test for selection to take school's own entrance exam at 13+. Pupils drawn from 170 different prep schools. Traditional 'feeds' are the Pilgrims' School on the doorstep, Horris Hill and Twyford. Entry to sixth form by way of an exam and interviews in February (for following September). No hurdle for boys already in the school.

Exit: Oxbridge as always – averaging over 50 a year for the past five years. Pupils go on to be lawyers, bankers, doctors, accountants, diplomats and backroom experts.

Money Matters: Underpinning parents through the recession has been stretching current considerable resources to the limit. One or two pupils even so have fallen by the financial wayside. Each hardship case considered on merits. Bursar has been heard to comment that the school is 'full of pupils who can't afford to be here'.

Seventy scholars, around six exhibitioners a year, plus a few bursaries for boys from Hampshire state schools, plus up to six music exhibitions and two other sixth form exhibitions. Five-star value.

Remarks: Traditionally and currently one of the best – if not the best – and brightest public schools in the country. Outstanding all round. Enormous muscle, both mental and financial. Far more all-round education than ten years ago; the remaining tendency towards ivory-towerishness may perhaps change with the new head.

WITHINGTON GIRLS' SCHOOL

Wellington Road, Fallowfield, Manchester
M14 6BL

TEL: *0161 224 1077* FAX: *0161 248 5377*

E-MAIL: office@withington.manchester.sch.uk

WEB: www.withington.manchester.sch.uk

✦ PUPILS: 630 girls, all day ✦ Ages: 7-18
✦ Size of sixth form: 140 ✦ Non-denom
✦ Fee-paying

Head: Since 2000, Mrs Janet Pickering BSc (forties). Educated at Bridlington High and Malton Grammar, followed by biochemistry at Sheffield. Late entrant into school teaching: did research, lectureship (Leeds and Bradford), motherhood and scientific publishing first. Previous post headmistress of St Bees (qv), and before that housemistress and deputy head at King's Canterbury (during its move to co-education – taught in the school since '86). Married to a biology teacher and textbook author, two teenage sons. Keen committee person. Academically a bit high-powered for St Bees – that shouldn't be a problem here, though. Took over from Mrs Margaret Kenyon, who was here from 1986.

Academic Matters: Seriously good teaching throughout, with computers all over, good careers department, with strong links to industry, and girls encouraged to arrange their own work-shadowing – embryo doctors do this very early. Lots of speakers, often parents, or senior hospital/university figures. State of the art language lab (two languages at same time and touch-screen operations). Exam results continue to be outstanding. Hardly needs more than two columns for its GCSE results – 90 per cent A★ and A. 92 per cent A/B grades at A level, maths, chemistry, biology, English and French the most popular. All girls do either three separate sciences or double award to GCSE. Girls regularly features in the Science Olympiads and win science prizes. Girls do original research for Royal Society at school level, and publish results. Very little streaming, maths and French only, maximum class size 26. League table note: almost all girls do general studies as an A level (most getting As) and this bumps up the school's position.

Games, Options, the Arts: Tennis outstanding still (usually Lancashire finalists), lacrosse (several county players). No pool, but super sports hall, with trampolines and viewing gallery. New all-weather pitches. Music super, three orchestras, wind band, jazz group, v inspirational staff (strong links with the BBC Philharmonic). Drama strong, clubs, etc, fabulous hall in the round, with lots going on (much done with Manchester Grammar, qv) plus house play competitions and visits to local theatres. Whole school humming with Manchester cultural contacts.

Good art, and ceramics, art rooms revamped as part of the Centenary Appeal, plus fabric design and textiles. Home economics, also revamped, and full of cooking and green-room activities when we visited. Art not much to the fore in exams. There are good charity links (Barnardos is tops), links with school in Kenya, clubs and masses of extra-curricular activities and trips hither and yon.

Background and Atmosphere: School founded in 1890 by a group of prominent Mancunians, whose original aims still hold good: to provide 'efficient and liberal education for girls: to make work interesting and stimulating in itself, eliminating prizes; to remain small; to stress the importance of Natural Science'. School is set in an oasis of green (building on this is forbidden by Founders' orders – but sports hall was OK.) Superb labs, and more being revamped, and new classrooms to come.

Pastoral Care and Discipline: Chain of support via form teachers, tutors in sixth form, formalised PSHE programme (timetabled), working up to girl's Personal Statement and Record of Achievement. Plus lots of speakers including the police. No written rules, other than 'Respecting other people and respecting self'. No detention, ad-hoc punishments, like sorting lost property. 'Has never sacked', 'no whisper of drugs, drink not a big issue'. A few anorexia problems, but school 'keeps an eye wide.'

Pupils and Parents: Ethnic mix, including Chinese (with parents at the university). Girls come from wide catchment area. Lots of university and medics amongst parents, good role models. Good parental contact. Old Girls include the first female director of Price Waterhouse in Manchester, C A Lejeune (Mrs Louisa Lejeune was one of the school's Founders), Judith Chalmers, Christine Rice, Catherine Stott.

Entrance: Selective – brains to die for. Own exam at seven, eight, nine or 11 (approx 26 come in from own prep school), plus 50-55 from outside. Over-subscribed three to one. Some places at sixth form: at least six A grade GCSEs needed for new entrants; WGS girls treated more leniently, but 'it is to be hoped they will have As in subjects to be taken at A level'.

Exit: A few leave after GCSE. All sixth formers go on to degree courses. Usually fif-teen or so to Oxbridge, rest scattered, mainly to old civic universities – Leeds figures largely, followed by Edinburgh.

Money Matters: 'Very reasonable fees', 'best value around, all our developments are based on northern thrift'. Fees £1,680 a term, with lunches and individual music extra. Had over a hundred assisted places, and governors' bursary scheme has been set up to replace (some of) them.

Remarks: Very strong stable girls' day school which thrives on the back of Manchester's cultural and educational resources. Highly sought after (and deservedly so) and old girls look back on their time here fondly.

WOLDINGHAM SCHOOL

Marden Park, Woldingham,
Surrey CR3 7YA

TEL: *01883 349431* FAX: *01883 348653*

E-MAIL: registrar@woldingham.surrey.sch.uk

WEB: www.woldingham.surrey.sch.uk

✦ PUPILS: 540 girls, 420 board, 120 day ✦
Ages: 11-18 ✦ Size of sixth form: 140
✦ RC ✦ Fee-paying

Head: Acting head Miss Diana Vernon. A graduate of Durham, and City PR firms; thence to teaching and head of sixth form at Downe House. Joined Woldingham as deputy head Easter 2000. Previous head Mrs Maureen Ribbins left the school at (it appears) the request of the governors and at very short notice in August 2000.

Academic Matters: Doesn't pretend to be a hothouse, nevertheless encompasses some high-fliers, a bulk of middle-of-the-roaders, and a few stragglers – 'all gifts are equal; we are here to identify talent'. About a quarter of the staff are male, including the deputy head. Hot on languages and all must take two modern ones (mostly French, Spanish, German) in addition to Latin or classical civilisation. One third of pupils do separate sciences, the rest dual award sciences in modern science block; very strong computer technology. Exceptional careers advice under Mrs. Bagley. Nine or ten GCSEs the norm; all must take RE, keen geography. English Lit. still the most popular A level, followed by business studies; art history and art next in line, maths fading fast. Art, French, maths and English account for most A*s at GCSE (in that order). Altogether very pleasing exam results, particularly given intake. Parents have, however, been known to move their v bright children to more academic establishments for extra 'stretching'.

Games, Options, the Arts: Strong tennis, also hockey, netball, athletics track, popular fitness studio. Sports centre opened in '95, financed by 6 per cent fees surcharge over three years. Lots of training in 'responsibility', eg leadership courses. Good debating, community service, D of E awards. Very strong art includes life-class, plus art trips to Florence, Amsterdam and Barcelona; photography. Art exam results excellent. Flourishing music – new music/drama centre opening in '99, including concert hall.

Background and Atmosphere: Glorious rural setting (with an extra 700 acres of rolling farmland), though suburbia only a few miles off. Immaculate leafy grounds, manicured topiary, etc. 'I never tell girls to hurry to class in such surroundings,' says Head. Formerly a Convent of the Sacred Heart (order founded in 1800 by French nun following turmoil of French Revolution – four elderly nuns still hanging on in school bungalows) and lay-based since '85. Transferred here from Roehampton in 1946 to spreading mellow late 17th-century (fire-damaged and partially rebuilt) chateau-style house (mentioned in John Evelyn's Diary) with sympathetic additions including luxury-motel-style upper sixth house. Senior girls eat with juniors housed in nearby more functional barracks-style addition (younger girls house own pets in Hamster Hall and Guinea Pig Gallery). Good food, lots of choice. Open, friendly, no-clique atmosphere. 'Ribbons' (prefects) elected by pupils (a coveted honour); senior girls can earn weekend and evening money manning reception, school bank and shop. Discos, etc, with Worth, Wellington, Charterhouse, Cranleigh; Upper Sixth can ask boys for dinner and cook it in own kitchen-diner. 'Flexible boarding' – weekly boarding particularly popular – and full boarding. Unstuffy spirituality with alternating C of E and RC confirmation years – 'this is no [St Mary's] Ascot,' comments a relieved mixed-marriage parent – under female chaplain from the RC Oxford Team Chaplaincy and visiting religious from nearby Wonersh seminary; leaving girls attend Mass with highly charged Ceremony of Commission.

Pastoral Care and Discipline: Reputedly 'not a whiff of drugs' in this steadily middle-class suburban community: 'We operate on trust, like a good home,' said outgoing head. No going to pubs, strict screening on videos, etc. Health education taught, plus visiting tellers of cautionary tales, eg reformed drug addict, HIV-positive man, Old Woldingham high-flier single mother.

Pupils and Parents: Half are Catholics; 15 per cent families living overseas; also v handy for Londoners. Ratio of day to boarding pupils 1:4. Breeds great loyalty among Old Girls; droves return to be married (at least 12 wedding bookings listed at any time, for which choir returns to sing), plus some to be buried alongside the nuns in school's own cemetery. Wide social mix encompasses lots of first-time buyers. Old Girls: Caroline Charles, Caroline Waldegrave.

Entrance: Currently very popular. Pre-selection day at 10-11 before CE. Only half a dozen fall at a fairly soft-edged CE and all siblings are automatically accepted. New parents' dinner and treasure-hunt plus lunch for all on parents' day, 'so they can compare problems and solve them'. Sixth form entry.

Exit: To medical school, business management, art courses, secretarial, teaching. Also gap year. Six to eight leave post-GCSE to sixth form colleges, etc.

Money Matters: Not short of a bob or two, in fact, coffers bulging (see land purchase above). Nine scholarships (some academic, others for music and art) plus internal scholarships for sixth form.

Remarks: An institution that we recently described as a truly super girls' boarding school in the liberal ecumenical RC tradition, left in splendid shape in 1997 by the previous head, has clearly suffered a major hiatus. Await developments.

WORTH SCHOOL

Paddockhurst Road, Turners Hill, Crawley,
West Sussex RH10 4SD

TEL: *01342 710200* FAX: *01342 710201*

E-MAIL: office@worth.org.uk

WEB: www.worth.org.uk

✦ PUPILS: Over 420 boys; about 75 per cent board ✦ Ages: 11-18 (there is no longer a Junior School) ✦ Size of sixth form: 140 ✦ RC ✦ Fee-paying

Head: Since 1994, Father Christopher Jamison OSB MA (forties). Educated at Downside and Oxford, where he read modern languages. Recently wrote a book on developments in the Catholic church since Vatican 11. Parents comment, 'He's good news, a doer.' One enthusiastic parent went further, and described him as 'good-looking, capable, keen on PR and broad-minded'. Father Christopher comments, 'Pupils in RC schools learn as much about how to be human as how to be RC.' Also comments he sees himself 'leading a community of learners into a changing world ... a unique animal with deep monastic roots and modern technological wings'.

Academic Matters: This place is not an academic ball of fire but is doing increasingly well with a very gentle intake. Staff of 50 teachers including eight monks, plus partnership with Dyslexia Institute plus own SEN staff. Combined or separate sciences at GCSE. Languages – Spanish (lots do this) with German, Italian as 'extras'. All take religious studies at GCSE. A level results more than commendable, with a good preponderance of A and B grades and few stragglers; most popular subjects are maths, history, theology, English and physics. Business, media, theatre studies etc on offer as well as the mainstream subjects. Father Christopher comments: 'We aim to make silk purses out of sows' ears.'

Games, Options, the Arts: Fairly games-orientated school with strong rugby tradition (acres of mud-strewn pitches) – ex-head boy capped for England school boys, and new keen deputy head. Sports hall, also seven-hole golf course. No CCF, but active D of E instead. Revival of music under director who favours early(ish) music – new theatre and music school in '99. Two plays and two rugby teams touring Australia in 2001. The school has recently expanded its IT provision, and is going at this with a will. School heavily into granny bashing – playing guitars at a school for the handicapped, manning soup kitchen in Brighton etc.

Background and Atmosphere: Original building is Lord Cowdray's late 19th-century house in 500 acres of rolling Sussex parkland, with many additions, plus painful-looking circular '60s weathered concrete Abbey Church ('UFO style,' says school). The school was originally founded in 1933 as prep school for Downside, became senior school in '59. Fagging outlawed in '95 (it was £10-£20 a term, fetching newspapers, vacuuming prefects' rooms, etc). All boys are expected to clean their own rooms. Benedictine ethos permeates. Very strong community/family feel. Gentle approach suits some but not others. School empties at weekends ('but not till Saturday night and there are activities for those still here', comments head). Non-stop social life 'incredibly social', commented a parent. One or two dissenting pupils however comment there's

'no life, not enough sport, and it's too small' (such dissenters usually leave after GCSE for life elsewhere).

Pastoral Care and Discipline: Lots of monitoring and strictish rules on going out so 'boys know where they stand'. Gatings for having boys in rooms after 11 pm and 'for playing canasta in prep', also 'suspension for smoking indoors'. Flexible exeats. Drugs policy with 'targeted testing' – 'the problem lies with what our students encounter outside school,' says head.

Pupils and Parents: 'Popular with island dwellers' says the head, 'from Jersey to St Lucia'. The rest live within an hour's drive. OB Harry Enfield, who apparently loathed it, and Peter Jonas, ex-Director of ENO, (who apparently loved it).

Entrance: Mainly at 11, 13 and 16. Interview for Junior House. At 11+ and 13+ entry tests in English, maths and verbal reasoning in the spring of the year of entry. For sixth form, interview, recommendation from the current school, and at least 5 GCSEs at grade C or above. No line is drawn between weak and strong: the school pledges to accept 'any pupil who would flourish here'. 'Resolutely' single sex and developing a partnership with Woldingham (the new head of Woldingham is a governor of Worth).

Exit: Almost all to higher education: ten per cent to Oxbridge: some to building, agriculture, business, arts foundation courses, the Forces. One or two post-GCSE to crammers and sixth form colleges.

Remarks: RC boarding school taking increasing numbers of non-Catholics. Boys coming from/going elsewhere comment that the school feels 'very nice, very friendly ... but limited' to quote one.

WYCOMBE ABBEY SCHOOL

High Wycombe, Buckinghamshire HP11 1PE

TEL: *01494 520381* FAX: *01494 473836*

WEB: www.wycombeabbey.com

✦ PUPILS: 534 girls, all board except for 30 day girls ✦ Ages: 11-18
✦ Size of sixth form: 153 ✦ C of E
✦ Fee-paying

Head: From September 1998, Mrs Pauline Davies BSc PGCE MEd (early fifties), married with two sons. Read botany and zoology at Manchester University. Previous post head of Croydon High, before that taught in 'a variety of schools'. Took over from Mrs Judith Goodland, who was here since '89.

Academic Matters: Hard work and exam success are what really matter here. The school picks children who enjoy work, and wherever you are, work is never far away. Girls confess they are worked like stink and report themselves 'exhausted' (ditto staff). High-powered common room – particularly unusual in a girls' school. Some long-standing staff, staff mainly female (one or two Old Girls), often earnest and usually immensely dedicated. Senior house mistress, Mrs Best, is 'absolutely super' according to a parent.

Exam results are as you would expect of a school which prides itself on taking only the academic cream: 90 per cent plus A★/A grades at GCSE; outstanding history by any standards at A level (twenty-six As out of twenty-six candidates), English Lit also excellent and very popular. No weak links. All take general studies. A good range of A

levels on offer, including classics, philosophy, drama and PE. Russian and Mandarin can be studied in the sixth form. Satellite TV for languages. Other exotic languages being taken by foreign nationals. Relatively large number taking Latin and Greek at GCSE – good department. No set prep periods: 'We like girls to work out how to use their time', except in the first year; after that, girls must fit it in during the day (using libraries, house studies, classrooms, not overseen). Separate and dual award sciences.

Games, Options, the Arts: Extras are taken seriously too. Everyone does design and technology and cooking (not examined). First-rate theatre in the arts centre (local artists put on exhibitions here, and theatre used by the outside world as well), a triumph of modern architecture rising above the lake. Seven pupils took art at A level in '97 – all got As. Good photographic department. Intensive music – 70 per cent of girls reach Grade V, many do better – chamber groups, orchestras, etc, and good singing. New music school and recital hall. Lacrosse played keenly (dozens and dozens of matches; lots of county and national players); also tennis (coaching round the year, very successful), with 24 tennis courts. A rich variety of societies – notices up all around the school about these, far more sophisticated than most schools – even went punting recently. Some excellent poets currently in the school. IT being upgraded.

Background and Atmosphere: Mildly castellated slightly grim grey stone Gothic (James Wyatt), decorated in pretty soft colours, set on the edge of High Wycombe, girdled one side by the wall so that four of the eleven boarding houses back on to an extremely busy road. Feels a bit small town. Houses are fiercely competitive; Lower sixth in charge of younger girls (so upper sixth can concentrate all their energies on A level), mixed-age dorms (actually rooms), but 11-year-olds live together in the junior house further up in hill. Another sixth form house, new(ish) coolly elegant, happily partially hiding the hot red-brick plain Clarence – excellent school-to-university stepping stone, with girls living in tens (study bedrooms), where they cook their own breakfast and supper (provisions laid on, plus weekly allowance for some fresh foods). Houses are interconnected, with one main sitting room. NB television not much watched: Fridays and weekends, with Neighbours videoed for bumper sessions. Regular visits to theatres, exhibitions, lectures (London, Oxford, Stratford). At the top end, increasing activities with boys' schools – drama, music, debating, shared lectures, etc, with Eton, Radley, Harrow, Abingdon and Winchester. 'Just enough,' sighed one girl wistfully. School founded in 1896 by Dame Frances Dove from St Leonards, Scotland, and faint links are retained with St Leonards (prayers are said, etc). Daily chapel. Atmosphere is definitely busy, with pupils going purposefully to and from classes calmly carrying heavy book bags.

Pastoral Care and Discipline: This is a 'grown up' place – where children are treated as adults and eg even 11 year olds are allowed into Marlow on school coaches (in groups with a member of staff). Self-discipline is the key. New head as fierce about smoking and drink as her predecessor, who said 'I suspend at once'. Revolutionaries are few and far between, tight pastoral system, backed up all down the line. Exeats either side of half-term means the whole school shuts down: pupils and staff both need the breather. 'Polite, gentle' children may have a hard time, reports a parent.

Pupils and Parents: Pupils from prep schools all over the south-east, particularly London and round the M25. Few now from further afield in the UK, but a small handful from abroad. ' ... Brains as the common denominator,' said a parent. The professional intelligentsia, civil servants, solicitors, city folk, the well-heeled upper classes. Girls are poised, stylish and often more mature than their peer groups elsewhere. Old Girls include Elizabeth Butler-Sloss, Elspeth Howe.

Entrance: Takes its academic prowess very seriously. Interested in performance rather than potential. At 11, 12 and 13, with 55 per cent at CE (the bottom line in a girl's weakest subject): 'They must be academically able, and most important, they must be able to cope – and still have energy and enthusiasm for all the rest.' Increasingly popular to come at 13. Entry at sixth form by own exam plus minimum eight GCSEs at C. Now offers up to 30 places to day girls – an expensive choice, given some very good day schools locally.

Exit: Around a quarter to Oxbridge, the others to top universities, Edinburgh popular, to read a variety of subjects – medicine and arts subjects popular, and then lots to the professions. Gap years are popular 'and well planned', say parents. NB a fair number leave after GCSE – to co-eds etc.

Money Matters: Several scholarships, including some at half fees. Bursaries for seniors' daughters/ grand-daughters.

Remarks: Famous girls' boarding school, resolutely ploughing its straight and single-minded furrow as an out-and-out academic machine. Produces highly articulate girls well prepared for the fast track.

WYMONDHAM COLLEGE

(PRONOUNCED WIND'EM)

Norfolk NR18 9SZ

TEL: *01953 605566* FAX: *01953 603313*

E-MAIL: wymcollege@aol.com

WEB: www.wymondhamcollege.co.uk

✦ PUPILS: 930 boys and girls; about 520 board (both sexes), 410 day ✦ Ages: 11-18 ✦ Size of sixth form: 310 ✦ Non-denom ✦ State; parents pay boarding fees

---

Head (Principal): Since 2000, Mrs Victoria Musgrove MEd FRSA (mid forties). Read English at Sheffield, education at Hull. Married to a teacher, four sons one daughter. Previously head of Blenheim High School, Epsom. Took over from Mr John Haden , who came here in 1992.

Academic Matters: Pupils set by ability in major subjects (25 per class). Notably good GCSE results considering the raw intake. Does well among the Norfolk league tables – indeed, the best GCSE results of any state school in Norfolk or Suffolk from '94 to '00 – not that that is overpoweringly difficult. It would be nice to see a few more A★s, though, and fewer Ds in maths and English. Average points per A level student 22 (including underperforming general studies) – a steady increase over the past five years. Maths now the most popular A level, and good. Next in line are English, business studies, biology, art, physics and design All students do at least three A levels and general studies . GNVQs increasingly popular. Learning support department.

Extremely good library, with over 14,000 useful tomes, large budget, excellent staff, and large collection of careers material that has been identified by the County as a Centre of Excellence, and deservedly so. 'Individuals expected to do well,' says the principal. Acquired Technology College status in '96.

Games, Options, the Arts: Plenty of playing fields, and good facilities (sports hall, indoor pool, etc). Keen games playing and matches against state and private schools throughout East Anglia. Regularly fields England caps; school has Sportsmark Gold Award. CCF continues to be strong – very unusual for a state school, possibly reflecting Service parents, and the school was USAAF hospital base during the war. Now developing a link with the Royal Anglian Regiment in Colchester. School is said to have produced more RAF pilots than any other school in the UK. Good art department – 'superb,' says principal, and the exam results bear him out. Good computer, video, animation facilities. New IT network with PCs in the houses. Enthusiastic drama. Had two students in the National Youth Choir recently, and three in the National Youth Theatre, plus school's concert band in the National Finals of Music for Youth. Gets a large percentage of distinctions in Associated Board music exams.

Background and Atmosphere: Founded in 1951 by Norfolk County Council Chief Education Officer Sir Lincoln Ralphs, who apparently designed the boarding houses with four separate staircases so that boys and girls could reside under one roof as though in a family. Cosy and clean. Genuine co-education. Heavy TV-watching school. Tangible commitment ('We chose to come here,' commented boarders). Atmosphere, as we have said before, is fairly steamy. Humble surrounding in wind-swept Norfolk. All

Nissen huts now gone bar the chapel/heritage centre and one store. Since opting out, atmosphere has changed to being brisk and purposeful with cheerful, dedicated, excellent staff, now dressed less in Crimplene, more in little Chanel-type numbers. Copies of RAF News and Norfolk Young Farmers handbook littered about in visitors' waiting room. There has been a reorganisation of the boarding in response to growing numbers. New boys and girls now spend their first year in Peel House, which is specifically for them, and provides a safe base from which to get to grips with this large institution. 17-year-olds in the lower sixth play 'key leadership role' in the 12-17 houses. There is a separate sixth form house for final year students.

Pastoral Care and Discipline: Staff very committed. Norwich, 12 miles away ('Not a Babylon,' commented a parent), a magnet for some boarders. Day pupils can arrive early in the morning and stay until 9 pm. Deals with problems kindly and wisely. Flexible, judges each case on its merits, but being on the wrong staircase means instant expulsion.

Pupils and Parents: All sorts. Claims to be socially classless. Growing number of students from the EU, in particular from France, Denmark, Greece, Germany and Spain (now fully integrated), also some UK passport holders from Hong Kong etc but most children are from Norfolk. Children of all ranks of RAF and Army, Colonels to airmen/ women (20 per cent of boarders). Slight tendency to unpolished manners – 'I would disagree, students are polite and charming' says the principal. Increasing number of ex-private school pupils (at all ages, including sixth form).

Entrance: No tests, but previous school report and interview. For sixth form A level entry – five subjects A-C at GCSE, and B grades in A level subjects. For Advanced GNVQs: four GCSEs A-C, including English and maths. Pupils have come from over 270 different schools over the years.

Exit: Approximately 77 per cent went on to take degree courses – ex-polys popular. Handfuls taking a gap year, retaking A levels, nursing training, etc. Some go straight to employment after GCSE.

Money Matters: Currently a 'foundation' school – and in control of the situation. School opted out in 1991, and operates on a £6.2 million annual budget. One of the relatively few state boarding schools in the country, with fee-paying element to make the boarding pay for itself – approximately one-third the cost of private sector equivalent (ie at the time of writing, around £5,200 per year). Norfolk County Council bursary scheme for some very low-income families and 'disadvantaged children' now abolished.

Remarks: Friendly, lively school which claims to be by far the largest state boarding school in Europe. Since opting out, has had lift-off. Well worth consideration if you are looking for a state school with boarding and a traditional ethos (and are not too concerned about social polish).

JUNIOR AND PREPARATORY SCHOOLS

ABBERLEY HALL

Worcester, WR6 6DD

TEL: *01299 896275* FAX: *01299 896875*

E-MAIL: postmaster@abberleyhall.co.uk

WEB: www.abberleyhall.co.uk

✦ PUPILS: 141 boys, 38 girls; 75 per cent board, the rest day. Girls from 1998 in the lower classes. Also pre-prep/nursery with 45 boys, 26 girls ✦ Ages: 7-13, pre-prep 2+-7 ✦ C of E ✦ Fee-paying

Head: Since 1996, Mr John Walker, BSc in psychology from Surrey (forties). Previous post was head of Bramcote (where he did not stay long), and before that he was head of studies at Pembroke House prep school in Kenya. Went into schoolmastering straight from school and took his degree on the wing. Open personality, open minded. Good with pupils and staff. Comments that the 'golden thing about a small school is small classes – not only can you see the problems, but you can always get on top of them'. Wife Janie fully involved with the school, particularly on the pastoral side.

Entrance: Informal interview, no exam. All-ability intake. A few scholarships and awards on offer.

Exit: Usually a good number to Shrewsbury (being local), several to each of Radley, Eton, Winchester, King's Worcester, Cheltenham; then Malvern, Marlborough and a wide range of others. Steady scholarship record.

Remarks: A training ground for the major public schools (governors include representatives of Shrewsbury and Winchester); aims to inculcate the character needed to succeed there, ie self-confidence, self-motivation and the ability to get on with others. Once a year, each pupil in the school prepares and gives a speech. Small classes (11ish). An impressive staff room and, say parents, 'very good at helping the weaker brethren get up to scratch, very structured.' Sets and streams, with forms given convoluted names so that academic hierarchies are disguised (a pupil might progress from 1BC to LR to Shell BP to Form 100 to Form 6). Teaching and prep combined in hour-long lessons; teaching time increased to total 30 hours per week. The entire span of British history is taught over three years. IT for all; recent investment in machines and networks. Languages strong and grammatical, with German for all in the top two streams; classics still strong, with Latin for all, and Greek as an option. Art and design a central part of the curriculum. Excellent library, much music-making. Keen sporting school (boys regularly put in for local and regional championships) but not so good that the boys don't learn to be good losers. Ricochet court, Astroturf sports hall, climbing wall, new 25 metre indoor swimming pool, and a new riding school.

The school is housed in a fascinating and remarkable Victorian country house, complete with fine crumbling stucco work, antlers on the wall, billiard tables, large gloomy Victorian paintings, huge drawing-room. Set in 90 glorious acres, overlooked by bizarre clock tower. Pre-prep is attached. Modern additions somewhat at odds with nineteenth-century architecture. Dorms run by friendly matrons, with cosy wooden bunks/beds; stuffed animals allowed but not universal; décor and plumbing showing their age (now much improved, says school). A full boarding school, as opposed to weekly boarding. All-in and all-out weekends, with some optional outs. Happy and busy atmosphere. No uniform still occasionally leads to cries of 'scruffy' from parents – but discipline is firm, and politeness is emphasised. Interesting mix of the liberal and the formal – high standards all round, and very lively extra-curricular departments, producing self-confident, articulate and really super pupils. Perhaps not for the wild, or wildly shy. No prospectus, see the school mag instead.

ABERLOUR HOUSE

Aberlour, Banffshire, Scotland AB38 9LJ

TEL: *01340 871267* FAX: *01340 872925*

E-MAIL: admissions@aberlourhouse.org.uk

WEB: www.aberlourhouse.org.uk

✦ PUPILS: 42 boys, 22 girls board;
10 boys, 13 girls day ✦ AGES: 7/8-13
✦ Non-denom ✦ Fee-paying

Head: Since 2000, Mr Neil W Gardner BA CertEd (forties), from the College of the Venerable Bead, Durham. Head-hunted from Ardvreck, (where he did great things, was highly popular, and regarded by some pupils as 'jolly good fun'). Before that was head of the wonderful King's School Junior School, Worcester. Had previously been head of English at Aberlour. Mr Gardner was educated in the Midlands, and spent a couple of years studying law before 'becoming addicted' to education. Loves teaching, and is married to Carol, who also

taught at King's School and is now effectively joint head. The Gardners have two children at university; they love Aberlour 'deep nostalgia for the place, we were here between 1980/90 and the children were brought up here'. Took over from Mr John W Caithness.

The Gardners are keen to 'strengthen the close relationship with Gordonstoun', they have a Joint Education Committee. Mr Gardner optimistically hopes to find time for his hobbies of bee-keeping and fishing.

Entrance: By registration, interview and assessment. Pupils usually stay over the weekend to be assessed and can be awarded scholarships with bursaries for the needy. Additional financial help may be on hand from Gordonstoun Foundation. Pupils come from all over: ex-pats with grannies, foreign nationals from exotic places – the Seychelles, Saudi, Jamaica, Bermuda and the BVI.

Exit: Mainly a feeder for Gordonstoun, but also to Loretto, Glenalmond, Merchiston, Fettes, plus a smattering down south.

Remarks: The school was founded by Kurt Hahn in 1936 at Wester Elchies as the prep school for Gordonstoun (qv). Aberlour House was bought in 1947 and whole school moved here in 1963. The school is set in fabulous rolling pine-clad countryside (on the malt whisky trail) well fulfilling the founder's decree that 'our youth should dwell in the land of health, amid fair sights and sounds and beauty'.

Good classroom conversions with passage leading to old stable block and fine hall, an envy making bowl of fresh fruit is put out daily and pupils help themselves at will. Other schools please note. Dorms under attack, vile wallpaper now a thing of the past, though not bunks. The Gardners aim 'to change the heart of boarding life and make it a wonderful experience, into something exciting. New house staff.

School run firmly along lines of Hahn's philosophy 'plus est en vous' (loose translation 'there is more in you than you think'); no class more than 18, superb CDT, computers everywhere and linked with Gordonstoun, and school uses big school's facilities. Music strong, including the clarsach and chanter (leading to the bagpipes). Music department with computer composition facilities, and plans for a CD under new director of music.

There are some gifted children, and some less so, small remedial department with two dedicated teachers. Staff have gained their qualifications from an amazing range of places, and there appears no difficulty in finding good ones. French and German taught by nationals. Masses of games, rugby, hockey, athletics, netball etc. Children can and do bring their own ponies, lots of serious expeditions, eight day riding expedition – 'Hoof Prints of Queen Victoria', backpacking at Cape Wrath: all jolly character building. Pretty upmarket, prefects, called 'helpers'. Children stand up when you enter the room, look you in the eye and say Sir; well that's the general idea anyway, though when we visited pupils weren't quite so quick on their feet as Mr Gardner would have liked.

Foreign exchanges (staff and pupils) with German sister school, other exchanges in the offing.

School has had several hiccups, but now back on form and filling up despite being miles from anywhere. Around 80 per cent of all pupils live within 70 miles (and that takes ages in this part of Scotland) with about 9 per cent from the rest of the UK. The prospectus information booklet has a wonderfully helpful list of who flies into Aberdeen and Inverness airports from where and a jolly list of hotels, B&Bs restaurants, taxis and activities for parents who might well consider combining their hols with taking the children back to school. Numbers distinctly down (111 at last time of writing to 87 this time) but signs of recovery. Perceived as being very much tied to the Gordonstoun ideal, which may not suit everyone.

ALLEYN'S JUNIOR SCHOOL

Townley Road, London SE22 8SU

TEL: *020 8693 3457* FAX: *020 8693 3597*

E-MAIL: juniorschool@alleyns.org.uk

WEB: www.alleyns.org.uk

✦ PUPILS: 224, 50/50 boys/girls, all day
✦ Ages: 5-11 ✦ C of E ✦ Fee-paying

Head: Mrs Bridget Weir CertEd (fifties), married to consultant engineer with two children. Previously head of St Hilary's Junior School, Sevenoaks, and educated at Tiffins, Kingston upon Thames, and Homerton. Teaches handwriting to littles and RE to older ones, likes to 'hear what they are saying' and hopes to give as broad an education as possible. Mrs Weir is the first head of this young school (it opened in 1992), 'all the mistakes are mine'. Her stated philosophy is that 'learning must be fun'.

Entrance: Name down a year in advance, usually doubly over-subscribed, assessment at 4+ and 7+ (a few places possible at 9+). Most children are local, but some come from further afield and have brothers and sisters in the senior school, JAGS or Dulwich College.

Exit: Almost all to Alleyn's (even though this is not an automatic route) and one or two to other local schools.

Remarks: The latest and much appreciated development in the Alleyn complex: connected to Dulwich College and James Allen's School via the Elizabethan actor-manager Edward Alleyn under Royal Charter of 1619. Very relaxed links between the three schools. Fabulous exciting designer school, with great feeling of freedom and open space tucked unobtrusively behind Alleyn's Music School, which both schools share – but with different teachers. Junior school also shares dining hall, games complex and swimming pool, etc. Own art room, hall, science labs. 18 staff, all chosen by Mrs Weir. French everywhere when we visited (lessons start at 5). A grown-up prep school with a cosy feel. Classes range from 16 upwards, head unashamedly keen on academic excellence, maths set for last two years. Some help can be given for dyslexia, and external tutors are on hand and children are given time off for 'extra help'. Children respectful and very polite. Altogether a useful place to start.

ALLFARTHING PRIMARY SCHOOL
St Ann's Crescent, Wandsworth, London SW18 2LR

TEL: *020 8874 1301* FAX: *020 8870 2128*

E-MAIL: admin@allfarthing.wandsworth.sch.uk

WEB: www.allfarthing.wandsworth.sch.uk

✦ PUPILS: 460 boys and girls, plus 45 children in the nursery class; all day ✦ Ages 3-11 ✦ Non-denom ✦ State

---

Head: Since 1979, Mrs Veronica Bradbury MBE (in '98) DipEd MA (early fifties); 'is she still here? I hope so!' said one with happy memories. Deputy head here five years before taking over headship. Married with two sons. Hugely respected and admired, energetic, outgoing, very get-up-and-go, knows all her children. Teaches 20 per cent timetable. 'Excellence for all,' she says, 'is the logo of the school – and I really do believe in that.' Has to remind herself sometimes 'I'm an educationalist, not a social service officer'. Very hands on in the school and absolutely determined not to be swamped by admin. Qualified Ofsted inspector.

Entrance: At 3 to nursery, or 5; also some at 6 and 7 (often from Clapham and Putney). Preference for siblings and near at hand.

Exit: Wide choice of 'good' local state schools, which are varied – 'foundation' (formerly grant maintained), selective, technology colleges, non-selective, also specialist schools. Also to fee-paying schools such as

Alleyn's, Dulwich College, King's College, Wimbledon, James Allen's Girls, Godolphin and Latymer.

Remarks: Outstanding example of a primary school. Creative disciplined dynamic atmosphere generated by super head and team of staff – 'my key resource' – mostly long-standing (parents love the continuity) but healthy trickle of new blood too – the head chooses carefully for 'the chalk face'. One trained plus two assistant staff per class (about 27-30 children in each, divided into smaller groups by ability). Awarded Beacon status for IT, leadership and management in 2000, the 'Investors in People National Standard' in '95, has won the National Schools ECO Award, and has been chosen to become a 'digital centre of excellence' by the local training and enterprise council (AZTEC). The school now has a computer suite of 20 Pentium machines, two scanners and three digital cameras, also 2 computers in every class – a truly impressive collection. ICT is a 'BIG ISSUE' says the head. Commitment to high standards is visible everywhere, work displayed throughout the school, classes make lovely books on outings/projects, etc. And the school has produced a pamphlet which is given to all parents called 'Excellence for All', setting out what amounts to a job description for parents, children and the school in the matter of educating the pupils (aimed at keeping everyone up to scratch). Big emphasis on reading, with teams of parents coming in daily to hear pupils' reading. Regular spelling tests, tables, etc. Individual progress monitored very carefully, slow-coaches slotted in for extra letter or number work in small groups (there is a full-time special needs teacher). Way above the national and borough average in English, reading, writing, maths and science. Extremely strong

links with parents (four on governing body). 'It has to be a partnership,' says Mrs Bradbury, admitting also that worst disciplinary problems are with a small minority of parents 'who need nagging to get right attitudes'. Large playgrounds outside. Ten clubs on the go, something on offer every day ('My children never leave school till 4.30,' said a parent), including athletics, languages (French, Italian, Spanish), choir, drama, science. Constantly take part in Capital Woman TV programme and Blue Peter. Children happy and motivated. Good social mix – middle class and the socially deprived with plenty of salt-of-the-earth in between. 'This mixture has never changed in my time here,' says the head. 'It's the geography of the area'. 30 per cent of mixed ethnic minorities. Truancy rate is negligible, excellent attendance record and no exclusions. Parents can't speak too highly of the place, and nor can we.

ARDVRECK SCHOOL

Crieff, Perthshire, Scotland PH7 4EX

TEL: *01764 653112* FAX: *01764 654920*

E-MAIL: ardvreck@bosinternet.com

WEB: www.ardvreck.org.uk

✦ PUPILS: 140 (split roughly 60/40 boys/girls); 100 board, 40 day. No weekly or flexi-boarding ✦ Ages 4-13(including Little Ardvreck) ✦ Inter-denom ✦ Fee-paying

---

Head: Since January 2000, Mr Patrick (Paddy) Watson MA PGCE (thirties) who comes to Ardvreck from Swanbourne Prep where he was housemaster and head of English. Educated at Charterhouse, followed by philosophy and theological studies at St Andrews, then PGCE at Reading, Mr Watson started his teaching career at Woodcote House, after a brief spell in the banking world. His wife, Sara, taught French at Swanbourne, and they come to Ardvreck with two young children (who are 'proper' boarders in the school) and the essential black labrador puppy – this time called Bracken.

Bubbly and enthusiastic, Mr Watson buzzes when he talks education, and is delighted to be able to do at least some teaching – scholarship class and third form. Children like him 'he's a nice head, but not as much fun as our last one, who was a bit like a used-car salesman' was one child's comment.

Entrance: Via nursery or pre-prep, but most come at 8+. Boarding in the last year no longer compulsory (but great majority do). Prospective pupils spend a day in school (or overnight if boarding) and wear school uniform 'so they don't stick out'. Head spends a long time interviewing parents, and gives all prospective pupils 'an academic assessment, not very difficult, but like to know where children are at'. He occasionally says no.

Exit: School claims it is no longer perceived as 'the prep for Glenalmond' even though it was started by a former Glenalmond master over a century ago and sends about half children there. A scattering go to Gordonstoun and Fettes and, interestingly, Oundle. Beyond that in ones to Scottish and English schools – more of this now than a few years ago. The 'steady handful of awards' continues.

Remarks: Little Ardvreck numbers well down since our last edition – school says

that they will stay this way – but main school numbers up a bit, especially boarding. School had a bit of a glitch, and is now said 'to be back on form again'. Purpose built Victorian school (1883), with swimming pool (rather grand, but in a polythene tent nonetheless), and a fairly ad hoc collection of classrooms (some a lot better than others) which straggle across the back of the hog, but work well. Little Ardvreck now gathered at one end of the hog, rows of green wellies everywhere.

Ardvreck has just had a mini building boom, and Mr Watson inherits a brand new combo-hall, with carpentry below, all singing and dancing above, cunningly perched on really quite a steep slope. Two senior houses to prepare boys and girls for public school, with mixed age dorms except for the last term when CE candidates bond (girls can and do their own washing). Dorms filled with climbing boots and rucksacks; school does three mini Barvicks each summer term, very popular. Fixed exeat every third weekend, Friday noon – Sunday 7.30pm, and great misery if the exeat coincides with any dorm's turn for the 'red room' (equal in hideousness of colour and popularity, and full of games).

Class sizes 15–16, no streaming till fourth form, then maths, followed by French in fifth. Two sister CE classes in sixth (RTQ = READ THE QUESTION), lots of scholarships and awards, but no honours board. Excellent learning support both for the bright and for those with dyslexia et al, plus two student teachers who help in class. Keyboarding skills on offer, and computers for teaching maths and English as well as more trad teaching; French from five, lyrical art room. Seriously strong orchestra – fifty play at assembly each Friday. Singing and drama outstanding, school regularly features in the ribbons at the Perth Festival.

Outstanding in the games front – all sports, all comers, though parents from other schools have been heard to mutter about trying too hard (still). Games pitches fairly well scattered on the flatter areas, Astroturf in the offing.

Selection of scholarships on offer. Head likes to 'discuss naughtiness' and 'work out what went wrong', 'it's a true family atmosphere'. Parents, a Sloane bunch if ever there was one, 'a close knit group of families', not too many first time buyers, with pupils 'tending to remain friends well into middle age'.

ARNOLD HOUSE

3 Loudoun Road, St John's Wood, London NW8 0LH

TEL: *020 7266 4840* FAX: *020 7266 6994*

E-MAIL: arnoldhouse.school@virgin.net

✦ PUPILS: 249 boys, all day ✦ Ages: 5–13
✦ C of E in theory, but all are welcome
✦ Fee-paying

Head: Since 1994, Nicholas Allen BA, PGCE, aged 47, educated at Bedales ('It taught me that you look at people as individuals'). Formerly head of Ipswich Prep School. Married with three children, two of whom attended Arnold House. Read history and archaeology at Exeter, and this is where his interests lie. Formal, pin-striped, very concerned for the welfare and reputation of the school. Not beloved by all the boys, but generally agreed to be a highly efficient head. ('He might seem a bit like the Demon Headmaster when you first

meet him,' said a parent, 'but he's actually very approachable if you have any concerns.') Teaches religious studies in years 6 and 8 – 'that is a good time to get to know the boys.'

Entrance: Put your son's name down before his first birthday (though the school will try to accommodate those less organised and families moving into the area). Head meets the parents and gives them a tour of the school when their son is about 2 1/2: 'This is an opportunity to form a mutual impression.' It is helpful, but not essential for parents at this stage to have views on potential senior schools.' At rising four, boys come in for half-hour group sessions of stories and nursery activities with head and head of junior school. The school takes into account reports from nursery schools as well as looking at how the boys interact, but it's probably more important that parental values are in line with those of the school, plus, 'I'm hoping I've identified those who really want to come here.' Head says he aims to 'produce a balance of parental professions, where they live, religion and nationality.'

Exit: A large proportion to London day schools especially Westminster, St Paul's and Highgate. Also boarding schools e.g. Winchester, Eton, Harrow. OBs include Sir Jonathon Porritt, Dr Jonathan Miller, Sir Crispin Tickell, Sir John Tavener, Lord Ackner, Lord Wolfson and Lord Woolf.

Remarks: An extensive building programme, due to finish in 2001, will give the school five new classrooms, a six-room music suite, a large ICT room and a new library. Light, airy classrooms, a gym used for assemblies (the school has a larger hall at its sports ground in Canons Park, near Edgware), science lab, sunny art room at the top of the school. Largish (for inner London) playground. The junior school, years 1 and 2, is kept as separate as possible to create a family atmosphere. Class size: 16 ('which makes it feel almost like one-to-one tuition,' commented a parent) with two classes in each year. The junior forms are divided by age. Setting from year 6 for maths, French and Latin; the school is considering setting in other subjects. A few of the brightest take up Greek. French from year 2; in year 8 boys spend a week in a French chateau. In recent years, at the end of the summer term, year 8 boys perform a French play written by the head. A part-time special needs teacher works with boys who need extra help up to year 5; after that, 'they tend to prefer support outside the school, and we have a network of people we can recommend'. One mother commented that in her opinion the school doesn't tackle dyslexia seriously. Her son has managed to keep up and is very happy ('which says a lot for the teachers') but doesn't get enough support.

The school is in a quiet side-turning off the A41, opposite the American School. Eight acres of playing fields, plus a large hall, at Canons Park. ('It is quite a long trek,' commented a parent.) Boys bussed there once or twice a week for football, rugby, hockey and cricket; matches on Saturdays. Gym, basketball, volleyball back at the school. 'It's great if your son's very good at games – not so good if he's just normal,' said a parent. Strong on art with plenty of paintings and ceramics on display, including delightful individual plaques designed and made by leavers. Most boys learn at least one instrument; several orchestras and choirs, with entry by audition and invitation. Plenty of drama. Some after-school clubs eg judo, chess, but 'boys in London lead busy lives – it's tempting for families to overload their children,' says the head.

The school code of conduct, written by the head, 'indicate[s] the school's expectations of civilised behaviour in the belief that good manners provide the foundation on which a happy community is built.' The school prefers remonstration to punishment, with 'far more rewards than sanctions. One tries to impress on the boys the value of civilised living.' School dinners still have a good reputation. Newly formed Parents' Association, composed of reps from each form, organises fundraising events, coffee mornings and cocktail parties. Weekly newsletter and termly parent-teacher evenings, though one parent commented that she didn't have much of a feel for what was going on – 'I rather feel that I'm kept at the gate.' Head says that parents are encouraged to get in touch swiftly if they feel there is a problem. Many rewards for achievement, and parents of high-flyers sing the school's praises, though a parent of an average-ability child commented: 'There should be more for those who aren't stars.'

School is pretty popular, especially amongst St Johns Wood-ites. Parents are mostly upmarket north London professionals; plenty of four wheel drives and Space Wagons around at collection time. Boys lively, very polite, very privileged ('Everyone has a mobile phone and all the latest gadgets' commented a mother). 'It's a typical English prep school – it turns out little gentlemen,' said a satisfied parent.

ASHDELL PREPARATORY SCHOOL

266 Fulwood Road, Sheffield S10 3BL

TEL: *0114 266 3835* FAX: *0114 267 1762*

E-MAIL: headteacher@ashdell-prep.sheffield.sch.uk

WEB: www.ashdell-prep.sheffield.sch.uk

✦ PUPILS: approx 115 girls, all day ✦ Ages: 4-11 ✦ C of E ✦ Fee-paying

Head: Since 1984, Mrs Jane Upton (fifties), brought up in Cumbria, further education in France, teacher training in Sheffield. Married, husband is deputy head of Silverdale School in Sheffield. Gentle, inspiring, tireless, forthright, sense of humour. Ambitious that the school should be 'excellent in what it does best', and for this reason has policy not to increase numbers radically. Runs the school by the seat of her pants – at her post or round about all hours, has no deputy. Comments that when she took on the job she had 'no idea how all-consuming and thrilling it would be'.

Entrance: Parents are interviewed 'to see how much they are doing and what they want.' The school looks for bright girls with supportive parents. Then child is interviewed and tested. Register any time.

Exit: Most to Sheffield High, Wakefield High. Also to eg Oakham, Cheltenham Ladies' College.

Remarks: Excellent as ever, and presided over by one of the best heads in the business. Rare commodity in this area – a 'proper' girls' prep school with the feel of a boarding school – doors open. at 7.30 am, teaching begins at 8.30 am and ends at 4.30 pm (afternoon tea included). Standard of handwriting excellent – five-year-olds turning in performances which would not discredit people twice that age – and school regularly wins competitions. Mrs Upton reckons to achieve 'very high standards', academically speaking. Acquisition of new mid-Victorian building behind the current site on Fulwood Road (nice views over Sheffield) has eased feeling of crowding. Recent developments include a large new music room with individual practice rooms, a vastly extended gym and a smart IT centre with ten new PCs and a dedicated teacher. Coaching given not only to those falling behind in the race, but also to the extra bright ('it is unfair not to'). Part-time special needs teacher comes in twice a week. Maximum class size – 22, average 17. Parents are doctors (local hospitals very handy), lawyers, landed and builders, etc. Children well behaved and good mannered, perhaps a bit lacking in zip, laden with briefcases and musical instruments. All children get chance to experience a week's boarding while in the school – ostensibly abseiling or whatever, but the 'hidden curriculum' being to introduce them gently to life away from home. School founded in 1948 as a Dame School by coal and steel baronet Roberts, now charitable trust. Cheery cherry red jackets and boaters with snowdrop crest – 'a humble flower, and the first sign of spring'.

ASHDOWN HOUSE

Forest Row, East Sussex RH18 5JY

TEL: *01342 822574* FAX: *01342 824380*

E-MAIL: headmaster@pncl.co.uk

WEB: www.ashdownhouse.co.uk

✦ PUPILS: around 140 boys, 75 girls, all board except for a few in their first year ✦ Ages: 7-13 ✦ C of E ✦ Fee-paying

Head: Since 2000, Andrew Fowler-Watt MA (late thirties). Educated at Eton and Cambridge (choral scholar). Previously head of St Edmund's Hindhead, and before that combined teaching English with running a theatre and singing professionally. Teaches English to the older children. Wife Vivienne (Zimbabwean) teaches scripture to the younger ones, and oversees domestic, catering and pastoral arrangements.

From a prep school family (father was head of Brambletye for 28 years). We hear v good things of him. Took over from the delightful Mr Clive Williams, who was here from 1974 and who will continue to be involved with the Château du Livet (see below).

Entrance: Names down 3 years in advance 'though one's lists are more volatile now'. Interview one year ahead. Roughly a third from London, a third overseas (a handful of foreign nationals), a third local. Entry usually at 8 or 9; a few later. Most important criteria is that children (and their parents) should be ready for boarding.

Exit: Mostly to smart boarding schools – Eton topping the lists. King's Canterbury,

Marlborough, Harrow, Winchester also popular destinations. NB – the school is only interested in girls who stay at the school until they are 13, 'Because girls too need the opportunity to lead – we like girls in the top slots at school'.

Remarks: A good traditional fashionable/sought after boarding prep school with safe, sound, happy, family feel, though not without a certain formality. School hums with activity (4 plays a year, a choral work, etc, etc), especially over lunch time. Very handsome Georgian house (listed grade 2★), soft grey stone, overlooking Downs, with much tactful building-on behind. Indoor swimming pool, classroom block and more dorms (the 'East Wing') opened in '94. School is expanding gently as more girls come in – eventual aim 60:40 boys:girls.

Lovely setting in rural acres, 'jungle' area for camps, etc. Strong on the games front. Good food eaten in huge dining hall, cafeteria style – 'A pity,' comment parents of young children; Mr Fowler-Watt says 'fair comment – but we do supervise what they eat carefully, and breakfast is now a formal sit-down occasion'. Keenly musical – around 175 play an instrument and portable instruments are often practised in dorms.

Reading rest period in theatre for all ages after lunch: 'Very difficult to get children to read nowadays,' moans the head. He reads to the youngest forms nightly, sitting in his study, his voice broadcast to their dorms. Children awaken at 7.15 to Radio 4.

Class size about fifteen, with streaming after two years, scholarship class varies in size from year to year. Learning support available. French very good, and has had a higher profile since the acquisition of a chateau in Normandy (the Château du Livet, near Falaise) which they occasionally let out to other schools. Pupils initially go to the chateau for two weeks, then spend half a term there. They have to fax French diaries back every day. Previous head and wife now live in and run chateau. Parents are invited to spend a weekend there while their children are in residence.

Becoming ever more co-ed. Unashamedly a boarding school.

AYSGARTH SCHOOL

Newton-Le-Willows, Bedale, North Yorkshire
DL8 1TF

TEL: *01677 450240* FAX: *01677 450736*

E-MAIL: enquiries@aysgarthschool.co.uk

WEB: www.aysgarthschool.co.uk

✦ PUPILS: 104 in the main school, 70 in pre-prep and nursery; 80 per cent plus board in the main school ✦ Ages: 3-13 ✦ C of E ✦ Fee-paying

Head: (Joint Headmasters): Since 1988, Mr John Hodgkinson MA (Cantab) (fifties). Previously housemaster at Uppingham. Married (wife, Hilary, helps in the school doing 'all the usual things'); three daughters. Since 1998, Mr P J Southall BA PGCE, previously head of history at Elstree. Married to Louise, three sons.

Entrance: By interview – all children are assessed before they join the school. No scholarships into school, but occasional bursary, including one from the Charles Leveson-Gower Memorial Fund. Siblings and Forces discounts.

Exit: Mostly to English public schools – Harrow, Ampleforth, Radley, Shrewsbury, Eton, Sedbergh, Uppingham, Rugby, Stowe.

Remarks: Once the automatic choice for Yorkshire toffs, but for several reasons (including the advent of day boys), no longer, and intake has widened and gone a bit down-market. Lovely grounds, purpose-built school with tower. Latin for all at nine and ten – though 'one or two drop off'. IT up to date. Very successful petite extra tuition teacher. Good carpentry, lively art, and head points lots of action on the music front, lots of distinctions, not to mention boys being taught the organ, the best play for Sunday morning chapel.

The first eleven were unbeaten for a (?record) 100 matches up to '95, then alas, lost one. Still going strong – only lost one in '99 due to 'arrogance and a woeful lack of concentration.' Full boarding, with exeats every three and a half weeks, Sunday exeats also if 'special family occasion'. Chapel every morning. Rest on beds after lunch for the youngest boys. Numbers up. Some happy reports from pupils, some less so.

BEAUDESERT PARK SCHOOL

Minchinhampton, Stroud, Gloucestershire
GL6 9AF

TEL: *01453 832072* FAX: *01453 836040*

E-MAIL: office@beaudesert.org.uk

WEB: www.beaudesert.org.uk

✦ PUPILS: 142 boys (of whom 45 board), 107 girls (of whom 24 board) Pre-prep 58 boys, 50 girls ✦ Ages: 4-13 ✦ Mostly C of E ✦ Fee-paying

Head: Since 1997, Mr James Womersley BA PGCE (forties) (aka Jumbo), educated at The Dragon, St Edwards and Durham where he read 'economics, history and rugby'. Previously at Eagle House, The Dragon, Emanuel (London), and a very popular housemaster at The Dragon where he taught maths and history. Married to Fiona who comes from a prep schooling family, they have three sons, all in the school. Mr W coaches rugby and athletics, enjoys walking, tennis and golf.

Relaxed and very much hands on, Mr Womersley has kicked the school back into contention, following a slight hiccup after the departure of the Keyte family who founded the school in 1908 and ran the place until 1995.

Entrance: Waiting lists for the pre-prep till 2003, automatic transfer to the main school via a basic assessment, 'not selective in anyway'. Pupils mainly local: Gloucestershire, North Wiltshire, Oxfordshire border etc.

Exit: Again, mostly local: Marlborough (scholarship), Cheltenham Ladies' College, Radley (scholarship), Rugby, St Edwards, and a wide range of others.

Remarks: School is perched at the top of a hideous wiggly drive up a hill on the edge of Minchinhampton Common surrounded by 12 acres of steeply terraced games fields, including an Astroturf and use of a further 12 acres on the Common. Splendid Victorian Gothic with many additions (sympathetic Cotswold stone at the front) filled with hunting prints and rows of graded green wellies. The school term follows the Badminton set (ie closes down for the Horse Trials).

Three-weekly reports on each child as opposed to just one at the end of term. Children are graded on their individual improvement, and marks are not read out for comparison. Great emphasis on self worth. Certificates of Effort handed out in assembly, when everyone claps. Three forms in each year, max 18 per form, but pupils set for maths, lang (Fr and Latin only) throughout and science in top forms – scholarships are important you see. Consistent learning support both one to one and in class throughout school. Music strong and ambitious, art good, drama on course.

Huge increase in younger staff, with accommodation currently being provided in rented cottages, plans afoot to convert the stables. New housemaster appointed, computers everywhere, each child has its own email, and all sciences computer-linked. Good CDT, and fabulous mega-gym with links to swimming pool tiled like a Roman bath. A new building programme is underway.

Day pupils usually opt to board in their senior years, flexi-boarding an option but absolute max is 75 boarders. Uniform throughout now rather a jolly green, with girls in black watch kilts.

Friendly happy school getting good results and turning out tomorrow's embryo Sloanes, not v street wise.

BEESTON HALL SCHOOL

West Runton, Cromer, Norfolk NR27 9NQ

TEL: *01263 837324* FAX: *01263 838177*

E-MAIL: office@beestonhall.co.uk

WEB: www.beestonhall.co.uk

✦ PUPILS: 105 boys and 70 girls. 110 board, 65 day ✦ Ages: 7-13 ✦ Mainly C of E ✦ Fee-paying

---

Head: Since 1998, Mr Innes MacAskill BEd (forties), formerly deputy head at Caldicott (qv). Teaches history in middle of school. Married to Sandy, three children. Took over from Mr John Elder (head from 1986), who left the school all singing and dancing.

Entrance: Entry tests in English and maths, but all children are seen about six months before entry. Subsequently they come (in groups of 12) to try out a day's timetable (and may 'try out' boarding).

Exit: Widespread (with most girls staying till 12+ or 13+). Gresham's has had by far the largest numbers in the past 3 years, followed by Oundle, Uppingham, Harrow and Norwich School; in ones or twos to a range of other good schools. OB – cricketer James Whitaker.

Remarks: A delightful happy family country school, mostly catering for proper country children (20 from London); half a mile from the sea, pleasant Regency white house plus additions, in 700 acres and surrounded by National Trust estates. Good facilities for everything, bright classrooms, art work – which is outstandingly good – framed and hung throughout the school, a joy to see. (new art centre opened in '96.) Very thorough teaching, and highly professional approach to preparing children for entry to senior school. Classes streamed in early years and set for final three. Remedial help given at no extra cost.

Good work goes straight to the head, as does the bad. Astonishing number of cups (120) and prize-giving every single term. Strong emphasis on drama (main stage is in the indoor sports hall). Huge amount of sport (and unusually varied for a prep school) with house matches as well as loads with other schools even as far afield as Scotland. Geographical position something of a disadvantage, with lack of local competition and long journeys for matches. The school is very successful however: won 24 titles of varying importance in '97, including seven-a-side rugby, cross-country national individual titles, cricket prep school finals, under 11 girls' hockey finals etc. Similar levels of success in later years – and girls' hockey team unbeaten in '99. Books everywhere, also magazines – public school mags, Focus, etc. Super common rooms (French bar football, mini billiards, etc). All children provided with a school cheque book for Church money, tuck, etc. Children allowed out in groups of three (to the beach, to the tiny town one-and-a-half miles away. 'It's an area you know they are safe in,' from a parent). Long (50-minute) morning breaks, for music practice (148 lessons a week, plus 13 music clubs etc), climbing trees, play, etc. Loads of clubs/activities for evenings and action-packed weekends. Children given duties – postman, sweeping up after lunch, etc. Long exeats (but fairly far between).

An outstanding little school, slightly over-full, deservedly popular with confident, happy children.

BELHAVEN HILL SCHOOL

Dunbar, East Lothian EH42 1NN

TEL: *01368 862785*, FAX: *01368 865225*

E-MAIL: belhavenhill@learnfree.co.uk

✦ PUPILS: 65 boys, 40 girls; 85 board, 20 day
✦ Ages: 7-13 ✦ Non-denom
✦ Fee-paying

Head: Since 1987, Mr Michael Osborne MA (fifties) educated at Radley and Cambridge where he read economics and qualified as an accountant. Considered by many to be 'the best teacher in Scotland'. Separated from his wife, who lives 'amicably' nearby with his two sons and daughter (in the school). Popular head, a Pied Piper, children love him – he knows his 32 times table, and 57 times table – 'well actually any times table'. Charming and enthusiastic, good at advising on senior schools, children keep up with him after they leave (and he writes back). Parents still comment that not all staff are up to head's high standard (head reports influx of good young teachers) and mutter about 'Michael showing his age'.

Entrance: No test, but register as soon as possible. Children spend a day at Belhaven the term before they come.

Exit: About four a year to Eton, three to Glenalmond; others to Harrow, Radley, Loretto, Ampleforth, Stowe, St George's Edinburgh.

Remarks: Scotland's school for toffs which specialises in sending the little darlings to public school in the South. Dubbed 'Hogwarts for Muggles' by the Evening News. Based in late eighteenth century sandstone house, with imaginative new additions and tower, ten new classrooms built on site. Pupils going on line, very ritzy' and (v new) computer room.

Streaming after first year, and class sizes down to 10/12. Scholarship stream; good remedial help on hand. Greek on offer, as are piping and roller blading; magnificent sports hall which adapts for school plays and air rifles (not both at the same time). Manicured grounds including two cricket pitches, 6 tennis courts, masses of Astroturf, a putting course and an eighteen-hole golf course 'over the wall'. Bracing sea air. Streams of unbeaten teams, regular trips to Hillend artificial ski slope, children encouraged to have their own bit of garden (the staff do not eat the produce in the holidays).

Boys' dorms upgraded, no more bunks, but still complaints that girls' house, which opened in 1996, is much ritzier – particularly the lavatories (how do they know?). Lyrical recent HM Inspector's report could have been written by Osborne himself. Parents and children incredibly happy, with masses of input from the parents – tranches of farmers/Charlotte Rangers from East Lothian, plus the usual quota of quite grand children and an increasing gang from South of the border – usually with Scottish connections. Non-Belhaven children have been heard to complain that they 'are a bit cliquey'. Numbers slightly up. Successfully co-ed since 1995.

BILTON GRANGE SCHOOL

Dunchurch, Rugby, Warwickshire CV22 6QU

TEL: *01788 810217* FAX: *01788 816922*

E-MAIL: enquiry@biltongrange.co.uk

WEB: www.biltongrange.co.uk

✦ PUPILS: 348 boys and girls including 125 in pre-prep. Around one third of children board ✦ Ages: 4-7 pre-prep; 8-13 prep ✦ C of E ✦ Fee-paying

---

Head: Since 1992, Mr Quentin Edwards MA (Oxon) PGCE (late forties), read English at Christ Church, Oxford, before taking on dual role of housemaster and head of English at Bradfield College. Chatty, energetic. Big on drama, producing/directing *The Tempest* when seen. Very proud of what 'his children' can achieve at such young age. Still gushing enthusiasm eight years into the job.

Not one to instil fear. Greets pupils by name: they stand aside to let him pass and call him 'Sir'. Demonstration of politeness though, not subservience. Openly warm, friendly. Likes pupils to reach own conclusions but strong on discipline when it's called for. Won't tolerate bullying or bad manners. Encourages parent participation as much as possible. 'It gives us a good excuse to throw a party.' Wife Maggie runs pre-prep on separate site. Forthright, efficient, very much boss of her own part of school. Head/husband 'visits' once a week for assembly. Great advocates for co-education which was introduced when they arrived. Parents toed line 'almost without exception. We both believe very strongly in co-education as being the proper way to bring chil-

dren up.' Have two grown-up children, 22 and 20.

Entrance: Early enquiries recommended. Non-selective but there is an entry test and interview. Popularity reflected in 23 per cent rise in numbers since 1995. More boys than girls – roughly 60/40. Starter's scholarships and open awards offered at 8+. Children with academic potential encouraged to apply. Artistic, musical, design, or sporting talent 'taken into account'.

Exit: Regular tests way of life here so shouldn't be fazed by major exams later. Roughly third of pupils leave for senior school at 13 with academic, sport or music scholarships. Rugby takes almost 45 per cent, other favourites include Oundle, Uppingham, Bloxham, Stowe, Oakham and Princethorpe.

Remarks: Stunning setting for this lovely originally Georgian red-brick school, on raised plateau with far-reaching views across surrounding countryside. Children can explore 2.5 acres of well-kept grounds with enviable freedom, though school occupies 150-acre spread in all. Founded in 1873, was once boys only with separate school for girls on nearby site. Now fully co-ed with pre-prep Homefield in former girls' school. All classes mixed but dormitories very much apart. Boys can never enter girls' dorms and vice versa. 'You must never make the mistake of thinking children are too young,' said the head sagely. Dorms recently decorated, largest has 11 beds (including bunks) with plenty of posters, own possessions on show.

Latin and French compulsory. Extensive range of extras include golf, sailing, scuba diving and fly fishing. 'We really give children a tremendously enriched experience here.' Average class size 14, with years streamed according to ability. Weekly spelling and tables tests for little ones, hour's homework a day when older. Pupils decide when to do it, as long as it's done on time. Supportive of slower learners and proud of achievements, but if more than extra hour a week needed, parents may be advised to seek more suitable school.

Education seen as more than just lessons. Pupils encouraged to be responsible for their actions, to take charge. 'We are genuinely a preparatory school. Our children arrive at their next school running.' Famous Old Boys and Girls include composer Sir Arthur Bliss and Independent columnist and humorist Miles Kington, also a number of Tory MPs.

Little evidence of mixing outside class. Pupils tend to opt for self-segregation at meal-times and so on. Well stocked library restored to original Pugin splendour (Pugin is the Victorian architect responsible for much of the school's regal interior) complete with computers and CD-ROMs and stacks of new books. Thousands spent on fresh stock each year thanks to healthy budget and money raised from book fairs. Dining room leads into pretty little chapel currently missing its fine old organ – the one Arthur Bliss first learned to play – which is undergoing massive restoration work. Classrooms bright, airy, functional. Bit of a rabbit warren with narrow corridors, twists and turns. Pre-prep cosier with lots of work on display. Good IT provision in 'both' schools.

Impressive art studio on main site, sports hall and 25-metre pool plus new all-weather outdoor courts. C of E school which welcomes all denominations but no-one gets out of going to chapel to kick start the day. Pupils from all walks of life. 'We're not snooty.' Broad curriculum in which PSHE plays important part. Bullying 'not an issue that concerns me,' says head. But well aware of it and can become a disciplinary matter. Very keen on adventure training. Teaches 'self reliance, tolerance, ability to cope with each other's weaknesses'. Also leadership training in sixth form gets them thinking about others' needs. As a result pupils come across as confident, not cocky.

Continuing tradition of Saturday school, lessons in morning and sport after lunch. Wednesdays time-tabled in same way. Not too many grumbles when children quizzed about this even from day boys/girls. 'That's just the way it is,' said one. As scholarships show, strong academically, but good too for science and design technology, ICT and drama. Children's production has featured more than once at Edinburgh's Fringe. Music department even has composition and recording suite. Teams fare well at most sports, but rugby disappointing since main opponents (like Dragon) now much bigger.

Real school for real kids. Not just for smart Alecs and Alices. Would also suit outdoors type as must get chilly up there in the winter. Feeling of real contentment in the wood-panelled halls and even at this age, pupils know exactly where they're going and what's expected of them. They seem only too happy to oblige.

BOUSFIELD PRIMARY SCHOOL

South Bolton Gardens, London SW5 0DJ

TEL: *020 7373 6544* FAX: *020 7373 8894*

E-MAIL: Jennifer.Selmes@bousfield.kensington-

chelsea.sch.uk

✦ PUPILS: 200 boys, 200 girls, all day ✦ Ages: 3-11 ✦ Non-denom ✦ State

---

Head: Since 1998, Ms Connie Cooling, MA DipEd (forties). Studied education management and the teaching of maths, has taught in a number of London schools rising to deputy head of Sherringdale primary school in Wandsworth before coming to Bousfield.

Entrance: Over-subscribed. Nursery place does not guarantee entry to reception. Priority given to brothers and sisters and to children who live nearest the school. 30 in September, 30 in January: 2 reception classes. 30 children in a class. Lots of European ex-pats. Broad social mix. Despite location, 33 per cent of children are eligible for free school meals (lots of temporary accommodation in Kensington).

Exit: One-quarter go to a wide variety of private schools – four to the French Lycee in 1999. State favourites are Holland Park, Shene and Elliott.

Remarks: Continuously and deservedly popular, much sought after primary school in a v useful central London location. Support from the Borough. Successful Ofsted inspection in '99. English is not the first language of about half of the pupils – over 30 mother tongues (Arabic and French chief among them). No school uniform but children are tidy with nice haircuts. Well run, fun, strong on parental involvement. Draws on parents' skills (actors, artists etc). Bousfield busily fosters the creative arts – music especially good, also art.

Head keen on 'achievement across the curriculum', good manners, minds about discipline (not a problem), and there is a homework policy obligatory for all junior classes – children throughout the school take work home regularly. Well-used and well-stocked libraries. Offers an early morning maths class but doesn't coach; buys in additional support for learning and behaviour difficulties. Children heading for private schools typically get extra boosting (for a year or more) from outside teachers on maths and English.

Classrooms bursting with colourful and creative project work. School is on the site of Beatrix Potter's childhood home, built in 1956 (and now a listed building), with light airy classrooms ('too small,' sighs the head) and grass play area, plus very large playground, the envy of private central London schools. Central body of the building consists of two large halls mirroring each other for infants and juniors, used for dance, productions, gym, assemblies. Ms Cooling oversees everybody and often 'goes walkabout'.

BRAMBLETYE SCHOOL

East Grinstead, West Sussex RH19 3PD

TEL: *01342 321004* FAX: *01342 317562*

E-MAIL: brambletye@brambletye.rmplc.co.uk

WEB: www.brambletye.com

✦ PUPILS: around 100 boarders, 50 day; 140 boys and 10 girls (beginning to go co-ed); plus pre-prep 'The Beeches', 50; boys and girls ✦ Ages: 7-13, pre-prep 3-7 ✦ C of E ✦ Fee-paying

Head: Since 1997, Mr Hugh Cocke (pronounced 'Coke') BA CertEd (forties). Wife Lucy very much involved in the life of the school – surrogate mother figure for junior boys and a 'great support to her husband'. Two school-age daughters at Benenden. Previous post – headmaster of Old Buckenham Hall. Before that taught at The Old Malthouse and Cheam where he was head of history and ran the cricket. Teaches religious studies. Family man, keen on games, music and 'children who are happy, alert and eager'. His philosophy: 'to give every child something to be good at'. Took over from the legendary Mr and Mrs Fowler-Watt, who reigned here from '69 and made the school one of the happiest in the land. No agonised cries when the new head came in – a feat, given the length of time the previous regime was in place.

Entrance: Book early, this is still a sought-after school. No entry test, but previous school fills in a telling form for pupils. Entry at 7-8 and sometimes places available later. Large number of children from London,

30-35 Brits from abroad, whose arrangements are looked after by Mrs Cocke.

Exit: To at least 17 different boarding schools each year – currently to Harrow, Charterhouse, Wellington, Winchester, Eton, Radley etc etc. Plenty of scholarships and awards. Pupils go on to a thrilling variety of careers – eg brain surgeon, importer of aloe vera, commercial flight simulator engineer, naval commander, prep school housemaster – to take a few at random.

Remarks: Cosy boys' boarding school setting out on the road to co-education – first girls '00. Not a hothouse but thinks of itself as 'quite academic' (senior schools note Brambletye boys are well grounded in most subjects). 7- and 8-year-old entry classes separately taught. Maximum class size: 18, average 14. Scholarship group is formed at 11. German and Spanish now taught as well as French. Set in lovely countryside (though just on the edge of East Grinstead), once the Abergavenny hunting lodge – and looks baronial, though the atmosphere is cosy in a grand kind of way: lots of polished wood and panelling and fires. Also junior boarding 'wing' attached to headmaster's house. Top-quality staff of long standing, and heaps on offer, including shooting, golf, fishing. Good music, with 85 per cent of children learning an instrument, tours to eg New York and Prague; impressive external exam results at different levels. Excellent art, with 4 art scholarships to senior schools in '98. New IT 'facilities' opened '97. Terrific theatre produces fine drama – productions every term involving all age groups. V full sports programme 'fearfully competitive', 'not good losers' say pupils in neighbouring schools. School magazine makes a good read – even bursts into poetry when it gets to the 3rd XV's match results. New sports hall.

New(ish) library with full-time librarian

on site – not nothing. The money – as usual at this school – comes from the school's own resources – including a donation from a grateful parent, 'The most expensive present we have ever had': (no appeals to parents, please note). Accessibility to London means strong parental involvement, with parents calling by with cake, etc, on a child's birthday. No weekly boarding, but school coach to Clapham and Victoria for exeats usually every fortnight. Manners are important, boys and girls very sparky and self-confident. Pastorally good.

BRAMCOTE SCHOOL

Filey Road, Scarborough, North Yorkshire
YO11 2TT

TEL: *01723 373086* FAX: *01723 364186*

E-MAIL: bramcoteschool@easynet.co.uk

✦ PUPILS: 83 (57 boys and 26 girls), full boarding except 7 day boarding and a few day pupils ✦ Ages: 5-13
✦ C of E Foundation ✦ Fee-paying

Head: Since 1996, Mr J Peter Kirk BSc (forties). Previous post housemaster at Glenalmond. Was in the navy before going into teaching, came out as lieutenant-commander and went to teach maths at Welbeck College, then to Marlborough. Married with two daughters. Keen on mountaineering, skiing, sailing, music.

Entrance: No entrance exam – all comers taken. Pupils come from all over Yorkshire and from 'outside' (by which the school means outside Yorkshire).

Exit: Traditionally two to three to Winchester (long tradition of links there), and to Shrewsbury (v popular recently), Radley, Uppingham, Sedbergh, Ampleforth, Queen Margaret's. Eton and Harrow now back on the list too. Four or five boys regularly get academic or music scholarships.

Remarks: Once a super all boys' traditional boarding school, now a full co-ed with day pupils and pre-prep. Sightings of happy parents: 'super, it deserves to be better known'. Founded just over a hundred years ago by Sir Samuel Servington Savery, whose brother George opened Harrogate Ladies' College. Traditionally more for children of professionals than landed compared with rival school Aysgarth (including relatively large number of MoD parents.) School has a tough time owing to geographical position – with the sea on three sides (not much catchment area,) and numbers somewhat reduced from when we last wrote.

Straightforward no-nonsense preparation for common entrance. Standards geared to high demands of Winchester entrance exam – Latin for all, except those doing 'Extra English', of which there are about 2 a year, and a full-time specialist teacher. Lots of basic grammar, Greek for scholarships pupils, solid grounding in traditional subjects. Streaming takes place from year 2, with vertical streaming to allow able children to do an 'accelerated course'. Excellent history, under John Horton, with charts on wall saying for example, 'important dates in 1909: Edward VII died; Bramcote played first match against Aysgarth'.

Academic class sizes a 'variable feast' – occasionally split forms, average around 13, maximum 16. Staff:pupil ratio 1:7. First years called 'Toads' (as it is kindly and at great length explained in the prospectus). The school admits that parents don't always like to think of their children as 'toads'.

Music: an impressive 100 per cent play 'at least one' instrument and practice takes place every day after breakfast and before lunch – 'there is plinking and plonking and scratching in every corner of the school,' as the previous head delightfully put it. School housed in what looks like a large red-brick seaside hotel up above the sea front. Do not be daunted – behind the facade everything is in good working order, with super playing fields, all on same site, and wonderful view of the sea from one or two of the dormitories. The school is sticking to 'full' ('seven-day') boarding, with some flexibility at the junior end – the head has argued this thoughtfully and persuasively, pointing to the opportunity to 'learn to live in a community' and 'develop friendships and acquire confidence – through tackling a challenging project'. Post-CE pupils are treated to a v active 'leavers' programme' which takes in trips to the Somme, building bridges out of spaghetti, going for 36-mile walks – you name it. In one corner of playing fields is a pavilion which used to belong to the North of England Tennis Club (a museum piece); steamy hot indoor pool, good indoor ball-bashing-about room, sports hall with cricket nets. Football, rugby, cricket teams all very strong. Girls coached by their own (female) specialist games coach – netball (under 11s unbeaten) and rounders fixture list, but also swimming, tennis, cross-country running, mixed hockey, riding etc on offer. All this, says head, on 'equal basis with the boys, with the possible exception of rugby football!'. School swaps the use of its sports fields with Scarborough Football Club in exchange for a professional coach from the club – good news.

BROOMWOOD HALL

Head office (and part of Lower School):
3 Garrads Road, London SW16 1JZ
Lower School:
74 Nightingale Lane, London SW12 8NR
Upper School:
192 Ramsden Road, London SW12 8RH

TEL: *Garrads Road: 020 8769 0119; Nightingale Lane:020 8673 1616; Ramsden Road: 020 8772 9400*

FAX: *Garrads Road: 020 8773 7428; Nightingale Lane: 020 8772 9417; Ramsden Road: 020 8772 9407*

E-MAIL: office@broomwood.co.uk

WEB: www.broomwood.org.uk

✦ PUPILS: Lower School: 340 boys and girls, 235 at Nightingale Lane and 105 at Garrads Road. Upper School 100 girls
✦ 4-8 Lower School, 8-13 Upper School
✦ Christian non-denom with special provision for RCs ✦ Fee-paying

Head (Joint Principals): Since 1984, Mrs K A H Colquhoun BEd DipT (thirties, pronounced cahoon), and her husband Malcolm, a Scotsman (whose sister is the Duchess of Argyll). They have two young children plus an older (step) child. Mrs C is considered by many to be daunting, and is most definitely imposing. Tremendously confident, open, very tall, an enthusiast.

Broomwood Hall and Northcote Lodge (qv) are owned by the Colquhouns, ie they are not run as 'charities'.

Head of Broomwood Hall: Mrs Colquhoun (see above), based at 3 Garrads Road. Head of Upper School Mrs

Elizabeth Heath BA. Head of Lower School Mrs Maureen Campbell MA.

Entrance: At 4, also at 7 and 8 by ballot weighted by distance from school. One-to-one interview for littles, tests for the older ones. Mixed ability. 'Family' policy – ie siblings are guaranteed a place, otherwise school picks names out of a hat. NB catchment area rules for 8+ children no longer apply – you don't have to be local, though most live in the fashionable bits of Wandsworth.

Exit: Boys (at eight) to London day schools (the great majority to Northcote Lodge) and to boarding schools including Cothill, Ludgrove. Girls to day schools eg JAGS, Streatham Hill and Clapham High, Wimbledon High, Francis Holland SW1 and to boarding schools eg Heathfield, Benenden, Tudor Hall, the St Mary's, North Foreland Lodge, Wycombe Abbey (though NB this list changes).

Remarks: The Colquhouns empire is expanding very fast in every direction. Broomwood Hall is charming and posh, set up by Mrs Colquhoun in 1984, and has grown (and keeps growing) successfully; now hotly sought after by south London parents. The Upper School, which is intended to become a full girls' prep school with perhaps half leaving at 11+ and the rest at 13+/CE, is at The Old Vicarage. The Lower School is split between two sites.

Maximum class size for 4-7s is 20; 8-13-year-olds, 15. Very traditional and structured in every respect, including setting and streaming, lots of emphasis on manners, friendly competition (cups galore, many donated by satisfied leavers' parents). Box for 'slips' of good behaviour marks, and (rare) poor marks. Termly school magazine, and a weekly 'What's on' leaflet. The junior school also pioneered a wonderful A-Z guide for parents (B is for Ballet, Bedtimes, Birthdays...) Extremely cheerful and friendly children, from Sloaney backgrounds.

School is a large plain Victorian house, once the HQ of SOGAT, with splendid garden and playground, enviable space. Homework guidance: parents must set the conditions, leave the child alone to work, and knock when time is up (no extra time allowed). In the upper school, all homework is done at school after school. Strict party rule: none during the week: 'It ruins two days, the day of the party and the day after.' Good system of swaps with Paris school for girls in class 6 ('It took me years to find the right school') – girls correspond for a year before, and exchanges sometimes continue for years ahead. 'I wish I had worked harder at French before I went to the Paris school,' commented a pupil. Latin (very popular) begins at 8. School has recently invested £100k in IT, 'the intention being to re-equip every 3 years'. Full time IT specialist currently engaged in integrating computers and IT into the curriculum. Throughout the school children are taught in ability groups within the same class. Mrs Colquhoun considers her main thrust is preparing children for boarding. 'It's important that they have a liking for themselves, and feel comfortable with themselves,' she says, adding that the academic side of school life is far easier to get right. 'I see my job as helping them to feel in control of their lives.' The school shares a remedial teacher with Northcote Lodge for 'moderate' learning disorders.

BUTE HOUSE PREPARATORY SCHOOL FOR GIRLS

Bute House, Luxemburg Gardens, London W6 7EA

TEL: *020 7603 7381* FAX: *020 7371 3446*

E-MAIL: mail@butehouse.co.uk

WEB: www.butehouse.co.uk

✦ PUPILS: 306 girls, all day ✦ Ages: 4–11
✦ Non-denom, predominantly Christian
✦ Fee-paying

Head: Since 1993, Mrs Sallie Salvidant BEd (fifties). Formerly head of the lovely Rupert House School, Henley-on-Thames. Has worked in the state sector; grown-up daughter teaching children with special needs abroad. Firm, matter of fact, straight down the line manner; the children adore her, and parents respect her. Believes 'all children have gifts and strengths, we value everyone'. Teaches citizenship to older children on a roving basis.

Entrance: Non-selective ballot entry at 4+; childrens' names may be registered from birth but only need to be in by September 30 of the academic year in which they are going to be 3. Open day for parents to see round the school, and an afternoon discussion of the workings of the 4+ and 7+ entries – don't miss these, as you don't get another chance to see the school unless you have a place.

Selective entry at 7+. Thirty-five places, school chooses from well over 100 girls (seen by 3 members of staff in groups of 10, testing and teaching – the school is quite secretive about what is actually involved in these tests ('guide line notes' are provided), but the emphasis is on initiative and inquiring minds and they are looking for girls who have a 'spark' that can be fired. Sisters get priority for places at 4+. Will keep a place open for your daughter if you are temporarily overseas – if you pay the full fees, including school lunch money.

Exit: Large numbers to St Paul's (20ish); also to Godolphin and Latymer (about 30 offers a year), and several elsewhere, half a dozen to boarding (Downe House popular). Regular awards won – including art and music.

Remarks: Still the reigning London academic girls' prep school, a position which is well deserved. An exciting place; lots of happy comments from parents: 'The best possible start,' said one. 'Children skip into school like Enid Blyteenies.' Senior school headmistresses also comment that the girls come up 'well prepared'. The system appears informal, but this is deceptive. Work comes back with remarks not marks, no streaming, no positioning, no weekly or termly tests – which can make parents twitchy at the top end of the school, although without reason – 'don't believe all the stuff about no competition, no streaming', commented a parent. 'The standard is very high indeed. My daughter is doing things at 8 I didn't do at an exceptionally academic school until 11 or 12'. Timed tests reserved for the last year. Classes changed and mixed every year.

Interesting mix of all abilities ('though you probably wouldn't choose to send a child here unless you had high expectations,' says the head). Specialist teachers for 8-9+ (unusual in a girls' prep). Much time (at no extra charge) is devoted to extra help if a child doesn't grasp spelling etc. Some 'marvellous' teachers, say parents.

Impressive science labs (and lots of hands-on), really lovely art, on show at every turn. Chess and debating societies, as well as the usual crafts, sports etc. Strongly musical, with all instruments (including trombone, saxophone and all the strings) taught in school hours; two general music lessons per week. Two choirs – senior and junior, and two orchestras – the main school one, and a 'training' one.

The school was founded in 1932 and is now housed in a purpose-built block built in the 1950s on land leased by the Mercers, rebuilt and refurbished in 1998. Glorious grounds, lots of space, sunny rooms overlooking a beech tree, with picnics in summer, a bright Wendy house for play, wonderful hot food with meatballs and sunshine tart a 'special favourite'. Large assembly hall acts as gym, dining and drama hall and looks out over senior St Paul's playing fields, which Bute House may use at allotted times. Unusually large library and own class libraries as well. New DT and art rooms. Fortnightly meetings for community discussions – children involved in helping at all levels, table-setting, litter-picking, etc. Drama, games and swimming clubs after school enthusiastically taken up. Parents are: political, arty, media, performers, not rich.

The school is firing strongly on all its many cylinders, much deserves its continuing success. Well worth bustling about to get into.

NB: the school is not – and never was – the prep school for St Paul's, despite its erstwhile name, proximity and notwithstanding the numbers of girls going on there – often doing well in academic scholarship stakes.

BUTTERSTONE SCHOOL

Arthurstone House, Meigle, Perthshire
PH12 8QY

TEL: *01828 640528* FAX: *01828 640640*

E-MAIL: heads@butterstone.freeserve.co.uk

WEB: www.users.zetnet.co.uk/butterstone/

◆ PUPILS: 53 girls board, 10 day; 9 girls and 7 boys in pre-prep; 42+ in nursery ◆ Ages: 4/5-13 (nursery for ages 2-5) ◆ Inter-denom ◆ Fee-paying

---

Joint Heads: Since 1998, Mr and Mrs Brian Whitten (both forties), Mr Whitten BA (Open University), CertEd, educated in the state sector in Yorkshire followed by Balls Park at Cambridge where he read Art History, comes from Queen Mary's, Baldersby Park where he was head of art. His wife Margaret, CertEd, was educated in the independent sector in Essex, followed by drama at Bristol; she comes from Queen Margaret's York where she was senior housemistress and taught drama. She now teaches English. Lacking traditional qualifications, though both have plenty of academic experience. School flourishing and happy. 'Gorgeous couple', comments a parent, 'they love the school, the girls, and Scotland'. They have three children, their younger son is at Glenalmond ('and very happy'). Took over from Mr Christopher Syers-Gibson.

Entrance: By interview, assessment if known difficulties. Some bursaries/scholarships on offer.

Exit: To all the posh schools: tranches to the South: North Foreland Lodge, Wycombe Abbey, St Mary's (Ascot and Calne), Tudor Hall, Oundle plus St Leonards, Kilgraston, Glenalmond and Gordonstoun.

Remarks: Numbers down in main school. The only all-girls boarding prep school in Scotland, a haven of horses, rabbits, music and happiness. Girls may keep their ponies at school – though they must share; fabulous new riding mistress, v popular; pony camp in the summer term. Tiny toffs' school with tiny classes encourages academic excellence. Girls, as you would expect, beautifully behaved with charming manners.

Fabulous resources, good computers, all learn at least one musical instrument, (17 on offer). Regular players in the local Perth festival. Art fantastic. Enthusiastic dancing of all kinds. English speaking board exams popular and compulsory subjects. Good remedial support, and enormous amount of parental backup. Run as an extended family this is a full boarding school, but no problem at all with exeats for granny's birthday or whatever. Part of stables recently converted to provide – amazing to relate, extra dormitories and a couple of classrooms.

After years in the wilderness, school is now financially secure and owns the building. Still the most popular school for little girls from all over Scotland. Nursery popular and flourishing.

NB Not to be confused with Baroness Linklater's *THE NEW BUTTERSTONE SCHOOL,* in Butterstone House, Dunkeld, Perthshire (Tel: 01350 724216, FAX 01350 724283); Head, Dr Bill Marshall, which for the 'educationally fragile' with most children being funded by local authorities. A useful place to know about if you have a child in need of special attention.

CALDICOTT

Farnham Royal, Buckinghamshire SL2 3SL

TEL: *01753 644457* FAX: *01753 647336*

E-MAIL: office@caldicott.com

WEB: www.caldicott.com

✦ PUPILS: approx 250 boys, 150 board (including all in the last 2 years), the rest day ✦ Ages: 7-13 ✦ C of E ✦ Fee-paying

---

Head: Since 1998, Mr Simon J G Doggart, former head of history at Eton. Took over from Mr M C B Spens, who left to go to Fettes. Heads and ex-heads Mavor, Silk and Morgan are governors of the school.

Entrance: Test and interview. Majority of boys live within an hour of the school.

Exit: To M4 corridor schools – Radley in particular, Harrow, Wellington. Also to Eton and Oundle in largish numbers.

Remarks: Highly structured traditional slightly buttoned up boys' prep school with emphasis on very serious, very hard work and boarding (though now there are a considerable number of day boys). Not as highly sought after as once it was, though luvvies like it. Founded 1904, moved in '38 to present site – now 40 acres of choice Home Counties surrounded by seas of computer commuters. Penultimate head Mr Wright instigated dynamic building programme and huge increase in numbers during his long reign – the result is large numbers of carefully thought-out purpose-built blocks – the new block, the 'new new block', the 'academic block', etc – all light and spacious and with noticeboards everywhere – more than at any other prep school we have visited and boys walk past them mesmerised. Very complicated streaming – 'I might die if you asked me to explain it,' said a boy. The object of the streaming, comments the head, is 'nothing to do with "pushing scholars" and everything to do with looking after weaker candidates'. A propos weaker candidates, their are two part-time specialist members of staff for (minor) learning difficulties, but this is not the place to send a dyslexic. Maximum class size 18. Setting as well as streaming. Dorms in long corridors and wings off corridors, numbered from 23 to 1 – very much in keeping with the logical structure of the rest of the school. Large light common rooms for boarders (slight feeling of them and us between boarders and day). Some accommodation for staff in yet another block of houses. Noisy dining room (the food has inspired wonderful poem in the school mag on the subject of mushy peas – '...As smelly as a rotten fish! Ma'am, mushy peas is my worst dish!'). Headmaster's study, masters' common room and admin slightly cut off from rest of the school. Strong keen rugby school – long tradition of this, and the wall is plastered with trophies. Hot competition from The Dragon and Papplewick. Art teaching still excellent – with two art teachers (mothers) with real hands-on technique. Early Ofsted report commented that the quality of learning was one of the major strengths of the school – 'satisfactory or better in more than nine out of ten lessons observed; it was good or very good in six out of every ten'. Good music facilities, including a piano which plays by itself like in Harrods. Drama traditionally strong – school patronised by clutch of actors' and media sons. A feature of school is a handful of Thai children, who can be seen learning English in corners (also Japanese, Chinese, Colombians etc – 'we like a "smallish" number of foreign nationals'.

Structured disciplined atmosphere has rubbed off on boys, who are kind and thoughtful but perhaps lacking in zip and in need of opportunities to let off steam. Ofsted report comments on the 'exemplary' behaviour of the children – we think it is possibly too good. Burnham Beeches – 700 acres of wild, wild woods – are on the doorstep, but not a place you would want to go on your own (panic). NB Mr Doggart has taken us to task for providing an inaccurate, unrepresentative description of the school.

CAMERON HOUSE

4 The Vale, London SW3 4AH

TEL: *020 7352 4040* FAX: *020 7352 2349*

E-MAIL: cameronhouse@lineone.net

✦ PUPILS: 65 girls and 50 boys, all day
✦ Ages: 4-11 ✦ C of E ✦ Fee-paying

Principal: Since 1980 Mrs Josie Ashcroft BSc. Mother of three, founder and owner of the school, charming and competent, teacher and psychologist by training. Taught at Thomas' and coached children privately before setting up her own school (here, initially called the Learning Tree and specialising in helping dyslexic children.)

Head: Since 1994, Miss Finola Stack BA PGCE (forties). Previously co-founder and co-principal of Finton House (qv). Three children in the school. 'Keen student' of karate (brown belt). Sensible, caring and thoughtful. Pupils (and parents) call her by her first name. Visits the senior schools her pupils are down for. Won't send a child to a school she hasn't visited.

Entrance: Put child's name down asap – at least 12 months before year of possible entry; visit the school at least a year in advance of child's entry. All pupils given an informal assessment (two hours, groups of 12) in the spring term; interview plus test at 8+. Active sibling policy.

Exit: Some boys (decreasingly) leave for traditional boys' preps at 8. Others transfer at 11 to City of London Boys', Latymer etc. Girls to St Paul's, Putney High, Francis Holland, Queen's Gate, Heathfield etc.

Remarks: Small school, now an established part of the London scene, a good place for children to learn self-confidence (at least 6 pupils have gone on to become heads of their subsequent schools) and pupils are not over-faced. Bright colours everywhere, walls well decorated with work and projects. 'The environment helps children think and become curious,' comment parents. Sense of creativity all around the place. Bouncy children: lots of laughter. Predominately local Chelsea children – lots of Euros – a number from Holland Park/Notting Hill (parents have organised a minibus).

Teeny playground (indeed, the whole outfit is dinky). French at 4, Latin at 10. Science extremely popular. Remarkably good (better than some much bigger schools) on visitors/talks, eg John McCarthy, drugs project – children are articulate and thoughtful, 'academically well prepared,' commented another head. A charity-minded place, with strong parental involvement. Good singing, ambitious drama. Clubs keenly attended after schools hours, outstanding karate taught by Mrs Lavender Ralston-Saul, one of Britain's few full-time female black belts (3rd Dan). Good sport despite lack of on-site facilities. Swimming from reception class. Maximum class size 18 (with 2 teachers); average size 15. Specialist teachers to help with dyslexia and dyspraxia – bright children only. Despite the lack of 'bigger school' facilities, it is a super school offering the sort of environment which makes one question the validity of the more 'rigorous' London junior schools.

CARGILFIELD SCHOOL

Barnton Avenue West, Edinburgh EH4 6HU

TEL: *0131 336 2207* FAX: *0131 336 3179*

E-MAIL: deocustode@aol.com

WEB: www.cargilfield.edin.sch.uk

✦ PUPILS: 83 boys, 38 girls; 20 board, 35 weekly board, 58 day. Pre-prep, Benbow House: 68 boys and girls. Nursery 24 boys and girls ✦ Ages 3-13 ✦ Non-denom ✦ Fee-paying

---

Head: Since September 2000, Mr Mark Seymour BA CertEd (forties), an historian and previously senior housemaster at Haileybury. Keen cricketer, and comes highly recommended. His wife Andrea has an honours degree in literature and media and has been involved in school PR – which will be a great boon. The Seymours have 3 young children; 10, 8 and 4. Interests include playing the drums, power-boating. Took over from Mr Andrew Sinclair Morrison, head from 1997.

Entrance: Bulging waiting lists for nursery and pre-prep, but numbers down by almost a third in main school; places pretty well guaranteed through pre-prep, but tests if learning difficulties suspected.

Exit: All the Scottish public schools, Glenalmond heads the list, but also Fettes, Gordonstoun, Loretto – much as you would expect. A trickle down South, Oundle popular. 22 'genuine academic awards', in last 3 years, eight last year.

Remarks: The departure of the previous head, Andrew Morrison, came as a surprise, though there had been several rather sour comments about the Fettes factor, and the resulting sharp decline in numbers. No matter, the facilities are superb for such a small school, and plans are afoot to build 'a new pre-prep building, new classrooms, swimming pool, dormitories and new staff housing'. All this to be financed by selling off yet more Cargilfield ground (albeit the wood behind the cricket pavilion which the staff probably never used but the children loved) and some staff housing.

Founded in 1873, the school moved to its purpose built site in 1899 (23 acres then, 15 now); recent additions have included an IT room, also DT and a stunning sports hall. Not enough 'proper' boarders, boys dorms forbiddingly like a fever hospital, though girls' ones cosier over head's house.

Pupils set and streamed, scholarship help as well as remedial on hand – Jan McAusland runs one of the best remedial departments in Scotland. Masses of options and activities – the pipe band is second to none. Bed and breakfast on offer as well as lots of bursaries. Discounts for MoD children, (v handy for Scottish Command), otherwise a mixed bunch of parents, some brash first time buyers.

The School does not feel that tired, but numbers remain low ('Edinburgh parents are a picky lot' said Andrew Morrison). Hopefully young Mr Seymour (as parents appear to call him) will inspire.

CHEAM HAWTREYS

Headley, Newbury, Berkshire RG19 8LD

TEL: *01635 268381* FAX: *01635 269345*

E-MAIL: office@cheamschool.co.uk

WEB: www.cheamschool.co.uk

♦ PUPILS: 140 boys, 90 girls; half boarding, half day. Plus pre-prep with 104 boys and girls ♦ Ages: 8-13, pre-prep 3-7 ♦ C of E ♦ Fee-paying

---

Head: Since 1998, Mr Mark Johnson, BEd (forties). A West Country product – educated at Buckland House, Devon, and Exeter School; got his degree at the College of St Mark and St John, Plymouth. His last post was as deputy headmaster at Summer Fields, where he was hugely popular. Nickname: Mr J (from his initials: MRJ). Bursting with enthusiasm and energy, slightly hail-fellow-well-met, describes himself as 'restless – I'm having a cheering up Cheam mission and I'm putting paint everywhere, I love challenge, I love to be busy.' Bubbling with ideas for and about the school. Does not (currently) teach, because he reckons it is more important for him to be seeing parents, potential and present. 'He's very parent friendly,' remarked one warmly, 'an overgrown prep school boy' said another. Married to Jane, a lovely bouncy lady, a classicist, who does a little Latin and

Greek teaching (NB Greek re-launched after a long lapse). Two daughters, both in the school. Took over from Mr Chris Evers.

Entrance: Informal tests – children spend one day at the school four terms before entry. First come, first served (but at the time of writing over-subscribed, so book early).

Exit: Boys to Marlborough (1 academic scholarship in 2000), Stowe, Harrow, Radley, and a number of others; Eton occasionally. Girls to St Mary's Wantage, Bath Royal High, The Abbey, Downe, St Swithun's; too soon to say for the increasing numbers staying on till they are 13. Most famous Old Boy: the Prince of Wales.

Remarks: Back on course as a vibrant and strong prep school after several years in the wilderness. Claims to be the oldest of all the prep schools, traces its history back to 1645. Set in well kept grounds, with an elegant terraced garden, the main house is partly by Detmar Blow. Lots of new buildings, and from November 2000 new classroom blocks will go up; plans for further expansion and improvements in the pipeline. The merger crisis with Hawtreys a thing of the past; two years ago the local pre-prep had to close and 'offered to merge'. Numbers have, therefore, shot up and the school is now choc-a-bloc. Day numbers have also shot up, and presumably will continue to increase as the local pre-prep children grow into the main school, 'But remember a lot of them insist on boarding in the last two years.' Large London contingent, and a few from overseas (one term, one year, EFL an option).

New and younger staff have been brought in, adding zest to staid older teachers. Setting and streaming in most subjects. Latin considerably beefed up, with a Latin reading competition now on the menu. Strong on outings and trips to provide hands-on teaching eg workshops at archaeological digs, French classes in Bayeux, environmentalists to the Wyld Court Rainforest, plus all the usual museum visits.

Music is on the up – now boasts four choirs; 90 recently performed Fauré's Requiem, helped by adults; keen drama for all ages and very good art displayed all over the school. Minimum TV. watching, reading period (Digest) after lunch; library poised to be re-housed and re-designed. Computer games rationed, digital games forbidden.

School day starts at 8.15 with daily Chapel, and all the children must say good morning and make eye contact with the head on the way out. Saturday morning school. Huge numbers (75) of extra-curricular activities, from copper etching to fly-fishing. No winter time table: throughout the year children work all morning, after lunch do more lessons until 3.30, then games. Games are big here, with matches and competitions at all levels, so practically everyone is in a team – and, by the way, they beat other schools. Competitive on the house front. Parental report that there are 'almost no games in the baby school – dancing – rather than anything physical, and no hockey in prep school proper, only football' – so perhaps not total perfection. Notice boards everywhere along passages and meeting places, bulging with information, lists, newspaper cuttings, news etc. The first notice to hit you in the eye as you enter the school asks: Are You Happy? Head's stated aim is to have 'blissfully happy children'. Manners well taken care of, and the school operates a fierce anti-bullying policy.

CHELTENHAM COLLEGE JUNIOR SCHOOL

Thirlestaine Road, Cheltenham, Gloucestershire GL53 7AB

TEL: *01242 522697* FAX: *01242 265620*

E-MAIL: ccjs@cheltcoll.gloucs.sch.uk

WEB: www.cheltcoll.gloucs.sch.uk

✦ PUPILS: 286 boys, 176 girls; 54 board, rest day. ✦ Ages: 3-13 ✦ C of E ✦ Fee-paying

---

Head: Since 1991, Mr Nigel Archdale BEd MEd (forties). Educated John Lyon School, Bristol University and Edinburgh University. Previously headmaster of Royal Wolverhampton Junior school and before that at the Edinburgh Academy junior school. Keen sportsman (swims or runs every morning). Three children, his wife is a teacher (career on hold). Came into a difficult situation with dwindling numbers, discontented parents and staff – and has turned the school around. Writes plays and librettos for children in spare time. He 'adores teaching and young children'. Keen on going for the individual's 'ceiling'. 'Smashing head,' commented a parent.

Entrance: At 3, 4, 7, also 11. Boarders from overseas, ex-pat families living abroad, and outlying areas of the Cotswolds.

Exit: Majority over the road to Cheltenham College (see separate entry), but also to smart schools elsewhere.

Remarks: Seriously super dynamic school previously all boys, now co-education at all ages, with lots going on and some fine teaching. High standards in many departments – especially good music (the choir tours regularly – World Tour 1996), also French (the 'martins pecheurs' start at three, with daily lessons) under excellent real French Madame. Lovely art, drama strong, and keen technological department (like big brother) with power boats being built and Apple Macs everywhere. Full-time staff to help dyslexics at no extra charge, also part-time staff for EFL (extra). Maximum class size: 20; from age nine, four sets in core subjects across each year group.

Splendid grounds and setting (across the A40 from the public school), and the school uses some of the senior school facilities.

First lesson at 8.15, and children can stay till 5.30pm. Full weekend programme for the boarders (technology department open, dry ski-slopes not far away, 'brilliant' 100-foot long model railway, etc). All boys housed in the main Victorian block, dorms now refurbished.

Careful balance for all children of organised extra-curricular activities (including popular Scout troop) and free time for children to organise as they will. Super (shallow) lake with paddle boats. Kingfishers pre-prep department opened '93 (chorus of delight from locals), very attractive and bright, cosy well-defined area within main junior school block.

CHRIST CHURCH PRIMARY SCHOOL

1 Robinson Street, Chelsea, London SW3 4AA

TEL: *020 7352 5708* FAX: *020 7823 3004*

E-MAIL: caz_sw3@yahoo.com

WEB: www.christchurch.kensington-chelsea.sch.uk

✦ PUPILS: 210 boys and girls, all day ✦ Ages: 5-11 ✦ C of E voluntary aided ✦ State

Head: Since 1992, Ms Anna Kendall BEd (forties). Formerly an adviser to the Royal Borough of Kensington and Chelsea, Camden and Westminster; before that a class teacher.

Entrance: Application by February for September as the child is rising 5. All other ages on an ad hoc basis. Priority given to i) children with siblings in the school; ii) children of families who are regular worshippers in St Luke's or Christ Church, Chelsea; iii) children living in the parish; iv) children of families who are regular worshippers in a neighbouring parish church.

Exit: Shene School, Greycoats, Elliot School, Pimlico School, Salesian College etc etc and about 20 per cent to private London day schools – Alleyn's, Emanuel, Dulwich, etc.

Remarks: Excellent primary school in super location tucked away in a quiet corner of Chelsea, with – by London standards – lots of space, including good-sized playground and extra area of garden/pond etc. Founded 1840, affiliated with local church-es (Helen Morgan-Edwards is now chair of governors). Cherry-coloured uniform. Bright classrooms. Class size 30 maximum. Approximately 50 per cent of pupils from Chelsea, the rest from Wandsworth, Westminster and beyond – mixed intake. Popular with media folk. Funded by a mix of government, local education authority and the church. Good science and technology provision. All children have experience with computers. Maths and English also good. French on offer after school, swimming to year 3. PE in much-used all-purpose school hall. Games keen and the school participates in inter-school competitions. Keen music. Recently awarded 'Beacon Status' by DfEE: means that they think it's in the top one per cent of state schools for excellence – though even here parents sending children to private schools usually opt for a year or two of coaching. Continuing good, happy reports from parents.

CLIFTON HALL SCHOOL

Newbridge, Midlothian EH28 8LQ

TEL: *0131 333 1359* FAX: *0131 333 4609*

E-MAIL: cliftonhall@rmplc.co.uk

WEB: www.cliftonhall.org.uk

✦ PUPILS: 115 boys and girls, plus 30 in nursery school ✦ Ages: 5-11, nursery 3-5 ✦ Non-denom ✦ Fee-paying

Head: Since 1987, Mr Mark Adams BSc (forties), who originally came to the school to teach science in 1985. His American wife, Nancy, is bursar and they have two children who have gone through the school and are now at George Watson's. Mr Adams was educated at Bloxham and Durham University and previously taught at Dulwich College, followed by 'a couple of years' supply teaching in Edinburgh'. Terribly pleased at how successful the school has become, fun; he takes time with his answers (you almost think he has forgotten the question) . Looks to produce 'confident children full of self-esteem'.

Entrance: Mainly through the nursery – a proper nursery school with many of the children wearing uniform, and a member of the Edinburgh City Partnership Scheme. Otherwise by assessment and interview.

Exit: The school follows the Scottish system and children leave at 11 for the big Edinburgh day schools ('whatever is the flavour of the month'); George Watson's, Merchiston, St George's, Stewart's Melville College & The Mary Erskine School, and George Heriots.

Remarks: This is an 'independent primary school' based in a magical Bryce house (classrooms and passages painted jolly pinks, blues and yellows) in 42 acres of child-inspiring grounds just off the Newbridge roundabout – the junction of A8, M8 and M9. A boon for parents to the west of Edinburgh who can either take advantage of the school bus which leaves Bathgate daily at 8am (and leaves the school at 5pm each evening), or drop their little darlings on the way into work in Edinburgh. The school opens at 8am and children can stay till 6pm, for after school club – two fresh staff who help with homework, etc. There are other clubs for judo, ballet, fencing, swimming et al until 6pm. Morning drop-off point for parents v sociable, with coffee on tap, and door to head's study open and school secretary on hand. Weekly menus handed out to all, so that parents don't cook the 'same for their tea'. Lots of parent participation. Bags, run by Philip and Pamela Bagnall, organise holiday courses throughout most of the Easter and summer holidays, and are doing the same at the long half term. (Hours from 8.15am to 5.30pm with a fine of a fiver every fifteen minutes if you are late in the evening). This is child care made easy.

Mr Adams started the nursery in 1987; the boarders were thrown out in 1995, since when numbers have risen and risen. Huge growth and conversion of out-buildings and former school flat under way, with a four-year expansion scheme in hand. Great facilities, computers and French from nursery; tiny classes, learning support both withdrawn and dual teaching, and 'learning enrichment' to encourage clever clogs who might otherwise be bored.

The main catchment area is West Lothian: Livingston, Linlithgow, Bathgate – Silicon Glen – 85 per cent or more first time buyers, ditto two working parents, and about 15/20 per cent single parents. Jazzy young staff, new deputy head September 2000. Mr Adams is keen to 'provide male role models', so all children learn to cook and a third of the staff are male.

Strong theatre, masses of music and peripatetic teachers. Children devised own punishment detail: 'if you are naughty your name goes in the book, if your name is in the book three times, then you get a piece of writing that you have to do at home and your parents have to sign it. If your name is not in the book, then you get a star'. So there. Tinies hold out hands and show off eagerly to Mr Adams (who has infinite patience); older children stand up when we enter a room and call him 'Sir'. Fees include almost all extras; trust fund on hand to pick up financial hiccups 'for a year or two', 'safety net', rather than 'safety blanket'.

'School is going places and it is growing'. Governors very bullish – so they should be.

COLET COURT

(ST PAUL'S PREPARATORY SCHOOL)

Lonsdale Road, London SW13 9JT

TEL: *020 8748 3461* FAX: *020 8563 7361*

E-MAIL: hmseccc@stpaulsschool.org.uk

WEB: www.stpaulsschool.org.uk/coletcourt/

✦ PUPILS: Approx. 440 boys, day (plus one small boarding house) ✦ Ages: 7-13 ✦ C of E ✦ Fee-paying

---

Head: Since 1992, Mr Geoffrey Thompson (early fifties), who has more qualifications than you ever dreamed of: BA from Newcastle in biology, MEd CertEd MI Biol CBiol, Fellow of the College of Preceptors, Fellow of the Linnaean Society. In other words, the man's a hotshot biologist. Also Fellow of the Royal Society of Arts. Educated (in the first place) at Hemsworth Grammar, West Yorkshire. Taught at Colet Court yonks ago. Appointed here following posts in senior schools – previous post = Head of Clevedon House School in Ilkley. Is responsible to the high master of the senior school – ties have been strengthened between the two as a matter of policy. Married to teacher. No children. House overlooking River Thames in the middle of school site.

Entrance: At 7+, 8+, 10+ and 11+ – these last two ages were mainly for assisted places, of which senior and junior schools jointly had a very large number, and are now a good route in for beady parents with kids at state primaries. Name down asap – list closed the November before the January exams. Intake of two forms of 18 at 7+ (makes for hot-house tutoring by pre-preps), plus two at 8+ = 4 forms in all. Test usually in January – maths, English and verbal reasoning, followed by interview for those weeded out by the exam. Children come mainly from pre-preps in Battersea/Clapham. Internal academic scholarships; music and choral scholarship offered to outsiders. NB parents must sign that St Paul's is their first choice of school on being offered a place at Colet Court.

Exit: Around 98 per cent to St Paul's (qv) – ten scholarships in '99; otherwise, one or two scholarships to Eton and/or Winchester etc.

Remarks: Truly horrendous ('says who', says the head) '60s buildings (architect should be shot) on fabulous site on the banks of the Thames. Redecorated classrooms. Music block in ex-Thames Water building with new furniture and new double glazed windows. The school remains one of the two most hot-swot academic preps in London – with Westminster Under – parents rightly viewing it as an entry to Mecca – St Paul's. Common room of academics, old and new, high powered. Around 11 women. Boys bespectacled and bulging with brains, mainly from professional families; keep the staff on their toes – withering scorn when one of them makes a floater. Class sizes 18 at bottom, 22 at top (max 24). Talk and chalk everywhere (mostly chalk). French from second year, Latin from the third. French assistant. ' Some' Greek for scholars. Set from third year in some subjects; in fourth and fifth year one scholarship class and three equal ability classes – setted in most subjects. ICT all through the school. The school has a specialist on the staff who assesses pupils with learning difficulties, and once a week someone comes in to tutor where necessary – though NB this is absolutely not the place for dyslexics. Games ' as strong as always' . School uses all the facilities of the senior school, which is on the same site – (NB Colet Court has more outdoor space by far than any other central London prep). The school plays all the usual games, twice a week – matches against Dulwich, Whitgift, Haileybury, etc. One boarding house with a handful of boarders, but if eg parents are away from home, boys can clock in for short periods on a B and B basis. Consistently produces good meaty poetry (look in the school magazine). Chess very strong – includes national players, excellent coaching.

Heavy academic atmosphere. Terribly terribly hard work with no let-up. Do not be tempted by the designer label unless your son is bright, keen and above all emotionally robust.

THE COMPASS SCHOOL

West Road, Haddington EH41 3RD

Tel: *01620 822 642* Fax: *01620 822 144*

E-mail: mb@compassschool3.freeserve.co.uk

◆ Pupils: 52 boys, 57 girls; all day
◆ Ages: 4–11 ◆ Inter-denom ◆ Fee-paying

Head: Since 1997, Mr Mark Becher (pronounced Becker) MA PGCE (thirties), educated at Queen Margaret's Academy Ayr, followed by Dundee University where he read Modern History, and PGCE at Craigie College of Education in Ayr (now part of Paisley University). Previously head of sport at Stewart's Melville College & The Mary Erskine School, and primary teacher at Edinburgh Academy where he met his wife (now a senior primary teacher there.)

Mr Becher, whom we met on his first day back in school following a coronary thrombosis, has overseen a considerable building programme during the summer, The Compass has the smartest office, cloakrooms and loos in the business, and has not only increased in number, but also in size. An open, engaging head, with a confidential manner, he teaches RE, Latin, history, and support teaches at all levels throughout the school.

Entrance: Children can come (and do) at any time, school uniform is sold in house, so children can come for an interview on Thursday and start the following Friday.

Exit: Children now regularly stay past the magic age of eight, with more leaving at ten or eleven, either to go to the Edinburgh independent day schools, the state sector, or off to trad prep schools as before. Belhaven, Butterstone, Loretto popular.

Remarks: The Compass is no longer the sleepy dame school it was. Started in 1963, and run by Mrs Alny Younger for years. French from four, extracurricular Latin at seven, with formal Latin at eight. Small classes in a still very cramped space, some learning support – currently with Sir David Clark, who was previously at The Nippers (Loretto Junior School). Stunning new attic development (the previous new build) houses older children with sag bags and a raft of computers. Lots more games and sport based at the 'properly run' local authority ground at Millfields', with regular changing rooms' and rugby, hockey and cricket matches a feature. Music and drama on the up, plus all the usual trad subjects.

Lots more first time buyers, with pupils coming from as far away as Duns and Dalkeith, lots from the farming community as well as business folk and landowners.

A popular little school, good ethos, good manners important with lots of parental input – the parents recently revamped the (tiny) playground. Problems with housing staff in expensive environment of Haddington. One can't help feeling that rather than spend good money adding piecemeal to the existing building the governors would not have been cleverer to buy afresh (after all most of the children are delivered by car) and sell the rather handsome former merchant's house for serious money. The governors, we are told, decided that the disruption, and change to the school's atmosphere, would not have been worth it.

COTHILL HOUSE

Nr Abingdon, Oxon OX13 6JL

TEL: *01865 390800* FAX: *01865 390205*

E-MAIL: office@cothill.oxon.sch.uk

✦ PUPILS: 250 boys; all board ✦ Ages: 8-14, plus day 'arm' for boys and girls ages 5-11 ✦ C of E ✦ Fee-paying

---

Head: Since 1976, Mr Adrian Richardson CertEd Oxon (early fifties). Popular with parents and boys, very experienced, very professional, respected by other heads. Tall and (too?) self-assured. Lovely wife Rachel (strong mother appeal), who still refers to 'our ghastly mad system of sending children away to board – so it must be as much like home as possible'. Three young children. School is brimful, and all boarding – a great rarity – 'But we're probably living on borrowed time.'

Entrance: Early registration advised. Interview plus assessment, 'to encourage and reassure, not to eliminate'.

Exit: Eton, Radley and Harrow, and one or two to other public schools such as Stowe, Marlborough.

Remarks: Very traditional prep school which suits some well and others not at all. Those it suits tend to be the top of the school's academic range (the range is quite a wide one). Family feel pervades – main building is large, white and uninstitutional, the way in is through the Richardsons' living quarters, where new little boys are allowed to play Lego, help cook, befriend the family's au pair etc. Cosy (huge teddy count) at all levels, despite deeply traditional approach. Vast numbers of clubs. Reading emphasis (a book by each boy's bed), two libraries (4,500 volumes in the reference library) plus classroom libraries.

Well-designed modern teaching blocks; lots of female staff (grannies and young). Three streams with maths workshops to 'sort problems'. School now has a whole extra 'year' to keep boys occupied who go 'late' to their public school (an increasing number) – much appreciated. Good CDT, art and choir. Rifle range and golf course. Boys divided into Greeks, Romans etc, competitive over obtaining good marks (generously given for good work, tidyness etc). One full-time member of staff and two part-time members to provide extra academic support for dyslexia and dyspraxia, but 'we do not advertise it' says the head, and 'The school doesn't really want to know about children with learning difficulties,' moaned a mother. (Understandable, given the pupils' traditional destinations.) Each boy must write a 'personal report' at the end of each term answering the school's questionnaire on which books he's read, his opinions on school life in general – staff, food etc. New purpose-built music room. Manners considered very important. Exeats minimum, boys kept busy at weekends, parents encouraged to visit for matches etc (suits Londoners), though complaints that 'only parents of match children' are allowed to attend.

Happy school (for most) doing a fine job, and viewed with envy by others: against the trend of the national drop in boarding numbers, here is a boarding-only school which is fuller than ever. However, it could be in danger of becoming a bit swollen headed, though head vetoes this, commenting '... we are only too well aware of our good fortune and daily marvel at it...' Château de Sauveterre (near Toulouse) was bought by the school in '89, 'the best thing we ever did'. Produces sour grapes comments from some other schools but all who take part are agreed it gets pupils chattering away unselfconsciously in French. As Mr Richardson comments, 'first and foremost they lose the fear of speaking French'. All boys spend at least one term out there, some of them two. Great for boosting their confidence on many fronts. Children (boys and girls) from other schools often come too. Teaching starts in English, moves into French (teaching staff now entirely French nationals).

NB Chandlings Manor, Tel: 01865 730771, five miles away, is the school's day pupil 'arm'. This typically Richardson venture was officially opened in '94 and quickly blossomed; now has 360 boys and girls aged 5-11; regarded as an excellent option by Oxford families. Boys can transfer to Cothill. Cothill sixth formers sleep at Chandlings (and feel very grown up to be a bus ride away from their juniors). Chandlings belonged to an Arab who built spread-eagle style on to the original manor house, indoor swimming pool, squash court, fine grounds etc.

COTTESMORE SCHOOL

Buchan Hill, Pease Pottage, West Sussex
RH11 9AU

TEL: *01293 520648* FAX: *01293 614784*

E-MAIL: cottesmore@compuserve.com

WEB: www.cottesmoreschool.com

✦ PUPILS: around 100 boys, 50 girls; all board
✦ Ages 7-13 ✦ C of E ✦ Fee-paying
(private limited company)

Head: Since 1971, Mr Mark Rogerson MA (fifties). Educated at Eton, read history at Churchill College, Cambridge. Taught at Wellesley House, Summer Fields and Windlesham (where he met his wife, Cathryn, who plays a vital supportive role in this family business.) Grown-up children.

Entrance: Not a problem. £400 deposit required one year before entry and retained until pupil leaves. One third of parents live abroad (but only around ten foreign children). Lots from London and the Home

Counties, a few Services' children. April and September entry (a rarity nowadays).

Exit: Girls to Benenden (largest number go here), Roedean, Sherborne plus co-ed public schools eg King's Canterbury, Marlborough, and a mix of other girls' schools. Boys to all manner of schools, including Charterhouse (by far the largest number have gone here over the past five years), Radley, Wellington, Harrow, Marlborough and King's Canterbury. Five or more scholarships a year. Recent survey shows boys have gone on to be City types, businessmen, medics, advertising and media men, policemen and sportsmen (eg pro rackets and polo).

Remarks: Family-run prep school (present head took over from his father, after two years of joint headship) with a jolly, friendly atmosphere. Splendidly grand house (architect was Lutyens' teacher) built in the 19th century for a French gentleman, whose fortune was based on ostrich feathers, which are painted on ceilings. Fine views and grounds, lots of (modern) cottages on site for staff. Maximum class size 17, average class size 14, two 'sets/streams'. Pupil: teacher ratio 9:1. Two part-time staff come in three days a week each to take care of special needs, including dyslexia and dyspraxia. All children do Latin and French; plus 'tasters' of Greek, Spanish and German after CE. Keenly competitive children. Excellent maths teaching, and national prizes to prove it. Small enough to be cosy, yet with a sense of space and tradition – oak-panelled corridors with rows and rows of school photographs. Not overly tidy. Boys and girls do everything, 'they're busy, busy, busy'. Much use of computers and the internet. The school wins a great many games matches, also keen and exceptionally good swimming. Riding, judo, very nice

music (eg *The King and I*, described as one of the school's 'most stunning productions'). Mini-billiard tables everywhere. 'Show ups' (for good work etc) get signed and seen and praise is liberal. Exeats every two weeks, when the entire school empties out: NB ex-pats should have handy relations/ guardians. Long 'catching up' period daily at breakfast time, when pupils can catch teachers, practise games, musical instruments, do prep. One of the four boarding-only prep schools left in England (historical note: there were eight when we last counted) – and the only co-educational one. One or two complaints from parents about disorganised pastoral care. Very low profile. Marketing note: the school had a whole bed with a teddy on it at an ISIS schools' fair.

CRAIGCLOWAN
PREPARATORY SCHOOL

Edinburgh Road, Perth PH2 8PS

TEL: *01738 626 310* FAX: *01738 440 349*

E-MAIL: mbeale@btconnect.com

WEB: www.craiglowan-school.co.uk

✦ PUPILS: 281 boys and girls, plus 30 or so in the nursery (it comes and goes). All day ✦ Ages: 5-13, 3-5 in nursery ✦ Inter-denom ✦ Fee-paying

---

Head: Since 1979, Mr M E (Mike) Beale BEd (fifties) educated 'at a grammar school in Dorset', followed by a BEd in Birmingham. His previously taught at Downside where he was head of economics and politics. 'The parent of a pupil' persuaded him to apply for the headship of Craigclowan and he has been here, happy as Larry, ever since. School has grown enormously under his reign, starting with just fifty children, rising via 140 plus new facilities to current size, which has been more or less static for the last ten years. Married to Angela, who acts as bursar, they have two grown up daughters. Busy border terrier, Breagh, 'my favourite pupil'.

Mr Beale is a lovely head. Confidential, loving to the children; during our visit trails of tinies came to have their work approved: stickers of mice on a mountain were issued to all, and the children put out their hands, had their hair ruffled and were alternately called 'honey pot' and sweetie pie'. 'I make it a rule always to stop and talk to children wherever they find me', and 'if they are happy to come and see me for praise, it is so much easier to come and see me when they have done something wrong – and then we discuss it'. No punishment for a first offence, but if it is repeated 'we get Ma and Pa in'. No actual teaching duties, just games, rugby and cricket – Mr Beale also fronts the ski team – trips to America as well as the Highlands.

Entrance: Children from all over the northern central belt; usually within forty minutes travel/thirty mile radius, middle class professionals, plus a toff or two. Large number of first time buyers.

Exit: To 14 different schools in summer 2000. 70 per cent go relatively locally, Glenalmond, Strathallan, Fettes, Merchiston, St Leonards, Kilgraston. 25 per cent down South; trickle to Eton, quite a few to Downe House ('Emma McKendrick likes our product'), plus Rugby, Stonyhurst, Ampleforth, QM York, Haileybury, Stowe.

Remarks: Cunning conversion of Victorian mansion set in 13 acres of undulating urban Perth overlooking the M90. Plans afoot to remove the rather tacky temporary classroom and build a mirror block to the rather grand clock-towered classrooms. Current speculation is whether, when the new Astroturf is put in and the land flattened, there will be sufficient fall to install a – very small – artificial ski slope. Tinies work in the main house, lining up either on yellow painted human or webbed feet at the main door. And we are greeted most excellently, by mini-tartaned creatures who escorted us with great aplomb to the head's office. Tartan everywhere.

Two tiny classes throughout, some streaming further up, but basically divided alphabetically, with those whose birthdays fall in the spring or summer term joining the school the summer term before their fifth birthdays. French from nine (though some earlier exposure), traditional teaching. Latin, computers; fantastic sports hall, fine art. Learning support for 'any child who needs help for any reason either for a long or a short term, and for the very able'. Two teachers for every year, plus trained support staff – we saw many children getting one to one attention in little work stages all over the main classroom block. Excellent staff. Part of the Comenious project, lots of foreign contact, as well as regular tours abroad.

This is a vibrant seven day a week co-ed day school, with classes on five days, and a mass of extra-curricular activity. Parents can (and do) leave their young at 7.50 am and collect them again at 6 pm. Lots of involvement with Perth festival; a film crew was auditioning when we visited. All singing and dancing.

CRANLEIGH PREPARATORY SCHOOL

Horseshoe Lane, Cranleigh,

Surrey GU6 8QH

TEL: *01483 274199* FAX: *01483 277136*

E-MAIL: themaster@cranprep.demon.co.uk

+ PUPILS: 174 boys, of which 44 board
+ Ages: 7-13 + C of E + Fee-paying

Head: Since 2000, Michael Roulston, CertEd BPhil MEd University of Ulster. Came here from Tokyo, where he transformed the limping British School into a thriving show-piece with infuriatingly long waiting-lists. Parents can't quite believe their luck that he's beamed down in rural Surrey. Married, one son at Cranleigh Prep, a daughter coming next year and a bigger child across the road at Cranleigh School.

Entrance: Through own test (maths and English) and school reports.

Exit: Most head off across the road at age 13 (no automatic right of entry, but only roughly one boy a year fails to make it;) about one in four to other schools (Charterhouse, Wellington popular).

Remarks: Happy but unexceptional and (currently) grubby prep school, undergoing short, sharp revamp. Promising refurbishment plan under way, to be finished in time for the school to go co-ed in September 2001. Girls will initially enter forms one (age 7) and five (age 11), but the school hopes to have even numbers of boys and girls within about five years. Good, traditional prep school virtues: teachers still sit with the boys at lunch, doling out grub and checking table manners. One and a half hours of games each day led by specialist games teachers. Good sports hall. Prep school uses some of the main school's facilities, especially the indoor pool. Forty-five minutes prep each evening, done in classroom under tutor's supervision. Cranleigh School is turning up the pressure to send over some music scholars at age 13, so music is getting a lot of attention (one music scholarship available at age 11). Saturday school every second week, with the boarders turfed out each intervening week-end for a 'compulsory exeat' (possibly not ideal for overseas parents). Exams every term. Excellent, detailed reports every month, with a place for the boy to write how he plans to improve the following month (poor souls).

DANES HILL SCHOOL

Leatherhead Road, Oxshott,

Surrey KT22 0JG

TEL: *01372 842 509* FAX: *01372 844 452*

+ PUPILS : 465 boys, 374 girls, all day +
Ages: 7 – 13, pre-prep (Bevendean)
$2^1/_2 - 7$ + Christian non-denom
+ Fee-paying

Head: Since 1989, Mr Robin Parfitt MA MSc. Two headships prior to Danes Hill, Mr Parfitt (fifties) has been at the helm of a school that has evolved from a small boys' boarding school into one of the largest independent co-educational day schools in the area. Friendly and down to earth according to parents, the children apparently think he is a 'lovely man'. Married to Angela (head of modern languages and domestic bursar), they have 4 sons (twenties) and are immersed in all aspects of life at the school.

Entrance: There are waiting lists at all entry levels so get names down early. Pupils come in at $2^1/2$, $3^1/2$, $4^1/2$ and 7. There are occasional spaces thereafter. No entrance tests for the pre-prep (known as Bevendean) but there is an assessment and interview at 7.

Exit: Both boys and girls at 13 (only a few leave at 11). Most popular choices are Epsom College, City of London Freemen's (Ashtead), Guildford High, King's Wimbledon, Royal Grammar Guildford, Hampton and Tormead. No formal links with any of these schools but the trend it would seem is for the academic and or sporty day school.

Remarks: A very large school that tries hard to maintain the tone and feeling of a small school. The pre-prep is separate from the main school and has its own dining room. Each section of the school, pre-prep, middle school and upper school has their own head who in turn reports in to Mr Parfitt. Different year groups have their own block of classrooms, yet they have access to all the facilities on offer. Some parents have misgivings about the increasing size of the school believing that it has already got too big and unwieldy.

The centre of the school is a large Victorian House, to which various buildings have been attached. Classrooms are mostly bright and clean. Unlike many prep schools that outgrew their original buildings in an explosion of ad-hoc additions, a great deal of thought seems to have gone into the planning and function of the buildings. The new dining room is a large, modern space that doesn't smell of boiled cabbage – a choice of hot or cold meals (plus vegetarian) is on offer and if you are to believe the sign 'school dinners makes you good looking'.

Danes Hill has a reputation as an academic hothouse, for example, there are 100 children in a one particular year group and 41 of them are in scholarship classes. The school feels that this academic hothouse label is not quite fair. For although they achieve excellent results this is, the school believes, because pupils are highly motivated and encouraged to learn. Some parents are unsure. They feel their children are pressurised but these same parents also accept that their children are generally happy. Just how good is Danes Hill academically? At key stages 1 and 2 the school gets better results than most. In the 1999-2000 academic year, nine pupils (aged 13) passed GCSE German with 5 A★s, 2 As and 2Bs, and 25 out of the 58 school leavers won awards to top senior schools.

Languages are a strength, with French, German and Spanish on offer. There is also a strong language support centre and fulltime staff are available to provide one-to-one support for children with dyslexia (mild) and dyspraxia. The new science block with its state-of-the-art laboratories is one which many senior schools would be proud to own. Pupils are set for most subjects from 8/9 years, and have a carousel system for non-academic subjects such as music, DT and drama.

Superb art at the school. Wonderful examples adorn all the walls with art taken as a mainstream subject. As a result, many prestigious art scholarships have been won to various schools. There is a flourishing drama department, which puts on several major productions every year in the 'Ark' – an imaginatively designed, multi-purpose theatre. The school offers a wide range of musical instruments for individual tuition. Four choirs, jazz band, orchestra and brass and guitar ensembles are all available for the would-be musician.

Sport is compulsory and there is lots on offer. Mainstream sports for boys are rugby, football, cricket, tennis and swimming, and for girls, netball, swimming, athletics, tennis and hockey (quite a few girls play football too). They are also national biathlon champions. Some parental grumblings here as many feel that the size of the school has outstripped the available sporting facilities. One says 'there are quite a few children who are good little players, but who never make the sides,' to which the head replies '98 per cent of children will have represented the school by the time they leave.' A wide range of clubs and activities are available, from sailing (Danes Hill hosts the IAPS regatta), dry-slope skiing, golf, archery, judo, chess, needlework, to horse riding.

Pupils come mostly from the upper middle-class set (professionals, investment bankers etc), with an odd celebrity here and there. Mostly British, although a few expats (American, South African, Asian) make up the mix. Catchment areas include Oxshott, Claygate, Esher, Weybridge, Leatherhead and Kingston.

Strong parents' association which provides the school with fundraising through social events (normally excellent by all accounts). Pick-up and drop-off times are a nightmare according to one parent, even though the school has a 'wonderful' fulltime security man who calls himself 'the fat controller' and helps with the traffic flows.

There is a strong pastoral care system in place. Clear anti-bullying policy and discipline issues are based on respect for others and good manners. Size is definitely an issue for those parents who feel that a survival of the fittest syndrome exists. However this is balanced by those who maintain that the size of the school enables it to offer something for everyone.

Fully co-educational, providing a good balance between the needs of boys and girls – no sense of this once being a boys only school. Ideal for the capable or self-possessed child. Not the school for the child who needs too much hand-holding.

THE DRAGON SCHOOL

Bardwell Road, Oxford OX2 6SS

TEL: *01865 315405* FAX: *01865 311664*

E-MAIL: dpd@dragonschool.org

WEB: www.dragonschool.org

◆ PUPILS: 453 boys, 174 girls. 206 boys and 65 girls board. Plus 118 boys and 85 girls, all day, in the pre-prep – Lynams – on separate site ◆ Ages: 8-13, pre-prep 3-7 (but nursery entry being discontinued, with more in at year 1) ◆ C of E ◆ Fee-paying

---

Head: Since 1993, Mr Roger Trafford MA (fifties), married to Cheryl, with two grown-up sons. Educated at Forest School, London, then Hertford College Oxford, a historian. Previously head of Clifton Prep, before that head King's College Taunton Prep, and before that head of English and housemaster at Colet Court. Accessible, moved his office to the middle of the campus (keeps door open). A beady-eyed wandering head, he turns up everywhere, in the classroom, on the games field. 'Never know when Trafford is going to come round the corner.' Knows school, little boarders have tea chez Traffords, and leavers' dinner in groups of 15. A super helpful head. Aims to give the children 'two feet to face the world', 'the world's getting tougher' and to develop their interests 'to the best of their abilities'.

Entrance: By early registration – embryos not OK – though immediate places available in exceptional circumstances (and in the middle of term for visiting profs to Oxford). Non-competitive academic assessment a year before entry, head sees parents, waiting lists. Easier to board than day. Takes occasional refugees from London hothouse preps – worth a try at odd stages. Lots of pupils from abroad, particularly Hong Kong and ex-pats. One of the schools which fields state school pupils bound for Eton. Tres chic little prospectus with Oxford blue cover.

Exit: To 95 different schools over the past few years, but most to Eton (has over 100 here at any one time) and St Edward's Oxford. Largish numbers to Marlborough, Abingdon, Radley, Magdalen College School; otherwise all over the public school shop, from Cokethorpe to Wrekin. Regularly wins squillions of scholarships for everything (30 in '00).

Remarks: Still one of the best, most exciting and charming academic prep schools in the country. This is a genuine co-ed (though girls say they feel like the minority they are), with boarding houses cleverly broken down to give a sense of belonging and a feeling of cosiness in what is, in fact, a large school. The school projects an image of informality – scruffy cords, the scruffier the better (bomber jackets only worn by day pupils), and even scruffier casuals after school. This laissez-faire attitude to outward appearances charms the children who feel that somebody somewhere is on their side. Underneath, however, the school is very disciplined with rigorous academic timetable and absolutely no messing about allowed in class. Terrific staff loyalty, all computer literate or trained in special needs teaching in the classroom.

'Learning Support' available (though this is not the place for severe dyslexics). Maximum class size 22, average 19. Seven streams in each year after the junior school, but school will fast stream a child up three forms (within their age group) if necessary (or drop). Maths, French and Latin setted separately. Top two (of seven) streams do Greek, German or Spanish in their last two years; Japanese, Mandarin and Italian available as extras. Masses of computers everywhere (produces own CD-ROM's) and more scheduled. Close links with school in Tokyo – pupils and staff regularly exchange and are plunged into Japanese school life.

Good music, with choirs, orchestras, boys' jazz bands etc. Some charming, unfettered art. State of the art theatre with grown-up sound box and lighting (operated by boys). Indoor pool with art centre above. Lots of options. Trips to eg Japan (has links with school there,) Calcutta, Barbados, Brunei.

Boarders have extra TLC in tiny houses (up to 20 pupils live with house parents, matron etc). Building new junior girls boarding house – against the trend. All meals moved to central feeding (new hygiene regulations, alas), but tinies will still have bun break and tea in houses. Horizontal tutorial system throughout. Top class pastoral care throughout. Day houses opened in '95. Masses of sports, traditional rugby, hockey, tennis, cricket, but also sculling (good at that), canoeing etc.

Enthusiastic at mainstream sports – words such as 'slow start', 'promising' and 'frustration' feature in the school magazine write ups. Terrific parental support, however. Teaching days usually end at 4.15, with activities thereafter. Punishments for class disobedience, the five-minute rule which can end in detention or copying out. Occasional sacking for theft or OTT.

Conglomerate of purpose-built blocks mingling with Victorian North Oxford, girls' boarding house opened September '94 by parental request. New girls' house in 1997. School bought another site in 1995 about a mile away (for pre-prep, v v popular). Children can play by the river when they have passed their 'clothes test' (two lengths of swimming pool in clothes). Lots of Dragon traditions, including Draconian (school mag), Christmas fair, Stooge's dinner. Favoured staff have nicknames, Smudge, Chips, Lofty, and were known as Ma and Pa, as were house parents (though some are called Sue, Ruth, Henrietta) but: 'we call them "Sir"', corrected a pupil. Fierce Old-Boy loyalty. A very exciting school to be at, and a place OBs are very proud to have attended, but don't send your daughter unless she is robust.

DULWICH COLLEGE PREPARATORY SCHOOL

42 Alleyn Park, London SE21 7AA

Tel: *020 8670 3217* Registrar: *020 8766 5525*

Fax: *020 8766 7586* E-mail: fva@dcpslondon.org

✦ Pupils: approx 820 boys, 795 day, 25 boarders ✦ Ages: 3-13 ✦ C of E ✦ Fee-paying

---

Head: Since 1991, Mr George Marsh MA (fifties), previously head of Millfield Preparatory School and before that taught for eight years at The Dragon School and ten years in state comprehensive schools. Tactful, beady-eyed and – rarer than you might think in this world – genuinely loves children and enjoys their company. Has 'softened' the approach to children here and introduced system of 'good show ups' in which children come to see him and get a star and a chat when they have done well – so they don't solely associate the headmaster with bad show ups. Five star head – 'the tops', said an ex-pupil.

Entrance: Through own excellent nursery school at three, otherwise at four or five, or into cosy, lively infants' school at seven (large intake) or eight. All children who are registered are assessed – numbers registered are restricted.

Exit: Around one-third to Dulwich College, fair numbers to Westminster, Tonbridge, Marlborough, Eton and other academic schools. Regularly gets lots and lots of academic and music scholarships.

Remarks: Absolutely wonderful academic prep school doing everything and doing it very well (and by the way, no relation to Dulwich College). Very large and much prized in South London. Not pressured (unlike Central London preps); some parents fearful of size – 'will my little cope?' - but they seem to love it after a week. Five streamed forms in each year from the age of ten (no streaming from seven to nine), average class size 20. Set on edge of leafy des Dulwich in unprepossessing houses, with asphalt playground behind. In recent years the school has added a multi-purpose building which would not disgrace a university, a 'magnificent new teaching block' which, reports head, is the envy of all the other local schools, new science labs and a language centre. Music is top class – all children can read music by the age of nine, lots of choirs (including one for parents) and school puts on ambitious and wonderful performances including eg the Mozart Requiem. Also super art department – imaginative work, tireless staff, good teaching and much display round the premises. Good school bookshop – mostly manned by older boys. Excellent maths, French and English teaching in particular. The school is a centre of excellence for design technology and information technology. Lots of clubs and activities; aforesaid parents deeply involved (not a school to patronise if you haven't got lots of time). Super deputy head is working wonders on the pastoral system. School has its own little boarding house – Brightlands – just down the road – 13 acres in woodlands with capacity for about 35 boys – weekly and flexible.

DUNHURST

(BEDALES JUNIOR SCHOOL)

Petersfield, Hampshire GU32 2DP

TEL: *01730 300200* FAX: *01730 300600*

E-MAIL: dunhurst@bedales.org.uk

WEB: www.bedales.org.uk

◆ PUPILS: approx 190 in Dunhurst; 80 in pre-prep Dunannie; boys and girls. Approx 60 board ◆ Ages: 8-13, pre-prep 3-8 ◆ Non-denom ◆ Fee-paying

Head: From 1998, Mr Michael Piercy BA (mid thirties), educated at Gresham's and Leicester – read English. Married, two young children, previously deputy head of Forres Sandle Manor. Interests sport, drama, music. Took over from acting head Mike Lucas who held the fort following the early retirement of the five star and much loved Heslops. A very tricky act to follow.

HEAD OF DUNANNIE: Since 1987, Miss Sarah Webster (forties), trained at the Froebel Institute, did MA in psychology, has taught in America, travelled in Africa and worked in France for two years. Came here from the Unicorn School in Kew. Top-class professional, dedicated and thoughtful.

Entrance: No testing of littles, but testing for Dunhurst from 8+ as they move on, almost automatically, to Bedales. Older children are tested for everything, come for 48 hours 'like a junior civil service exam' and spend a night or two boarding and getting to know the school. Entry at 8, 9, 10 and 11 and occasionally at 12 (so now you know).

Exit: Bedales, apart from one or two. The school does not specifically prepare for common entrance.

Remarks: Under the last heads was a five-star prep school. Interregnum between previous heads leaving and new head arriving was unsettling. For the first time in our memory, one or two real complaints – including it's 'cliquey', child 'not happy', 'school's gone downhill' – and disappointed comments continue to come in.

Still, however has many excellent qualities. As the majority of pupils go on to Bedales, the school is not stuck in the strait-jacket of common entrance (for those who want to go elsewhere, almost all schools will make adjustments for the difference in curriculum). No streaming, setting for maths only; at 11+ start secondary curriculum. Good maths staffing. Biggest class is 22; art etc, not more than 12; lower down the school the class average is 18. Follows national curriculum in some subjects, shadows in others to keep curriculum as broad as possible, eg might spend a fortnight studying the Bayeux tapestry.

Art, music and design and technology are all timetabled (all excellent) and form integral part of school life – not shuffled on to sidelines. Pupils have three supervised music practice sessions a week (148 out of 170 now learn an instrument). Eleven-year-olds do prep in study periods which are timetabled (shades of Dalton method – or 'all at sea' as one mother put it) and keep their prep recorded. Each child at 11/12 has a tutor and individual sessions each week going through their whole work file – so, by the time they get to Bedales they should be able to work on their own. There is no formal competition, no public marks or lists posted up. Good PE facilities (use of Bedales where necessary). Other preps pour

scorn on Dunhurst's (lack of) prowess on the games field – but not with reason, as pupils 'can be keen as mustard and you've got to cater for it' and they have been known to do brilliantly. Pupils can seem a little spoilt. One boys' boarding house and one girls' known as 'wing'. New junior boarding wing for 8-9 year olds opened in '00 and already full. All children involved in local charity work. Lots of trips, particularly in the summer, eg to Edale (sic, coincidence).

Meanwhile, Dunannie is still super. Four and a half teaching staff plus four assistants, two members of staff to each class. Some specialist help providing individual lessons in maths and English. Class size 'approx 20'. Carefully structured timetable from 8.30-12, then 'more free-flowing afternoon'. One of schools to take part in the Nuffield Design and Technology project, and this is excellent in both schools. Good library, classrooms, Wellington boots kept at eye level (so they don't get kicked around). Own garden (and gardens for children to cultivate), large sand pit, adventure playground (designed by the children).

EATON HOUSE THE MANOR

58 Clapham Common Northside, London

SW4 9RU

TEL: *020 7924 6000* FAX: *020 7924 1530*

E-MAIL: EatonHse@aol.com

✦ PUPILS: Pupils: 130 boys. Plus pre-prep with 255 boys and girls (and nursery 60 boys and girls) ✦ Ages: 8-13, pre-prep 4+ to 8, nursery 2- to 4+ ✦ C of E ✦ Fee-paying

Head: Since 1993 Mr Sebastian Hepher BA (mid-thirties), previously taught at Eaton House near Sloane Square, and has taught in both state and private senior schools. Gentle, straightforward, enthusiastic, married with a young daughter in the nursery school here, and a baby son. Keen reader. The Hephers have a house in the south west of France, which they go to 'whenever we can.'

Entrance: Put names down early (at birth for the nursery) – entry at 4½ on a first-come first-served basis. At 7½ or 8 ;by assessment (English and Maths are what matter) – either taken at previous school or on an individual basis as and when. No automatic entry from the school's own pre-prep. Scholarships for 8 year olds: 1 academic, 1 music, 1 sport.

Exit: At 8 to Ludgrove, Summer Field, Sunningdale; also Northcote, Westminster Under, Colet Court, Dulwich College Prep School, King's Wimbledon Prep. At 13 all over the place – Latymer, City of London, Dulwich, Wellington, Marlborough, Stowe, Bryanston, Eton, Radley, Harrow, Alleyn's, Westminster, King's College Wimbledon.

Remarks: Younger brother school of the old established (1857) Eaton House School near Sloane Square (pre-prep only, for boys ages 5-8): boys at both branches wear the same holly green and red uniform. Mr and Mrs Harper are Principals at both these schools, (also The Vale, in Elvaston Place is part of their empire). The Manor was set up in 1993, and took a while to get seriously established. Now it is definitely a first-choice school, well run and happy, with prep., pre-prep and super nursery school all on site. Distinguished main Georgian house, with Victorian additions plus newly purpose built block behind, with attractive courtyard. Previously part of South Bank Polytechnic (ie lots of teaching devices already in place), and before that a prep school. Acres of green with Clapham Park just across the road. Children mainly from Wandsworth, Clapham, Stockwell; the school runs a bus service to/from Eaton Gate, another from Parsons Green.

Pre-prep uses the same excellent teaching methods as its older brother school across the Thames – i.e. children are taught in small groups within the class according to their ability (which is mixed). Pre prep and nursery (both super) are round at the back of the school, the latter smelling deliciously of baking the day we visited).

At 8 boys are streamed, two parallel classes per year group, Latin for all at 8, specialist teaching staff in every subject from second year in prep. Small special needs department, with its own tiny classroom. Lots of male teachers, average age of staff 35 (several with public school teaching experience). Thorough teaching throughout, big emphasis on reading. Supervised homework option from 4 till 5 p.m. every day. Light bright classrooms, and good equipment, big gym, theatre. Keen games. Busy extra-curricular programme, with lots of clubs (including clay-pigeon shooting and photography) – this is a work hard, play hard school. Boys appear industrious and cheerful, and not over-pressurized – but it is competitive place. House system, cups galore. Plenty of parental involvement. Popular with parents – 'Just the right balance of tradition and spark' according to a father.

EDGE GROVE

Aldenham, Hertfordshire WD2 8BL

Tel: *01923 855724/857456* Fax: *01923 859920*

E-mail: headmaster@edgegrove.indschools.co.uk

Web: www.edgegrove.co.uk

✦ Pupils: around 150 boys, 75 board, 75 day
✦ Ages: 8-13 (Also 130 mixed from 2-7 in St Christopher's Edge Grove) ✦ C of E
✦ Fee-paying

Head: Since 1997, Mr J R Baugh, BEd (forties), formerly head of Solefield School (a prep school in Sevenoaks). Educated Aldenham School, and St Luke's College, Exeter; taught geography at Haileybury. Married to Wendy (fully involved in school life); two girls. Keen on sports (esp soccer). Keen IAPS committee man. Nice line in ties. Took over from Mr Jolyon Waterfield, whose father was co-founder of the school.

Entrance: Registration and non-competitive testette three terms before pupil is due to come into school. About a third of pupils come from school's own pre-prep. Most pupils from within a one-hour radius of school. Over 10 per cent of parents living abroad.

Exit: A rich mix. Most currently to Harrow, then to Oundle, some to Haileybury, Uppingham and nearby Aldenham, some to Eton, then all over the place.

Remarks: Low-key prep boarding school with increasing day element. Fine seventeenth-century building and grounds in apple pie order. Formerly the property of J P Morgan. Whole atmosphere of the place is more like a country house party than a prep school. Largest dormitory an elegance of wood panelling – and hence no posters. Wood floors, bags of spit and polish and flowers, no carpets. Head and family live 'over the shop', five-star gardener has cottage in grounds. Back of buildings less prepossessing than front. Good modern science block; computer centre, music centre etc. Two form intake, then streaming at age ten or eleven. Full-time learning support teacher, plus two part-time assistants. Maximum class size 18; average 16.

Keen ski club. Enthusiastic music – three-quarters of pupils participate. The new head concurs with the school's long-running conviction that 'the important thing is being part of a team and getting on with other people' – an approach which is less common in prep schools than you might think. Pupils have exquisite manners.

EDUCARE SMALL SCHOOL

12 Cowleaze Road, Kingston-upon-Thames
KT2 6DZ

TEL: *020 8547 0144* FAX: *020 8546 5901*

E-MAIL: educaresmallschool@btinternet.com

WEB: www.educaresmallschool.org.uk

✦ PUPILS: 41 boys and girls ✦ Ages: 3-11
✦ Non-denom ✦ Fee-paying

Head: Liz Steinthal (fifties) CertEd MA, ex state school deputy head. Hands-on teaching of 5-11's. Husband, Peter is bursar 'in his spare time', resulting admin creaky but serviceable. 3 grown-up children muck in as required. Head's mother does legendary baking for PSA and reading support.

Entrance: Mostly first come, first serve. Kindergarten: 'Don't even need to see the child, but of course it's nice for them'. From 5: Meeting with parents and child. Special needs can be met, although several applicants (gently) refused. Dyslexia well supported.

Exit: Kindergarten leavers to state primaries (many stay on). At 7, state primaries or local independents with alternative reputations. At 11, Head actively works with parents to 'find a school that suits the individual'. 'It's a hard act to follow' (leaver's mother).

Remarks: Self-declared 'School for the future'. Holistic approach with equal emphasis on physical, social, emotional and academic development. Charitable trust established 1997. Maximum 50 children.

Individual learning programmes taught in small groups. Fees kept to a minimum, allowing access to largest possible cross section of pupils. Bursary scheme funds 1 full time place. No school uniform.

Froebel-trained teacher leads kindergarten in structured play, much socialising, basic numeracy and literacy. Well-equipped classroom, exciting home made props, own computer. Gentle transition to the upper school 'when the time is right for the child'.

The Head, a classroom assistant and one teacher take two classes in the school hall. Teacher's post has, one suspects, seen more changes than wanted in 3 years. Fourth incumbent brings specialisation in primary science.

Curriculum covers everything expected, although no RE (appeals to minority faith / no faith circle). School assembly focuses on physical well being and the practice of warm up exercises drawing on aikido, tai chi and Alexander technique. Pupils engage in daily 15 minutes semi-meditative 'quiet time'.

Peripatetic teachers offer weekly French, Music and Alexander technique. Parents help with tennis coaching, craft, reading, and cookery. Extra-curricular parental activities include plumbing, DIY, gardening and soft furnishing.

No typical Educare parent. School attracts everyone from the X reg. Mercedes brigade to those who are more financially challenged. Common link is that they are committed to alternative style education. A few might have gone conventional prep school route, won over by the humanity of it all. Appeals to foreigners particularly Americans; 5 ESL pupils.

Housed in a converted 19th Century Baptist chapel of some charm, in a singularly charmless area of North/Central Kingston, amidst run down housing and light industrial estates, minutes from the railway station. Very Manhattan: multi-painted walled car park, security-gated playground with vibrant collaged perimeter wall, planted tyre mound, and 10-foot mosaic totem pole. 'It always seemed sunny there' (ex-pupil).

Designed and decorated interior, some parental comment that space inside and out might prove insufficient to absorb the energy of livelier youngsters. Weekly PE takes place off-site; church hall in winter and local rec. in summer.

Atmosphere of positive reinforcement; reward stickers abound. Firm but fair exclusion from the group meets wrong doers, never a raised voice, nor a harsh word. Healthy eating policy (fruit, no chocolate crisps or juice) and enjoinment to drink plenty of water.

You will either love it or hate it. Not a school for those wanting their children sitting in rows learning their tables. A broad education in its widest sense Children able to achieve full potential, excellent creative work from all ages. School turns out pupils dripping high self-esteem and happiness.

ELSTREE SCHOOL
Woolhampton, Reading, Berkshire RG7 5TD

TEL: *0118 971 3302* FAX: *0118 971 4280*

E-MAIL: office@elstreeschool.freeserve.co.uk

WEB: www.elstreeschool.demon.co.uk

✦ PUPILS: around 200 boys. 100 board, 100 day. Pre-Prep: around 65 boys and girls
✦ Ages: 7-13, pre-prep 3-7 ✦ C of E
✦ Fee-paying

Head: Since 1995, Mr S M Hill MA (Cantab) – read geography and education – (fifties), previously a housemaster at Malvern College. A big man with a sporty background – soccer and tennis blue – and a sense of humour (we think). Super wife, Jane, who is 'much involved in the school'. 'Very proud indeed' of the school's tutoring and pastoral care system.

Entrance: No test. 25 per cent from London, a few from abroad, rest from the Thames Valley.

Exit: Bradfield, Eton, Harrow, Marlborough, Radley; and a number of other well-known schools.

Remarks: Traditional prep school in fine Queen Anne country house with stylish additions (designed by Basil Spence) – lots of play space, woods, tennis courts, marvellous classrooms, dorms, dining room, etc, log fires in the hall in winter. Streaming, setting for senior classes, good teaching for dyslexics and EFL (four part-time staff). Reasonable scholarship record. French continues a special strength, good DT and computers all over the place. Marks for effort first.

God very important – assembly for morning prayers, quiet period observed nightly for reading – and particularly Bible reading (more than one-third of the boys ask for Scripture Union notes); good manners high on the list too. Lots of games – rugby, football and hockey throughout the two winter terms as well as squash, shooting and golf on own course. Strong tennis. New sports hall '99. Good art and music (boys design the stage sets themselves for the annual musical). Strong on extra-curricular activities, with astronomy (real 12-inch reflecting telescope). Wonderful Form 4 exercise, 'Ye Olde Rubbish', reproduced in school magazine. Too many day boys now for boarding comfort, but parents of day pupils are warmly enthusiastic about the school, and the influx of day pupils has made it a livelier place.

NB Pre-prep, HOME FARM SCHOOL opened in 1993, in lovely eighteenth-century farmhouse in the grounds, proved popular at once; staff here headed by Mrs Evans. Good reports reach us.

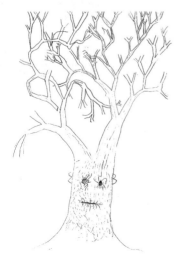

FALKNER HOUSE

19 Brechin Place, London SW7 4QB

Tel: *020 7373 4501* Fax: *020 7835 0073*

E-mail: falknerhs@aol.com

♦ Pupils: 140 girls, all day ♦ Ages: 4-11, also co-ed nursery, ages 3-4 ♦ Christian non-denom ♦ Fee-paying

Principal: Mrs Flavia Nunes, a star. Keen sailor. Famously talkative. Catholic. Founded the school in 1954, was the driving force behind it, and now plays a supportive role as a partner with her daughter.

Head (and the daughter in question): Since 1999, Mrs Anita Griggs BA PGCE (mid forties). Educated Queens College, London and York universities, taught economics at St Paul's Girls' School. Mother of four. Succeeds her elder sister, Mrs Jacina Bird, who was head from 1988. Mrs Griggs strongly supports the ethos that the school is 'one big family', and that it runs in her blood, she was brought up in the school.

Entrance: Girls tested at age three or four, and 'only the bright ones' are picked. Mrs Griggs firmly believes it is possible to winkle out brains at this age, though comments that 'she may well miss many highly competent girls.' Worth trying for a place later.

Exit: To London day schools eg Francis Holland (both), Godolphin and Latymer, St Paul's, More House; fewer now to boarding schools, but 25 per cent to eg Wycombe Abbey, St Mary's Calne.

Remarks: Housed in two large, light, gracious, prettily decorated red-brick buildings behind Old Brompton Road, with playground in front. Solid phalanx of very experienced staff, plus one or two younger. Inspired music – almost every child learns an instrument and some two. Art appreciation for all. French from the start. Latin from age of nine (grammatical approach). Spanish. Excellent grounding in three Rs. Part time learning support – and learning difficulties are regarded as 'par for the course' – a very comforting approach.

Head keen that 'parents should appreciate their child's own strengths and weaknesses by observing work done at home.' Homework help and clubs available after school. All girls taught computer/keyboarding skills. 'Early' and 'late' Bird system (in honour of the previous head) – children can be dropped by eg fathers driving in from suburbs at seven-thirty, and left after school till six-thirty at night. Bliss for overburdened mothers. Maximum class size 'usually' 20. No streaming or setting. Despite posh image, school accepts from all backgrounds and all are welcome. Mrs Griggs' study is at the top of the house, away from the hurly burly, but the door is always open. Lunch is served in tiny basement room (a miracle). Lots of nice little touches.

Much thought goes into the school day and opportunities grasped, courtesy of extensive networking (eg the purchase of a garden square-ette 120 yards away – super secret garden). Some games on site, but pupils transported by bus to sports centres, and sport taken seriously. Good noises from parents.

FARLEIGH SCHOOL

Red Rice, Andover, Hampshire SP11 7PW

TEL: *01264 710766* FAX: *01264 710070*

E-MAIL: ofice@farleighschool.co.uk

WEB: ourworld.compuserve.com/homepages/
farleigh

+ PUPILS: 290 boys and 110 girls; 110 boarders (boys and girls, more full than weekly), rest day + Ages: 3-13 + RC + Fee-paying

Head: Since 2000, Mr John Allcott. University in Exeter and Oklahoma. Comes from being head of the junior schools at King's School, Worcester, and before that ('82-'95) a teacher at Ampleforth. Married to Cecilia (who is active in the school); three children (two at Farleigh, one at Ampleforth). Governor = Rosemary Groves of Marlborough.

Entrance: At 7/8 children need to be well grounded in the basics; plus a letter from previous school.

Exit: To a mixture of Catholic and non-Catholic schools – Ampleforth, Marlborough and Sherborne the top choices, Eton, Harrow, Canford, Radley in there too. 14 scholarships in '00.

Remarks: Formerly a boys' Catholic prep school, now turning into a co-ed all-purpose day/boarding school. Good for middle of the road. Solid learning support centre with full time qualified co-ordinator and helpers caters for dyslexia/dyspraxia and the requirements of the very able. Some excellent teaching, and staff popular with parents and pupils, also eight dogs on the staff. Children divided into three or four sets of 7 to 18 pupils each (varies with subjects). Average class size 16. Encouragement and praise generously given; stars allotted for effort. French at 8, Latin at 9. Super art; new Acorn Risc PCs, lesser computers 'cascaded down' to other departments. Lots of sport, and splendid modern sports hall with lots of natural light (unlike most); also good music centre. Not a rich school but financial whizz on the governing board. Former head revamped and moved the library in 1995 – re-organising books, methods, above all 'getting children to know how to use the resources'. Library tables set up with chess boards, at time of our visit, ready for play by club members. Fine Georgian country house with many later additions (mostly inherited from former incumbents – Red Rice School). Handsome stucco work, fireplaces, fine proportions, polished wooden floors, whole house light and airy, charmingly painted in shades of yellow and blue (school colours). 60:40 ratio RC to non-Catholics: Christian values very much underpin the ethos. Entire school attends Mass on Friday; voluntary attendance on daily basis. Dorms (named after Saints) alive with teddies and jolly duvets. Girl boarders admitted for the first time in '94 (nineteen weekly, eleven full as we write) – making this more of a co-ed enterprise. Lovely grounds of 50+ acres and specimen trees. Lots of activities and clubs – the speciality of deputy head Philip Watts, (prep-school born and bred, son of co-founder of Moor Park), many day pupils stay till 5.30 or later every day. A happy place, with pleased parents.

FELTONFLEET SCHOOL

Byfleet Road, Cobham Surrey KT11 1DR

TEL: *01932 862264* FAX: *01932 860280*

E-MAIL: pcw@feltonfleet.co.uk

WEB: www.feltonfleet.co.uk

✦ PUPILS: approx 300 in total (two-thirds boys, one-third girls). 47 boarders (boys only), rest day. Nursery and pre-prep with approx. 70 boys and girls.
  ✦ Ages: 7 – 13, pre-prep 3 – 7
  ✦ mainly C of E ✦ Fee-paying

Head: Since September 2000 Mr Phillip Ward BEd (forty but looks younger). Educated at Reigate Grammar School and Exeter University. Spent 17 years at Uppingham (he is a huge fan) working his way up the ranks to senior housemaster. Married to Sue, who plays an active wife of the headmistress role. Two children both at Feltonfleet. Succeeds Mr David Cherry who had been headmaster since 1990. Mr Cherry was responsible for ridding the school of its 'boot-camp' image, introduced girls and turned Feltonfleet into a popular local school. Mr Ward intends to go one step further and make it 'a leading edge prep school'. He is one of the new breed of polished and personable young headmasters. Switched on to both marketing and education he realises that if the school is to hit the big time nationally he has to get rid of its macho image and broaden its appeal – not least to girls. Although an enthusiastic sportsman (he is keen to boast about the school's sporting prowess) he wants to see less time spent on sport – he is looking for quality rather than quantity – and more on culture and creativity. He is also aiming to give more attention to the children 'who are not in any of the teams and who never get seen doing anything'. Boarding for girls is on his agenda.

Entrance: Difficult due to the small numbers and long waiting lists. Early registration required, but it is always worth regularly checking whether there are odd places available. Entrance at 3 for nursery – no tests – but according to Mr Ward 'if the child is obviously a dribbler and has no desire to learn creatively' then it may not be the right school. Most children from the pre-prep go on to main school, but there are places for outsiders although it becomes selective at 7+, requiring an entrance test and interview. Mr Ward comments that the school 'is not an academic hothouse' but a pupil must show clear evidence of being socially and educationally aware.

Exit: Boys mainly at 13. Popular choices locally include Royal Grammar Guildford, King's College Wimbledon and City of London Freemen's. Nationally, they head for schools such as Bradfield, Wellington and Tonbridge. School only been co-ed for about five years so too early to see any trends develop for girls. Girls mostly leave at 11 (in Surrey most of the girls senior schools have their main intake at 11 rather than 13). Locally, girls have gone to the big name private schools Tormead, Guildford High, Sir William Perkins's and Surbiton High.

Remarks: A small school with big ambitions under its enthusiastic new head. The pre-prep is known as Calvi House and is set quite apart from the main school. Run by the superbly capable Mrs Jan Preece who can keep parents and children in check with a single glance.

The main school is housed in a hodge-podge of buildings, all emanating from a central Jacobean manor house. Classrooms vary from modern and airy to old and a little scruffy. The hours are long for a prep school (8.15am – 5.30pm), it makes for some very tired children but they get used to it, and much of the homework is completed during these hours which many parents find an added bonus.

Academically, Feltonfleet is strong and holds its own against many of the bigger schools. In 2000, the school leavers managed to snare some useful scholarships, which included the maths scholarship to Harrow, academic scholarships to Royal Grammar Guildford and all-round scholarships to Tonbridge and Epsom.

Children are streamed for Maths and English at 8+ and again at 10+. Class sizes are small, with the max being 14. All do Latin from age 9 but may drop it later on. French is compulsory from age 3 and much is done in the way of trips and events to foster interest and the spoken word. Not a school which specialises in learning support but there are some children with conventional and moderate learning difficulties.

Flourishing drama department. Musically, the school puts on three concerts every term (junior, middle and senior sections of the school) and every child is encouraged to play an instrument as well as sing in the choir. A bit ho-hum – there are some parental mutterings about boring material and teaching style. Mr Ward has heard the musical rumblings and intends to 'give relentless support to this area'.

Traditionally, a very sporty boys school. Girls' sport is still at a Cinderella stage but it is on the up. A full time girls' PE specialist has been appointed. 'In three years time, girls' sport here will be one of the strongest' says Mr Ward. Indoor swimming pool could do with smartening up. Superb new sports hall offers a great deal of scope for new games activities, including basketball and badminton.

Some parents do not chose the school because they feel it is still too macho and not suitable for timid or shy boys or girls. Other parents in the school have the opposite view and praise the pastoral care. 'The nurturing aspect is one of the school's strengths' says a parent. Parents are a mix, but are largely professional and well off. Mr Ward describes them as 'typically Surrey'. Active parents' association. Usual car park battles – too little parking, not enough time- but no major dust-ups. You take your life in your hands as you drive across a very busy road to get to the school, but once inside it is a green and pleasant environment with happy pupils.

FINTON HOUSE SCHOOL
171 Trinity Road, London SW17 7HL
TEL: *020 8682 0921* FAX: *020 8767 5017*

E-MAIL: fintonhouse@zoo.co.uk

✦ Pupils: 102 boys, 160 girls, all day ✦ Ages: 4-11 ✦ Non-denom ✦ Fee-paying

---

Head: Since 1996, Miss Emma Thornton MA Cantab PGCE (thirties). Previously deputy head at James Allen's Prep School (where she was wonderful) and before that head of Upper School at Finton House. Known as 'Miss Emma'. Jolly. Popular with parents. Succeeded the widely respected Miss Terry O'Neill, co-founder of the

school, and Finola Stack, now head of Cameron House.

Entrance: Much sought after. Non-selective. Put names down early. Places appear in later years, always worth checking. 3 special needs places a year.

Exit: Some move to 'the country' before 11. Some of the boys leave at 8+ for boys prep schools (Northcote Lodge, Eaton House, Dulwich Prep, Kings). School happy to prepare for 8+ exams (there are many that won't). At 11+ to wide variety of day and boarding schools (Putney High, Wimbledon High, JAGS, Francis Holland, St Mary's, Ascot, Woldingham, Benenden, Port Regis, Dulwich etc).

Remarks: Smallish school with strong family feel and parent-friendly atmosphere. Children are local to Smart Wandsworth. Parents all seem to know each other. Recently expanded to accommodate a third class per year group. Two handsome and well-proportioned Victorian houses sensitively adapted for school use, light rooms, good library, lots of stairs (would be difficult for children with physical disabilities). Good sized playground. Unflattering, rather dreary uniform for girls. Classes are of mixed ability, within which there is a great deal of individual teaching. In one year there are 9 separate spelling groups. All the staff know all the children extremely well. French throughout the school. Music department notably strong with music tuition for all pupils plus individual lessons. Active after-school clubs. Useful, no-nonsense magazine, which, for once, feels as if it is for the children and parents rather than for PR. The school is known for being one of the few private schools to integrate special needs pupils and offers 3 places a year to special needs children (epilepsy, Down's syndrome, partially sighted, profoundly deaf etc) who are fully integrated, as far as their disability will allow, with the rest of the class. The school's team of therapists and special needs assistants (a staggering 12 full-time and two part-time) means that children with learning difficulties can be helped on site on a one to one basis (many schools claim this, few actually deliver). Be warned, like most private schools, there is a charge for extra help and it can add up. School used to have a problem keeping boys at 8+ (a common problem for co-eds that stop at 11 and not 13) but the Head has worked hard to encourage them to stay and there is now a fully co-ed class at 8+. Much sought after. Happy, well-rounded children. Emphasis on individuality and results without pressure is its forte.

FRANCIS HOLLAND JUNIOR SCHOOL

Graham Terrace, London SW1 8JF

TEL: *020 7730 2971* FAX: *020 7823 4066*

E-MAIL:office@francishollandsw1.westminster.sch.uk

WEB: www.francishollandsw1.westminster.sch.uk

✦ PUPILS: around 170 girls, all day ✦ Ages: 4-11 ✦ C of E ✦ Fee-paying

---

Head: Since 1984, Mrs Molly Bown DipEd (fifties), elegant, sparky, on the ball. Came to teaching late, her first career was as a ward sister. Grown-up son and daughter (husband works in the medical world). Turned the school around. 'I'd seen really good schools and knew what I wanted.' Has chosen some excellent staff to work with her. Encourages girls to 'say what they think – I tell them they don't have to agree with me, I want to know their views,' and also emphasizes manners. Some complaints that she passes problems on to head of senior school instead of dealing with them herself.

Entrance: At 4. Children are 'tested' in January for the September term: causes problems for parents whose daughters are offered places at other schools the previous October. Mrs Bown and staff see 100 for 24 places (potential is sought).

Exit: About two thirds go into the senior school (via London Schools Consortium exam).

Remarks: Strong girls' pre-prep and prep school with happy children (if one or two ruffled parents), in the centre of London, with senior school on site across the playground (very useful for extra space). Modern block with large, light and bright classrooms; computers, PE, pottery and some art, also music done in the senior school. Pictures on the wall everywhere, and slogans such as 'Jolly Jennifer eats juicy jellies'. French from eight. All girls are reading by the age of six; very regular spelling homework (help for learning difficulties, but they rarely crop up). Sound basic 3 Rs. Too traditional for some. Very strong project work – as strong as any we have seen – involving research encouraged from eight-year-olds onwards. Girls choose a composer to write about, or choose from a range of inventors, scientists, pioneers, and are guided towards source material, a regular weekend homework, and madly popular, eg World War II for which they get in locals to speak from experience and go and grill the Chelsea Pensioners, etc. They also learn to talk about their subject to the rest of the class for five minutes. Not surprisingly, these children are articulate and fearlessly tell adults of their interests and work. Science club popular.

Good mixing with senior school, sixth formers come over to hear reading, etc. The head reckons the children don't need remedial teaching, but as there are two staff to each class, she can whip them out and train up at odd moments as necessary. Girls in 'houses', as per main school, so children of all ages mix. Plays and music and charity fund-raising galore. Some complaints that parents don't feel they have direct access to the staff (head disputes this), and find, to their surprise, that the prep school 'is not autonomous'.

GARDEN HOUSE SCHOOL

53 Sloane Gardens, London SW1W 8ED

TEL: *020 7730 1652* FAX: *020 7730 0470*

E-MAIL: gardenhs@aol.com

✦ PUPILS: approx 270 girls, 100 boys (number of boys growing); all day ✦ Ages: girls 3-11; boys 3-8 % Non-denom % Fee-paying

Head (Principal): Since 1973, Mrs Jill Oddy BA = owner/ administrator. A five star mover and shaker, with a keen eye for the main chance. Has recently bought a school in New York.

Head (OF UPPER GIRLS): Since 1998 Mrs Janet Webb, CertEd, took over from Mrs Rosemary Whaley who was here from 1993. Runs school jointly with the v popular Mrs Wendy Challenor, CertEd Froeb,

who has been head of the lower girls since 1988.

Heads (OF BOYS): Since 2000 Mr Magoo Giles (pastoral) and Mr Simon Poland (academic).

Entrance: At three and four, later if/when places arise (always worth a try). Pupils come in from dear little local nurseries eg Young England, Smallies, Knightsbridge Kindergarten, etc. Entry test one year before entry. Long waiting lists; put down name asap. NB in common with other inner London preps, charges astronomic fee on firm offer of place – £950 at time of writing; not the sort of ethics that you hope for in a school, but it concentrates parents' minds wonderfully.

Exit: Boys: Northcote Lodge v popular. Girls to Downe House, Heathfield, Francis Holland SW1 and a clutch of gentle girls' schools.

Remarks: Dear little girls' prep school in central London – stone's throw from Sloane Square. The school has recently mushroomed out into new ventures, with a separate site in Pont Street for the boys (see below). Girls: Charming main house – carpeted, flowery, light with nooks and crannies for individual tuition, pretty pictures on walls, friendly and gentle atmosphere. Big drawback is it looks out onto buildings on all sides, there is no good daylight, no outside space, and communal gardens a no go most of the time – it's off to Battersea Park or Burton Court (nicknamed Poo Park) etc for games (minibus). Little science lab in the basement and top-class science teacher. Meals also in basement – cramped but perfectly OK. Parallel classes for girls all the way up the school. Size of classes 15-20. Maths set. Ambitious parents have been known to take out their children half-way up the school for less charming more 'stretching' establishments – rumblings of unhappiness about staff in recent years – but the school has countered this with a 'scholarship class' getting four to six assorted awards a year (to Tudor Hall etc). Special needs teacher comes in four days a week. Investigative maths – puzzles, learning to think for themselves. 'Serious' work from the word go. French at four, French nationals on tap. Parents are doctors, architects, solicitors/American bankers (many Sophies and Charlottes), lots of siblings. Clubs after school. Lots of poetry. Homework 'club' till 5 pm every day.

Boys' School: 26/28 Pont Street, SW1X 0AB Tel: 020 7589 7708, Fax: 020 7589 3733. Lots of space when we visited – nice big rooms, albeit a fair amount of it in the basement. Lots of sport including fencing and judo. New computer/media room is based here too for both sexes. Average class size is now 15. Could be a very jolly solution for central London parents, and has loads of American appeal (looks, not pushy, designer label, v English, glam staff, raising children to be young ladies in well kept premises.) Prep boys: four rooms in a church in Sedding Street.

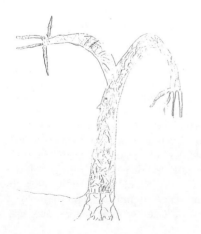

GEORGE WATSON'S PRIMARY SCHOOL

Colinton Road, Edinburgh EH10 5EG

TEL: *0131 447 7931* FAX: *0131 447 7931*

E-MAIL: d.mcgougan@watsons.edin.sch.uk

WEB: www.watsons.edin.sch.uk

✦ PUPILS: 431 boys, 360 girls; also 100 in the nursery; all day ✦ Ages: 5-12, nursery 3-5 ✦ Non-denom ✦ Fee-paying

Head: Since 1989, Mr Donald McGougan DipEd (forties), educated at Campbeltown Grammar School, then Moray House. Unmarried. An internal appointment: was form teacher then deputy head before achieving this post. No thought of 'trying to produce a typical Watsonian: not all in the same mould'. Wants children to be happy and clamps down on bullying. Chuckles. Aims to produce 'well-educated children who excel in every possible area'. A wandering head, 'pops into the odd classroom': assisted by a 'timetabled wandering gang of three assistant heads (one of whom doubles as form teacher) and two deputy heads'. Nothing escapes their notice. Head teaches each of the six Primary Seven forms.

Entrance: At five and every term thereafter if space available – can take next day if ditto. Assessment and test at five, eight-year-old tests tied to the National Curriculum – an indication of potential. Serious waiting lists at five and 11 (state schools). No automatic transfer from nursery: no special bias in favour of FPs' children.

Exit: Very occasional leakage at eight to traditional prep or public schools (they usually go at 13 anyway), most go on to the senior school (qv) unless outside circumstances dictate otherwise.

Remarks: Very large, but cosily encampused on George Watson's mega site, surrounded by, and with use of, all senior school facilities. Shares labs, science and technology, home economics, but own music staff and modern language staff. Clubs for everything, orchestra from age eight, pipers, also Brownies, Guides, Computer Club, and for art and drama, etc. etc. Hockey, jogging, cross-country, sports hall, etc. Classes vary in size from 22 in Primary One, to 25/6 in Primary Seven. Famous with the senior school for teaching dyslexics: 'the Cabin', as the learning centre is called, is without rival in Scotland. Full- and part-time teachers, pupils either receive support teaching in the class or go for individual lessons at the Cabin. Support staff are constant throughout. Nails its colours to the mast in the prospectus with the headline 'we believe that learning should be fun' (less common a belief than you might think).

GLENDOWER PREPARATORY SCHOOL

87 Queen's Gate, London SW7 5JX

TEL: *020 7370 1927* FAX: *020 7244 8308*

E-MAIL: office@Glendower.Kensington.sch.uk

WEB: www.Glendower.Kensington.sch.uk

◆ PUPILS: around 185 girls, all day ◆ Ages: 4-11 ◆ Inter-denom ◆ Fee-paying

Head: Since 1986, Mrs Barbara Humber BSc (forties). Previously at Colet Court, where she was head of science for nine years. Very keen that girls should be taught science and provided with the same facilities as boys. Comment to parent: 'we are a very social school'.

Entrance: At four and a half; also ten places for seven-year-olds. All potential pupils are interviewed (though not IQ tested). Put names down early.

Exit: All at 11. The majority to London day schools – largest numbers of places accepted at Godolphin and Latymer and St Paul's recently; also a fair number to boarding, largest numbers to Wycombe Abbey and Downe House.

Remarks: Girls' prep school in smart inner London which enjoyed years of great popularity as a result of its reputation for 'stretching' pupils and for being rather hotter on science than most of its nearest rivals. In these matters however other schools have caught up, if not overtaken, Glendower, which is consequently, though still popular, no longer flavour of the month.

Structured teaching starts at an early age – French at four, setting at nine, combined science for all at eight. Girls do electronics and soldering – in spare time as well as class; Latin at ten for all, computers used from four onwards. Some 'support teaching' offered in English and maths.

Very cramped premises, with children spilling out into the hall and stairways and every inch of space used to the hilt. Expansion plans in hand. Class sizes: up to 22 in lower school (each class has one qualified teacher and one assistant); upper school 14-16 pupils. Staff are young, keen and otherwise switched-on. Good music. Delightful art – fresh, and without the dead hand of the teacher in it. Lots of visits and lectures, clubs after school five days a week. Teams win most netball matches, and IAPS netball and swimming champions in '99 – they use Imperial College swimming pool. Active Parents' Association. Startling purple uniform. Glendower progressed from a dame school (founded in 1895 – recently celebrated its centenary) to a well-established jumping-off place for academic senior schools. All school lunches are vegetarian – and served in classrooms (tablecloths etc laid out by girls), with 'a lingering smell of cauliflower,' reports a parent.

GODSTOWE PREPARATORY SCHOOL

Shrubbery Road, High Wycombe, Bucks
HP13 6PR

TEL: *01494 529273* FAX: *01494 429001*

E-MAIL: headmistress@godstowe.org

WEB: www.godstowe.org

✦ PUPILS: 123 boarders, 214 day girls. Also pre-prep of 118 boys and girls, all day ✦ Ages: 7-13, pre-prep 3-7 ✦ C of E ✦ Fee-paying

---

Head: Since 1991, Mrs Frances Henson BA PGCE (forties), previously deputy head of Thornton College, educated 'in the maintained sector' in Lancashire, followed by a history degree at Warwick, and PGCE at Nottingham University. Teaches history, and positively lit up when we asked her if she still did. Lives in the grounds with husband who works in educational publishing, and two teenagers. Able. 'Loves this age group'; pupils greet her without shyness – despite the somewhat ritualistic 'Good morning Mrs Henson,' she greets both staff and pupils by name. Quietly spoken, firmly efficient, fun and proud of the place.

Entrance: Not a selective school. Entry at 7 or 8 for the main school. Currently the place is full on all fronts, 'and another boarding house is being considered'. Apply early. Academic scholarships at 8 and 11.

Exit: Pre-prep boys usually to trad boys'

boarding at eight. Girls to major senior schools, including Wycombe Abbey, Cheltenham Ladies' College, Downe House, Benenden etc etc. Most take CE at 13, with scholarships and exhibitions on all fronts (19 in '00). Small trickle to state sector at 11.

Remarks: The first girls' boarding prep in the country, purpose-built 1900 (with later extensions). Magical new music school (with spectacular views across the graveyard) and serious re-vamp of older buildings, particularly the dining room. Brilliant use of very hilly ground on outskirts of High Wycombe, assault course and outdoor activity areas. Four boarding houses, one for weekly boarders. Masses of activities at weekends, plus clubs and options. Excellent PSHE in place and girls get lifestyle course after CE that includes lectures from representatives of The Body Shop.

Pre-prep has expanded hugely; now has new separate buildings. French from age four. Latin or Spanish at ten. Classes 'subtly' streamed. Maximum class size 18, scholarship stream. IT, art, marvellous textiles, and ceramics, fantastic music (long tradition of this) with masses of girl-inspired concerts. Dyslexia help on hand, with one-to-one help where necessary, regular spelling and reading help available. EFL also available, though only about 5 per cent foreigners (not counting ex-pats). Some MoD parents. School is very much on form as a day school with boarders in the background – 'the only good one [ie girls' prep] in the area' say parents.

THE HALL SCHOOL

Crossfield Road, Hampstead, London NW3 4NU

TEL: *020 7722 1700* FAX: *020 7483 0181*

✦ PUPILS: around 430 boys; all day ✦ Ages: 4-13 ✦ C of E ✦ Fee-paying

Head: Since 1993, Mr P F Ramage MA (fifties). Educated at Warwick School and Cambridge – Historian and cricket blue (he describes himself as 'quite gamesy'), keen on the theatre, and on antiques. Previous post was as head of St John's Northwood, before that he was at Bedford Prep ('for six happy years'); started his teaching career in the senior school of UCS so, in geographical terms, he says, he has 'come full circle'. A good egg. Mrs Ramage, who is a splendid soul, is involved in admin and social matters in the school – a very present help ('she is everything', comments Mr Ramage). They have three grown up boys. Deputy heads are Ros Bond (junior), Craig Watson (middle) and Garry Pierson (senior school). After rocky start to the nineties, the school is once again in good safe hands, and ones which are unlikely to move before retirement. Mr Ramage is a twinkly soul, calming, with a great sense of humour, warmth for all under his care – including the tinies – who says modestly that really all he has had to do so far is 'bring some stability to the place'. Mr Ramage is a mixture of enthusiastic but laid back – perfect for this school. He also projects an air of confidence, much appreciated by one and all.

Entrance: You must register early to stand a chance – at birth if possible, but certainly by the time the child is two, though it is always worth approaching the school for gaps at odd moments. The school registers the first 125 names which come in – to avoid taking registration fees under false pretences (registration fee a modest £50, however). Children come from all the local pre-preps – Stepping Stones, Broadhurst, Phoenix, the Children's House in Islington etc. Fees are just over £2000 to £2,450 a term.

Exit: More on average to Westminster than anywhere (there are apparently more boys from The Hall at Westminster than from any other prep school), after that Highgate, St Paul's, Eton, Harrow, King's Canterbury, Winchester etc. Got four academic and four music scholarships to major schools in '00. Plenty of famous OBs, including Stephen Spender, who bequeathed a bijou gem to the school including the line: 'It would be such a hackneyed (sic) thing; I must not write about the spring'. Among distinguished former heads (of the junior school) was E H Montauban, who was one of the founders of Stowe (parents of Hall boys subscribed for the first library here).

Remarks: A highly academic prep school which has, in the few years of Mr Ramage's reign, climbed back into its position as numero uno assoluto academic boys' prep school in North London, and well worth bustling about to get into. The school is on two sites – tinies 4–8 in a nice light house surrounded by playground in Buckland Crescent. The head's house is above the shop here, so he gets to know the littles particularly well, treading among the trail of scarves and pink blazers which litter the junior school (but not the senior school – older boys think they are 'cissy'). New building opened in '98 to serve as middle school, with form room-based teaching (but using specialist facilities of the senior school). The building also has an underground car park (hallelujah) and new all-purpose hall. Major building projects underway in the senior school.

The 'senior' school (and note there is a very firm line drawn between it and the junior school) in Crossfield Road has a very school-boyish atmosphere. Bags of effervescence, a strong smell of science stinks as you walk through the front door, was not all in the best of decorative order – well-scuffed surfaces everywhere, and not exactly a pretty sight – but better now. There is however some excellent art on the walls (really impressive), fine music (four scholarships to senior schools last year) and good IT in the basement where the boys get to grips with basic principles and obviously find it very refreshing after the academic grind (and it is a bit grind-y). There is a constant state of unpeaceful co-existence in the road, (thoughtless double parking), but recent purchase should help relieve pressure on space. Class sizes show 'a little flexibility': fifteenish in the class but 'it could be eighteen'. 'No nothing' in the way of setting until 10, then setting for maths and English. At 11, for the first time, 'we identify a "quicker form"'. Two parallel forms. Occasional drop-outs who can't take the pace move to calmer establishments. Very occasional complaints re lack of encouragement and advice for pupils.

There is a wonderful and mad keen computer man – Mike Fitzmaurice, who has survived the successive heads, and another enthusiast in the shape of Mr Gilbey-Mckenzie, who is in charge of the scholarship form, particularly keen on drama – every form, incidentally, puts on a play, and drama is on the timetable even at the top of the school – set against current affairs (sound idea). Latin for all at nine, Greek as a club activity. Science for all – investigative work goes ahead of the course. Endless patience is taken with those who fall by the wayside, and the school is very astute at spotting those with problems at home – both these things are great and unexpected strengths of the place.

The school uses the Wilf Slack Ground at Finchley for games – twice a week (soccer, cricket etc), and reports it has become very good at fencing: number one among prep schools at time of writing, beating even Sussex House. Parents are north London high powered barristers, media, etc (big Jewish contingent), with a surprising number of fathers at the top of their professions with much younger wives. Traditionally a very demanding difficult lot. However, Mr Ramage appears to be totally in control of the situation.

The school was started in the 1880s by Francis John Wrottesley, who as a 'father of a growing family of boys,' decided the best way to educate them was to start his own school. From this time it has grown in strength and distinction – get a copy of One Hundred Years in Hampstead for a fascinating read – even includes some of the school songs (Carmina aulariensia).

HANFORD SCHOOL

Childe Okeford, Blandford, Dorset DT11 8HN

TEL: *01258 860219* FAX: *01258 861255*

E-MAIL: hanfordsch@aol.com

WEB: www.hanford.dorset.sch.uk

✦ PUPILS: approx 110 girls; all board ✦ Ages: 7-13 ✦ C of E ✦ Fee-paying

Head: (Joint Heads): Since 1995, Mr and Mrs McKenzie Johnston (Mrs 'M-J – emjay') (late forties) who took over from the Sharps and run the school with Miss Sarah Canning MA (late sixties), who is still very much present, running things, looking after the ponies and generally being splendid. 'Sarah', as she is known, owns the school and is the daughter of Clifford Canning, the distinguished head of Canford, who started Hanford with his wife, Enid. Mr (Lt Col, though he's dropped that) M-J read economics at Cambridge and was a professional pongo, and ended up teaching at Shrivenham before coming here where, he says, he can hardly believe it's work. Mrs M-J is an occupational therapist – and so doesn't teach. Sarah at the moment still lives in the school, while the M-Js are in 'Fan's House' (a not too special building in the grounds), but the idea is that eventually they will move into the school, with its lovely drawing room. The MJs appear to be the perfect couple for the job – he is fun, enthusiastic and she is an exceptionally warm and friendly soul, totally 'unhead-mistressy', brilliant at being with the children and at treating them as human beings.

(Some parents have complained that she treats them as children.) Mrs MJ is an OG of the school. They have three daughters, one in the school.

Entrance: All are welcome. Pupils are very English, a combination of locals, girls from the south and west, Londoners in need of real country life, and numerous families posted abroad (26 Services' children at last count). One teeny music bursary – the Helen Smith award.

Exit: Mainly to good girls' boarding schools in the south, including Sherborne Girls (always a good number here, and regular scholarships), Marlborough. Regularly gets scholarships to division one girls' schools. Increasingly girls are staying on to 13+, and not just those going to co-ed schools – is it parents keeping tender flowers in a younger environment, or just the saving on fees?

Remarks: One of the nicest if not the nicest boarding school in the country, with a gentle, kind, friendly, enthusiastic, if slightly twee, gloriously happy-go-lucky, genuinely family atmosphere. A place you can feel absolutely confident leaving your ewe lamb in, with the knowledge the school will probably do a better job of looking after her than you would yourself, and almost as a side issue, give her a thorough grounding in CE subjects, and a fun time with it. Some outstanding staff, all very experienced (if anything too little turnover) and indeed one of the cooks who died a few years ago having cooked Christmas lunch was in the school for OVER FIFTY years. The head gardener is eighty-three.

Excellent French under Mrs Boulton who champions the French series 'Il etait une Grenouille' – the pupils are usually way past the standard of their senior school by the time they leave, and all articulate, with good pronunciation. There are three streams, and setting within those streams can split right down to one pupil if necessary – 'we're desperately flexible,' says Mrs MJ. Maximum class size is 15 at the moment. No EFL but the school has a full-time remedial teacher, who helps with any difficulties.

The art was outstanding under Ann Babington, producing work which would not disgrace an art foundation course in a wide variety of disciplines – wonderful sculptures in particular; appears to be continuing so under Lucy Yemenakis (a professional potter). Good grounding in technique, but this does not dampen the pupils' creative excitement. Computers came nowhere in the general scheme of things when we last visited, but the MJs report they are 'moving into' them, with eleven PCs and IT from the fourth form up, and they are connected to the Internet but 'computers do not drive our teaching'.

Sport is top class, under Bedford-trained Sarah Butt, who was head of PE at Downe House and captain of the England lacrosse team. The school regularly wins everything (in particular, short tennis) and again, although they do not train teams ('you train the school') very thorough teaching is given, though when we visited the whole school had actually been tobogganing. Gym club v popular, outside in summer; visitors arrive to find girls standing on their heads.

Excellent pastoral care – 'it's all done by trust', kindness and common sense rule. There are 'no punishments' says Mrs MJ, but they get SYRs – (serve you rights) if they do something silly. These could involve writing down some truly boring long poem while everyone else is having fun. Pupils are labelled (and re-labelled every week with great excitement by their peers) according to their good manners – starting with 'Piglets' (the bottom) and scaling the heights to 'Royal guest'. There are no fixed exeats 'so parents can choose', no uniform (except for games) and basically 'no changes' says Mrs MJ, from the previous regime.

A terrific feature of the school is the large numbers of furry Thelwellian ponies they own (22 at last count) – all can ride and they have a covered riding school. The ponies, by the way, have walk-on parts in the school plays which are memorable, and all take part. and there is a wonderful wardrobe room. The school takes the shabby chic look to an art form. The main building is a glorious 1623 manor house (instantly seductive to parents and children) in an antique landscape (Iron age barrows, Roman fort remains, rolling Dorset countryside). Inside, lots of polish, wonderful old rugs, slightly peeling paint, well-worn wood, and the dorms are quite Spartan – some have carpet, otherwise you're lucky if there's a rug. Old iron bedsteads groaning with teddies 'as many as they can fit in' says Mrs MJ. In the garden, there is an enchanting chapel in beautiful grounds, and the veg garden supports the school, except for potatoes. Teaching is done in a series of what feel like rabbit hutches – a bit sad and squashed looking, though no one seems to care. Pupil numbers on the up.

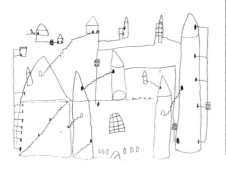

THE HIGH SCHOOL OF

GLASGOW JUNIOR SCHOOL

27 Ledcameroch Road, Bearsden, Glasgow G61 4AE

TEL: *0141 942 0158* FAX: *0141 570 0020*

E-MAIL: hsogjs@globalnet.co.uk

WEB: www.hsog.demon.co.uk

✦ PUPILS: 159 boys, 165 girls. Nursery 54 boys and girls. All day ✦ Ages: 4-10 ✦ Non-denom ✦ Fee-paying

Head: Since 1974, Miss Eileen Robertson MA CertEd (fifties), educated at Perth Academy, Edinburgh University and Moray House. Has total autonomy with staff appointments. 'In the classrooms all the time.' Aims to 'educate the whole child'. Much admired.

Entrance: At three and a half or four. Waiting lists, though vacancies may become available throughout the school. Priorities to siblings, FPs' children, then rest of the field.

Exit: Automatic transfer to senior school and almost all do.

Remarks: The Glasgow prep they all –with good reason – fight to get into. Umbilically attached to the senior school (see separate entry) and it often feels as though the tail is slightly wagging the dog. Elegant Victorian house almost totally surrounded by cunning collection of additions. Classrooms off buttercup yellow main passage with cosy area for tinies, and room upstairs for learning support.

Group teaching, aggressively academic. Tinies start to learn at four. Good learning support that carries through to senior school. Computers in classroom, IT strong, French everywhere when we visited – no Latin.

Junior school shares senior school facilities, bussed to Anniesland for rugby, hockey and swimming at Allander Centre. Lots of (good) music, and drama being built up. Very strong local support, Lord Macfarlane of Bearsden (FP) is Honorary President of the school (not to mention former chairman of Distillers') and much in evidence. Lots of first-time buyers. Kindergarten opened in '96, extension added '97. After school care for pupils has recently been introduced – pupils looked until after 6pm. Middle-class bias, doctors, lawyers, and high work ethos.

HIGHFIELD SCHOOL

Liphook, Hampshire GU30 7LQ

TEL: *01428 728 000* FAX: *01428 728 001*

E-MAIL: office@highfieldschool.org.uk

WEB: www.highfieldschool.org.uk

✦ PUPILS: 110 boys, 84 girls; 100 boarders, 94 day pupils. Brookham pre-prep on site, 118 boys and girls ✦ Ages: 7-13, pre-prep 3-7 ✦ C of E ✦ Fee-paying

---

Head: Since 1999, Mr Phillip Evitt MA (early 40s). Educated at Kimbolton School and Cambridge (history and PGCE).

Taught at Monmouth School, and then at Dulwich College for fourteen years. Teaches history. Married to Joanna, solicitor and homeopath; four young children at Brookham and Highfield. Succeeded Mr Nigel Ramage, head from 1993.

Entrance: By registration and interview, must be up to scratch on their reading and writing; visit school for informal test. Most from within A3 corridor from London. Many ex-pats and Services' children.

Exit: Recently to reasonably nearby schools such as Marlborough, Bryanston, Charterhouse, St Swithun's, Eton, Wellington, Canford, Bedales etc.

Remarks: Purpose-built redbrick conglomerate in 175-acre grounds. Lots of woods, cows, pats, pets. Traditional chapel, good games hall, a theatre (hideous hard benches now destined for the bonfire), drama in Chapel and Assembly as well as a school play each term. Music thriving and head of music composer in his own right. New library and junior house recently revamped. New classrooms and IT room. Tennis courts good and floodlit hockey in winter. Outdoor swimming pool.

Girls dorms jollier than boys, but posters and own duvets everywhere. One boys' dormitory – Wellington – has a canon firing a canon ball through a hole in the wall, and a large shark bursts into the boys' changing room. Recently installed central heating and hot water system throughout school. new light central atrium. Superb art, and art centre opened by Penelope Keith in '95 – head of art a practicing artist.

Takes 'some children who have dyslexic problems and one or two dyspraxics' – 'extra English' department of three teachers provide learning support (extra). Maximum class size 18, three forms in a year, streamed from year 5. Latin timetabled, Greek as a hobby. Games on computers in free time. 'A thrust to raise academic standards is further underway.' Daily reports for slacking. Serious naughtiness equals no sweets on Wednesday. 'Quite a few' first-time buyers. Boarding no longer compulsory.

HIGHGATE JUNIOR SCHOOL

Cholmeley House, 3 Bishopswood Road, London N6 4PL

TEL: *020 8340 9193* FAX: *020 8342 8225*

E-MAIL: Jsoffice@highgateschool.org.uk

WEB: www.highgateschool.org.uk

✦ PUPILS: approx 370; plus 130 in co-ed pre-prep; all day ✦ Ages: 3-7 pre-prep; 7-13 prep ✦ C of E foundation ✦ Fee-paying

Head (The Master): Since 1992, Mr Simon Evers BA in English, CertEd (early fifties). Previously head of Worksop College prep, before that wide-ranging experience from VSO to trainee booking clerk in Cooks. One of teaching dynasty – four brothers, all teaching or having taught, grandfather was housemaster at Rugby, father was head of Sutton Valence. Laid back (some parents say 'too laid back'). Married with two sons – wife helps in school. One of the head's first changes on being appointed was to move his office from top of school into the body of the kirk, where all rush past. Members of staff commented in the early days that perhaps he could be tougher on discipline – but clear code of conduct long since established.

Entrance: Main points of entry are 3 (v v popular – get your place early), 7 and 11 (though try any time). Entrance exam in January and February for September. Some from local primary school, St Michael's.

Exit: All are 'expected' to transfer to Highgate Senior School – see separate entry.

Remarks: Junior school for Highgate in grounds of senior school which has increased in popularity in recent years owing not just to geography but also to increased success of the senior school. Good sports facilities (uses the senior school facilities), including the 18 fives courts (not surprisingly, the junior school beats everybody at fives). There is housing for a proportion of the staff – an enormous draw in this expensive area of north London. Super green rolling country-like site between Highgate Village and Kenwood – cluster of buildings grouped round the playing fields of main school, with lots of room. Shares dining hall – modern light block with good choice of food, tinies eat in separate room. Uniform reverses colours of senior school.

Streaming and setting from 11, but no year places and no form places – assessment twice a term for attainment and effort. School has nice relaxed feel of an establishment which exists for education rather than cramming for CE. Form tutors are first contact with parents, parents collect tinies from classroom. Very popular pre-prep housed in separate bizarre-looking building tucked away, formerly a boarding house; 7-9-year-olds also have their own quarters – Field House – super form rooms of 16 or so – three forms at seven plus, four at 11 plus. Average class size 18, with 16 in years 3 and 4, rising to 21 in years 7 and 8 (maximum size). Parents have reported a 'bit of bullying' from time to time – otherwise good reports. School has anti-bullying code, and 'circle time' – a time of self-assessment when pupils can express their feelings and thoughts honestly. Pupils sons of local professionals, some actors. Largish numbers of ethnic minorities, including Jewish, Muslim. John Betjeman was taught here by T S Eliot. Inspired art master. Computers easily accessible lining walls in classrooms – and all boys in the top half of the school have their own computers at home – v useful for project work. Lots of nice touches – eg younger boys change in classroom, leaving pile of clothes on each desk to avoid chaos of changing rooms.

HILL HOUSE INTERNATIONAL

JUNIOR SCHOOL

17 Hans Place, London SW1X 0EP

Tel: *020 7584 1331* Fax: *020 7591 3938*

✦ Pupils: up to 1,100 (currently 1067): 700 boys, 400 girls; all day ✦ Ages: 4-13 ✦ Non-denom ✦ Fee-paying

---

Head: Owner and founder in 1951, Colonel H S Townend OBE MA (Oxon) (ninety in 1999 and STILL GOING). Educated at St Edmund's, Canterbury, read maths and science at Oxford, followed by a diploma in French, German and Italian. An educational institution. Enormously charming and fun, the Colonel wears his years well, claims 'never to sleep in England, only on an aeroplane or in Switzerland,' where he spends half of every week running the Swiss side of Hill House.

Runs school without secretarial or bursarial help, takes a dim view of Schools Inspectors – considers their reports not worth reading (ditto guides, we guess). Colonel Townend has no intention of either retiring or dying, but if he did his son Mr Richard Townend (late fifties) (Westminster School, Lausanne University and the Royal College of Music), who teaches music in the school, would take over, assisted by his very able wife, Janet (Saffron Walden Teachers College, Cambridge).

Entrance: Idiosyncratic entry process- one of the very very few London private schools which puts the childrens' needs before its own. Is often a very present help to parents arriving at odd moments from abroad (but don't count on a place). The school is open to parents every weekday, between 8 and 9 am (nowadays you can ring to make an appointment); prospective parents may tour the main school on Wednesday after assembly. After assembly in Pont Street Church Hall they are introduced (or not, as the case may be) to the Colonel to whom they hand a green slip of paper with their child's name, date of birth and required date of entry. Two weeks later they are sent an official confirmation, which is followed nearer the proposed entry date by an information pack. The school has four terms or quarters, starting in January, April, August and October; but the Colonel will admit any child at any time, as the need arises, if he sees fit.

Exit: As you would expect, some to trad prep schools at eight, but otherwise boys to Westminster, St Paul's School, Dulwich College, Harrow, Eton, Stowe, etc., and girls to More House, Francis Holland, St Paul's Girls, JAGS, Benenden, Cheltenham Ladies', Downe House, etc. NB parents report that – understandably – the school does not prepare children for prep school entrance exams at 7+.

Remarks: A unique school: people love it or loathe it. Colonel Townend is Hill House, terrific emphasis on challenge, sport, almost 50 per cent pupils foreign (Americans in particular find it easy to relate to). School scattered around Knightsbridge and Chelsea, chronically short of space (no we're not says Richard T,) with different ages in different locations, and crocodiles of orange and brown knickerbockered children (girls can opt for culottes or skirts) moving in orderly (or not) file, hands behind backs, to swim at Chelsea Baths, play sport (lots of it) at The Duke of York's Barracks, or Hyde Park, or in the local church hall. Buses for almost everywhere else, though the Bentley shooting break is also labelled 'school bus'.

Lots of young (pretty) staff, many from South Africa, New Zealand and Australia, all called 'tutor'; fast turnover a thing of the past, says Richard T: 'most staff have been here for over five years.' Staff paid small sum for attending evening meetings. Each department has its own head. V cosy buildings in Flood Street, Milner Street, Pont Street, Cadogan Gardens (380 children) and Hans Place. School fondly nicknamed 'Hell House'. All buildings self-contained, with own dining room, etc. Tiny classes at bottom rising to no more than 12 at top – pressure now descends heavily during the last two years. Traditional, rigorous teaching, giving a good grounding in main stream subjects. All children learn to sing (full time choral animateur) and three-quarters learn an instrument; pianos and music rooms everywhere. Computer lessons for all in last six years, and much staff use of laptops. Good science, languages, art, etc. Special help for those needing extra English. HRH Prince Charles here briefly. Huge eclectic mix. School opens daily at 8 am and closes by 1 pm on Friday. Usual punishment is detention after lunch on Fridays (their only free time), though little children sit cross-legged on floor outside head of department's door instead. Junior department super, girls hived off for entrance exams at 11 or 12 and, in the main, taught separately from the boys. Twenty 'Uppers' (8/12 – girls or boys separately) spend four-week periods at the Swiss base of the school, in Glion above Montreux, with lessons as normal during the week and skiing or water skiing at weekends. Last two years v hard work for the Brits, as lots of foreign nationals have left to slot into their own schooling systems.

HOLMEWOOD HOUSE

Langton Green, Tunbridge Wells, Kent
TN3 0EB

TEL: *01892 860000* FAX: *01892 863970*

E-MAIL: admin@holmewood.kent.sch.uk

WEB: www.holmewood.kent.sch.uk

✦ PUPILS: 510 boys and girls (290 boys, 220 girls); 20 weekly boarders, the rest day ✦ Ages: 3-13. ✦ Inter-denom ✦ Fee-paying

Head: Since 1998, Mr Andrew S. R. Corbett MA (forties). Educated at Marlborough, and Edinburgh, where he read history of art. Previous post – head of King's College School, Cambridge (though not a musician). Tall approachable, a man of action, wife a teacher, two young daughters. Before that director of studies, head of history and housemaster of a girls' house at Port Regis, and before that head of history at The Hall. A distinguished career. Took over from Mr David Ives, who was head here from 1980. NB School was put on road to fame and fortune by the famous Mr Bairamian.

Entrance: At 3 and 4 for nursery and pre-preps (no tests, but 'very occasionally we advise parents that children have serious problems that we are not equipped to deal with'). Also at 7 and 8 (and some at 11), with school's own tests.

Exit: To Tonbridge, Sevenoaks, Eastbourne College, King's Canterbury, St Leonards-Mayfield most frequently. Impressive collection of scholarships and awards every year.

Remarks: Strong academic prep, moving into a new regime. Boarding numbers have continued to decline, and full boarding ended in 2000. From year 5 Saturday morning school (almost always followed by matches), and day pupils stay till 6 or 7pm most evenings for prep and sports.

Every department ticking away, staff (loads of them, all ages, vociferous) are fantastically committed, well paid, energetic, some inspired – and not all everyone's cup of tea. An interesting bunch however – the former head has been busy collecting from all over, eg Natalie Clarkson ex-Olympic gymnast, Chris McGovern ex-Lewes secondary school history head where he lost his job for allowing some pupils to do the Scottish History exam, as well as the English History exam, and now part of team re-writing the history curriculum for our schools. Good New Zealanders etc, adding extra dimension – as do a handful of foreign students (TEFL lessons given) including Russians/Ukrainians – but will depart when boarding ends. Excellent remedial department (run by fully trained ex-parent) helps children via special brain gym as well as more conventional methods.

Streaming from year 3, but increasingly setted at older ages. Homework in principle done at school. Pupils bright and bouncy, well aware of high expectations but outward going and playful. Wonderful CDT. Good science labs with tiered seating for lectures/demonstrations. Lovely art, heaps of IT, well-used and well-stocked library with full-time librarian – rare in a prep school. Lots of teams for games – but not known as a strong sports school.

School founded post war, privately owned until the last head took over. Went co-ed in 1989; recently-built pre-prep. Decimus Burton house, boys and girls dorms recently modernised. Live-in house-parents in flats adjacent to the boarding houses. Other buildings tagged on at sides and back – a mish-mash. New music block opened '96 and 400-seat theatre opened in '97. Opening in '01, a 25 metre swimming pool and a rifle range. Good views at the back and playing fields, but an unlikely setting on the edge of executive homes estate.

One of the most expensive preps in the country, much sought after, and producing outstanding academic results.

HONEYWELL JUNIOR AND INFANTS' SCHOOL

Honeywell Road, Battersea, London SW11 6EF

TEL: *020 7223 5185 (Junior school)*

020 7228 6811 (Infants) FAX: *020 7738 9101*

E-MAIL: office@honeywell.wandsworth.sch.uk

✦ Pupils: around 360 boys and girls in junior school; 325 in infants' school; day ✦ Ages: 3-7 (infants); 7-11 (junior) ✦ Non-denom ✦ State, foundation

---

Head: Since 2000, Mr Duncan Roberts BEd DipEd NPQH. Read education and history at London, Previously deputy head and acting head here. Keen on music, sport and the cinema. Took over from Mr Dick Cooper, who was here from 1992.

Entrance: Via Infants' school – entry here guarantees a place in junior school. Harder to get into than some of the private schools round here – oversubscribed, waiting lists. It helps to live in the right catchment area. 'Occasional' vacancies for older children.

Exit: To Wandsworth foundation schools, a third to private schools in South London, Alleyn's, Dulwich, Emanuel, Whitgift and Trinity. Most popular state schools are Graveney, Burntwood and Elliott.

Remarks: Described by the head of a public school in London as 'the best prep school in South London'. Huge old purpose-built building, with its own tarmac playground; new all-weather pitch. Disciplined, well structured. Follows National Curriculum. Comes way above national average in standard attainment tests for 11 year olds (eg national average for English = 75, Honeywell 90). Lots of attention given to less able. The school has its own teacher specialising in the teaching of dyslexic children, and is running an experimental dyspraxia programme, which, says the head, 'looks like being very successful' – a pioneer in this field. Maximum class size 30; overall teacher/pupil ratio nearer 1:20. Two computers per class. Jolly art department – produces some good work. Also hot on music – this is one of the very few schools to offer free tuition, and to loan instruments (recorder, violin, 'cello). Lots of clubs, sport. Nursery class caters for half-day and all-day attendance. Happy reports from parents. Large contingent of satisfied middle class parents who comment 'if you can get into Honeywell we see no point in going anywhere else'.

HORDLE WALHAMPTON SCHOOL

Lymington, Hampshire SO41 5ZG

TEL: *01590 672013* FAX: *01590 678498*

E-MAIL: jb@walhamp.demon.co.uk

WEB: www.walhamp.demon.co.uk

✦ PUPILS: 337 (more boys than girls) of whom 210 in the main school (inc 69 boarders), 127 in pre prep ✦ Ages: 7-13, pre-prep 2-7 ✦ C of E ✦ Fee-paying

Head: Since 1998, Mr Henry Phillips BA (forties), educated at Harrow, worked as a stockbroker in the City before doing an Open University degree in English. Deputy head at Summer Fields, then head of Hordle which subsequently amalgamated with Walhampton (see below). Jolly, positive, decisive – popular with the children, 'He's a dab hand with the young,' according to a mother. Not everyone's cup of tea. His wife Jackie teaches PSHE, helps with girls' games, and is a matron. The Phillips have three children who are all in the school.

Entrance: At 7 (no assessment), or at 8 with assessment one year before entry; lots of children come in from the bulging pre-prep. Book early for the nursery. Popular with the army (a large contingent of Services' children from both schools), civil service, a solid contingent from the Isle of Wight (as day pupils or as weekly boarders).

Exit: To a wide variety, mainly the Wessex private schools, Canford, Clayesmore, Dauntsey's, King Edward's Southampton, Talbot Heath, a trickle to Winchester (there is a special board in the hall), Godolphin, Downe House.

Remarks: Has settled down after the shenanigans surrounding the merger of Hordle and Walhampton in 1998. Based in a splendid Norman Shaw adaptation of an earlier Queen Anne building (some original cornices, plaster work and wood carving are still in evidence) – ie, at what was Walhampton. The chapel is in the old music room, and the school has a huge entrance hall with roaring log fire and acres of parquet floor, elsewhere there are utilitarian additions, including a rather grim refectory dining room, however food is good. Wonderful grounds – almost a hundred acres – with ornamental lakes and fine trees.

Ponies (bring your own), sailing, and masses of options available. Numbers rising again after the '98 hiatus; school definitely runs as a boarding school with a very full timetable, this is attractive to day children who very often don't leave until 6.10 after 'activities' have finished. There are lots of these.

Little boys board at the Lodge, seniors in the main house and girls in the Clockhouse, all in cosy bright dorms. Extremely good pastoral care at all stages. Quite a hierarchy with 'patrols' and 'patrol leaders', and responsibilities accordingly ('everybody wants to be a 'patrol leader' explain the children). Sound rather than inspired teaching throughout, not many young staff: 'They could do with fresh young blood,' complained a father. Setting in maths and English from the age of seven, and setting in all subjects at the age of ten/eleven. Maths is a particular strength, Latin holds its own ('I fought to keep it' says the head), but no Greek, German recently introduced at the top end, and French from four onwards. Very good remedial help (but severe cases are not accepted). More IT than at our last visit, but thin on the ground compared with some schools. Library in line for a make-over, currently looks unloved. Particularly good woodwork, and some lively art. Excellent nursery and pre-prep, purpose built, with huge demand for places. Light and slick buildings, and bright purposeful staff. Quite a contrast to some down-at-heel areas of the main school, which the new energetic head has begun to sharpen.

HORRIS HILL

Newtown, Newbury, Berkshire RG20 9DJ

TEL: *01635 40594* FAX: *01635 35241*

E-MAIL: enquiries@horrishill.demon.co.uk

WEB: www.horrishill.com

♦ PUPILS: around 120 boys 100 boarders, 20 day boys ♦ Ages: 8-13 ♦ C of E ♦ Fee paying

---

Head: Since 1996, Mr Nigel Chapman BA (fifties). Previously senior-head at Lockers Park, educated at Felsted and London University. Married to Lindsay, three children. Keen family man. Mrs Chapman is fully involved in the school on the boarding and domestic side. 'He's going to be good', commented head of a nearby prep school. Took over from Mr M J Innes who taught here for a record thirty-five years, eighteen of them as headmaster.

Entrance: By registration. No entrance examination but 'little placing test' and it is sometimes gently suggested, but not insisted, that a boy might do better at a school more geared to remedial teaching.

Exit: Ten-year breakdown of where boys go on to shows Winchester top of the list with 59. Eton second, (57) – some record, Radley third (31). Increasing numbers to Marlborough. Some every year to Milton Abbey. OBs: Richard Adams, Richard Noble.

Remarks: A famous country prep school (nickname by boys 'Horrid Hell') which has managed to hang on to its traditional feel while softening the edges of discipline, environment, etc. A super place. One of few academically successful boys' prep schools at which boys have time to play with model aeroplanes, etc, have regular pit stops for 'cocoa' and generally behave like little boys rather than potential Derby winners. That said, the school works and plays hard. No horizontal streaming but school adopts the 'filtering' approach and boys are constantly on the move upwards which, says the head, 'keeps everyone on their toes'. Average rate of movement is once every two terms. Good remedial help.

Outstanding art department under Ian Keen (and keen is the word). Over 90 boys learn one musical instrument, eighteen learn two and two learn three. New director of music from Abberley – 'a real inspiration,' comments head. Whole room dedicated to wonderful model train set – pride and joy. Squash courts, very keen footie and cricket but not doing quite as well as thy have done at the moment. Pupils playing Horris Hill from other schools comment they're 'vicious'.

Classrooms recently done up. Average class size 11.9. Sports hall doubles as theatre – keen drama here. No speech day, no motto – 'no humbug', to quote the founder, who was an (ex) master of Winchester aiming to train up boys for entry to that school (date of foundation 1888). Both boys' and masters' houses are dotted around the grounds, which are pleasant and spacious, though main school building is of such hideous Victorian red brick that at one time the prospectus featured it heavily camouflaged with snow.

HUTCHESONS' JUNIOR

SCHOOL

44 Kingarth Street, Glasgow G42 7RN

TEL: *0141 423 2700* FAX: *0141 424 1243*

✦ PUPILS: 800 boys and girls ✦ Ages: 5-11
✦ Ecumenical ✦ Fee-paying

Head: (Rector) Mr John Knowles, as for the senior school, with acting depute rector Mrs Lorna Mackie DCE.

Remarks: This is an enormous junior school, in the most fabulous original Victorian academy, think green and cream tiles, think fabulous carved oak assembly hall, think huge sunlit classrooms (three of the old ones now converted into two), spacious, full of light, full of child inspired art with a super old fashioned gym. Exciting new build now houses the tinies, serious academic work here. One intake a year (but see above), all children assessed, 120/150 apply for 81 places.

French from six, serious little faces doing proper science, with male as well as female staff and lots of specialist staff. Computers all over, good learning support.

Reduced playground means timetabled breaks, main gym at senior school (bussed) but ten minutes' walk away, and bussed to Auldhouse for games.

Sibling discounts, in line with main school and after school club till 5.45 pm when pupils can do homework (costs extra in the evening, but early drop-off not a problem). Note five-year-olds only do a half day for the first term.

Most children go on to senior school, having learnt how to work (with a vengeance). Super – only snag is the parking, but school have 'a working arrangement' with the local supermarket (who built on what was the girls' sports ground – if you follow) and a 'certain number' can park there.

IBSTOCK PLACE

Clarence Lane, Roehampton,
London SW15 5PY

TEL: *020 8876 9991* FAX: *020 8878 4897*

E-MAIL: registrar@ibstockplaceschool.co.uk

WEB: www.ibstockplaceschool.co.uk

✦ PUPILS: 630; 300 boys and 330 girls; all day
✦ Ages: 3-11 junior school, 11-16 senior school ✦ Non-denom ✦ Fee paying

Head: Since 2000, Ms Anna Sylvester-Johnson BA PGCE (forties). Took over from Mrs Franciska Bayliss, who was here from 1984.

Entrance: At 3 and 11 – book very early, there are long waiting lists – entry is relatively unselective. Sibling policy.

Exit: At 8 or 11 for local mainstream schools eg Hampton, Latymer, and Godolphin and Latymer for girls; Pupils also go on to school's own senior school. Apres GCSE, Pupils go on to a wonderfully wide choice including Latymer Upper, Hurtwood House, KCS Wimbledon, Westminster

Remarks: School founded in 1894 in West

Kensington as the demonstration school of the Froebel Educational Institute, propounding the educational principles of Friedrich Froebel, the German educationalist (d. 1852), pioneer of kindergartens and women teachers. Main principles are: that each child is a unique and essential human being, who develops by and through his own actions; that young children should learn through constructive play; that the mother is the child's first teacher and that close links should be fostered between home and school. Most mainstream schools have now incorporated these salient points, making the Froebelian principles less revolutionary than it once was. Indeed the liberal progressive image has faded considerably.

Both kindergarten and primary classes are bursting with energy and excitement. Busy children, walls full of work, colour everywhere – a very rich environment. Strong sense of inter-relatedness of subjects. Work in the early years is topic-based, with emphasis on projects. A place where you know your child will get an excellent educational start. Unstressed environment, but perhaps a bit crowded. Articulate children.

Set in six green acres, on the edge of Richmond Park. From the age of 9, children are taught in the main building, a large Queen Anne-style house (designed by Chesterton, founder of the estate agency). Good facilities. Senior school stops after GCSE. Good staff:pupil ratio, emphasis on 'social skills' – open dialogue, getting on with people, communication.

In our view, the strongest part of the school is the junior school; however, the senior school works well for some and may be a solution. Changes afoot with the new head.

JAMES ALLEN'S PREPARATORY SCHOOL

(JAPS)

East Dulwich Grove, London SE22 8TE

TEL: *020 8693 0374* FAX: *020 8693 8031*

E-MAIL: sarahh@jags.demon.co.uk

WEB: www.jags.demon.co.uk

✦ PUPILS: 108 boys and girls in Lower School, 187 girls in Middle School, all day ✦ Ages: 4-7 Lower School, 7-11 Middle School ✦ C of E ✦ Fee-paying

---

Head: Since 1992, Mr Piers Heyworth MA PGCE (forties). Educated at Marlborough and Christ Church, Oxford, where he read English and founded the Oxford Survival Society (keen on environment). Previously celebrated head of English at JAGS, and appointment here an unusual and inspired choice – there's even more scope for his enthusiasm. Comments that the school takes 'a hundred and ten per cent of my time'. 'A good front man' commented his previous headmistress at JAGS. Married in '98 Sarah Russell, who teaches at neighbouring Alleyn's Junior School. As school recently expanded to double the size, most of the staff are his own appointments.

Entrance: From 'a hundred different nurseries', mainly in Dulwich and Clapham. Selective entry test in December and January for September, teachers watch out for 'adventurousness of spirit'. Followed by interviews.

Exit: In all 24 scholarships in '99 (a brilliant par for the course) including twelve to JAGS (qv). Boys at 7 go on to Dulwich, Dulwich College Preparatory School, Alleyn's Junior School etc.

Remarks: God's gift to the people of Dulwich. Part of the same foundation as JAGS etc, and consequently very well funded. Formerly the prep department of JAGS, has now spread its wings, with IAPS membership, co-education (up to 7) and an identity all of its own. On two sites – littlies in Gothic mansion down the road, 'Middle School' tucked beside JAGS, with large extension opened in '93 to include large sports hall, and super user-friendly library with own librarian – light and much used. Separate IT room, IT is being 'firmly incorporated in all subjects'. Timetabled computing for all (National Curriculum), large sunny science room. Specialist staff in a wide range of subjects – a tremendous strength. Brilliant 'immersion' French from age 4, with Mlle Pascale Bizet, who speaks entirely in French and so far children have not cottoned on to the fact she speaks English as well – lots of fun games, impeccable accents, and by the time these children leave the school they will need special fast stream to keep up the good work. French taught in half classes in the middle school by another French specialist, who also teaches some other subjects (eg drama) in French. Eighteen per class in lower school, rising to 24 in middle school, though most classes have two members of staff and can be split. Consequently 'we feel no need for setting or streaming'. Year 6 pupils took the national curriculum Key stage 2 in '97 and came out considerably above other IAPS schools. Brilliant art teacher, ex-Jackanory producer Mrs Pauline Carter, who earns her salary several times over in art prizes won by the school. Drama strong (head keen and experienced). Fifty-five clubs after school, and a staggering 170 pupils turn up for 'Saturday School' – brain child of staff member Miss Beverly Sizer – music, drama, dance from 8.30 am till 1.30 – wonderful way for pupils to work off excess energy, and parents to get to Tesco's in peace. Active parents' committee with 'maths for parents'sessions from time to time, curriculum evenings, social events etc. Three part-time qualified specialists provide one-to-one tuition for the small proportion of children ('often the brightest') needing it – special rooms set aside for this. School absolutely full of fizz, top-class staff, strong all round. Has to be contender for one of the two best London preps south of the Thames.

KENSINGTON PREPARATORY SCHOOL

596 Fulham Road London SW6 5PA

Tel: *020 7731 9300* Fax: *020 7731 9301*

E-MAIL: enquiries@kenprep.gdst.net

WEB: www.gdst.net/kensingtonprep

✦ Pupils: 275 girls; all day ✦ Ages: 4-11
✦ Non-denom ✦ Fee-paying

Head: Since 1993, Mrs Gillian Lumsdon MEd (fifties), previously head of Whitford Hall Prep School in Bromsgrove. Married (husband is a lawyer) with three grown-up children. Educated at Oxford High School and read pharmacy at Nottingham

University and more recently an MEd at Warwick University. Mrs Lumsden was for many years a pharmacist and was a 'latecomer to teaching'. Competent, openminded, enthusiastic, good sense of proportion; parents blow hot and cold about her, though. Hobby is choral singing. Her opinion is that the keeping up of a good academic standard is 'the place we have in the London scene'.

Entrance: Register child's name up to the time of testing age 4 ('they are supposed to have registered by the end of June'). NB no advantages given to early registration, and no charge for registration (unusual). Main entry is at 4+ following a group assessment twelve months before proposed entry (parents must visit the school first). Entry at 7 is now phased out, which, says the head, should make for slightly more flexibility at other uncharted ages where vacancies do sometimes occur, always via testing.

NB parents have complained to us in the past about the over-bearing behaviour by the school on the whole question of entry, but no recent reports of this. Children come from 40+ different nurseries and currently, owing to the move, from a huge area, but this will change. Some pupils from state schools, but generally young ones because the older they are the harder they find it to come up to speed.

Exit: The majority to London day schools: – St Paul's, City of London, Francis Holland Clarence Gate, Godolphin and Latymer, Putney High; also an increasing number to boarding schools, eg Wycombe Abbey.

Remarks: A school which has changed out of all recognition since it moved in '97 from fash Kensington to its present site in the back end of the Fulham Road, and will continue to change as parents/staff face the fact that this is an entirely different affair. Formerly cramped old-fashioned, with gentle well-behaved young ladies – despite current head's headway into 'opening the school up'. Now she has achieved that aim with one bound – girls are still friendly, but livelier, more hail-fellow-well-met, holding their heads higher, expanding happily into the wonderful new space. 'We are much more of a Trust school now' says the head.

The building was formerly a convent school (the Marist Convent) and there is still a lingering smell of nun, but goodo solid large purpose-built block (1960) with large open space (by London prep school standards), trees, birds tweeting etc. Extremely contented and steady staff. The head 'treats the children as people, not just as "little girls"', commented a mother. Standard of work is high, and teaching is good old-fashioned with mirabile dictu English grammar taught, and Latin in final year to help with the structure of the language. Discipline important (though no longer the feeling that this is oppressive). Firm emphasis on spelling and handwriting, with examples of best work stuck up on the wall to encourage the troops. Setting for maths only in penultimate year. Specialist teaching from the age of 8. A little fun French from the start – nursery rhymes, singing etc, but not so much as to leave the children treading water at their next school. Classes of 20 children. School lunch is compulsory – no lunch boxes – 'if there's a dietary need, we deal with it'. Netball can now be played on site (floodlit courts donated by parents); swimming currently in Putney. Keen music, with lots of room to practise and sing. Kensington Prep was the first of the G(P)DST schools to be founded, and has recently celebrated its 125th anniversary. It is the odd one out, being now, for historical reasons, a junior school only, but we are assured the Trust is 'firmly committed' to keeping the school.

Not everyone's choice – 'too big', 'lacking in imagination', 'quite ordinary', 'exam-centred', 'staff not caring enough about individuals' are some of the comments we have received – but many local parents find it just the ticket.

KING'S COLLEGE SCHOOL

West Road, Cambridge CB3 9DN

TEL: *01223 365814* FAX: *01223 461388*

✦ PUPILS: 190 boys, 95 girls. All day bar 34 boy boarders (including 16 choristers and 6 probationers) ✦ Ages: 4-13 ✦ C of E ✦ Fee-paying

---

Head: Since 1998 Mr Nicholas Robinson BA (early forties). Educated at Worth, read English at Anglia Polytechnic and then took a PGCE in maths at Goldsmith's College. Then a master and housemaster (for twelve years) at Worth. A bachelor.

Took over from Mr Andrew Corbett, head from 1993, who went to Holmewood as head.

Entrance: At 4, 7, 11. Fairly broad intake, from the average plus to the v bright. Annual choir auditions. Assessments at 7+ and above. Around 30 per cent children of academics, offspring of farmers and business people. Both the pre-prep (which opened in '92) and the dyslexia unit are over-subscribed, so register early.

Exit: Largest numbers to the Perse (boys and girls), followed by the Leys. Also Oundle, Uppingham, Eton, other local(ish) schools, and one or two to St Paul's, Westminster, Winchester, Millfield etc. Girls leave at 11 and 13. Twenty or so scholarships and awards most years. Fascinating list of Old Boys include Orlando Gibbons, Michael Ramsey, Christopher Tugendhat, John Pardoe, Professor Andrew Wiles (solved Fermat's Last Theorem).

Remarks: One of the two top prep schools in Cambridge (the other is St John's), in glorious surroundings, ancient buildings, trees, space, river, beauty everywhere. The two schools fluctuate in the popularity stakes. Exceptional music – of course – school provides choristers for King's College (a splendid sight in their gowns, top hats and stiff collars). King's choristers are of world renown, and still best known for Nine Lessons Carol Service. Choristers are well used to being in the public eye, sophisticated (and unspoilt) over making recordings, travelling etc. Well integrated with the rest of the school – not unusual for a chorister to be also an academic scholar. Music obviously plays a major role in school life, with 147 children learning one instrument, 79 learning two and there are no less than 29 visiting music teachers etc – and a good record of associated board exam successes solid from grade 1-5 (and some higher). Some staff of long-standing; stimulating high standards of teaching in all areas – and somewhat taken for granted by one and all. Staff somewhat other worldly and not clamouring for change. Pupils help decision-making within school via a committee; regular visiting speakers. Development work well under way: includes, among other things, a much needed purpose-built IT room. Sports all happening – but they 'keep a sense of proportion about results;' chess on the other hand – constant winners.

Dyslexia unit with two full-time specialists catering for up to 30 'bright dyslexics', all of whom have been assessed by an educational psychologist. Also an 'English Plus' teacher, who teaches one to one on a tutoring basis. Fields state pupils destined for Eton scholarships. Maximum class size 22, average 18.4. Children set for maths and French in year 5; streaming from year 6. Five-minute walk over to King's; founding of this school dates back to 15th century, though premises are undistinguished redbrick 19th century. Atmosphere is definitely friendly, liberal, informal, pretty scruffy even. Notwithstanding, rigorous academic and music standards underpin all this; place with a long tradition of pupils being happy.

KING'S COLLEGE JUNIOR SCHOOL

Wimbledon Common, Southside, London SW19 4TT

TEL: *020 8255 5335* FAX: *020 8255 5339*

E-MAIL: jsadmissions@kcs.org.uk

WEB: www.kcs.org.uk

◆ PUPILS: 461 boys; all day ◆ Ages: 7–13
◆ Anglican (other faiths welcome)
◆ Fee-paying

Head: Since 1998, Mr John A Evans BA (early fifties). Educated Priory Grammar School, Shrewsbury and at universities all over the shop – Bangor, Sorbonne and Cambridge. Promoted from the senior school. Taught modern languages, French and German. Senior housemaster then senior master in 1992. No longer married, two children, including one in the senior school. Interests – music, reading, France and Germany, theatre etc. Took over from Mr Colin Holloway, who reigned supreme here since 1976.

Entrance: Difficult. Takes 36 boys at 7 and another 36 at 8, some at 9, 10 and 11. Four classes in each year group. All boys interviewed. Weed out boys who have been over coached. There are some bursaries. Early registration advisable. Boys come from mainly local private (eg Squirrels) and state (eg Bishop Gilpin) schools and there are coaches from all over SW London.

Exit: Boys go on to the senior school (qv) (gaining most of the scholarships, academic and musical), although two or three per year may go elsewhere.

Remarks: A busy, bustling school. On the same site as the senior school, neatly tucked at one side. Heart of its main building was once Tudor-y Victorian, brutally destroyed and built over in the 1960's, but softened, face-lifted and altogether improved in the '80s, and the grey and beige impersonal corridors have now been enlivened by pupils' work/paintings/maps, posters. Good library and quite terrific emphasis on reading (lists galore). Some subjects taught in subject rooms. Most facilities (science, art, music, sport, dining hall) are shared with the senior school. Indeed some staff, unusually, teach both age groups, 'certainly very challenging,' says the head of art. Acquired Rushmere in 1992, the large handsome Georgian house which backs on to the main junior school building (divided by a garden and now a jolly playground), bought from the sculptor David Wynne, and the home base for the 7- and 8-year-olds who have a quiet, low key start with cosy classrooms and their own dining room which doubles as the hall. At 8+ life gets much busier. From 10 onwards boys are setted in French, maths, Latin and, unusually, music which is extremely strong. Touch typing in the IT room for 7- and 8-year-olds. Maximum class size 26. Not the place for dyslexics. Lots of clubs; chess and debating keen. Some nice art and wonderful creative writing. Drama hall (shared with senior school) has tiered seats that fold and run to the wall at the press of a button so that six ping-pong tables come into their own every lunchtime. School does consistently well in tennis and cricket. Recent First XI tour to South Africa was hugely fun. Recent concerns by parents about bullying are being addressed and the school holds workshops for parents to discuss any relevant issues. Broad social mix, strong Asian contingent. Bright red blazers. An outstanding prep school, with excellent standards in absolutely everything. Perhaps a bit of smug complacency in the place at the moment.

KNIGHTON HOUSE

Durweston, Blandford, Dorset DT11 0PY

TEL: *01258 452065* FAX: *01258 450744*

E-MAIL: tigmooney@aol.com

✦ PUPILS: 105 girls. 80 board, 25 day. Pre-prep with 41 children, including 19 boys. Nursery for 10 ✦ Ages: 7-13, pre-prep 4-7, nursery 2+-3+ ✦ C of E ✦ Fee-paying

---

Head: Since 1997, Mr Tighearnan ('Tig') Mooney MA DipEd, previously second master of Lathallan School. Mrs Mooney

runs the games and was previously head of modern languages and PE at Lathallan. Both are young and 'go ahead', and come from a dynamic school. Determined to keep the Knighton House 'X' factor. Open door policy in operation – much appreciated. Parents are making very enthusiastic noises here, not only over Mr Mooney, but also Mrs Mooney, who, they report, is 'a hugger', and 'mad keen on games' and has, in the space of one term, got the girls winning all their netball matches – very good for morale. Deputy head has taught in London – helps keep an eye on the coal face.

Entrance: Via pre-prep, or at 7 or 8 (informal interview plus report from previous school). Ponies accepted after a trial period: 'Mine was expelled after three weeks for kicking', said a girl.

Exit: At 12 or 13 mainly to Sherborne, Bryanston, St Mary's Shaftesbury, Godolphin etc. Reasonable record (and building up) of awards and scholarships. Pre-prepper boys go on mainly to Sandroyd, and the Old Malthouse.

Remarks: Charming, happy, unassuming, country school for girls with family atmosphere. A village school, set in marvellous Dorset country (originally founded by Christopher Booker's parents), with many not-so-hot-looking later additions. The building programme is all managed out of fees, and includes a smart music school, an all-purpose gym/assembly/performance hall, also a splendid dining room (small tables, emphasis on manners). Good food with loads of home-grown veg and fruit. Good teaching in all areas (but bear in mind this is not an academic hothouse), and occasional use of nearby Bryanston's facilities (the swimming pool, riding in their grounds). Girls greatly encouraged to read; breadth considered important. Regular internal curriculum reviews. Reports every two weeks. There is a good mix of ages in the common room. Music a special strength – head of music Simon Twistleton gets a special mention – with 15 peripatetic music staff, high standards chorally and instrumentally (80 per cent of pupils learn an instrument). Girls fund-raise seriously. Sport improving rapidly (under 12 Dorset netball champions in '98) lots of outdoor life, keen riding. Increasing numbers of girls stay on until 13, and there is a boarding house with housemistress for senior girls. Red dungarees (which fade to pink) are the uniform, 'We love them.' Girls are friendly, mutually supportive, natural and unspoilt, many from country homes. As we said before, this is a school where girls can stay relatively unsophisticated until they are 12 or 13. Breeds contented parents and some charming pupils. Good noises from Dorset – firing on all cylinders and v happy.

LADY EDEN'S SCHOOL

39/41 Victoria Road, London W8 5RJ

TEL: *020 7937 0583* FAX: *020 7376 0515*

E-MAIL: ladyedens@clara.net

✦ PUPILS: 165 girls; all day ✦ Ages: 3–11
✦ Christian based but non-denom
✦ Fee-paying

Head: Since 1996, Mrs Judith Davies BA MA (fifties). Educated GDST, Open and London Universities. Super lady, brisk, open, warm, totally competent, knows what she's about, adores children. Her office doubles up as reference library. Has spent the last twenty five years in senior schools with junior schools attached. Previously deputy head of Bromley High School, where she is still missed. Married to a university lecturer, with two grown up sons. Reads with pre-preps, 'Otherwise, I'm on hand for anybody and everything.' Trained and experienced Schools Inspector.

Entrance: At $3^1/_2$ only – put names down early. Waiting lists close at 12 per year. No formal test (Mrs Davies is 'absolutely against' testing at this tender age); occasionally places may occur later, places offered subject to testing and interview. Preference given to siblings.

Exit: Half to day schools, half to boarding schools – eg St Paul's, both Francis Hollands, Wycombe Abbey, Downe House, St Mary's Ascot, Heathfield.

Remarks: Seriously good, highly structured, upmarket little school. Founded in 1947 and still privately owned (by Lord and Lady Eden, who live above the shop but play a background role while keeping a close eye nowadays). Lots of smart names on the notice board, for prospective parents to see. The school is housed in light airy rooms in a converted pair of Georgian houses near Kensington Gardens. Rooms often double up – the dining room also used for art, teeny weeny playground.

Highly structured on the academic front, with specialist teaching in all subjects from 9 years old up. Maths do especially well ('excellent' said Ofsted). Huge recent investment in ICT. French from the age of 3; Latin for the top two years, scholarship class at this stage. Children are now taught in small groups (one of Mrs. Davies' innovations), and each class now has an assistant (often Oxford or Cambridge graduates waiting to do their PGCE), so as to pay close attention to the individual. One of the rare schools that can and does give help to the very able. Reading is pushed, so children are comfortable with it, and parents come in on a rota system to listen.

Madly keen drama. Music has 'gone woomf' according to parents, Mrs D encourages it like mad 'because it teaches all the skills – discipline, attention, precision.' Wide choice of instrumental lessons in school, choir tour to Belgium in 1999. Head firmly believes in stretching girls through extra-curricular activities, 'to encourage their interests and commitment,'she says, adding 'A little bit of pressure does no harm – but over pressure does'. Professor Parkins for fencing; Vacani for ballet – though at year 3 this changes to modern dance. Sports programme recently much expanded, and PE every day. Weekly news letter. General knowledge keenly fostered. Houses introduced 1998 (giving an edge to games), with the girls choosing female writers – Mansfield, Austen, Bronte, Alcott Prizes for everything – altogether, a confidence building environment.

LAMBROOK HAILEYBURY SCHOOL

Winkfield Row, near Bracknell, Berkshire
RG42 6LU

Tel: *01344 882717* Fax: *01344 891114*

E-mail: info@lambrook.berks.sch.uk

Web: www.lambrook.berks.sch.uk

✦ Pupils: 189 boys and 22 girls, 53 board. pre-prep 72 boys and 22 girls
✦ Ages: 4¹/₂-13 ✦ C of E ✦ Fee-paying

Head: Since 1999, Robert Deighton BA (fifties), educated at Wellington and Durham, and comes to the Lambrook Haileybury conglomerate after a career in advertising which he abandoned when he sold his agency at the age of forty. He then spent ten years at Cothill ('doing everything from driving the mini-bus to running their boarding house at Chandlings on Boars Hill'), followed by two years as head of Bruern Abbey.

A charismatic head, natty in double breasted grey hopsack and tasselled loafers – bit of a change from the regular diet of M & S blue shiny – he giggles a lot, 'it helps to have a mentality of a nine-year-old'. 'The bad joke of the week' is dead popular, with mini Mars bars for the best/worst, 'but it has to get a groan'. 'Why were the English cricket team given lighters as presents? Because they kept losing their matches'. A new bug, he claims this is the quickest way to get to know the boys, who stop him everywhere to tell him 'the latest one'. Head tries to teach 'about three times a week.'

Loves the school, loves the job, sells himself well. Into man management, inspires great loyalty (one of the Cothill staff followed him to Bruern and on to Lambrook Haileybury and matron is ex-Cothill as well). Sells the school well too, 'we major on weekly boarding' and has 'done the rounds' of the London pre-prep proclaiming the advantages. 'Any boarding actually', from the odd day or two to total immersion. 'You name it, we can do it'. Recent inspector's report declared him 'benign but firm'. Married to Olivia, a trained actress who turned her hand to starting a day school in Oxford. She and their Westie (black lab too old and fat for the stairs) read Harry Potter at bedtime. Moles tell us that 'she is the power behind the throne and can be pretty tough', on the moles we suspect. Two grown up sons – Summer Fields and Wellington – and a daughter teaching at Eaton House.

Entrance: From local primaries and own popular pre-prep. Numbers have increased from 295 to 325 this year, so presumably a spot of poaching as well; children can and do come at any time, half term, relocation, whatever, 'as long as there is space'. High percentage of first-time buyers.

Exit: Impressive collection of scholarships to Eton, St Paul's, Charterhouse, Wellington, Bradfield, Haileybury and Reading Bluecoats – 'bright boys and well taught' plus the odd senior girls' school.

Remarks: What a transformation. When we last visited this was a dreary little school, a Marie Celeste with falling numbers (and we took with us an Old Boy who hadn't been back for over forty-five years and 'didn't see much difference'). Lambrook and Haileybury Prep school amalgamated in '97 when school moved 'seamlessly' to the 40 acre Winkfield Row, and the Haileybury site on the edge of Windsor was put on the market – Persimmon are now building little boxes. The cash-rich combined school is flourishing, numbers have increased, facilities have improved, the new science and IT centre is up and running – the new baby house in production, the leisure centre in pipe line and there is still money in the pot. Girls are trickling in through the pre-prep, and working their way up the school, but this is a softly-softly operation, and the school is basically boy orientated with 'the occasional girl'. Tiny classes, average 16 with three parallel classes in pre-prep rising to four parallel in September 2001, the projection is 450 children by 2003/4. Could take 80/100 boarders. The grounds are terrific, boy-inspiring woods for camping, plus squash, tennis, swimming, golf – could be a country club rather than a prep school. The most vicious sleeping policemen we've seen anywhere.

Academically impressive, computers everywhere, revision on computers. Very comprehensive learning support division (after all, head comes from Bruern) with double teaching where necessary from Australian stooges. Greek for the gifted, public speaking practices, and lots of options. Drama timetabled and masses of music. At least three quarters of the children play at least one instrument, and the choir is seriously good; they provide trebles for Eton and are currently producing their own CD, lots of rehearsals, but lots of trips and jollies too. Original school buildings have had a lick and a promise and the dorms have been painted and carpeted, but they really need radical surgery to get the place totally up to scratch. The head maintains that the food is 'cracking', and jolly good it looked too, but the painted panelled walls of the dining room looked too old fashioned for words despite being covered in pupil paintings. The older library and chapel were far more the thing.

Thriving school, with an enterprising head who seems to have his market well sussed out. Boys' school with a small but fast increasing number of girls – on the up.

LATHALLAN SCHOOL

Brotherton Castle, Johnshaven, by Montrose,

Angus DD10 0HN

TEL: *01561 362220* FAX: *01561 361695*

E-MAIL: office@lathallan.com

WEB: www.lathallan.com

✦ PUPILS: 62 boys, 50 girls; 60 day, 10 full board + flexi-boarding (62 max); plus kindergarten with 60 children ✦ Ages: 5–13, kindergarten 3–5 ✦ Inter-denom ✦ Fee-paying

---

Head: Since 1998, Mr Peter Platts-Martin BA PGCE (forties), educated at King's Canterbury and London University where he read history and PE, comes to Lathallan after King's School Bruton where he ran the girls' sixth form boarding house. (Lathallan governors seem to have a passion for appointing senior school housemasters). Head still teaches history and religious studies, and coaches rugby, hockey and squash. Wife, Abigail, a former Wren officer happily prettying up dorms; three children in the school and a dog called Kendall.

Mr Platts-Martin comes to the school after a period of some turbulence, during which time many of the last headmaster but one's better schemes were overturned. The kindergarten used to take tinies from two, nappies not a problem and had an eight o'clock drop off point and a six o'clock collection – a godsend for parents working in Aberdeen.

Entrance: From local primaries and own kindergarten, some ex-pats with handy grannies.

Exit: Mostly to Scottish public schools, Glenalmond tops, plus Strathallan, Fettes, Merchiston, Loretto, St Leonards, a tiny dribble to the south. Having said that, the school got the top 'all round scholarship' to Uppingham last year – 'we worked hard to get it'.

Remarks: 'Good all-round school', small classes (14 the norm), high staff pupil ratio (1-7), boys sleep in main castle block, with girls cosily ensconced above the servants' quarters. Great improvement here, with better heating throughout. Classroom block in the old stables which also houses the kindergarten has been revamped and more staff, particularly sports specialists, employed (Rob Wainwright an Old Boy). Provision for 'mild dyslexia only', with children withdrawn from class and 'kicked up to speed'. Impressive art and IT, computers everywhere, lots of music. At a recent concert 60 children volunteered. Parents very supportive – joint Scottish country dance sessions with children and lots of participation. Daily coach and two minibus service to and from Stonehaven and Aberdeen (25 miles away). Weekly boarding is now a popular option; there is no school on Saturday mornings. First time buyers from the Aberdeen business community slightly less in evidence since the oil slump.

Set in own 62 acres of woodland, with

ten acres of playing field overlooking the North Sea and own beach (bracing) 'wonderfully clean air, safe and v healthy environment' says the head. Excellent games and been thrashing all-comers; flourishing pipe band, they played at Balmoral last year. Lots of trips and links abroad.

Popular and good local prep and pre-prep where 'joining in is de rigueur'; we share parental concerns that the children might be a bit over-stretched.

LOCKERS PARK

Hemel Hempstead, Herts HP1 1TL

TEL: *01442 251712* FAX: *01442 234150*

E-MAIL: secretary@lockerspark.herts.sch.uk

✦ PUPILS: 119 boys, around 55 board
✦ Ages: 7-13 ✦ C of E ✦ Fee-paying

Head: Since 1997, Mr David R Lees-Jones (early fifties). Educated at Stowe and Manchester University, where he read music. Previous post, head of Marlborough House. Has also taught at Bramcote and at Epsom. Likes outward bound-ing and motor racing. Says the high point of his career was 'conducting the Verdi Requiem'. Married – wife Katharine teaches some French and is a physiotherapist. Three children, one at university, one at Charterhouse, one at Abbots Hill. Second Headmaster: since 1983, Mr Roger Stephens BA (fifties), educated at Repton and Durham. Small jovial bachelor, every inch a schoolmaster, organises the day-to-day running of the school plus pastoral side, teaches the top end. Has been teaching at Lockers since '67

and has been a 'tower of strength', says Mr Lees-Jones – providing the continuity 'so lacking in many of our style of establishments today'.

Entrance: No problem. At 7 or 8, with a one-to-one test, fairly wide ability range. All boys are encouraged to board at 11 (until recently they were required to do so – the decision is now made by the parents).

Exit: Ask for remarkably clear breakdown of leavers' destinations over last 10 years for full picture. Harrow continues to be popular; Rugby and Stowe steady. Scholarships solid, given intake, including one or two music awards annually to strong music schools.

Remarks: Popular local choice, plus full boarding. A small traditional slightly old-fashioned prep school purpose built in 1874, in pleasantly rural setting despite nearby city and suburbs. Links with founding family (Draper), but the school is now a charitable trust and for historical reasons has two heads.

Noticeably friendly boys, very much listened to by staff, who are friends with them. CE always in sight. Maximum class size 16, but usually 14. At time of writing had 20 being given support for learning difficulties. Very well-thumbed library, technology and computing integrated. Boys move up by ability allowing two years at the top for scholarship stream. Strong music – all boys play the violin for a short time at least; extremely good singing.

Neither rich nor smart – though it has been fashionable. Impressive list of Old Boys includes Lord Mountbatten (excellent classroom block named after him), also Keith Joseph, Paul Channon and the Nawab of Pataudi. Keenly sporting, with French windows looking out onto slightly sloping playing fields – 'annoying for visiting teams,' admit the boys gleefully. Good drama. Chapel plays a central role. Firm discipline, but also a free-range outlook, boys are good at expressing themselves in all manner of ways. 'Bicycles, skateboards, scooters, tree-climbing, camp building, expeditions and remote controlled cars will be the scene this term for the boys when they are not otherwise busy with more pressing matters,' says head, who comments 'I like each day to be an exciting and sensible experience.'

LUDGROVE

Wokingham, Berkshire RG40 3AB

Tel: *01189 789881*

Web: www.ludgrove.com

✦ Pupils: 195 boys; all board ✦ Ages: 8-13
✦ C of E ✦ Fee-paying

Joint Heads: Since 1972, Mr Gerald Barber MA (late fifties), and Mr Nichol Marston MA (ditto). Both educated at Eton and Oxford, both from prep school backgrounds: Mr. Barber is the third generation to run the school (now a charitable trust), Mr Marston's father was headmaster of Summer Fields. Mr Barber previously taught at Mowden in Sussex, where he met his wife Janet (the Barbers have three grown-up children, one of whom (Simon) is teaching at Ashdown House and will return to Ludgrove in due course). All three are charming, friendly, and popular with parents and pupils. Parents and heads are immediately on Christian name terms. Mr

Barber comments his biggest challenge is 'to prepare boys for the highly competitive modern world and yet retain a firm set of moral values'.

Entrance: No exam, but reasonable standards essential. Names need to be registered at birth.

Exit: Eton feed. As always, almost two-thirds to Eton; also Harrow, Radley, Stowe.

Remarks: Has always been among the top ten posh prep schools in the country. Despite unselected intake, the school continues to get large numbers of boys over the Eton hurdle by dint of professionalism by staff and sheer hard slog – boys trained up like racehorses.

Breeds tremendous loyalty and has large numbers of old boys' sons (who find the place unchanged in essence), very much a choice for Eton families, aristocrats and royals. Having survived the young princes, the school has not changed its ways one jot, except perhaps to be even more leery of outsiders (and this says much). Royal blight a thing of the past.

Homely, a bit scruffy and some battered old desks. Cosy, friendly, understated, unpressurised and in some respects laid-back, with a strong family feel. Large country house (only one hour from central London) with masses of later additions and conversions, in fabulous 130 acres. Loads of woods for camps and free-range games, with most pitches out of sight. Very strong games, lengthy fixture list. The Victorian-Tudor house contains all the main school rooms and dorms (bathrooms with 16 baths surprised the Children Act Inspectors, now replaced with modern shower blocks). Sick children use Barber children's bedrooms in isolation if needs be. Traditional – old-fashioned – in every respect, with sensible care, minimum fuss (and uniform) and lots of emphasis on manners: 'We're always banging on about table manners, and the importance of considering others.' Good food, lists of all boys' names on boards in the dining room (spills out into the conservatory).

Excellent pastoral care; boys have access to telephones and e-mail, all problems channelled through staff, mainly Mrs Barber (called Ma'am by the boys, as are all the female staff). There are regular exeats from Friday midday till Sunday evening.

School fully networked since we last went to press. Teaching throughout is very traditional. Maths teaching 'brilliant' say parents; three 'teaching support' teachers now employed – 'a big help' say parents. Huge sports-hall-theatre, clapboard chapel, computer room, squash and fives courts, tiny indoor swimming pool (the next on list for updating) and new art, CDT and pottery rooms in converted cowsheds.

Most boys happy as larks, and good reports from parents continue to reach us. Gives parents a huge sense of security and confidence.

THE MALL SCHOOL

185 Hampton Road, Twickenham, Middlesex
TW2 5NQ

TEL: *020 8977 2523* FAX: *020 8977 8771*

E-MAIL: tmacd@btinternet.com

✦ PUPILS: 285 boys; all day ✦ Ages: 4–13
✦ C of E ✦ Fee-paying

Head: Since 1989, Mr T P A MacDonogh MA (fifties) (pronounced MacDunner).

Educated Winchester and Cambridge, previously deputy head of Berkhamsted Junior School. Keen musician, teaches IT, Latin and religious studies, emphasizes school as a community.

Entrance: First come, first served with the main unselective entry in September – there is a waiting list so book early. Thereafter, including at 7+ and 8+, subject to test. Feeds include Jack and Jill, The Pavilion Montessori, Sunflower Montessori, Cellars Montessori & Marble Hill Nursery, The Falcons and Broomfield School – the list changes year by year.

Exit: Wide selection, mainly day, in particular King's College Wimbledon, and Hampton, and St Paul's; also a dozen or so to high powered schools outside the area eg Winchester, Eton, Harrow. Gets an average of eight academic awards per year.

Remarks: Traditional prep school ('Mall' pronounced short as in 'shall') with unusually informal and friendly atmosphere. Maximum class size 24, average 20, but in the final year boys are in three or four sets (smallest grouping for those who need most attention), and the scholarship class where they spend two years. Little ones are 'mothered' for three years, six-year-olds' computer is programmed for them, and there is a multi-media computer in all junior classes, (five year olds know how to use it quicker than their teacher); senior department networked, all have e-mail and internet access though 'thank goodness the four-year-olds are not using it yet'. Reception class bakes, sews and learns joined-up writing (the head says he's not sure this last part is strictly true). Cosy plus trad in a nice balance all through the school. Remedial help for minor cases. Strong sport now, especially swimming and rugby; music also good (two choirs, two orchestras). Lots of plays. Lively. Good on clubs and projects – with boys queuing up before 8 o'clock (Daddy drops them off) to get stuck into their activities (table tennis is popular). Judo, fencing, chess, computing, carpentry all on offer. Considerable amount of new building in the last three years has greatly improved the facilities, classrooms and space; new science and music block opened in '97, swimming pool in '99. As we have said before, there is notably strong rapport between parents and staff, intimacy and warmth the keynote of the school. Happy reports from parents. And: 'Nothing else like it around,' comment parents clamouring to get boys in. Very hard working but: 'I would hate us to be considered pressurised,' says head.

MALSIS SCHOOL

Cross Hills, North Yorkshire BD20 8DT

TEL: *01535 633027* FAX: *01535 630571*

E-MAIL: admin@malsis.fsnet.co.uk

WEB: www.malsis.com

✦ PUPILS: around 130 boys. 40 girls. 65 board, the rest day ✦ Ages: 7-13, pre-prep 3-7 ✦ C of E ✦ Fee-paying

---

Head: Since 1998, Mr John Elder MA PGCE (forties). Previous post head of Beeston Hall (since 1986), where he was brilliant (a member of Beeston staff came with him). Educated Lathallan and Cranleigh, plus St Andrews and Edinburgh Universities and UEA. Teaches maths and scholars English. Dutch wife, Hanneke

teaches wee ones scripture and one form maths. Three children. Took over from interrex David Pighills (brilliant ex-head of Strathallan), following very short tenure of previous head.

Entrance: Spend at least one day in school and do tests in maths and English. No longer Yorkshire only – Wales, Cheshire, Lancashire, to Somerset, and Services families.

Exit: Shrewsbury remains popular. Also to Sedbergh, Uppingham, Oundle, Glenalmond, Giggleswick. One or two to Eton, Ampleforth, Radley etc. About ten awards/scholarships a year, including a couple for music.

Remarks: Prep school founded (in 1920) by a teacher from Giggleswick. Has been through vicissitudes of fortune recently, including changes of head. Has however in the not-so-distant past been very strong and sparky, and could well become so again under hotshot new head. Day boys have to be in school by 8.30am and stay till 6.15pm – -though most will stay on for clubs etc. Marvellous John Piper War Memorial Windows in Chapel, plus the flags which used to hang on the Cenotaph in London. Chapel converts to hall/theatre. School housed in flamboyant Victoriana, with many additions. Light airy classrooms. School now tarted up (and not before time). Outstanding 'Victorian' ceilings and cartoons all over by Cedric (who used to be the carpenter). French from nine, plus Latin from eight and Greek from ten 'available.' Small classes (average 12) and dedicated staff. Pet shed in front garden. English has been outstanding under Roger Beaufoy (now part-time). Good and active special needs unit, with visiting staff from Harrogate Dyslexia Institute. Superb facilities – music school, art centre, IT, Astroturf.

Good drama. Masses of outdoor activity (school surrounded by fells), including long-distance hikes, as well as soccer, rugger (traditionally very strong), cricket, golf. Large sports hall, plus proper gym and swimming pool and communal showers beside the changing area. Staff live mainly within ten minutes, so lots of busy weekends. Head sees all good work; lots of 'effort prizes' for everything from work to granny bashing. Pre-prep (opened '96), housed in redesigned surplus building next door to main school – new building from 2001. Turns out splendid well-rounded chaps. Old Boys include Simon Beaufoy (who wrote The Full Monty), John Spencer and Bernard Gadney (captains of England rugby XV), Martin Taylor (Barclays Bank), Lord Robinson. Started to go co-ed in '98.

MALTMAN'S GREEN

Gerrards Cross, Buckinghamshire SL9 8RR

Tel: *01753 883022* Fax: *01753 891237*

E-MAIL: office@maltmansgreenschool.bucks.sch.uk

✦ Pupils: 380 girls, all day ✦ Age: 3-11
✦ Non-denom ✦ Fee-paying

Head: Since 1998, Miss Julia Reynolds BEd, who comes from being head of the Old Vicarage, Richmond. A private person. Took over from Mrs M Evans, who was here from 1988.

Entrance: By assessment and visit; to nursery at 3, also 4, 5, 7 and other ages – a very mobile local population results in vacancies popping up all the time. Children (with very rare exception) automatically move up the school.

Exit: A good area for grammar schools with eg Dr Challoner's and Beaconsfield High. Also to a number of top boarding schools, seemingly different ones each year, eg Wycombe Abbey, Queenswood, St George's Ascot, Queen Anne's Caversham. All girls leave at 11+.

Remarks: Very popular all day school. Housed in what looks like just another grand stockbroker's pile in ritzy suburban belt of Gerrards Cross, tile floors gleaming with polish. Subject teachers for everything at 8+. Good design technology which has been flourishing for some time, smart science and technology building and ICT room. Enthusiastic gymnastics, with girls winning all manner of medals. Art department an Aladdin's cave. Some help for mild dyslexia. Average 14-20 in a class.

Busy, happy, bright place, ditto children who are confident and outward going, zooming about in their purple uniform. Good food. Good on trips and outings. Eleven well-kept acres, with outdoor heated pool, adventure playground etc. Girls can come in early for breakfast and stay late for tea if it suits their families.

MILBOURNE LODGE

Arbrook Lane, Esher, Surrey KT10 9EG

Tel: *01372 462737* Fax: *01372 471164*

✦ Pupils: 200 (too many, in the head's view), mostly boys, but about 20 girls; all day ✦ Ages: 7/8-13 ✦ C of E ✦ Fee-paying

---

Head: Until 2000 and since 1949, Mr Norman Hale MA (seventies), who deserves an entry in the Guinness Book of Records, and is looking fitter and more active than ever. A National Living Treasure. Says he occupies his spare moments with expensive holidays and trips to Annabel's, where he has been known to bump into parents. Has seriously glamorous wife, who in a weak moment last time said she was in charge of 'buns, bursar and bogs' – an excellent description. Both Mr and Mrs Hale have phenomenal amount of energy (in our view) and work with giant enthusiasm for the school which, incidentally, is owned by them – an inspiration to us all, and a good sense of humour and proportion with it. The only head we have seen going round clutching Kennedy as though his life depended on it. Mr Hales was educated at Shrewsbury and Lincoln College, Oxford, where he read history. The Hales live on the site, through a little wooden gate from the playground. Still active behind the scenes, and to some extent on stage.

From 2000, Graham and Gillie Hill, who have 'been in the wings for some years.' Mr Hill, who read English at University College, Oxford, was head of Danes Hill, Oxshott, just down the road, for 17 years. Mrs Hill is much involved with the school, eg as registrar and general 'mum' to the children.

Entrance: Register asap, but this part of the world has a shifting population, so always give it a try especially at odd entry times. Stiff test, but, said previous head, if you are at all worried, the thing to do is to come and visit the school informally with your infant and the school will give him/her an OK to go ahead (or not). Some children come from Milbourne Lodge Junior School (Tel 01372 462 781, but which has no connection with the school) and 20 other pre-preps roundabout. Some by schools' own bus from Putney, Wimbledon and ports of call at the top of the A3. Also some 'transplants' from other schools in the area, and refugees in need of cramming.

Exit: Consistently gets as many scholarships per head as any other prep school in the country – over an enormous number of years, year in year out. Not just any old scholarships either, but Winchester, Eton (top scholarship '97), Harrow, King's College Wimbledon etc. Girls now go not only to Roedean and Wycombe Abbey but also Marlborough (top scholarship in '97) etc.

Remarks: In terms of scholarships, this is probably the most successful little prep school in the country. It is a day school, but feels very like a traditional boys' boarding school, with a few girls thrown in for good measure (mostly sisters of boys in the school). The success appears to be due to rigorous unrelenting attention to the academic subjects set in Common Entrance, by staff who manage to make the hard work (slightly) fun: 'I say, "I want to be entertained,"'says the head, 'Let's have fun in the classroom'. Staff have their sleeves rolled up and ooze hairy arms and strong minds. Surprisingly short on homework compared with most London preps 'because we do the teaching here'.

The day starts early, and for the older children, doesn't finish till 6pm or later – 'whenever I've finished with them,' says Mr Hale. There are A and B streams – two classes of 24 for the tinies (thus proving that small classes are not everything), going down to about 18 or 16 in the higher classes – the head is quite flexible about this. Latin for all from the start, and Greek for the A stream from the third year (eleven-year-olds, Greek for Beginners) – the school is one of the last outposts of classics, and this in itself finds favour with the academic public schools, who recognise the need for the little dears to have some demonstrable mental discipline. Physics comes as a light relief after this under the brilliant teaching of Miss Carroll, who was formerly in the state sector. Computers are creeping in at last – 'whisper who dares, there is even a network at the top of the main building.' Miss Carroll looks sternly at one which looks as though it has been made to stand in the corner for bad behaviour 'we run it,' she says, 'not vice versa'.

Lest you get the impression that it's all swot and no sport, let it be said the whole school does games every afternoon (football, rugby, cricket, some tennis, fencing, golf) – thought to be part of the secret of school's success. There is also a 5 minute run-round between lessons, and the place hums with the energy of 200 children letting off steam at all available moments. The school has the most wonderful games fields – rolling acres stretching out towards the wild, wild wood of Ardbrook Common (mature broad-leaved trees, excellent for dens and things). This comes as a surprise after the rather unprepossessing approach to the school – up a suburban-looking cul de sac, set about with modern houses.

Extra-curricular activities are what go to the wall in the quest for academic excellence – not that the school doesn't get the odd music scholarship, but you feel this is more because of pressure from home rather than in-built music timetabling. Some good poetry in the school magazine, however, eg: The alarm rings – morning – My last few moments. Curled up like a croissant... No gym, but heated swimming pool. CDT is done as a concentrated course once CE is out of the way. There is also an absolute minimum of Nissen-hut type extra buildings – and again, no plans for any building expansion as we write. The school is housed in a cramped but pleasant-looking suburban gothic building. New large classroom for upper sixth form – to replace amazingly squashed but 'lucky' old one.

The original school was founded by the father of Woodrow Wyatt in a house up the road. The prospectus (all one page of it) is laconic in the extreme. Pupils are solidly from the professional classes (and an actor or two) and go on Oxbridge and thence to be upstanding citizens, particularly fat salaried ones – doctors, surgeons, lawyers etc. Parents are ambitious sushi/BMW belt, who are quite likely to have moved into the area to be near the school, though some children commute huge distances from London. Both parents and staff (and there are some very long-serving of the latter) comment that this is a one-off place, inspiring, charismatic, managing to get the results without over-punishing little spirits. For what it sets out to do, it is hard to fault, and even has a new caterer.

MILLFIELD PREPARATORY SCHOOL

(formerly EDGARLEY HALL)

Glastonbury, Somerset BA6 8LD

TEL: *01458 832446* FAX: *01458 833679*

E-MAIL: office@millfieldprep.somerset.sch.uk

WEB: www.millfield.co.uk/prep

✦ PUPILS: 500, boys and girls. Around 60 per cent board, the rest day ✦ Ages: 7-13 (junior school); (also pre- prep in middle of Glastonbury, ages 4-8) ✦ Inter-denom ✦ Fee-paying

---

Head: Since May 2000, Interregnum; Mrs Sara Champion, deputy head, is holding the fort. From 2001 the head will be Mr Kevin Cheney (fifties). A Millfield senior school housemaster in the '80s, Mr Chency became head of Trinity School Teignmouth in 1986, and head of Cranmore Prep in 1992. Married to Hilary, four sons.

Entrance: Exam in January for entry in September, loads of scholarships; otherwise interview and report from previous head.

Exit: Mostly to Millfield, but a smattering elsewhere.

Remarks: Large by prep school standards, used by National Association for Gifted Children and well known for dyslexia. Good ratio of staff to pupils, strong on sport. Logistically quite a distance away from Millfield proper, a charming site, surrounded by truly rural farms. Not possible to comment at the moment.

MOOR PARK

Ludlow, Shropshire SY8 4EA

TEL: *01584 876061* FAX: *01584 877311*

E-MAIL: moorpark@netmatters.co.uk

WEB: www.moorpark.shropshire.sch.uk

✦ PUPILS: 260; 147 boys, 113 girls; 74 board, ✦ Ages: 3-13 ✦ RC (but only one-quarter are Catholics) ✦ Fee-paying

---

Head: Since 2000, Mr Neil Colquhoun MA (fifties), educated at Eton and Trinity, Oxford (history). Beak then housemaster at Eton (teaching history, Latin, Spanish, divinity and French) and then (briefly) at Lathallan until arrival at Moor Park. Married (to Rosie, who will be active in the school), four boys (the youngest 15). Sport and music feature highly in his CV; has house in Ardnamurchan. Not a Catholic, but committed to 'developing the Catholicity that is such a vital part of the Christian ethos'. Took over from Mr John Richard Badham, the charming, loose-limbed, and naturally chaotic former head.

Entrance: Tests for children 'if necessary' entering at 7+ and 8+. Not highly selective.

Exit: In order of popularity Shrewsbury, Spain (the country), Bedstone, Malvern College, Christ's College Brecon, Moreton Hall, Hereford Cathedral, Wrekin and Cheltenham (both). A few to the great Catholic boarding schools.

Remarks: Chirpy, relaxed prospectus a breath of humanity among all the marketing-speak. The school is as nice as it sounds.

Founded in 1964 in large country house in fine (if somewhat untidy) grounds; the setting for some of the scenes in 'Blot on the Landscape'. Enjoyed rapid growth, a period of decline, and recently substantial growth again; firmly solvent but not rich. In response to the decline in boarding and long-distance parenthood generally, the school has recast itself from its original UK-wide mission to a local flexi-boarding school serving the surrounding fifty miles or so. Good facilities generally. Activity/hobby session for children between 5.30pm and 6.30pm, games sessions every weekday, child minding for the juniors until 6.30pm, and lots to do on Saturdays; day pupils welcome to board for the odd night or stay over weekends, twenty/thirty pupils in school on the average Sunday.

Children given plenty of encouragement under head's aim to 'stretch not drive' them. Some setting from year 5, but otherwise almost all move up the school together. Literacy and numeracy support from a small team, for the dyslexic and for those coming from some state schools; English teachers trained to spot those who need help. Class sizes max 18. Art fine and all over the school. Good drama, music ('on the up' report parents, 'especially the choir'), and strong on games (best teas for miles around). School has been the first nationally in the St David's Shield Shooting Competition. Cross-country trophies too.

The Catholic proportion of pupils has diminished steadily, but the school remains committed to maintaining a Catholic ethos throughout; observances are necessarily relaxed, though. Lovely chapel in the old ballroom. Good pastoral care, all houseparents are married, award winning PSHE scheme (when it comes to the ticklish subjects, parents are told exactly what is being taught each week so that they are not caught unawares). Boys' dorms are cosy, girls' quarters are recently refurbished and exceptionally comfy. Extended family atmosphere; children who are ill overnight are given beds in the head's flat, pupils' pets' menagerie (bunnies, hamsters, rats etc, but no cats or dogs) heated to a better standard than the dorms. The story about some parents being shown round by a boy with his pet rats balanced on his shoulder is true.

NB expect changes with the new head: 'likely to be more focused, but hopefully will not lose its charm' is the official line.

MOUNT HOUSE SCHOOL

Mount Tavy, Tavistock, Devon PL19 9LJ

TEL: *01822 612244* FAX: *01822 610042*

E-MAIL: mounthouse@aol.com

WEB: www.mounthouse.devon.sch.uk

◆ PUPILS: 175 boys, 80 girls; 100 full boarders ◆ Ages: 7-13; plus own pre-prep for boys and girls ages 3-7 ◆ C of E ◆ Fee-paying

---

Head: Since 1984, Mr C D Price BA (fifties). Educated Clayesmore and Open University – read English. Was previously assistant headmaster at (what was) Cheam. Teaches geography and English. Hobbies – sailing, model railways, sport and the 'latest boys' crazes'! An enthusiast who carries all before him. Boys appear to regard him as a human being – a rare state of affairs, in our observation, which speaks volumes for his talent as a teacher. Tireless in promoting school to outside world. Steady back-up from wife Sue – who does everything from running the clothing shop to serving match teas and 'loves it'. Their son teaches at Summer Fields (qv), his daughter, an ex prep school matron, is married to a Summer Fields housemaster. Some useful governors, including headmasters, accountants, surveyor, David Owen's sister, and the editor of the Dragon Book of Verse (who teaches at Eton).

Entrance: From local and far-flung corners of the West Country (notably Plymouth Hospital), plus newcomers to the West Country abandoning London for life in Devon and work on the web. Some Services' children (though fewer of these) and others 'from Elgin to Penzance', not to mention from Hong Kong, Dubai, Singapore (diplomats, bankers etc). School runs an 'Escort' service to and from London and the airports. Interview, assessment and test.

Exit: Average ten scholarships/exhibitions a year. Pupils go on to eg King's Taunton, Marlborough, Sherborne, Bryanston, King's Bruton, Winchester, Eton, Radley, Millfield and Kelly College. First girls off to Downe House and Cheltenham Ladies'. OBs: Ed Bye (producer of Jasper Carrott etc), Philip de Glanville, David Owen.

Remarks: School still billed as the best in the west by senior school headmasters – 'nothing to touch it for miles,'said one. Girls do not appear to be adversely affecting the place. Particular strengths are the intangible unquantifiable qualities – politeness, friendliness, the children look you in the eye, hold their heads up – confident without being cocky. A particularly safe, kind and very special place. Main building is glorious old manor house overlooking Tavistock with a view – on a good day – to Cornwall. Super site, with river running through the bottom of the playing fields (school has riparian rights) and surrounded by Dartmoor (tendency to mists and gloom). Music, which was always enthusiastic, now has the great Brian Armfield as head of department – a brilliant teacher, inspirational, much loved by children. Much encouragement and diligent practice, practically everyone learns an instrument, and music scholarships are won from time to time. New music school being built. Keen games school and will travel miles for a match with traditional preps such as Caldicott and Papplewick. Strong on natural history – not surprising, with so much scope for study on the doorstep – also keen adventure activities (climbing, caving, canoeing, you name it). Pupils streamed and setted in English and maths, and are turned out well prepared for their public school. Maximum class size 16, average 12-13; two or three streams a year. Few staff changes. Smart sports hall, with a full-size tennis court and two squash courts in it, also CDT centre. Sunday chapel a bit of a feature here – much attended by parents still, and regularly corrals first division public school headmasters to preach the sermon. Parents by and large professional – lawyers, accountants, medics (one or two who work in London but have weekend cottages in the area), Services etc. Pre-prep department opened in '96. Traditional teaching, has the use of many of the main school's facilities. Full boarding: two exeats each term plus three Sundays out. 'We never have a child left behind at an exeat' says head. Girls admitted since '96 (there is now a waiting list for them); pre-prep full too.

MOWDEN HALL SCHOOL

Newton, Stocksfield, Northumberland
NE43 7IP

TEL: *01661 842147* FAX: *01661 842529*

E-MAIL: lb@mowden.northumbria.sch.uk

WEB: www.mowdenhall.co.uk

✦ PUPILS: 90 boys, 75 girls (130 boarders, 35 day) ✦ Ages: 8-13. Plus pre-prep and nursery with 85 boys and girls ages 3-8
✦ C of E ✦ Fee-paying

Head: Since 1991, Mr Andrew Lewis MA (fifties), educated at Marlborough, and Magdalene College, Cambridge. Oodles of quiet charm, a mathematician, he teaches all ages in the school (a rarity these days), some maths, some RE. A very keen sportsman (Rugby fives half blue). Taught at Stanbridge Earls, was a housemaster at Repton before coming here. Carolyn, his wife, has bags of energy and participates on all the school's fronts, including helping children with learning difficulties. They have four children.

Entrance: Wide ability range, no exam or test, three term entry. Children from all over Northumberland, Scottish borders, also Cumbria and Yorkshire.

Exit: Largest numbers to Sedbergh, RGS Newcastle, Oundle, Uppingham Shrewsbury and Gordonstoun, though Eton, Harrow, Rugby etc feature. Twenty-nine awards in last three years; top scholarship to Rugby in '00.

Remarks: Good and traditional prep school with lots going on, efficiently run in an old country house with many additions and conversions. Splendid setting with fine views, up a long drive with sleeping policemen. Not a rich school, but as a result of energetic fund-raising and good management, it has good facilities. The latest acquisition, and a wild success, is a part share in Sauveterre, the chateau near Toulouse, originally bought by Cothill (see entry under Cothill). Eleven/twelve year olds go for a full term. Boarding still very popular, and head notes 'high proportion of parents who start their children at the school with no thoughts that they will become boarders – but who then allow them to board at Mowden and go on to send them to boarding public schools.' All children (however local) must board for their final two years.

Jolly atmosphere, a family school with a nice balance of discipline and freedom. Good food in the agreeable dining room (with staff seated at each table), children on rotas to clear plates. Pre-prep unstreamed, eighteen per year; first year of main school two streams of thirteen; from then on three streams of twelve, the top being the scholarship stream. Good and imaginative teaching at all levels. Light bright classrooms, with loads of work on display, and heaps of encouragement on hand. Scholars at the top end only, younger ones may do two years. Good library, with a pupil-written (all ages) suggestions book. Brilliantly converted science, art and technology centre in the stable yard (very busy at club time in evenings and over week ends) and super art. Keenly sporting – particularly successful at rugby and girls' hockey. Many matches are played on tour as the school is fairly isolated. New swimming pool, a covered heated version (no diving) takes over from the old outdoor pool. Weekend life is kept busy and full, with lots of expeditions, outdoor pursuits of all kinds (madly popular), lots of staff on hand (staff accommodation dotted about the grounds, good for attracting teachers).

Three-weekly exeats (Thursday evening till Monday evening), but no half term in Lent.

Nursery has been tacked on (by parental demand, and moved here from another venue). Pre-prep continues to flourish.

All round, the school is in good heart and doing well; jolly good parental noises. Not a concentratedly academic place – its ambitions and the abilities of its children are both wider than that.

NEWCASTLE PREPARATORY SCHOOL

6 Eslington Road, Newcastle-upon-Tyne NE2 4RH

TEL: *0191 281 1769* FAX: *0191 281 5668*

✦ PUPILS: 290 day boys and girls (two-thirds boys, one-third girls) ✦ Ages: 4-13 ✦ Plus 40 children ages 2-3 in the kindergarten ✦ C of E ✦ Fee-paying

---

Head: Since 1988, Mr Gordon Clayton, MA (early fifties). Educated at Bede School, Sunderland, and Christ's College, Cambridge, where he read natural sciences. White haired and jovial, a schoolmaster to his fingertips. Married with three children.

Entrance: At 4 (no tests), and at 8, via test and assessment.

Exit: Boys go on at 11 and 13 to the Royal Grammar School, Dame Allan's and The King's School Tynemouth. Girls leave at 11

for Central Newcastle High, Dame Allan's and Newcastle Church High School, with a few to La Sagesse and Westfield School.

Remarks: Traditional prep school with pre-prep and kindergarten attached, long established (1885). Has been through rocky periods (there were only 67 pupils, all boys, when Mr Clayton took over), but these days it is firmly entrenched as the first choice for parents wanting sons to go on to the RGS and daughters to the Central High. Regular contingents of bright Asians, including Japanese (Nissan cars are here). School bus runs all the way to/from Alnwick (about one hour). Other preps in Newcastle, Newlands Prep and Ascham House, are both in Gosforth.

Three-and-a-half terraced houses interconnected at various levels, every room crammed with colourful work and art. Cosy feel, slightly stuffy: very much an urban setting, in need of fresh air and greenery. Staff include experienced grannies and enthusiastic beginners. Broad intake, with two parallel classes, no streaming, no setting. French starts at four, and is well taught, 'Children love to mimic,' comments the head. Daily French lessons for nine year olds, Latin starts at ten. Around nineteen children per class. Small playing field on site, otherwise facilities are not far off and the school takes sport very seriously. Chirpy yellow and dark grey uniform and cheerful children. Some angst – among staff and parents – that 'children won't/don't read enough', (boys especially), despite school's valiant drive to encourage reading. Emphasis on computers at all ages, available even to tots. 'Too much computing,' muttered one parent. Keen boys edit and produce their own broadsheet newspaper, the accent on sporting activities.

NEW COLLEGE SCHOOL

Savile Road, Oxford OX1 3UA

TEL: *01865 243657* FAX: *01865 209 116*

E-MAIL: office@newcollegeschool.fsnet.co.uk

WEB: www.newcollegeschool.fsnet.co.uk

✦ PUPILS: 135 boys, all day ✦ Ages: 7-13
✦ C of E ✦ Fee-paying

Acting Head: Mrs P F Hindle MA (Oxon) PGCE. Previously deputy head, and at the school since 1993, is holding the fort while a successor is sought to Mr J Edmunds, who was here from 1990 and has left to pursue literary projects. Governors – the Warden and Fellows of New College.

Entrance: School runs a week of testing in January for six-year-olds – they come in groups of six with their friends to school, are tested in maths and English, play with construction equipment etc – ie it is selective, especially given geographical position. Potential choristers have voice trial in February aged eight, and pay reduced fees.

Exit: Magdalen College School, Abingdon, St Edwards are still by far the most popular choices. 20 scholarships (including 1 music award) in the last two years – ie, about a third of the leavers. Winchester no longer popular despite foundation link. OBs = Richard Seal, Ian Partridge, Andrew Lumsden, Howard Goodall (composer – Black Adder, Red Dwarf etc), Ian Fountain (pianist), etc etc.

Remarks: Feels like an elderly indigent relation, clinging to the coat tails of big brother – the mighty foundation of New College, in whose shadow the school squats. Do not, however, be put off by the unritzy surroundings, the standard asphalt playing ground and functional classrooms. Energy was breathed into the place by the former head, and by head of music Dr Roger Allen, who, according to a delighted parent, is 'fabulous, has opened up the music so that whereas before it all revolved round the choristers and college, now there are all sorts of events for the rest of the school' – including a regular St Matthew Passion and St John Passion – with help from parents.

Meanwhile choristers singing all manner of wonderful things, particularly early music, under direction of New College's choir master, Dr Edward Higginbottom, who came in '76, has seven children (some in the school), wears a Rupert Bear scarf and treats the children as adults (too adult?). 'I see it as an enabling job,' comments Dr Higginbottom, 'to get out of them what they can do.' Constantly on Classic FM and in their Top Ten.

Saturday morning is all devoted to culture – the head has taken this out of the weekday curriculum, so children can do four out of seven or eight options, eg drama, pottery, art, music. Soccer can be dropped at the age of nine – 'we're very civilised here'. Uses New College playing fields just across the road. Weeny gym. Long rather naff trousers for all pupils. Despite choristers, boarding is no longer. Parents mainly lawyers, doctors, dons. Teaching traditional – three Rs. One class in each year group all taught together – ie, no streaming or setting, until the last year (8) which has a scholarship class. Maximum class size 25, average 20.2. Good, friendly low-key small Oxford prep with happy reports from parents. Awaiting news on the new head.

NEWTON PREPARATORY

SCHOOL

149 Battersea Park Road, London SW8 4BX

TEL: *020 7720 4091* FAX: *020 7498 9052*

E-MAIL: admin@newtonprep.london.sch.uk

✦ PUPILS: 230 boys, 220 girls, all day ✦ Ages: 3-13 ✦ Non-denom ✦ Fee-paying

---

Head: Since 1993, Mr Richard Dell MA (fifties). Came late to teaching. Left school at 16, discovered books at 21, attended an adult education college in early 20's, went up to read PPE at St John's, Oxford when he was 27. Former head of Penrhos in North Wales. Approachable, down-to-earth, and extremely popular with parents. Teaches philosophy to all children from year 5.

Entrance: Highly selective at 3+ and 4+. All applicants sent to educational psychologist at parents' own expense. 40 places offered to top 40 IQ scores. Operates a 'sibling policy' – they are admitted if at all sensible. School becoming increasingly popular so average IQ rises each year. Easier to get a place higher up the school, room then. From year 2 psychologist's report and half-day assessment. Scholarships available from year 1.

Exit: To Francis Holland (both), Alleyn's, JAGS, Latymer Upper, and a range of other schools. St Paul's and Westminster expected to feature more in the future, but Newton parents tend not to follow the herd.

Remarks: Markets itself as the school for high ability children. Initial rocky beginning when staff jumped ship en-mass to the now defunct Octagon School in 1994. Everything has now calmed down and the school is flourishing. Large Victorian purpose-built building (high ceilings, long corridors) situated in the no-mans land between Battersea and Nine Elms, almost opposite Battersea Dogs Home. New additions are light and spacious. New gym in 1999, plans for a swimming pool soon: permanent building work. School is not short of money.

Emphasis on academics. Four classes of 20. French from nursery. Maths setting from year 1, English setting from year 2, specialist teachers from year 4. Latin from year 5. Teachers are enthusiastic and some teaching is inspiring. Special resource unit run by 4 part-timers for children of high ability and dyslexics. Tremendous art. Lots of wonderful brightly coloured papier-mâché figures floating around the school. Good library, generous book allowance. Trying hard with sport; some games on site. Games teachers are an ex-rugby international and an ex-British gymnast.

Wide geographic mix produces larger social mix than other SW schools. School catchment area stretches into the far reaches of Streatham and beyond. Lots of media types. Attracts first-time buyers. Scholarships available, unusual for a junior school. Children appear happy and keen to learn. A popular school with parents, though some worry that their child has only proven to be above average, not brilliant, and so may suffer in the class as a result.

NORLAND PLACE SCHOOL

162-166 Holland Park Avenue, London
W11 4UH

TEL: *020 7603 9103* FAX: *020 7603 0648*

✦ PUPILS: 150 girls, 90 boys (to age 8 only)
✦ Ages: 4-11 ✦ Non-denom ✦ Fee-paying

Head: Since 1996, Mr David Alexander BMus (thirties), educated at Grosvenor High School, Belfast and University College, Wales. Musician (violin) and keen glider. Thoughtful, not pushy, quietly humorous. Parents blow hot and cold over Mr Alexander, the hot describe him – approvingly – as 'understated' and 'approachable'. A keen door-step head, relaxed and in control of the situation. Married to Valerie who works in the City, in insurance.

Entrance: At 4 years old – put babies names down at birth. First come, first served, NB still no tests, but special cases for children of Old Girls and Boys, also siblings. Occasional places later – worth a try.

Exit: Mostly to London day schools, academic or otherwise. Some to boarding.

Remarks: Back on form as a popular Holland Park pre-prep + prep choice. The former head, Mrs Garnsey, is still the owner, but has moved to the country, and 'keeps in touch regularly'. Rise in the fashion stakes also helped by Ken Prep shifting its premises out of the area. Several staff changes with new emphasis on youth including two competent young recruits (just ex-Durham), plus good student back up, some cuddly oldies stayed put, so did the

renowned head of gym, Stephanie Price; three men on the staff, the rest women. Music department has been given a big boost – with three choirs and a newly constructed music room round the corner in Queensdale Road. Director of studies newly introduced: 'badly needed' according to a parent with three children here, 'teaching and curriculum are co-ordinated now'. Two parallel forms of mixed infants – summer babies and winter babies, then boys and girls segregate and boys prepare for prep school entrance. No-nonsense approach to teaching prevails with homework throughout (sample for four year olds: finding four things beginning with the letter 'M'). Three special needs teachers come in from outside. Girls set in English, maths and science in the last three years; no Latin, but French from the age of four. 'We're proud of being an academic school without being selective,' says the head.

School founded in 1876, and is popular with successive generations. The three houses comprising the school are (still) a veritable rabbit warren of stairs, landings, and inter-connecting rooms. Well worn, crammed conditions typical of central London – crowded tidy classrooms have clearly marked cardboard boxes (for teaching materials), files, books, art, work stacked on shelves, notice boards with plenty on them on every wall. Gym has lunch tables stacked down one end and transforms into the dining room. Children can be dropped off at 8.15am, keen clubs (recorder, violin, country dancing, games) after school ends, except on Friday when estate cars, piled high with dogs, au pairs and provisions, scoop the children up and head off towards the M40 or M3. Mr Alexander has installed a library, (previously bookshelves in individual classrooms), done away with the educational psychologists' tests for four year olds (cries of 'hurrah' from parents), introduced twice termly news letters, and re-instated the school mag.

NORTHCOTE LODGE

26 Bolingbroke Grove, Wandsworth Common, London SW11

TEL: *020 7924 7170* FAX: *020 7801 9027*

E-MAIL: secretary@northcotelodge.org.uk

✦ PUPILS: 158 boys, all day ✦ Ages: 7-13
✦ C of E ✦ Fee-paying

Joint Principals: Since 1984, Mrs Colquhoun BEd, and her husband Malcolm. See entry on Broomwood Hall (prep). School is privately owned by the Colquhouns. Head: Since '98, Mr Paul Cheeseman BA (fifties). Did French studies at Warwick University. Experienced prep school teacher – came here by way of Hereward House in North London, and before that was at The Hall, Orwell Park, Port Regis, Ashdown House and an educational consultancy. A keen traveller. Qualified cricket coach, and hockey. Unmarried. Took over from Mr Bain.

Entrance: 40 boys taken in at 8+, tested in November before September of arrival. Boys from Broomwood Hall have priority. All round ability sought, not just academic strength.

Exit: To a fair spread of schools. Bradfield, Bryanston, Eton, King's College Wimbledon, Marlborough, Tonbridge and Wellington among them.

Remarks: Opened in '93 as a 'sister' school to Broomwood Hall, providing much needed more gentle trad prep south of the river, particularly appealing for parents whose children might find the high profile London prep schools daunting. School not yet an IAPS member. Parents from Wandsworth, Clapham, Putney, Fulham, Chelsea etc. Games four afternoons a week on Wandsworth Common. Keen karate. School housed in purpose-built 1870s building, with extra block for science, gym and art. Remedial teacher and IT teacher. Good IT provision. Smallish library. Children may arrive at 7.45am. Prep done at school so no homework. Lots of after school activities.

THE OLD MALTHOUSE

Langton Matravers, Swanage, Dorset
BH19 3HB

TEL: *01929 422302* FAX: *01929 422154*

E-MAIL: office@oldmalthouseschool.co.uk

WEB: www.oldmalthouseschool.co.uk

✦ PUPILS: 115: 85 boys (50 board, 35 day in main school + Pre-prep 30 (including 14 girls) ✦ Ages: boys 3-13, girls 3-9 ✦ C of E ✦ Fee-paying

Head: Since 1988, Mr Jonathan (Jon) Phillips BEd (forties), previously deputy head at The Downs, Wraxall. Educated at Canford School and St Luke's College, Exeter. Teaches junior French and PSHE to boys in their final two years. Very proud of school, enthusiastic and fun. Married (Sally)

with two children, James and Georgina.

Entrance: At seven or eight into the prep school, register early, own entrance test. Pupils 'mainly Dorset', five or so arrive via the London train and the same number 'from abroad'.

Exit: Two distinct camps here: major public schools (Winchester, Eton) and local(ish) schools such as Bryanston, Canford, Sherborne, Milton Abbey.

Remarks: Slightly surprising entrance off main street, but delightful converted Old Malthouse (dorm still called 'Granary'). Splendid multi-purpose hall with music rooms below and adjacent. Solid tradition of a scholarship stream, but also caters well for less able. Maximum class size currently 18, average 10. Some help for special needs. The school has a well-run exchange system (parents and boys are enthusiastic) with a French school in Normandy – boys spend ten days on their own in French families and attend French lessons. Teachers exchange too. Very structured, discipline includes cleaning silver, mucking out mini-buses and extra work. Boys say 'Sir', stand up etc, table napkins. Dining hall (lovely old benches) doubles for assembly and chapel on Sundays, when the dining hatch to the kitchen converts to an altar.

No longer the Spartan place it used to be; outdoor swimming pool has replaced 'Dancing Ledge', but lots of boyish activities abound – target shooting in old gym at break, clay shooting, karate, cookery and outdoor pursuits. Also good crop of school-boy howlers/jokes in the school magazine. Good games pitches in school's 15-acre grounds, including one all-weather area for tennis and hockey. Cricket teams doing well at the moment. Senior boys and 'Captains' ('OMH' prefects) have own room with 'toyes' (curtained off private work areas), where they do their assignments as preparation for life in their public school. This is a good small school, with a friendly atmosphere. Boys only – and as such now rather a rare beast. Works well – satisfactory reports.

ORWELL PARK

Ipswich, Suffolk IP10 0ER

TEL: *01473 659225* FAX: *01473 659822*

E-MAIL: headmaster@orwellpark.demon.co.uk

WEB: www.orwellpark.demon.co.uk

✦ PUPILS: 151 boys, 46 girls; around 149 board ✦ Ages: 3-13 ✦ Inter-denom ✦ Fee-paying

---

Head: Since 1994, Mr Andrew Auster BA DipEd (forties), previously head of The Downs School, Colwall, and before that director of music at Shrewsbury. Keen rugger player (played for English Universities, Durham, Cambridge and Gloucester RFC), accomplished musician. Gentle voice and manner belie the inner steel. strong social conscience. Aston Villa supporter though parents include Ipswich Town board members and players. Married with three children. Wife Liz greatly involved in school.

Entrance: By registration, thence by screening. Not difficult.

Exit: Harrow, Oundle, Gresham's, Haileybury, Westminster, Felsted etc.

Remarks: Famous East Anglian boys' prep school which has gone the usual route of taking girls (since '93) and creating a pre-prep. It is becoming increasingly local in feel. Not a swot shop, but initial extremely strong emphasis on spelling, tables, reading (the first activity of the day). Member of staff 'in charge' of special needs. Maximum class size 16, average class size 12. Sets/streams from third year and scholarship group from fifth year. Children kept busy at all hours and given heaps of opportunities – they build all kinds of things, sail well, play games four times a week (enough girls to be county champions at hockey, netball and tennis), use the army-built confidence (ie assault) course etc. The school has its own observatory (manned by local astronomy club) with a 10-inch refractor telescope and radio station. Lovely art studios; good music, pianos all over the place, and dozens of music practise rooms in the cellars. Busy clubs (including radio club), lots of options: free time is one, 'but you can't always choose that'. Library with bean bags (excellent idea – more schools are now copying), IT room open at all times. Glorious setting, overlooking the River Orwell, an attractive, dignified large Georgian-style house in mellow red brick with turn-of-the-century additions including brick skin; beautifully proportioned rooms, set in 105 acres of parkland. Dormitories user friendly. 'Formal family' meals in the large dining room. Immense, ritzy facilities. School has perhaps not quite the same energy it had in the late '80s, early '90s; pupil numbers are on the up, though. Children traditionally sons of landed gents and farmers, but intake now very considerably broadened; several from abroad. OB James (Lord) Prior.

PACKWOOD HAUGH

(PRONOUNCED HAW)

Ruyton-XI-Towns, Shrewsbury, Shropshire

SY4 1HX

TEL: *01939 260217* FAX: *01939 260051*

E-MAIL: enquiries@packwood-haugh.co.uk

WEB: www.packwood-haugh.co.uk

✦ PUPILS: 145 boys, 75 girls, 130 boarders, 90 day ✦ Ages: 8-13. Plus small pre-prep department (opened '93) ages 4-7 ✦ C of E ✦ Fee-paying

---

Head: Since 2000, Mr Nigel Westlake LLB PGCE (forties). Studied law at Exeter, qualified as a solicitor, then taught at Sunningdale until 1990 when he took his PGCE at Exeter. Taught at The Old Malthouse (qv, deputy head, head of English), and Aldro School, Surrey before coming to Packwood as deputy head in '98. Gentle, committed. Teaches English, French and drama; coaches rugby, cricket, squash (strong sporting interests). Unmarried. Has already been active in broadening the clubs and weekend programmes, and classroom reorganisation. Says that 'life at Packwood must be flexible and varied enough to enable each child to flourish', and that each child should leave Packwood 'with a strong sense of Christian values, and the courage to stand up for what is right'. Took over from Mr P J F Jordan, who was head from 1988.

Entrance: Short informal assessment – maths and English; academic scholarships sometimes awarded. Help for the needy. Children from Shropshire, Cheshire, Wales,

London and also from places abroad.

Exit: Boys mainly to Shrewsbury, with good numbers to Eton and Ellesmere (the local school of choice for the less academic); girls principally to Cheltenham Ladies' and Moreton Hall; ones and twos to a wide range of other schools. Good track record of gaining serious awards – academic, music and art – at good schools. School mag (unusually well written and presented – a must-read) full of ads from top girls' schools in pursuit of pupils).

Remarks: Academic but unpressurised, traditional country prep school. Boarding numbers, which had dropped dramatically, now rising again. Boys and girls work hard – they can be found doing so in their free time in small happy groups all round the school – and play hard too. Good learning support department. Careful streaming. High standards, but no sense of pressure cooking. Staff very prep-schoolish, several good old hands. Pupils openly nice to each other; a refugee from a London prep commented she couldn't believe how kind and caring and gentle it was, after London.

The outlook is broad – something for everyone to shine at, and a good choice (fifty plus) of options and activities (ballroom dancing is the most popular). Sensible use of free time. Keenly sporting – boys and girls do well in wide variety of sports; pupils allocated to 'Sixes' for school competitions. Astroturf pitch floodlit for after-dark games. Swimming pool covered (at last). Music and art much in evidence; IT, art and drama playing their part within other subjects.

Original sandstone house and farm buildings encrusted with additions and corridors; the '60s buildings seriously unhandsome, but recent ones (eg handsome purpose-built boarding house for the girls, run by charming former head of science plus

wife) much nicer. Boys' dorms in the main building with a cuddly matron on each landing. Grounds sweep away down the hill – a fine setting. Famous topiary of the Apostles in the garden bears more resemblance to a dozen steak-and-kidney puddings. Flourishing pre-prep.

PAPPLEWICK

Ascot, Berkshire SL5 7LH

Tel: *01344 621488* Fax: *01344 874639*

E-mail: saraht@papplewick.org.uk

Web: www.papplewick.org.uk

◆ Pupils: 200 boys. 150 board, 50 day. All must board by 11 ◆ Ages: 7-13 ◆ C of E ◆ Fee-paying

---

Head: Mr Rhidian Llewellyn BA DipEd (early forties). Educated at Pangbourne College, followed by University of London (where he read history), previously taught at Arnold House, and The Dragon, where he was a housemaster. Friendly, confident and fun. His wife, Sue, an interior designer, is in charge of housekeeping, and teaches art to the boys. Head teaches English and General Paper to scholarship boys, but would probably rather be playing, coaching or watching cricket (despite his keen horsey background – uncle is Harry of Foxhunter fame). Not everyone's cup of tea, though. He also edits the seriously challenging school STAG mag. Ably helped by his black labrador, Orlando. New chairman of governors, Mr Peter Rotheroe, who dealt wisely with recent bullying case, report parents, and school as a whole 'treated it as a nasty disease'.

Entrance: Non-competitive entrance exam: apply early. 60 per cent from Berkshire, around 20 per cent from overseas (about half ex-pats, half 'real' foreigners), the rest from London and 'wherever'.

Exit: Good record of scholarships/awards, academic, art and music over the years. More boys go to Eton than anywhere else.

Remarks: Prep school, which has celebrated its fiftieth anniversary as a boys' only proper boarding prep school (not a lot can claim this) with a considerable amount of harking back to past and not so distant triumphs. (Be sure to ask for up to date information as well.) Continuing stories of inspired teaching; small classes and brill computing and CDT facilities (and output). Help for dyslexics now comes from the Helen Arkell Dyslexia Centre. Maximum class size 17, average class size 12. Streaming and setting. Latin for all. Staff must stay late twice a week, most live on campus (and those that don't are housed by school locally) and boys now allowed out 'most Sundays' as well as official three exeats a term (including half term). Sunday afternoons are devoted to mega-activity time, with all staff on duty – day off in lieu during the week. Good with tricky children. Mr Llewellyn says his cleverest appointment was that of Father Eddie Phillips-Smith as Chaplain (previously at Edgarley Hall, where pupils still speak fondly of his 'wicked' (pupil-speak = top class) assemblies, eg turning scrambled eggs purple. Campus feels a bit suburban cramped, perhaps owing to position on the main road. Cars and games pitches all tucked into thirteen-acre site opposite Ascot No 7 car park, with lots of activities on heath and in nearby Windsor Great Park. Music keen, particularly choral. New sports hall and music school (including fourteen individual practice rooms) '98. Swimming pool, local riding. School's pride and joy is media centre with full-blown recording studio, pre-set camera markings on floor and regular Sunday am broadcasts on Radio STAG. Boys wear short trousers till their tenth birthday and must board for their last two years, which helps keep the proper boarding school 'feel' of the place. Super matron, formerly at The Dragon. Classrooms and dorms higgledy-piggledy throughout with cunning extending chapel. Twenty-four-bed dorms tucked under the eaves much the most sought after (ie 24 good bounces). New carpets, some bedrooms cramped, shabby furniture, ditto bathrooms. Local parents can and do use squash courts, tennis courts etc, good parent teacher contact but no Association. Friendly camaraderie, 20 per cent first-time buyers. Two 50 per cent scholarships annually. Strong sense of cheerful Christianity and well-organised and happy children. Good vibes. Breeding ground for headmasters.

PEMBRIDGE HALL PREPARATORY SCHOOL FOR GIRLS

18 Pembridge Square, London W2 4EH

TEL: *020 7229 0121/2* FAX: *020 7792 1086*

E-MAIL: pembridgehall@talk21.com

✦ PUPILS: 250 girls, all day ✦ Ages: 4+ – 11 ✦ C of E ✦ Fee-paying

Head: Since 1995, Mrs Laura Marani CertEd (finds it irrelevant to disclose her age). Has been deputy head here since 1986, and is widely respected and approved of both by staff and parents. Now she carries on the work of the redoubtable Mrs Elizabeth Collison, who took the school from 94 to over 250 pupils during her reign. Married with two grown-up daughters, who have been 'through the London system, and that's a great help' says Mrs Marani.

Entrance: Complicated. Two entry dates per annum (now a rarity): September (for those born between September and February) and January (for those born between March and August). Definite places are offered to the first five children registering for each month (applications should be in before the child is SIX WEEKS OLD), and thereafter up to five girls per month are put on the waiting list (which usually closes 6-8 months after birth). Girls may then be added to a supplementary waiting list (the father of a two-and-a-half-year-old was being given the bad news when we visited!). Twenty-three girls join the school at each intake, few are taken later, though occasional spaces do arise.

Exit: Most to London day schools; between a quarter and a fifth of the children go to smart boarding schools.

Remarks: Pleasant site in generously proportioned London square. School founded 1979. Tinies are taught by a teacher and full-time assistant for first three years, and classes hopefully 'fall away' down to about 20 by upper school (7-year-olds). Staff to pupil ratio 1:11. Classes mixed, not streamed (and totally integrated by upper school); French from eight, daily. Computers throughout. Special needs catered for in rather jolly room at top of house, girls often want to have reading difficulties to go there. Whole school in cunning conversion of former police house, music rooms under the pavement, science lab on the roof, and a super great hall in the basement for gym and drama, which Pembridge Association also uses. Science combines with CDT – put an electric circuit in your doll's house. Much use of local facilities: Avondale Park, Linford Christie Stadium and Perks Field (the Royal helipad) for rounders. Girls use the Square gardens after lunch. No catering on site, girls bring packed lunches and there was a competition running when we visited for the most imaginative.

Ethnic backgrounds mixed, but most children are British, with smart contingent. Very successful, very popular girls' prep and deservedly so. Low profile, now under steady leadership. The only worry, say strive-y London parents, is: are the children 'stretched' enough? Others celebrate this rare non-pushy girls' school.

THE PILGRIMS'SCHOOL

The Close, Winchester, Hampshire SO23 9LT

TEL: *01962 854189* FAX: *01962 843610*

E-MAIL: pilgrimshead@btinternet.com

✦ PUPILS: around 200 boys. About 75 full/weekly board, the rest day and day boarding ✦ Ages: 7/8-13 ✦ C of E, but caters properly for RC ✦ Fee-paying – includes 38 choral scholars on half fees

---

Head: Since 1997, Dr Brian A Rees BA BD DipMin PhD (early fifties). A Canadian, left school at 16 to go banking, to university (McGill) to study child psychology, computing and religious studies, then a masters' degree and doctorate in divinity at St Andrews, Scotland. Trained as a priest in Canada, doctorate in Church history, curacy in Canada, then sent to Bedford School as chaplain, then housemaster, then head of Bedford Preparatory School, where his charm and enthusiasm for PR wowed potential parents. Soft spoken, clear eyed, still very much a priest. Married to Susan. Has made substantial changes to the fabric of the school (see below). Wants boys to feel glad each morning, and to have a sense of accomplishment each evening. School owned and governed by the Chapter of Winchester Cathedral; head and bursar of Winchester College are also governors (and Dr Rees has common room rights at the College.)

Entrance: Voice trials for choristers and quiristers in November or by individual appointment at other times, aged 7-and-a bit to under 9. One audition for both; parental views on the different musical and life styles (public and committed for Cathedral, private for College), and different vocal requirements (bigger, purer for Cathedral, top line in full for College), usually decide who goes where; no difference in kudos. 'It is expected that successful candidates will stay at the school until 13; the first year is regarded as probationary.' Half boarding fees for these, plus means-tested bursaries if needed. Test at seven plus for ordinary mortals, in English, maths, perceptual and verbal reasoning, and 'other such tests and activities as may prove helpful in determining readiness to begin at The Pilgrims'.' – a 'fun morning for the candidate.'... School looks for all-rounders as much as scholars. Day places oversubscribed. Put name down a couple of years early, at least.

Exit: Up to half to Winchester (40 awards here in nine years). Otherwise hither and yon, to eg King Edward's Southampton, Sherborne, Eton, Charterhouse, Canford, Marlborough – in particular to schools offering music scholarships – 56 of these in the last nine years.

Remarks: Traditional little prep school in the most glorious site in the shadow of Winchester Cathedral (tourists milling round). School (and its previous incarnations) originally for the 22 choristers who sing in the Cathedral. Present incarnation of school founded in 1931 to add 'commoners' and turn what had been a choir school into a 'proper' prep; the 16 quiristers (pronounced kwiristers) who have sung in Winchester College Chapel since 1383, joined the school in 1965.

Music understandably strong – 185 boys learn at least one instrument, and music scholarships are regularly won. Two choirs of its own 'They emerge', said a mother, 'as little professionals.'

French from year 3, Latin from year 6. Streaming, setting and differentiation within years and subjects. Timetabled computing, satellite French. An impressive staffroom – a good many young and female, good teaching; large numbers of Oxbridge graduates teach in the school, head wants teachers to be the best in the UK at their disciplines. Careful not to overcook those not headed for Winchester or Eton. Assessment card filled in for each pupil every three weeks – keeps close tabs on progress, has EP's reports on many.

School has a bit of a 'split' feeling as choristers go in one direction, quiristers to Dr Christopher Tolley in another, and the rest eg to assembly. School day for day pupils = 8.15-4.40, then, after first two years, hobbies (known as 'Commoners' Hour' – as the singers are singing at this point) till 6.15, supper 6.25, then prep. Choristers begin at 7.15 – singing with the larks. Maximum class size 18. Very keen games – 12 sports teams out on the average weekend.

Uniform Lovat-green sweaters, grey trousers. choristers wear red, quiristers blue. Buildings an interesting squashed hodgepodge from wonderful medieval Pilgrims' Hall, in which pilgrims were thought to rest from their exertions at St Swithun's shrine (now the school hall – note the ancient hammer beam roof) to impressive new buildings put up to house classrooms, labs, IT etc. Swimming pool 'The Puddle' next to courtyard. New small concert hall, where pupils put on concerts at their own initiative. As you might expect from the head's background, IT, internet, e-mail and music technology all now top notch.

Dormitories in middle of school, no longer Spartan – lots of furry animals, the nicest showers we can remember seeing. Twenty-eight also sleep in the 'quiristers' house' that is just down the road. Music

rooms and practice cells in what was probably the stables – incredible old oak. Team games important – fields up to twelve teams at the weekend. River in the grounds – senior boys have fishing rights.

Boys bright-eyed, lively, smart and courteous. A fine school all round

---

PORT REGIS

Motcombe Park, Shaftesbury, Dorset
SP7 9QA

Tel: *01747 852566* Fax: *01747 854684*

E-MAIL: office@portregis.com

WEB: www.portregis.com

✦ PUPILS: 330 boys and girls (57 per cent boys), 260 board, 70 day ✦ Ages: 7-13. Plus pre-prep (around 50 boys and girls ages 3-7) ✦ C of E ✦ Fee-paying

---

Head: Since 1994, Mr Peter Dix MA (Cantab in classics) and BA (Natal University) (forties). South African, he worked for a short time in the City before taking up teaching. Previous post: sixteen years at King's Canterbury, the last five as a housemaster. Keen sportsman, humorous, a sensitive soul hiding behind a slightly bland exterior. Keenly aware that people are the most important aspect of a school, strongly believes in team work. Hot on emphasising the positive, heaps enthusiastic praise and encouragement on children. Teaches Latin five or six periods each week. Attractive wife, Liz (they are a double act), with a BA in fashion and textiles, teaches textile design here. Two children (one on her gap year).

Entrance: Not academically selective. Book a year in advance. Academic, music, gymnastic, and all-rounder scholarships awarded.

Exit: Bryanston for around one quarter of the latest leavers, also Marlborough, Canford, Sherborne, Eton, Millfield, Sherborne Girl's and a wide range of others – a recent survey shows that since the current head has been here children have moved on to 69 different schools – excluding state and overseas – of which 29 are co-ed and 40 single sex). Very good record of academic and art scholarships.

Remarks: Co-ed country prep school humming with activity and with fabulous facilities, bucking the trend by increasing boarding numbers. Set in rolling Dorset parkland, the main house was originally built for the Duke of Westminster. This main building has been facelifted inside since our last visit (paint and lay out), 'so the contents now match the packaging' claims Mr Dix. Huge staff increase – ratio is now 6:1 pupils:staff (is this a record?), staff a mixture of young and old, with a low turnover. Average class size is 15, streaming from 8 and setting from 10, Latin at 10 for some, 11 for others. General knowledge and current affairs part of the weekly timetable. Head keenly aware that the child is the father of the man, and puts much emphasis on motivating children so that they believe in themselves. Head insists school is for low-flyers, not just high-flyers: 'the modestly under-powered are welcome here'. Mild to moderate learning difficulties well dealt with by good help on hand (one full-time and nine part-time teachers). EFL. Currently 30 foreign nationals in the school, and 90 children from overseas. Chaplain taken on recently, school has its own tiny chapel and uses the local church from time to time.

Houses have colourful dorms, bright carpets and duvets, boarding facilities all cosied up since our last visit, and everyone must be in their house by 7.55pm, with the last half hour as reading time in bed. Bean bags all over the library, however, not very sophisticated reading schemes or literary criticism compared with some schools we have visited. Hobby time every day – a vast choice.

Sport could well be your main reason for sending your child here – it is just fabulous, with games every day, teams at all levels, (colts, mini colts, fourth XI) 'So good for boosting confidence and self-esteem,' from a parent. Girls sports now taken very seriously (complaints that 'it was just the boys' previously), under 11 national netball and hockey champions, also very strong on rounders and gymnastics. Drama keen – notable recent production *Lark Rise to Candleford*.

Children choose their own tutor when they are 10 (and hang on to him/her until they leave), and head has instigated a firm whole-school attitude to nurturing. New building opened September 2000 housing dining room and kitchens. Head terribly keen on meal times ('my father was a hotelier'), and insists on no queues, on leisurely meals, on staff and children sitting together so that table talk and manners are taken care of. Pre-prep has waiting lists – most of the children come on to the main school.

Atmosphere is informal, friendly, fun. Everyone appears to be on-the-go all the time – staff and pupils, and plenty happens at week ends. Which said, the school appears to have calmed down somewhat since our last visit (no bad thing?).

QUEEN'S GATE JUNIOR
SCHOOL

133 Queen's Gate, London SW7 5LF

TEL: *020 7589 3587* FAX: *020 7584 7691*

E-MAIL: principal@queensgate.org

WEB: www.queensgate.org

✦ PUPILS: 130 girls, all day ✦ Ages: 4–11
✦ Non-denom ✦ Fee-paying

Head: Since 1998, Mrs Nia Webb BA PGCE, who comes from the senior school; took over from Mrs Ann Karol who was here from '87. Works closely with the principal, Mrs Holyoak (see entry for Queen's Gate School).

Entrance: Put names down early (preference given to grand-daughters/daughters of Old Girls, and sisters). Children spend a morning in the school a year in advance of their entry to make sure they will 'fit in'.

Exit: At least a dozen per year move on up into the senior school (qv), others choose other London day schools or board. Horses for courses – and the school puts no pressure on pupils to move on to the senior school.

Remarks: Delightful and busy school – the walls bulging with pupils' work, loads of clubs and extra-curricular activities to be enjoyed – including cooking, sewing, music. Clever grouping of children and use of staff enables them to work at their own pace. Remedial help for those in need, but every single child takes a turn with the specialist teacher so 'no-one feels odd'. French

from the age of four, Latin for all at ten, computing from eight. Some worries that it's not academic enough at top end.

Excellent use of space (eg the entrance hall lobby turns into a quiet corner for reading when needed). The junior school has its own front door and it takes up a comfortable chunk of the ground floor; plus use of some of the senior school facilities, eg science laboratories, music rooms, computer room etc. School flowers brought in by class rota. No garden or playground, but two roof terraces, and daily walks and lots of games and keen gymnastics. Strong PTA and parental links (loads of Old Girls' whose own mothers were here). Minimal uniform (Harris navy blue coat, knitted wool hat; blazer and boater; plus games clothes). Lively and cosy. Collection time (double parking) a real bore for passing traffic.

RIDDLESWORTH HALL
SCHOOL

Diss, Norfolk IP22 2TA

TEL: *01953 681246* FAX: *01953 688124*

E-MAIL: riddlesworthhall@pobox.com

✦ PUPILS: 41 girls (13 full, 8 weekly boarders, the rest day) plus 20 boys and girls in the nursery and 8 in kindergarten
✦ Ages: 8–13, pre-prep and nursery, 2–8
✦ C of E ✦ Fee-paying

Head: Since 2000, Mr Colin Campbell BA (forties), educated at King George V School, read philosophy at Sussex. Previously at Belmont School in Surrey.

Wife – Julia – is an authority on Phono-Graphix and runs pre-prep and remedial departments; two daughters. Hobbies include mountaineering and sailing. Took over from Mr David Dean, who was here from 1997.

Entrance: Registration and interview.

Exit: Mainly at 13, usually to a broad spread of single-sex schools, Tudor Hall, North Foreland Lodge, Queenswood, Benenden, Gresham's, Oundle, Framlingham, Hethersett Old Hall etc.

Remarks: Used to be one of the Allied Schools, who decided to close it – resulting in a precipitous fall in numbers. Rescued in April '00 by Colonel Keith Boulter, owner and head of Barnardiston Hall, Haverhill, and the Reverend David Blackledge. Posh little school with a family feel to it – being nice and good manners all matter here – set in a distinguished Georgian-style listed stately home (the original building was destroyed by fire, and re-built in the Edwardian era) with glorious grounds and lovely trees in an unspoilt deep country area (down the road from Diss). But the grandeur is made cosy, with log fires burning in several rooms, including the library, where there is a welcoming mixture of bean bags and old leather sofas.

Some teaching rooms pleasantly set around courtyards. French particularly well taught, and starts at the age of five. Maths streamed for one year; good IT, rather dark dingy science lab in the basement, but clearly an area where a lot goes on. Some help for individuals who need it (dyslexia, dyspraxia and so on), given in slightly gloomy rooms; also EFL – this school is a popular choice for girls from the continent doing a term or two. Not the place for academic high-flyers with ambitious parents.

Strong music (the harpist practises in the head's study), and lovely art. Little puppet theatre (in one of the classrooms) and a good collection of puppets. Weekend programme has been beefed up by the head (complaints in the past that it was little better than a baby-sitting service), with day children gradually attracted to spend time in school on Saturdays and Sundays. Tap, ballet and modern dancing, Brownies, riding, and sailing in the summer are all popular. Wonderful adventure playground.

Fabulous indoor swimming pool, with a good swimming team, and games are taken seriously. So is drama: dressing up boxes for theatrically minded children dotted about the place. Gym doubles up as theatre. Smashing home economics department, sprouting budding cooks.

Boarding children sleep in small groups in jolly rooms, huge cuddly animal population and outdoors there is a mass of hutches for rabbits, gerbils etc. The dining room seats children (rota seating) with staff who dish out. Bread and butter pudding is everybody's favourite. Thriving nursery – known as the Wigwam. Most famous Old Girl: Princess Diana.

'Please don't let the recent change of ownership downgrade your write up – it's still the lovely country girls' prep it always was – and the new money/management should give it new opportunities' said a local. We hope so too.

ROKEBY SCHOOL

George Road, Kingston-upon-Thames, Surrey
KT2 7PB

TEL: *020 8942 2247* FAX: *020 8942 5707*

E-MAIL: hmsec@rokeby.org.uk

✦ PUPILS: 350 boys, all day ✦ Ages: 4-13
✦ C of E ✦ Fee-paying

Head: Since 1999, Mr Michael Seigel MA (forties). Educated at St Paul's and New College, Oxford; a classicist. Married, wife an education consultant, two children. Took over from Mr Roy Moody, who was head from 1985.

Entrance: At 4 (first come, first served subject to 'an informal assessment in a group play situation') and also at 7 via tests. Put names down early.

Exit: King's College Wimbledon, St Paul's (often with scholarships); also Charterhouse, Epsom, Eton, Winchester, Westminster, Dulwich and others, mostly high-powered. A very distinguished record of scholarships, including art and music.

Remarks: Traditional and forward-looking prep school. Enviable setting, almost like a country prep, in a very leafy part of Kingston, golf courses more or less all round. Founded in 1877 and has been going strong ever since. Became an educational trust in the 1960s, and the school belongs to a charitable company with current parents as members. The main building was the childhood home of John Galsworthy – built in the collegiate style in red brick with steeply pointed eves, and subsequently a large number of newer buildings, added to and adapted often. Good facilities throughout, two science labs with good space and light; strong design and technology. Loads of specialist teachers, and specialist teaching rooms for the top two years. 24 per class maximum (average 21 up to 11, twelve thereafter). Scholarship class for the last two years. High expectancy all round and boys work hard, formal teaching and regular testing – 'The boys thrive on it' said a father. Heavy emphasis on maths and English through all stages. Latin for all from 8/9 and always a clutch of clever boys doing Greek too. The head keeps a Red Book where pupils' names are recorded for exceptionally good work. Cups and prizes for just about everything. 'The school is best for the brightest boys,' commented the mother of a middle-of-the-road child wistfully. Specialist help for dyslexia, dyspraxia and – unusually – speech therapy, 'particularly useful at the junior stage' said the former head. Good food provided by a catering family. Unusually lively debating society, the Athenaeum, organised and run by the boys; good range of well attended activities – music groups etc. Sports hall and Astroturf on site, and two large split level playgrounds at the back of the school where the boys roar about – occasional reports of 'too much and a bit rough' from parents of (delicate?) boys reach us. Super sports grounds nearby. Keenly sporting – with lots of Saturday matches. Ambitious theatre and good music: lots of this, including regular singing competitions, three choirs, and lots of small groups play to the rest of the school. An additional music room is a recent addition. The pre-prep is self contained and purpose built (recently overhauled) with its own playground plus adventure playground – and appears to produce cheerful and fearless chaps. Junior

Rokeby has its own principal, but Mr Seigel is head of the whole enterprise.

ST ANSELM'S PREPARATORY SCHOOL

Bakewell, Derbyshire DE45 1DP

TEL: *01629 812734* FAX: *01629 814742*

E-MAIL: headmaster@s.anselms.btinternet.com

WEB: www.anselms.co.uk

✦ PUPILS: 185, including one-third girls. About two-thirds board – 90 per cent in later years. Also nursery/pre-prep of about 60 boys and girls ✦ Ages: 7-13, pre-prep 3-7 ✦ C of E ✦ Fee-paying

Head: Since 1994, Mr Richard Foster BEd from St Luke's, Exeter (early forties). Previously head of Pembroke House, Kenya (a school which has produced two heads for English preps in recent years). Married to Rachel – who helps run the school with him, they are in charge of all the boy boarders. Three young children, one still at the school. NB almost all the governors have (had) children in the school.

Entrance: By registration. Non-selective.

Exit: Impressive scholarship and exhibition list (bumper year '00 – half the year group) – most to good strong schools, Repton, Oundle, Rugby etc. Non-scholarship leavers go to as wide a range of schools as any prep school we know – Lady Manners, Uppingham, Worksop College, Sheffield High, Shrewsbury, Queen Margaret's, Wycombe Abbey, Wrekin, Derby Grammar, Denstone, Eton, Tudor Hall, Kimbolton – and this is only half the list.

Remarks: Site tucked up behind Bakewell church, overlooking fields of sheep and cows. Well-designed purpose-built blocks. School is only on to its fifth head since it started in 1888 – gives the place a totally family feel and the head's house is practically in the middle of the school, with toys and treasured possessions scattered about. Three girls' boarding houses, a little way down the road, all run by married couples, with small groups of children in them. The school has an outstanding record of academic success (given mixed intake), partly attributed to the staff-pupil ratio, with classes of an average of 12, and partly to that precious commodity which boarding schools have in abundance – time. The heavy schedule is, the head admits: much harder on the day children. Busy schedules with well designed trips to France, serious music (music scholarships to Oundle and Rugby recently). Pupils are children of doctors, lawyers, businessmen (no longer the very nice farmers) and some ex-pats. Dedicated and gentle staff, including classicists and linguists. Terrifically keen computer department. Pottery outstanding. School streamed after the first intake, but St Anselm's is definitely not a force feed. Philosophy pervades to learn what trying is – 'when you are 40 down in a match...' Sport on 'only' four afternoons a week, options otherwise. Main games rugby, football, hockey and 'mad keen' cricketing school – staff/parent XI goes on tours. Deserves to be better known. 'Good at getting the less academic up and running,'said a neighbouring headmaster.

ST ANTHONY'S SCHOOL

1 Arkwright Road, Hampstead, London NW3

TEL: *020 7435 0316* FAX: *020 7435 9223*

✦ PUPILS: 280 boys, all day ✦ Ages: 5-13
✦ RC ✦ Fee-paying

Head: Since 1994, Mr Nigel Pitel BA PGCE (forties), a historian, educated at Ampleforth and Oxford, married with two daughters and a son. Took over from his uncle, Tim Patton, who reigned here for 32 years, who finally transferred his shares into Trust, and took off to 'blow fire and run street theatre in Ireland'. Nigel joined St Anthony's in 1986 and was joint head '92-'94. Earnest, committed and caring. Wears Austin Reed jackets, but nevertheless he pledges to continue his great-grandfather's ethos 'that learning must be fun'. Comments (in response to our questioning) that his biggest challenge is without doubt 'trying to help our weaker students' over the intensely competitive 'hurdle' of getting into the major London day schools. Also comments a propos this that there is a need for another private senior school in North London. The school is privately owned, and Nigel is the fourth generation headmaster.

Entrance: Interview two terms before arrival. Boys admitted at any time if place available, and come from as far away as Islington, though most are fairly local.

Exit: Primarily to London day schools – Highgate, University College School, Westminster, City of London, St Paul's – and only occasionally to boarding schools, and almost never to 'proper' prep schools.

Remarks: School split between Junior School to nine in Fitzjohn's Avenue, and Senior School in Arkwright Road, nearby. Marvellous facilities for a London school: heated, covered swimming pool, good CDT, fish pond, and lots of play area. Junior school recently expanded, Portakabins removed, dining area extended and smell of cauliflower banished. School very firmly a jeans (with tie) place – though Nigel has tightened the dress code – 'but in no way will we become a grey school'. The school now employs four part-time specialist learning support teachers who provide over 40 hours of teaching a week (at no extra cost to parents – commendable). Academically, children are stretched. Teaching is imaginative and streamed at the top. Average class size 18. Staff are known by their first name, and classes are called eg '6G' = Six Gerald. 'Guys' get a huge choice of extra-curricular activities (chess, stained-glass making, producing their own 'playettes'). Hobbies, with 20 different activities, are after school and are on offer on different evenings of the week. Excellent creative writing. Boys have their horizons broadened 'minds blown with the excitement of it all': currently masses and masses of mime and theatre, with art in all directions intermingled with a really serious 'strong moral and spiritual dimension'. (Antonians, incidentally, are not noted for prowess on the games field.) Senior boys compose their own prayers; mass is celebrated at school three times a term. Strong anti-bullying policy. Great emphasis on self-motivation. Both sex education and the 'major survey on pot, speed, the barbiturates, cocaine, acid and heroin' are detailed in the prospectus. No bells ring. Curriculum revamped but Nigel has no thoughts of drastically changing this most unusual school – prospective parents either love it or loathe it. The staff have a rock band, and musical happenings are known as GAWs or Groove Awhiles. Sisters can only be green with envy.

ST AUBYNS

Rottingdean, Brighton, Sussex BN2 7JN

TEL: *01273 302170* FAX: *01273 304004*

✦ PUPILS: around 100 boys and girls; approx. 35 board or flexi-board ✦ Ages: 7-14. Plus own pre-prep with about 55 children ✦ C of E, Non-denom ✦ Fee-paying

Head: Since 1998, Mr Adrian Gobat (pronounced 'Gobar') BSc PGCE (early fifties). Educated at Hereford Cathedral School, St Andrews University (physics) and St John's Oxford for his PGCE. Previous post was one of two heads of the amalgamated prep schools Hordle and Walhampton, but owing to a governors' kerfuffle left and ended up here. Previously at Hurstpierpoint College Junior School, before that worked with older children at Cheltenham (housemaster) and Abbotsholme. Described by parents as 'a lovely man'. Married to Mary, with four children. Interested in hill walking, camping, sea swimming, theatres etc etc. Took over from Mr Julian James, who was here since '74 and created a community which was altogether special. RIP the school dog Perkins, who was very much part of the success story. Sic transit gloria canis. The end of an era.

Entrance: By assessment, interview and report from previous school.

Exit: St Bede's, Brighton College,

Eastbourne College, Stowe, Tonbridge and a scattering of others; Eton, Radley and Harrow, which used to take lots from here, not much in evidence in the last few years. Reasonable record of scholarships.

Remarks: Excellent reports on new regime – a happy, vibrant place. Follows on the major changes of moving from single sex (boys) to co-ed, and tacking on a flourishing pre-prep (good Ofsted report already). French, Latin and maths setted from eight; in final years either in scholarship classes or CE classes. Full-time Hornsby-trained special needs teacher plus a part-timer, helping with dyslexia etc and with EFL. Maximum class size 16 (average 14). Good links with France and French boys, also Spaniards, in school. Super art. Currently winning fencing prizes. Under Mr and Mrs James, pupils were charming, confident, articulate and looked you in the eye – it was the perfect place to send a child in need of confidence-boosting, and had a very special safe and happy atmosphere; Mr Gobat shows every sign of maintaining it.

School on the edge of the sea (which, if you think of it, is a geographical disadvantage as far as catchment area is concerned – fishes only), in village with playing fields rising up the hillside behind. Super matrons – dormitories a bit Spartan (but reported redecorated summer 2000, and carpeted indeed), but immaculate and gleaming. Wonderful iron bedsteads, cheerful, seaside wooden architecture. A slightly grimbo chapel (entire school disagrees with this description), small and full of memorials to the war dead. Some recent building improvements.

Flexible arrangements on boarding to suit parents and individual pupils. Alternate Saturday morning school and Saturday afternoon games for one and all. Proud of their sports record. Do not be put off by humble surroundings and slight old-fashioned feel.

ST CHRISTOPHER'S SCHOOL

32 Belsize Lane, London NW3 5AE

TEL: *020 7435 1521* FAX: *020 7431 6694*

E-MAIL: admissions@st-christophers.hampstead.sch.uk

✦ PUPILS: around 230 girls; all day ✦ Ages: 4.5-11 ✦ Non-denom ✦ Fee-paying

---

Head: Since 1992, Mrs Fiona Cook (fifties), has been at the school 17 years, previously teaching maths, computers and science. Educated mostly in America. Interests: hiking, reading, computers. 'If anything goes wrong (with the school's new computer network) I'm landed with it.' Grown up son. 'Very English, very reserved, dry sense of humour,' commented a mother. Both parents and staff describe her as 'distant', but she gets on well with pupils: twice during our tour first-years stopped her for a chat.

Entrance: Children born September – February start at 4^{1}/2+ and stay for 7 years; March – August birthdays start at 5+ and stay for 6 years. Despite the almost-universal North London penchant for taking girls at 4, has no intention of changing the policy. 'I believe in nursery schools. And it's almost impossible to assess children at 3. They can be hopelessly shy then but amazing a year later.' List for assessment closes at 80, first come first served. Assessment mostly on a one-to-one basis by head and educational psychologist, but trying out some limited group assessment in 2001. Younger siblings nearly always admitted: 'We can advise that the child is unlikely to cope, but it's up to the parents to decide.' Occasional vacancies higher up, but not filled after year 4.

Exit: To all the major North London girls' day schools eg North London Collegiate, South Hampstead High, St Paul's Girls, City of London Girls, Channing, Francis Holland and some smart boarding schools. 'The girls try for three schools each, and they generally get offers from all of them,' says the head.

Remarks: Small, high-achieving girls' prep. 'Very confident girls, used to getting what they want,' said a mother. Class size: 18. Strong family feel, sheltered, informal, girls mostly dressed in tracksuit trousers and sweatshirts. 'The school has a feeling of controlled but bubbling energy,' said a mother. Large, airy Victorian building with separate classrooms for years 4-6. New library and computer building – 18 computers, all linked up to central network – designed in Scandinavian style with light wood and big windows. One parent commented that 'The girls utterly adore all the teachers.' Specialist teachers throughout for French, music and PE, and for all subjects in the top three years, at which point the children move from classroom to classroom for different subjects. Some muttering about pressure and loads of homework in years 5 and 6, but head denies this and insists that it never goes above 40 minutes a night. No scholarship class and no competition within the classroom. Highly praised remedial teaching (with no stigma attached) for the small minority – mostly younger siblings – who aren't highly academic. 'They've done everything they can to help my daughter', said one grateful parent. Very strong on art and music – 'We have very bright children, so we don't need to be eyes down all the time – we have time for all these other things.' 80-90 per cent learn at least one instrument. Junior and senior orchestras and choirs, plus chamber choir. Several non-art teachers (eg DT) are also trained in fine art, much top quality work on display around the school. Less emphasis on PE. Cramped site allows netball and short tennis, plus rounders. Swimming in year 3 only. All girls do British Amateur Gymnastics Association awards. Much care goes into choosing appropriate senior schools. 'Mrs Cook pointed out my daughter's personality and character and gently directed us towards the school that would suit her.'

Parents mostly affluent 'something in the City' or similar North Londoners. ('Can be a bit precious,' comments a fellow-parent.)

ST JOHN'S COLLEGE SCHOOL

Grange Road, Cambridge CB3 9AB

TEL: *01223 353532* FAX: *01223 315535*

E-MAIL: registrar@sjcs.co.uk

WEB: www.sjcs.co.uk

✦ PUPILS: around 240 boys, 200 girls. 50 boy and girl boarders, 390 day ✦ Ages: 4-13 ✦ C of E ✦ Fee-paying

---

Head: Since 1990, Mr Kevin Jones MA (early forties), plus unfinished thesis on how best to acquire knowledge and preserve creativity. Educated Woolverstone Hall (state boarding) and Caius, Cambridge. Previous post – deputy head in the school and before that head of drama and English at the Yehudi Menuhin School. Married with one son who has just left the school, and one in the kindergarten. A thinker, good with children. Nice sense of humour. Comments, a propos parental observation that the school is a high pressure zone, that this is not so, he thinks, and that 'the most precious thing we can give to our children is their childhood'.

Entrance: Getting in is Cambridge prep Valhalla. Name down embryo on. No testing at three-plus = 'ridiculous' – but test at seven. Yearly scholarships for up to five boy choristers a year. Means-tested scholarships and bursaries at 11+ for outstanding academic, music, artistic or all-round ability.

Exit: Every year gets clutch of scholarships to strong music schools – Eton, Tonbridge, Uppingham, Winchester. Also gets academic scholarships, not to mention art IT, DT and sports awards (28 awards from 50 leavers in '00). Sends up to one third of boys to The Perse School, Cambridge, also sends pupils to Oakham, Westminster, Rugby, Radley, Oundle, King's Canterbury etc, and one or two East Anglian schools. A few girls leave at 11+ usually for The Perse Girls' and St Mary's Cambridge, the rest generally opt for co-educational boarding at 13+.

Remarks: Wonderful prep school in a dreamy city – well worth bustling about to get in. Feels like a honeycomb of schools – kindergarten department in separate house, 'so it feels like home'; five-to-eight-year olds are in a wing of the smart tailor-made Byron House, which was refurbished and reopened in 1990 to replace a multitude of Portakabins, and provides not only classrooms, but smart hall/gym, drama studio, DT, music department etc for tinies. A bit of a squash, say parents, particularly for younger pupils. Older pupils in a house next door; boarders live above the shop with their own private recently refurbished and upgraded quarters – part of the £2 million building development (you name it, they've got it, from indoor swimming pool, to junior library and new music school with individual practise rooms, song school and concert room). Adjacent property acquired and recently redeveloped provides gardens, an arts facility and a lecture theatre; space freed up in old buildings used to expand ICT etc. Claims to have (and we would not dispute it) best computer facilities of any prep school: whole school networked in '98; two computer labs, and two networks of PCs for the four- to nine-year-olds. (Plus laptops.) More important – the school has the staff to go with them: all teachers and classroom assistants are trained in IT in-house to the skill level achieved by leaving pupils (ie v high). Recognised as the National Expert Centre for all prep schools for design technology and information technology. Head's aim is to 'meet individual needs of each child, so the most (and least) able children get what they need', and with that in mind he has come up with a number of developments: study skills (teaching children the skills of individual learning) now an integral part of the curriculum; advanced tutorial system, with one member of staff responsible for 'knowing all there is to know' about no more than ten children and their families; reporting system that allows parents to be 'fully involved' in their children's education. Also 'individual needs department' – qualified specialists backed by educational psychologist on staff. Approximately 20 per cent of pupils at any one time receive help with a 'learning difficulty'. Head hopes that a parent's comment that 'The school's fine if you can cope, but no fun for the strugglers' no longer applies – places immense emphasis on children's happiness, the need for fun and laughter,

and training teachers (wish more did this).

Jolly red uniform. High calibre of teachers who draw all that is best and most original from pupils. Classes never more than 20 and these are subdivided in senior years to make classes of 12-18. Choristers under tutelage of organist Christopher Robinson. Terms now fit in with other schools and not university terms as hitherto. Most helpful, flexible school day/week includes weekly boarding, 'day' boarding (ie until 8.15pm) and 'staying on' (until 6.00pm) – a miracle for working parents. No longer Saturday morning school, but sports coaching and optional activities. Although this is not a professional games school, it has lots of sporting options with good coaching including real tennis and rowing (has produced national real tennis champions). Also the usual sports – rugby, hockey (for the girls), etc and head points out the school has produced county players in these sports as well as netball, cricket, racquets, athletics and swimming.

ST PAUL'S CATHEDRAL

SCHOOL

New Change, London EC4M 9AD

TEL: *020 7248 5156* FAX: *020 7329 6568*

E-MAIL: admissions@spcs.city-of-london.sch.uk

WEB: www.stpauls.co.uk

✦ PUPILS: 100+ boys, including 38 choristers (15 a side plus 8 probationers); choristers board, the rest day ✦ Ages: 8–13 plus pre-prep – up to 45 boys and girls, ages 4–7 ✦ C of E, but ' all are welcome' – though ' better if choristers are Christian' ✦ Fee-paying (but choristers get their tuition fees paid)

Head: Since 2000, Mr Andrew Dobbin (forties). Educated at Uppingham and Emmanuel College, Cambridge, where he read English, architecture and fine art. Taught at prep schools, then King's Canterbury where he was a housemaster and head of drama, running the King's Week Festival. Passionate about all arts. Escapes at weekends to Shropshire, where he has an eight acre garden-to-be. Took over from Mr Stephen Sides, who has gone to be head of Northbourne Park.

Entrance: Preliminary assessment at 4+(waiting list here); academic test and interview at 7+. Choristers also have voice trial at 7+ and 8+ in November, February and May. Any RCs are 'cleared with Westminster Cathedral' (brownie points). Four-year-old entrants; we 'might kick them out at seven'. Pupils come from Dallington, Charterhouse Square, the Mary Rose Barbican Playgroup, Stepping Stones, Green Gables etc.

Exit: Girls head for Francis Holland, City of London, Cavendish, The Lyceum; day boys go to City of London, Highgate, Forest; or to a varying range of boarding schools eg Uppingham (the celebrated Anthony Way is here). Choristers were not getting enough choral scholarships to high powered music schools (eg one to Eton '97), but better now.

Money Matters: Bursaries up to full fees available for choristers.

Remarks: A prep school which is beginning to flex its muscles in an area described by one and all as an 'educational desert' – the City and round about. Parents and the Dean and Chapter (the latter form the governing body of the school) are being dug in the ribs by the head who says he is 'quite good at selling the school'. There have also been a fair number of staff changes over the past three to four years. The school lurks in the eastern shadow of the mighty Cathedral with buses swirling past, non-stop traffic, very central, very hemmed in, but the amount of space is not bad by inner London standards. The school has a garden for juniors, a quad for bashing balls about in, and the choristers can skateboard actually in the grounds of the Cathedral after hours – a great place to let off steam among the tombstones. Enormous ambitious (re)building programme now completed, funded by the Dean and Chapter of the Cathedral – 'the Cathedral dominates all our lives', comments the head. Most of the rebuilding is to make room for the pre-prep, which gets a nice, light airy wing with lovely (if rather too close up) views of the Cathedral. Main school is packed around the quad, with a business-like boarding house to one side. Accommodation here is warm and comfortable, though lacking in extra rooms for playing in – all meals etc are taken in the main school building – 'the boys go here to sleep'. The boarding master is 'me', says the head. There are two qualified nurses; the head of science also lives in, and the head of PE. There is a wonderful bouncing castle on the site – 'excellent for boys to let off steam after evensong', and lots of esoteric clubs in the lunch hour and after school, such as Star Trek, home modelling, War Hammer, musical composition, fencing (they're usually beaten by the Hall at this, which is no disgrace however). All do Latin from ten, French from four, Greek is an option. Class sizes 15-20, maximum 20. Single stream. Not a place for dyslexics, though specialist help 'can be called in'. All do games once a week, though school admits games might be a weakness. Music is of course the school's raison d'être. Organist and director of music in the Cathedral John Scott is in charge of the choristers' music, and has lifted the choir into the first division of choir schools, making a merry and musical sound, every eye on the conductor all the time, and no help from amplifiers at time of writing. The choir is currently recording all the psalms from the St Paul's psalter – a massive labour of love. So far the school has mostly avoided the pot-boiling end of recording. The choristers have the usual exhausting regime, plus tours of eg Brazil, and have the usual slightly white pinched weedy look to them. Theory of music perhaps not as hot as performance – but all choristers take GCSE music at 13. New director of music for the school has improved the excitement level in music for non-choristers. The school magazine does a good line in acrostics and other gems, eg: 'S', Scott, Sides, Sutton, Stanford in G, 'T's Tallis, Truro, Treleaven's for tea, 'U' is for Unison, Praise the Almighty…'

ST PETER'S EATON SQUARE CE PRIMARY SCHOOL

Lower Belgrave Street, London SW1W 0NL

TEL:*020 7641 4230* FAX: *020 7641 4235*

E-MAIL: stpeaton@rmplc.co.uk

✦ PUPILS: 266 primary and 50 nursery (intake 10 per term to the nursery and 40 per year to the reception class). All day ✦ Ages: 3-11 ✦ C of E ✦ State – voluntary aided

Head: Since 1992, Mr John Wright BEd in education with geography and mathematics (fifties). Previous career in state system in London Borough of Merton and in Beaconsfield. Keen on music, especially opera, gardening, also travel planning. Fantastically thorough and efficient and makes a real point of knowing his pupils, his staff and the parents well. Keen on 'the corporate ethos' and has a real talent for 'getting us to work as a team,' said one teacher, not to mention encouraging parents to help. Comments dryly that the school's overall intake 'helps provide an environment well-matched to the society in which our young people will enter when they leave school'.

Entrance: Register name after first birthday for the nursery, and after the second for the reception class. Visit school. Priority given to children whose parents attend St Peter's Church; children with siblings in the school; children whose parents attended the school; children baptised as Anglicans etc etc. Always oversubscribed at early levels, and there is no automatic transfer (but some priority) from nursery to reception classes. Offers are made eleven months before a pupil is due to take up a place.

Exit: To local state schools, particularly Greycoat Hospital, Lady Margaret, Pimlico, London Nautical etc. Thirty per cent to private schools – Christ's Hospital, JAGS, Godolphin & Latymer, Clapham Hill and Streatham High etc.

Remarks: Super central London primary school, which got a deservedly glowing Ofsted report. Good social mix – 'everything from duchesses to dustmen and politicians', in the words of the previous head; 'a very broad spectrum of socio-economic backgrounds', comments the present head. Loyal parents and PTA (good fund raisers, these), exceptionally committed and dedicated professional staff. Terrific swimming school (all except nursery and reception use nearby Queen Mum's Sports Centre pool every week) – and continues to hold all the Westminster trophies and children regularly compete at county level. Good music, and getting better all the time. Keen computers – and computer centre opened '98 and IT timetabled. Competent special needs provision. Maximum class size thirty (several classes less than this). No streaming. French now an 'option' – with parent-organised club after school on Wednesdays, staffed by members of the Les Petits Marionettes – a start. Food reported to have improved (was ghastly). Maintenance of school supported by London Diocesan Board. Every inch of the school is used, with cunning time-tabling and doubling up of rooms for various purposes. Jolly shouts from the playground (playtimes are staggered – a clever move), with a regular

supply of mothers overseeing fair play. Library recently rehoused organised under the leadership of a rota of mums. School first mentioned in survey carried out by the National Society for Promoting Religious Education in 1864-7, sited in Eccleston Place. Moved to present building in 1872 on a site given by the Marquess of Westminster. Assumed its present form in 1949. Visited by HM Queen in 1972 (centenary year) and by HM Queen Mum in '95. Strong links with St Peter's Church, and the clergy pop in and out (Church very high Anglican – so high, in fact, that a passing arsonist mistook it for Roman Catholic and burned it down not so long ago). Super nursery opened in '92 in the crypt of the Church, now on site. Morning or afternoon sessions, with groups of 25, with a gem teacher, a nursery nurse and two helpers – not nothing. Alas, this is (of course) a pretty windowless crypt, but has lovely 'areas' for different activities. Drawback of the main school is that it is very cramped for space (though NB, many local private schools are even more cramped) and playground can be horrifically noisy and bursting at seams at break time. Children are not 'pushed' academically – but with two thirds of pupils reaching level 5 in year 6 they are well well ahead of national expectations; good '97 Ofsted report.

ST PHILIP'S

6 Wetherby Place, London SW7 4NE

TEL: *020 7373 3944* FAX: *020 7244 9766*

E-MAIL: info@stphilips.demon.co.uk

WEB: www.stphilips.demon.co.uk

✦ PUPILS: 95 boys, all day ✦ Ages: 7/8-13
✦ RC ✦ Fee paying

Head: Since 1990, Mr H Biggs-Davison MA (early forties), educated St Philip's, Downside, Fitzwilliam College, Cambridge, where he read geography – and came straight back to St Philip's to teach in 1978. Aims to run an 'even more excellent little prep school and develop it, not in terms of expansion but as a place'. Seriously good looking. Good at recruiting and good with children. Open. Recently won the school's annual Conker Competition. Wife is the one with ideas.

Entrance: Standard not difficult, but over-subscribed like everywhere else. Several tests, but priority is given to Catholics.

Exit: A variety of schools including the London Oratory, the Oratory (Reading), St Benedict's Ealing, Westminster, St Paul's, Dulwich, and out-of-London boarding schools eg Ampleforth, Harrow.

Remarks: Central London Catholic prep school – could be a solution. Housed in large redbrick Kensington building. Cramped classrooms but wonderful leafy and muddy playground which runs the whole length of the block. Maximum class size twenty; top form streamed. Kensington

Dyslexia Centre provides teachers for dyslexics/dyspraxics (school will accept pupils with learning difficulties). Pupils a riot of different nationalities – Italians and Portuguese, restaurateurs etc.

ST RONAN'S SCHOOL

Hawkhurst, Kent TN18 5DJ

TEL: *01580 752271* FAX: *01580 754882*

E-MAIL: info@stronans.kent.sch.uk

WEB: www.stronans.kent.sch.uk

✦ PUPILS: 165 boys and girls. A third boarders, two thirds day. Pre-prep: 65 boys and girls ✦ Ages: 7-13 (girls often move at 11) ✦ Pre-prep: 45 boys and girls, ages 2¹/₂-7
✦ C of E ✦ Fee-paying

Head: Since 1998 (but was in the school before this as teacher and head designate, learning the ropes), Mr Edward Yeats-Brown MA (thirties), who was a boy here, and after a short spell in the City, taught at Yardley Court where he met his wife Joanna (appears cuddly, but teaches judo). Four young children. Mild, intense, musician. Deputy heads: Mr John Buckles and his wife Sandie.

Took over from Sir John Vassar-Smith ('Charming Johnny'), who was here since 1970, at which point the school was family-owned. Sir J took over from his father 'Sir Rich'. New head maintaining the style and tradition including the boast 'You choose the school, and we'll get them there.'

Entrance: By interview. No exam, but pupils have to be of fairly good standard (if only because of that rash promise), but nonetheless cover a wide ability range. Pre-prep (still under the highly competent wing of Linda Smith), 'the puppies', now come in at age three, and there is even a teeny nursery class for two-and-a-half-year-olds. Girls can stay till eleven, or beyond if all agree that that would be for the best, and this is on girl/parent driven demand (35 per cent of upper 9s are now girls).

Exit: About two-thirds of pupils go on to public schools, of which Eton, King's Canterbury and Tonbridge are currently the most popular, Harrow, Sevenoaks, Wycombe Abbey and Benenden also feature. About a quarter of public school entrants gain scholarships. One third go to local grammar schools, principally Cranbrook. No CE or 11+ failures since 1990.

Remarks: Spiritually a home from home, a relaxed and informal school where teachers are approachable, mud is unremarkable, dogs are numerous, and boys pour in and out of the head's room to use the computers. Physically, a somewhat higgledy-piggledy encrustation on an impressive red-brick pile that was built from the proceeds of OXO.

A school which aims to develop each individual rather than impose a style. Academic achievement is valued; notices celebrating recent scholarships appear all over the school. Maximum class size 18, average 10-12. Good art. Latin taught as major subject from early on, traditional methods of teaching – grammar, syntax, the lot. Recent IT invasion now has computers all over. Vertical streaming: pupils stay in each class for three terms, but can move up at the end of any term if results justify; the top scholarship class offers a broad education for those who have surpassed the requirements of CE.

Day boys are included in everything (prep ends at 7.30pm every day) and most ask to board sooner or later. Children sleep and eat with their own age group. Saturday morning school, afternoon matches. The buildings are still quite recognisably a turn-of-the-century generous-hearted rich man's house. Acres of parquet; Lino flooring in corridors and classrooms now replaced by carpet; warrenous servants' quarters and basements, all pleasantly battered and much loved; splendid one-time ballroom (with sprung floor and painted ceilings) doubles up as theatre, reading room, billiard room, indoor football room etc. Stable block refurbished to provide space for art, music and labs. The chapel, which features every leaver's name and destination enrolled on boards, is used every morning and every evening for ten minutes. Dorms with themes, eg the nautical dorm has info on Morse code, flags and knot tying corner. OBs include Piers de Laszlo and cartoonist Sir Osbert Lancaster, whose Latin master used to tear up his sketches and demand prep instead. Popular with the Services and professions – 'Volvos, not Rolls-Royces'. Walls everywhere groaning with photographs of teams down the years: 'played 8, lost 8' at football records the fact that hockey is king here. Shooting and golf – they have their own course – also popular. Long tradition of muddy games in the woods. Cross-country runs on the school's own 247 (c)hilly acres.

Currently feels like a boys' school, with a few girls in it, but this will gradually change as feeder pre-prep grows up. Numbers on the up. Fine for chatty individuals who think work is fun, with parents who don't mind mud and mess. Combines wonderful very special family atmosphere with good results, and not above sending for mum if child ill and mum handy.

ST VINCENT DE PAUL
PRIMARY SCHOOL

Morpeth Terrace, London SW1P 1EP

TEL: *020 7641 5990* FAX: *020 7641 5901*

✦ PUPILS: 260, all day ✦ Ages: 3-11 ✦ RC ✦ State – voluntary aided

---

Head: Since 1986, Mrs Eileen Z Weller BEd. Previously acting head, before that, head of St Patrick's Kentish Town.

Entrance: Must be practicing Roman Catholics, priority given to those living in parishes of Westminster Cathedral or Pimlico.

Exit: Cardinal Vaughan, The London Oratory, St Thomas More, Sacred Heart Hammersmith etc.

Remarks: Super primary school in the shadow of Westminster Cathedral, with large (for Inner London) playground much coveted and occasionally used by other local schools. Main building designed by Street. God and the Church very important here – the school's mission statement starts 'The vision of our school is to create a warm, loving, learning environment, to live the Gospel and to enable each individual to realise their full potential'. Stuffed with local Spanish and Portuguese waiters'/cleaners' children. Large basement – plenty of room for brownies etc – good library. Shot to brief fame when ex-education minister John Patten revealed his child was here and he had put his daughter where his job was.

SANDROYD

Rushmore, Tollard Royal, Nr Salisbury, Wiltshire SP5 5QD

TEL: *01725 516264* FAX: *01725 516441*

E-MAIL: sandroyd@dial.pipex.com

WEB: www.eluk.co.uk/sandroyd/

✦ PUPILS: 150 boys, 110 board, 40 day ✦ Ages: 7-13 ✦ C of E ✦ Fee-paying

---

Head: Since 1994, Mr M J (Mike) Hatch MA AFIMA (fifties). Educated at Wells Cathedral School, and Trinity College, Oxford. Mathematician; keen cricketer. Previously housemaster at Sherborne, before that was at King's Canterbury. Married to Christine, who has pursued her own teaching career, and now teaches here; two grown up children, one a teacher.

Entrance: Requires fluency in reading, writing and arithmetic, assessment nine months before entry.

Exit: To Sherborne, Radley, Milton Abbey, Bryanston, Marlborough; a scattering elsewhere.

Remarks: Very traditional old-fashioned prep school in imposing Pitt-Rivers family house, open fires (well guarded) and marvellous long hall focus of school with benches for all and super oak furniture everywhere and amazing grounds (70 acres in middle of Rushmore estate) beautifully kept. Three-quarters of staff live within the Park. Boys terribly polite, say 'Sir', and stand up as soon as you appear, both table napkins and firm discipline. Punishments include emptying bins or being deprived of free time. Survived its trauma (previous head left following a sex scandal) amazingly well, handled with speed by the governors, and helped by the unquestioning loyalty of parents, of whom, by the way, over a third are in the Services.

Several boys keep their ponies here (stables have been rebuilt), pets, bikes and gardens. Reassuring keenness for 'traditional' boys' pastimes – Lego, sandpit, board games. Day boys introduced in '95 (all at the lower end of the school), maximum now raised from 10 to 25 per cent and fully taken up at great speed – a sign of the times. Still however clinging to full boarding for those in their last two years. New form for seven-year-olds established in '98.

Whole school under same – somewhat sprawling – roof, with super swimming pool built to celebrate school's centenary in 1988. Computers all over, CD-ROMs, strong art, very good music (three choirs, orchestra) and drama. God important, boys attend chapel three (used to be five) days a week. Delicious food. Busy on the sports fields (boys often play seven days a week). Remedial teaching for about 20 per cent with mild dyslexia, dyspraxia etc: three part-time qualified teachers, who have their own rooms in recently formed unit; boys usually taught on a one-to-one basis; Alexander technique where beneficial, plus touch typing tuition available. Otherwise classes streamed after two years. Maximum of 16 per class (average 12), staff pupil ratio of around 1:7. Senior boys spend their final year in a separate wing, in study bedrooms ('It's great!', they agree), with their own common room area, computer, telephone etc. A complaint or two of bullying, and of parents 'not being made to feel welcome'.

Good social mix. Most children from Wessex, 10 per cent OBs' sons. OBs include the Lords Avon, Carrington and Snowdon, also Sir Ranulph Fiennes and Sir Terence Rattigan. V v popular locally.

SARUM HALL

15 Eton Avenue, London NW3 3EL

TEL: *020 7794 2261* FAX: *020 7431 7501*

✦ PUPILS: 165 girls (including pre-prep); all day ✦ Ages: 3-11 ✦ C of E ✦ Fee-paying

Head: Since 2000, Mrs Jane Scott, previously deputy head of St Paul's Cathedral School. Took over from Lady Smith-Gordon, head since 1984.

Entrance: No tests. Places offered after interview with parents.

Exit: Mainly to day schools – all the North London ones, eg North London Collegiate, South Hampstead High, Queen's College Harley Street, Francis Holland, Channing; also City of London School for Girls and St Margaret's, Hampstead; one or two to smart boarding schools.

Remarks: Solid small school that grounds the girls well in all the basics. Strong emphasis on 'core subjects' especially reading – sadly not the learning of poetry that there used to be. Senior schools remark on the fact that girls arrive well taught and keen, which speaks volumes. 'We are ambitious for them,' says the head, but pressure appears minimal. Maximum class size 21, smallest classes (in top year, which is split) – 10-12. No provision for special needs. IT from age four from a full-time specialist.

Physical education (gym, games or dancing) every day. Garden play area covered with sensible rubber flooring, contains netball court doubling as four short tennis courts. The school moved in '95 to what is currently the only new purpose-built private preparatory school for girls in London, and opened its own pre-prep in this new building

---

SUMMER FIELDS

Oxford OX2 7EN

Tel: *01865 454433* Fax: *01865 459200*

E-mail: SummerFields.School@btinternet.com

Web: www.summerfields.oxon.sch.uk

✦ Pupils: 250 boys, 240 boarders, 10 day ✦ Ages: 8-13 ✦ C of E ✦ Fee-paying

---

Head: Since 1997, Mr Robin Badham-Thornhill BA (forties). Educated at Cheltenham and Exeter, where he read economics, politics and history. Previously head of Lambrook. Interested in hockey, cricket, golf, reading (especially biographies) and wine-tasting. Wife Angela very involved in school and, amongst other things, helps show round all prospective parents; two daughters aged 15 and 12. The school's first head appointed from outside the school. Believes in a breadth of education – 'interests and disciplines learnt at prep school are with you into adult life' and excellence in everything – 'if the boys are going to do something, they should aim to do it well.' Firmly refutes criticism that the school is an academic hothouse. 'There are some very able boys and the other boys are taught

well'. Took over from five star head Mr Talbot-Rice who was here for years and years.

Entrance: Put names down early: this is one of the very few boarding prep schools that is full and with a waiting list despite the national anti-boarding trend. Once a very upper-class establishment, now a mixed bag with a lot of 'Fulham Aga parents – know what I mean?' said a parent. Entry assessment two terms before the boys are due to join the school.

Exit: Eton feed – 50 per cent here – and has had five or six Eton scholarships in one year (annually celebrated with feasts on the lawn) though only one or two recently. Radley and Harrow the most popular choices after Eton.

Remarks: Out and out feed for Eton, and very successful at this. Set in 60 acres (feels less) in suburbs of north Oxford, founded in 1864, main building a large bow-windowed house with many additions, almost all of them attached. Facilities are exceptionally good, including the Wavell building, large and light, for art (which is excellent), science, and technology, and ICT room – the school now has lots of good computers, music technology etc. School hums with activity. Brilliant equipment everywhere and the sports hall is splendid, with a rifle range, three squash courts, two fives courts, a climbing wall. Outdoor theatre. The former gym has been converted into a theatre and concert hall.

Elsewhere classrooms are bright and light (17 per class), and teaching is evidently a pleasure to the teachers and the taught: curiosity, interest and a desire to learn is the norm. Some staff of notably high calibre. Boys not all geniuses by any means – plenty of the average as well as the very clever, all of them very fully stretched. The school is particularly good at gearing the less academic up and getting them into Eton. Good too with boys requiring learning support. Boys are competitive, but not unpleasantly so, work and play very carefully monitored; lots of tests, lots of homework. Scholarship classes set apart for the last two years, almost invisible streaming from the start. Emphasis on reading (main library is very grown up, more like a public school) with two reading periods per day, one after lunch, overseen by hovering masters; the second before lights out. More female teaching staff now, and handfuls of very pretty, very young, matrons – wowing fathers and staff alike. Chapel plays a major role (keen organists nip in to practise whenever they can), the altar cloth embroidered with what could be taken as the school's motto: 'A good seed brings forth good fruit'. School has the use of a château (near Caen) – boys have a ten-day stay in their third year, and two weeks in their fourth. School staff accompany them over, and there is a young couple plus assistant based in Normandy all the time.

Sport is extremely strong. Indoor and outdoor swimming pool (the boys swim every single day), 9-hole golf course and splendid adventure playground – 'You name it, it's there and the boys do it full throttle,' said one parent who knows his son finds holidays and home offer rather less. Music also strong – choir sings in a cathedral most years, and recently performed in Paris and Germany.

Cosy homely dorms have individual bedside lights and wallpaper, fine dining hall (food is good – sausage and mash highly recommended) with portraits of the great and good, mostly Old Boys, including Macmillan and Lord Wavell. Day boys ('whose numbers will not increase,') are often dons'sons. Exeats have recently been slightly increased, to general cries of delight. Without doubt a very strong boarding prep school, and for the boys, this is where networking begins

SUNNINGDALE SCHOOL

Dry Arch Road, Sunningdale,
Berkshire SL5 9PY

TEL: *01344 620 159* FAX: *01344 873 304*

E-MAIL: headmaster@sunningdaleschool.co.uk

✦ PUPILS: 100 boys, all boarding except 2
✦ Ages: 8-13 ✦ C of E ✦ Fee-paying

Head: Owned and run, since 1967, by the well-known Dawson twins (sixty-five) – a national institution. Nick Dawson is head (the bachelor). Tim Dawson is deputy head (married with four practically all grown up children). Mrs Tim Dawson is in charge of the domestic side. Twins educated at Eton and spent two years in the Green Jackets. Very charming, delightful 'old school' headmasters. Both do a full teaching week. No plans to retire just yet but the next generation Mr Dawson is in the pipeline, presently an assistant housemaster at Harrow.

Entrance: At 8+ ('they settle in better at this age') from a wide variety of pre-preps all over the country including Scotland. Some from London but not as many as expected given the proximity to the London SW postcodes. Also happy to take boys at 10 or 11 from day schools.

Exit: 60 per cent to Eton, 25 per cent to Harrow, 10 per cent to Stowe. One or two to Marlborough, Radley, Charterhouse,

Ampleforth, Shiplake, Wellington and Milton Abbey.

Remarks: Small cosy old-fashioned prep school. A large country house with lots of add-ons including new-fashioned classroom blocks furnished with old-fashioned wooden 'lift-up lid' desks. Attention given to individual academic needs. Much movement between classes. A brighter boy may end up doing two years in a top class which gives him a tremendous advantage at Common Entrance. Well-behaved boys juxtaposed with seemingly informal teaching staff. One arrived at his lesson with his dog, another carried a cup of coffee into the class. 74 per cent learn a musical instrument. Active chess club with a part-time chess teacher. Lots of sport including Eton fives. Full boarding and unlikely to change. Pastoral care has improved dramatically, fierce matron has gone. Present matron is kind and cosy. Carpeted dorms for younger ones (piles of teddies on the beds), cubicles for the older boys, hot chocolate offered as a reward for tidiness. A large communal bathroom with eight miniature-sized cast-iron baths with claw feet – new shower block too. Boys allowed to walk the Dawson's dogs in the grounds (wonderful at cheering up a homesick child). Good hearty food. Those sitting on headmaster's table get offered cheese after their pudding. Boys have happy, cheery faces with sparkling eyes. Excellent manners and well disciplined. Lots of praise too. Popular with a certain kind of parent, and the Dawsons like it that way.

SUSSEX HOUSE

68 Cadogan Square, London SW1X 0EA

Tel: *020 7584 1741* Fax: *020 7589 2300*

✦ Pupils: 180 boys; all day ✦ Ages: 8-13
✦ C of E ✦ Fee-paying

Head: Since 1994, Mr Nicholas Kaye MA ACP (forties). Read English at Cambridge. Previous post – deputy head of the school – has been here for yonks. Has also taught in Ethiopia and runs a Trust there. Unmarried. Bags of mother appeal. Rides a bicycle. Ambitious for the school. A shrewd operator. Keen on Victoriana – and has undertaken tremendous restoration work and renovations to the school's superb redbrick Betjemanesque building, including the original ballroom. Even keener on music, and regularly conducts concerts, a serious amateur, and directs the St Mary Magdalene Church Music Society. Lives above the shop – a great perk.

Entrance: Own paper taken at Sussex House, plus interview. £500 deposit required when place is accepted.

Exit: Eton, St Paul's, City of London, Westminster, Harrow, Winchester, Stowe, Latymer, Marlborough and a few others.

Remarks: Mellow prep school in the wonderful elegant surroundings of Cadogan Square, also owns an annexe round the corner which houses music school and gym. 85 per cent of staff are Mr Kaye's appointments – strong new heads of department, some imaginative teaching. Three small sixth forms (13) – one a scholarship class; some unlikely candidates do well. French for all from the start, Latin from second year, optional Greek. 'Clinics' in main subjects, where boys can ask for extra help in the lead-up to common entrance without fear of holding up the rest.

Spectacular art all over the school – current craze is architectural models. Terrific music, including choral and orchestra. School well known for prowess in the fencing world – U12 and U14 national champions. Games programme uses nearby Royal Hospital and Battersea pitches. Football on a winning streak. Games are 'taught', and not just 'taken'. Voluntary football on Saturdays. NB no playground, but occasional limited use of Cadogan Square. Weekly services in St Simon Zelotes round the corner (whose vicar is the chaplain). A good place for self-confidence.

THOMAS'S
28-40 Battersea High Street, London
SW11 3JB

<small>BATTERSEA BRANCH:</small>
T EL: *020 7978 0900* F AX: *020 7978 0901*
<small>KENSINGTON BRANCH:</small>
T EL: *020 7361 6500* F AX: *020 7361 6501*
<small>CLAPHAM BRANCH:</small>
T EL: *020 7326 9300* F AX: *020 7326 9301*

E-MAIL: <battersea@thomas-s.co.uk>

(For Kensington or Clapham amend appropriately)

✦ P UPILS: 485 boys and girls in Battersea; 210 boys and girls in Kensington; approx 350 boys and girls in Clapham, all day ✦ Ages: 4-13 (Battersea); 4-11 (Kensington); 4-11 (Clapham) ✦ C of E ✦ Fee-paying

---

Principals/Owners: Mr and Mrs David Thomas (and now their sons too). Whizzo entrepreneurs both, enthusiastic, tireless, courageous and much deserve their great success. Vice-principal (from 1996) is Miss Jill Kelham CertEd, previously headmistress of Thomas's Battersea. Son Ben is now headmaster of the Battersea branch (see below) and son Tobyn is director of administration for all the schools – sorting out transport, maintenance etc. Mr Thomas = ex-Gurkha, hot on property – family has acquired three top-class sites.

Mrs Thomas is alive with ideas, eye for detail and design, and the one who started it all in a church hall in Pimlico. NB involvement of the Thomases means that – unusually in these tricky times – the school heads can get on with the business of running the school, untroubled by PR and other marketing matters.

Head of Battersea Branch: Since 1999, Mr Benjamin Thomas BA (thirties) who comes from the Kensington branch where he was appointed as head in 1996 amid much brouhaha and cries of nepotism. Liked by parents, after this difficult start. Educated at Eton and Durham University, taught at a school in Lesotho, worked for Barings (left before it collapsed). Replaced Mr Andrew Sangster, head since 1996, who departed ahead of time (to be a rural vicar). Energetic, enthusiastic, keen on chess and debating. His wife Carol also has long experience of teaching. Two sons.

Head of Kensington Branch: Since 1999, Miss Anne Charlesworth BEd (thirties), who joined in '91 as head of the lower school (at time of writing on maternity leave.)

Head of Clapham Branch: Since 1993, when the branch opened: Mrs Carol Evelegh DipCE (thirties), who has been with the Thomases for years, in all their ventures. Fizzy with long blonde hair, Scottish upbringing and says she would rather not be described as a Miss Jean Brodie (it's tempting). Not a favourite with all parents – some find her nervy and too pushy for the childrens' good.

Entrance: Treat the three schools as one school on three separate sites, advise the Thomases (not to mention two kindergartens – one in Pimlico, and one in wonderful site on river in church crypt in Battersea). Name down asap; 'assessment' at four, exam after that. Hefty deposit required on accepting a place (£950 at time of writing – not returnable till child leaves the school and no interest paid on it). Automatic transfer from Kensington to Battersea at age 11. School 'keen to take siblings – very few turned away'. NB this can mean few places available for outsiders.

Exit: A few boys leave at seven and eight to go to all-boys' prep schools. Otherwise go to London day schools or smart boarding – Harrow, Eton, Wycombe Abbey etc etc. Some complaints from parents that the advice on choice of senior school is limited.

Remarks: School founded in 1977 by the empire-building Thomases (see above) – went from strength to strength through the eighties, main school now housed in ex-grammar school on rat run in Battersea – dignified old red brick, with softening touches of carpets and flowers and curtains provided by Mrs Thomas. The Battersea building is large by London prep standards (unlike the Kensington branch, which is two large formerly private houses and has a cosy more nursery feel to it). Thomas's was the people's choice for London prep education for many years, not least because, unlike most rival establishments, it was co-ed. Expansion has changed this, and the schools have slid a bit in the popularity stakes, though still able to pick and choose.

Clapham branch housed in old girls' grammar school – a magnificent redbrick building which must appear daunting to five-year-olds coming from cosy nurseries. Made user-friendly, however, inside by elbow grease and inspiration – budding interior designers should take a good look, particularly at magnificent school hall. Unusually strong PTA stuffed with terrifyingly ambitious parents. High expectations and good emphasis on non-exam work, though day is still highly structured. Projects from age eight, French from five, Latin for all at nine years old, streaming from eight onwards. By age eight the only subject-taught classes are French and science,

Around 20 per class. The school is very keen to organise remedial help (billed direct by therapist to parent). Recently, reports a parent, a whole class were deemed in need of such help... Lots of extra-curricular activity fitted into long school day – computing, ballet, swimming, lots of clubs and exercise. Battersea has three-quarters of an acre of playground, with pitches marked out everywhere, a gym, assembly hall/theatre, masses of labs etc (the grammar school legacy). Good food. Lots of enthusiasm and bright, cheerful children. Children bussed everywhere – the Kensington lot have science lessons in their last year in the Battersea building – better facilities and 'it gets them used to the place for when they move,' say the staff – and children say they are chuffed to be in with the seniors.

NB Probably best not to send your gentle retiring flower to Battersea or Clapham, though locals comment Clapham children are 'beautifully behaved' in the street.

TREVOR-ROBERTS

55-57 Eton Avenue, London NW3 3ET

TEL: *Senior 020 7586 1444, Junior 020 7722 3553*

FAX: *Senior 020 7722 0114, Junior 020 7483 1473*

✦ PUPILS: 175, 95 boys, 80 girls; all day ✦ Ages: 5-13 ✦ Non-denom ✦ Fee-paying

---

Head: Since 1999, Mr Simon Trevor-Roberts BA (forties) (son of the founder Christopher Trevor-Roberts LVO who established the school in its present premises (it moved from the Vale of Health) in 1981, and remains in the school as a teacher and as principal), educated at Westminster, formerly headmaster of the junior school, and 'lovely' according to a parent. Simon shares his father's conviction that 'self-esteem and confidence are what make for happy children... Confidence is 80 per cent of learning – perhaps more, it's easily destroyed.' The headship of the junior department has passed to Amanda Trevor-Roberts MA (thirties), Simon's sister, who has taught at the school for five years.

Entrance: Main entry is now at 5 but some places are available at other ages, by interview (children and subsequently parents).

Exit: Wide range of day and boarding schools.

Remarks: Despite shedding its original tutorial tag and now officially a prep school with its own pre-prep, the school has overtones of a 'tutorial' establishment at the top end. Staff, an unusually close-knit team, are all in the business of getting children excited about their work – and getting them to work. 'In fact, we get them more interested in studying, not just working.' Non-competitive, no orders, no public marks – but half term reports and all progress exceedingly carefully monitored. Some children arrive here as refugees from other schools where they were wobbled, lost concentration, turned work shy etc. 'And they get made whole,' commented a mother. No streaming, but classes can be divided into smaller groups for certain subjects. Maximum class size 22, average 18. No form teachers after fourth year, but subject teachers all the way. All six main subjects taught every day. No remedial unit, but one specialist teacher who sees pupils in need 'for an hour or two a week'. Fees £2,900 a term at time of writing.

Large Edwardian houses with good-size

airy rooms (some folding doors open to double the space for plays, assembly etc); well-designed black folding furniture. New computer room is used to support subjects, teach word-processing. Bright dining rooms and good food. Rubberised playground used for outdoor teaching, and theatre, also games, ie basketball and soft hockey (this is not the place for a football-mad boy, though there is now a weekly football club using a local pitch, and popular with Pupils). No matches against other schools, however. PT every day; swimming (at Swiss Cottage) twice a week, plus fencing, rowing and netball clubs. Head is very insistent on children becoming self-reliant, thus for homework there is no notebook, no parental monitoring, no telephoning around. The neighbouring house (bought from Eton College and previously a school for the blind) is used by the junior department ages 5 to 8. As well as housing their classrooms, science laboratory, and dining room/gym there is also an art room and music room used by the whole school. Music plays an important role throughout the school, and children arrive to piped classical music (programme written up in the hall) every morning at assembly with mini playlets, poetry reading etc. Continues to get good reports from parents. The only real contender as a strong co-ed prep in North London.

TWYFORD SCHOOL
Winchester SO21 1NW
TEL: *01962 712269* FAX: *01962 712100*

E-MAIL: admissions@twyfordschool.org.uk

WEB: www.twyfordschool.schoolzone.co.uk

♦ PUPILS: 225 in prep school, of which 70 girls (20 girl boarders) the rest boys, mostly day; 80 in pre-prep, of whom around 40 per cent girls ♦ Ages: pre-prep 3-8; prep 8-13 ♦ C of E ♦ Fee-paying

Head: Since 1997, Mr Philip Francis Fawkes MBA CertEd (forties). Educated at Embley Park (where he also taught and set up junior school), and Keele University, where he took his MBA in education – a rare commodity 'and it shows', commented a parent at his previous school appreciatively. Previous post was head of Lathallan prep in Scotland, which he took from a somewhat small and sleepy underfunded establishment to perhaps the most dynamic prep school in Scotland, by dint of 'man management' and 'marketing skills', not to mention use of Pavlovian techniques to get parents through the door. Senior coach for the national Cricket Association, former chairman of selectors for the Hampshire Schools' Cricket Association under 19 XI. Assisted by his wife Jane and dogs – RIP Daisy the Yorkshire terrier, long live Kristy and Bonnie. One daughter. Took over from the colourful Mr Richard Gould, who was here from '83.

Entrance: Children come for a day's informal assessment in the November before they are due to come into the school. Threshold for passing this deliberately set not too high – register early for safety.

Exit: A third to Winchester, almost as many to King Edward VI in Southampton, the rest to Canford, Wellington, Bradfield, Marlborough, Harrow, the Winchester state schools (which are good), and hither and yon.

Remarks: Still regarded by locals as probably the friendlier more fun of the two top prep schools in this area and this looks unlikely to change in near future. Interesting place – goes back to the middle of the seventeenth century and its current C of E foundation for the 'sons of middle class persons' to 1809 – school lays claim to being the oldest 'proper' prep school in the country. Bags of riveting history (see Shades of the Prison House by the Rev R G Wickham). Wonderful list of OBs, including Hubert Parry, Douglas Hurd, not to mention Thomas Hughes, author of Tom Brown's Schooldays. Pupils formerly upper and upper middle class, now a wider mix. School motto Vince Patientia, that has been lovingly translated and engraved above fireplace as 'Dogged as does it', and picture depicting the hare and tortoise (headmaster's tie sports a tortoise, second head's a hare). Streaming into three sets at nine, and two CE sets plus a scholarship set from ten. No class more than 18, smallest 10. Science taken seriously; French from a young age, Latin for all. Other languages may be available, but there again, they may not.

Top-class art department and evidence of pupils' work on walls cheerfully all over the school. Music traditionally strong, with three choirs (sings from time to time in Winchester Cathedral), jazz band, three orchestras – not bad for a small school. Large light music room with sound-proof studio, overlooking playing fields, below which squats an open-air amphitheatre. Pleasant 20-acre country site close to Winchester, which includes the original old school hall (wood panelling and the vibes of centuries of schoolboys). Fairly scruffy. Charming chapel. Excellent swimming pool and sports hall, good coaching. Strong on games for the boys. Those who aren't much good at rugby no longer, alas, do 'shinty' – a form of hockey. Cricket still strong however. Each pupil has a 'tutor' responsible for overall welfare, and keep the same one throughout. Weekly sessions with tutor to record state of play. Eternal vigilance on teasing so that it is not allowed to develop into bullying. Houses – Wasps, Mosquitoes etc. Pupils on the whole are cheerful, bouncy, casual and school appears to achieve delicate balance between learning and allowing boys to be boys with shirts hanging out etc. Dining hall with long tables and benches – anyone can sit anywhere, but pupils must ask to leave table. Fax machine and e-mail used for pupils to keep in touch with parents (and the statutory telephone, of course). Traditional and in some areas old-fashioned school which still has a feel of a boys' boarding school, though it is now overwhelmingly day. Girls (first let in 'around '87') progressing from the rudimentary stage of being honorary boys and playing football etc. Happy noises, and the head has good track record.

WELLESLEY HOUSE

Broadstairs, Kent CT10 2DG

TEL: *01843 862991* FAX: *01843 602068*

E-MAIL: wellesley.office@lineone.net

WEB: www.wellesley.kent.sch.uk

✦ PUPILS: 98 boys, 60 girls. 132 board (including 52 weekly boarders), 26 day ✦ Ages: 7-14 ✦ C of E ✦ Fee-paying

Head: Since 1990, Mr Richard Steel BSc (early fifties), previously head of York House School. Has three children, and wife (a trained teacher) is 'everybody's mummy'.

Entrance: Interview, occasionally assessment as well. Buses from Essex and Victoria Station via the M25.

Exit: King's Canterbury currently the popular choice (boys and girls), followed by Eton, then Tonbridge. Harrow and Benenden also feature.

Remarks: Classy and traditional prep school. Continues to get good results without pushing the children (fairly rare). Can cope with mild dyslexia 'broadly speaking'. Maximum class size 17; average 12. Children streamed into two or three groups (depending on year) and setted in some subjects at top end of school.

Sunny redbrick buildings set in 15 acres of manicured games pitches surrounded by suburban sprawl of Broadstairs, and one mile from the sea. German, Spanish and Greek are options. Good facilities, including heated indoor pool, also impressive music, art and pottery complex. New science /ICT block. Lots of hobbies/activities, wonderful carpentry, keen sewing, current affairs, extra music. Library recently refurbished and re-equipped.

Excellent games/sports, with especially strong cricket: four times winner of the National Prep School Under 13 knock out championships in the '90s; both captains of the '97 Eton-Harrow match were OBs of the school. Keen golf (a pro from Sandwich comes weekly). Girls' hockey currently strong, and school has won the National Rounders Competition twice.

Girls have their own house across the games field, cramped, cheerful, and very feminine. Dorms throughout refurbished and beds painted in bright colours (pine with 'personal drawers'). Animal complex a recent addition. Children are friendly and chatty. Popular with City and establishment – lots of smart and successful parents. Small school atmosphere, and lots of charm. Chapel used every morning. A happy school, and good reports reach us from a number of parents.

WESTBOURNE SCHOOL FOR

BOYS AND GIRLS

50-54 Westbourne Road, Sheffield S10 2QQ

TEL: *0114 266 0374* FAX: *0114 267 8203*

E-MAIL: info@westbourneschool.co.uk

WEB: westbourneschool.co.uk

✦ PUPILS: 230, 20 per cent girls (40 per cent in reception;) all day
✦ Ages 4-16 ✦ Non-denom ✦ Fee-paying

Head: Since 1984, Mr Colin Wilmshurst BA from Open University (fifties), promoted from assistant, formerly at Crawfordton House (Mr Wilmshurst's father in law started Crawfordton, and Mr W was a pupil there). Studied educational psychology and the arts. Qualifies for all the adjectives used to describe a good head – friendly, approachable, experienced, with understanding, full of good ideas and much liked by the pupils and the locals. Hobbies: archaeology, model cars and ancient postcards. Mrs Wilmshurst used to help in the school but is now a psychotherapist outside the school. The head has been seen from time to time on TV, including the Esther Rantzen show. Some loyal staff – six people represent more than 110 years of service at time of writing.

Entrance: First come first served; exam for senior school. Interview with head and form teacher. Fees reasonable, and discounts for siblings.

Exit: Fifteen scholarships in last three years (about par for the course) – to Worksop College, Repton, Gresham's, two to Trent, Birkdale, Eton. Some of these scholars dyslexic. Most pupils used to go on to public school, now increasingly they are headed for local schools (or stay here for GCSE.)

Remarks: The best 'proper' prep in Sheffield, and indeed for miles around – now beginning to take girls (from '98) and to offer GCSE: too early to judge how this will affect things. Atmosphere is a good mix of friendliness, fun and hard work. Outstanding French language teaching from reception onwards, with French assistants speaking nothing but French in class most of the time (immaculate accents). Mixed ability intake. No streaming until 11 – one class intake before that, though classes split into half groups for various lessons. Excellent support staff for coaching pupils up to standard – used by 'even the brightest', says the head – for any specific problems. One full-time SEN teacher (included in fees) plus two 'almost full-time' dyslexia teachers (extra). The school has had the National Under 15s Dyslexic Arts Champion for two years running, and its work with dyslexics has attracted much media attention. Worth moving into the area for this.

Pleasant light wing of classes for tinies, with books thoughtfully arranged in tiers at the height you might expect pupils to help themselves. Large asphalt playground which can get a bit overheated – the staff room overlooks it, however (nice cosy old chairs) and a watchful eye is kept. Acquired the neighbouring Ashdell House in '00, doubling the school's capacity. The site is in Sheffield Hallam, on the hill in what has been described as the 'greatest academic concentration in any mile in Europe' – with two universities within easy reach and countless schools. The change of name to

'Westbourne School for Boys and Girls' projects (even if subconsciously) the image of a non-privileged, non-elite establishment (no bad thing in Sheffield, which is David Blunkett's stronghold). Nice touches – breakfast is offered to all (including parents) from 8 am, which has been a big hit with families where both parents work. Parents are professionals – medics in particular – even the occasional football manager. There are clubs etc. after school and a creche till 5.30. The head has a 'headmaster's surgery' twice a term so people can get at him without having to make an appointment. Every Friday there is a 'good work assembly'. Games is serious business – with specialist games teacher – on site until the age of 8 then the school uses Sheffield's prestigious Abbeydale Sports Club – every child is an associate member of it.

WESTMINSTER CATHEDRAL
CHOIR SCHOOL
Ambrosden Avenue, London SW1P 1QH

TEL: *020 7798 9081* FAX: *020 7630 7209*

E-MAIL: emailwccs@aol.com

PUPILS: 96; (between 20 and 30 choristers, all board), the rest day ✦ Ages: 8-13
✦ RC ✦ Fee-paying

Head: Since 1995, Mr Charles Foulds BA (early forties). Previously at Stonyhurst in various posts, his last one as assistant headmaster with special responsibility for discipline (no mean task). Easy to get on with, outspoken and sensible. Four children.

Read modern languages at Swansea and Durham; wife, Elizabeth was at the Royal Academy of Music. Can communicate with the boys on their own level, there is every sign they judge him to be just the ticket.

Entrance: Too many ramifications to explain, but basically by exam and interview at 7+ around Jan/Feb. Choristers have separate entry procedure, with voice trials normally in Feb, and academic assessment at the same time.

Children come from eg Eaton House, The Vale, Wetherby's, Falcons, Eaton Square etc. You do not have to be RC to join the school – a third of the school is not (but NB all choristers are RC).

Exit: A pretty catholic mix, now more to top ranking public schools, both RC and not (Westminster, Ampleforth, Downside, Worth etc). Currently getting a good number of music scholarships to strong music schools (nine most recently – seven won by choristers, two by day boys).

Remarks: The cramped school buildings ('spacious', says head) with tarmac playground are umbilically linked to Westminster Cathedral (you can get through to the school via a little door behind the high altar). School founded in 1901 to provide choristers for the new Cathedral, reconstituted in '77 and provided with board of governors etc, and subsequently day boys grafted on and school became more than just a choir school. The library – which was criticised in the Ofsted report – belongs to the Cathedral, and still feels very dusty, full of old tomes and not boy-friendly. The other criticism from Ofsted – the IT provision, which, compared with switched right-on prep schools was almost non-existent – is making headway, with a smart new IT room. Apart from these matters of fine tuning, it's all go. Enthusiastic, confident boys who get endless practice standing up and performing (musically) in front of adults. Excellent French, a super chaplain, the most terrifyingly imaginative pictures lining the walls on the way to the art department, depicting monks in black chalk with ecstatic obsessed faces and when you get to the art department it's jolly, light and the requisite model aeroplanes swing from the ceiling. Teaching is traditional in nature (indeed, some have said it is over-traditional). The biggest class is 22, the average is 19. As they move up the school there is streaming in the last two years. Special learning teacher comes in three times a week. Games twice a week (three times a week for the tinies) and the school has some use of Vincent Square, but Battersea Park is the main games place.

The choristers have the usual horrendously long day, which they appear to cope with amazingly well. All choristers are boarded in two light dormitories, with posters squashed on the walls (not much wall space each). They sing mass four days a week in the Cathedral (and twice on Sundays), and this is the most important part of their activities, says the headmaster.

The master of music is Martin Baker. Boys produce a wonderful, clear, robust and merry noise, though it is difficult to tell the quality of the voices, as the amplification in the Cathedral would flatter a bullfrog (head queries this). The choristers obviously overshadow the rest of the school's musical activities – it is after all why the place is there – but in the way of many choir schools, most of the rest of the school is dragged up (musically speaking) to a level way above the average and practice sessions go on all day in every cupboard and corner. The head has a flat in Ambrosden Avenue (cheek by jowl with MPs) which makes it

handy for him to have supper with the boarders, matrons etc.

We would agree with Mr Foulds that what strikes you first here is a sense of community. Added to that, a minuscule chapel for the boys and staff right in the middle of the school makes a very definite statement about the priorities of the place. This is still definitely an old-fashioned, traditional prep school on which the Roman Catholic Church leans heavily, but the result is a place of strength, warmth, and, particularly in matters of music, excellence.

WESTMINSTER UNDER SCHOOL

Adrian House, 27 Vincent Square, London SW1P 2NN

Tel: *020 7821 5788* Fax: *020 7821 0458*

E-mail: under.school@westminster.org.uk

Web: www.westminster.org.uk

✦ Pupils: 250 boys; all day ✦ Ages: 7–13
✦ C of E ✦ Fee-paying

Head (The Master): Since 2000, Mr J P Edwards, who succeeded Mr G Ashton MA, the master since 1992, who died suddenly in May 1999.

Entrance: Probing and competitive entrance exam (taken at the school), with 160 boys chasing 40 places at 8+. Lists left open until near the exam; no need to sign on a dotted line that you wish your son to proceed to Westminster School, 'the Great School'. At 10+ and 11+ smaller entries, often of boys from primary schools. Substantial numbers of Asians ('and English, and French, and American...'). Some boys travel for miles as the map in the school hall shows. Had 62 assisted places (which pupils could carry through to the senior school) – loss appears not to have meant loss of primary school children, 'a substantial number of bursaries have been awarded'. Music bursaries of up to half fees to incoming 11+ or boys of that age already in the school. There will be entry at 7+ from 2001.

Exit: 48 out of 60 typically go on to Westminster School. The others go to Eton, Winchester, City of London etc. Approximately twenty-five boys sit the Challenge and three or four usually gain Westminster scholarships.

Remarks: School marches strongly on, with continuing favourable comments from most parents (one or two disgruntleds). One of the three top central London boys' academic prep schools. Exceptionally high standards of teaching throughout. Outstanding English under Mrs Gillian Howarth. Terrific emphasis on reading, with inter-house competitions, where the boys declaim poetry and prose. Sciences and classics also immensely strong: growing boys developing intellectual curiosity satisfied and fed. A large new computer room with RM machines, with older boys belting out sophisticated projects, totally computer literate – school famous for this. Latin started in year 6 (10+). Part-time member of staff for special needs. Class size normally 22. Two scholarship classes chosen and set aside in the last year only, up till then classes work on parallel lines, with a minimum of streaming (relatively gentle start). Many more than will actually get scholarships are part of the scholarship classes and sit the exams, 'because many boys can profit from advanced teaching', and CE would seem humdrum. (Also Westminster and Eton like this arrangement as it gives them a better insight into boys' potential.) Music of a high quality – and lots of it: (it occupies the entire basement, head of department plus assistant head, and 20 peripatetic teachers). Choirs and orchestra, jazz ensemble, chamber group etc. The school provides choristers for St Margaret's Church, and boys regularly win music scholarships to Westminster and elsewhere. Lovely art and pottery, incredibly enthusiastic drama performed in an eyesore of a hall (soon to be redeveloped). Over the road is Vincent Square (shared with Westminster School), the envy of nearby central London preps and used for breaks, twice weekly games sessions. 'Not enough sport,' a regular complaint. Weekly swimming and PE. School building (previously a hospital) is well loved, well worn, well used. Dingy basement hall for dining, plays etc. During lessons you could hear the proverbial pin drop; out of lessons, the place shakes with noise, rush and high spirits. Occasional grouse from parents, who are liberal with praise on the academic front, that the boys don't 'absorb much social polish at school'. Parents a complete mixture of well-off and badly-off, public school and first-time in the fee-paying sector.

Extra-curricular activities are a big strength – very strong on outings and trips – exchange with a school in Marseilles, annual trip to Pompeii, and eg walking in Scotland, choir tour to South Africa, art trip to Florence, the results of staff enthusiasms and receiving strong support from parents and boys. Sophisticated debating at the top of the school. Being bright is not enough: robustness an essential ingredient for boys to flourish here.

WINCHESTER HOUSE SCHOOL

Brackley, Northamptonshire NN13 7AZ

TEL: *01280 702483* FAX: *01280 706400*

E-MAIL: office@winchester-house.org

WEB: www.winchester-house.org

✦ Pupils: 135 boys, 60 girls; 80 boarders (50 of whom are weekly), 108 day pupils ✦ Ages 7-13, plus pre-prep with 75 boys and girls, ages 3-7 ✦ C of E ✦ Fee-paying

---

Head: Since 1997, Mr Jeremy Griffith BA PGCE (early forties). Educated at Horris Hill and Winchester. Previously taught at Horris Hill and Windlesham, and was a housemaster plus at The Dragon. Married to Lindy – BEd – who currently fronts the youngest class in the main school. Two children, both currently in the school. A linguist, he teaches IT and scripture to the scholars. Friendly, totally approachable and disgustingly young-looking. Took over from the long-serving Richard Speight, with whom, sensibly, he shared his first term.

Entrance: 'Preferably' in September, though some flexibility still. Day Pupils move up via hugely popular pre-prep (Tel: 01280 703070), others come for an informal test. Most boarders come from within 100 mile radius. Some 'professional b & b' but usually only to encourage boarding.

Exit: Mostly to schools within a 100-mile radius – Rugby, St Edwards, Oundle, Uppingham, Stowe, Bloxham etc. Girls to Tudor Hall, Downe House, Malvern Girls, Wycombe Abbey etc. Has had a good collection of awards over the years.

Remarks: Traditional co-ed prep school, predominantly boys, with weekly and full boarding but majority day, based in a converted Victorian hunting lodge with a chapel and (mini) billiard room/library in an earlier Tudor building. The school was founded in 1876, and moved to its present site in Brackley in 1923. Very much a local school, and popular as such. Keen games, athletics meetings here a great favourite. Thriving well-run pre-prep and nursery over the road, with the playing fields, sports hall and tennis courts. Library block and IT centre attached to the main building. School's appearance brought up to scratch by the head. Sound teaching on all fronts, including Greek for the brightest, strong classics and maths for scholars. The headmaster, as a linguist, 'is keen to develop languages, with the possibility of a second language'. Some remedial help for dyslexia – co-ordinator is director of studies (but also trained in special needs). Maximum class size twenty, average around fifteen. Setting in all subjects (two sets) from age eight on. Potential scholars grouped together for all subjects in final two years.

WINDLESHAM HOUSE SCHOOL

Washington, Pulborough, West Sussex

RH20 4AY

TEL: *01903 873207* FAX: *01903 873017*

E-MAIL: office@windlesham.com

WEB: www.windlesham.com

✦ PUPILS: 270, including about 110 girls. All board. Plus pre-prep with 60 boys and girls ✦ Ages: 7-13, pre-prep 4–7 ✦ C of E ✦ Fee-paying

---

Head: Since 1996, Mr Philip Lough (pronounced lock) MA (forties), educated at Sherborne and Trinity College, Oxford. Keen sportsman (cricket and golf), modern linguist (French), married to Christine, also a modern linguist, she teaches French to the pre-prep, PSHE to older children. A super couple, warm, energetic and relaxed, good listeners. They have three children (none here). Both are from teaching families. Mr Lough was formerly a housemaster (C2) at Marlborough (spent seventeen years there in various capacities).

Entrance: Via interview, and testing at 11. Lots from London and the south east, about a third local, and ninety from overseas, mainly ex-pats, around 15 non-nationals (quite a tradition of French and Spanish children coming for a term or year or so, all by word-of-mouth). 45 Foreign Office children – fewer than formerly but still more than any other school. Three term entry. Wide ability range.

Exit: To over sixty different schools in the last five years, co-ed and single-sex, with a good record of scholarships. Most popular currently are Bryanston, King's Canterbury, Marlborough; some to Eton, Winchester etc. Also local schools, eg Ardingly, Hurstpierpoint, Cranleigh.

Remarks: Recovered from a rocky ride at the end of the long and wonderful reign of the much loved heads, Mr and Mrs Malden (see historical note below). Numbers back up, and head says the current overall figure is 'the right one, the maximum permitted under the school development plan, and where we want to keep it'. Pre-prep now up to capacity too. Once they join the prep school they may be day pupils for one year only, thereafter they must board. Pupils are set in most subjects, high expectations, with lots of project work. Good links with Europe, all pupils learn Spanish for two years, German is an option as an 'activity', Latin at 10+ for the brighter pupils, extra English or subject support timetabled for the rest at this point. Scholarship class at the top (two years for some). Science labs (previously dingy) have been re-sited and re-vamped, under the excellent Mr Ashley Butlin (wears a Mr Happy tie), who involves the children in hands-on work practically all the time. Special needs department, with good help for dyslexics and dyspraxics; also EFL. Outstandingly good art under the hugely popular Mr David Yeomans (this is probably the only prep school to hold its own exhibition in an upstairs Bond Street gallery, courtesy of a parent). Textiles, design, pottery as well as painting are stunning. Gym and swimming taught in small groups. General refurbishing programme has now reached (at last) the dining area and dormitories. Very full weekend programme. Flexible exeat system (just two 'all-in' weekends), and children allowed out on Sundays: the school runs a weekly Sunday bus service back to Windlesham School leaving Putney at 6pm. Splendid and distinguished old redbrick house on the Downs near the coast, set in sixty acres, amid masses of games pitches, tennis courts and a new seven hole golf course opened in '97 by Bernard Gallacher: see the snappy latest school mag, designed to look like Hello. Historical note: School founded (elsewhere, and at the request of Dr Arnold of Rugby) in 1837 by the Malden family, who owned and ran it until a few years ago when it became a charitable foundation named The Malden Trust in their honour. The famous and much loved Mr Charles Malden, who retired in '94, was the great-great-grandson of the founder. Claims to be the first single sex prep school to go co-educational (1967).

WOODCOTE HOUSE

Windlesham, Surrey GU20 6PF

Tel: *01276 472115* Fax: *01276 472890*

E-mail: n.h.k.p@btinternet.com

Web: www.woodcote.cjb.net

✦ Pupils:104 boys, of whom 12 day boys, who 'usually board after a year or so'
✦ Ages: 8-13 ✦ Non-denom ✦ Fee-paying

Head: Since 1989, Mr Nick Paterson BA (forties), educated at Westminster and Exeter University. Called 'Mr Nick' by one and all. Runs the school with the help of Mrs Nick and his parents Mr and Mrs Mark, who themselves ran the school for 30 years before him. Mr Nick's grandfather bought the school in 1931 when it was going 'but only just'. It is now a private limited company. Super wife, with older children, and they have one son at public school. Mr Nick comments (in answer to our question) that his biggest challenge is continuing to instil a code of good manners, fair play and unselfishness in the face of a deteriorating situation nationally.'

Entrance: Send for what is still one of the smallest prospectuses in the country (though Ludgrove and Sunningdale come close), small 'because it is vital they (the parents) come and see us with the boy, and really we must get on pretty well'. Always prepared to talk to parents right up to the last moment. Takes new boys in at the beginning of all three terms.

Exit: Biggest numbers to Sherborne, Radley, Bradfield, Shiplake, Charterhouse, Harrow, Wellington, plus a dozen others.

Remarks: Super little school where each boy is carefully cocooned so that the shock of leaving 'nursery environment' will not be too much. Main problem might be the shock of leaving Woodcote for their public school. Exeats every third week, though ex-pupil commented it was more fun staying at school during an exeat than going home because they did all sorts of nice things like playing golf with the Paterson family. Monthly magazine, also minuscule but extremely informative, yearly magazine which kicked off last year on the very first page: 'Food. Always the most interesting part of any small boy's day'. Keen chess, bridge, fishing, calligraphy, and nice old-fashioned boy things, such as making model aeroplanes, and less old-fashioned things such as 'Warhammer' (the head is appalled at the cost). Set in its own thirty acres, which includes some attractive woods, the main building is Regency and elegant but delightfully worn at the edges, with additional modestly built classroom blocks round the back and charming little chapel across the lawn, made of corrugated iron (painted black) and wooden inside. ('Buildings like hen houses,' said one visiting parent disappointedly.) Barbour and/or Husky part of the uniform, corduroy trousers and a rather dreary brown sweater or school sweatshirt.

Lots of golf played (on site), and cricket, squash (uses courts up the road), rugger and shooting. Head concentrates on placing boys in the school of their parents' choice rather than on getting scholarships – though they got two top ones in '00. Small and very competent remedial unit – recommended by special needs organisations for dyslexia and dyspraxia. Fully-qualified teacher who works in a small unit – some 10 per cent of the boys receive help – EFL teacher available three afternoons a week.

One or two gems among the staff including the super dynamic head of science, and the archetypal schoolmaster, Colin Holman, assistant headmaster, who has been here for yonks and lives in the lodge and, amongst other things, looks after the grounds lovingly. Development programme means school now has science lab, computer centre, art and music block, even new changing rooms (not before time, some might say), also Astroturf hockey pitch/tennis courts and telescopic swimming pool enclosure. About one-third are sons of soldiers or ex-pats (Services, Gulf etc but no Foreign Office at time of writing), one-third London or local and a third from 'far afield'. One or two Thais (long-standing tie with Thailand), a few 'Europeans' (by which they mean not British). One of a dying breed – the family-owned school – and, unlike some, by and large it works. Continuing good reports.

YARLET SCHOOL
Yarlet, Stafford ST18 9SU

Tel: *01785 286 568* Fax: *01785 286 569*

E-mail: enquiries@yarletschool.co.uk

Web: www.yarletschool.co.uk

✦ Pupils: 85 (60 boys, 25 girls) in the main school, 60 in the pre-prep, 10 in the nursery ✦ Ages: 2-3 nursery, 3-7 pre-prep, 7-13 main school ✦ C of E/inter-denom ✦ Fee-paying

Head: Since 1989, Mr Richard S Plant MA (early fifties). Potteries born and bred. Studied English at Pembroke, Cambridge; worked for a couple of years at Wedgwood, the famous pottery company, and then joined Yarlet. Cheerful, enthusiastic, still a schoolboy; clearly loves the job, the place and the children; likely to be here until retirement. Teaches history to the top three forms, and leads the choir in song. Married to Sue, an elegant lady of perfect taste and sanity, much involved in the life of the school; three grown-up children.

Entrance: By interview. Waiting list, but not that long.

Exit: Boys to Shrewsbury, Repton, local day schools and the occasional one to other notable boarding schools. Girls – too early to say. Two art scholarships (Shrewsbury, Uppingham) in '99, four in '00 (Repton,

Shrewsbury, Denstone) and one academic scholarship to Newcastle.

Remarks: Founded 1873, occupying a grand old house with fine views to the east and the A34 roaring away to the west, with various later additions and a dear little green tin chapel (God important). Dormitories bright and airy, plenty of furry animals; schoolrooms full of pupils' work and other decoration; a well used feel; colours cheerful and well chosen.

Once a traditional boys' boarding school, but now going co-ed throughout, and focussed on its local day market. Some still board – and are well looked after by staff at weekends; 'occasional boarding' available but not much used except by those practising for senior school. Pre-prep full to bursting, features the Perkins Cup for Effort; new building opened in '99 by Baroness Trumpington, and thus assured of great success.

A very sporting school – six days a week for all without exception – so Sunday is the only day off. Good pitches (including an Astro), but indoors facilities on the basic side. Boys' cricket and football strong, also girls' netball. Won the Staffordshire under-twelve county cricket final in '00 and the under-eleven final in 1999 – with sides that included two ten/nine-years-olds. Good athletics, cross-country.

Shows a proper disregard for turning the heating on for cold days in autumn – staff huddled round the fire at break, hands clasped round coffee mugs; boarders sleeping in their dressing gowns.

One form a year, so mixed teaching but brighter pupils can jump a year and so spend their last two years in the scholarship class. Dyslexia support available from the Stone Dyslexia Unit (in the neighbouring town of Stone). Pupils friendly, articulate, active. Staff a chirpier lot than usual; good art and lively English (there's a poetry reciting competition every year for all – proper poetry too). Drama present but not overly so; ditto music – new director of music from '00. Well-stocked computer room, increasingly part of teaching life.

MAPS

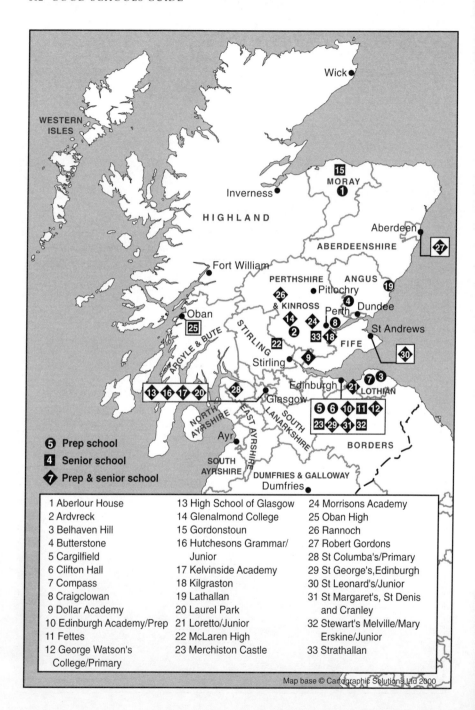

5 Prep school
4 Senior school
7 Prep & senior school

1 Aberlour House	13 High School of Glasgow	24 Morrisons Academy
2 Ardvreck	14 Glenalmond College	25 Oban High
3 Belhaven Hill	15 Gordonstoun	26 Rannoch
4 Butterstone	16 Hutchesons Grammar/	27 Robert Gordons
5 Cargilfield	Junior	28 St Columba's/Primary
6 Clifton Hall	17 Kelvinside Academy	29 St George's, Edinburgh
7 Compass	18 Kilgraston	30 St Leonard's/Junior
8 Craigclowan	19 Lathallan	31 St Margaret's, St Denis
9 Dollar Academy	20 Laurel Park	and Cranley
10 Edinburgh Academy/Prep	21 Loretto/Junior	32 Stewart's Melville/Mary
11 Fettes	22 McLaren High	Erskine/Junior
12 George Watson's	23 Merchiston Castle	33 Strathallan
College/Primary		

Map base © Cartographic Solutions Ltd 2000

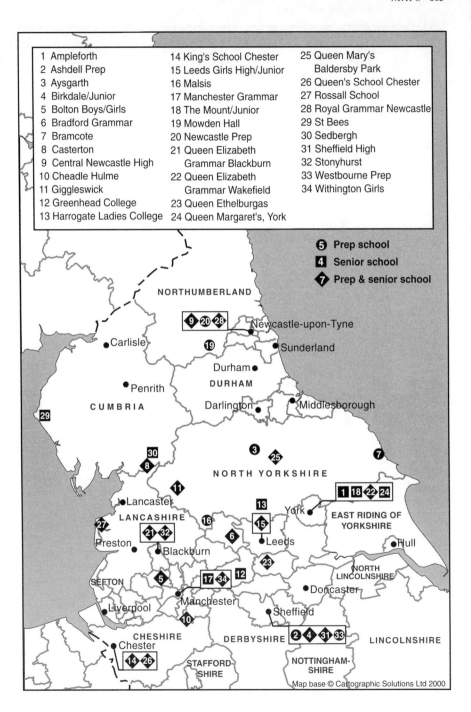

1 Ampleforth
2 Ashdell Prep
3 Aysgarth
4 Birkdale/Junior
5 Bolton Boys/Girls
6 Bradford Grammar
7 Bramcote
8 Casterton
9 Central Newcastle High
10 Cheadle Hulme
11 Giggleswick
12 Greenhead College
13 Harrogate Ladies College
14 King's School Chester
15 Leeds Girls High/Junior
16 Malsis
17 Manchester Grammar
18 The Mount/Junior
19 Mowden Hall
20 Newcastle Prep
21 Queen Elizabeth
    Grammar Blackburn
22 Queen Elizabeth
    Grammar Wakefield
23 Queen Ethelburgas
24 Queen Margaret's, York
25 Queen Mary's
    Baldersby Park
26 Queen's School Chester
27 Rossall School
28 Royal Grammar Newcastle
29 St Bees
30 Sedbergh
31 Sheffield High
32 Stonyhurst
33 Westbourne Prep
34 Withington Girls

Prep school
Senior school
Prep & senior school

Map base © Cartographic Solutions Ltd 2000

1 Abberley Hall	15 Cherwell	28 Haileybury
2 Abingdon	16 Cothill House	29 Headington/Junior
3 Aylesbury Grammar	17 Dean Close/Junior	30 Hills Road
4 Bancrofts	18 Dr Challoner's Grammar	31 King Edward's Birmingham
5 Beaudesert Park	19 Dr Challoner's High	32 King Edward VI High
6 Bedford/Prep	20 The Dragon	33 King's College School
7 Beeston Hall	21 Edge Grove	Cambridge
8 Bilton Grange	22 Felsted	34 King's Worcester
9 Bloxham	23 Framlingham	35 The Leys
10 Burford School	24 Godstowe Prep	36 Lockers Park
11 Caldicott	25 Gresham's	37 Lord Williams's
12 Chelmsford County High	26 Haberdashers' Aske's Boys/	38 Magdalen College School
13 Cheltenham College/Junior	Girls; Boys Prep/Girls Lower	39 Maltman's Green
14 Cheltenham Ladies' College	27 Haberdashers' Monmouth	40 Malvern College

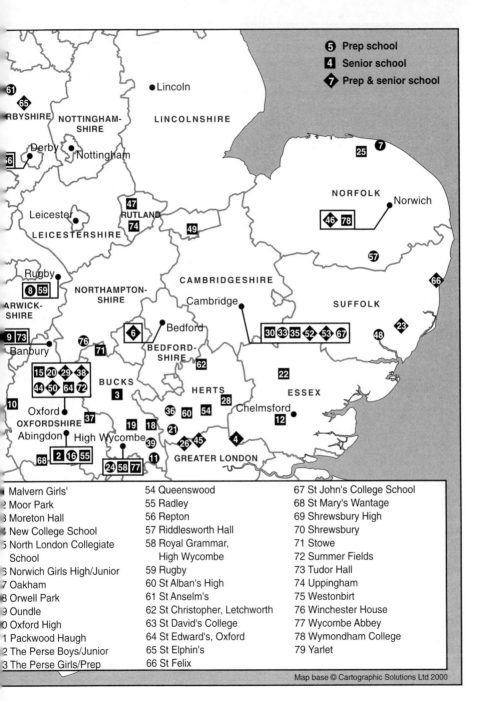

Key:
- ⑤ Prep school
- 4 Senior school
- ◆7 Prep & senior school

Malvern Girls'
2 Moor Park
3 Moreton Hall
4 New College School
5 North London Collegiate
  School
6 Norwich Girls High/Junior
7 Oakham
8 Orwell Park
9 Oundle
0 Oxford High
1 Packwood Haugh
2 The Perse Boys/Junior
3 The Perse Girls/Prep

54 Queenswood
55 Radley
56 Repton
57 Riddlesworth Hall
58 Royal Grammar,
   High Wycombe
59 Rugby
60 St Alban's High
61 St Anselm's
62 St Christopher, Letchworth
63 St David's College
64 St Edward's, Oxford
65 St Elphin's
66 St Felix

67 St John's College School
68 St Mary's Wantage
69 Shrewsbury High
70 Shrewsbury
71 Stowe
72 Summer Fields
73 Tudor Hall
74 Uppingham
75 Westonbirt
76 Winchester House
77 Wycombe Abbey
78 Wymondham College
79 Yarlet

Map base © Cartographic Solutions Ltd 2000

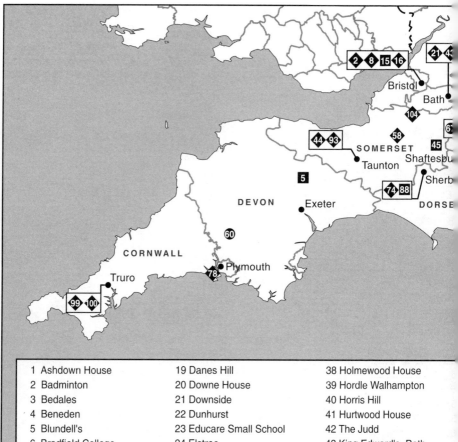

1 Ashdown House	19 Danes Hill	38 Holmewood House
2 Badminton	20 Downe House	39 Hordle Walhampton
3 Bedales	21 Downside	40 Horris Hill
4 Beneden	22 Dunhurst	41 Hurtwood House
5 Blundell's	23 Educare Small School	42 The Judd
6 Bradfield College	24 Elstree	43 King Edward's, Bath
7 Brambletye	25 Epsom	44 King's College, Taunton
8 Bristol Grammar	26 Eton	45 King's School, Bruton
9 Bryanston	27 Farleigh	46 The King's School,
10 Canford	28 Feltonfleet	Canterbury
11 Charterhouse	29 Frensham Heights	47 Kingston Grammar
12 Cheam Hawtreys	30 Godolphin	48 Knighton House
13 Christ's Hospital	31 Guildford High	49 Lady Eleanor Holles
14 City of London Freemens	32 Halliford	50 Lambrook Haileybury
School	33 Hampton	51 Lancing College
15 Clifton College	34 Hanford	52 Ludgrove
16 Clifton High	35 Harrow	53 The Mall
17 Cottesmore	36 Heathfield	54 Manor House
18 Cranleigh/Prep	37 Highfield	55 Marlborough College

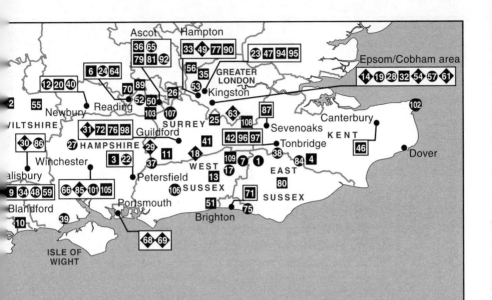

Prep school
Senior school
Prep & senior school

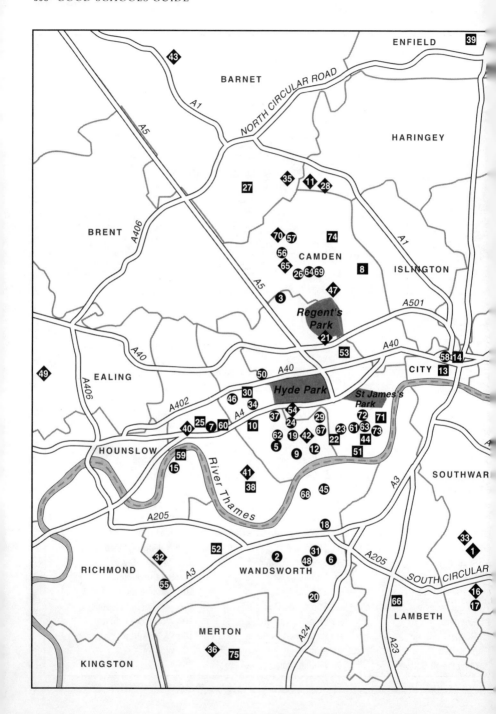

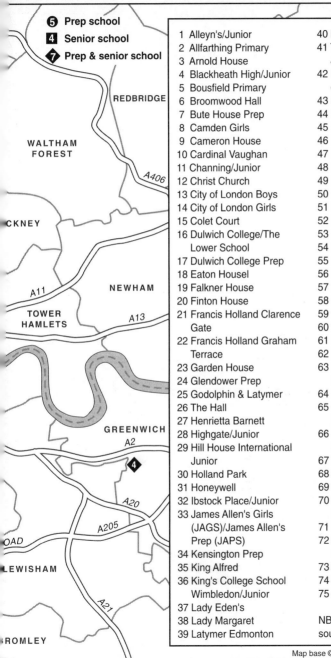

⑤ Prep school
④ Senior school
⑦ Prep & senior school

1 Alleyn's/Junior
2 Allfarthing Primary
3 Arnold House
4 Blackheath High/Junior
5 Bousfield Primary
6 Broomwood Hall
7 Bute House Prep
8 Camden Girls
9 Cameron House
10 Cardinal Vaughan
11 Channing/Junior
12 Christ Church
13 City of London Boys
14 City of London Girls
15 Colet Court
16 Dulwich College/The Lower School
17 Dulwich College Prep
18 Eaton Housel
19 Falkner House
20 Finton House
21 Francis Holland Clarence Gate
22 Francis Holland Graham Terrace
23 Garden House
24 Glendower Prep
25 Godolphin & Latymer
26 The Hall
27 Henrietta Barnett
28 Highgate/Junior
29 Hill House International Junior
30 Holland Park
31 Honeywell
32 Ibstock Place/Junior
33 James Allen's Girls (JAGS)/James Allen's Prep (JAPS)
34 Kensington Prep
35 King Alfred
36 King's College School Wimbledon/Junior
37 Lady Eden's
38 Lady Margaret
39 Latymer Edmonton

40 Latymer Upper/Prep
41 The London Oratory/ Junior
42 Lycée Français Charles de Gaulle
43 Mill Hill/Junior
44 More House
45 Newton Prep
46 Norland Place
47 North Bridge House
48 Northcote Lodge
49 Notting Hill & Ealing
50 Pembridge Hall
51 Pimlico
52 Putney High
53 Queen's College
54 Queen's Gate/Junior
55 Rokeby
56 St Antony's
57 St Christopher's, London
58 St Paul's Cathedral Choir
59 St Pauls Boy's
60 St Pauls Girl's
61 St Peter's Eaton Square
62 St Philip's
63 St Vincent de Paul Primary
64 Sarum Hall
65 South Hampstead High/Junior
66 Streatham Hill & Clapham High
67 Sussex House Prep
68 Thomas's
69 Trevor-Roberts
70 University College School/Junior
71 Westminster
72 Westminster Cathedral Choir
73 Westminster Under
74 William Ellis
75 Wimbledon High

NB Lady Eleanor Holles on southern England map

REDBRIDGE
WALTHAM FOREST
A406
CKNEY
A11
NEWHAM
TOWER HAMLETS
A13
GREENWICH
A2
④
A20
A205
OAD
LEWISHAM
A21
ROMLEY

Map base © Cartographic Solutions Ltd 2000

Index of Schools